Research
in Practice

Research in Practice

Applied methods for the social sciences

Edited by

Martin Terre Blanche, Kevin Durrheim,
and Desmond Painter

UCT
PRESS

Research in Practice: Applied Methods for the Social Sciences

University of Cape Town Press (Pty) Ltd
Private Bag Rondebosch
7701 Cape Town
South Africa

First published 1999
Reprinted 2004 Includes Moonstats CD and User Guide
Second revised edition 2006
Reprinted 2009

ISBN 978 19197 1369 4

Photographic credits:
pp. 478 & 528 – courtesy of Alex Butchart
p. 273 – courtesy of Ashley Clements
p. 3 – courtesy of David Goldblatt
P. 332 – Robin Hutton
pp. 308 & 527 – courtesy of Neil Lightfoot
p. 532 – courtesy of Njabulo Ndebele
p. 471 – courtesy of Kathryn Smith
pp. 275, 280, 298, 413, 416, 472, 478, 528 – courtesy of Centre for Peace Action, Unisa
p. 126 – courtesy of Centre for Violence and Reconciliation
Cover images and other images individually specified – Rodney Barnett

Every effort has been made by the publisher to obtain permission to reporduce the various
images in this book. Where it has not been possible to trace the copyright holders, the publisher
would be pleased to hear from them, so that the omission can be rectified in future editions.

Project manager: Sarah O'Neill
Editor: David Merrington
Cover design: Pumphaus Design Studio
Designed and typeset in Palatino BT 10/12 by Lebone Publishing Services
Printed and bound in the Republic of South Africa by

Contents

Preface

Research methodology must be one of the most ardently disliked of social science courses, and it is easy to see why: Students who enjoy critical academic debate find themselves having to conform to a set of narrow scientific conventions; those who appreciate the linguistic and cultural dimensions of their discipline are expected to make sense of arcane statistical procedures; and those who thrive on applied, practical work are fed a thin diet of hypothetical examples. As students, we experienced some of these frustrations and observed the debilitating effects they had on our friends, many of whom came to believe themselves to be irredeemably incompetent at, or unsuited to, research work.

Fortunately, the world of social science research, as we have since come to know it, has proven to be anything but narrow and restrictive, and in this book we try to convey some of our excitement in discovering this. Research methodology is one of the most fiercely debated fields in the social sciences today, and, rather than a single scientific orthodoxy, it is now characterised by a proliferation of radically divergent philosophies and techniques. This has not changed in the six years since the first publication of this book, and to make sure this second edition is as contemporary and vibrant as the first, we have invited the original contributors, consisting of more than forty researchers from across the South African research spectrum, to update their chapters in the light of changes in both the social science research environment and South African (and global) society. All chapters have been updated to reflect the most recent scholarly literature, and to include fresh illustrative material and exercises. A number of chapters have also been extensively rewritten, while a number of new contributors have been invited to write new chapters or participate on the reworking of existing chapters.

One of the original aims of this book was to provide students with clear paths through the world of research, by structuring the material in terms of both the research process, and in terms of the major paradigms drawn on by researchers. In order to facilitate this process even better, we have changed the structure of the book in this second edition. Rather than the original three sections focusing on the research process, applied settings, and advanced techniques and approaches, the book is now divided into four sections. The first still provides a broad overview of the research process, while the second and third sections provide thorough overviews of qualitative and quantitative research approaches respectively. The reason for this is not to entrench the idea that qualitative and quantitative approaches cannot be used in conjunction, but to enable easier use of the book by grouping together topics that were scattered across different sections.

Not only do social science research methods now provide scope for creative work ranging from sophisticated statistical modelling to cultural critique, the work has also moved steadily away from disengaged ivory tower enquiry to applied action research. By making use of numerous real-life examples, illustrative boxes, and entire chapters devoted to particular fields of applied research, we hope to equip students not only with the conceptual and practical tools to carry out particular research procedures, but also with a sense of what it means to be a professional researcher in South Africa today. In addition, therefore, we still devote a whole fourth section to research in applied settings.

Among the many fields where social science researchers already play a leading role are public health, road safety, education, advertising, marketing, government policy formulation, political activism, and personnel selection and development. For those already involved in such fields, we trust that this book will provide a compendium of useful new methods and procedures. For those about to embark on a research career, or considering it as a career option, we hope that the book will help you take the first step towards becoming a professional researcher.

Martin Terre Blanche, Kevin Durrheim, and Desmond Painter
January 2006

Contributors to chapters

Arvin Bhana
Human Sciences Research Council

Kevin Durrheim
University of KwaZulu-Natal,
Pietermaritzburg

Gill Eagle
University of the Witwatersrand

Karima Effendi
Senior features writer, Associated
Magazines

Brandon Hamber
Associate, INCORE, University of Ulster

Graham Hayes
University of KwaZulu-Natal, Durban

Andrew M. Kaniki
National Research Foundation

Anil Kanjee
Human Sciences Research Council

Kevin Kelly
Rhodes University, CADRE

Graham Lindegger
University of KwaZulu-Natal,
Pietermaritzburg

Desmond Painter
Stellenbosch University

Yogan Pillay
Department of Health

Charles Potter
University of the Witwatersrand

Tyrone Pretorius
Monash University

Kopano Ratele
University of the Western Cape

Linda Richter
University of KwaZulu-Natal,
Pietermaritzburg

James Sey
Independent researcher, Wits School of the
Arts

Thabani Sibanda
University of the Witwatersrand

Mario Smith
Stellenbosch University

Henry Steel
Stellenbosch University

Martin Terre Blanche
University of South Africa

Colin Tredoux
University of Cape Town

Sheila Tyeku
Council of University of the Western Cape

Mary van der Riet
University of KwaZulu-Natal,
Pietermaritzburg

Douglas R. Wassenaar
University of KwaZulu-Natal,
Pietermaritzburg, and South African
Research Ethics Training Initiative (SARETI)

Contributors to special inserts

Rashied Ahmed
University of the Western Cape

Kim Baillie
University of KwaZulu-Natal,
Pietermaritzburg

Ray Basson
University of the Witwatersrand

Alex Butchart
World Health Organisation

Vaughan Dutton
University of KwaZulu-Natal,
Pietermaritzburg

Zaynab Essack
University of KwaZulu-Natal,
Pietermaritzburg

Melvyn Freeman
Department of Health

Nolwazi Gasa
Medical Research Council

Dev Griesel
University of KwaZulu-Natal,
Pietermaritzburg

Derek Hook
London School of Economics

Kevin Kelly
Rhodes University, CADRE

Lance Lachenicht
University of KwaZulu-Natal,
Pietermaritzburg

Catriona Macleod
University of Fort Hare

Mpfariseni Nembahe
University of the Witwatersrand

Mike Quayle
University of KwaZulu-Natal,
Pietermaritzburg

Robin Palmer
Rhodes University

Xolani Sithole
University of KwaZulu-Natal,
Pietermaritzburg

Wendy Smith
University of KwaZulu-Natal,
Pietermaritzburg

Lu-Anne Swart
Unisa Institute for Social and Health
Sciences & Unisa–MRC Crime, Violence and
Injury Lead Programme

René van Eeden
University of South Africa

Jacob Wambugu
University of KwaZulu-Natal,
Pietermaritzburg

Lindy Wilbraham
University of KwaZulu-Natal, Durban

Merridy Wilson
University of KwaZulu-Natal,
Pietermaritzburg

Acknowledgements

This book has in many ways been a collaborative effort, and we are grateful to everybody who contributed, both officially and unofficially. In particular we would like to thank Mike Greyling, Rene van Eeden, Vasi van Deventer, Linda Richter, and Lance Lachenicht for their suggestions and advice, Glenda Younge, Rose Meny-Gibert, Fiona Wakelin, Sarah O'Neill, and David Merrington of UCT Press for their professionalism and unstinting hard work in getting the manuscript into press, Neil Lightfoot, Gerald Williamson, and Rodney Barnett for permission to use visual material, and the many colleagues and students who over the years have inspired us with the quality of their research work. Finally, we thank our partners and families, Alex and Shea Durrheim, and Helen, Ruth, and Sarah Terre Blanche, and Claire Haggard, for their support.

Section

1

The research process

chapter

1

Histories of the present:
social science research in context

Martin Terre Blanche
University of South Africa

Kevin Durrheim
University of KwaZulu-Natal, Pietermaritzburg

We start this book about ways of producing knowledge in the social sciences with a photograph – an objective 'capturing' of an event – and with three equally convincing but widely disparate 'readings' of that event (see page 3). The readings that researchers seek to give of the social world have much in common with the three accounts: They consist of factual statements, knowledge claims, and moral judgements that refer to an empirical reality while simultaneously setting up the conditions through which that reality can be known.

Consider the Staff Reporter's account. It is based on empirical observation of events and an interview which, when written up in the factual style of a newspaper report, cannot be read as anything but true. However, after reading the other two accounts, we may begin to suspect that such truths are partial and conceal as much as they reveal. For example, why does the Staff Reporter not mention gender or race issues at all, and why are the particular ways in which the photograph frames the event not mentioned?

Just as versions of the world are continually being produced and contested in the arena of everyday life, so, too, social science research produces multiple accounts. These seek to describe the world, but they also seek to undermine competing accounts, and to achieve a multitude of other effects such as advancing the career of the author, justifying certain actions, and influencing policies. Understanding how this is done is the job of methodology.

All research accounts are based on empirical data, and this is what methodology textbooks properly focus on. However, we can only partially understand accounts of the world by referring to the facts (just as the 'Miss Lovely Legs' photograph tells only part of the story), and we must look beyond empirical evidence to the background knowledge that makes the evidence believable.

Smith-Collins would reject the reporter's account, not because she or he got the facts wrong, but because these were not interpreted in their proper context, which Smith-Collins would say is a context of patriarchy. Equally, Nkosi would probably label Smith-Collins's account naive, as she fails to note the constructed nature of the photograph itself. Returning full circle, the Staff Reporter would say that the other two accounts read too much into a straightforward event that happened at a Boksburg shopping mall in January 1974. What distinguishes these accounts is not accuracy of observation – a distortion in the way the authors saw the photograph – but the background knowledge against which they made sense of their observations. Background knowledge tells us what exists, how to understand it, and – most concretely – how to study it. In the social sciences, the various forms of background knowledge are called paradigms.

Photo: David Goldblatt

'Last night Charmaine du Preez was crowned Miss Lovely Legs Boksburg for 1974. Charmaine is a 2nd year student at Sukses Secretarial College and says her hobbies are reading, watching films and gym. Charmaine said that she was thrilled that the judges chose her out of so many deserving competitors and would try her utmost to live up to everything expected of her during her reign.' (Staff Reporter, *Boksburg Times*)

'Although one does not want to further denigrate the participants in such contests, nor ascribe personally malign motives to those who consume these images, the political implications of such "cattle parades" are inescapable: women are turned into objects in a male-dominated world. Such practices are the visible manifestations of an all-pervasive patriarchal culture.' (Patsy Smith-Collins, *International Journal of Feminist Studies*)

'In this photograph Goldblatt again explores the semiotic (and now perhaps even nostalgic?) possibilities of 1970s suburbia, so fetchingly oblivious of the larger political forces playing themselves out in the context of apartheid South Africa. The careful juxtaposition of the fore-grounded white participants and the predominantly black audience plays with the irony of white culture as the object of black consumption.' (Mandla Nkosi, *Art World*)

Paradigms in social science research

A commonsense understanding of science – and one shared by some philosophers of science – is that progress occurs through a process of falsification: incorrect theories are rejected on the basis of empirical evidence, leaving, over time, correct theories that stand for truth. In this understanding, scientific research is an objective, logical, and empirical activity, and scientists, in their research, should adhere to the logical and empirical procedures outlined by the hypothetico-deductive model of science.

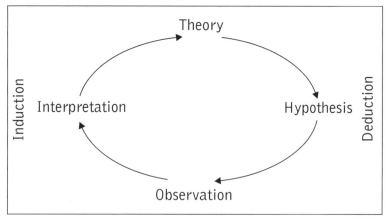

Figure 1.1   The hypothetico-deductive model

According to this model, scientists begin their research activity with a theory about the nature of the world. For example, one theory posits that the interior of South Africa was uninhabited when the first colonists arrived, and that there were no African settlements south of the Fish River at the time. Theories of this nature are general truth statements that scientists put to empirical test by deriving hypotheses about particular observations. The process by which hypotheses are derived follows principles of deductive logic; that is, drawing conclusions about particulars from knowledge of the general. Thus, a scientist would hypothesise that, if it is true that the interior of South Africa was uninhabited (a general statement), then it should also be true that there were no African settlements in the Knysna region (a particular conclusion, which must be true if the theory is true). Next, the scientist subjects the hypothesis to empirical test by exploring the Knysna region with a team of researchers and looking carefully for any evidence of pre-colonial African settlements. So the hypothesis is put to empirical test. An inductive logical phase then ensues, when the findings are interpreted and the theory adjusted to fit the newly discovered facts. Sometimes, as in the case of the theory that there were no African settlements south of the Fish River, the theory is disproved and has to be rejected.

The beauty of this model is that it is a kind of machine. Provided we go on rigorously framing hypotheses derived from theory and subjecting them to empirical test, we are assured of moving closer and closer to the truth. Over time, all false theories will be rejected.

There can be little doubt that the hypo-thetico-deductive model, or something like it, does operate in scientific practice, and that it actually works to produce successively closer approximations to a true account. For example, although researchers observed a sudden rise in the incidence of lung cancer in the early twentieth century, they were uncertain about its cause. In 1927, Kennaway and Cook discovered carcinogenic compounds in coal tar, and speculation about the cause of cancer ranged from the effects of tar in roads to smoking and other lifestyle changes that occurred in the twentieth century. Gradually, research evidence accumulated to show that smoking caused cancer. In 1938, Dr. Raymond Pearl of Johns Hopkins University reported that smokers do not live as long as non-smokers. By 1964, in the light of over 7 000 research studies, the US Surgeon General released a report noting that the average smoker was about 10 times more likely to get lung cancer than the average non-smoker, and attributed this to carcinogens in tobacco smoke, including

Health warnings on cigarette packs

cadmium, DDT, and arsenic. This research informed political activism, which led to anti-smoking policy in countries around the world. Today, despite protestations by tobacco companies and misleading advertising about low-tar cigarettes, we know that smoking causes cancer.

Although the hypothetico-deductive approach has been the dominant model of science during the twentieth century, it is now widely accepted that there is more to social science than this. The philosopher of science Thomas Kuhn (1962) was the first to argue that progress through falsification only operates in periods of 'normal science', when the kinds of question that can be asked and the proper ways of answering them are generally accepted. In Kuhn's view, such periods are followed by periods of 'paradigm conflict', when different systems of understanding (paradigms) compete for ascendancy in the scientific community. Because paradigms differ in terms of the questions they consider legitimate and the scientific methods they endorse, there is no way of empirically adjudicating between them – they are said to be 'incommensurate', meaning that, much like the three reports on the Miss Lovely Legs competition, they simply talk past one another.

'In large degree the sciences have been enchanted by the myth that the assiduous application of rigorous method will yield sound fact – as if empirical methodology were some form of meat grinder from which truth could be turned out like so many sausages.'
(Gergen, 1985, p. 273)

In the long run, paradigms come to be discredited and supplanted by new ones (Kuhn called this a 'paradigm shift') not because they have been shown to be false, but because they no longer speak to the concerns of practising scientists.

The danger of subscribing to the hypothetico-deductive method as a complete explanation of the way in which science works is that it disguises the 'perspectival' nature of the knowledge it produces. Just as each of the perspectives on the 'Miss Lovely Legs' photograph could be further developed through a process of rigorous proof and refutation but could never be shown to be more true than any of the others, so too are the scientific truths produced through the hypothetico-deductive model perspectival and bound to a particular paradigm.

Pretending that social science research operates from within a single paradigm leads to an exclusive focus on technical issues such as accurate measurement and proper research design with no concern for the wider context within which knowledge is produced. Kurt Danziger (1986) labelled this kind of position 'methodolatory', and one can see traces of this in many methodology textbooks in the social sciences.

In this book, we take the view that the hypothetico-deductive model, and the various technologies of knowledge production that flow from it, are useful tools for the social science researcher, and that it is worth the effort to learn how to use them properly. However, to be more than mere technicians, social science researchers also need to have a good grasp of the wider social and political forces that continually produce new knowledge of all kinds. In particular, they need to understand the nature of the major paradigms that influence social science practice today.

Paradigms are all-encompassing systems of interrelated practice and thinking that define for researchers the nature of their enquiry along three dimensions: ontology, epistemology, and methodology. **Ontology** specifies the nature of reality that is to be studied, and what can be known about it. **Epistemology** specifies the nature of the relationship between the researcher (knower) and what can be known. **Methodology** specifies how researchers may go about practically studying whatever they believe can be known.

'What differentiated these various schools [of scientists supporting different theories of the same phenomena] was not one or another failure of method – they were all "scientific" – but what we shall come to call incommensurable ways of seeing the world and practicing science in it. Observation and experience ... cannot alone determine a particular body of such belief.' (Kuhn, 1962, p. 4)

Table 1.1 Positivist, interpretive, and constructionist paradigms

	Ontology	Epistemology	Methodology
Positivist	• Stable external reality • Law-like	• Objective • Detached observer	• Experimental • Quantitative • Hypothesis testing
Interpretive	• Internal reality of subjective experience	• Empathetic • Observer subjectivity	• Interactional • Interpretation • Qualitative
Constructionist	• Socially constructed reality • Discourse • Power	• Suspicious • Political • Observer constructing versions	• Deconstruction • Textual analysis • Discourse analysis

The three dimensions of paradigms shown in table 1.1 constrain one another.

If a researcher believes that what is to be studied consists of a stable and unchanging external reality (e.g., economic laws, cognitive mechanisms, the law of gravity), then she or he can adopt an objective and detached epistemological stance towards that reality, and can employ a methodology that relies on control and manipulation of reality. The aim of such research would be to provide an accurate description of the laws and mechanisms that operate in social life. You may recognise this as a positivist approach.

If, on the other hand, the researcher believes that the reality to be studied consists of people's subjective experiences of the external world, she or he may adopt an intersubjective or interactional epistemological stance toward that reality and use methodologies, such as interviewing or participant observation, that rely on a subjective relationship between researcher and subject. This is characteristic of the interpretive approach, which aims to explain the subjective reasons and meanings that lie behind social action.

Finally, if the researcher believes that reality consists of a fluid and variable set of social constructions, he or she may adopt a suspicious and politicised epistemological stance, and employ methodologies that allow the researcher to deconstruct versions of reality. This is characteristic of constructionist research, which aims to show how versions of the social world are produced in discourse, and to demonstrate how these constructions of reality make certain actions possible and others unthinkable.

In contrast to the deductive emphasis of positivist research, interpretive and constructionist research typically prefers an inductive approach (see figure 1.2). Here, the researcher starts with a set of vague speculations about a research question and tries to make sense of the phenomenon by observing a set of particular instances. Say, for example, you were interested in studying the thoughts going through the minds of clinically depressed people. Rather than starting out with a firm theory of this phenomenon (as in the hypothetico-deductive model, see figure 1.1), it would be better to conduct a series of interviews with a clinically depressed sample. After an initial set of interviews have been analysed, you will start to see common themes and patterns emerging. Now, armed with this emerging theory and understanding, you could conduct a second set of more focused interviews and refine your understanding.

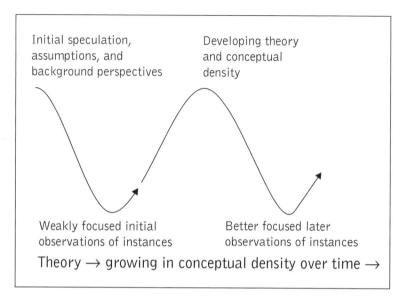

Figure 1.2 Inductive research proceeds through iterations

We can illustrate these different paradigms by considering research about differences among 'race' groups in South Africa. Working in the 1950s, Danziger (1963) asked young people to write essays about what the future meant for them. He interpreted the responses to indicate that black people's hopes and aspirations for the future were rooted in collective action because apartheid laws made it very difficult to fulfil many personal goals (e.g., tertiary education). This was broadly interpretive research, as Danziger was interested in the subjective worlds of his research participants – their meanings, hopes, and aspirations – and tried to understand this by empathetically interpreting the meaning of what they said. He developed his understanding inductively, trying to make sense of the autobiographical stories the youth wrote.

Contrast this with the numerous studies that have measured the attitudes that various South African 'race' groups have toward each other. In reviewing this literature, Foster and Nel (1991) conclude that 'blacks, strictly speaking, do not evidence a "racist" attitudinal pattern at all, in contrast to whites who do' (p. 154). These studies were positivist in the sense that, using objective measures, they aimed to establish the existence of definite social facts (i.e. patterns of intergroup attitudes) and did so in a distanced and quantitative manner. Much of this research adopted a deductive, theory-driven approach, as researchers entered the field to collect data 'armed' with theories and measures of what constituted racism.

Finally, consider Durrheim and Dixon's (2001) analysis of newspaper articles that commented on racial segregation on South African beaches. Their research shows how seemingly politically neutral concepts – for example, good manners – are used to construct beaches as the exclusive preserve of white families. This was a constructionist study

Paradigms help to determine the questions researchers ask about constructs such as 'race', and how they go about answering them.

to the extent that the researchers described a socially constructed reality (different 'race groups', each with different kinds of 'manners') through a critical analysis of texts, and showed how these constructions made particular sets of practices (e.g., racial segregation) possible in post-apartheid South Africa.

The above are examples of interpretive research conducted in the 1950s, positivist research in the 1960s to 1980s, and constructionist research in the 1990s. It is not the case, however, that South African social scientists first practised interpretive research, that this paradigm was later supplanted by positivist research, or that constructionist research is now the reigning paradigm. Contrary to Kuhn's initial ideas about paradigms (which were based on his studies of the natural sciences), paradigms in the social sciences often coexist. To the extent that there has been an historical progression, most social scientists in the twentieth century initially operated within a positivist paradigm, with interpretive research gradually becoming more prominent since the 1960s and constructionism being the most recent development. Today, positivist ideas still inform most social science research projects.

Have a look at the three faces representing different paradigms and artistic styles. Which face most resembles the kind of researcher you would like to be?

Positivism/realism

Interpretive research/ impressionism

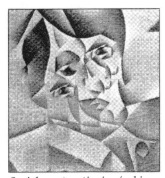

Social constructionism/cubism

Because different paradigms exist simultaneously, it is possible for the same researchers to draw on more than one paradigm, depending on the kind of work they are doing. Nevertheless, many researchers conduct most of their research within a single paradigm, in the same way that artists typically prefer a certain style. If one were to compare the three paradigms to artistic styles, positivism would resemble realism, interpretive research would be like impressionism, and social constructionism would be the equivalent of cubism. Can you see why? Like different styles of art, each paradigm has a different look and feel, and researchers gravitate to one or the other paradigm because it fits in with the sorts of things they can identify with, not because one is better than the others. Thus positivism may suit those who are after objective facts, interpretive research may suit those who care about the meanings people attach to such facts, and social constructionism may suit those who wonder how the social world gets constructed in the first place as one which contains 'facts'.

The changing face of research

The word 'research' conjures up images of white-coated scientists working in a laboratory, but of course this is no longer what most social science research is about. As we have seen, other paradigms, other 'faces', are now available to the social science researcher. Even the positivist paradigm, which is traditionally associated with stereotypical images of science, has evolved to allow for sophisticated forms of applied nonexperimental work.

Not only is research no longer confined to the laboratory, but it is also increasingly breaking through other boundaries, such as those between the traditional academic disciplines (sociology, psychology, anthropology, and so on), as well as the boundaries between academic and popular knowledge. In particular, two kinds of border are currently in the process of being redrawn by social science researchers: those between pure and applied research, and between scientific and non-scientific knowledge. Rather than research as a form of aloof reflection, we are now increasingly dealing with research as a form of **action**; and rather than scientific knowledge being something apart from and above other forms of knowing, we now have researchers having to join in the rough-and-tumble of the **politics of knowledge**.

Research in action

The twentieth century saw the rise of the global market economy, and with this has come increasing pressures on universities to move away from the traditional liberal arts education (emphasising the languages and humanities) toward providing an applied and technical education in the sciences, commerce, and medicine. Across the world, governments have reduced subsidies for the social sciences and humanities, and, as a consequence, universities have been forced to scale down courses in many of the less obviously 'useful' subjects.

The teaching of social science research at universities plays an interesting role in this regard. Although research training does not focus directly on preparation for an institutionally defined occupation (e.g., a nurse, lawyer, doctor, or psychologist), it does equip students with a range of applied skills that can lead to a career as a professional researcher. As is described in section 4 of this book, social science researchers now play key roles in business, medical, and community contexts, where their practical and theoretical skills are highly valued. Among other activities, researchers are now involved in evaluating social programmes, community activism, policy development, clinical and public health research, media and market research, and social and psychological assessment. In each of these contexts, researchers engage in a large variety of activities, ranging from traditional quantitative data gathering and analysis to facilitating group processes and becoming involved in political activism. Thus, to a large extent, social science research has managed to keep alive the liberal arts ideal of a generalist education while also responding to demands that universities 'deliver' students with specific marketable skills.

Research is about creating new social realities, not just about studying old ones.

The evolution of universities from repositories of knowledge and centres for debate to 'factories' for the production of skilled professionals should not, however, be seen exclusively as a (reluctant) submission to market forces. The transformation of universities has also occurred in the context of a profound shift in the way that the relationship between knowledge and action is theorised. Where knowledge and action were previously seen as two quite separate domains, it is now accepted that by investigating social phenomena we also simultaneously change the nature of those phenomena, so that research becomes a creative activity as much as a form of objective enquiry.

When we start asking questions about phenomena like domestic violence, unemployment or sexual 'deviance' and proceed to answer them from within one paradigm or another, we have already intervened simply by flagging them as social facts worthy of study and as susceptible to being better understood through a particular kind of enquiry. By collecting research material from research participants, we intervene further, as the participants are bound to pick up particular ways of looking at the phenomenon from us, even as we seek to collect data from them. Finally, publication of our research findings is an explicit intervention, as it changes not only the way a phenomenon is understood but also the way in which the social practices that hold the phenomenon in place will be acted upon in future.

Consider, for example, maps of the world, such as the two reproduced here. Like much social science research, maps aim to represent the world. In representing the world, however, they also achieve a number of other ends. Representations in social science and cartography are forms of action, and representational practice is thus also a form of intervention.

The first map is a traditional world map, used for many centuries, and derived by the mechanical application of entirely unbiased and objective cartographic procedures. However, it introduces certain distortions, such as showing the southern continents as far too small

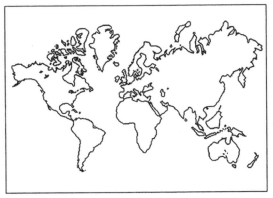
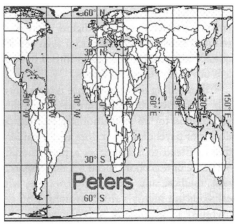

Two representations of the world

relative to the northern continents. For example, North America appears to be considerably larger than Africa, whereas in fact it is smaller – 19 million square kilometres as against Africa's 30 million square kilometres. The second map is (in some ways) a more accurate representation. Devised by the German historian Arno Peters, it is also based on the objective application of cartographic procedures, but is more accurate in its depiction of the relative sizes of the continents, showing Africa as being considerably larger than North America.

However, since a two-dimensional representation can never do justice to a three-dimensional object, the Peters projection has to be less accurate in other respects, for example in reflecting the relative distance between different points on the earth. Both maps show Europe at the top and Africa at the bottom, whereas a globe travelling through space of course does not have a top or a bottom. These various distortions, although perhaps not intentional, have encouraged people to accord undue importance to the northern colonial powers relative to the south.

The realisation that knowledge making is in itself a form of intervention has led to an increasing emphasis on planning and executing research in such a way as to make explicit provision for the way in which the research is to fit into its real-world context, and you will see traces of this approach throughout this book. As you read through the chapters, note how research is often designed and implemented in close cooperation with organisations and communities, and how much thought is given to the manner in which the results will be publicised and used once the project has been completed. When research stops being a purely academic pursuit and becomes a form of action, it finds itself in the arena of the political, and has to become attuned to political considerations as much as to questions of technical excellence.

The politics of knowledge

Scientific research has long been portrayed as occurring on a different plane from that of politics, and it is true that the quality of research can be compromised when political interference occurs. This happened, for example, to the Human Sciences Research Council (HSRC), which, in the view of some, was for many decades manipulated by the apartheid government to conduct research supportive of its policies (see Cloete, Muller, & Orkin, 1986). Less easy to spot are the kinds of politics operating *within* scientific research, even when it tries to keep itself apart from politics.

Recall the hypothetico-deductive model presented earlier, which operates like a kind of knowledge-making machine by constantly refining theoretical understanding through a process of empirical testing. We have said that this model works well within a particular paradigm, but that it is rarely useful in adjudicating between different paradigms. Another weakness of the model is that it describes what happens within the 'context of justification' but not the 'context of discovery'.

Talking about research from within the context of justification is to tell only half the story.

The **context of justification** refers to the arena of objective scientific observations and deductions, such as we find in the course of scientific work in the field or the experimental laboratory. Some histories of science, most methodology textbooks, and most literature reviews restrict themselves to tracing the logical succession of hypotheses and evidence that occurs in this context. They tell a history of ways in which incorrect hypotheses were or could have been eliminated with well-designed scientific method.

The context of justification stipulates methods for the production of 'solid evidence' on which to base our knowledge.

The **context of discovery**, by contrast, is the social and subjective world of scientists as human beings, with particular histories, experiences, values, and beliefs. The rules of scientific objectivity have little value here – what counts are researchers' private convictions about what kinds of question are worthy of being asked, and their social ties to friends, social groups, political agendas, and fellow researchers. Danziger describes it as follows:

> What unites individual contributors is not simply their common possession of the same logical faculties and their common confrontation with the same external nature. Their social bonds are a lot more complex than that. They are related by ties of loyalty, power and conflict ... The fundamental issue in research is not whether the lone investigator can verify his hypotheses in the privacy of his laboratory but whether he can establish his contribution as part of the canon of scientific knowledge in his field. In other words, the issue is one of consensus, and consensus is not entirely a matter of logic. (Danziger, 1990, p. 3)

Spotting when political interference occurs in the context of justification is relatively easy, a notorious example from the social sciences being Cyril Burt's fraudulent research on the genetic basis of intelligence (see Fletcher, 1990). However, it is far less easy to know when unwarranted interference has occurred in the context of discovery, as this context is constituted by the subjective, interpersonal, and political interactions among people. For example, the research done at the National Institute for Personnel Research (NIPR) during the apartheid years was mostly technically sound within the context of justification (i.e., data were properly collected, analysed, and interpreted), but, with hindsight, it is easy to see that researchers were strongly influenced by the political context of the time (the context of discovery) to ask only certain kinds of question (Terre Blanche & Seedat, 2001). For example, they often asked 'How can black workers be assigned to different job categories to make industrial companies more efficient?', but seldom asked 'How can companies be transformed so as to employ more black managers?'

It is quite possible that today's social science researchers will similarly be judged as having been coopted into current political agendas, such as those of racial reconciliation and national reconstruction. It may in fact be impossible for researchers not to participate in the political agendas of the day – by supporting, opposing, or even trying to ignore them. While it would therefore be unreasonable to expect that researchers should operate outside the realm of politics, one can justifiably expect them to be able to give an account of the way that their work relates to larger political forces. Appealing to the hypothetico-deductive model as a description of what one does as a researcher is not enough – it is to pretend that one can be immune to political influences. Being able to account for one's work in terms of broad research paradigms of the sort outlined earlier is better, as it marks the beginning of critical reflection on the unspoken assumptions by which one operates as a researcher.

Class, race, and gender have a powerful impact on the way in which research is conducted.

In addition, it is important to become aware of the way in which social science research comes from an intellectual tradition that is predominantly white, male, and instrumental – that is, it is focused on achieving mastery and control over the social world, in the same way that natural scientists have laboured to master the worlds of physics and biology. However critical one may be of this, by becoming part of this research tradition it is almost inevitable that one's work will start to reflect certain stereotypically Western ways of viewing people from the 'developed' world differently from people in 'developing' and 'underdeveloped' countries, and men differently from women. Throughout this book, we have sought to remain alert to such issues, and have also included chapters dealing explicitly with issues of class, race, and gender in research.

Finally, a consciously reflective stance towards one's own research should include an awareness of ways in which the practice of academic knowledge making has been transformed in the postmodern era. We have already spoken about the ways in which the university has become subservient to the needs of the market economy, and to this can be added the transformation of that economy from agriculture and manufacturing to information production. Because so many more sectors of society are now involved in the 'information business', there has been a flattening of knowledge hierarchies so that academic knowledge is no longer automatically privileged over the kinds of knowledge produced by grassroots organisations, the mass media, 'alternative' therapists, cults, consultants, politicians, religious leaders, and cultural commentators of all sorts.

We might decry the inaccuracy of the information that sometimes comes from such sources (including from some academic researchers), and be grateful that the hypothetico-deductive model provides us with the machinery for exposing some of the more extreme and harmful falsehoods. However, researchers would do well to accept that the quest is no longer only for truth, which is in any case always temporary and perspectival, but also for 'performativity'. The purpose behind research is not only 'How can we be more accurate in our findings?', but also 'How can we produce findings that have an impact on the social ecology of knowledge?' To do this, we need concrete applied skills – and much of this book is concerned with imparting such skills – but we must also be able to stand at a critical distance from those skills and what they enable us to achieve (and not achieve). We have therefore included reflection on such issues throughout the book, together with a chapter that deals specifically with research and the politics of postmodern knowledge production.

Box 1.1

The truth is out there

(Vaughan Dutton, University of KwaZulu-Natal)

Research conducted by SAMP (South African Migration Project) shows that some things everybody perceives to be true are actually false. These myths and realities about cross-border migration show the power of scientific research (adapted from McDonald et al., 1998).

Myth 1. Every poor and desperate person on the African continent wants to get into South Africa. Reality: By and large, people from the region prefer their home country to South Africa. This preference was expressed in terms of raising a family, and access to basic resources like land, water, and housing.

Myth 2. People are jumping the borders in their millions, using whatever means necessary to get into South Africa. Reality: Movement across the South African border is not nearly as corrupt or chaotic as one might expect from press coverage. Well over 90% of the people interviewed crossed the border at formal immigration posts using formal modes of transportation.

Myth 3. Cross-border immigration has largely negative implications for the source country. Reality: Although research has identified negative effects of migration, most immigrants considered it to have had a positive effect on them personally, on their family, on their community, and on their home country.

Myth 4. Governments and people in the region expect South Africa to throw open its doors to whoever wants to enter. Reality: Most immigrants question the legitimacy of borders that were created during the colonial era, but nevertheless feel that the South African government should be able to restrict the number of (im)migrants allowed into the country and that it should also have the right to deport people in a humane manner.

Myth 5. Conditions in the region will only get worse and, unless South Africa takes a tougher stand on immigration policy, the country will continue to be inundated with 'illegal aliens'. Reality: The people most likely to immigrate are economically active single young men. They are likely to possess documents permitting migration, to have some education, to have family in South Africa, and to have been in South Africa before. These are not the kinds of circumstance that are associated with people leaving their homes in droves to go to South Africa.

Finding your way through this book

This book has been written with a number of aims in mind, conscious of the manner in which the technical, political, and applied aspects of research overlay one another. At one level, these aims arise through reflections on knowledge production, some of which have been considered above. At a more material level, the aims of this book reflect the fact that the authors are located in the African continent, and more specifically in a country with wide racial, class, and gender divisions. The kind of politics and the types of application and issue to which technical expertise is brought to bear by the authors of the various chapters all speak to the contemporary concerns of developing countries. We believe that this makes the book a good deal more vibrant and exciting to read and study than the standard American 'blockbuster' text.

The book consists of four sections. Section 1 introduces the reader to a range of important decisions that precede and follow the actual business of data collection and analysis. These are decisions about formulating a research question, doing an information search, designing a study, considering the study's ethical dimensions, writing a research proposal, and deciding where and how publication of the study's results will be done. Section 2 offers a closer look at research in a positivist mode. It follows the process of quantification from decisions about sampling and measurement to discussions of various aspects of quantitative research design, and it provides overviews of descriptive, inferential, and multivariate statistical techniques. Section 3 focuses on research in a qualitative mode, looking at both interpretive and constructionist approaches. The section starts with a general overview of the similarities and differences between these two paradigms, before progressing through the stages of qualitative research design and data collection, and discussing both general and paradigm-specific techniques of data analysis.

Whereas sections 1 to 3 introduce the research process in general terms, section 4 shows how the research process unfolds in a variety of actual research settings in South Africa, including clinical, community, and policy settings. This section also introduces research orientations that are more explicitly informed by political considerations, such as feminist, Marxist, and postcolonial approaches. The chapters have been written by scholars and active researchers who have made liberal use of local examples to illustrate the material they cover, as well as to alert the reader to the debates, issues, and developments taking place in their areas of practice.

Exercises

1. Like all publications, this textbook operates both in the context of justification and in the context of discovery. Consider what the social forces are that bind together the authors of this book. What kinds of author do you think may have been excluded from the

book and why? Which universities are likely to prescribe the book, and what are the political and academic consequences of this?

2. This book frames research methodology within the context of applied research practice in South Africa. Can you think of other ways in which the book could have been framed and what the consequence of such framings would have been? (Hint: Scan one or two American methodology textbooks in your library and see how they differ from this one). Scan the daily and weekly newspapers. What natural or social research is reported? How do you think media reporting affects the scientific credibility of the ideas or raises matters of social values?

3. What kinds of problem do people in your community face, and how do you think research may help them? What kind of research do you think needs to be done? What would you do with the research findings?

Key readings

Bitterkomix
This series of comic books (new editions are available from most leading bookstores; back orders and an English compilation available from Bitterkomix Pulp, PO Box 564, Stellenbosch 7599, South Africa) captures the dark underbelly of white South African culture with more devastating accuracy than any social science research project is ever likely to do.

Feyerabend, P. K. (1988). *Against method*. (Revised edition). London: Verso. This is a classic and controversial critique of the scientific method. On the basis of a detailed investigation of 'scientific progress' (especially in the natural sciences), Feyerabend develops a counter-intuitive argument that science limits rather than fosters knowledge production.

Neuman, W. L. (2005). *Social research methods: Qualitative and quantitative approaches*. (6th edition). Boston, Massachusetts: Allyn & Bacon. Research methodology textbooks are big business in the United States, and there are very many products on offer, all impressively packaged but most simply recirculating the same tired old ideas and techniques. Neuman's text stands out from this crowd because it takes theoretical issues seriously and covers both quantitative and qualitative techniques critically and in some depth.

2

Doing an information search

Andrew M. Kaniki

National Research Foundation

A research project does not exist in isolation, but must build upon what has been done previously. Therefore, before embarking on a project, a researcher should review previous work in the field. Such a review commonly encompasses recently published research, but could also include a review of historical and oral material.

A literature review, used in the widest sense of the word, involves the identification and analysis of information resources and/or literature related to one's research project. This process includes identifying potentially relevant sources, an initial assessment of these sources, thorough analysis of selected sources, and the construction of an account that integrates and explains relevant sources. Research proposals (see chapter 5) and research reports (see chapter 6) both rely heavily on such a literature review.

Information searching has its own rules, demands specific skills of the researcher, and must be done systematically. It involves developing a search strategy in which specific criteria are used to identify information sources and to access and select relevant literature. The more systematic the search process, the greater the chance of finding information relevant to the research. In this chapter we will discuss the purposes of doing a literature review, how to develop and execute an information search strategy, and how to develop your own literature database.

In this chapter, we use the term literature broadly to refer to all kinds of information, including books, journals, electronic materials, and oral information.

Purposes of a literature review

A literature or information review puts your research project into context by showing how it fits into a particular field. A number of more specific purposes of a literature review can be identified.

Identifying knowledge gaps and developing a research problem

In the next chapter, we discuss the importance and role of a carefully formulated **research problem**. Without an identified research problem that is important enough to warrant investing a researcher's resources, there would be no need to conduct research. Furthermore, to be practical, the identified research problem has to be clearly stated with explicit parameters.

While a research problem may be conceived from personal observations and experiences, most researchable problems are identified through reading or examining previously published historical, theoretical, and empirical work.

A literature search is used at two levels to identify a research problem. First, a wide reading or examination of literature helps a researcher identify the general problem area. Often, the research problem identified at this level is general and vague. One of the most common

Research problems can be derived from personal experience, from a reading of the literature, or from a survey of issues considered important by communities or organisations.

Try to find a small, specific, and concrete research problem.

mistakes made by novice researchers is to proceed with the rest of the research process (as described in the rest of this book) immediately after establishing the general (but vague!) research problem. The result is that the researcher discovers when it is too late that the problem is too large to handle, too small to make a worthwhile contribution to the field, or already over-researched by others.

To avoid these difficulties, a research problem needs to be sharpened, crystallised, and clearly stated by the researcher. This is achieved at the second level of literature review, which involves further reading and assessment of the literature. Here, the researcher examines the literature closely with the aim of understanding a research problem better and setting parameters on a research question.

Consider a researcher who is interested in 'services for the mentally ill in South Africa'. Over the years, she or he may have observed that mentally ill patients appear to receive inferior care in comparison to persons suffering from other ailments. For the researcher to develop a focused research problem out of this general area of concern, it would be necessary to consult various information sources. An information search would help to refine the research problem by bringing the researcher up to date on the current state of mental health service in South Africa, the amount of information available on the topic, gaps in the literature, and related issues of concern.

Identifying a theoretical framework

Refining a research problem involves identifying a theoretical framework upon which to base the research. As Bless and Higson-Smith have argued, 'theory serves as an orientation for gathering facts since it specifies the types of facts to be systematically observed' (1995, p. 23). This is so because the elements or variables of a theory are logically interrelated, and, if relevant theory exists, hypotheses or research questions can be deduced based upon particular relationships between these elements.

Identifying issues and variables related to the research topic

Reading the literature helps the researcher to focus on important issues and variables that have a bearing on the research question. For example, the researcher interested in services for the mentally ill may find that there are many aspects to this problem, and that one aspect particularly interests her, namely how mental health personnel seek out and make use of information.

From discussions with people involved in mental health work and from reading the literature, the researcher may also start to think that a specialised information system for mental health personnel would enhance the quality of care. To develop such a system, however, the researcher needs to have a better understanding of the information-seeking behaviour of mental health personnel, and also an understanding of the 'use of information sources and information itself among mental health personnel'.

Some of the specific variables or issues she might identify from her literature search would include:

- information sources and channels used,
- information (provision) timeliness,
- information accuracy and appropriateness, and
- information accessibility and availability.

A literature review involves more than merely citing as many sources as possible. It should highlight pertinent literature and contribute to the field by providing a novel and focused reading of the literature. A common mistake made by student researchers is to try to include every source they come across in an effort to impress the reader of a research proposal or report. In addition to providing a focused reading of an area, a literature review must be well structured and systematically presented. Rather than jumping from one issue to the other, each topic should be carefully developed and all topics that are considered in the review should be arranged into a structured argument.

A literature review should be organised around a particular theme, and is written from the perspective or standpoint of the reviewer.

Box 2.1

Types of literature review

There are a number of 'standard' types of literature review, each of which gives a particular reading of a body of literature. A literature review could include a focus on one or more of the following:

- **Historical reviews** – these consider the chronological development of the literature, and try to break the literature down into phases or stages of development.
- **Thematic reviews** – these are structured around different themes or perspectives in the literature, and often focus on debates between different 'schools'.
- **Theoretical reviews** – these trace theoretical developments in a particular area, often showing how each theory is supported by empirical evidence.
- **Empirical reviews** – these attempt to summarise the empirical findings, often focusing on different methodologies used.

Identifying conceptual and operational definitions

An important aspect of the research process is to provide clear and unambiguous definitions of key concepts. A review of the literature provides a researcher with sources for 'generating' or picking up definitions of key concepts that need to be operationalised in the study. In the case of the mental health researcher, it would be necessary to clearly define concepts and parameters such as 'information-seeking behaviour', 'information use', and 'mental health personnel'. From a literature search the researcher may, for example, discover that mental health personnel are a far more diverse group than thought at first, and include in a definition allied mental health personnel, clinical psychologists, community mental health personnel, mental health care teams, mental health clergy, mental health counsellors, minority mental health personnel, psychiatric nurses, psychiatrists, psychotherapists, and student volunteers in mental health. If there are widely accepted definitions of concepts in the literature, the researcher would usually be well advised to use these definitions rather than generate her own definitions. After all, one of the purposes of standardising definitions of concepts or variables in a field is to ensure communication and understanding among one another within a knowledge field.

Identifying methodologies

A review of related literature may reveal a number of diverse methodologies that have been employed by others to study similar problems. Obviously, the more a method has been tested and adjusted for use in studying a specific problem, the more reliable it will be. However, the researcher should also be alert to new and interesting methods that may appear in the literature.

Don't read journal articles just for their findings; also focus on the methods used.

Developing and executing a literature search strategy

A literature review involves identifying relevant literature or sources of relevant information (bibliographic access), physically accessing the most relevant literature (document delivery), reading and analysing these works, and writing up the literature review. Some fields of research in the social sciences have generated a great deal of literature, while others have very little. Whatever the amount of literature in your field, a literature search should be well-planned and systematically executed. A literature search involves developing a search strategy, identifying information sources, and using these sources to retrieve relevant information.

Refining key concepts

Developing a search strategy involves two tasks: (1) identify key concepts that describe and set the parameters of the research topic, and (2) identify relevant information sources to search. As a first step, a researcher could generate an intersection set of highly relevant literature by searching for literature that includes all aspects, concepts, or variables he or she has identified. The more refined the research topic, the more refined the search strategy is likely to be; and the more refined the search strategy, the more efficient the search for literature.

An intersection set is a collection of information sources (e.g. journal articles) that each refer to all the key concepts in which a researcher is interested.

After the mental health researcher we have been considering has identified key concepts, an intersection set of literature can be developed by identifying literature that discusses all of the following, for instance: (1) information-seeking behaviour, (2) information use,

(3) mental health personnel, and (4) South Africa. Books, articles, or other sources of information that fall within this intersection set would constitute the **core literature** relevant to the researcher's topic. Although the researcher may also want to look at articles dealing with only one of the four concepts, it is often a good idea to start by looking at the core literature, as this contains work most similar to one's own.

You may well find that your initial search for core literature yields nothing, or only one or two sources, in which case you will have to start refining the search, for example, by looking for literature dealing with some, but not all, of your key concepts. For instance, you may find that a specific search for 'mental health personnel' may yield little or no hits. You may therefore need to search under a more general concept of 'mental health'. Another technique is to identify all possible synonyms or near synonyms of your preliminary key concepts, together with semantically related terms. Use your knowledge of the subject to generate synonyms, or refer to **controlled vocabulary** lists, such as a subject thesaurus, for example the *Thesaurus of psychological index terms* (Walker, 1997), or lists of subject headings (e.g., *the Library of Congress subject headings*). The services of an information professional, such as a librarian, are useful here, as they have knowledge of a wide range of controlled vocabulary lists.

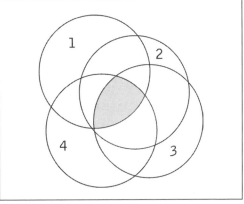

Figure 2.1   The intersection set (shaded area), containing the core literature on information use among mental health workers

It's not what you know, but who you know

Box 2.2

Developing a sophisticated and well-defined search strategy can be much enhanced by making use of the assistance of professional information workers, such as librarians. Some South African university libraries are well-staffed with competent personnel who are available full time to assist students with literature searches, but even if your university library is understaffed it is still a good idea to try to establish a professional relationship with some of them. Almost invariably, they can point you to literature you would never have thought of on your own. However, it is important that you should be able to develop a basic search strategy yourself, because you know best what you want to study.

If the mental health researcher in our example approached a librarian, the latter could help to look up synonyms for keywords in the *Library of Congress subject headings* (2003). Synonyms, near-synonyms, and semantically related terms for 'mental health personnel' include allied mental health personnel, clinical psychologists, community mental health personnel, mental health care teams, mental health clergy, mental health counsellors, minority mental health personnel, psychiatric nurses, psychiatric nursing, psychiatrists, psychotherapists, and student volunteers in mental health. Searching for these terms in addition to 'mental health workers' greatly increases the researcher's chances of finding relevant literature.

Box 2.3

Browsing

Sometimes the most useful literature is found not through a carefully planned and executed search, but simply by browsing around the shelves in your library. If you have found a reference to a particular book and go to collect it from the library shelf, take some time to look at other books nearby. Several of them may be relevant to your research project. If you have noticed that many of the most useful articles for your project come from a particular journal, browse through back copies of that journal. It does not take long to scan the index pages of five or even ten years' worth of most academic journals.

Executing the search

In addition to generating relevant concepts and identifying keywords, a researcher needs to know where to search for sources of information most likely to yield literature about the topic at hand. The first place to go is usually a library catalogue, which lists all the books, journals, and other materials that the library has in its collection. Although some libraries still use card catalogues, most South African university libraries use computerised catalogues such as the Online Public Access Catalogues (OPACS).

Box 2.4

Catalogues – big and small

Are you frustrated with the limited number of books and journals kept in your university library? Fortunately, South African libraries are increasingly starting to work together to offer a better service to students and academics. If your university has a small library, you could find books in a larger library's catalogue and then ask your library to get the books for you through an interlibrary loan.

Even if you cannot actually get hold of the books, it could be useful to know what is available elsewhere. Many library catalogues can be accessed via the internet, for example, the Unisa library (www.unisa.ac.za) or the Library of Congress in the USA (www.loc.gov). Another catalogue that is worth searching via the internet belongs not to a library, but to the world's largest bookshop – Amazon.com (www.amazon.com). Local bookshops such as kalahari.net (www.kalahari.net) are also worth searching, as is Google Book Search (books.google.com), which allows full text searches of a large and growing collection of books.

There are several ways to search for relevant information in a library catalogue. You can search by author if you know who wrote the particular book you are looking for. It is also useful to search by subject, using the concepts and keywords developed in the search-strategy stage to identify relevant information. A manual catalogue requires you to look up each concept separately, but a computerised catalogue allows you to enter all search terms at once, indicating how they are related by using boolean logic, which simply entails using words like 'and' and 'or' to link the keywords to search for (see box 2.5). If you are interested in feminist work on violence in South Africa, for example, you might search for books that contain information on feminism AND violence AND South Africa.

Box 2.5

Boolean searches

Novice researchers often use computer catalogues and indexes to search for one keyword at a time. By using several keywords together and linking them with simple boolean operators such as AND, OR, and NOT, you can increase the power and efficiency of a search enormously.

Function	What it means	Example
AND	All terms must be present	Mental health personnel AND information services
OR	Any of the terms can be present	Mental health personnel OR clinical psychologists OR psychiatric nurses OR psychotherapists
NOT	The terms must not be present	Mental health personnel NOT student volunteers
Adjacency	Terms must be next to each other	'South Africa'
( )	Lets you group functions	(Mental health personnel OR clinical psychologists) AND (information services OR mental health libraries)

These are the most frequently used boolean operators, but most computer catalogues also allow for others that make even more sophisticated searches possible. Note that different systems treat boolean operators differently, so be sure to check the system's help file. For example, some systems (including the Google search engine) interpret adjacency as meaning the same as AND. In such cases, if you want to search for references where certain terms occur next to each other, you usually have to put the words in double quotes, e.g., "South Africa".

Box 2.6

Bibliographic sources

Behrens (1994, pp. 115–117) lists the following key bibliographic and abstracting sources for the human and social sciences. Some of these sources exist in both printed and electronic form:

- Business and economics: ABI/INFORM, Wilson business abstracts, Economic literature index, *Journal of Economic Literature*.
- Communications: Communication abstracts.
- Criminology: Criminal justice abstracts, Criminal penology and police science abstracts.
- Education: Australian education index, British education index, Review index in education, ERIC, Education index, Canadian education index.
- Geography: Geo abstracts.
- History: Historical abstracts.
- Library and information science: Information science abstracts, Library and information science abstracts, Library literature.
- Philosophy: Philosopher's index.
- Political science: International political science abstracts, Political science abstracts.
- Psychology: Index medicus, Medline, Psychological abstracts.
- Social work: Social work research and abstracts.
- Sociology: Applied social science index and abstracts, Social science index, Sociological abstracts.
- Multidisciplinary: Dissertation abstracts international, ERIC, Index to South African periodicals, Readers' guide to periodical literature, Science citation index, Social sciences citation index, Social sciences index.

In addition, there are several electronic databases specific to South Africa available online. Perhaps the most important is the South African Bibliographic and Information Network (SABINET) Online, which contains a large variety of databases both international and national in coverage. Other databases are the SA Cat, which contains items available in Southern African libraries, and the Index to South African Periodicals (ISAP) by the National Library of South Africa, which contains articles (with abstracts) from South African journals.

Another important source of local research information is the Nexus Current and Completed Research Projects Database of the National Research Foundation (NRF) (www.nrf.ac.za/nexus). Your university library may not be able to give you access to all of these, but it is likely to have at least some of the key ones available.

One shortcoming of library catalogues is that they list only the titles of journals and not the titles of the articles contained in each journal. Fortunately, there are many printed and electronic indices in which one can use keywords to find references to specific journal articles. A good place to find literature on psychology, for example, is in Psychological Abstracts or its electronic version, PsychLit. Bibliographies and indices of this sort help to identify literature by providing full references for selected articles, citation details and, in some cases, abstracts or reviews of the literature (see box 2.6 on the previous page). Once again, it is advisable to consult an information professional (librarian) for the appropriate and existing indices, bibliographies, and abstracts in your field.

A two-step procedure is used to search bibliographies or indices and abstracting sources. First, one finds information about relevant articles by searching the databases using sets of keywords. Second, one has to get physical access to the material, which is known as document delivery. Usually it just means getting the book from the shelf, but it could involve ordering the material from another library (interlibrary loan) or downloading it onto disk (if it is an electronic document). Of course, you would not actually want to get hold of every book or journal article identified from your search – look at the titles and (where available) abstracts and get only those that seem to relate strongly to your research topic.

Photo: Rodney Barnett

Remember that, in addition to printed and electronic sources of information, you can also gather background information by talking to people.

Searching the internet

The internet has become an all-purpose tool for gaining access to scholarly and 'popular' information. Many library catalogues and other academic databases can be accessed without restriction via the internet, and an increasing number of highly regarded academic journals are published and actual full documents are accessible and available via the internet. There are a variety of sites that allow anyone to search for and freely access articles published in academic journals. One good starting place is Stanford University's Highwire Press (www.highwire.stanford.edu), the largest repository of free, full-text, peer-reviewed academic content – almost a thousand journals and well over a million free, full-text articles. If your research involves medical issues, PubMed (www.ncbi.nlm.nih.gov/entrez/query.fcgi?db= PubMed) is an invaluable resource, containing over 15 million citations from MEDLINE and other life science journals for biomedical articles dating back to the 1950s. If your focus is on African issues, try African Journals Online (www.ajol.info) which allows searches of two hundred and twenty African journals. There are various other services on the internet making it possible to search for journal articles and other scholarly material, such as www.scholar.google.com, www.bubl.ac.uk, and www.findarticles.com. Look around for the service that best meets your research needs.

In addition to formal academic databases, many non-academic databases can be accessed freely via the internet. Many South African and overseas newspapers, for example, have internet archives containing articles from previous editions. Although the material available from such sources does not carry the same weight as academic books and articles, it is permissible to cite them in a literature survey and they can provide useful leads to other material.

Another approach is to use a general internet search engine such as www.yahoo.com or www.google.com to search the entire internet. Because there is so much potentially relevant material, it is particularly important to try and specify exactly what you are after – use synonyms and boolean operators to broaden or narrow your search until you find a useful subset of links. General internet searches of this nature typically produce material of very uneven quality, but not uncommonly include links to serious repositories of information set up by scholarly researchers, research institutes, and academic departments. Just as there are conventions for referencing books and journal articles in research reports, so there are standard techniques for referencing web pages (see chapter 6).

Much of the more popular material found on the internet is not suitable for formal inclusion in a literature survey, but it can help to give you a feel for important issues in a field. For example, there are popular sites dealing with most medical and psychological conditions

Why not visit the internet home pages of several local and overseas universities, and see how their courses (for example, in social science research methods) compare to what happens at your university?

where you can get a quick overview of current scientific and 'alternative' therapies. If your research is concerned with popular culture or group processes, internet searches can provide you with a rich source of data and background information (see Schiano, 1997; Smith & Brant, 1997).

Some journals publish the email addresses of the authors of articles. If you would like to comment on the article or if you have some query, you could email the author directly. But be careful not to impose, as many academics do not have time to engage in long email correspondence.

Developing a working bibliography

The purpose of literature searching is to identify and examine the relevant literature. It involves generating a file of literature that appears to be relevant to the topic, reviewing the literature, and making notes of the most relevant material. It also involves discarding literature that is considered to be irrelevant. In creating a database of the relevant literature, it is advisable to use a proper referencing technique right from the beginning of the literature searching process. First, this saves time when writing a research report because full details of the reviewed literature are available on your referencing system. Second, fewer referencing errors are likely to occur in the course of writing the research report because you will more than likely use the same referencing technique used at the time of literature searching, and with which you will have become very familiar. Third, compiling a reference list (see chapter 6) at the end of a research report is made easier, because selected references can simply be transferred from your database into the report.

Adopt a standard system of referencing and summarising all articles you read.

A bibliographic database can either be handwritten or kept on a computer. If you do not have access to a computer, it is a good idea to use index cards. These are easy to handle and can be carried with you (to the library, for example). Individual cards are used for each reference and can be filed and re-filed as more items are added to your database. Data from these cards can be transferred to a computerised database if you so wish.

Whatever referencing style you use, the following bibliographic data should be entered on the index cards or the computerised database. For a book, put the full names of the authors, full title and subtitle of the book, editors and translators (if any), edition of the book (if not the first edition), number of the volume and total number of volumes (if the book is a multi-volume work), series name (if book is part of a series), place of publication (cite only the first city if several are listed), publisher, and year of publication.

Box 2.7

Managing your own bibliographic database
(Mike Quayle, University of KwaZulu-Natal, Pietermaritzburg)

Managing literature for a research project can be a nightmare. Keeping track of literature that you are searching for, that you have on order, or have on file requires administration skills that many researchers lack. Additionally, the task of formatting in-text citations and generating a correctly formatted and complete reference list is, for most, a chore that distracts from the more enjoyable aspects of writing up research. Even more onerous is the task of converting references from one format to another for different audiences. For example, a paper may initially be submitted to a journal that specifies a Harvard referencing format where the author and date are cited in-text, referring to an alphabetical reference list at the end (e.g., APA format). If the article is rejected, it may be resubmitted to a journal that requires Vancouver format where a superscript number is used to refer to a reference list presented in order of citation. Converting referencing formats manually can be a tedious and exacting task.

Fortunately, these literature-management tasks may be facilitated by various software packages, including Bibliographica, Biblioscape, Citation, EndNote, GetARef, LaTeX/BibTeX, Library Master, Papyrus, ProCite, Reference Manager, Refs, Scribe, and WriteNote. Excitingly, for cash-strapped students and academics alike, work is proceeding on Bibus – an open-source (i.e., free) bibliographic management package designed to integrate with OpenOffice – an excellent open-source office-suite that gives Microsoft Office a run for its money. Download Bibus bibus-biblio.sourceforge.net.

These software packages do not work by magic. Learning to use them and creating and maintaining a bibliographic database requires some effort, but they certainly take a great deal of the drudgery out of maintaining bibliographic records and formatting citations and references correctly in documents.

For a journal article, put the authors' names, title of article, title of journal, volume number, issue number or month (if available), year of publication, and the starting and ending page numbers.

In addition to the above information, the researcher may also keep a record of the source of the material included in the working bibliography. This is helpful in case she or he needs to re-check the references or details of the item and re-read the item in the future. Details may include the use of library classification numbers or call numbers. A review of literature involves not only identifying and accessing relevant literature, but reading, analysing, and keeping notes about the identified literature. Your notes about the book or journal article should also be part of each index card. Ideally, this should include information about both the content of the paper and the research methods used.

In addition to bibliographic cards or computer records, many researchers also find it useful to make photocopies of selected journal articles, but be careful not to photocopy hundreds of articles indiscriminately or to photocopy more than you are legally allowed to copy.

Conclusion

A literature review involves the process of identifying literature relevant to the topic of research, studying that literature, and actually writing the review. This can form part of a larger empirical study, but can also be a worthwhile project in itself. We live in an age of information, and often what is required from the researcher is not more findings but an ability to integrate and synthesise the overwhelmingly large volume of information already available on a topic. Skills of the kind needed to do a good literature survey are valued not only in academia but also in the world of applied research, and these skills form the foundation of good research practice.

Exercises

1. Find out what the 'Delphi technique' involves, what a 'geographical information system' is, and how a 'foresight exercise' is conducted. To find out:

    (a) Check the subject index of textbooks on methodology.

    (b) Do a search of your library catalogue and get the appropriate books from the shelf.

    (c) Search for the concepts on the internet.

    Which one of these three methods was quickest? Which provided you with the most useful information?

2. Search for and download off the internet some current South African discussion documents about science development and technology. Try the websites of the South African Government Communication Service, the Department of Arts, Science, Culture, and Technology, and the Human Sciences Research Council. Also try the websites of national associations, such as the Social Sciences Research and Development Forum, and the Consortium of Human and Social Sciences in South Africa.

3. Apply your knowledge of search strategies.

    (a) Use, for example, one of the sources listed under the 'Biblio-graphic sources' section of this chapter.

    (b) Determine your keywords and establish synonyms.

    (c) Determine the use of boolean operators for the specific search engine and execute your search.

Key readings

Hart, C. (1998). *Doing a literature review: Releasing the social science research imagination*. London: Sage.

This accessible text offers advice on how to find existing knowledge on a topic, analyse arguments and ideas, map ideas, arguments, and perspectives, produce a literature review, and construct a case for investigating a topic.

Memering, D. (1983). *The Prentice Hall guide to research writing*. Englewood Cliffs, New Jersey: Penguin.

This book provides useful chapters on developing a search strategy, searching for literature and information, analysing the resources, and evaluating the evidence. It also contains useful ideas on taking notes, summarising information, generating records or literature entries, and keeping the working bibliography.

Whiteley, S. (Ed.). (1994). *The American Library Association guide to information access: A complete research handbook and directory*. New York: Random House.

This book is a one-stop reference to finding information in libraries and from other sources. It has a strong American bias, but much of the material applies to the South African situation as well.

Research design

Kevin Durrheim

University of KwaZulu-Natal

A **research design** is a strategic framework for action that serves as a bridge between research questions and the execution or implementation of the research. Research designs are plans that guide 'the arrangement of conditions for collection and analysis of data in a manner that aims to combine relevance to the research purpose with economy in procedure' (Sellitz, Jahoda, Deutsch, & Cook, 1965, p. 50). It is the designed and planned nature of observation that distinguishes research from other forms of observation. In everyday life, people make sense of the world through observation. We have all observed that the steam from a kettle is hot, and do not need scientists to tell us this. Journalists, too, observe events – for example, soccer matches, crowd protests, and political corruption – and report their observations in newspapers. Research differs from everyday observation because research observation is planned. Such planned research is termed **systematic observation**, because it is guided by concrete research questions and a research design. The researcher seeks to draw coherent and plausible conclusions or inferences from her or his observations, and thus plans observation to ensure that it will fulfil the purposes of the research. Designing a research study has often been compared to designing a building. There are a number of reasons why it is a good idea to plan a house before actually building it. Without a plan to work from, builders will be making ad hoc decisions as they build, and could easily forget to include a toilet or sufficient windows. Also, the builders may start constructing a very large house, only to run out of money and bricks and be forced to abandon the mansion as an incomplete shell. Like building plans, research designs ensure that (1) the study fulfils a particular purpose, and (2) the research can be completed with available resources.

Figure 3.1 shows the crucial role that research design plays as a bridge between the research question and the execution of the research. Research may be viewed as a process consisting of five stages:

- stage 1: defining the research question,
- stage 2: designing the research,
- stage 3: data collection,
- stage 4: data analysis, and
- stage 5: writing a research report.

A research design should provide a plan that specifies how the research is going to be executed in such a way that it answers the research

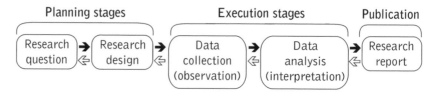

Figure 3.1   The research process

question. Designing a study involves multiple decisions about the way in which the data will be collected and analysed to ensure that the final report answers the initial research question.

In figure 3.1, you will note that bi-directional arrows link the five research activities that make up the research process. The dark arrows (on top) indicate that the research process is made up of a **sequence of activities**, beginning with the research question and ending with the report. One normally begins a research project with a research question, then develops a design that will answer the question, and finally conducts the research and writes up the findings.

By emphasising a model of research as a progressive sequence of events, some researchers describe designs as 'architectural blueprints' (Bickman, Rog, & Hendrick, 1998; Mouton & Marais, 1990). According to this understanding, research designs are (1) fixed and specified in advance of execution, and (2) defined by technical considerations. Just as one would not change an architectural blueprint once building has started, in this understanding of research, designs are developed in full and then implemented. The term 'architectural blueprint' also carries connotations that designs are developed on technical grounds. The blueprint of a building, for example, is developed according to principles of civil engineering to ensure that the construction is sound. Similarly, research designs should be developed in accordance with scientific principles to ensure that the findings will stand against criticism. In this model, the answer to the question 'What research design are you using?' would be something like 'I will use a randomised, double-blind, experimental design'. This design is technical – that is, it employs scientific technologies of randomisation, double-blind techniques, and experimental manipulation – and it is specified fully in advance and merely implemented in the research setting.

Although there is nothing wrong with understanding research designs as blueprints, there are other legitimate research designs that cannot be defined in these terms. Qualitative researchers in particular propose designs that are more open, fluid, and changeable, and are not defined purely in technical terms. According to this view, research is an **iterative process** that requires a flexible, nonsequential approach. The light arrows in figure 3.1 reflect the iterative nature of research. Although one begins by proposing a research question and developing a design, things can change when the research is being carried out, and there may be good reasons why one would want to change the original design. This means that it is not only technical considerations that are used in developing a design, but that pragmatic considerations may well influence the final research design.

Suppose we set out to investigate the efficacy of the Department of Health's Aids prevention campaign, in which television and newspaper advertisements are used to encourage safe-sex practices. We decide to use a randomised survey research design of dwellings in the Eastern Cape to determine the impact of the campaign in rural

Practical issues that only become apparent when the researcher begins the investigation (e.g. lack of material resources and high illiteracy rates in rural areas) as opposed to technical considerations (e.g. the scientific validity of randomised surveys) can prompt the researcher to reflect upon and change a research design.

areas. However, before spending millions of rands on an expensive survey, we first interview a group of clinic nurses to help us construct a questionnaire. We find from the nurses that there are no television sets in the area, and very few people read newspapers. This information would lead us to change our original research design – it would be pointless to conduct the survey – and perhaps even to change our research question. Instead of seeking to determine how effective the advertising campaign was, we may investigate alternative means to communicate health messages in rural areas. Rather than viewing research as a sequence of activities, this example shows why one would want to use iterations in research, changing research designs and even research questions once the research has begun to be implemented.

There has been much debate about the nature of the research process and the type of research design that is most appropriate for the social sciences. Some experimentalists and quantitative researchers argue that flexible and pragmatic designs are nonscientific, and that bias may be introduced when designs are modified during the execution stage of research. Qualitative researchers, on the other hand, argue that fixed, technical designs (blueprints) are restrictive and unsuited to much exploratory and inductive research, which does not begin with general theories to be tested. Lincoln and Guba (1985) go so far as to say that some qualitative designs 'cannot be given in advance; it must emerge, develop, unfold' (p. 225). This is because the research questions and focus may change in the light of new ideas that emerge from early observation and analysis. In this book, we understand design as a **strategic framework**, a plan that guides research activity to ensure that sound conclusions are reached. Depending on the purpose of the research and the orientation of the researcher, a design may vary along a continuum, from inflexible and technical blueprints on the one hand to flexible and pragmatic guides for action on the other hand (see figure 3.2). The blueprint specifies exactly how the research will be carried out, while the flexible guide for action specifies an iterative process in which the researcher will engage. For example, instead of specifying the questions to be covered in an interview in advance of the research, a researcher could list some themes to be covered in the interview, and state that precise questions will be developed after consultation with key informants (i.e., persons who know the context well), and will be refined during the first few interviews. Most research falls between the two extremes of the continuum as experimentalists often adjust their designs (e.g., to the availability of measures), and qualitative researchers specify in advance certain data collection methods (e.g., the use of interviews).

As strategic frameworks for action, research designs should specify a series of activities which will ensure that valid conclusions can be drawn from the research. A flexible and pragmatic research design cannot be an excuse for not providing a detailed strategic framework or for producing invalid or unsound conclusions. Far from being an easy way out, fluid and pragmatic designs make for very demanding research, as the researcher must continually reflect on the research process and, by making difficult decisions, refine and develop the research design throughout the research process to ensure valid conclusions.

Blueprints			Flexible guides
Experiments	Field experiments	Ethnographies	Case studies
Surveys			

Figure 3.2 Varieties of research design

Principles of research design

In developing a research design, the researcher must make a series of decisions along four dimensions: (1) the purpose of the research, (2) the theoretical paradigm informing the research, (3) the context or situation within which the research is carried out, and (4) the research techniques employed to collect and analyse data (see figure 3.3). Multiple considerations that derive from these four dimensions must be woven together in a coherent research design in a way that will maximise the validity of the findings. The strategic framework (research design) that links the research question to the execution of the research is developed through a process of reflecting on issues relevant to each of these four dimensions, to produce a coherent guide for action which will provide valid answers to the research question. This process of reflection is guided by two principles of decision making: design validity and design coherence.

'The aim of a research design is to plan and structure a given research project in such a manner that the eventual validity of the research findings is maximised.' (Mouton & Marais, 1990)

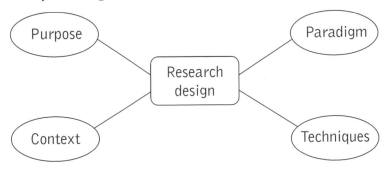

Figure 3.3 Four dimensions of decision making in research design

Design validity

Traditionally, research in the social sciences has been restricted to one paradigm (positivism), has used a standard set of research techniques (including experimentation and surveys), and has approached research contexts or settings with the main purpose of controlling them. This made research design a technical exercise, but restricted the complexity and scope of the decision making. Complexity in design was attributed to 'the experimenter's lack of complete control' (Campbell & Stanley,

1966, p. 1), a situation that could be managed by identifying and controlling a set of **validity threats**. These include extraneous factors which could influence the outcome of the study and confound interpretation of the results. In this tradition, research designs are blueprints, employing a set of standard technical procedures to control for or eliminate validity threats.

Design decisions are made by identifying and eliminating **plausible rival hypotheses**. These are possible alternative interpretations of the research findings. Rival hypotheses refer to causal factors, other than those the researcher sets out to investigate, that could have brought about the research results. By identifying and controlling for plausible rival hypotheses, the researcher is eliminating sources of invalidity in the research. Say we conduct a study and we find that young males are more likely than young females to be injured in motor vehicle accidents. Say we then conclude that men are bad drivers because they are more impulsive than women. Can you identify any alternative explanations for the results besides male impulsivity? What about other factors such as alcohol consumption? Men drink and drive more frequently than women, and it may be this rather than impulsivity that 'explains' the findings. To eliminate this plausible rival hypothesis, we should do one or more of the following: (1) review previous research on gender differences in impulsivity to establish whether men are indeed more impulsive than women, (2) measure impulsivity of the individuals in our sample and compare accident rates among men and women with similar levels of impulsivity, or (3) control for alcohol usage by studying only those male and female drivers who had no trace of alcohol in their blood at the time of the accident.

Thinking about plausible rival hypotheses is a general principle of decision making in designing research. Although it is historically associated with positivism, the principle of looking for plausible rival hypotheses is a way of checking the validity of all kinds of research. All researchers should ask themselves whether their research is designed to give valid and believable conclusions, or whether the conclusions could be explained by factors that the researcher has not taken into account.

Principle 1: Achieve design validity by identifying plausible rival hypotheses and eliminating their impact. Plausible rival hypotheses are eliminated when unexplained variables that influence the findings are either (1) controlled to remove their presence, or (2) measured (observed) to determine their influence.

Design coherence

The increasing legitimacy of research paradigms other than positivism has expanded the decision-making process. No longer is it only threats to validity that should be considered, but also the **coherence of the design**. Design coherence is achieved when the decisions from each of the four different domains shown in figure 3.3 fit together with an internal logic. Design coherence is a broader construct than design validity. Whereas design validity is concerned with an important set of research objectives – that is, correct causal attributions – design coherence is concerned about whether a study will be able to achieve a broader set of objectives, including answering research questions (which may not be causal) or fulfilling other pragmatic demands, such as community development. Researchers achieve coherent designs by ensuring that the research purposes and techniques are arranged logically within the research framework provided by a particular paradigm.

Suppose that a researcher adopts an interpretive paradigm to investigate the experience of motherhood. The researcher plans to collect qualitative data by interviewing mothers in the context of their homes while they are interacting with their children, and employs techniques of qualitative data analysis to produce findings. This design is coherent because the techniques of sampling, data collection, and interpretation, as well as the context of the study, 'fit' within the logic of the interpretive paradigm and with the purpose of the research. Interpretive research emphasises rich experiential data (as opposed to causality), and this research is designed to produce this kind of data. Although the uncontrolled environment of the interviews may undermine the validity of the study from a positivist perspective, from an interpretive perspective this context is the key to valid research.

Principle 2: *Achieve design coherence by ensuring that the research purposes and techniques are arranged logically so as to 'fit' within the research framework provided by a particular paradigm.*

Principles 1 and 2 are not opposing principles. Both principles aim to ensure a level of consistency between the researcher's paradigmatic assumptions, the purpose of the research, and the eventual conclusions. This consistency is achieved when the research activity produces data that provide valid answers to the research question. Research coherence is, however, a broader concept that accommodates research designs with different (i.e., nonpositivist) understandings of validity. Although there may still be debate between researchers working within different paradigms regarding what a good research design should look like, there should be a wide degree of consensus among different researchers subscribing to the same paradigm regarding a good research design.

Making design decisions

In planning an investigation, the researcher must make a series of decisions about the way that the research questions can best be answered by the investigation. The researcher must find a compromise between the ideals of good research and the numerous practical constraints that present themselves in real-life research settings. Design decisions relate to the four dimensions of decision making that were considered in figure 3.3, and the researcher approaches these decisions with a view to developing valid and coherent research designs.

Paradigms

As we discussed in chapter 1, paradigms are systems of interrelated ontological, epistemological, and methodological assumptions. Paradigms act as perspectives that provide a rationale for the research and commit the researcher to particular methods of data collection, observation, and interpretation. Paradigms are thus central to research design because they impact both on the nature of the research question – i.e., what is to be studied – and on the manner in which the question is to be studied. In designing a research study, the principle of coherence can be preserved by ensuring that the research question and methods used fit logically within the paradigm. If a researcher planned to study the experience of motherhood from an interpretive perspective, the use of an objective scale to measure experience would betray positivist commitments and make for an incoherent research design. In this case, the researcher could achieve design coherence either by adopting a positivist ontology (e.g., identifying mothers with different styles of attachment) or by using methods such as interviews, which allow the researcher to understand mothers' experiences through shared interaction.

Do not ask questions from the perspective of one paradigm and then try to answer them from the perspective of another paradigm.

Since positivism has been somewhat of an orthodoxy in the twentieth-century social sciences, most accounts of research design did not consider design coherence. Instead, research design was considered as a set of tactics to ensure that the methodology used in research fitted logically within a positivist paradigm. However, since all paradigms rest on untestable (metaphysical) assumptions, none can be incontrovertibly right. What is important is that researchers recognise that their findings and conclusions are embedded in paradigms, and employ research designs that are coherent. This will go a long way towards achieving the final aim of all research: persuasiveness.

Questions to ask about paradigms

1. What paradigm do you personally find appealing?
2. What paradigm do you think best fits the research question?
3. Is there a coherent fit between the paradigm that you are using and the research design?

Purpose

By specifying the nature of reality that can be known, paradigms provide broad frameworks of research purpose. They do not, however, define precisely the purpose of a specific research study. In developing a research design, the researcher must ask two further questions about the research purpose: Who or what do you want to draw conclusions about? And what type of conclusions do you want to draw about your object of analysis?

The object of study

In defining the object of a research study, the researcher is specifying who or what they want to draw conclusions about. There are typically two aspects of these 'objects' of study that are worth defining: (1) the units of analysis that are the focus of investigation, and (2) the variables, which are features of these objects that are to be observed or measured.

1. Units of analysis

Babbie (1989) distinguishes between four different **units of analysis** that are common in the social sciences: individuals, groups, organisations, and social artifacts. Social artifacts are the products of human action (e.g., newspaper articles, or San paintings) and forms of social interaction (e.g., university graduation ceremonies). It can be difficult deciding which unit of analysis is being investigated. Loyalty, for example, could be investigated as a property of individuals (e.g. politicians), groups (e.g., sports teams), organisations (e.g., churches), or social artifacts (e.g., marriage ceremonies). Although there are no clear boundaries between these different units of analysis, the researcher must ask on which aspects of loyalty their research will focus. Is it individual emotive and cognitive processes, inter-individual processes within groups, or organisational structures? Does the researcher want to compare these processes across different individuals, different groups, or different organisations?

In devising a research design, the researcher must scrutinise the research question to determine precisely what the object of study is.

The units of analysis have an impact on sample selection, data collection, and the types of conclusion that can be drawn from the research. If organisations are the unit of analysis, the researcher should sample across different organisations. If letters to the editor of a particular newspaper are the unit of analysis, the researcher should sample across different letters. Similarly, even if data are collected from individuals, the type of data that is collected will depend upon the unit of analysis. Individuals can be studied as individuals, as members of groups, or as representatives of organisations.

Individuals, for example, could be asked about their loyalty in different situations (individual units of analysis), about the development of loyalty in their soccer team before different matches (group unit of analysis), or about the manner in which their employers reward loyalty (organisational unit of analysis). Design coherence is achieved by matching the sampling and data collection strategies to the units of analysis.

Logical errors may arise when the object of investigation – i.e., the unit of analysis – does not correspond with the conclusions of the research. The **ecological fallacy** is one such error in reasoning.

This occurs when a researcher investigates one unit of analysis, and then draws conclusions about a different unit of analysis. If our study finds that groups in threatening situations show aggressive tendencies, we would make an error to conclude that threatened individuals will be aggressive. Groups and individuals are different units of analysis, and different processes may operate when each is

The ecological fallacy involves drawing conclusions about a unit of analysis different from the unit studied.

under threat; rather than being aggressive, threatened individuals may show signs of fear and flight.

2. Variables

If someone asks you what you are researching, you need to say more than what your units of analysis are. You need to specify the features of these objects you are going to observe. These features of objects that we observe in research are termed variables. A **variable** is defined as a concept that can take on two or more values. Loyalty is a variable, since individuals differ in the degree to which they are loyal, and their loyalty differs across situations. Age, household income, and blood alcohol level are all examples of variables, because they are properties of objects that can take on different values. Variables are measured, so that scores indicate the amount of an attribute a unit has.

Box 3.1

Types of variable in research design

A crucial part of designing a study is to define different kinds of variable:

- Independent variable (IV) — the hypothesised causal variable.
- Dependent variable (DV) — (measured) variable whose value depends on the value of the IV.
- Mediating variable (MV) — variables that influence the relationship between the IV and DV.
- Extraneous variable (EV) – nuisance variables that are unrelated to the research but affect the DV.

The relationship between these variables is shown in the design below, in which a researcher hypothesises that the time it takes for HIV to convert to full-blown Aids (the dependent variable) is determined by poverty (independent variable) because of nutrition quality (mediating variable) which is associated both with poverty and sero-conversion (the reproduction of HIV). Note that the researcher has also specified a number of plausible rival hypotheses, extraneous variables, which are also possibly associated with both poverty and sero-conversion, and which would need to be either measured or controlled.

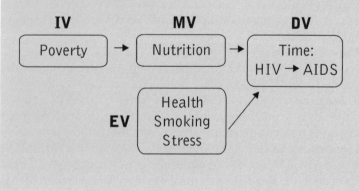

When describing a research design, it is often useful to distinguish between two kinds of variable – dependent and independent. In an experiment, the **independent variable** (IV) is the variable that the experimenter manipulates to determine its effects on the **dependent variable** (DV). So, in an experiment on the effects of alcohol on driving ability, alcohol usage is the independent variable and driving ability the dependent variable (it is thought to depend on alcohol usage). Some researchers also use these terms in nonexperimental research – for example, a study on the strength of the relationship between intelligence (IV) and university marks (DV) – but they are less useful in such cases as it is frequently unclear which variable should be considered to be dependent and which independent.

There are a number of different features of the objects of investigation which are typically measured as variables.

Properties of objects – These may be divided into conditions, orientations, and actions (see Mouton & Marais, 1990). Conditions refer to objective descriptions of individuals (e.g., age, sex), groups and organisations (e.g., size, structure) and social artifacts (e.g., appearance, size) and are relatively stable. Orientations are perspectives such as attitudes and organisational policy. Actions are behaviours such as smoking and violence. Many studies aim merely to describe these properties of the objects under investigation.

The object of a research study is defined by specifying the kind of information that is to be collected from particular units of analysis.

Time – Although beginning researchers often take single observations, introducing a time factor will improve the quality of the research. Longitudinal studies (also called diachronic research) involve the observation of the units of analysis over a period of time. The aim here is to determine changes in the properties of the unit of analysis over time. Repeated measures during experimental studies identify change by comparing pre-test measures, taken before an intervention, with post-test measures of the same variables taken after the intervention.

Groups – Comparative studies involve the observation of different groups of units. For example, research may aim to compare males and females, school sports teams and professional sports teams, African countries and Asian countries, or letters to the editor of a conservative and a liberal newspaper.

Situations – Research may involve the observation of the units of analysis in different situations. For example, the loyalty of sports teams after winning important matches may be compared with their loyalty after losing.

Precisely what information about which units of analysis is to be collected is determined by the research question, and the researcher must design the study in such a manner that the information which is collected can answer the research question. Suppose a researcher wishes to investigate changing attitudes towards people's loyalty as they develop through childhood, adolescence, and adulthood. In this study, individuals would be the unit of analysis, orientations (i.e., attitudes) would be the property of study, and a longitudinal study would be the most appropriate.

It is often not possible to specify variables so precisely at the early stages of qualitative research. In inductive approaches to research, the focus is typically on a number of instances, which are conceptually relevant to the research question. The aim of this research is eventually to identify concepts and variables that will be the focus of the research report, but which will emerge only in the process of doing the research. Consider the example of the researcher observing mother–child interactions. The focus in the early stages of the research is on listing different kinds of behaviours – e.g., smiling, eye contact, kissing, crying – which will only later be conceptualised as variables such as 'bonding', 'frustration', and so on.

The type of study

The purpose of a research project is reflected in the types of conclusion the researcher aims to draw or the goals of the research. What do the researchers wish to attain through their study? There are three different ways in which types of research have been distinguished: (1) exploratory, descriptive, and explanatory research, (2) applied and basic research, and (3) quantitative and qualitative research.

Exploratory, descriptive, and explanatory research

This distinction focuses on the **goals** of the research. **Exploratory studies** are used to make preliminary investigations into relatively unknown areas of research. They employ an open, flexible, and inductive approach to research as they attempt to look for new insights into phenomena. For example, exploratory research, perhaps interviews with key informants (people who manage shelters, etc.), could be used to identify the kinds of health and safety challenges facing homeless people living in the area where you stay. **Descriptive studies** aim to describe phenomena. Whereas exploratory studies generate speculative insights, new questions, and hypotheses, descriptive studies aim to describe phenomena accurately, either through narrative-type descriptions (e.g., interviews with homeless people about their experiences of threat and fear), classification (e.g., documenting different types of risk that homeless people face), or measuring relationships (e.g., between health status and length of time living on the streets). **Explanatory studies** aim to provide causal explanations of phenomena. Experimental and quasi-experimental designs are used to determine whether one variable (e.g., smoking) causes another (e.g., cancer).

In developing a research design, the researcher must consider whether the aims of the research are mainly exploratory, descriptive, or explanatory, as this will impact on the type of study to be conducted. Exploratory studies are designed as open and flexible investigations. They adopt an inductive approach as the researcher makes a series of particular observations, and attempts to patch these together to form more general but speculative hypotheses. Exploratory research designs should detail how the researcher plans to collect information and where she or he will look for this information. Descriptive studies seek accurate observations, and the research design should focus on the validity (accuracy) and reliability (consistency) of the observations, and the representativeness of sampling. Explanatory studies are designed to identify causality, and the focus of the designs should be on eliminating plausible rival hypotheses.

It is important to know, however, that there is no consensus in the social science research community about exactly what counts as exploratory, descriptive, and explanatory research. Because qualitative research is open-ended, many positivist researchers believe that qualitative research is always exploratory, leaving the work of accurate description and explanation to more rigorous quantitative research. Interpretive and constructionist researchers, however, contend that qualitative research can be used not only for exploratory purposes, but also to formulate rich descriptions and explanations of human phenomena.

Applied and basic research

This distinction refers to the uses to which the research will be put. The findings derived from **basic research** are typically used to advance our fundamental knowledge of the world. Such knowledge takes the form of general theories about the operation of psychological, social, and physical processes (e.g., conformity, or epilepsy) and events (e.g., outbreak of civil war, or 'nervous breakdown'). Basic research is used to refute or support these theories. The findings derived from **applied research**, in contrast, have an immediate practical application. Applied research aims to contribute towards practical issues of problem solving, decision making, policy analysis, and community development.

Applied and basic researchers often study the same phenomena, but approach the study from different perspectives. Consider the social problem of homelessness. A basic researcher may design a study about the causes of homelessness by investigating the relationship between homelessness and the economic policy, degree of urbanisation, and literacy rates of different countries. The purpose of this research is to make general theoretical claims about the social processes that underlie homelessness. The applied researcher, on the other hand, would approach the topic to determine whether a new policy towards homeless people – e.g., the policy of arresting homeless people (which was adopted by the Cape Town Traffic

How could research be used to intervene in social conflict?

Department in 1995) – is working or not; or whether it is being properly implemented by the police. The purpose of this research is to provide information about some form of social action (as opposed to theory) with the aim of providing decision makers with information to facilitate decision making.

Box 3.2

Beyond basic and applied
(Alex Butchart, World Health Organisation)

The idea of a distinction between basic and applied research leads to claims that certain kinds of (basic) knowledge exist in a pure, academic form above the factional interests of organisations or communities. Conversely, the basic–applied distinction can be used to silence theoretical critique by labelling it 'ivory tower' research or an exercise in navel gazing. An alternate set of categories has been developed in public health research to represent the ways in which pragmatic and theoretical concerns operate at different levels of generality. In this view all research is action-oriented (and therefore applied), but can be divided into three types. **Fundamental research** aims to increase knowledge about questions of scientific significance that may lead to the development of new technologies (e.g., theories of aggression leading to violence prevention). **Strategic research** generates knowledge about specific needs and problems (these include specific social conditions and systems) with a view to eventually solving or reducing the problem through further development and evaluation. **Intervention development** and **evaluation research** create and assess intervention technologies of all types, such as health policies, social technologies, vaccines and drugs, and environmental interventions.

In developing a research design, the researcher must consider whether the purpose of the research is applied or basic. This can usually be determined from the research question: Does the research question aim to answer a theoretical question that is deemed important by a discipline in the social sciences (basic research), or does the research question seek to answer a practical question deemed important by a policy maker, organisation, or community (applied research)? The answer to these questions will impact on the research design by determining the level of generalisation that the research aims to attain. In contributing towards theory, the findings of basic research should ideally be generalisable across a wide range of different contexts. Applied research aims only to generalise the findings of a study to the specific context under study in order to assist decision makers in drawing conclusions about the particular problems with which they are dealing. The difference in the desired level of generalisation between applied and basic research impacts on many aspects of design, including population selection and sampling, and observation and measurement.

Quantitative and qualitative research

The distinction between quantitative and qualitative research marks a series of differences in approaches to research. At the most surface level, quantitative and qualitative researchers base their conclusions on different kinds of information and employ different techniques of data analysis. Quantitative researchers collect data in the form of numbers and use statistical types of data analysis. Qualitative researchers collect data in the form of written or spoken language, or in the form of observations that are recorded in language, and analyse the data by identifying and categorising themes. These surface differences in method mark deeper differences in orientation. Qualitative methods allow the researcher to study selected issues in depth, openness, and detail as they identify and attempt to understand the categories of information that emerge from the data. Quantitative methods, in contrast, begin with a series of predetermined categories, usually embodied in standardised quantitative measures, and use this data to make broad and generalisable comparisons.

A qualitative investigation of homelessness, for example, could begin by attempting to determine how people experience living on the street, or could study autobiographical accounts of how individuals 'ended up' being homeless. On the basis of interviews and possibly participant observations, the researcher would attempt to build up a detailed picture of the life stories and experiences of homeless people. A quantitative investigation of homelessness would start out with measures of variables that the researcher deemed relevant to homelessness, for example, levels of education, achievement motivation, mental illness. Standard measures of these variables could then be applied to large samples to determine, for example, the factors that distinguish homeless people from the rest of the population. What the standardised measure loses in depth and detail of understanding, it gains in facilitating comparisons between different groups of people. Quantitative and qualitative research have differing strengths and weaknesses, and constitute alternative, not opposing, research strategies.

Quantitative and qualitative research have differing strengths and weaknesses, and constitute alternative, not opposing, research strategies.

Deciding whether to use quantitative or qualitative research has many implications for research design: it has a variety of consequences for sampling, data collection, and analysis. This decision is made after considering the purpose of the research and the type of data that will achieve this purpose. Qualitative research is naturalistic, holistic, and inductive (see table 3.1). If the research purpose is to study phenomena as they unfold in real-world situations, without manipulation, to study phenomena as interrelated wholes rather than split up into discreet predetermined variables, then an inductive, qualitative approach is required.

In planning a research project, the researcher must make decisions regarding all three of the ways in which types of research are distinguished: (1) exploratory, descriptive, and explanatory, (2) applied and basic, and (3) quantitative and qualitative. These decisions are interrelated. Although exploratory, descriptive, and explanatory goals may be achieved in either applied or basic research, it is common for basic research to have explanatory goals that facilitate theory development. Similarly, although exploratory, descriptive, and explanatory goals may be achieved with either quantitative or qualitative research, qualitative research is more commonly used to inductively explore phenomena, and to provide 'thick' (i.e., detailed) descriptions of phenomena.

By considering both the object of study and the type of study that is implicit in a research question, the researcher begins to make explicit decisions about the way in which the research will be implemented. Such reflection on the purpose of the study should be guided by the principles of validity and coherence. The object of study and the type of study should fit logically within a particular paradigm of research and inform decisions about the techniques to be used in implementing the study to ensure valid findings.

Table 3.1 Themes of qualitative inquiry	
1. Naturalistic	Studying real-world situations as they unfold naturally; non-manipulative, unobtrusive, and non-controlling; openness to whatever emerges – lack of predetermined constraints on outcomes.
2. Holistic	The whole phenomenon under study is understood as a complex system that is more than the sum of its parts; focus on more complex interdependencies, not meaningfully reduced to a few discreet variables and linear, cause–effect relationships.
3. Inductive	Immersion in the details and specifics of the data to discover important categories, dimensions, and interrelationships; begin by exploring genuinely open questions rather than testing theoretically derived (deductive) hypotheses.

Adapted from Patton, 1990, p. 40.

Questions to ask about purpose

1. What are your units of analysis? About whom/what do you want to draw conclusions?
2. What information do you require about these units of analysis? Can you identify independent, dependent, mediating, and extraneous variables?
3. What type of study is best suited to answering the research question? Are the goals of the research exploratory, descriptive, or explanatory? Are the findings to be used for applied or basic purposes? Is the kind of information required and the analytic strategy to be followed quantitative or qualitative?

Techniques

A research design should provide an explicit plan for action. This should include the techniques that will be employed in executing the research. These are divided into three categories: sampling, data collection, and analysis. Research designs should provide detailed and extensive information about all three aspects of the research. 'Architectural blueprints' will specify exactly the sample size and sampling technique, the measurement instruments, and the types of data analysis. Designs that are developed as flexible guides will state explicitly which procedures will be adopted to determine the method of sample selection, observation, and analysis. In addition, flexible guides should detail how decisions will be made, and provide a rough outline of possible options that are likely to be implemented. Although these topics will be considered in greater detail throughout the book, we will consider here how decisions about paradigms and purpose impact on technique selection.

Sampling

Sampling is the selection of research participants from an entire population, and involves decisions about which people, settings, events, behaviours, and/or social processes to observe. Exactly who or what will be sampled in a particular study is influenced by the unit of analysis. If your research question was about household poverty, you would select a sample of households, but if your question was about poverty and homelessness, you would select a sample of individuals.

Who or what will be sampled in a particular study is influenced by the unit of analysis.

The main concern in sampling is **representativeness**. The aim is to select a sample that will be representative of the population about which the researcher aims to draw conclusions. Representative samples are especially important in descriptive surveys that are used to estimate accurately the properties of populations. To achieve representativeness, researchers draw random samples. A second concern is the **size of the sample**; a very small random sample may be quite unrepresentative, and the same is true for a large nonrandom sample. The researcher must ensure that the sample is large enough to allow him or her to make inferences about the population. Just how large a sample should be depends on the type of study conducted (experiment or survey) and on numerous measurement and statistical criteria (see Lipsey, 1998). Often, sample size is determined in part by practical constraints – e.g., how many people does the researcher have access to, how much money and time are available for the study, and so on. A more detailed discussion of sampling in quantitative research is presented in chapter 7.

Rather than insisting that samples should be representative, qualitative researchers ensure that their findings are transferable – i.e. they help to understand other contexts or groups similar to those studied.

Types of research that are less concerned with statistical accuracy than they are with detailed and in-depth analysis – e.g., interpretive and constructionist research, qualitative research, and exploratory research – typically do not draw large or random samples. Various types of purposeful (i.e., nonrandom) sampling may be used. The researcher may select a few information-rich cases, including critical cases (theoretically important cases), extreme cases (e.g., extreme liberals and extreme conservatives), or typical cases (i.e., common or average cases).

Box 3.3

Types of sampling

1. Convenience sampling:
   - selecting participants who are available, without any prior rationale;
   - nonrepresentative → cannot generalise;
   - used in experiments, where (universal) processes are supposedly examined.
2. Random sampling:
   - every case in the population has equal chance of being (randomly) selected ;
   - representative → generalise;
   - used in surveys.
3. Purposive sampling:
   - cases selected for theoretical reasons → good examples of the phenomenon;
   - for example, select extremely depressed people to study processes of depression;
   - used in qualitative research.

The researcher must justify why a particular sampling strategy suits the particular research study. Although an in-depth study of the life stories of a few homeless people may not be generalisable to all homeless people, there may be strong grounds for arguing that their experiences of alienation are transferable to other people living on the margins of society. These types of argument are particularly convincing when the researcher has used a technique called **sampling to redundancy**. This involves not defining one's sample size in advance, but interviewing more and more people until the same themes and issues come up over and over again. The sample has achieved redundancy in the sense that no new information can be gained from increasing the sample size. You can read more about sampling for interpretive research in chapter 13.

As a general rule of research design, it is better to focus your research question in such a manner that you can explore in detail a small instance of a phenomenon rather than attempt to study a large issue with an inadequate sample. In a study that investigated how rural African women experience university life, Brown (1997) decided to conduct in-depth interviews with a number of women in their first year of university. Instead of trying to select a large random sample from all universities, technikons, and colleges in South Africa, which would have generated mountains of interview data, she decided to focus on the experiences of 11 such women – determined by sampling to redundancy – on a single university campus. This allowed an in-depth investigation of their experiences within a single context – an English-speaking, historically white, and liberal campus. Although her findings are not representative in a statistical sense, her research showed many of the conflicts that such students experience around language and culture, and suggested issues that are likely to be transferable to similar contexts.

Data collection

Data are the basic material with which researchers work. Data come from observation, and can take the form of numbers (numeric or quantitative data) or language (qualitative data). To draw valid conclusions from a research study, it is essential that the researcher has sound data to analyse and interpret. Just what is meant by sound data is a matter of debate, and is an issue to which we will return on many occasions throughout the book. There is widespread agreement that data should be valid – i.e., data should capture the meaning of what the researcher is observing. If the researcher is investigating alienation, whether the researcher uses a quantitative scale to measure alienation or interviews individuals about their experience of alienation, the data should capture the meaning of the concept of 'alienation'.

This, however, is where agreement between researchers ends. Positivist researchers prefer to use quantitative measures that predefine the objects to be studied (see chapters 7 and 8). Interpretive, and especially constructionist, researchers maintain that the meaning of phenomena varies across contexts, and they adopt a more inductive approach to data collection, investigating how categories of observation emerge in context (see chapters 13, 14, and 15). Positivist research generates predefined observational measures through a twofold deductive process: **conceptualisation**, that is, defining a construct (e.g., alienation) in abstract terms according to its theoretical meaning; and **operationalisation**, that is, translating this theoretical definition into observable indicators of the construct. Validity is defined by the extent to which the operational definition is a true reflection of the conceptual definition. In addition to measurement validity, positivist research aims toward measurement reliability. Reliable measures are stable in the sense that they consistently give the same information repeatedly when used under similar conditions (see chapter 7).

Many qualitative researchers reject 'reliable', 'objective' measures as invalid. They argue that social phenomena are context-dependent, and that the meaning of whatever it is that the researcher is investigating depends on the particular situation an individual is in. Feeling alienated in the context of one's family may be completely different from feeling alienated among one's peers at school. Instead of predefining alienation in abstract (theoretical) terms, many qualitative researchers approach observation inductively without being constrained by predetermined categories. In qualitative research, rather than using a measurement scale as an instrument of observation, the researcher is the instrument of observation. Data are collected either by interviews or by observing and recording human behaviour in contexts of interaction. These particular observations are then categorised into themes, and a more general picture of the phenomenon under investigation is built up from particulars. Qualitative researchers still seek valid observations. Validity, however, is not defined in terms of the extent to which the operational definition corresponds with the construct definition, but by the degree to which the researcher can produce observations that are believable for herself or himself, the subjects being studied, and the eventual readers of the study.

In developing a coherent research design, the researcher should take great care in describing strategies of observation that fit in with the research paradigm and the research purpose. Positivist research values objective, usually quantitative, measures. These can be used to measure the responses of large samples of people, and thus facilitate generalisation, group comparisons, and statistical analysis. Qualitative methods of data collection – observation and interviewing – are favoured by researchers working within the interpretive and constructionist paradigms. These methods permit rich and detailed observations of a few cases, and allow the researcher to build up an understanding of phenomena through observing particular instances of the phenomena as they emerge in specific contexts.

Analysis

Many of the chapters in this book are concerned with various techniques of data analysis. Data analysis issues should be carefully considered when designing a study, since the aim of data analysis is to transform information (data) into an answer to the original research question. A careful consideration of data analysis strategies will ensure that the design is coherent, as the researcher matches the analysis to a particular type of data, to the purposes of the research, and to the research paradigm.

As a general rule of thumb, never proceed with a study unless you have a good idea how you will analyse the data.

Data analysis procedures can be divided into quantitative and qualitative techniques. Quantitative techniques (chapters 9, 10, and 11) employ a variety of statistical analyses to make sense of data, whereas qualitative techniques (chapters 14, 15, and 16) begin by identifying themes in the data and relationships between these themes. From a design perspective, it is important to ensure that the type of data analysis which is employed matches the research paradigm and data, and can answer the research question.

Questions to ask about techniques

1. How should the sample be collected (and what size should the sample be) to ensure that the study can answer the research question in a convincing manner?
2. What specific measures, interview questions, or observation techniques will be used to collect data? Is it important to have 'objective' measures or should the categories of analysis 'emerge' from the data?
3. What specific quantitative or qualitative techniques of data analysis should be applied to the data? Do the data allow such techniques to be used?

Situations

Research always takes place in a specific context. Researchers can take very different attitudes towards this context. Some ignore context altogether and disregard the impact of context on the findings. Others attempt to control and manipulate the context to determine the influence that these manipulations have on the responses of the research participants. Still others acknowledge the impact of context on human and social behaviour and attempt to study these as they occur naturally in context.

Experimental research goes to great lengths to control and manipulate the context of the research. Often, experiments are conducted in highly controlled conditions in order to eliminate extraneous variables (e.g., differences in temperature, lighting, or noise) that might impact on the subjects' performance and thus influence the outcome of the study. Experimenters also purposefully manipulate certain aspects of the situation to determine whether this manipulation impacts on the subjects' behaviour. For example, two groups of subjects may be asked to complete a measure of self-esteem in exactly the same experimental laboratory. In one group, the experimenter acts as a threatening, dominant character; while, in the second, the experimenter acts as a kind and caring character. The two groups are treated exactly the same in all other regards. If the two groups score differently on self-esteem, the experimenter can conclude that it was the experimental manipulation which caused the differences in the scores.

Experimentation and other kinds of positivist research, such as surveys, have been criticised for ignoring the social nature of the interaction that takes place in research with human subjects. Critics have highlighted two kinds of influence:

- **Experimenter effect** – The researcher can give subtle clues about the way in which she or he expects the subjects of a study to respond (Rosenthal, 1966). If a black experimenter, for example, asked white subjects to complete a measure of racism, their responses could easily be influenced by what they think the experimenter expects (i.e., nonracist responses).

- **Demand characteristics** – Certain features of the research setting can impact on the findings (Orne, 1962). If subjects are asked to complete a questionnaire measuring their attitudes towards alcohol, one would expect quite different responses if this was completed in an experimental laboratory, in a bar, or in a church.

Box 3.4

Whose research?

(Robin Palmer, Rhodes University)

In this chapter, we have presented the process of designing a research project as a series of logical decisions made by a researcher. This is a useful way of thinking about the principles of research design, but, in practice, researchers often do not plan research on their own but in consultation with colleagues and others who have a stake in the research. Sometimes the key to a successful outcome lies not so much in technical design excellence, but in managing the complex political situation within which the research occurs. The Dwebe project is a case in point.

The forests and shoreline of Dwebe and Cwebe on the Transkei coast have been for many years sites of struggle over the rights to the abundant natural resources which are found there. Not long after the annexation of the Transkei a hundred years ago, these two remaining areas of the type known as the South Coast Forest were declared protected areas, and placed under the jurisdiction of the Department of Forestry. Over the years, some of the households that dwelt in the reserves were removed, yet the neighbouring communities continued to have access to resources in the form of building materials, emergency grazing, medicinal plants, and seafood. This relationship changed after Transkeian 'independence' in 1976. Declared as nature reserves, the forests and adjacent coastline at Dwebe and Cwebe were fenced, game was introduced, and the areas were placed off-limits to the impoverished communities that depended on their resources.

During the years of negotiation, but especially following the 1994 elections, the communities waited for the restrictions on access to the reserves to be lifted. Towards the end of that year, when there was no response to their representations, they planned a series of invasions to coincide with the spring tides. Bearing agricultural instruments, hundreds of villagers descended on the rocks of the intertidal zone and rapidly denuded them of mussels and other edible organisms. Others stripped botanical resources from the forests. It was not normal behaviour – the local Xhosa-speakers are traditionally respectful of nature – but rather a form of protest, and it worked.

The protest drew the attention of nature conservationists, the media, and government. Community Conservation Committees were established and joint management of the reserves set in motion. A research project – the Dwebe Project – was born out of the concern of some of the conservationists to reconcile community needs with conservation, and to act as facilitators in this process. But issues of access to the reserve were soon eclipsed by the possibility of ownership, not only of the communal lands around the reserves, but of the reserves themselves. The earlier removal of households from the forests

Photo: Rodney Barnett

provided the basis for a land claim which was henceforth pursued in accordance with the provisions of legislation passed in 1994 relating to land restitution.

The restitution process was actively promoted at grass-roots level by a land NGO and its consultant, who appeared to regard the joint management process and its proponents as a source of distraction from the struggle for ownership. In 1996, following a meeting called by consultants, to which representatives of the Dwebe project were not invited, the community representatives formally requested that the Dwebe Project suspend its activities until the land issue was resolved.

By October 1997, the land claim, both in the communal areas and in the reserves, was granted in principle. A key condition for the transfer of rights from the state to a trust representing all the stakeholders, however, is that there be a management plan for the reserves and delegation of their day-to-day management to a responsible agency, in this case, the same conservation authority which has managed it up to now. In short, joint management in principle and in practice was a condition of the land claim. Through the suspension of the Dwebe Project and the neglect of joint management, valuable time was lost, and now the finalisation of the Trust and its consideration of lucrative leasing deals in the reserves is being delayed for want of the experience and understanding needed from all parties to provide the Trust with a viable management plan in a conservation area.

At Dwebe and Cwebe, a major environmental crisis was met with a variety of interventions: initially politicians and media people as well as senior conservationists; later, and over a longer period, an interdisciplinary research team concerned with a variety of conservation and community-related matters and an NGO consultant furthering the land claim. It is not surprising that the complementarity of these interventions escaped the local community leaders and allowed them to be persuaded that the land claim should take priority for a time. They themselves had been in an 'us and them' conflict relationship with the reserve management for years and were bound to be suspicious of joint management and anyone who promoted it too enthusiastically. Land restitution, by contrast, was a policy of the government all of them had recently voted for – a way of making amends for historical injustices and empowering local people that everyone could identify with. Their oppositional model was readily projected onto the outsider interests – the academic researchers and the NGO furthering the land claim. Yet, as was apparent to all in the end, joint management and the land claim were never antithetical processes in this conservation area, but key elements in a reform process that needed to be run in tandem for it to succeed.

Precious time in this fast-track process to resolve conflict and conserve the environment had been lost; the baseline studies of the communities and the local flora and fauna had to be postponed; the fruits of such research were not available in time to feed into the Trust process and, more generally, into development planning for the entire area.

While multidisciplinary research promises to yield information which is of value in finding solutions in contexts such as this, close facilitation of the research process – including adequate consultation with all those who have a stake in the outcome – is crucial. Unless the research process itself is 'owned' by all parties involved, it is likely that lack of cooperation, resistance, and rejection of research findings will continue to bedevil field research designed to address conflict situations in development areas.

Although controlled experiments are useful in determining causality – that is, whether a change in one variable causes a change in another variable – they suffer from a number of problems. In addition to experimenter effects and demand characteristics that may have an unknown impact on the outcome of the experiment, it is often impossible to generalise the findings of experiments to real-world settings. Because experiments take place in controlled and artificial environments, their applicability to real-world settings is uncertain. For this reason, qualitative researchers prefer naturalistic forms of enquiry (see table 3.1). Although qualitative data can be collected in controlled settings that may or may not involve manipulation of one or another variable, many qualitative researchers prefer to investigate behaviour as it unfolds naturally in a setting. Naturalistic inquiry is a nonmanipulative, unobtrusive, and noncontrolling form of qualitative research that is open to whatever emerges in the research setting. The researcher, for example, as a member of a football crowd (investigating crowd behaviour), may conduct unobtrusive investigations, unbeknownst to the subjects. The aim of such research is holistic: to investigate the complex system of interrelationships that develops in particular situations – e.g., the relations between the players and the crowd – without isolating and manipulating specific variables.

In developing a research design, the researcher should consider what she or he is going to do in the research situation while observations are being made. The first question to ask is: Will the researcher be physically present in the context, and what impact will this have on the findings? Researchers are not present in mail surveys or when studying archival material such as newspaper articles or court records. This means that the race and gender of the researcher will not influence the findings, but it also means that the subjects cannot ask for clarification if they do not understand a question, or that the researcher cannot probe for further information. On the other hand, the researcher is present in experimental research and in contexts of naturalistic observation. If the researcher is present, will the participants know that they are being researched? Subjects will act more naturally in situations where the researcher is unknown, but there may be practical or ethical reasons why the researcher cannot remain unknown. For example, it is unethical to observe patients at a hospital without their knowledge and permission.

Decisions about the role of the researcher in the research situation are influenced by the paradigms and purposes of the study.

If the researcher is guided by positivist thinking, she or he may assume that it is stable laws that are being studied, and could disregard the impact of the researcher on the results. Gravity, for example, does not work differently when it is being researched. Interpretive and constructionist researchers, on the other hand, believe that experiences and meanings can only emerge in social interaction, and depending on what type of interaction is of interest to the researcher – i.e. naturalistic interaction, or interaction between researcher and subject – the researcher may choose to be either obtrusive or unobtrusive.

The second question to ask is: Will the experimenter manipulate and control features of the research context? Once again, the answer to this question is influenced by the paradigms and purposes of the study. Positivist research seeks to control and manipulate variables, whereas most interpretive and constructionist research does not. Most explanatory (causal) research seeks to control the research environment, whereas some descriptive and all exploratory research does not.

The role of the researcher in the research situation and the degree of control and manipulation exercised by the researcher will have an impact on the whole study and will influence and be influenced by the types of research technique that are employed. If the researcher, for example, aims not to intervene in the context at all, unobtrusive participant observation or archival research techniques will be employed. This will influence the unit of analysis, as the researcher will have to sample behaviours or pieces of text, which in turn will influence data analysis as the researcher will have to employ qualitative analytical techniques.

Questions to ask about situations

1. Does the research question require experimental control and manipulation to identify causal factors?
2. What impact could the researcher and setting have on the results?

Conclusion

A research design is a plan for action that is developed by making decisions about four aspects of the research: the research paradigm, the purpose of the study, the techniques to be employed, and the situation within which observation will take place. Research is an immensely creative activity, and there are many different forms of research resting on different combinations of paradigm, purpose, technique, and situation. Ethnomethodological research for example, is influenced by the interpretive paradigm, but aims to manipulate variables – a situational intervention normally associated with positivism. Positivist research can use qualitative methods, normally associated with interpretive research, while social constructionist research may attempt to explain causality, a purpose normally associated with positivism.

In spite of the potential for creativity in research design, there remains a constraining relationship between paradigm, purpose, technique, and situation: Certain paradigms advocate certain purposes, which in turn encourage particular techniques and situational arrangements.

With all these competing influences, contingencies, and comple-ments, making design decisions can be challenging. Design decisions should be made according to the principles of coherence and validity. In designing a study, the researcher should engage in two reflexive strategies. Both involve proposing practical strategies for the implementation of the research, and then subjecting these to questioning. First, the researcher should seek to identify and eliminate plausible rival hypotheses in an effort to attain a valid research design. Second, the researcher should strive for design coherence by asking how the research paradigm, purpose, and techniques should fit together logically so that they complement each other. You can do this by answering each of the questions in the boxes above with a view to determining (1) how the answers to the different questions fit together, (2) how the answers relate to the research question, and (3) how the answers relate to the ability to produce persuasive research findings. Each decision should be made to ensure that the results of the study will provide valid and believable answers to the research question.

Exercises

1. The Department of Correctional Services has recently tendered for research to explain the increasing suicide rate among prison inmates. Design a research study to investigate this question. Break into small groups. Let one group design a study from an interpretive paradigm, a second group design a study from a positivist paradigm, and the third group design a study from a constructionist paradigm. Compare the designs and discuss what kinds of question each design is likely to be able to answer.

2. Ezemvelo KZN Wildlife (formerly the Natal Parks Board) has received a number of complaints that their nature reserves are overcrowded. Design a study to investigate overcrowding in nature reserves. Break into two groups. Each group should devise a specific research question and design a study to answer this question. One group should design a quantitative study while the second group designs a qualitative study.

3. A political scientist seeks to determine the reasons why countries under threat of war tend to adopt conservative styles of political leadership. Design a study to investigate the relationship between threat of war and styles of political leadership. Break into two groups. Each group should devise a specific research question and design a study to answer this question. One group should design an experimental study while the second group designs a survey.

Key readings

Bickman, L., & Rog. D. J. (Eds). (1998). *Handbook of applied social research methods*. Thousand Oaks, California: Sage.
This text provides an overview of the state of the art of applied research design. It is particularly useful in the manner in which it considers which techniques best fit the research question, the context, and the available resources.

Campbell, D. T. (1988). *Methodology and epistemology for social science*. Chicago, Illinois: University of Chicago Press.
This book contains a collection of papers on various aspects of methodology that were written or co-authored by Donald Campbell, whose contributions to methodology in psychology have been broad and far-reaching. In addition to an autobiography, the book contains

chapters on measurement, experimental design, and applied social research.

Denzin, N. K., & Lincoln, Y. S. (Eds). (2005). *Handbook of qualitative research.* (3rd edition). Thousand Oaks, California: Sage.
This comprehensive handbook of qualitative research methods considers all aspects of qualitative research, including research design. It is particularly strong in considering how paradigms impact on method.

4

Ethical issues in social science research

Douglas R. Wassenaar

South African Research Ethics Training Initiative (SARETI)
School of Psychology, University of KwaZulu-Natal, Pietermaritzburg

The essential purpose of research ethics is to protect the welfare of research participants. **Research ethics**, however, involves more than a focus on the welfare of research participants and extends into areas such as scientific misconduct and plagiarism.

Ethical review is increasingly becoming mandatory for social science research globally. In South Africa, most leading universities require that all social science research involving human participants be reviewed by an independent **research ethics committee (REC)** before data collection can commence (Israel & Hay, 2006). Similarly, many editors of leading international and local social science journals are requiring authors to furnish proof of ethics approval before a research article will be considered for publication. In 2003, the Human Sciences Research Council (HSRC), the largest social science research organisation in Africa, instituted compulsory ethics review for all research with human participants (see www.hsrc.ac.za). Although the above illustrates that there are increasing concerns with research ethics at institutional level globally, research ethics should be a fundamental concern of all social science researchers in planning, designing, implementing, and reporting research with human participants. The growing institutional priorities accorded to research ethics by large institutions such as science councils, universities, and academic journals should not distract individual researchers from their fundamental obligation to treat research participants ethically and not as simple means to researchers' ends.

Research ethics should be a fundamental concern of all social science researchers in planning, designing, implementing, and reporting research with human participants.

The new *South African Health Act* (Act 61 of 2003, Chapter 9, section 71) stipulates that an independent accredited research ethics committee must approve all research with human participants. **Research ethics guidelines** were published shortly after the act was promulgated (Republic of South Africa, 2004b). At the time of writing, it is not clear whether they were intended to apply to social science research unrelated to health research. A specific international guideline has also been drafted for social science conducted in the context of health research (Jesani & Beraji, 2000).

History of research ethics

Most accounts of the history of research ethics attribute the growth of research ethics to the aftermath of the atrocities committed by Nazi medical researchers in Germany during World War II. The trial of several Nazi doctors in Nuremberg was followed by the publication of the Nuremberg Code in 1948 (Amdur, 2003). This code emphasised the importance of individual informed consent in all research with human participants in order to prevent the recurrence of abuses by scientists in the name of research.

The Nuremberg Code is rather restrictive regarding persons who could not consent to research, and the World Medical Association published the more detailed Declaration of Helsinki in 1964, last revised in 2000 (Amdur, 2003). Numerous other guidelines and ethical codes for researchers have been published since World War II, and

Dr Mengele of Auschwitz

most of these focus on biomedical research. However, many disciplines in the social sciences have also developed codes of ethical conduct for researchers, and these include psychology, sociology, anthropology, history, and nursing (Calahan, 1988). In South Africa, some universities conducting biomedical research have RECs dating back to the 1960s. The South African Medical Research Council (MRC), was one of the first to implement mandatory ethical review of all its research, and published the first edition of its research ethics guidelines in 1977 (Israel & Hay, 2006; see also www.mrc.ac.za/ethics/ethicshuman.htm). Compulsory review of social science research in South African institutions has not been systematically surveyed, but it is probably true that social science research ethics did not enjoy much attention institutionally in this country before the 1990s.

Many disciplines in the social sciences have codes of ethical conduct for researchers. These include psychology, sociology, anthropology, history, and nursing.

As in medicine, increased awareness of the importance of ethics in social science research has been driven in part by outrage caused by particular studies. (For an overview of research abuses in medicine, see Amdur, 2003; Emanuel, Crouch, Arras, Moreno, & Grady (2003), Part I). Some examples are mentioned briefly here. Probably the best-known controversial study in social science was Milgram's obedience experiment (Amdur, 2003; Blass, 1999), in which participants were led to believe that they were inflicting lethal electric shocks on other people. In reality, the shocks were not really being delivered, but if they were they would certainly have been lethal. The research participants and many in the scientific community were distressed when they learned that participants had been deceived, and also that they had been encouraged to administer what could have been fatal shocks if they had been real.

Another well-known case was Zimbardo's simulated study of the tensions between prisoners and warders. Zimbardo's student participants began to assault each other as conditions in the study rapidly began to resemble a real-life situation (Blass, 1999). In a 1955 study of jury decision making, a jury was audio taped while it considered a case, believing their deliberations to be *in camera*. When it became known that the deliberations had been recorded by a researcher, there was a public outcry (Amdur, 2003). In a study in the 1970s of casual homosexual encounters, which became known as the 'tearoom trade' study, the researcher covertly observed sexual meetings in a public park, then recorded participants' car registration numbers, traced their residential addresses, went to their homes, and interviewed them about some other information in order to profile the characteristics of persons involved in the 'tearoom trade'. This study thus involved intrusive monitoring of public and private behaviour, as well as deception about the nature of the interviews conducted (Amdur, 2003).

Many of the major ethical guidelines for researchers were developed because of specific abuses of research participants. Although the worst of these were in biomedical studies, psychosocial research has also involved abuse of research participants.

Although it could be argued that none of the above examples equals the nature and extent of the atrocities committed by the Nazi doctors, or the tragedy of the Tuskegee syphilis study (Brandt, 1978; see box 4.1), all of these studies involve ethical violations of one type or another.

While some might argue that the eventual benefits to knowledge outweigh the discomforts of a few participants, research ethics since World War II has strongly emphasised that the ends of research do not justify the means. Research participants' dignity and welfare should always transcend the interest of the research.

Research participants' dignity and welfare are more important than the research.

Box 4.1

The Tuskegee syphilis study

In 1932, the US public health service funded a study to examine the effects of syphilis. There was no effective treatment for syphilis at the time, and the long-term effects of the illness had not been clearly described. The study enrolled over 300 male syphilis sufferers from an impoverished rural area in Alabama where the prevalence of syphilis was known to be high. There were 200 matched uninfected controls. It is uncertain whether the men knew they were in a natural history study involving no treatment, and there is no clear record of informed consent. They were subjected to various examinations and medical procedures. Penicillin, an effective treatment for syphilis, became available during the course of the study in the early 1950s, but the men in the study were not informed of this, nor were they given this treatment as it would undermine the scientific purpose of the study.

Their condition was allowed to worsen and many of the men died. After public exposure, the study was stopped in 1972 and it led to the development of national research regulations in the USA in 1974. Survivors and families of the deceased were awarded compensation, and President Bill Clinton issued a formal presidential apology for the Tuskegee syphilis study on behalf of the US government in 1997. (Amdur, 2003; Brandt, 1978)

Resistance to ethical review of research

The growing emphasis on the ethical review of social science research should not go unexamined, and, like many other areas of academic activity, it is an area of vigorous and critical debate (see box 4.2). In general, it is useful to distinguish between principled objections to ethics review and pragmatic objections. The main principled objection to ethical review comes from those who might argue that the imposition of ethical constraints on research is a curtailment of academic freedom. This is a fallacious argument that is only true if academic freedom is construed as the freedom to pursue any academic line of enquiry using any methodology, without consideration of the welfare of the research participants (Herrera, 2003). Academic freedom sanctions freedom of intellectual enquiry, but cannot sanction particular research methodologies which may impact on the dignity and the rights of others. Other principled – and partially pragmatic – objections to the ethical review of social science research include the fact that the systems of review for social sciences are generally derived from biomedical review (Cribb, 2004; Hoeyer, Dahlager, & Lynöe, 2005; Israel, 2004). Social science researchers may thus be asked questions about their research proposals that are entirely irrelevant to social science research (e.g. tissue sampling) while other key social science nuances (e.g. confidentiality of institutional or community identity) may be missed.

A major review of the ethical review requirements for social and behavioural research in the US has made several recommendations to move the ethical review process in the social sciences away from those for biomedical research, in order to suit the key ethical issues in social science as opposed to biomedical research – although some remain shared. In general, most social science research carries lower risks than biomedical research, and the focus should be on ensuring voluntary informed participation and addressing threats to confidentiality (National Research Council, 2003). With regard to the ethical review of research, it has been proposed that there should be clearer performance indicators for Research Ethics Committees to determine whether in fact they do significantly improve human protections (Emanuel, Wood, et al., 2004; National Research Council, 2003).

Box 4.2

The ethics committee: A problematic starting point

Ethics committees are not without problems or criticism against them. Such committees may assume that researchers will behave unethically unless prevented from doing so, and there are also institutional dynamics that shape their decision making. Ian Parker (2005, p. 18) argues that there are four reasons why ethics committees are problematic for some qualitative research.

- Quantitative: Most ethics committee members have very little training or exposure to qualitative research and so they judge proposals against positivist and quantitative criteria. Good qualitative research is often treated with suspicion.
- Normative: The committee will try to anticipate the outcomes of your research, and will prevent new forms of research whose outcomes fall outside these predictions.
- Bureaucratic: The endlessly expanding checklists of ethics criteria 'always fail to capture exactly what it is you want to do.'
- Routine: By getting researchers to conform to its rules, an incompetent ethics committee can put an end to creative thinking.

For Parker and many other researchers, there may be occasion to resist conventional thinking about ethics to undertake good moral-political research activity. For example, you may need to use deception to gain entry to research a corrupt and abusive police department. On the other hand, while it might be easy to conceal the identity of your research participants, some participants may feel that they are being denied their voice by this practice, and may want to be identified.

The important lesson from these critics is that we should not view ethics guidelines as rules to be applied in an unthinking manner. Rather, we should aim to do sound moral-political research, exposing bad practices, and protecting and empowering participants as far as we can.

Pragmatic objections to ethics review are much less complex but may nevertheless be intense. Many objections concern the time delays involved in obtaining ethical review, as RECs typically meet monthly at best. Typically, about 50% of proposals are returned for amendment (Jelsma & Singh, 2005) and corrections to proposals may require resubmission in a subsequent month. Researchers need to factor the ethical review process into their research timelines. More seriously, some researchers may feel that RECs are not competent in their review of the technical aspects of the study, or in some cases even of the ethical aspects of the study. This second point illustrates the fact that REC members have an obligation to be trained in research ethics, and that RECs should have access to advisors who are competent in methodological aspects of the studies they review. If researchers themselves are more competent in the ethical aspects of research, their protocols are less likely to be returned for revision by research ethics committees (see box 4.3).

Research ethics is a field of lively debate.

The more carefully researchers address ethical issues in designing their studies, the less likely they are to be frustrated by the decisions of an ethics committee.

Box 4.3

Training for research ethics committees

Poorly trained RECs lacking in confidence are likely to err in a conservative direction to minimise their exposure to risk, and may thus withhold approval of well-designed, complex, and potentially controversial studies. In this regard, there are several global initiatives to build the capacity of REC members, led primarily by the Fogarty International Center at the National Institutes of Health in the USA, and the Wellcome Trust in the UK. The European Union is also contemplating funding research ethics training programmes globally. There are currently two Fogarty-funded research ethics training centres in South Africa – SARETI at the Universities of KwaZulu-Natal and Pretoria, and IRENSA at UCT (see www.shsph.up.ac.za/sareti.htm and www.irensa.org). These programmes also enrol researchers for ethics training, and not just REC members.

Researchers and members of research ethics committees at an international research ethics training course held in Durban.

Most training courses for social scientists in South Africa have not paid particular attention to the ethics training of researchers. This contributes to resistance by researchers to the process of ethical review, which is fundamentally a system of peer review. Peer review is a practice accepted by all *bona fide* researchers who seek research funding and publication. Ethics review is an analogous process that, if competently conducted, can add value to the proposed study and prevent or reduce harm to the participants and adverse consequences for the researcher. There is nevertheless vigorous debate about bioethics and the ethics review process (see Stevens, 2000), which at worst is seen as an interfering layer of obstructive bureaucracy, and at best adds ethical safeguards to well-designed and carefully considered research designs. Ideally, ethical review should be done quickly by a committee including persons trained in research ethics and familiar with social science methodologies. The purpose of RECs is to promote the ethical conduct of research, not to obstruct scientific progress and discourage innovative researchers. There is a dual obligation on RECs and researchers fully and frankly to address the ethical dimension of all research if participants are to be protected from harm.

A further pragmatic criticism of ethical review committees is that, after approval of studies, most committees do not have the resources to monitor post-approval studies, meaning that much of the ethical compliance is based on the researcher, with little real involvement by ethics committees in ensuring compliance with the approved protocol (Weijer, Shapiro, Fuks, Glass, & Skrutkowska, 1995).

Exemptions from ethical review

It is difficult to think of a study that does not have ethical implications. However, there are some classes of study that in most countries would be exempted from ethical review, although the guidelines are not unambiguous (Pritchard, 2001). The clearest case for exemption applies to studies that do not involve human participants and/or are based on information that is already in the public domain. For example, an analysis of newspaper reports on suicide is exempt, as would be a meta-analysis of published studies on childhood sexual abuse. A study of university graduation statistics by race group would not require review if based on data released in public reports by South African universities. Certain organisational evaluation and quality-control audits are exempt from review, though these become complicated if considered for publication and individuals or institutions are identifiable. Research based on data from personal clinical or institutional records, however, although not engaging with human participants directly, is not exempt from review. (Some US guidance on classes of research exempt from review is available at www.ohrp.osophs.dhhs.gov/humansubjects/guidance/decision charts.htm).

Philosophical principles guiding ethical research

Although there are several approaches to ethics (see Fulford, Dickenson, & Murray, 2002), there are four widely accepted philosophical principles that are applied in various ways to determine whether research is ethical (Beauchamp & Childress, 2001). This approach has become known as **principilism**. There are also several variations of these philosophical principles. Furthermore, different codes of conduct and ethical guidelines for researchers give different emphases to these four philosophical principles, so the field can be bewildering to the newcomer because these principles are not rules and need to be thoughtfully applied to specific situations.

*In addition to four basic ethical **principles** applicable to research – respect for persons, beneficence, non-maleficence, and justice – there are also several research ethics codes that are used to guide researchers.*

Autonomy and respect for the dignity of persons

This is the philosophical principle most clearly linked to the Nuremberg Code, and it finds expression in most requirements for voluntary informed consent by all research participants. Protection of individual and institutional confidentiality is also an important operational expression of this principle. The identity of communities should also be protected in particular circumstances (see American Academy of Pediatrics, 2004)

Nonmaleficence

This philosophical principle supplements the autonomy principle and requires the researcher to ensure that no harm befalls research participants as a direct or indirect consequence of the research. It must be noted that harms can include wrongs (Macklin, 2002) – someone may not be harmed by certain research, but they may nevertheless be wronged. For example, if someone were covertly to observe your private behaviour and never disclose any details to anyone, you would not be harmed but you would nevertheless have been wronged. Similarly, deception is fundamentally wrong (Macklin, 2002) and should be avoided wherever possible through careful consideration of alternative research designs (Herrera, 2000). Research should avoid and minimise harms and wrongs.

Beneficence

This philosophical principle obliges the researcher to attempt to maximise the benefits that the research will afford to the participants in the research study. In combination with the above principle (nonmaleficence), beneficence finds expression in research ethics in risk/benefit determinations, where researchers and ethics committees have to consider the relative risks of a proposed study against any benefits that the study might directly bring to participants or to society through knowledge gained. Note that, in this determination, the payment of research participants is not considered a benefit. In other words, risks cannot simply be offset by the payment of large sums of money to participants – the benefits of the research must be more direct – such as better access to health facilities, better skills, better knowledge of the topic in question, and so on.

Justice

Justice in general requires that people receive what is due to them. Justice in research is a complex philosophical principle, and in general it requires that researchers treat research participants with fairness and equity during all stages of research. Thus, for example, justice applies to the fair selection of research participants. Selection of participants should not be based on convenience. It could, for example, be argued that in most social science research the burdens of the research are borne by the participants while the benefits accrue to the researcher, who gains degrees, publications, prestige, promotion, etc., while the circumstances of the research participants remain unchanged. Justice also requires that those who stand to benefit from the research should bear the burdens of the research, and vice-versa. This means, for example, that interventions should not be experimentally applied to populations who in future would be unable to benefit from such interventions if the study were to find the intervention effective. Justice requires that researchers have some responsibility to provide care and support for participants who may become distressed or harmed by a study.

While the above four philosophical principles are important and almost universally accepted, there are alternate ethical frameworks that can be mentioned briefly. These include virtue ethics, feminist ethics, the ethics of care, and cross-cultural ethics (Beauchamp & Childress, 2001; Cole & Coultrap-McQuin, 1992; Fulford, Dickenson, & Murray, 2002). All of these are currently engaging with research ethics, and making research ethics a vibrant field of intellectual activity and practice. In the African context, there is increasing debate about whether the four principles are acceptable in a continent in which communal concerns are weighted as heavily, if not above, individual values (Mkhize, 2004). It is hoped that these debates will nurture the evolution of a more indigenous and nuanced approach to research ethics in the African setting.

The elements of ethical research

The practical implications and application of the above four philosophical principles to applied social science research are not self-evident. Recent works have attempted to spell out the ethical obligations of researchers more pragmatically and operationally than has to date been clear from the four philosophical principles or available ethical guidelines.

The most useful of these recent works was published by Emanuel, Wendler, Killen, and Grady (2004). Although this framework was developed to guide clinical researchers conducting externally sponsored research in developing countries, its key components are relevant and useful to social science researchers working in developing countries, whatever their funding sources are, if any. Emanuel et al. (2004) state that their framework, unlike many current international ethical codes, is not driven by a recent scandal, is structured to match the process of research design, implementation, and reporting, and furthermore embeds within it the four principles and their operational implications. It is also compatible with most international guidance documents that can provide more detail on some of the specific elements set out below. The framework is based on eight *practical* principles (not to be confused with the four *philosophical* principles outlined in the previous section), each of which has several operational benchmarks, some of which are mentioned in each section below. The eight practical principles are collaborative partnership, social value, scientific validity, fair selection of study population, favourable risk/benefit ratio, independent ethical review, informed consent, and ongoing respect for participants and study communities.

These broad principles, if considered carefully and applied together, are likely to enhance the ethical standing, and, probably, the scientific value of research. No single principle is more generally important than any other, although not all of them are applicable to every conceivable research design. The framework is designed to provide researchers and REC members with a coherent set of considerations and benchmarks against which to evaluate the ethical merits of a particular research proposal. An adaptation of Emanuel et al.'s (2004) principles is outlined briefly below, with a special emphasis on their relevance to social science research. Many of these practical principles will be familiar to social scientists, as they reflect values inherent in much social scientific research.

An ethical framework should be accessible to researchers, and structured to deal with the various stages of implementing a research project.

Collaborative partnership

This dimension requires researchers to ensure that the research they are conducting is developed in collaboration with the target community or population (see, for example, Diallo, Doumbo, Plowe, Wellems, Emanuel, & Hurst, 2005). Ideally, such research should be driven by an expressed community need and should involve the community in planning the focus and purpose of the research, participating in the research, and sharing the benefits of the research. The research should also be sensitive to the values, cultural traditions, and practices of the community (see Molyneaux, Wassenaar, Peshu, & Marsh, 2005). Benefits from the research should also accrue to the participating community and not just to the researchers.

The researchers and the research method should be sensitive to the values, cultural traditions, and practices of the community.

Social value

The research should address questions that are of value to society or particular communities in society. The research should specify who the beneficiaries of the research will be, and in what way they might benefit directly and indirectly. The problems being studied should lead to knowledge and/or interventions that will be of value to the participants and/or society.

Box 4.4

How to apply for ethical approval

In South Africa, different institutions may have different procedures, but there may be common elements to them. Each REC should have standard operating procedures — these should be transparent and available to researchers on request. In general, the stages in obtaining ethical approval are roughly as follows:

The researcher, either alone or as the head of a research team, drafts a research proposal. A good proposal includes a review of relevant literature which justifies the need for research on the area under study, and justifies the particular research method being proposed (see chapter 5). The proposal should include a section in which the researcher considers and discusses the ethical issues she has identified in her proposal, and what she plans to do to resolve these.

The researcher must submit the proposal to her local institutional ethics committee (REC) for review. In some institutions, it should be submitted for scientific review and approval first. A specific application form must be completed, depending on the institution. The full proposal must accompany the application, along with a copy of the questionnaire, test, or interview schedule that will be used in the study. A copy of the information sheet for participants and the consent form (see box 4.5) should usually also accompany the application.

The REC will review the proposal and may come to any of the following decisions, which it will communicate to the researcher in writing:

- Approve the proposal. Written approval, often with an approval number, will be issued to the researcher.
- Provisionally approve the proposal but request the researcher to provide some minor additional information or make minor changes to the proposal or documentation. Such minor issues are usually

Scientific validity

The design, methodology, and data analysis applied in the study should be rigorous, justifiable, and feasible, and lead to valid answers to the research question. Unreliable and/or invalid methods are unethical because they waste resources, yield invalid and unusable results, and expose participants to risk and inconvenience for no purpose. Poor science is unethical. Methodology should be rigorous, appropriate, and systematic whether quantitative or qualitative designs are being used. The competence of the researcher and his or her research associates to undertake the research and its subcomponent tasks are also important components of this ethical dimension. Some restrictions or under-powering of sample size are acceptable if the purpose of the research is partly educational, such as junior postgraduate research projects and certain master's level projects conducted under supervision.

Poor research design is an ethical issue because it can lead to invalid results and an unnecessary waste of resources and participants' time.

then approved by the chair of the committee and need not await a further committee meeting. Some RECs invite the researcher to be present during the review so that clarifications can be made immediately.

- Suggest amendments to the proposal, or some aspect of the proposal, and request the resubmission of certain documents to the full research ethics committee.
- Reject the proposal in its submitted form. In such cases, the committee must provide written justification for its decision. The researcher may discuss the decision of the REC with the chair of the committee or may ask to attend the next meeting of the committee to appeal the decision of the committee and defend the proposal.

Different institutions have different procedures for dealing with appeals by researchers who are dissatisfied with an REC decision. In South Africa, the new Health Act allows researchers to appeal to the National Health Research Ethics council if they are dissatisfied with the decision of an accredited REC.

After approval, the researcher may proceed with the study and must adhere to the procedures and methods in the approved proposal. If it becomes clear that deviations are necessary for reasons that could not be anticipated earlier, the amendments must be brought to the attention of the REC.

The REC may monitor the study to ensure that the protocol is being adhered to and that participants' welfare is being ensured.

The researcher should inform the REC when the study is completed. If the results of the study are submitted to a reputable peer-reviewed journal, the editor will usually ask for written proof of ethical approval. The researcher should ideally send a copy of any publication arising out of the study to the REC.

Fair selection of participants

The population selected for the study should be those to whom the research question applies. Convenience samples should be avoided unless in pilot research or studies intended primarily for education of trainee researchers. Vulnerable populations should not be exploited or used merely because they are accessible to the researcher (Eckstein, 2003). Those most likely to benefit from the outcomes of the research are those who should bear the largest burden of the research.

Try identifying possible harms or risks to your research participants.

Favourable risk/benefit ratio

Researchers should carefully identify all the possible risks, harms, and 'costs' of the research to the participants, and specify means to minimise such risks and costs so that the risk/benefit ratio is favourable. Contingencies should be developed to deal with foreseeable harms or discomforts associated with research, such as access to competent counselling facilities where interviews elicit traumatic material, etc. The payment of money for participation in research, while not unethical, is not to be factored into offsetting risk (see Dickert & Grady, 1999). However, money may be paid to participants to reimburse them for their travel and other costs. The best way of balancing risks and benefits is to minimise risks and to maximise the benefits the research might generate for participants in relation to the research question. Benefits to society, as distinct from benefits to participants themselves, are a secondary but important consideration in determining the risk/benefit ratio.

Payment of money to research participants is not considered a benefit to offset risks.

Independent ethical review

An independent and competent research ethics committee should subject all protocols to independent ethical review prior to commencement of data collection.

Such review is analogous and complementary to scientific **peer review**. Competent ethics review should maximise the protection of the participants and enhance the quality of the research. There is as yet no standardised application form for ethics review of social science in South Africa, and there is considerable variation in institutional requirements. Some institutions exempt some postgraduate research from review; this is questionable in view of the fact that the status of the student is not a determinant of whether the study is likely to do harm or not (Ashcroft & Parker, 2003; BPS, 2003). The ethics committee will review scientific elements of the study, but it will do so to determine whether the methods are appropriate and carry risk of harm or likelihood of benefit, and it will consider alternate, less risky methods of addressing the research question (see box 4.4).

Informed consent

Historically, **informed consent** has often been seen as the only determinant of the ethicality of research. In this framework, it is only one of eight determinants of ethicality in research. Participants may not, for example, legally consent to research known to cause harm without accruing benefits. The standard components of consent are (a) provision of appropriate information, (b) participants' competence and understanding, (c) voluntariness in participating and freedom to decline or withdraw after the study has started, and (d) formalisation of the consent, usually in writing (see box 4.5). This means that researchers must provide potential participants with clear, detailed, and factual information about the study, its methods, its risks and benefits, along with assurances of the voluntary nature of participation, and the freedom to refuse or withdraw without penalties.

There is some data to suggest that historically oppressed groups do not perceive participation in health research as voluntary (Barsdorf & Wassenaar, 2005), and this should be surveyed further in the social sciences. Signed consent is not necessary if the risks of harm are very low, and if the signed consent form constitutes a potential breach of confidentiality (Amdur, 2003). Research with minors is ethically and legally complex and should, as a rule, be done only with the consent of legal guardians and the assent of the minor if risks are acceptable (Leikin, 1993; Schenk & Williamson, 2005). The degree of risk involved in the particular study and the maturity of the child influence whether or not independent adolescent consent is acceptable. Risks also have to be weighed against direct benefits of participation. Permission to conduct research in a school or other institution does not substitute for obtaining the informed consent of parents or guardians. Particular care and special precautions need to be taken in obtaining informed consent from vulnerable populations, including but not limited to psychiatric patients, prisoners, members of disadvantaged groups, illiterate persons, persons in impoverished rural settings, and persons in crisis situations such as natural disasters, warfare, or refugee situations. In some settings, it is appropriate to seek permission from gatekeepers of particular communities (e.g., village elders) to conduct research with a particular population, but such permission in general is not a substitute for informed individual consent.

Ongoing respect for participants and study communities

This principle requires that participants be treated with respect during a study, that their individual information remains confidential (Easter, Davis, & Henderson, 2004), and, in some cases, that communities are not identified with research that may attract harms through foreseeable stigma and discrimination (American Academy of Pediatrics, 2004). In extended studies, the informed consent process should be repeated, and monitoring of harms should be carried out. In addition, there are increasing international concerns about what happens to participants and communities once the research is over. There is an increasing sense that researchers at the very least have an obligation to make the findings available to the host community in a format that is relevant and appropriate, and empower that community with the knowledge that has been collected. In intervention research, the experimental group should be ensured some continued access to the successful interventions, and the intervention must be made available to any control groups that were involved. This has budgetary implications but prevents exploitation of participants for the sake of the career and prestige of the researcher. At the very least, researchers should consider these issues and make whatever arrangements are within their means or powers of advocacy to recommend. There is also the question of the nature and degree of obligation that researchers might have to assist participants with other problems that they become aware of in the course of their research – this is dealt with by Belsky and Richardson (2004) under the rubric 'ancillary responsibilities', full discussion of which is beyond the scope of the present chapter.

Consideration and thoughtful implementation of these eight practical principles will increase the likelihood that research is ethical and that knowledge is gained without avoidable harms to participants, without whom knowledge cannot be created.

There are increasing concerns about what happens to participants and communities once the research is over. Researchers should at the very least consider making research results available to the study population in some appropriate format.

Box 4.5

Sample consent form

(To be adapted for individual projects/circumstances/needs)

Hello, I am _____ I am from (*organisation/university X*). Our organisation is asking people from your community to answer a few questions for our research (*adapt as needed*), which we hope will benefit your community and possibly other communities in the future.

(*Organisation/university X*) is (*state type and purpose of organisation*), and we are conducting research regarding _____ We are interested in finding out more about _____ We are carrying out this research to help _____ (*adapt for individual projects*) (*Add a few more lines here on the purpose of the study.*) The purpose of this research is to _____

The results of the study will be released in a (*specify: scientific paper, thesis, conference presentation, etc*). No personally identifiable details will be released, only averaged information.

We have chosen you and your household (*adapt*) because we are stopping at every (*xth*) house in this neighbourhood and asking all the adults (*adapt*) in the household to respond to a few questions. We are doing this in a number of different areas in the country, and, after combining all people's answers, we hope to learn more about _____ which will help us make useful recommendations to the relevant authorities and organisations.

Please understand that **your participation is voluntary** and you are not being forced to take part in this study. The choice of whether to participate or not is yours alone. However, we would really appreciate it if you do share your thoughts with us. If you choose not to take part in answering these questions, you will not be affected in any way whatsoever. If you agree to participate, you may stop at any time and discontinue your participation. If you refuse to participate or withdraw at any stage, there will be no penalties and **you will not be prejudiced in any way.**

I will not be recording your name anywhere on the questionnaire, and no one will be able to link you to the answers you give. Only the researchers will have access to the unlinked information. All individual information will remain confidential.

The interview (*adapt: questionnaire etc.*) will last around (*X*) minutes (*this is to be tested through a pilot*). I will be asking you a few questions and request that you are as open and honest as possible in answering these questions. Some questions may be of a personal and/or sensitive nature. You may choose not to answer these questions. I will also be asking some questions that you may not have thought about before, and which also involve thinking about the past or the future. We know that you cannot be absolutely certain about the answers to these questions, but we ask that you try to think about them. When it comes to answering these questions, there are no right and wrong answers. When we ask questions about the future we are NOT interested in what you think the best thing would be to do, but what you think would actually happen. (*Adapt for individual circumstances.*)

If I ask you a question which makes you feel sad or upset, we can stop and talk about it. There are also people from the local Department of Health/university (*adapt*) who are willing and available to talk with you/assist you with those things that upset you, if you need any assistance later. If you need to speak with anyone after I have left, a professional person can be reached at the following telephone number _____

If possible, our organisation would like to come back to this area once we have completed our study to inform you and your community of what the results are and discuss our findings and proposals around the research and what this means for people in this area.

If you have any other questions about this study, you may contact (*name*) at (*institution*) by (*phone/fax/email details*).

If you have a complaint about any aspect of this study, you may also contact the ethics committee of (*institution*) at (*phone/fax/email*).

(The above section should be in a 'tear-off' format that can be kept by the participant. The researcher should keep the sections below.)

CONSENT

I hereby agree to participate in research regarding _____ I understand that I am participating freely and without being forced in any way to do so. I also understand that I can stop this interview at any point should I not want to continue and that this decision will not in any way affect me negatively.

The purpose of the study has been explained to me, and I understand what is expected of my participation. I understand that this is a research project whose purpose is not necessarily to benefit me personally.

I have received the telephone number of a person to contact should I need to speak about any issues that may arise in this interview.

I understand that this consent form will not be linked to the questionnaire, and that my answers will remain confidential.

_____

I understand that, if at all possible, feedback will be given to my community on the results of the completed research.

_____

_____   _____

Signature of Participant   Date

(This introduction and consent form, as well as the questionnaire, must be translated – and verified by back translation – into the first language of participants.)

Additional consent to audio or video recording:
_____

In addition to the above, I hereby agree to the audio and/or video recording of this interview/ evaluation (*adapt*) for the purposes of data capture. I understand that no personally identifying information or recording concerning me will be released in any form. I understand that these recordings will be kept securely in a locked environment and will be destroyed or erased once data capture and analysis are complete.
_____

_____   _____

Signature of Participant   Date

(With acknowledgement to the University of the Witwatersrand, Johannesburg, and anonymous members of the HSRC Research Ethics Committee, on whose forms this adaptation was based.)

Ethics in qualitative research

It is often mistakenly assumed that **qualitative research** is exempt from ethical considerations or review. Arguments presented are that the method is conversational and that data analysis attempts to preserve the integrity of the data collected. However, participants in qualitative research are entitled to the same protections and respect as those in quantitative research. Qualitative interviews should be done only with informed consent, explicit confidentiality agreements, and the application of a rigorous analytical process to ensure that valid and supportable conclusions are drawn. Qualitative interviews carry far more potential to cause subjective distress in participants than most quantitative methods, and this must be carefully addressed in the risk/benefits section of the protocol. In short, all eight principles above apply to qualitative research. For specific guidance and commentary on the ethics of qualitative research, see Amdur (2003), Cribb (2003), Ramcharan and Cutcliffe (2001), and MRC (2001).

Qualitative research also involves many ethical issues.

Focus groups are a popular methodology in social science research, but they present complications concerning confidentiality, as the researcher cannot guarantee that all group members will treat the information of other persons with the respect it deserves. This should always be pointed out in consent forms for focus group research, and the researcher should undertake to make focus group members aware of the importance of confidentiality. All participants should be encouraged to maintain confidentiality and be briefed about the confidentiality risks in advance.

Focus groups may involve problems with confidentiality, as the researcher cannot guarantee that participants will maintain confidentiality.

Photo: Rodney Barnett

Particular care should be taken to respect the rights of special groups.

Other issues

Apart from and complementary to the issues above, social scientists are expected to observe the highest levels of scientific and professional integrity, and avoid falsification, fraud, and plagiarism, as well as abuse of employees, students, or research participants in any way that takes advantage of the power of the research position or which compromises the researcher's objectivity. There is extensive literature on each of the above that cannot be detailed here. As much research is carried out by trainee researchers under the supervision of academic researchers (see Ashcroft & Parker, 2003), the issue of co-authorship with students in student research will be touched on briefly here. The British Psychological Society Guidelines on authorship (Game & West, 2002) stipulate that the default position is that the student should always be the first author of a publication emanating from the student's research project. The supervisor should be second author, even if the study was undertaken as part of the supervisor's larger field of study, and/or the supervisor's funds and/or equipment were used. Both parties, preferably at commencement of the project, should always agree upon authorship in writing. Changes can be negotiated later as specific circumstances warrant. The onus would be on the supervisor to show that the student's efforts were insufficient to qualify for first authorship.

Supervisors and students should enter into explicit early agreements about possible publication and authorship. The default position is that the student should be the first author of the work unless there are compelling reasons for this not to be justifiable.

Conclusion

Ethics in social science is currently not as well developed as it is in the biomedical sciences, and is not without some controversy. Research ethics is a field of vigorous debate and complexity, and this is to be desired. Research ethics, as has hopefully been shown above, is neither slavish rule obedience nor blunt bureaucratic interference with scientific progress. Research ethics review is fundamentally concerned with assuring that the dignity of human participants is respected, and is not abused or violated in the search for knowledge, scientific progress, or, more mundanely, for career advancement. Science is not value-free, and research ethics strives to make the value component of research more explicit. Efforts need to be made to increase the ethics education of social scientists at undergraduate and postgraduate levels. Systems of ethical review for social science should be sensitive to the particular risks and methodologies of the social sciences, and not just emulate biomedical structures and procedures. Researchers enjoy considerable power to sway public and professional opinion, and these powers must be exercised responsibly and with sensitivity to the issues covered in this chapter. Ethical sensitivity can enhance the value of research practice if seen as congruent with the common goal of most social scientists – the understanding and betterment of human existence.

Researchers enjoy considerable power to sway public and professional opinion, and these powers must be exercised responsibly and with sensitivity to the welfare and rights of research participants.

Acknowledgement: Comments from Cathy Slack on this chapter are gratefully acknowledged.

Exercises

1. Deception in research: Psychology has involved many studies in which participants were deceived about the true purpose of the study. A researcher wants to study the personal hygiene of a group of hospital nurses by placing a hidden video camera so that hand-washing behaviours can be observed. Consult the eight practical priniciples described in this chapter and (a) identify some of the ethical issues associated with this design, (b) describe some ways of trying to improve the ethics of this study, and (c) think of some alternate research designs that might answer the study question and eliminate the need for deception.

2. Research in rural settings: A researcher wishes to study child-rearing practices in rural communities. The study involves interviews and video recording of families interacting with their children. The researcher employs a member of the community to assist with the process. Should individual informed consent be obtained from each of the persons interviewed and recorded on video? What are the possible risks and benefits of such a study? Should the researchers offer to let the community know the results of the study?

3. Personal financial management study: A researcher wishes to study ways in which new graduates manage their personal finances. Statistics suggest that many new graduates overspend and fail to repay their study loans, resulting in spiralling debt and credit blacklisting. The researcher plans to approach major banks to ask them to disclose the accounts of new graduate clients so that these can be tracked for one year to identify spending patterns. It is hoped that the results of the study will inform financial management training programmes for undergraduates and thus benefit future graduates. The researcher assures the banks that no personally identifiable details about the banks or their clients will be recorded or revealed in any reports arising out of the study. Should this study be approved? What are the ethical issues involved?

4. Adoption study: A researcher believes that placing institutionalised children in carefully selected foster homes will benefit their physical, intellectual, and emotional development. She obtains a large grant to conduct a longitudinal study in which half of a group of 100 children is randomly placed in foster care and compared with the 50 children remaining in institutional care over a five-year period. Consult the eight practical principles and make recommendations for each benchmark that would make this study ethical.

5. Victims of business collapse: An economics researcher is interested in the impact of the collapse of a large corporation. The business closed down and the directors were charged with fraud. Employees lost their jobs and their pension funds, and investors lost their

investments. At least two suicides were linked to the financial and personal consequences of the collapse. The economist plans to conduct qualitative research using interviews and focus groups with a sample of affected employees and investors. Consider some of the ethical aspects of this research, applying the eight components of ethical research, and make recommendations that you feel would ensure that the study is ethical.

Key readings

Cribb, R. (2004). Ethical regulation and humanities research in Australia: Problems and consequences. *Monash Bioethics Review, 23*(3), 39–57.
This paper outlines some of the problems that social scientists experience with certain forms of ethical review, especially when conducting qualitative research.

Emanuel, E., Wendler, D., Killen, J., & Grady, C. (2004). What makes clinical research in developing countries ethical? The benchmarks of ethical research. *Journal of Infectious Diseases, 189*, 930–937.
This paper presents a novel framework for conceptualising and operationalising ethical issues in research. It sets out eight general principles, and articulates several benchmarks for each. The framework matches the sequence of designing and implementing a research proposal and is more 'user friendly' to researchers than most ethical guidelines and philosophical principles.

Hoeyer, K., Dahlager, L., & Lynöe, N. (2005). Conflicting notions of research ethics: The mutually challenging traditions of social scientists and medical researchers. *Social Science & Medicine, 61*, 1741–1749.
This paper contrasts biomedical and social science notions of research ethics, and articulates some of the different scientific and political issues that characterise each field. The authors recommend that ongoing dialogue be initiated to reconcile these apparently different disciplinary attitudes towards research ethics. (It is hoped that this chapter bridges some of these tensions.)

5

Putting design into practice:
writing and evaluating research proposals

Mary Van der Riet
University of KwaZulu-Natal, Pietermaritzburg

Kevin Durrheim
University of KwaZulu-Natal, Pietermaritzburg

Research designs exist in research practice. At the end of the day, it matters not so much what the researcher planned, but what was done when the research was carried out. Most often, the first step in starting a research project is to convince others of the importance and feasibility of the research. A research proposal is therefore more than a plan for research, but is a persuasive document that should help to get your research project off the ground. Types of research proposal correspond to types of design, and proposals can vary from architectural blueprints to flexible guides. Proposals that take the form of blueprints specify in advance every detail of how the study will be conducted. Proposals that take the form of guides provide a rough picture or framework of what will be done, and state explicitly how decisions will be made during the research to ensure that the study is coherent and the findings are valid.

There are two aims of any research proposal. First, the proposal should be used to guide the researcher in carrying out the research. A research proposal must be a concrete and practical guide for action. It should give the researcher sufficient detailed information regarding all aspects of the implementation of the research. Second, the proposal is a means of communicating the research plan to others. Research proposals are usually evaluated by others – a contractor, research supervisor, funding agency, or academic peers – and in writing a proposal you should take into account what kind of evaluator will read it. Besides stating how the research will be executed, the proposal should convince a reader that the research is important or worthwhile, scientific, and ethical.

The margin notes in this chapter contain student experiences of proposal writing with hints and tips.

Why write a research proposal at all? The research proposal is important for conceptualising the research process, and writing it helps the framework of your research to emerge. It forces you to think about what the focus of the research is, how you are going to carry it out, and why it is important. Before this process you have an idea of what you want to do, but these ideas are actually made concrete in your research proposal. MERRIDY

Structure of a research proposal

There is no standard format for a research proposal, and proposals can vary in length from one page to a 50-page document. We have included two brief sample proposals at the end of this chapter (see boxes 5.5 and 5.6). We recommend that you read these boxes first, before continuing with the chapter. We have also provided a commentary evaluating these proposals to illustrate the critical decisions one needs to make in the proposal writing process. The proposals relate to quite different kinds of research – an experimental, quantitative survey, and a qualitative study – and we consider each to be an effective persuasive document within its field. However, as with almost all actual proposals, each also has certain weaknesses, and in reading through the rest of the chapter, we will invite you to identify these weaknesses, as well as the strengths, of each proposal. In providing the commentary on the proposals we illustrate the way in which proposals are 'read' by a reviewer. Box 5.1 illustrates the issues evaluators of proposals consider when they examine each section of the proposal. Remember that you often don't know enough about the research context or problem before the research process to write a perfect proposal. The key is to find a way of writing about the research so that it identifies your decision-making process – so that it balances what you don't know with ideas about how you will address particular problems.

Box 5.1

Research proposal assessment form

(University of KwaZulu-Natal, School of Psychology, Pietermaritzburg
Honours research project proposals: Guide for assessment)

The purpose of a research proposal is to present a conceptual overview
and detailed plan of the student's intended research. Students were
given an outline of the structure of the proposal with guidelines.
These guidelines have been used to construct the following framework
for assessing the proposal. Please make comments according to this
framework. Comments will be shown to students as feedback on this
proposal writing process.

Name of student:	Name of supervisor:	
Structure of the proposal	**Guidelines given to students**	**Comments**
Introduction (about 10–15 lines)	A brief account of the research and reasons for conducting it. Is the research topic introduced and motivated?	
Review of literature (1 or more pages)	A brief argument for the thesis based on a preliminary review of the literature. References must be included and cited in APA format. What literature provides support and evidence for the intended research? What is the gap in the literature that the research will address?	
Aim and rationale (about half a page)	A clear and explicit statement of the aim/s in conducting the research, including what the question/s is/are that are to be investigated.	
Methodology (about 1 page)	A detailed description of how the research will be conducted (literature on methodology should be cited). What type	

	of **research design** will be used and why? **Sample/ sampling**: Who will the subjects be and how will they be accessed? What sampling technique is to be used? What is the size of the sample? Motivate all of these. What **data collection techniques** will be used and why? What **instruments** will be used and why?	
Data analysis (a couple of paragraphs)	How will the data be analysed? Specific processes must be described, referring to available methods and literature.	
Ethical considerations (a few paragraphs)	What ethical considerations will arise in the project? How will they be addressed? Has the student adequately addressed ethical issues?	
Time line	A detailed breakdown of deadlines by which each stage of the project will be completed.	
Budget/costs	A detailed estimate of the likely costs of each stage of the project, and where funding might be obtained.	
Anticipated problems	Outline of anticipated problems in doing this project, and a proposal of how these will be dealt with.	
References	A brief list of appropriate references in APA format.	

Additional comments:

There are eight central issues that should be considered in any proposal. These are listed below. These issues might be structured in a research proposal in slightly different ways depending on the type of proposal; for example, is it a proposal submitted for an academic thesis, or is it a research tender?

1. Project title

The proposal should include a carefully crafted title that communicates the purpose of the research and guides the reviewer's expectations. Bear in mind that the title is one of the searchable components of the final research document, be it a thesis, project report, or journal article. Titles should be short and interesting, and provide information about the project's content. A title is too long if you can delete some words without real loss of meaning. What could you improve about the titles of the proposals in boxes 5.5 and 5.6?

2. Research purposes

The purpose of a study is normally explained in three stages: (1) a general statement of what the research aims to discover, (2) an account of where these aims come from, the importance of the findings, and a rationale for the research, and (3) specific hypotheses or questions that the researcher is investigating in the particular study.

Research aims – These specify and **operationalise** the focus of the research. This should be a brief and concrete statement of what the research plans to investigate.

Research rationale – This provides reasons why the research is being conducted. The rationale can be theoretical (basic research) or practical (applied research). The research rationale is normally developed alongside a review of some central ideas in the relevant literature. The purpose of such a review is to show that the proposed study is part of a broader context of academic enquiry. It will neither repeat work that has already been done, nor is it completely unrelated to anything that has gone before. In a proposal written for purposes of university study (such as a proposal for doing a master's or doctoral thesis), it is usually necessary to demonstrate a more thorough familiarity with the literature than for contract research (i.e., research that has been commissioned by some company or organisation).

Hypotheses – Hypotheses are a re-statement of the research aims in terms specific to the study being conducted. They should follow logically from the rationale and literature survey. If the aim of a study is to investigate processes of social control at play in Parliament, the hypotheses should be more specific. The researcher should state what aspects of control are being investigated (e.g., the role of the Speaker), and the kinds of question being investigated; for example, does the gender of the Speaker influence the processes of social control? These hypotheses and questions should emerge from the rationale and literature review. Are the hypotheses in box 5.6 linked to the literature reviewed in the box? Proposals for interpretive or constructionist research projects usually do not have formal hypotheses but should nevertheless contain a specific formulation of the research question (see box 5.6).

3. Sampling

The sampling strategy to be followed should be explained in detail (for details on how sampling works, see chapters 7 and 13). (1) How will the sample be selected (random selection or purposeful sampling), and why is this method of sampling appropriate to the study? (2) What are the characteristics of the required sample (e.g., male schizophrenics, political leaders), and why are they required? (3) What sample size is required, and how will the final sample size be determined? For interpretive or constructionist studies, sampling will be described in less technical terms than for positivist studies. It is nevertheless essential to give a clear indication of the scope and extent of the proposed data collection, and why this is justified. Note the different sampling strategies in boxes 5.5 and 5.6.

4. Procedure

Explain the practical arrangements that will be made to give effect to the sampling requirements of the study. How will entry be gained into the site where the research is to be conducted (important in naturalistic observation, but also in surveys and interviews)? How will you obtain the assent of research participants (see chapter 4 for the details about informed consent procedures)? In the case of institutions such as hospitals or schools, has permission been granted or how will it be obtained? Discuss the kind of relationship to be established with subjects (e.g., an experimental scientist or unobtrusive participant observer) and, if appropriate, the kinds of intervention (controls and manipulations) that will be used.

5. Methods of observation/data collection

Give a detailed account of how the data will be collected (interviews, observations, tests, questionnaires). If measurement instruments are being used, their names and source references should be stated, and their appropriateness to the study, reliability, and validity should be explained. Appropriateness could be seen as the degree of fit between the aim of the research and the data collection technique. How does the data collection technique assist you in achieving your research aim? If interviews are to be used, the purpose of the interviews, the style of the interviews (in-depth, focus group, structured), and some typical interview questions should be given. If observation is to be used, the focus of the observation and the observation recording techniques should be explained. Are these sufficiently explained in boxes 5.5 and 5.6?

Defining a topic too broadly leads to a long proposal and creates difficulties in knowing what to say in the proposal and what to leave out, how large the sample should be, who to include, etc. Narrow down and focus the topic.
CHITRA

Think of the proposal as a 'funnel', going from the broad to the specific. This helped me to know where I was going and how each part fitted into the rest of the proposal.
SILVIA

6. Data analysis

What will the researcher do with the data once it is collected? This question should be answered in as much detail as possible. Although providing a detailed account of the data analysis in advance is not always possible, if the researcher does not know what to do with the data once it is collected, it is likely that the research question is still unclear, the research has not been well planned, and the researcher could easily collect too little, too much, or inappropriate data. A quantitative research proposal should include an account of which statistical procedures will be employed to analyse the data, and explain why these are appropriate. A qualitative proposal should explain which kinds of qualitative method of analysis will be used (e.g., grounded theory, content analysis, or discourse analysis) and why these are appropriate. Do not just give a label (such as 't-test' or 'discourse analysis'), but explain how the analytic method will be used. The method of data analysis should also fit with your research design and research paradigm. Is this done sufficiently clearly in boxes 5.5 and 5.6?

> *Whatever you write in the proposal must be justified: why this sampling/data collection/data analysis method chosen for this study? You need to write to convince the reader that your project is valuable and that you have thought through each aspect of your study carefully.*
> *CHITRA*

7. Costing

A well-planned research study will anticipate the resources that will be used in completing the project. These resources include time (how long will it take to complete the project?), human resources (will assistants, interviewers, or statistical consultants be needed?) and money (how much will it cost for printed materials, consultation, paying assistants, technical equipment, and so on?). This part of the proposal is usually more detailed for grant and funding proposals than it might be in a proposal for academic purposes. The proposal in box 5.6 contains a costing section. Does the research seem too expensive?

> *Writing the research proposal forces you to think about every aspect of your study, before you conduct it. By doing this, potential problems may be highlighted and then you can think of ways to resolve these before they actually happen.*
> *CHITRA*

8. Anticipated problems

Finally, the proposal should anticipate any problems that may be encountered in conducting the research, and suggest ways in which these will be overcome. Problems could be practical (e.g., gaining access to the site and participants) or methodological (e.g., with a sensitive topic, you can expect many incomplete questionnaires). See if you can find the problems anticipated by the researchers in boxes 5.5 and 5.6.

Tender advert

Box 5.2

 Health Systems Trust

Call for tender applications

ID   20010215

By   RHRU (Reproductive Health Research Unit)

Summary   The Research, Monitoring and Evaluation Task Team
            that provides technical expertise to the South African
            National Aids Council is calling for tender
            applications.

Story   The Research, Monitoring and Evaluation Task Team
            that provides technical expertise to the South African
            National Aids Council is calling for tender
            applications. The tender deals with the need for a
            research inventory, which is necessary to enable the
            government to have a database of all the HIV/Aids
            research undertaken so far and identify areas that have
            been neglected or overlooked. Those interested should
            submit their tender to the Research, Monitoring and
            Evaluation Technical Task Team by March the 9th
            2001. The tender should demonstrate an understanding
            of the field and should outline the proposed
            methodology, timeframe, and budget. It is anticipated
            that a full-time researcher will be required for
            approximately 4–6 months. Funds available for this
            tender will be in the region of R80 000.00. For further
            details please contact:

            The Reproductive Health Research Unit, at www.
            rhru.co.za

            The Medical Research Council, at www.mrc.ac.za

            The Health Systems Trust, at www.hst.org.za

Evaluating designs

Earlier it was suggested that research proposals are often evaluated by an external source – the contractor, research supervisor, funding agency, or academic peers – and proposals should therefore be viewed as persuasive documents. The proposal should convince the reader that the research is important or worthwhile, scientific, and ethical. Designs can be evaluated for their persuasiveness along two main dimensions: rhetorically and scientifically.

The rhetoric of the proposal

Research proposals are **persuasive documents**. They aim to convince funding agencies to finance the research, convince contractors to employ a research consultant, and convince supervisors to enrol students for higher degrees. The proposal should therefore be written in a concise and persuasive style. Communication in the proposal should be clear, the argument should flow, and ambiguity should be eliminated.

Besides these general stylistic points relating to good writing, research proposals should be tailored to suit a particular audience. If the proposal is to be evaluated by a policymaker, it should be written in a language that can be understood easily by a nonscientific audience, and it should highlight the practical importance of the research (refer to exercise 4 below). If the proposal is to be evaluated by a scientific panel, it should be technically precise. In addition, the researcher should know whether the scientific panel will be using positivist (statistical) criteria for evaluation, or whether they are open to other research paradigms (including qualitative approaches). This knowledge should influence the language used in writing the proposal and the types of justification given for the study. Spend some time finding information about the person or institution that will evaluate your proposal (visit their website etc.). This will allow you to tailor the proposal to their criteria of evaluation.

Two aspects of a research proposal are particularly important in convincing an audience: the **rationale** and the **costing**. The proposal should be written up so that it convinces the reader that the research is important and worthwhile, in the sense that it answers the set of questions that the reader wants (or thinks should be) answered. The rationale for the study should clarify the importance of the research, and the rest of the proposal should show clearly how the research plans to answer the research question raised in the rationale. The section on costing is important because, besides being convinced of the importance of the research, the evaluator needs to be convinced of the study's feasibility. Is the study do-able, within a certain time period and within a certain budget?

If your proposal is clearly written up and succeeds in convincing the evaluator that the research is both important and feasible, you are likely to attract funding, be awarded a contract, or be admitted towards a higher degree. Good luck!

The science of the proposal

The most important way in which designs are evaluated is according to their scientific merit. If a design is not scientific, it will not provide the kind of answer to the research questions that evaluators require, and will thus not be rhetorically persuasive. The word 'scientific' is used here in a broad sense, referring not only to the criteria promoted by positivist research but also those associated with interpretive and constructionist approaches. Traditionally, a design was considered scientific if the results satisfied positivist criteria. If we are to consider research from other paradigms as scientific, we need to introduce a new criterion of evaluation – coherence – and modify the meaning of the other criteria.

Coherence refers to the degree to which the various elements of the design fit together within the framework provided by a research paradigm. This issue has already been considered in detail in the previous chapter. Coherent designs are like logical arguments: The different parts of the design – paradigm, purpose, techniques, and contextual arrangements – must match each other and fit together to form an integrated whole (see chapter 3). Coherence is bounded by a particular research paradigm. A set of research practices coherent in one paradigm may not be coherent in another. This should not worry us (although it may worry some traditionalists). The important thing to bear in mind is that the proposed research practices should fit the paradigm you are using.

In addition to evaluating a research proposal according to its coherence or fit, it is evaluated according to whether it is likely to produce findings that are valid, reliable, generalisable, and conclusive. As they stand, however, these qualities are not applicable to nonpositivist paradigms. In the discussion below, therefore, we expand the meaning of these qualities of good research as suggested by Lincoln and Guba (1985). Kvale (1996) also provides a conceptualisation of generalisability, reliability, and validity in ways appropriate to qualitative research.

The most difficult part of writing the proposal was the rationale section. We had to show a clear justification, derived from our literature review, for such a sensitive study. In a society that prides itself as gradually attaining a 'colour-blind status' we had to be careful and clearly come up with an informed motivation for a study on segregation in post-apartheid South Africa. JACOB

Box 5.3

Types of validity

Internal validity – The extent to which causal conclusions can be drawn.

External validity – The extent to which it is possible to generalise from the data and context of the research study to the broader populations and settings.

Measurement validity – The extent to which the constructs in the research question are successfully operationalised.

Interpretative validity – The extent to which the appropriate conclusions are drawn from the data.

Statistical validity – The extent to which the study has used an appropriate design and statistical methods of analysis.

Validity/credibility

In its broadest sense, validity refers to the degree to which the research conclusions are sound. To evaluate the validity of your proposed research, you should think about your anticipated findings and conclusions and ask yourself: 'How could I be wrong?' There are many different areas of research where validity may be threatened (see box 5.3). Although all these types of validity are important in research, their relative emphases may vary depending on the nature of the research questions. Explanatory research typically values internal validity over external validity, whereas descriptive surveys value representativeness and generalisability of the findings.

Generating plausible rival hypotheses is a general tactic to ensure the validity of a research design. Ask yourself the question 'Are there any other factors that might explain the results that I anticipate?' There are too many different threats of validity to list here, and there are many different techniques to ensure validity in each of these areas. Quantitative researchers and experimentalists normally design studies by identifying a set of specific validity threats in advance, and then controlling for these (see chapter 8). Such researchers normally use tried and tested measures, experimental arrangements, and statistical techniques to ensure that accurate conclusions can be drawn from the research results.

Qualitative investigators have two problems with this understanding of validity. First, they find it impossible to identify and rule out specific validity threats before doing the research. Second, social constructionists reject the idea that research findings can be accurate reflections of reality. Nevertheless, qualitative researchers maintain that some research is better than others, and they suggest that research can be evaluated according to its credibility. Credible research produces findings that are convincing and believable (see chapter 16).

Again, plausible rival hypotheses are used to establish the credibility of the research by identifying factors that challenge the conclusions. However, 'rather than trying to deal with alternative possible causes or validity threats as variables, either by holding them constant or comparing the results of differences in their values [i.e., measuring them] ... [qualitative researchers] deal with them as events, by searching for clues as to whether they took place and were involved in the outcome of the research' (Maxwell, 1998, p. 93). Qualitative researchers thus understand plausible rival hypotheses as events to be understood, not variables to be explained. Positivist researchers view validity threats as nuisance or extraneous variables that can be controlled and eliminated. Many qualitative researchers, in contrast, adopt a naturalistic orientation and believe that 'nuisance' variables are an integral part of real-world settings, and, instead of eliminating them, they try to find out what impact they have on the outcomes of the study. If they had an impact and this was not noted, misleading conclusions could be drawn. The credibility of qualitative research is established while the research is being undertaken. The researcher continually looks for discrepant evidence to the hypotheses she or he is developing as a means of producing a rich and credible account. One way of doing this is to use triangulation, employing many different research methodologies (e.g., quantitative and qualitative) to find out whether this provides discrepant findings.

Generalisability/transferability

Generalisability (also called external validity) is the extent to which it is possible to generalise from the data and context of the research study to broader populations and settings. Generalisability is especially important when (1) researchers want to make universal theoretical claims, or (2) researchers aim to describe populations. Positivist researchers often assume that they are studying the laws of behaviour in experimental settings. Generalisability is important because these laws are assumed to be universal laws that operate in the real world, not only in the experimental laboratory. Experiments are often conducted in natural settings (these are called field experiments) to ensure that the findings are applicable to real-world settings (i.e., are generalisable outside the experimental laboratory). Generalisability is also important in survey research, but here generalisability refers to other samples and populations, not to other situations or contexts. Surveys use representative samples to ensure that descriptions of samples can be used to describe populations.

Some interpretive research aims to explain and describe common and widely shared categories of human experience. Generalisability is also important for these studies. Constructionist researchers, on the other hand, begin by noting that meanings are highly variable across contexts of human interaction, and do not seek generalisable findings.

In qualitative research, the most difficult part for me was to state my research question at the beginning. Qualitative research is always a journey and it's hard to know at the beginning where I'll end up. Qualitative research also involves a constant review of the literature, so the way I see something, or understand it, changes too. JACQUI

Box 5.4

Working with others in the research process

The construction of a research proposal is a daunting task for the novice researcher. In academic contexts, one usually works with a supervisor. In other contexts, you might write the proposal as part of a team. Conceptualising the research problem and deciding on an appropriate research design is a process and it involves much debate and negotiation. Some university departments and faculties require students and supervisors to sign a contract outlining supervisor–student obligations and responsibilities. Besides the bureaucratic function of such a contract, clarifying several issues with your supervisor or research team is recommended.

1. Set deadlines together with your supervisor, or with your research team, for engaging in the research process. See the time line in box 5.5. When will you implement and complete each stage of the research process; that is, the review of literature, your methodology section, your data collection, and your data analysis?

   When you first start your research proposal, the whole research idea is quite overwhelming and daunting. You are just pulling together your ideas about your research and trying to find out where you are going to go with them, but at the same time you need to be able to conceptualise all the details at once. For example, when you first have to start writing your literature review you have to be able to think about where you are going and what you need to say. You have to know the research that is available in enough detail to decide what to include and what to leave out and how this affects what you need to say. This is quite overwhelming and, for me, one of the most challenging

It's good to understand the construction of the proposal, and the research, not as something that is set in stone, but as more of a process. It changes, and during the write up this involves going back and forth. SILVIA

Instead, they argue that research findings should be transferable. Transferability is achieved by producing detailed and rich descriptions of contexts. These give readers detailed accounts of the structures of meaning which develop in a specific context. These understandings can then be transferred to new contexts in other studies to provide a framework with which to reflect on the arrangements of meaning and action that occur in these new contexts. For example if one learns about the experiences of terminally ill patients in hospital settings, are these transferable to the experiences of terminally ill patients in doctors' surgeries (Silverman, 2000)?

Reliability/dependability

Reliability is the degree to which the results are repeatable. This applies both to subjects' scores on measures (measurement reliability) and to the outcomes of the study as a whole. Individuals will score *parts of the research proposal process. It's probably the stage where I felt that I needed supervision the most!* SILVIA

2. Give your supervisor drafts of sections of the research as they are completed. Developing an academic writing style is like an apprenticeship, and receiving feedback is a crucial part of fine-tuning your ideas. Discuss dates for your submission of drafts to your supervisor. Students provide useful advice:

Start writing! You might think you understand and know where you are going in your head, but it is only when you actually start writing that you realise what you know and don't know! When your proposal seems overwhelming and you are getting confused trying to piece these ideas together, it's best to write them down anyway. Writing sometimes helps to tie the confusing bits together. SILVIA

I learnt that it is extremely important to write several drafts of your proposal. You learn from your mistakes, so the more drafts you write the more you engage with your research proposal and the better it becomes. MERRIDY

I learnt that proposal writing is a skill that has the potential to be developed with practice and effort. ZAYNAB

It helps to have more than one person (besides your supervisor) read your proposal. Another reader might look at your proposal and provide useful feedback that you and your supervisor might not have thought of, which could then be incorporated into the study. CHITRA

3. Discuss publication possibilities with your supervisor and potential author issues. What could be published from your study? What journals could your study be published in? Who will be the main author?

similarly on reliable measures on numerous occasions. Similarly, the same set of results will be obtained repeatedly in replications of the study if the study is reliable. Since positivists believe that they are studying a stable and unchanging reality, reliability is a highly valued criterion that indicates the accuracy and conclusiveness of the findings.

Interpretive and constructionist researchers, on the other hand, do not assume that they are investigating a stable and unchanging reality and therefore do not expect to find the same results repeatedly. On the contrary, they expect that individuals, groups, and organisations will behave differently and express different opinions in changing contexts. In place of the criterion of reliability, they propose that findings should be dependable. Dependability refers to the degree to which the reader can be convinced that the findings did indeed occur as the researcher says they did. Dependability is achieved through rich and detailed descriptions that show how certain actions and opinions are rooted in, and develop out of, contextual interaction. Dependability is also achieved by providing the reader with a frank statement of the methods used to collect and analyse data.

Pilot studies

Conducting research involves costs and it is always a good idea to conduct a pilot study before implementing the final research design. Pilot studies are preliminary studies on small samples that help to identify potential problems with the design, particularly the research instruments. The results of pilot studies can also be included in the introduction to the research proposal. This will help to convince the reader that the research has been carefully planned and thought through, and will result in a scientifically sound study.

Conclusion

Researchers take great care in designing studies that will produce valid and reliable results. Although the quality of the design is apparent only from the actual conduct of the study, the design is usually written up first in the form of a research proposal. The purpose of the proposal is to convince others of the value of the research study, and to guide the researcher in conducting the study. This chapter has considered two ways in which research proposals are evaluated: rhetorically and scientifically. A good research proposal will satisfy accepted criteria along both of these dimensions.

Box 5.5

An investigation of the rationalisation of segregation at a local university

(Jacob Wambugu, Kim Baillie, Xolani Sithole, and Wendy Smith, Research master's class, University of KwaZulu-Natal, Pietermaritzburg)

1. Aims and objectives

This study will investigate how students perceive and rationalise 'racial' contact at a local university. We will study the way in which students describe, evaluate, and justify forms of racial segregation/ integration in their residences and the university campus in general.

2. Rationale

It is possible, in two very brief paragraphs, to provide a solid rationale for a research study. In contrast, the proposal in box 5.6 contains a longer 'literature review'. Be careful not to be over-inclusive in providing literature to support your argument. The central issue is to use the literature to make your argument persuasive, not to cite research for the sake of it.

Research in the USA has demonstrated the remarkable tenacity of segregation (Goldberg, 1998). Segregation in residence, employment, and education remains as widespread today as it was in the 1940s and 1950s (Massey & Denton, 1993). Are similar patterns of 're-segregation' occurring in South Africa after political and legislative transformation? It would appear that the process of *legislative desegregation* in SA has not translated into the *desegregation of social places*. Similarly, in SA universities, divisive racial differences are exacerbated (Washington, 1996) by university policies such as separating students racially into 'classified' residences. It is a sad irony that the liberal, historically white universities, which in the 1980s opposed segregation and apartheid, are now racially segregated. Segregation may have been outlawed, but we observe it in all aspects of university life, among and between staff and students.

This paragraph highlights the central issue and the focus in this study: segregation and social places. It locates the problem theoretically, and in previous studies, and identifies how it relates specifically to the context under study: a South African university setting. This paragraph is an example of the rhetorical nature of a proposal. It poses a question and proceeds to persuade the reader about the significance of answering this question.

The first aim of this study is to investigate student descriptions of racial segregation/integration in the social context of the university. The specific research question related to this issue is: How do students describe their practices in terms of segregation?

Box 5.5 continued

Although some proposals might only get to the aims at the end of the rationale, this paragraph concludes with a statement of the first aim of the study, drawing a direct link to the problem articulated. It then states the specific research question which operationalises the aim.

How is it possible for segregation to remain a *de facto* socio-spatial reality when its legislative and political base has been stripped away? Goldberg (1998) argues that social segregation has changed fundamentally since legislative desegregation. The 'new segregation' is not monolithic, but class based; it is governed ideologically, not by law, but by personal preferences. In this view, the way in which segregation is sustained as a social-spatial reality is by cognitive and ideological rationalisations. The rationalisations people provide for segregation, the reasons they give for segregation, are the discursive structures that preserve segregation (Buttny, 1991; Durrheim & Dixon, 2005). In the USA, for example, 'whites' seek out racially exclusive places because of their preferences for associating with people like themselves, sending their children to good schools, and staying in quiet neighbourhoods. Of course, as Goldberg (1998) argues, these preferences are ordered by the dominant discursive culture and terms.

The second aim of the research is to explore the way in which students explain and rationalise segregation at a local university campus. We are especially interested in describing the way in which students 'position themselves' in the moral field of segregation and racial contact. The specific research question is: How do students account for, justify, and criticise their own actions, and the practices of those around them?

The second aim of the study, and its related research question, are identified. In contrast to a quantitative experimental design, this study does not have specific hypotheses, but it does have clearly articulated research aims and specific research questions.

3. Methodology

Methodology is the study, or 'metatheory', of method, as distinct from the particular method you adopt in your study. Harding (1987) argues that one should attend to methodology in terms of epistemology (philosophies of knowledge, knowers, and knowing), and theory, to distinguish research paradigms. This methodology section contains the sample, procedure, methods of data collection, and data analysis components of the proposal.

The analytic focus of the investigation is on discourse. We describe rationalisations by studying the 'words that people use to describe simple everyday actions and states', for these, as Edwards and Potter (1993, p. 23) argue, 'carry with them powerful implications for the causal explanations of those events'. Qualitative methodology is most appropriate.

> Some proposals will contain a particular statement about the research design of the study, for example, that it is an experimental, or an interpretive, study. In this proposal, the researchers have highlighted that it is a qualitative, discursive study, which will use a focus group method.

We will be using focus groups and the discursive approach of Potter and Wetherell (1987) to investigate the meanings, opinions, ideologies, and experiences of the student body.

Sampling

The sample will be selected from the racially segregated residences at the local university. An initial 'scoping' (Terre Blanche & Durrheim, 1999) or orientation to the context will take place by speaking to people within the residences. Purposeful sampling will be used to select 'information-rich cases' (Patton, 1990), in the form of key informants. Once initial key informants have been identified at each residence, a snowballing technique will be used to recruit participants.

> The researchers should also provide some indication of how this sampling method will affect their research results. For example that a snowball sampling approach does not facilitate generalisation of the findings, but that this is not the central purpose of the study.

This means that the key informants will facilitate the recruitment of volunteers to participate in the focus group.

> Although qualitative studies do not utilise the concept of reliability in the same way as quantitative studies, if a reader wishes to replicate this study, there must be sufficient information about how the key informants were identified. Specific information about how the purposive sampling will be carried out will help evaluators of the proposal understand the potential threats to the findings of the study.

Homogeneous samples of different 'race' groups will be used to study each racial subgroup in depth. The groups will be selected as follows: two groups of black students (from two 'black' residences on campus); two groups of Indian students (one group of those living at home; one group of those living in a residence which has many Indian students); two groups of white students (one group from a racially mixed university residence, and one group from a student house); two groups of foreign black students (one group who live in student houses with white students, and one group who have only lived in the country for 6–12 months); and one group of black and white

Box 5.5 continued

students living in a racially mixed student house. The foreign student and mixed student house groups will be 'deviant' cases for purposes of comparing the rationalisations.

> Although the researchers provide a partial rationale for the types of focus groups, they have not clearly explained why selecting their sample from these different types of residential settings relates to their question. They could make this more explicit and explain, for example, why foreign students living in the country for different lengths of time would illustrate something significant in relation to their research question.

Nine focus groups, each with six to eight participants, will thus be conducted.

Procedure

After the participants have been recruited, they will be invited to participate in the focus group and asked to sign informed consent forms (attached in appendix 1). The focus group interviews will take place in convenient venues (preferably a quiet place in the residence). They will be audio recorded, and the transcribed conversations will make up the data set.

Methods of data collection

As mentioned above, the main form of data collection will be through focus groups. Focus groups allow for the interaction of participants (Stewart & Shamdasani, 1990) and provide a discursive forum suited to the aims of this study.

> The method of data collection is identified, and a brief rationale and reference for this method is provided.

Each focus group will be made up of six to eight participants and two facilitators, all of the same race. Grouping students together in specific racial groups, with a same-race facilitator, will help to facilitate discussion of issues of race. The size of these focus groups is guided by Stewart and Shamdasani's (1990) suggestion of an ideal focus group size (6–10 people), and potential constraints on obtaining participants. The discussions will last for approximately 1½ hours.

> This section provides detailed information on (and a motivation about) the size of the sample, and practical issues about the way in which the group will be conducted.

The discussion will be largely unstructured, but a number of preset questions and probes will be used to guide the discussion (see appendix 2).

General topics to be covered in the focus groups are outlined and the reader is referred to the proposal's appendix (not included in this textbook) for details of the questions to be used.

These questions have been guided by the two research aims identified above.

It is important to link the data collection process to the overall rationale for the study. Evaluators might want an explanation of how the research questions were generated. Were they constructed by the researchers? If so, how can they be certain that these questions will address the overall research question? Were the questions based on the literature reviewed? Are the questions ones which have been used in a previous study? Concern about this issue is related to *measurement validity* – the extent to which the constructs in the research question are successfully operationalised (see box 5.3).

Three general topics of conversation will be covered: participants' descriptions, evaluations, and explanations of segregation.

Data analysis
The recorded focus group discussions will be transcribed verbatim and analysed using the methods of discourse and rhetorical analysis (Edwards & Potter, 1992; Potter & Wetherell, 1987).

The researchers identify, and reference, a method of data analysis, and indicate the kinds of issue which will be primary in conducting the analysis of the data. Are you, as a reader, clear about how the data analysis will be done? A detailed account of the data analysis might not always be possible, but the researchers need to know what they are going to do with the data.

We will analyse the way in which accounts and evaluations of segregation/integration are constructed, and the functions and rhetoric of these constructions. We will identify counter themes and dilemmas in talking about individual and collective segregation on campus. We will also explore whether there are any systematic differences in the accounts of 'black', 'white', and foreign students. *NVivo* (a qualitative data analysis software package) software will be used to facilitate coding and analysis of the data.

4. Ethical considerations

Dealing appropriately with ethical issues is fundamental to any research study. These issues could be addressed in the 'Procedure' section of the proposal or at the end of the proposal, as is done here. See chapter 4 for further information on ethical dimensions of a proposal.

Box 5.5 continued

Informed consent

The aims and purposes of the study will be verbally explained, in detail, to the participants when they are first approached. All volunteers will be asked to sign an informed consent form immediately before the focus group (attached in the appendix). This form will relate to issues of confidentiality, nonmaleficence, and beneficence, detailed below.

Confidentiality

Because of the sensitivity of the issues to be discussed, the participants will be assured of confidentiality. This will be achieved by safely storing the audiotapes of the focus groups, so that no one apart from the research team will have access to these materials. All participants will be referred to by pseudonyms in all published reports. In addition, focus group participants will be asked to respect the confidentiality of the focus group by not divulging details of the discussions to others.

Nonmaleficence and beneficence

Since the issues of racism and segregation are sensitive, the following steps will be taken to ensure that no harm comes to the participants: Participation will be voluntary, participants will be free to leave at any stage during the process, they will be debriefed at the conclusion of the focus group, and individuals will be invited to contact the researcher after the interview if they need to discuss any sensitive issues. In terms of beneficence, quality research into segregation on campus can contribute positively to a transformation and 'diversity management' policy at the university.

5. Practical issues

Timeline

Implicit in this timeline is an indication of how the researchers understand the nature of each of the stages in the research process. It provides the evaluator with an idea of the scope, and the expected duration, of the project.

Activity	Length of time								
Note that in the research process some of the activities run concurrently. Note that a substantial time has been given to the data analysis and the report writing process of the study. Given the conceptual nature of qualitative research, this is often the most time-consuming part of the study.									
Research proposal	6 weeks								
Draft and pilot interview schedule		2 weeks							

Run focus groups (including pilot)	3 weeks					
Data analysis – coding		3 weeks				
Data analysis		7 weeks				
Report writing						3 weeks
Submit first draft						Due date
Submit final report						

Anticipated problems

It is anticipated that finding people to take part in the study might be a problem due to the sensitive nature of the topic under study. To counter this, the snowball sampling procedure will be used to identify groups of friends or acquaintances that are willing and interested in taking part in the research.

6. References

Providing references to the documents cited in your proposal is crucial. They are an indication of the types of theoretical and methodological resource you are using. Depending on the context of your proposal-writing process, there are various formats for citing references. In academic proposals and journal articles in psychology, we use the American Psychological Association (APA) format. Other disciplines might adhere to a different referencing style You need to find out which method of referencing is appropriate for your context.

Buttny, R. (1999). Discursive constructions of racial boundaries and self-segregation on campus. *Journal of Language and Social Psychology, 18*, 247–268.

Durrheim, K., & Dixon, J. (2005). *Racial Encounter: The social psychology of contact and desegregation.* Hove, Sussex: Psychology Press.

Edwards, D., & Potter, J. (1993). Language and causation: A discursive action model of description and attribution. *Psychological Bulletin, 100*(1), 23–41.

Goldberg, D. T. (1998). The new segregation. *Race & Society, 1*(1), 15–32.

Massey, D., & Denton, N. A. (1993). *American apartheid: Segregation and the making of the underclass.* Cambridge, Massachusetts: Howard University Press.

Patton, M. Q. (1990). *Qualitative evaluation and research methods* (2nd edition). Newbury Park, California: Sage.

Potter, J., & Wetherell, M. (1987). *Discourse and social psychology.* London: Sage.

Stewart, D. W., & Shamdasani, P. N. (1990). *Focus groups: Theory and practice.* London: Sage.

Terre Blanche, M., & Durrheim, K. (Eds). (1999). *Research in Practice: Applied methods for the social sciences.* Cape Town: UCT Press.

Washington, K. (1996). Liberalism and liberationism: Education and inequity in South Africa. Online at *www.digitas.harvard.edu/~perspy/old/issues/1996/apr/southafr.html*

Box 5.6

Stereotype activation and university access programmes: preparing students with one hand and holding them back with the other?

(Zaynab Essack, University of KwaZulu-Natal, Pietermaritzburg)

1. Literature Review

> Note that this literature review lays out the groundwork for the research rationale. It does not just summarise literature for the sake of it.

When evaluative tests of knowledge, ability, achievement, and skill are utilised in educational settings, mean differences in test scores are often observed between different racial, ethnic, or gender groups (Sackitt, Hardison, & Cullen, 2004). Stereotype threat theory accounts for this discrepancy by suggesting that negative stereotypes may undermine the performance of some groups of students (Steele, 1997).

Stereotype threat theory has three fundamental premises (Altermatt & Kim, 2004). First, individuals are conscious of society's negative stereotypes about them or the groups to which they belong. Second, the individual then feels pressurised not to confirm the stereotype, particularly in situations in which the stereotype is made salient. Third, this pressure may lead the individual to inadvertently confirm the negative stereotype.

> These two paragraphs clearly indicate the theoretical framework on which the research is based.

In South Africa, access programmes have been developed to increase access to higher educational institutions for students from disadvantaged backgrounds. These programmes were initiated in response to the decades of inequality entrenched by apartheid 'Bantu Education'.

> This part of the paragraph outlines the context of, and background to, the problem.

They offer disadvantaged students, who fail to satisfy university entrance criteria, the alternative of completing the programme as a means to prepare them for the challenges of higher education. The majority of disadvantaged students are African students who attended ex-Department of Education and training (DET) schools. This focus on disadvantage by many access programmes may unwittingly perpetuate stereotypes of intellectual inferiority in these students.

> Here the researcher outlines the 'problem' behind the research.

If such a 'sting in the tail' exists, then it is essential that interventions are designed and implemented in ways that minimise the extent to which negative stereotypes about their target populations are generated and/or made salient.

> Here the researcher outlines the practical value of the proposed research.

Social psychologists maintain that it is those individuals most invested in a particular domain who are most likely to be vulnerable to the pernicious effects of stereotype threat (Conaway, 2005). Domain identification is the degree to which an individual's self-regard is dependent on the outcomes he or she experiences in the domain (Steele, Spencer, & Aronson, 2002). While only a few studies have included domain identification as a variable, these studies have found that the effects of stereotype threat are most strong among those who are highly domain identified (Steele et al., 2002).

> The researcher further elaborates on theoretical notions relevant for the study.

In other words, somewhat ironically, the theory predicts that stereotypes are most disruptive for individuals who have strong domain identification. In the case of a university access programme, this might be a student from a disadvantaged high school who has outperformed her peers, perhaps has even been the top of her grade, and has been accepted into a bridging course at the university.

> The relevance of the theoretical concept to the context is explained.

Her family might be proud of her achievements and she has strong aspirations for her future studies. Unfortunately, according to stereotype threat theory, it is these students with the most commitment, and, perhaps the most academic potential that are most at risk from the negative consequences of stereotype activation.

2. Research purposes

Aims

This study has two central aims: first, to test the central element of stereotype threat theory, viz., the role of domain identification in mediating threat outcomes; second, to provide recommendations to the access year programme about the implementation of academic support at University X, based on the findings from this study, with a view to improving the delivery of such services.

> The researcher outlines the two main goals of the research. Note how these aims 'flow' from the literature review.

Rationale

The central element of stereotype theory has yet to be thoroughly empirically tested with the majority of studies estimating, rather than measuring, domain identification directly. Therefore this study

Box 5.6 continued

addresses a gap in the research. A critical evaluation of the implementation of access programmes will also provide valuable information for programme development and improving the delivery of such services.

> In the literature review above, the researcher has provided a theoretical rationale for the research, and highlighted specific problems. Here the researcher briefly restates the rationale.

Hypotheses

> In contrast to the proposal in box 5.5, this proposal clearly outlines the research hypothesis, which is a succinct and explicit statement of expectations to be tested.

The study aims to examine the hypothesis that access programme students, who are highly domain identified and experience negative domain-related stereotypes, will suffer performance decrements.

> By the end of this section of the proposal, one should be able to move very logically into the methodology – to explain how one will answer the research questions.

3. Methodology

Research design

This field experiment will employ a between-groups design with access programme students as the experimental group and mainstream students as the control group.

> Here the researcher clearly identifies the study as using an experimental, quantitative design. She briefly outlines the main steps in the research, further illustrating the research design.

End-of-semester academic performance in the *Africa in the World* course (a module completed by both mainstream and access students) will be used as the dependent variable, and domain identification and perceptions of stereotyping will be the independent variables.

> Dependent and independent variables are isolated.

This will permit comparisons of domain identification, stereotype threat, and academic performance among all students in order to determine whether stereotype threat and domain identification impact on academic performance. The extent to which students are domain identified will be measured using a multidimensional measure of general and specific domain identification developed for this purpose.

Sampling

> The researcher identifies, and provides a rationale, for a particular sampling strategy. Providing a reference for the technique enables the reader to access more detail about this strategy if necessary.

Purposive sampling is often used when looking for particular types of participants (Durrheim, 1999), and is used to obtain a representative sample by including typical groups in the sample (Kerlinger, 1986).

> It is questionable whether purposive sampling will yield a representative sample. Refer to chapters 7 and 13 for more detail on sampling.

The sample will consist of both access programme students and mainstream students enrolled for the *Africa in the World* module. Participants will be both male and female, 18 years and older.

> The researcher should provide a rationale for the gender and age characteristics of the sample. She should also indicate the sample size. Relative sample size and the fit between the characteristics of the sample and the research question have an impact on the validity of the research.

Procedure

During the first week of courses, we will measure domain identification of all students in the *Africa in the World* module, and thereby partition both mainstream and access-programme students into domain identified and non-domain identified. To track changes in domain identification over time, measures of domain identification will be taken on one further occasion during the semester. Final course marks will be collected at the end of the semester, and will be matched, via student numbers, with domain identification scores. A measure of perceptions of stereotyping will be administered to students at the beginning of the second semester.

> This detailed statement of procedures will act as a guide as the research is conducted.

Methods of data collection

New measures for domain identification will be constructed for the study specific to the domain at hand; i.e., academic study.

> The researcher must be specific about how these measures will be constructed. If new forms of assessment/measurement are to be used, and they have not yet been piloted or standardised, this raises potential threats to the reliability and validity of the research.

The measure will consist of ranking tasks and scaling tasks.

Box 5.6 continued

An evaluator would probably want to ask: Why these kinds of task? What rationale does the researcher have for a focus on these tasks and not others? How is this decision supported by other research?

Item analysis will be employed to evaluate the reliability and internal consistency of the measure.

The researcher could also elaborate on potential threats to validity.

A measure of perceptions of stereotyping will be constructed by the researcher. This will assess student's experiences of stereotypes about intellectual inferiority, their positive and negative evaluation of stereotypes, and their perceptions of other people's stereotypes of them.

Both the domain identification measure and the perceptions of stereotypes measure will be administered to the sample in the form of a questionnaire.

These measures should first be tested in a pilot study.

Data analysis
Quantitative data will be produced and analysed using multiple regression techniques.

The researcher clearly identifies the statistical techniques which will be used to analyse the data.

Measures of domain identification and perceptions of stereotype threat will be the independent variables, and academic performance will be the dependent variable. Multiple regression, which models multivariate relationships, will be used to find a linear combination of independent variables that predicts a dependent variable (Tredoux, 2002).

Structural equation modelling will be used to determine the relationship between stereotype threat, domain identification, and academic performance. Finally, t-tests will be used to explore differences between access and mainstream students in their susceptibility to stereotype threat and their degree of domain identification.

Here the researcher elaborates on what will be done in the process of data analysis: what relationships will be examined and what tests will be used to explore these relationships.

4. Ethical considerations

Although the researcher highlights ethical issues at this point in the proposal, they could also be raised in the section on the research procedure. For a detailed discussion of the ethical dimensions of a research proposal, see chapter 4.

Beneficence and nonmaleficence

Since the study measures performance indirectly (from student records), participating students will only be aware that domain identification is being measured. The measure of perceptions of stereotypes will be implicit so as not to activate stereotypes that could negatively influence their performance. Therefore the study poses no risks to the individual participants.

> It is possible that the researcher underestimates the risks of the research which may raise self-doubt in the minds of the participants.

However, if the expected effect is observed, students who have high levels of domain identification and are performing poorly as a result may be referred to counselling, or even be given the opportunity to participate in support groups which have been shown to successfully ameliorate the effects of stereotype threat (Steele, Spencer, & Aronson, 2002). In addition to this, the results will be of high value to the South African society.

> Justice concerns are an important aspect of the ethical dimensions of a study.

Confidentiality

The data from the study will only be available to the research team. None of the access programme management or staff will have access to the data. The data will be stored by the supervisor.

> Data management and storage is an important part of ethical practice.

However, anonymity cannot be guaranteed because student numbers are required to provide links to academic performance (i.e., first semester results). In spite of this, the risk to students is minimal because linking student numbers to student names and their domain identification and experience of stereotype scores is complex.

Informed consent

A preface outlining the research, its voluntary nature, and issues of confidentiality will be included on the questionnaire.

> The process of informing the participants about the research and obtaining their assent should be detailed. Any information sheets or consent forms used in the research should be attached as an appendix.

Dissemination of research

Research results will be made available to the access programme management. There is also the potential for results to be published in popular and academic press.

Box 5.6 continued

5. Practical issues

Costing

Below are some of the items that might need costing. There might also be costs for payments made to participants, transport to the research sites, subsistence for field trips, and costs for equipment such as video/audio tapes. In a qualitative study, one might also have costs for transcribing interviews and translation.

Survey	1 questionnaire of 4 pages x 80 copies = 320 @ R0.30 per page 1 questionnaire of 4 pages x 80 copies = 320 @ R0.30 per page 1 questionnaire of 2 pages x 80 copies = 160 @ R0.30 per page	R240.00
Research assistance	Research assistant 5 days at R150/day Research assistants might be needed to administer the questionnaire, process the information, and enter it into a computer data-analysis program. Research assistants are usually paid an amount per day or per hour, based on their qualifications.	R750.00
	Statistical consultation Some research skills could be bought in.	R2 000.00
Reference material	Literature searches	R300.00
	Books/literature purchases This may include interlibrary loans, costs for buying journal articles online, etc.	R1 150.00
Consumables	Photocopying	R300.00
	Computer and data consumables This may include hiring computer facilities, buying software, etc.	R2 000.00
	Production of final reports You need to think about possible forms of dissemination of your findings, e.g., presenting a paper at a conference, publishing a paper, and/or writing a report. 3 x 100-page draft copies @ R0.30 per page 2 x 100-page final copies @ R0.30 per page	 R90.00 R60.00
	Publication costs Many journals require an author to pay a fee when submitting an article for publication.	R2 500.00
	Conference attendance	R4 000.00
Subtotal		R13 390.00

Overhead	@ 5%	R669.50
	This figure allows for miscellaneous costs that cannot be anticipated. Some institutions may require an institutional overhead cost in addition to this 5%.	
Total cost		R14 059.50

Anticipated problems
We anticipate some difficulty accessing the entire sample due to absenteeism, etc. Therefore data collection will occur on successive days to ensure that all participants are sampled.

Anticipated research outputs
This study may provide important information for the conceptualisation and management of access programmes at University X. At the same time, it tests an important hypothesis in stereotype-threat theory and should have good potential for publication.

References

Altermatt, E. R., & Kim, M. E. (2004). Getting girls de-stereotyped for SAT exams. *Education Digest, 70*(1), 43–47.

Conaway, C. (2005). A psychological effect of stereotypes. *Regional Review: Federal Reserve Bank of Boston, 14*(3), 40–41.

Durrheim, K. (1999). Research design. In M. Terre Blanche & K. Durrheim (Eds.), *Research in practice,* (pp. 29–53). Cape Town: UCT Press.

Kerlinger, F. (1986). Sampling and randomness. *Foundations of behavioral research,* (pp. 109–122). New York: Holt, Rhinehart & Wilson.

Sackitt, P. R., Hardison, C. M., & Cullen, J. M. (2004). On interpreting stereotype threat as accounting for African American–White differences on cognitive tests. *American Psychologist, 39*(1), 7–13.

Steele, C. M. (1997). A threat in the air: How stereotypes shape intellectual identity and performance. *American Psychologist, 52*(6), 613–629.

Steele, C. M., Spencer, S. J., & Aronson, J. (2002). Contending with group image: The psychology of stereotype and social identity threat. *Advances in Experimental Social Psychology, 34,* 379–440.

Tredoux, C. (2002). Multiple regression. In C. Tredoux & K. Durrheim (Eds.), *Numbers, hypotheses and conclusions: A course in statistics for the social sciences,* (pp. 338–363). Cape Town: UCT Press.

We acknowledge the contributions of Merridy Boettiger, Zaynab Essack, Silvia Maarschalk, Jacqi Marx, Chitra Ranchod, and Jacob Wambugu to this chapter.

Exercises

1. Van der Merwe (1996, p. 285) claims that 'a well-formulated problem actually already contains the answer or solution'. This has implications for the design of research proposals, which should then state in advance details of the research question and techniques, as well as the solutions. While this may be appropriate for positivist research, many qualitative researchers would question the wisdom of such an approach. Explain why.

2. Provide a critique of the research proposal presented in box 5.5 (the qualitative study). Design a quantitative study to investigate the same research question. Develop a time frame and budget for the original study.

3. Provide a critique of the research proposal presented in box 5.6 (the experimental, quantitative study). Design a qualitative study to investigate the same research question. Develop a time frame and budget for the original study.

4. Imagine that you will submit a proposal to a policy maker rather than a research supervisor. How might the rhetoric of a proposal in response to the tender advert in box 5.2 differ from that of the proposal in box 5.6?

Key readings and resources

Ries, J. B., & Leukefeld, C. G. (1998). *The research funding guidebook*. Thousand Oaks, California: Sage.

This book introduces the reader to the competitive (and sometimes lucrative) world of applying for research grants. Although much of the text is devoted to a consideration of practical issues of managing research grants, it provides a very useful account of proposal writing.

There are also many resources on the internet, for example:

- The Qualitative Social Research Forum (QSR Forum) provides access to information about qualitative research and QSR software. It can be accessed through *www.forums.qsrinternational.com*.

- The Forum for Qualitative Social Research (FQS) is a free, peer-reviewed, multilingual **online journal** for qualitative research, and can be found at *www.qualitative-research.net/fqs/fqs-eng.htm*. Try accessing Roth's (2002) article outlining the process and problems he experienced in submitting a research proposal.

- You could also explore joining various **internet discussion groups** which provide a forum for you to discuss and raise questions about your research process. For example:

- Participatory Research email discussion list (PRA) is an email discussion list devoted to the topic of participatory community development. It is affiliated with the Participatory Initiatives Home Page at *www.tdg.uoguelph.ca/~pi*, an internet site listing resources on participatory approaches to change.

- Systems in Evaluation Discussion List (EVAL-SYS) can be found by looking for EVAL-SYS and 'post to the list' on the following site: *www.evaluation.wmich.edu/archives/index.html.*

- Community-based Participatory Research (CBPR) is an email community created to serve the growing network of people involved and interested in CBPR and other types of community–academic research partnership. The participants include people from community organisations, colleges, and universities, public and private funding agencies, decision makers, and policy makers. Access the list through *www.mailman1.u.washington.edu/mailman/listinfo/cbpr*.

6

Publish or perish:

disseminating your research findings

Karima Effendi

Senior features writer, Associated Magazines

Brandon Hamber

Associate, INCORE, University of Ulster

Social science researchers live in a competitive world in which the number and perceived quality of publications largely determine one's standing in the community. An inadequate publication record can prevent one from gaining promotion or from having a contract renewed, so that the situation quite literally becomes one of 'publish or perish'. Apart from the stress this obsession with publication causes for individual social scientists, it can also be to the detriment of the scholarly community when it leads to a proliferation of trivial work published in journals and books.

Publication is nonetheless an integral part of being a social scientist, and it can be practically and theoretically important. In this chapter, we present some tips on how to knock your work into the kind of shape that could get it published. We also try to show that publication can be more than an afterthought tacked onto your research. Publishing is in fact an exciting and creative process, and need not be limited to the usual academic forms such as journal articles, but can happen in newspapers, magazines, conference presentations, the internet, and video, or through graphics and posters of various kinds. Not all research is suitable for journal publication, but almost all research should be – and normally is – publishable in one form or another.

Different forms of publication

The aim of publication is to change the world, even if only in a small way, by sharing the results of a study with others. In this sense, all published research is a form of action research – research that actively intervenes and changes phenomena (see chapter 19). You should decide about publication and action outcomes early on in the research process. If your research is aimed directly at changing something in the community or organisation you are studying, you may want to use local and interactive forms of publication (e.g., meetings and workshops). If it is aimed at influencing public perceptions, you need to think of how best to present your research in the mass media (e.g., newspapers, radio, television, or the internet). If you plan on dealing with issues relevant to a particular professional group (e.g., Aids workers, trade unionists, or teachers), you could consider publication in newsletters, journals, and magazines catering for such groups. Of course, if your work is potentially of interest to other social scientists, you could opt for publication in an academic journal.

Consider a research project that focuses on the working conditions of farm labourers, the results of which indicate that the labourers are working under very poor conditions. What forms could the publication of these findings take? First, the results could be reported back directly to the farmers and labourers who participated in the project – in written form or through meetings and workshops (especially if illiteracy is high). This may encourage the participants to debate the results among themselves, and could prompt the labourers to organise into some sort of lobby group or union aimed at

Publication is a creative process. You don't have to be limited by narrow definitions of what constitutes publication. Researchers often don't publish their work because 'writing up' feels like an additional burden after a long research project. Why not work on a shorter publishable version of your work as you go along?

improving their conditions. The findings could also be summarised in the form of a report that could be sent to government, or to non-governmental organisations (NGOs) working on farm labour issues. Such a report may aspire to improving the conditions of the labourers by highlighting and prioritising the key problems faced by the labourers. The report could make specific recommendations at a policy level, as well as recommendations that local government officials could take up in the short term. Perhaps the public is unaware of the poor working conditions revealed by the research. In this case, a newspaper feature may be a useful form of publication to heighten public awareness of the issues and pressure government to change its policies. You could also start a blog to discuss the issue. It also may be worth writing up the research in an academic journal. This could highlight the fact that a limited amount of research is being done in the area, and help flag important issues for other researchers to study. Imagine also that a specific technique, say a new translation method, was used in the research process, and this proved successful. It may be useful to share this with other researchers. The general rule of thumb is to match the type of publication to the audience you want to inform and to the effects you want to achieve.

> A blog (or weblog) is a website that is updated on a regular basis, structured in reverse chronological order so that the most recent information is listed first. It can be a good way of keeping people informed about a research project as it unfolds.

Internal publications

Internal publications are generally distributed within the environment where one works, and can include briefing documents and preliminary research findings. Consider a research institute that undertakes a project assessing, over a two-year period, the stresses experienced by single mothers. Every few months, it may be useful to summarise the data that have been collected, and to distribute this to colleagues for internal discussion. Such discussion can help shape future research, provide those working in the institute with current information, and inform other areas of your colleagues' work or interactions with different organisations.

An internal report should be an easy read – short, to the point, and structured. You should also set aside time to discuss the report with people in the organisation and solicit suggestions about how you could proceed with the project. Internal reports can usefully be broken into the following sections:

- a brief review of the research project (objectives and expected outcomes),
- the current status of the research project (work undertaken to date),
- key findings to date (using tables and lists to summarise findings),
- key issues for consideration (implications of issues raised by the study),
- future concerns (issues that may need to be addressed in the future, such as research issues and logistical concerns, e.g. transportation issues or funding questions), and
- a time frame for completion of the research project.

Popular publications

These types of publication are distributed to a wider audience than internal publications. They can be aimed at others working in your field of interest or at a broader audience, and include publication in newsletters, periodicals, newspapers, magazines, and e-journals. Publication in newsletters or periodicals is usually undertaken to further interest in a certain field, to summarise research findings, or to inform others of the type of work being undertaken on a certain topic. Newsletters of professional organisations or small publications that are read by others in your field can be a useful place to publish, as they not only inform other professionals of your work, but can be a good way of 'networking' (i.e., making contact with others undertaking similar work to yours).

Articles in newsletters or periodicals are generally about 2 000 words in length and can be structured in the following way:

- a brief introduction to the topic and summary of the article,

- a summary of the research process (how the study was undertaken),

- key results (what the study has found) – if the article reports work in progress, this section should focus on the research objectives and method,

- implications and areas for future study.

If you find yourself unable to 'translate' your findings into popular language, this could be an indication that your work has not been sufficiently and clearly conceptualised.

You should consider using bullet points, tables, and lists to summarise key issues. This will highlight key points and make the article easier to read. Two or three quotations strategically placed in the article can help drive home central points.

Newspaper, magazine, and internet articles can be written to publicise research findings or to stimulate public debate, and can play an important role in lobbying for change or sensitising the public to a critical issue. Magazines would more likely be interested in a 'human-interest' feature, while e-journals tend to be more flexible and so your article could be quite opinionated. In both instances, though, you should back up your story with evidence from your research. It takes practice to write a good newspaper article, especially one that summarises a great deal of research data. Such an article is normally about 600 words, and for this reason it is critical that you select only one idea or one key fact that you will discuss in the article. Although you may feel that this will not do justice to your research, complicated articles will be rejected by newspaper editors.

Consider the following advice before writing a newspaper article:

1. Before you begin writing, select one basic idea or fact that you want to convey to the public and make this the focus of the entire article (even if you are allowed more than 600 words).

2. Consider beginning the article with an example or an anecdote. If you are writing about the impact of HIV and Aids on the South African workforce, you could begin the article with a human story.

For example, 'David, a young lawyer from Johannesburg, was first diagnosed HIV positive two years ago ...'

3. State explicitly the theme of the article and its significance, to inform the audience why they should read the article – for example, 'Due to the growing incidence of HIV and Aids within South Africa's workforce, it is critical that we assess more closely the HIV and Aids policies of companies.'

4. Give a brief summary of the research process, but be very selective and avoid technical terms.

Eldo's Bekgeskiedenis, *which was published by Unisa Centre for Peace Action, is an example of a popular newsletter read by both community members and professionals interested in preventing violence.*

5. Elaborate on the theme by using the key research result that you decided would be your main focus.

6. Conclude by explaining the implications of the research for society and the reader; and suggest a future course of action – for example, 'Thus we can see HIV/Aids does not discriminate. It can affect people at all levels of employment and requires a multi-pronged prevention campaign.'

Research reports and policy publications

Research commissioned by an organisation invariably requires a written report. Such reports should be clearly structured and logical in their format, but can vary a great deal in length and structure depending on the requirements of the commissioning organisation. It is a good idea to get clarity on the scope and structure of the report at the very beginning of a project, so that both parties know what to expect. You could also agree on the need for a series of smaller interim reports or meetings, and it is almost always a good idea to arrange for one or more meetings at the end of the project, during which questions arising from the report can be addressed. If you plan to publish some of your findings in other places (e.g., a journal article), negotiate this with the commissioning organisation at the outset.

Research reports often have policy implications – companies, organisations, or government departments may decide to change their rules and procedures in response to your findings – and reports are frequently specifically commissioned with policy changes in mind (see chapter 20). In such cases, policy recommendations should be emphasised, with somewhat less emphasis given to the findings and research methods used. A policy report should typically include the following:

1. **Executive summary** – This short summary (1 or 2 pages) should be self-contained, and readable without reference to the full report. Policymakers are usually busy people who do not have time to read a full report, and will use the executive summary to familiarise themselves with the research and develop policy on the basis of its recommendations.

2. **Introduction** – A brief introduction should summarise the aim of the research and provide an outline to the report.

3. **Method** – This section should be written in a nontechnical manner, and should provide an overview of the research process and the techniques and measures employed. It could conclude with a section on the way in which the data was analysed.

4. **Results** – The results and their implications should be presented in point form for easy reading.

5. **Recommendations** – A detailed list of recommendations and key conclusions should be the main section of the report. Recommendations should be clearly stated and backed up by the research.

Community feedback meetings

Although verbal reports are not usually thought of as publications, they are a legitimate way of disseminating research results. Meetings, workshops, and similar forms of feedback are useful for three reasons. First, they provide an opportunity for checking interim results and conclusions before rushing into print. Second, they provide a means of communicating the findings to people who may not be highly literate or who would not normally take the trouble to read a research report. Third, they help to extend ownership of the project to include other stakeholders (e.g., research participants and community members), beyond the researcher and the commissioning institution .

By participating in meetings and workshops, interested communities may have a say in the research project, comment on drafts of the report and the final report, and suggest suitable forms of publication. In some cases, feedback meetings and workshops are more than interim measures on the way to a final report, and become the primary means of publication.

If you choose this form of publication (perhaps in conjunction with conventional forms of written publication), there are of course many pragmatic issues that you will have to deal with. For example, exactly how much control should you, as expert researcher, maintain over the project, and how should you deal with political and other differences in organisations and communities? You can read more about these issues in chapters 18 and 19.

Alternate forms of publication

Research results can be disseminated in many different ways, and you need not feel constrained by conventional ideas about what constitutes a publication. Forms of publication that have been used with great success include videos, dramatic performances, cartoons, and training manuals.

The internet provides a means of disseminating material to a wide audience at low cost. It is easy to set up a website containing material such as your curriculum vitae or background information about the organisation you work for, publication lists, details of research work in progress, journal-style articles, photographs, and so on. Most word processors now allow

What made my pain worse was that Buntu and I were not sharing our grief. Buntu was just interested in getting the body back. We started to drift apart.

This is also a common thing, Nomvula. It is usually easier for women to grieve because they are allowed to show their feelings more than men. It is acceptable for women to express their fears and emotions. But many people think men shouldn't do the same thing. You must remember that, because men and women are brought up differently, they often grieve in different ways.

An extract from Death of a Son *by Njabulo Ndebele (1996), a training manual based on many years of research on dealing with grief.*

you to create documents in a format suitable for web publishing, but it could still be worth your while to consult with an expert on technical and style issues.

There are two golden rules for publication on the internet. First, do not allow your or your organisation's website to stagnate – keep adding new material, revising old material, and refining the way in which different parts of the site are linked together. Second, look for ways to link your site to the wider community of knowledge on the web – both academic and nonacademic. For example, if you do research on ecotourism, you could ask selected South African tourism sites and international academic sites on tourism to include a link to your site. The process of fitting your site into a network of related sites will also help you to understand better where you may be duplicating work already done by others and where you are contributing unique perspectives.

The internet is now the world's most-used research tool. When news breaks (worldwide) the internet is often the first port of call for producers, editors, and writers who are seeking and contributing information related to that news piece. News of the US war on Iraq first broke on the internet and related anti-war protests were successfully organised globally via the internet. The more you are published on the internet, the greater your chances of being further published in other media formats. Find ways of getting your publications to people without their having to actively look for them. If, for example, you are sufficiently disciplined to produce a monthly emailed newsletter on a topic that you are actively working on (e.g., prisoners' rights), you will soon start building up a list of subscribers and contributors. More recently, the blog (short for 'weblog') has become a popular way of keeping people informed of individuals' work and research.

A website is an ongoing project, not a once-off achievement.

Academic publication

Methodology textbooks sometimes give the impression that academic publication is the only legitimate means of disseminating research results. Although we take a wider view of publication, we recognise that academic publication provides an important forum for debating theoretical issues, informing fellow researchers of new research techniques, and building a base of knowledge for future research. Postgraduate students at most universities are obliged to become involved in academic publication (e.g., submitting a thesis or research report), and if you are planning an academic career, such publication is likely to become one of your main activities.

The four most common forms of academic publication are theses, conference papers, journal articles, and books (or book chapters). We will discuss these briefly, and then move on to a more detailed consideration of the structure of a journal article.

There are many excellent books on scientific writing (e.g., Sternberg, 1993) and a good number devoted specifically to the process of writing a **thesis** (e.g., Mauer, 1996; Mouton, 2001), and we strongly urge you to read these if you have to hand in a research report, thesis, or dissertation as part of your studies. Also take careful note of your university's requirements in terms of format, style, and length. Theses are bulky, and are written over an extended period, so one of their most common weaknesses is inconsistency – e.g., a mismatch between the stated aims of the research, the literature survey, and the way in which data were actually collected and analysed. Thinking of your thesis as an expanded journal article can help to keep it more tightly focused.

Presenting a **conference paper** is perhaps the best way to gain entry to the world of academic publishing. Many conferences welcome student participation, either on an equal footing with established academics or in a special 'student stream'. Although most conferences require that you submit an abstract (or sometimes a proposal or complete paper) for evaluation, you can be fairly certain that your paper will be accepted for presentation provided the abstract deals with one of the conference themes and is reasonably well written.

Box 6.1

Publishing tips

- **Be audience friendly**. Evaluate everything you write through the 'spectacles' of your audience. Would your audience be interested? Why? Ask a few people to comment on what you've written. Make sure your information is directly relevant to your topic.
- **Be accurate**. Be precise in your descriptions and in the presentation of your data and information.
- **Be convincing**. Justify your argument with quantitative data and sound arguments using qualitative information. Quotations from key informants can also be helpful.
- **Be brief**. Be as succinct as possible without sacrificing content. Information overload in the modern world means that well-structured and condensed work always gets more attention.
- **Be selective**. All research produces enormous quantities of information, so be selective in the material you choose to publish. Remember that you can choose to publish different aspects of your research for different publications and for different effects.
- **Be presentable**. Reports to organisations may be quite extensively formatted (e.g., colour illustrations and cover pages), but manuscripts for journal publications should be relatively modest. Carefully proofread the final version of the document, do a spell check, and make sure that all references are correct. A sloppy presentation does not inspire confidence.
- **Be ethical**. Do not use material (e.g., an interview transcript or responses to a questionnaire) unless your research subjects have given permission to do so. Preserve your subjects' anonymity if this was promised.

Conference tips

Box 6.2

- When preparing a paper for a conference or a presentation, write out a full version of your paper before the conference, even if this is not required by the conference organisers. This will ensure that you know exactly what you want to say, and can be the first step towards a further publication (e.g., in the conference proceedings or as a journal article). Do not read out the paper at the conference – give a talk based on the paper. It is usually best, particularly if you are new to public speaking, to make use of slides or other visual aids. These can include the main headings of your talk, interesting (short) quotations and graphs or other illustrations. A common mistake is to use lettering that is too small to be legible to the audience.
- Find out exactly how long you will have to speak and practise to see how much you can fit into this time – it is usually a lot less than you think. Conferences often fail to run to schedule, so expect further cuts in the time available to you.
- Do not try to cover too much ground in a conference paper. Make two or three (small) points in the presentation.
- Often the most interesting part of a conference paper is question time, even though it can be quite intimidating if some of the questions appear to be critical of your work. It is a good idea to think up possible questions that may be raised, and to prepare 'model answers' to these.
- If you are averse to public speaking, consider submitting a poster instead. Most conferences now have interesting poster displays, and time is usually set aside for people to view the posters and discuss their contents with the authors. A poster presentation has much the same academic status as an orally presented paper. You may also want to consider other interesting presentation formats, such as dramatic presentations, workshops, and round-table discussions. Conference organisers are usually quite open to such suggestions.
- One of the most important functions of conferences is networking – the opportunity to meet other people working in your field of interest, and to start setting up collaborative relationships. So, do go to the after-conference party and other conference functions.

Writing a **journal article** and getting it published is a little more difficult. From your literature survey, you are likely to know already which journals may be suitable for you to publish in, but ask around and have a look at the list of periodicals kept by your library – there may be possibilities there that you had not thought of. Journals vary considerably in status, with the most highly regarded international journals also generally being the most difficult to get into. Even small journals are usually quite strict about what they publish. Journals used to be available only in libraries, but now most are published online too, and some are only available electronically. Most reputable journals are 'peer reviewed', including those that are published on the internet. This means that the editor of the journal will send your manuscript to two or more anonymous reviewers, usually 'blind' reviewers (i.e., they do not know the identity of the author). This can take a long time – several months – after which you will receive a reply either accepting the article as is, asking for some changes, or rejecting the article. It is very rare that an article is accepted without modification, and in most cases the author should try to improve the article in the light of the reviewers' comments.

As with conference papers, it can be a good idea to co-author your first article with one or more established academics. Try and agree early on who will be first author (also sometimes called the senior author), who will be second, and so on. If your co-author does most of the conceptualising and writing of the article, it would not be unusual for her or him to be first author, even if the article relies on research work you have done. However, if you did most of the writing up and the co-author (e.g., your thesis supervisor) just helped you to refine it, you are entitled to be first author. Most universities have policies on authorship – consult these if you anticipate problems.

Reviewers vary greatly in how prompt they are and how much useful feedback they provide. Don't expect too much and you won't be disappointed.

The structure of a journal article

Knowing how to structure a journal article is useful not only for getting an article published in an academic journal but also because most forms of academic publication are structured in roughly the same way. There are no fixed rules about structure – different journals have their own requirements, and authors are often allowed considerable scope for creativity – but there are a number of standard (implicit and explicit) features to journal articles.

The title

The title should convey the gist of your research. It should not be too lengthy (five or ten words should suffice). You can usually leave out words like 'study', 'investigation', and 'research'. So a title such as 'A research study investigating the relationship between crime and unemployment' could do without the first four words. At the same time, the title should not be so brief that it becomes obscure, so 'Crime and unemployment' is probably not enough – say what aspects of crime and unemployment are being considered, for example, 'The relationship between violent crime and unemployment in the Cape Peninsula'. After reading the title of an article, the reader should have a fair idea of the article's main focus. It can also be useful to begin a title with a short catchy phrase, for example, 'Do sleeping dogs lie? The psychological implications of the Truth and Reconciliation Commission in South Africa', or 'Off the rails: An analysis of the causes of violence in the railway strike of 1987'.

Many more people will see the title of your article than will read the article, so it is worth putting some effort into getting the title right.

Abstract

An abstract is a summary of the main points made in your article and is typically about 200 words in length (but check the requirements for the journal you're submitting to). The abstract usually contains a brief account of the objective of the study, the methods used, the most important results and conclusions, and the significance of these conclusions. It should be possible to read the abstract on its own, without reference to the article itself. So, if possible, do not use phrases such as 'a relationship was found between levels of basic service provision and the number of women on local councils' but rather say what the relationship was, for example, 'levels of basic service provision were found to be higher for local councils with a substantial number of female members.'

An abstract summarises an article. An introduction orientates the reader by contextualising the research problem.

Introduction

The word 'introduction' is not usually used as a heading, but most articles start with an introduction. This should contextualise the research, giving the reader a good idea of what you will be investigating, and it should be engaging, so that the reader wants to find out more. The following is a useful structure:

- State the broad research question and why it warrants investigation.
- Explain how the problem being investigated fits into a bigger theoretical, academic, historical, or practical framework.
- Briefly review previous literature that addresses the research problem. Indicate how your research follows or diverges from previous studies. Avoid summarising each publication separately – show how the publications relate to each other and how they relate to your research problem.
- Provide a clear and specific statement of your research question. In the case of quantitative research, you may want to present this as a formal hypothesis. In the case of qualitative research, explain what questions you aim to answer. Avoid having too many hypotheses or questions – keep it simple.
- Conclude with a very brief summary of the article, showing how it answers your specific research questions.

If your introduction is fairly lengthy, you may want to consider using subheadings to break it into more manageable parts.

Method

The method section explains the approach you have used to gather and analyse your data. State in broad terms what kind of approach you used and why, and then present a detailed description of the procedures you followed. This should give sufficient information to enable somebody to replicate the study.

The instruments used to collect data should be described in detail. In qualitative research, you should explain how focus groups or interviews were conducted, how they were arranged, and what questions were asked. Properties such as reliability, validity, scoring, and relevance of all quantitative research instruments (e.g., standardised tests or questionnaires) should be explained.

The sampling strategy should be reported. Do not just say that it was a 'stratified random sample', but explain how this was done. For qualitative research, explain why you chose to interview certain people and not others. In all cases, report the sample size, and describe the participants who took part in the study – provide demographic details of age, gender, and other relevant variables. Provide descriptive statistics (e.g., mean age) for samples of more than ten.

The procedures you followed to collect the data must be explained. If you conducted a house-to-house survey, explain how field workers were trained, how many field workers visited each house, at what times of the day this was done, and in what sequence questions were asked.

Explain how you analysed the data. Do not simply give a technical label (e.g., multiple regression, or discourse analysis), but explain how the statistical procedure was applied (e.g., which dependent and independent variables were included in the regression and what form of regression was used) or how the qualitative analysis was structured and executed.

Results

Present the main findings of your study in the results section. For quantitative research, make use of tables and graphs to illustrate your results, although the results section should be more than just a list of tables. Include only tables with relevant information, and take care to explain what the figures in each table mean. Structure the results section so that it provides direct answers to your research questions and so that central questions are answered first, followed by any supplementary questions flowing from these. Although the purpose of this section is to present the results, not to interpret them, a certain amount of interpretation is necessary so that the reader can understand what the results mean. For example, rather than only giving the results of a t-test, you may want to say something like 'Contrary to the hypothesis that professional athletes would obtain higher motivation scores than social athletes, no significant difference was found between the two groups ($t = 1.04$, $p = 0.22$, $df = 38$)'. In the case of qualitative research, you are likely to want to include even more interpretation, and may even elect to combine the results section with the discussion section.

Discussion and conclusion

The final section of your article affords you the opportunity to give your insights into the research and to state to what extent the study has succeeded or failed in answering your research problem. The structure of this section would vary depending on whether you have used a separate results section. If you do not have a results section (as often happens with qualitative research), then this is where you would include a brief analysis of the most important results of your study, and proceed to discuss the significance of these results. Try to present this analytical discussion in an interesting and accessible way – it should not be too abstract or alienating for your reader. If you have included a results section (as is usual with quantitative research), your discussion would focus on the meaning and implication of your results. Make sure that the discussion and interpretation of the findings are consistent with your analysis in the previous section. Indicate how your findings are similar to or different from other important studies in the field. Finally, conclude by stating the implications of your study in terms of new findings and different perspectives the paper has introduced, and make brief suggestions for further research in the area.

The concluding section of an article is a good place to note limitations of the study and ways in which these can be overcome in future research.

References

Your article should conclude with a list of references that you have consulted and cited in the text. There are many different systems of referencing. Look at articles published in the journal for which you are writing to see what the format requirements are, and then stick to these with 100% consistency. Also double check that all references cited in the text are included in the reference list and that there are no references in the reference list not cited in the text. It may be useful to use a referencing software package such as EndNote, ProCite, or Refworks (see chapter 2, box 2.7).

Box 6.3

Different referencing styles

There are wide differences in referencing style across academic disciplines and journals. It is essential that you consult the journal webpage or read the 'instructions to authors' in the front or back of a journal before you submit an article for possible publication. This usually contains not only referencing guidelines but numerous other style requirements, together with an indication of the sort of article that the journal is likely to publish. There are also several general style manuals for referencing purposes available in most South African academic libraries, including the *Publication manual of the American Psychological Association* (APA, 1994) and *The Chicago manual of style* (University of Chicago Press, 1993). For tips on how to reference electronic publications, consult *Electronic style: A guide to citing electronic information* by Li and Crane (1993). The reference software mentioned above can also help with this, as most have the various styles built into them and can generate the layout for you automatically.

Attachments

Most journals prefer that you do not include graphs, illustrations, and tables in the text, but attach them to the end of the article. In this case, indicate where in the text the material should be placed (e.g., 'Figure 1 about here'), and attach the material at the end, making sure that it has an unambiguous caption.

Conclusion

If the graphs, illustrations, and tables are not your own work, ensure that you have permission to use them.

Journal publication is highly valued in the academic world, and in this chapter we have considered some generic publication guidelines. We have also suggested that there are many other ways of communicating your research results to people who are in a position to act on them. Effective publication is a skill that takes time and practice to get right, and it is only by trying out various different modes of publication that you can really get a feel for what works for you.

Research that makes a difference – extract from Truth and Reconciliation, *a booklet published by the Centre for the Study of Violence and Reconciliation (1996).*

In addition to trying your hand at different kinds of publication, you can also form alliances with others in getting your work into the limelight. We have spoken, for the most part, as if you have to go it alone, but in fact there are many others (such as fellow students, people with special skills in the community, sympathetic staff members at your university, or your thesis supervisor) who can collaborate with you in producing high-quality material. If you are good at writing things up, but less so at data collection and analysis, consider working with others who have a complementary set of skills. Increasingly, work in the social sciences is done in collaboration with others, and being sole author of a publication is but one of the options available to you.

We have also emphasised the importance of thinking about publication as soon as you start with a research project. Not only are you likely to publish more – and in more appropriate ways – if you include publication in your research plans, but the feedback processes will result in the research itself becoming more relevant and worthwhile.

Individuals and groups continually generate large amounts of useful knowledge, not only through carefully designed research projects but also in the process of their daily work. Think, for example, of the practical knowledge of how to deal with human problems generated by a group of nurses in a rural clinic, or by members of a church congregation. Unfortunately, such knowledge is seldom recorded and published so that others may benefit from it. If we make a practice of thinking of publication as a main outcome of a study, rather than as a vague possibility to be considered at the end of a project, we can start to unlock such knowledge and conduct research that truly makes a difference.

Exercises

1. Select an article from an academic journal and discuss the following questions with fellow students:

    (a) In what ways does the structure of the article confirm or contradict the guidelines given in this chapter for structuring a journal article? Where the article deviates from our recommendations, does this weaken or enhance the impact of the article?

    (b) What other forms of publication would have been appropriate for the material covered in the article?

2. Start a blog with other students in the class reflecting your research interests. Update it regularly with links and information about your work and progress on various projects. Use it to debate ideas among yourselves; make it a fun learning forum. Encourage others to comment on your blog. Try to keep it updated until the end of the academic year.

3. Go to the library and look up journals with titles beginning with *'The South African Journal of ...'* in your and other related disciplines, such as *The South African Journal of Sociology*, or *Psychology*. Ask these questions: Are local researchers in your subject working on similar topics to those being covered in your courses? If not, in what ways are they different? Has anyone from your institution published in the journal in the last year or two? If not, ask them why.

4. Browse around the *Conference Alerts* website (www.conference alerts.com) to see what national and international meetings and conferences are scheduled on different topics for the next six to twelve months. Consider presenting a paper or a poster at one of these conferences, perhaps together with an established academic or with fellow students.

Key readings

Becker, H. S. (1986). *Writing for social scientists: How to start and finish your thesis, book or article.* Chicago: University of Chicago Press.

Haag, D. E. (1996). *Guidelines for writing a dissertation or thesis.* Vanderbijlpark: Vaal Triangle Technikon.

Jay, R. (1995). *How to write proposals and reports that get results.* New York: Prentice Hall.
A good hands-on guide to writing research reports and proposals for maximum impact.

Kennedy, G., Moen, D. R., & Ranly, D. (1993). *Beyond the inverted pyramid: Effective writing for newspapers, magazines and specialized publications.* New York: St Martin's Press.
Indispensable if you plan to publish your research in the popular media.

Mauch, J., & Birch, J. (1993). *Guide to the successful thesis and dissertation: A handbook for students and faculty.* New York: Marcel Dekker.
There are literally hundreds of books that deal with how to structure a thesis or journal article and, more importantly, how to survive the process of writing it. We have found this text particularly helpful.

Mouton, J. (2001). *How to succeed in your master's and doctoral studies.* Pretoria: Van Schaik.
A very useful local text, packed with useful tips about managing a postgraduate research project. It divides the process into eight steps: getting started, selecting a supervisor, scanning the field of study, developing the research proposal, drawing up a research resource checklist, undertaking a comprehensive review of the literature, conducting the fieldwork, and organising and writing the thesis.

Mulenga, D. (1997). *Knowledge, empowerment and social transformation: Participatory research in Africa.* Atlantic Highlands: Zed Books.
An overview of issues and key initiatives in empowerment research in Africa – useful background if your research is being 'published' by means of community meetings and workshops.

Quantitative research techniques

7

Collecting quantitative data:
sampling and measuring

Kevin Durrheim
University of KwaZulu-Natal, Pietermaritzburg

Desmond Painter
Stellenbosch University

Historically, social scientists have favoured quantitative over qualitative data. Researchers preferred to *measure* things such as malnutrition, life expectancy, depression, etc., rather than to ask people for their opinions or experiences about such matters. Quantitative data enables researchers to say things such as 12% of children under five years of age in South Africa are malnourished, life expectancy is 46.5 years (data from the World Bank, www.worldbank.org), and 5% of the population is clinically depressed. One of the reasons why researchers have preferred quantitative data is the widespread acceptance of the positivist paradigm. Researchers believed that there were a whole lot of facts in the world to be collected by means of objective quantitative measures. They rejected qualitative research because, they claimed, it was open to bias. Today, we realise that qualitative research can tell us a great deal about the experience of poverty and depression and people's perceptions of the poor and depressed. However, there remain many good reasons for using quantitative data. Importantly, good quality quantitative data and statistics allow us to make comparisons of different situations. From the statistics, where would you prefer to live – South Africa, Zimbabwe (life expectancy, 36.7 years), or Cuba (life expectancy, 77.3 years)?

The social science canon tells us that quantitative research has two primary strengths: the findings are **generalisable** and the data are **objective**. This is not strictly true, as is evident from the many disputes about statistics. For example, whereas the World Bank says life expectancy in South Africa is 46.5 years, the American Government's CIA says South African life expectancy is 43.3 years, and the South African Medical Research Council estimates 52.5 years. In this chapter, we show that generalisability and objectivity are not standards, but are ideals to which we strive in quantitative research. The extent to which results are generalisable – that is, reflections of events in large populations – is dependent on the way in which the sample was selected. The extent to which the results are 'objective' is dependent on the way in which the phenomenon under investigation is conceptualised and measured.

Generalisability and objectivity are ideals towards which we strive in quantitative research.

Sampling

You have probably come across opinion polls conducted by newspapers, magazines, websites, and radio stations about current issues. An internet poll on the News 24 website (www.news24.co.za) might, for example, ask whether the national soccer coach should be dismissed or not. Such a poll will typically tell us that, say, 69% of people demand that the coach be dismissed, while 31% say he should be retained. This is then interpreted not as a distribution of views that is peculiar to the particular people who submitted responses, but as an indication of the opinions of a broader group of people – all South Africans, perhaps, or all the readers of the website. The opinions of those who have access to the internet and who bothered to click in their responses are in other words treated as *representative* of the views of South Africans in general.

The practice of inferring things about a broader category of people or things from observations of a smaller subsection of that category is a central component of social scientific research. While inferences like these are made possible by the various statistical theories and techniques discussed in following chapters of this section of the book, they depend for their validity on the method by which the cases to be observed are selected. This process of selecting cases to observe is called **sampling**.

In the example of the News 24 poll, the people who responded are referred to as a sample. The sample, in turn, is compiled from and (ideally) represents a larger group, referred to as a population. A sample, then, is quite simply those units or **elements** that are included into a study. The **population** is the larger pool from which our sampling elements are drawn, and to which we want to generalise our findings. Theoretically speaking, the population encompasses *all* the elements that make up our unit of analysis. In the case of a smaller population, such as all learners registered at a particular school in January 2006, it is possible to select our sampling elements from the population directly. In many instances, however, this is simply not possible. How, for example, can you ever have access to *all* South Africans at a particular time, or even to *all* used-car dealers currently doing business in the Bellville area? For this reason, a distinction is made between the population as an abstract category and the actual form in which the population becomes accessible to us. The latter is called a **sampling frame**, and can include a list of registered used-car businesses, a computer printout of all learners registered at a school in January 2006, or a telephone directory. Because the sample is drawn not directly from the population but from the sampling frame, it is vital that the sampling frame is as close an approximation of the population as possible.

Of course, the sampling frame will rarely be a *perfect* representation of the population. Say we use telephone directories as a sampling frame of a population defined as all residents of Cape Town in 2005; this will exclude people who only use cellphones from our sampling frame. Can you think of a few reasons why this kind of exclusion might introduce bias into our study?

Let us return to the example of the internet poll. Polls like these often specify not only their results, but also the overall number of responses they managed to get. Why is this? You would probably agree that you would more likely take such a poll seriously if 1 863 out of 2 700 callers, rather than 59 out of 87, called in to demand the coach's dismissal – even though the result in both scenarios is 69% in favour of dismissing the coach. You would probably sense that, if a poll claims to say something about the views of South Africans in general about the soccer coach, then the larger the number of opinions gathered the better, and you would not be wrong if you thought this. But while the size of a sample is indeed crucial, it is not sufficient to give a sample the kind of scientific credibility it needs. Indeed, our imaginary poll will not easily withstand scientific scrutiny. Can you see why not?

A sample is representative of a population if elements in the sample have been randomly selected from a 'sampling frame' listing everybody in the population.

For sampling to be scientific, it requires careful thinking not only about how many elements should be included for observation, but which elements should be included and *how* they should be selected. As already indicated, quantitative researchers are not interested in the particularities of the elements in a sample, but in the way that these elements together represent a broader population and make it possible to account for variations in that population. From a quantitative and particularly a positivist perspective, a good sample enables us to make claims, expressed in terms of statistical probabilities, about a population without having studied all the constituent elements that make up the population. (Qualitative researchers, in both interpretive and constructionist frameworks, take a different approach to knowledge production and thus they also approach sampling differently. You can read more about this in chapters 12 and 13.)

Probability sampling

Random number generators allow you to specify the amount of numbers you want (e.g., 10) from a range (e.g., 1–100).

Effective sampling ensures that the elements selected for a sample accurately resemble the parameters of the population they were selected from. How would one go about selecting a sample from a university with 12 000 registered students? The ideal way is to use a process called random selection. **Random selection** means that each element (in this case student) in the sampling frame has an equal and independent chance of being selected for the sample. Let us say we attain a numbered list of all 12 000 students. We decide to include 1 200 students into our sample (see box 7.1 for a discussion of sample size). To ensure that each student is randomly selected, we can make use of a random number generator. Random number generators are included in many statistics packages, including Moonstats, which comes with this book.

One can also find free and easy-to-use randomisers on the internet (see www.randomizer.org), or one can make use of a spreadsheet like Microsoft Excel.

Once a list of random numbers is generated, each random number is matched to the corresponding number on our sampling frame (the numbered list of students), and thus selects one student to the sample. The 1 200 students selected in this way will be our sample. We now have what is called a **simple random sample**: each element had exactly the same chance of being selected, and the selection of each element was independent of the selection of a previous one.

Box 7.1

Sampling ratios and sample size

As a rule of thumb, a sampling ratio (i.e., sample size/population size multiplied by 100) of about 30% is required for small populations of approximately 1 000. A sampling ratio of about 10% is needed for a moderately large population of approximately 10 000, a sampling ratio of approximately 1% for large populations of approximately 150 000, and a sampling ratio of 0.025% for a very large population of approximately 10 million. This means that a researcher would draw a sample of size n = 300 from a population of 10 000, n = 1 500 from a population of 150 000; and n = 2 500 from a population of 10 million. As you can see, the larger the population, the smaller the sampling ratio required to achieve the same degree of accuracy.

Your sampling would not have been random if you had simply selected the 1 200 students from the undergraduate psychology classes or students sitting in the cafeteria. Why not? First of all, only undergraduate psychology students had a chance to be included into the sample, leaving many thousands of students without any chance at all. Selection thus depended on external criteria – being an undergraduate psychology student, and one that attends lectures! While it is possible that the 1 200 students we selected represent the parameters of the population, we cannot be sure. We have, for example, inadvertently excluded postgraduate students from your sample; and what if there are significantly fewer black and male students in psychology than in the university as a whole?

Simple random sampling is an example of **probability sampling**. It is not the only form of probability sampling, and we will discuss some other strategies below. The key component of probability sampling is the already mentioned idea that each element in a sample frame should have a known, calculable chance of being included into the sample. This requirement has nothing to do with wanting to be fair. Rather, it makes it possible to use the branch of mathematics called **probability theory** to determine to what extent a sample represents the parameters of a population. Clearly, a random sample will seldom *exactly* mirror the broader population. Our university population may consist of 55% female students. If we had to select two samples, one may have consisted of 52% female students and the other of 57%. This is referred to as **sampling error**, but with probability sampling it is possible to compute sampling error and control for its effect.

When doing sampling, ask yourself: What is missing? How does my sample differ from my population?

Systematic sampling

Simple random sampling can be a very laborious process, and is in fact seldom used in practice. Systematic sampling presents an easier and more convenient alternative strategy. Rather than selecting each element randomly, the principle in systematic sampling is that we calculate a fixed distance (n) between elements and then systematically select every n-th element on the list to be included in our sample. This fixed distance is called the **sampling interval**, and is easy to calculate. We simply divide the sampling frame size by the size of the sample. For a sample of 1 200 out of a sampling frame of 12 000, the interval is calculated like this: 12 000/1 200 = 10. In practice, we select the first element randomly, and then select every 10th element until we have a sample of 1 200.

Systematic sampling is a quick and convenient way of selecting individuals from a sampling frame, but can result in a biased sample.

In the case of a sampling frame on which elements are randomly listed, systematic sampling will be no less accurate than a simple random sample. It is also an appropriate sampling strategy when our sampling frame is not available as a physical list. We might, for example, not have a list of all the used-car dealers in Bellville, but we can still randomly select a starting point in the main road and then proceed to select every third dealer for inclusion in our sample.

Box 7.2

Sampling error

Statistical laws of probability apply to all probability samples. These laws allow researchers to calculate the degree of error associated with using a sample to estimate a property of a population. If you have a simple random sample from a clearly defined population, the mean score of this sample on any variable will be an unbiased estimate of the population – but not necessarily a perfectly accurate one. There is always error associated with using sample properties to estimate population parameters, and if we were to select a second random sample of the same size, it is likely this would give a somewhat different sample.

Probability samples have the major advantage of allowing the researcher to determine the degree to which different sample estimates (e.g., means) will differ from each other and from the true population parameter. This estimate of possible error associated with sampling is known as the sampling error, which should always be reported with survey results. Another way of reporting survey results is to use the convention of reporting **confidence intervals**. A confidence interval is an interval of scores within which we can say with 95% confidence that the true population parameter falls. Table 7.1 reports 95% confidence intervals for estimating population proportions from sample proportions. If we aimed to determine what proportion of South Africans are left handed, we could use this table to show how the accuracy of our sample estimate would increase as our sample size increases. For example, if we select a sample of 500 people (of

The most important potential source of bias one has to be aware of when doing systematic sampling is that the list functioning as a sampling frame might be ordered according to a particular pattern or principle – that is, if the list is not itself random. If the list is, for example, compiled in the sequence Male-Female, and we select every fourth element, it is quite likely we might end up with a sample that consists of only men or only women.

Stratified sampling

Stratified sampling is used to establish a greater degree of representativeness in situations where populations consist of subgroups or strata. To ensure that a sample adequately represents relevant strata, the sample is not drawn randomly or systematically from the population or sampling frame as a whole, but from each of the strata independently. We can use one of two strategies, namely proportionate and disproportionate stratified sampling. In the former we select the same proportion of individuals from each stratum as there are in the population. Let's say our sampling frame consists of 'foreign' and 'South African' university students, and we decide to sample proportionately from each of these two strata. If there are 1 000 whom 90% respond to our question) and we find that 13% are left handed, the table shows that we can conclude with 95% confidence that the true proportion in the population lies between 10.4% (13 − 2.6) and 15.6% (13 + 2.6). If we select a sample of 1 200 subjects and 90% respond, we can conclude with 95% confidence that the true proportion in the population lies between 11.3% (13 − 1.7) and 14.7% (13 + 1.7). The table shows that, as the sample size increases (either through selecting bigger samples, or increasing the response rate), the sampling error decreases, and our sample properties become more accurate estimates of population parameters.

Table 7.1 Sampling of error at the 95% confidence level

Sample size	Response rate									
	95%	90%	85%	80%	75%	70%	65%	60%	55%	50%
500	2.0	2.6	3.2	3.6	3.8	4.0	4.2	4.4	4.4	4.4
600	1.7	2.4	3.0	3.2	3.6	3.8	4.0	4.0	4.0	4.0
800	1.6	2.2	2.6	2.8	3.0	3.2	3.4	3.4	3.6	3.6
1 000	1.4	1.8	2.2	2.6	2.8	2.8	3.0	3.0	3.2	3.2
1 200	1.3	1.7	2.1	2.3	2.5	2.6	2.7	2.8	2.9	2.9
1 500	1.1	1.5	1.8	2.1	2.2	2.4	2.5	2.5	2.6	2.6

Note: Values in this table assume that nonresponse is random.

foreign students and 11 000 South African students, our aim is to have our sample reflect these known proportions. We may decide to sample 100 foreign students. In proportion to this, we should sample 1 100 South African students.

If we want to make inferences about strata separately from the population as a whole, especially in cases where a particular stratum is important to the research project but too small in relation to the bigger population to allow for meaningful statistical analysis, we can use disproportionate stratified sampling. In this option we in effect oversample for some of our strata. One way of doing this is to compute a sample ratio for each of the strata separately (see box 7.1 for an explanation of sample ratio). To return to our university example: we could inflate the proportion of foreign students in our final sample by selecting 30% of them and 10% of the South African students.

If we now want to draw inferences for the population as a whole, rather than about the strata separately, we need to restore the original proportions. This can be done in one of two ways. First, we can oversample each of the other strata by the same proportion as the smallest stratum. Second, we can weight our data to re-establish the correct proportions. In the above example we have oversampled for foreign students at the ratio of 3:1. To end up with the right proportions, we weight each of the South African students by three.

To select elements from the different strata, we will use either simple random or systematic sampling. Stratified sampling is thus not as much a departure from the sampling principles already discussed as it is a modification of these to ensure a better correspondence between samples and stratified populations.

Cluster sampling

In many instances, especially when studying very large populations, a sampling frame may not be available. Let's say our population consists of all residents of Pietermaritzburg Msunduzi. We can decide to use telephone directories as a sampling frame, but this is likely to produce a very biased sample. An alternative is initially to divide the population up into more manageable groups of elements, called **clusters**, and then to select further clusters from these, in multiple and progressive stages, until we are able to select the actual units we wish to study.

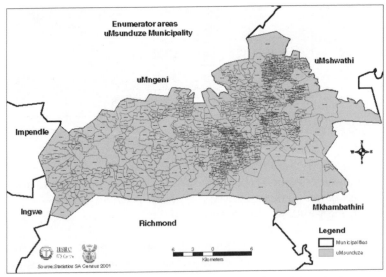

Figure 7.1 Map of enumerator areas, Pietermaritzburg Msunduzi

In the case of the municipality of Msunduzi, there is clearly no complete list of residents. Yet, people live in different **enumerator areas**, streets, and households. These can be treated as clusters, because they contain the elements we ultimately wish to study – individual residents. Cluster sampling allows us temporarily to treat these clusters as sample units themselves, in order to create a more manageable but still fairly representative pool from which our eventual sampling elements will be drawn.

Using a map like the one reproduced here as figure 7.1, we can compile a list of enumerator areas. Using a random, systematic, or stratified sampling strategy, we can select a calculated number of these areas. Our next cluster may be blocks, in which case we will now treat them, not enumerator areas, as our next sampling unit. We can repeat this process with streets, then households, in order to finally make a list of all individuals who live in the selected households. We will now have a sampling frame from which we can draw a random, systematic, or stratified sample of Msunduzi residents. While this is a frequently used sampling method, and often the only one practically possible, one should remember that each stage of sampling introduces errors, thus increasing the overall sampling error.

Nonprobability sampling

Probability sampling is touted as the preferred method because it allows generalisation to populations. In practice, however, probability samples are expensive and difficult to obtain, and so the vast majority of research in the social sciences – and almost all student work – relies on non-probability samples. **Nonprobability sampling** refers to any kind of sampling where the selection of elements is not determined by the statistical principle of randomness. Researchers often use **convenience samples** of undergraduate students or people who volunteer to participate in the research. They also make use of **purposive samples**, which means that sampling depends not only on availability and willingness to participate, but that cases that are typical of the population are selected. If we wanted to study people who work as interpreters in health-care settings, we could contact local clinics, NGOs, and hospitals and find interpreters who are willing to participate in our study. We may even ask these interpreters to direct us to their colleagues. This process of gradually accumulating a sufficiently large sample through contacts and references is called **snowball sampling**.

In many situations, these nonprobability samples are more than adequate for the research purposes. Qualitative researchers typically work with – and actually prefer – small nonrandom samples of information-rich cases that they can study in depth (see chapter 13). To study depression, they would prefer to study a small group of very depressed people rather than a random sample of people from the population.

What, though, is the value of nonprobability samples for quantitative researchers? Nonrandom samples can be very useful for testing theory about processes that are considered to be universal. Most experimental studies use small nonrepresentative samples to explore physical or mental processes. Most medicines that we use were first tested on small groups of volunteers, and not random samples of the population. The reasoning is that, if the medicines have harmful effects on these individuals, they are also likely to have harmful effects on others. So, nonrandom samples can be useful for testing theories – such as the new drug is not harmful to humans. Quantitative science often develops by way of replication. Say you do a study on a group of first-year psychology students at your university, showing that ideological conservatism is related to racism. Someone in Zimbabwe

Nonrandom samples can be useful for testing theories.

tests the same hypothesis with a group of students there. Another study is done in the USA with new army recruits. Gradually, over time, as evidence from a number of different nonrandom samples is produced, we develop confidence in the theory.

Measurement

How tall are you? How old are you? How much do you weigh? These are common questions, which most people can answer. The answers to these questions are all remarkably alike: they are all numbers. I am 1.72 metres tall, 89 years old, and weigh 83.6 kilograms. So my reply to the three questions is quantitative. The proper response to such questions is to give a number that *describes* basic features about yourself. It seems so obvious that we often don't give these numbers a second thought – except in so far as my being 89 signals my approaching death, 1.72 metres tall indicates an average height, and 83.6 kilograms shows that I am overweight. The numbers themselves, though, seem like accurate representations of my height, age, and weight.

If someone asked how I know these facts about myself, the answer would be equally obvious: I measured them of course. I measured my height with a tape measure, my age in terms of calendar years from my date of birth, and my weight on a bathroom scale. **Measurement** has become such a part of modern life that nearly everything is measured nowadays – for example, intelligence, daily calorie intake, attitudes, knowledge, gross domestic product, alienation, and suicide rates. Quantitative indices are used to represent a vast array of social and individual objects, events, and processes, both tangible and intangible.

Defined formally, measurement consists of rules for assigning numbers to objects in such a way as to represent quantities of attributes (Nunnaly, 1978). This definition may be broken down into three components:

1. **Rules** – The process for assigning numbers should be explicitly stated, standardised, and generally agreed upon by the scientific community. The rules for assigning numbers to height are so consensual and obvious – use a standardised tape measure – that they are often not explicitly stated. The rules that are used to assign numbers to intelligence, the consumer price index, 'brain waves', and social alienation, however, are less obvious and need to be explicitly stated. Usually, a standardised and widely accepted measure of these constructs is employed to ensure that others agree that the numbers do in fact represent the quantities that they are supposed to.

2. **Attributes of objects** – Objects are things in the world, including brains, individuals, societies, cultures, and so on. Such objects have attributes, which are particular features an object may have along various dimensions. Brains have attributes of weight, chemical composition, and being alive or dead. Individuals have attributes such as intelligence, height, and personality. Societies have attributes such as literacy rates, population growth, and levels of authoritarianism. When we measure objects, we normally attend to particular attributes of the objects, and measure these.

3. **Numbers to represent quantities** – Measurement involves assigning numbers to objects to represent how much (i.e., the amount) the object has of a particular attribute. This involves establishing quantitative relations among objects on particular dimensions. Although my mother and I have exactly the same intelligence, when measuring height I ignore this and attend instead to the attribute 'height'. The aim is to represent in numbers, using an explicit set of rules, how much each of us has of the attribute (e.g., we each stand barefoot against the doorpost while my father marks with a knife our height on the post). I have 1.72 metres of height, whereas my mother has 1.89 metres of height. My mother has more of the attribute, height, than I do.

The above definition of measurement is illustrated in figure 7.2. We have four objects – A, B, C, and D – which may be individuals, nations, groups, or brains, that we wish to measure by placing them on a quantitative scale reflecting how much of an attribute each object possesses. The attributes could be attitudes towards the death penalty, democratic values, spelling ability, and so on. To achieve this aim, we need a rule by which we can assign numbers to the objects that will allow us accurately to represent where they stand relative to each other in terms of how much of the attribute they possess. In figure 7.2, the measurement should reflect the fact that D has most of the attribute and A the least, and the difference in amount of the attribute between B and C is less than the difference between C and D.

> *Measurement allows us to differentiate between objects on the basis of the relative amount of the shared attribute they possess.*

Measurement has been the most fundamental aspect of social science research for more than a century. Measurement has allowed researchers to turn abstract phenomena into quantitative variables. This translation of phenomena into variables facilitates research in two ways. First, numbers provide a means by which the objects being investigated can be classified and arranged in a systematic way according to the amount of a certain characteristic they possess. Once the phenomenon 'intelligence' has been translated into a quantitative variable (i.e., IQ scores), individuals can be arranged from most intelligent to least intelligent, and can be classified as 'genius', 'normal', or 'feeble-minded' on the basis of their IQ scores (see Lea & Foster, 1990). Second, numbers may be manipulated by mathematical operations. By borrowing mathematical systems and applying them to measured attributes, researchers can do things with the phenomena under investigation that would otherwise be impossible. A simple adding operation allows the researcher to combine the intelligence scores of a group of people into one score. Statistical operations then allow the researcher to determine whether this group – e.g., children involved in traffic accidents – is less intelligent than the population as a whole, or whether individuals from different countries have the same intelligence. These are powerful reasons to quantify and measure, and scientific research may be defined in terms of measurement and mathematics.

> *'Scientists develop measures by stating rules for the quantification of attributes of real objects; they borrow mathematical systems for examining the internal relations of the data obtained with a measure and for relating different measures to one another.' (Nunnaly, 1978, p. 10)*

(Adapted from Nunnally, 1978)

Figure 7.2 Measurement involves placing objects on a quantitative scale

In addition to evaluating measures in terms of conceptualisation, operationalisation, reliability, and validity, we should ask about their practical effects. What are the positive and negative political consequences of treating intelligence as if it were a measurable variable? What are the consequences of treating infant mortality as a measurable variable?

The assumption in this kind of research is that it is possible to know what reality is really like, and all that researchers have to do is ensure that the numbers they use to represent reality correspond with the nature of the attributes being measured. This is achieved through the four processes discussed below: **conceptualisation**, **operationalisation**, **validity**, and **reliability**. Careful conceptualisation, operationalisation, and validity checking ensure that a measure (e.g., an IQ test) quantifies a real attribute of an object. Establishing reliability is a way of ensuring that the rules we use to assign numbers to quantities of the attribute are based on objective laws.

Conceptualisation

Measurement begins with conceptualisation. Since we can only speak about the attributes we want to measure in language, the first task is to clarify conceptually what we mean by the attribute we wish to measure. Conceptualisation is thus the theoretical task of defining what it is we are measuring. By the end of the conceptualisation process, the researcher should have developed a conceptual definition – a definition in abstract theoretical terms – of the attribute being measured. What does 'conservatism' mean? If conservatism is the thing we want to measure, we must begin by developing a *clear*, *explicit*, and *specific* definition of conservatism.

Although we have talked about measuring attributes thus far, social scientists generally are concerned with measuring constructs. **Constructs** are attributes that have been conceptualised and defined in language, and which have been theoretically elaborated in terms of how they are related to other constructs. The attributes of people, societies, and organisations that social scientists wish to measure – e.g., morale, cohesion, maturity, learning ability – are first viewed as systematically organised sets of ideas; that is, as *constructs*. These constructs are then refined and developed into a conceptual definition.

Develop a conceptual definition of your construct by drawing on everyday and academic understandings of the construct and by 'testing out' your definition on different situations and individuals.

How does one develop a conceptual definition? First, it is recommended that the researcher begins by exploring the everyday understanding of the construct. When Durrheim and Foster (1995) set out to develop a measure of conservatism, they began by consulting a dictionary and thesaurus, where they found that 'conservative' was defined as (1) averse to rapid change, and (2) moderate, avoiding extremes (*Concise Oxford Dictionary*). There thus seemed to be two aspects to conservatism: resistance to change and moderation. While these everyday definitions help initially in gaining an understanding of the concept, they are often inadequate since they lack detail, or are vague and inexplicit.

The second step in developing a conceptual definition is to consult the scholarly literature (see chapter 2) to see how other researchers and academics have conceptualised the construct. Here you may encounter two possible difficulties: you may find either very little literature on the topic or a vast overload of literature. If there is little literature on your topic, you will need to consult some related theory, and from there develop a working definition (i.e., a definition that can be revised) of the construct. In their study of school bullying, for example, Palmary and Barnes (1998) found very little literature on bullying, so they turned to theories of intergroup processes and gang behaviour to define bullying as a process whereby children achieve social identity through derogating and attacking outgroup members. This was an initial working definition that was developed and refined through exploratory research. At the other extreme, the researcher may find a wealth of (often contradictory) literature on the topic. In such cases, the researcher must either sift through the various definitions of the construct to develop a clear and unambiguous definition, or borrow such a definition (if one exists) from another researcher. In scanning the literature on conservatism, Durrheim and Foster (1995) found that the construct had been highly contested over the years, with some authors defining it from a Marxist perspective as support for the capitalist open market, some defining it as resistance to political change, and others defining it as a set of ideological beliefs, including racism, authoritarianism, and religious fundamentalism. In the end, Durrheim and Foster developed a South African measure of conservatism by following the lead of other researchers, who developed a clear and explicit construct definition of conservatism as a collection of beliefs in four different areas: social inequality, political and economic conservatism, religious conservatism, and punitiveness.

The final step in conceptualisation is to test your definition mentally by applying it to specific contexts and judging whether it misses certain aspects of the construct. Does the definition of conservatism cover religious fundamentalism? (Yes.) Does the definition of conservatism cover the beliefs of various political parties and conservative groupings in society (e.g., the AWB)? (Yes.) Does the definition cover the beliefs of people you know to be conservative? Give the definition to some friends or colleagues and ask them to see whether you have missed anything. Through this exercise, Durrheim and Foster (1995) found that there seemed to be two different units of analysis involved: individuals or collectives. 'Conservative' could be used to describe individual people or groups, nations, and organisations. Because they wanted to measure individual rather than collective levels of conservatism, they restricted their conceptual definition to individual beliefs in the four areas.

Conceptualisation is the first stage of measurement. During this stage, it is essential that the researcher develops a theoretical and conceptual definition of the construct that matches the attribute to be measured. In developing a good conceptual definition, the researcher ensures that the attribute being measured has a sound theoretical grounding. In sum, a good conceptual definition is a clear and explicit description in language of an attribute that exists in reality.

Once the conceptualisation phase has been completed, positivist measures increasingly take on the appearance of objectivity, and it is easy to forget that they start from contested conceptual foundations. Researchers should therefore take particular care to apply standards of rigorous scholarly enquiry to this early stage of the research process.

How would you determine which of the people you know would support each of these symbols?

It is important to remember, though, that it is very difficult to tease attributes apart from related attributes (e.g., conservatism from capitalism). Thus, while clear conceptual definitions go a long way towards rooting a construct in reality, sceptics point out that attributes are often conceptualised very differently by different authors. Conservatism, for example, is defined quite differently by pro-capitalist and Marxist researchers. In this, we are back with what we said in the introduction to this chapter: Rather than simply being things that can be found, described, and observed, attributes are produced as constructs, and are human creations that are developed through theoretical labour by individuals with particular values.

Operationalisation

After you have developed a working conceptual definition of a construct, you need to translate the linguistic meaning of the conceptual definition into observable indicators of the construct. That is, you should ask yourself how you plan to measure the construct empirically. This is called an **operational definition**. The operational definition defines the construct in terms of specific operations, measurement instruments, or procedures through which it can be observed. The principle here is to ensure that your operational definition corresponds with your conceptual definition.

There are usually many ways to measure a construct. The best measure is the one that fits most closely with the conceptual definition.

Durrheim and Foster (1995) operationalised conservatism by developing a bank of items that represented either conservative or liberal practices and beliefs, and asked research participants whether they believed in them, were uncertain, or did not believe in them. The beliefs and practices were divided into four groups: religious (e.g., nudist camps, legalised abortion, divine law), political and economic (e.g., mass action, strikes, big business, socialism), punitiveness (e.g., strict rules, censorship, moral training), and inequality (e.g., social equality, social welfare). Note that these items corresponded with the four dimensions of conservatism incorporated by the conceptual definition. Also note that the questions were asked in such a way that they tapped individual beliefs. These items were selected from other scales of conservatism, as well as conservative beliefs that the authors thought were particularly relevant in the South African context of that time (e.g., mass action and legalising dagga). This measure, which they called the South African Conservatism Scale, was a good operational definition because it generated observable indicators (i.e., individual responses) that reflected their conceptual definition of conservatism (i.e., individual beliefs in the four dimensions of conservatism).

Scale construction is a very important feature of measurement in the social sciences. **Scales** are developed to measure, *inter alia*, knowledge, attitudes and beliefs, sentiments, and judgements. (Chapter 22 provides a detailed discussion of scale development.) A scale is a measure of a construct that comprises one or more indicators of the construct. These indicators are summed into a score depicting the intensity, direction, level, or potency of the variable being measured. The score that an object (e.g., an individual or national economy) obtains on each item of the scale is added together to form the summed scale score. The summed scale score for each object (i.e., whether the score is high, moderate, or low) then indicates how much of the attribute that object possesses.

Constructs, however, are not operationalised only by scales; they can also be operationalised by indices. An index number is formed by transforming social and individual indicators (i.e., numerical facts) in such a way that irrelevant factors are controlled or eliminated in developing a numerical estimate of a particular attribute of an object (Campbell et al., 1981). Literacy rates are index numbers because they are expressed as the number of persons per 100 that are literate. Here the number of literate people in each country (i.e., a social indicator) is divided by the number of people in the country (and multiplied by 100) to control for differences in population size, thereby making the literacy rates across different countries comparable. Thus, although South Africa and Cuba have different population sizes, and different numbers of illiterate people, we can compare their literacy rates. Indices can show up some rather surprising things about the quality of life in different countries. For example, although South Africa is wealthy in comparison to Cuba, Cuba has a higher adult literacy rate than South Africa, and the literacy rate among females in many African countries is half that of males. Scales and indices are both very important ways of operationalising constructs in the social sciences, and, although they are derived in slightly different ways, they can be treated similarly in data analysis.

Operationalisation involves linking the world of ideas (concepts) to observable reality. The attribute we want to measure is first translated into a conceptual construct, and this construct is then translated into observable indicators of the construct (either by scales or indices). In each case of translation, the researcher must ensure that the elements before and after translation correspond with each other. If the attribute being measured is firmly theoretically grounded in a conceptual

According to UNICEF statistics, in 1990, the adult literacy rate in South Africa was 80 per 100 for males and 79 for females, while in Cuba it was 95 for males and 94 for females. In Niger, the literacy rate was 18 for males and 5 for females.
(www.unicef.org/sowc96/swc96t4x.htm)

definition, which is then accurately expressed in observable indicators, these observable indicators can be said to measure real attributes of objects.

Box 7.3

Common indices

(Vaughan Dutton, University of KwaZulu-Natal, Pietermaritzburg)

Indices are used in a variety of applications and disciplines. It is unusual to venture into any field without coming across an index of some kind. Here are some examples:

- **Gross domestic product** per capita. Average expenditure per citizen in a particular country.
- **Body mass index** (BMI). Height/weight ratio, computed by dividing a person's weight in kilograms by the square of her or his height in metres. People with BMI scores between 19 and 22 live longest. Death rates are inevitably higher for people with BMI scores of 25 or above.
- **Brain capacity index**. The ratio of brain weight to body weight, used to compare the intelligence of different animal species.
- **Gini index**. A measure of inequality of distribution of total income in a country's population.
- **Human development index**. Composed of scores for gross domestic product, health, and education; allows comparisons of social development to be made across countries.
- **Vocabulary richness index**. The number of unique words found in every 1 000 words in a text.

The relation between measures, operational definitions, conceptual definitions, and attributes can be illustrated through the example of an iceberg. By far the largest part of an iceberg is submerged, invisible below the water, while only a small part of the iceberg protrudes above the water. The visible part above the water is similar to the

operational definition – the observable indicators of a construct. The measurement instrument is like the tip of the iceberg because only a small subset of observable manifes-tations is eventually included in the measurement instrument. The part of the iceberg below the water can be likened to the conceptual definition. We cannot see the attributes that we want to measure directly, but we know, theoretically, that they must be there. However, even though we have a theoretical understanding that there is a submerged part to an iceberg, we do not know exactly what it looks like. Similarly, our operational definition and measurement instrument cannot measure exactly the construct we are really interested in. Researchers are thus very careful in developing conceptual and operational definitions, and in checking whether the observable indicators do indeed measure the attribute. This checking procedure involves the theoretical and empirical exercise of corroborating the measurement validity of the instrument.

Validity

There are many types of validity. What we will be discussing here is **measurement validity**, which is *the degree to which a measure does what it is intended to do*. This means that the measure should provide a good degree of fit between the conceptual and operational definitions of the construct, and that the instrument should be usable for the particular purposes for which it was designed (Carmines & Zeller, 1979). If an intelligence test consists of items that accurately reflect the conceptual definition of intelligence, the test may still be a valid indicator for only some purposes (e.g., predicting school performance). It may not necessarily be valid for other uses, such as predicting adult income. To establish measurement validity, the researcher must determine whether the instrument provides a good operational definition of the construct, and whether the instrument is suited to the purposes for which it will be used. Testing the validity of a measure involves a number of theoretical and empirical tasks that are roughly associated with three related kinds of measurement validity: criterion-related validity, content validity, and construct validity.

Criterion-related validity

Criterion-related validity is the degree to which a measure is related to some other standard or criterion that is known to indicate the construct accurately. This form of validity is established by comparing the measure with another measure of the same construct, called the **criterion measure**. Suppose that, because of changes in South African society, a researcher sets out to develop a new measure of racism that can detect covert and subtle forms of racism now prevalent in the country. To establish the criterion-related validity of this measure, the researcher would need to undertake the empirical task of determining whether this new measure is related to other measures of racism. When Duckitt (1991) developed a South African Subtle Racism scale, for example, he checked that the scores on this scale were related to (1) other scales that measured racist attitudes and racist behaviour, and (2) support for particular political parties (ranging from racist to anti-racist parties). If the Subtle Racism scale (see box 7.4) is indeed a measure of racism, it should correlate with other criteria for racism. There are two types of criterion-related validity that are distinguished by temporal positioning of the criterion measure in relation to the measure of the scale which is being validated. As the names indicate, **predictive validity** is established by correlating a measure with some future event,

The following are some other popular ways of operationalising constructs: Instruments – alpha rhythms (brain waves) as measured by an EEG machine are used as an indicator of anxiety. Galvanic skin response as measured by skin conductivity is used as an indicator of stress. Signs and symptoms – sunken eyes are used by primary health care workers as a sign of infant dehydration. Talking to oneself is popularly believed to be the first sign of 'madness'.

whereas, in **concurrent validity**, scores on the new instrument and the criterion measure are collected at the same time.

The term criterion-related validity sometimes misleads researchers into thinking that they can test their newly developed measure against some kind of incontrovertible criterion. Criteria are themselves also measures. Both the Subtle Racism scale and voting preference are measures of racism, and the fact that they are related does not prove either to be valid. It does provide suggestive evidence, though.

1. **Predictive validity** – Predictive validity is established by determining whether the measure predicts future events that are logically related to the construct. To establish the predictive validity of the Subtle Racism scale, Duckitt (1991) could have determined whether, during the 1994 elections, people who scored high on the scale actually voted for (as opposed to indicated that they supported) conservative political parties (e.g., the Freedom Front), and if people who scored low on the scale actually voted for historically anti-racist political parties (e.g., the ANC). Because of the racially divided nature of South African politics, voting behaviour is logically related to racism. Predictive validity could also have been established by determining whether people who scored high in the scale actually engaged in racist talk or actions during the six months following the study. Of course, there are many practical difficulties in establishing predictive validity, as the researcher may not be able to monitor the future behaviour of a large group of subjects to determine whether their scale scores predict their behaviour. In other contexts, though, predictive validity is easy to establish. Since the economic records of different countries are available, an economist could determine whether a new index of economic performance predicts the future inflation rate of a sample of countries.

Predictive validity is important in many applied contexts, and scores on measures are often used to make decisions about future performance. Predictive validity is routinely assumed, for example, when matric marks are used to predict university performance, or when companies employ people on the strength of their psychometric scores (e.g., intelligence and personality). Often, though, measures are used in applied contexts for purposes for which they were not designed. They thus have little predictive validity, leading to incorrect decisions that impact greatly on the lives of individuals (e.g., being refused entry into university, or being turned down for a job on the basis of poor matric results).

Establishing that a measure can be used to predict future events is a strong indication of its validity.

Another form of predictive validity is called criterion-groups validity. Here, the researcher selects a group of people (or countries or organisations) who have characteristics that are logically related to the measure, and determines whether group membership predicts scores on the measure. The validity of the Subtle Racism scale could be established by determining whether members of racist organisations (e.g., the AWB) score high on the scale while members of anti-racist organisations (e.g., IDASA) score low on the scale.

2. **Concurrent validity** – The second type of criterion-related validity is concurrent validity, the degree to which a new measure is related to pre-existing measures of the construct. There are many different

measures of racism, each using different items and response formats. To establish the concurrent validity of the Subtle Racism scale, Duckitt tested whether scores on his new scale were related to scores on other measures of racism. Of course, since the new scale was constructed to measure aspects of racism that were not assessed with the earlier measures, we cannot expect the different measures to be perfectly correlated. Duckitt encountered this problem when he used Ray's (1976) Anti-Black Attitude scale as a concurrent measure of racist attitudes. Ray's scale was developed at a time when highly racist opinions were commonly expressed by whites in public. Duckitt (1991) had to change some items on this scale because they were 'likely to be offensive to subjects' (p. 235) in the 1980s, when his study was conducted. Although the two measures of racist attitudes were very different, both measured racism, and were expected to be related to each other (even if not very strongly). In fact, Duckitt found that the individuals who scored high on the Subtle Racism scale scored higher on the Anti-Black scale than individuals who scored low on the Subtle Racism scale. The two scales were related (correlated), providing evidence of concurrent validity.

Content validity

Content validity is established by determining the extent to which a measure reflects a specific domain of content. Content validity is particularly important for tests of knowledge. When preparing an examination question paper, for example, the lecturer must ensure that all the material covered in the course is represented in the exam. If the exam includes questions on only four chapters out of a twelve-chapter textbook, the exam is not valid, and may be a misleading measure of students' knowledge. A student who studied hard and understood the material from the eight unexamined chapters may well fail the exam, when in fact the student had a very thorough knowledge of 67% of the textbook. Establishing the content validity of abstract constructs such as conservatism and subtle racism is a more difficult task because these phenomena do not have a predefined and restricted content that can fit between the covers of a textbook. The researcher must work towards content validity when developing the measure. This is done by (1) specifying the content area covered by the phenomenon when developing the construct definition, (2) writing questionnaire or scale items that are relevant to each of the content areas, and (3) developing a measure of the construct that includes the best (most representative) items from each content area. In developing their measure of conservatism, Durrheim and Foster (1995) followed these three steps by defining conservatism as consisting of beliefs in four content areas, generating an initial pool of approximately 30 items in each of the four content areas, and then selecting the most representative item from each area to make up the initial version of the scale. Selecting the good, 'most representative' items is a matter of

Whereas an empirical investigation is required to determine the criterion-related validity of a measure, conceptual and theoretical labour is required to determine whether the measure has content validity.

judgement. It is best done by the consensus method, where the researcher approaches others in the academic community to see whether the measure and the construct definition fit.

Duckitt's Subtle Racism Scale

This scale consists of 10 items in Likert scale format. Complete the scale by circling one of the five response options available for each item.

1. Given the same education and opportunities, blacks should be able to perform as well as whites in any field.
    1 Strongly agree **2** Agree **3** Neutral **4** Disagree **5** Strongly disagree
2. It would be unfair if greater expenditure on black education were to be funded by the white taxpayer.
    5 Strongly agree **4** Agree **3** Neutral **2** Disagree **1** Strongly disagree
3. Given favourable conditions, it is quite possible that black majority rule could result in a stable, prosperous, and democratic South Africa.
    1 Strongly agree **2** Agree **3** Neutral **4** Disagree **5** Strongly disagree
4. Only equality between black and white can in the long run guarantee social peace in this country.
    1 Strongly agree **2** Agree **3** Neutral **4** Disagree **5** Strongly disagree
5. The large-scale extension of political rights to blacks will inevitably lead to chaos.
    5 Strongly agree **4** Agree **3** Neutral **2** Disagree **1** Strongly disagree
6. The wealth of this country is almost entirely due to the hard work and leadership of the whites.
    5 Strongly agree **4** Agree **3** Neutral **2** Disagree **1** Strongly disagree
7. Although black living conditions should be improved, it is crucial for the stable development of the country that whites retain political control.
    5 Strongly agree **4** Agree **3** Neutral **2** Disagree **1** Strongly disagree
8. It is important that drastic steps be taken to ensure a far more equitable division of wealth in this country.
    1 Strongly agree **2** Agree **3** Neutral **4** Disagree **5** Strongly disagree
9. If all races were permitted to mix freely they would probably live in peace.
    1 Strongly agree **2** Agree **3** Neutral **4** Disagree **5** Strongly disagree
10. It is almost entirely best for all concerned that interracial marriage not be allowed.
    5 Strongly agree **4** Agree **3** Neutral **2** Disagree **1** Strongly disagree

Get your total score by adding up the numbers next to each word you circled. The lowest possible score is 10 (non-racist), with 50 (racist) the highest. Suppose you get a score of 15. This is called your raw score. Is 15 a high or a low score? Does it indicate that you are racist or not? In chapter 9, we will see how to answer such questions by translating raw scores into standard scores, which are used to compare your performance to that of a group of other people.

Construct validity

Establishing the construct validity of a measure involves both theoretical and empirical work: determining the extent to which a measure of a construct is empirically related to other measures with which it is theoretically associated. Construct validity differs from criterion-related validity because we are here seeking relationships between different theoretically associated constructs, not between two different measures of the same construct. Construct validation involves three steps: (1) specify a set of theoretical relationships between constructs, (2) test these hypotheses empirically, and (3) interpret the pattern of relationships in terms of how they clarify the construct validity of the measure. To find support for the construct validity of the Subtle Racism scale, Duckitt (1991) followed these three steps. From his review of the literature, he knew that racism is theoretically related to conservatism and to authoritarianism. The theory of the authoritarian personality (Adorno et al., 1950) provides a detailed model of the relationship between the three constructs of racism, authoritarianism, and conservatism. To test the construct validity empirically, he asked a group of research participants to complete measures of conservatism and authoritarianism in addition to the Subtle Racism scale. The measures of authoritarianism and conservatism are not direct measures (criterion measures) of racism, and neither scale contains any references to race groups. Duckitt found both scales to be strongly correlated to the Subtle Racism scale, suggesting that his measure of racism did have construct validity. This form of validity is called convergent validity, since it tries to determine whether scores from different measures converge or are related to each other. Campbell & Fiske (1959) have argued that researchers should also attempt to establish the **discriminant validity** of measures. In this case, measures that are theoretically unrelated to each other should not be empirically correlated, and, if strong correlations are found, the validity of the measure is placed in question. Since racism is theoretically unrelated to gender, males and females should not score differently on the scale. If the Subtle Racism scale was found to be empirically related to gender, this would question the validity of the scale. The scale may well be a measure of some gender-related trait and not racism.

Establishing a measure's convergent and discriminant validity will show whether it has adequate construct validity.

In sum, there are three broad categories of validity in terms of which a measure should be evaluated before the researcher can have confidence that the operational definition of a construct corresponds with the conceptual definition. Although the three types of validity have been discussed separately, they tend to complement each other in practice. If a measure has content validity, it is more likely to be related to other measures of the same construct (criterion-related validity), and is more likely to be related in theoretically predictable ways to other associated constructs (construct validity). The aim of checking the measurement validity is to ensure that the conceptual definition of a construct corresponds with the attribute being measured, and that the operational definition corresponds to the conceptual definition.

You will recall from the iceberg example that it is not possible to properly match the conceptual and operational definition of a construct. This means that, even though we have closely examined the validity of a measure, we can never be absolutely certain about its validity. What we can know is that an accumulation of evidence from a number of studies provides support for our belief in the validity of a measure. Also, we should not think that validity is an abstract property of a measure. Validity relates not only to the properties of the measure, but also to the purposes to which the measure is put and the context in which the measure is used. The Subtle Racism score of the managing director of a large company, for instance, may not be a good indicator of whether or not the company endorses an affirmative action policy, because the scale was not designed either for these predictive purposes or for use in the context of the post-1994 South Africa.

Reliability

Reliability refers to the dependability of a measurement instrument; that is, the extent to which the instrument yields the same results on repeated trials. In classical measurement theory, it is assumed that any score (X) that an individual 'object' (e.g. a person) obtains on a measure is made up of the true score (t) and an error score (e). Thus $X = t + e$. The true score is the amount of the attribute that the individual object has, whereas e is the error involved in measurement.

There are two sources of this error. First, measurement involves **random error** that is due to random disturbances in performance on the measure. These disturbances mean that an individual's score on the measure would be higher than their true score on one occasion but lower than their true score on another. Although you know exactly 70% of your research course work, because of daily fluctuations in performance, it is quite likely that by chance you would get 72% in the exam on one occasion but 67% on another. Although random error causes measures to be undependable, it is not a big problem. Mathematically it can be shown that, with sufficient trials on the test, the higher scores and the lower scores would cancel each other out, and, if we added the scores on the different trials together, we would get a good estimate of the individual's true score. Scales are usually made up of many items so that the random error on the individual items cancels out when all the items are added into a final scale score.

A second form of error, systematic error, is more problematic. **Systematic error** is nonrandom bias that impacts on the reliability of a measure. Suppose that an ambiguous question was used to measure an attribute. For example, to measure political and economic conservatism, the item 'Viva comrade Mandela, Viva' would be ambiguous because people would not know exactly what the item meant. On one occasion a person might view the item as a communist slogan that they reject, but on another occasion they may view the item as a friendly acknowledgement of a beloved president, and may support the slogan. This is an unreliable item because it does not elicit dependable responses, and may underestimate the conservatism of certain groups, who interpret the item in one way, but overestimate the conservatism of other groups, who interpret the item another way. The researcher should reduce systematic error by careful measurement design. There are a number of different ways in which the researcher can test whether a measure is reliable. They all follow a similar logic: If, on a number of different testings, the scores on a test correlate, we can assume that the test is dependable.

Test-retest reliability

Test-retest reliability is the reliability of the instrument over time. This form of reliability is tested by measuring individuals on the same instrument on different occasions and determining whether the scores correlate. What is meant here by 'correlate' is a matter of degree. To test that a bathroom scale is reliable, a single individual could weigh herself on a number of occasions and see whether the same weight is indicated. Since individual weight fluctuates slightly over time, we would not expect the exact same scores on each occasion, but we would expect very slight changes in weight on different occasions if the scale was reliable. In contrast, the test-retest reliability of an attitude scale is normally investigated with a reasonably large sample of subjects, and correlation in this context is indicated by how strongly the scores on both occasions are associated. As a general rule of thumb, a correlation coefficient (see chapter 9 and glossary) of greater than $r = 0.80$ is normally considered adequate for attitude measures, but this is not a hard-and-fast rule. This correlation coefficient indicates that individuals who score high on one occasion tend also to score high on the second occasion. We use a large sample to control for the large amount of random error present in attitude assessment. We can control this random error mathematically with a large sample, as the random fluctuations above the true scores for some individuals cancel out the random fluctuations below the true scores for other individuals. We can then determine whether the scores correlate across the sample.

Parallel forms

There are methodological problems with using the same test on two different occasions. When people complete a measure on one occasion, this often influences their performance on the measure on the second occasion. If you wrote an examination, and then wrote the same examination three days later, it is likely that your practice in the first exam will improve your performance in the second exam. Although researchers try to leave a large time period between administering the test and the retest, it is possible that real change in individual attributes could occur if the gap is too long. For this reason, test-retest reliability is often not appropriate, and researchers turn to parallel forms. These are measures which are exactly equivalent to each other. Instead of administering the same test on two different occasions, the researcher tests the dependability of the test by administering the two equivalent (parallel) measures of the attribute on the same occasion. Since the

Depression typically comes and goes within a matter of weeks. If we therefore administer a depression test to a group of people on two occasions three months apart, it will appear as if the test is unreliable when in fact the test is merely reflecting actual changes in depression. Conversely, if we administer a spelling test to a group of people on two occasions, five minutes apart, the test will appear to be very reliable, but in fact consistency of responses from one occasion to the next might simply be due to people remembering their answers.

measures do not have the same items, it is unlikely that scores on the one will influence scores on the other. If the scores on the two tests correlate strongly, we can assume that the items differ only in respect to random fluctuations, and that the tests are dependable measures of the construct.

Split halves method

The parallel forms method is wasteful since the researcher must construct two different tests, only one of which is retained as the true measure. A more efficient way of testing reliability is to construct a single measure made up of a number of items, and then divide these items randomly to make up two parallel halves. Reliability is then assessed by the strength of the relationship between the two halves. Since the halves should be equivalent, bar random error, people who score high on one half should also score high on the other half. The correlation between two halves of a test represents the reliability of half the test and is an underestimate of the reliability of the whole test. To correct for this, a mathematical formula, the Spearman-Brown formula, is used.

You can find the Spearman-Brown formula in most statistics books.

Internal consistency

It is possible with the split halves method that there may be systematic differences between the two halves of the test. There are many ways in which a measure can be split in two, and it is unlikely that they will all be equivalent. Internal consistency measures of reliability do not rely on either parallel forms or the splitting of tests, and are the most common measures of reliability. Internal consistency is estimated by determining the degree to which each item in a scale correlates with each other item. This is similar to determining the association between a series of different split half tests, and it controls for possible systematic differences between one half of a test and another. Internal consistency is normally determined mathematically by some formula that estimates the average inter-item correlation. Most statistical programs give estimates of internal consistency. Cronbach's coefficient alpha – a number that ranges from 0 (no internal consistency) to 1 (maximum internal consistency) – is the most common estimate. Although an acceptable internal consistency depends on what is being measured, as a general rule of thumb, questionnaire-type scales with an alpha value of greater than 0.75 are considered reliable (internally consistent).

Although one tests the reliability and validity of a measure for different reasons, the two constructs are related in some manner. If a measure is unreliable, it cannot be valid. If it gives different results on different occasions (i.e., is unreliable), at least one set of results must be incorrect (invalid). On the other hand, a measure can be reliable without being valid, because the reliable score may not assess the attribute being measured. The bathroom scale may be a reliable measure of weight, but it is an invalid measure of how fit I am. This illustrates, once again, that validity is related to the use to which measures are put, whereas reliability is purely a property of the measure.

Reliability is a necessary but not sufficient condition for validity.

Levels of measurement

Relations between numbers in a mathematical system often do not correspond with the relations between attributes being quantitatively represented by numbers. Numbers are abstract symbols that obey mathematical laws, but when these mathematical laws are applied to the quantities they are used to represent, absurdity often results. For example, when punching data into a computer, we might label all male subjects '1' and all female subjects '2'. It is a common (and legitimate) practice to use numbers to identify different groups of subjects: 1 is used to represent the attribute 'maleness'; 2 is used to represent the attribute 'femaleness'. However, once we start performing mathematical operations on these numbers absurdity results, because the mathematical relations between numbers do not correspond with the relations between attributes of things. Mathematically, it is perfectly legitimate to subtract 1 from 2 to get 1, but it is absurd to say that subtracting a female (1) from a male (2) results in a female (1). The attributes do not correspond with mathematical structure. Positivist researchers get around this problem by distinguishing between four levels of measurement – nominal, ordinal, interval, and ratio – each with appropriate mathematical applications. These four measurement scales help the researcher decide which mathematical operations can be performed on numbers, by ensuring that 'the structure of the method for mapping numbers (assigning scores) to observations must be isomorphic to some numerical structure which includes these operations' (Siegel & Castallan, 1988, p. 23).

- **Nominal** – Nominal measures indicate only that there is a difference between categories of objects, persons, or characteristics. Numbers are used here as labels to distinguish one category from another. For example, numbers can be used as category labels to distinguish between different categories that make up the variables Sex (male and female), Religion (Protestant, Catholic, Jew, Muslim) and Psychopathology (schizophrenic, manic-depressive, neurotic). We can label males 1 and females 2, but it would make no difference if we labelled females 1 and males 2, or females 1 and males 0. All the numbers do is distinguish individuals in one group from individuals in another. No mathematical operations $(+, -, \times, \div)$ or mathematical relations $(<$, less than; $>$, greater than) may be performed with these numbers because the attributes which are represented by them do not allow such operations. Although we can add or multiply 1 and 2, we cannot add or multiply the attributes Protestant and Catholic.

  Nominal variables that can take only one of two possible values – such as gender (male or female) and handedness (left or right) – are called dichotomous variables.

- **Ordinal** – Ordinal measures indicate categories that are both (1) different from each other, and (2) ranked or ordered in terms of an attribute. When we label developing countries '1', and developed countries '2', we are not only distinguishing between them but also marking the fact that developed countries have more of the attribute 'economic development' than developing countries. The same holds true when we label university grades A, B, C, D, or when we label opinions strongly agree, agree, disagree, and strongly disagree. With ordinal measures, we may perform mathematical relations ($<$, $>$), but not mathematical operations ($+, -, \times, \div$). Just because $2 = 2 \times 1$, we cannot say that developed countries (2) have twice as much economic development as developing countries (1). We can only say that they have more economic development. The differences between the amounts of the attributes that objects have do not correspond with the mathematical differences between the numbers that are used to represent these amounts. When the horses come in first, second, and third at the races, the numbers 1, 2, and 3 are measured on an ordinal scale and do not tell us how far the second horse was behind the first horse (i.e. the distances between the horses). The intervals between the numbers on an ordinal scale are meaningless, and therefore no mathematical operations can be performed on these numbers.

- **Interval** – Interval measures are the first true quantitative measures, because, in addition to marking difference and rank, the differences or distances between any two numbers on the scale are meaningful. This means that the difference between two scores is a reflection of the difference in the amount of an attribute which the two objects have. Temperature, measured in degrees Celsius, is measured on the interval scale, and a difference between 18 degrees and 20 degrees will be exactly the same as the difference between 25 degrees and 27 degrees. Most measures in the behavioural sciences (e.g., IQ scores, scores on attitude scales, and knowledge tests) are considered interval measures. In addition to performing mathematical relations ($<$, $>$), we may also legitimately perform the mathematical operations of addition and subtraction ($+, -$) with these numbers.

- **Ratio** – Ratio scales have all the properties of interval scales, but, because they have a true zero value (which interval scales don't have), the mathematical operations of multiplication and division ($\times$, $\div$) may also be performed on these scales. Since the variable Age has a true zero value – that is, at the moment when an individual is born she or he has zero of the property 'age' – we can say that a 40-year-old person is twice the age of a 20-year-old person. Interval scales do not have a true zero point. Although someone may get 0 out of 100 for an exam, this does not mean that the person has zero of the attribute 'knowledge'. Thus, we cannot say that someone who got 80% has twice as much knowledge as someone who got 40%. It is generally only physical properties – e.g. time, length, weight – that have real zero points and are thus measured on ratio scales. However, for most practical purposes in social science research, variables measured on the interval and ratio scales can be treated similarly.

These scales of measurement (nominal, ordinal, interval, and ratio) have been most influential in decision making since they were first introduced by Stevens (1946), because they determine the kind of statistical (mathematical) analyses which can be performed on the data. As discussed in chapter 9, the rule of thumb is to use parametric statistics to analyse variables measured on the interval and ratio scales, but different, nonparametric, statistics for variables measured on the nominal and ordinal scales. This ensures that the kinds of mathematical operation performed on the numbers correspond with the structure of the attributes being represented by the numbers.

Beyond levels of measurement

Box 7.5

The idea of 'levels of measurement' or 'measurement scales' has been heavily criticised from a number of different angles. A central line of critique focuses on the common assumption that the scale types depend on the nature of the variable being measured and the type of measure used. For a variable to be on a ratio scale, for example, it must have a real zero, and it must be measured with a sensitive instrument that can detect fine distinctions between amounts of the attribute being measured. Some critics suggest that the level of measurement has nothing to do with the nature of the variable or the measurement instrument, but the use to which the numbers will be put. According to Velleman & Wilkinson (1993), 'data that appear to have one type [of information] in fact hide other information' (p. 69). They suggest that the levels of measurement and mathematical operations that we can perform on data depend on our research questions. For example, the number of cylinders that motor cars have is usually considered an ordinal variable. We have cars with 4, 6, 8, and 12 cylinders driving on our roads, and the numbers tell us which cars have more or less cylinders. However, we can treat Numbers of Cylinders as a nominal variable when we ask the question 'Are there differences in fuel consumption between 4- and 6-cylinder cars?' When we ask the question 'Has the average number of cylinders in South African cars increased over the past 20 years?' we can calculate means, and treat the variable as an interval variable.

There are both principled and pragmatic critiques of the concept of levels of measurement. For example, there have recently been suggestions from statisticians that the use of parametric and nonparametric statistics often does not make any difference to the results. Despite this, levels of measurement retain their entrenched position in the methodology syllabus. The continued prominence of the 'levels' can be attributed to the fact that they provide a simple set of rules by which researchers can make decisions about which forms of data analysis to use. We recommend that these four levels of measurement should guide statistical decision, but that researchers should also 'break the rules' on occasions when this best fits the research question.

Conclusion

This chapter has explained how to collect quantitative data. We mentioned in the introduction that generalisability and 'objectivity' are important ideals for which quantitative researchers strive. With regard to generalisability, we discussed different sampling methods, attending to both probability and nonprobability sampling. With regard to the 'objectivity' of measurement in quantitative research, we first discussed the importance of conceptualisation, operationalisation, and validity-testing. The aim of these activities is to ensure that our operational measures accurately represent the real attributes of social and psychological 'objects'. We then discussed reliability, which is a way of checking the dependability of a measure. Finally we saw that, before analysing numerical data, researchers must decide on which measurement scale their variables are measured. This will ensure that the mathematical properties of the numbers correspond with the amounts or levels of the attributes being represented by these numbers.

Exercises

1. Using Moonstates and www.randomizer.org, create a list of 30 random numbers, with 1 as lower limit and 1 000 as upper limit (i.e., a sample of 30 from a sampling frame of 1 000).

2. Draw a systematic sample of n = 10 using your class as a population.

3. How many students drink Coca-Cola on your campus? Which sampling method would you use, and why, in order to answer this research question?

4. Consider Duckitt's Subtle Racism scale as reproduced in this chapter. Evaluate the validity of the scale as a measure of racism in today's context.

5. Design a 10-item scale to measure attitudes towards sexual harassment among university students. Focus particularly on conceptualisation and operationalisation. Suggest ways in which you could go about evaluating the validity and reliability of the measure. (You may want to have a look at chapter 22.)

6. Read through a newspaper and identify at least ten different variables that are quantified. Write these down and decide whether they are nominal, ordinal, interval, or ratio variables.

Key readings

Babbie, E., & Mouton, J. (2001). *The practice of social research*. (South African edition). Cape Town: Oxford University Press.
  This South African edition of a classic research textbook deals with sampling theory, probability theory, and various sampling methods.

Carmines, E. G., & Zeller, R. A. (1979). *Reliability and validity assessment.* Beverly Hills, California: Sage.

This short text is written in an approachable style and has been widely cited. It considers in a clear and applied manner all the main issues in assessing validity and reliability.

Nunnaly, J. (1978). *Psychometric theory.* (2nd edition). New York: McGraw-Hill.

This text is a classic that has been revised on numerous occasions. It provides a comprehensive introduction to the theory and practice of measurement. Although it has a psychometric focus, it is applicable to measurement generally.

Siegel, S., & Castallan, N. J. (1988). *Nonparametric statistics for the behavioural sciences.* (2nd edition). New York: McGraw-Hill.

This book's main aim is to provide a detailed account of the use of nonparametric statistics. In addition, however, it includes a detailed discussion of measurement scales, and defends the use of nonparametric statistics for most applications in the social sciences.

8

Evaluating research design

Colin Tredoux
University of Cape Town

Mario Smith
Stellenbosch University

Modern societies invest a great deal in empirical research, and we look to such research for answers to many of our important problems and questions. What are the causes and cures of cancer? What is the probability of contracting HIV from a single instance of unprotected sexual intercourse? What effect does malnutrition have on infant cognition? Is it safe to genetically engineer food crops? A casual flip through your newspaper will show that we do indeed place a lot of faith in empirical research. There is merit in asking how this 'science worship' has come about (see chapter 1), but, in this chapter, we will assume a position within this tradition and address the central question of how to decide whether particular pieces of research are sound. The goal is to outline a way of thinking that allows us to evaluate empirical research. Although our focus is social science research, this way of thinking can be considered a general approach that is useful for evaluating all kinds of research.

We will see that there are two central questions that have to be asked of any research design:

1. Are the conclusions drawn by the researchers sustained by the research itself?
2. Are the conclusions true in general?

Asking these questions of any particular piece of research can give powerful insights, and open up many avenues of enquiry. Box 8.1, for example, applies this way of thinking to government interventions around road safety, and shows that we should not leap to conclusions before we can answer the two key questions.

What is research design?

The term 'research design' is widely used in the social sciences, particularly in disciplines that champion experimental methods. However, there is a lot of hype around the term, and it is too frequently taken to mean a fixed set of procedures and methods that constitute a sort of 'periodic table' of the social sciences. It is perhaps better to take a more fluid view, and to think of a research design as a plan or protocol for a particular piece of research. The plan defines the elements (e.g., variables, participants), their interrelationship, and methods (e.g., sampling, measurement) that constitute the piece of research (see chapter 3).

Planning a research design involves thinking about the adequacy of the piece of research. The main task is to specify and combine the key elements and methods in such a way as to maximise validity. This is fine in theory, but very difficult to accomplish in the practical world. Research budgets are typically very limited, and the social and material worlds can be quite unruly! There are costs involved in doing research, and there is therefore a trade-off between the attempt to attain maximum validity and the costs involved in doing so. Research design can be viewed, then, as a kind of cost–benefit balancing; it is a plan for a piece of research that is constructed to maximise the validity of its findings, subject to the costs and practical difficulties of doing so (see Mouton & Marais, 1990).

It is clear from this definition that the notion of validity is central to the way in which we think about research design. Although there are very deep questions that we can ask about this notion from a philosophical point of view, social scientists tend for the most to ignore these questions, and posit two fundamental kinds of validity in relation to research designs. Particular studies must be interrogated with respect to each of these. (Note, however, that many other kinds of validity are

Box 8.1

Road safety interventions

Most people in the modern world live in large cities, and these cities have over the past century become fundamentally dependent on motorised transport. However, this modernisation has brought with it a major new cause of human death and suffering: traffic accidents. South Africa is no exception – during 2004, approximately 10 530 people were killed on South African roads. The number of fatal crashes increased by 291 (2.84%) from 10 239 people in 2003 to 10 530 people in 2004. The estimated cost to the economy in 2004 was in the order of R8.8 billion. Governments all over the world have recognised this problem, and from time to time introduce measures that are aimed at addressing it. Thus, a blitz on 'drunk driving' is frequently conducted over the December holiday season, since some 50% of accidents reportedly involve 'drunk drivers' (at least in South Africa). The effectiveness of this intervention is typically measured by whether a global indicator, like total number of road deaths, has declined in the period in which the intervention occurred. During the late 1990s, the South African Department of Transport mounted a programmatic intervention known as Arrive Alive. (For further details, see the project's internet home page: www. transport.gov.za/projects/alive)

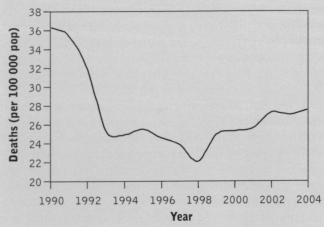

Figure 8.1 Fatalities on SA roads over a 15-year period

identified in relation to psychological measurement. These are set out in some detail in chapter 7).

Internal validity

If a study possesses internal validity, then its findings are said to follow in a direct and unproblematic way from its methods. It is said to 'sustain' its findings or conclusions. A very simple way of conceptualising internal validity is in terms of a classic form of logical argument called the syllogism. Consider the following arguments:

Over thirty years ago, Donald Campbell (1969) published a landmark paper 'Social reforms as experiments', in which he argued that many interventions of this kind can, from an analytic point of view, be treated as (social) experiments. Adopting such an analysis can tell us whether the change in the critical index can reasonably be said to show the effectiveness of the intervention, and whether it is reasonable to expect the intervention to be successful in different implementations. One of the points Campbell made is that government authorities are very quick to interpret any positive movement on the critical index as evidence in favour of the intervention. However, this is not sufficient evidence, since there are usually dozens of plausible alternative explanations for this movement. In the case of road safety indices – usually the total number of fatalities, or the total number of fatal accidents – we can expect there to be random variation over time. Or, to put it another way, we can expect the number of road fatalities to vary in the absence of any systematic intervention on the part of government. Figure 8.1 reports fatalities on South Africa's roads over the year period 1990 to 2004, and shows that there was substantial variation in this period. If we had introduced a traffic intervention programme in the latter part of 1995, we may have been incorrect in concluding that the change in numbers of fatalities and fatal accidents was due to the intervention. Policymakers need to show that any observed changes are greater than those we expect just by chance fluctuation. Even if it does seem reasonable to attribute the observed changes to the intervention, we should ask questions about the generalisability of the intervention and the findings. Are the changes permanent? What happens if we modify the nature of the intervention (e.g., we discover that we cannot afford to mount repeated large-scale road blitzes, and have to mount smaller scale operations in future)? The point is clear. When social policymakers interpret results from large-scale 'social experiments', they ought to carefully consider the 'internal' and 'external' validity of their experiment, and the research evaluating it.

Argument 1		Argument 2	
Premise 1	Your lecturer is a Rastafarian.	Premise 1	Your lecturer is a man.
Premise 2	All Rastafarians smoke dagga.	Premise 2	Some men are philanderers.
Conclusion	Your lecturer smokes dagga.	Conclusion	Your lecturer is a philanderer.

There is no doubt that if we concede the truth of both premises for argument 1, we must accept the conclusion that your lecturer smokes dagga! The argument is internally valid, even though its conclusion may in a real sense be false (because the premises are untrue). However, if we concede the truth of both premises for argument 2, the conclusion does not follow, and we should reject it outright, regardless of the truth status of the premises.

The logic of deduction corresponds with internal validity in the sense that the particular conclusion reached in the study should follow from the logic of the design.

An internally valid research design is directly analogous to argument 1. Findings can be sustained by the logic of the design if all the details specified by the design are adhered to. Continuing the analogy to argument 1, internally valid findings may have no basis in reality; it is quite possible to make findings in a laboratory that are not true in any way of the world outside the laboratory. The distinction between the internal validity of a study and the applicability of the results to real-world settings corresponds with the distinction between effectiveness and efficacy in clinical research (see chapter 21).

It is worth illustrating this point with an example. Imagine that we are testing the effect of a new wonder drug on stomach ulcers. To do this, we give a group of monkeys the drug, and another group a placebo treatment. We find that the drug reduces ulcers substantially. This result might not be generalisable to human beings – it might do nothing at all for human beings – but it does work on monkeys. The experiment is internally valid, given the terms of reference of the experiment.

Internal validity is a key consideration when formulating a research design, and researchers will spend a lot of time attempting to ensure that any results arrived at are sustained by the design itself, and cannot be explained by alternative considerations (or 'rival hypotheses', see chapter 3). Certain kinds of research lend themselves better to achieving strong internal validity, though, and it may be necessary to compromise the internal validity of a design to some extent if we are to address certain questions. Internal validity is typically strong for experimental studies conducted in laboratories, where it is easy to hold constant conditions to ensure that the observed results are the singular outcome of an intervention. However, some questions are not amenable to this. For example, any effect of ageing is difficult to answer with an experimental study (e.g., 'How does ageing affect memory ability?') Can you see why?

External validity

A study has external validity when its findings or conclusions can be generalised beyond the confines of the design and the study setting. If the findings are true for all humans, and for all operationalisations of the measures used in the study, then the study possesses complete external validity, but this is unlikely ever to be the case in practice. Indeed, it would be an unusual study that aimed for such extreme generalisability! On the other hand, it would be pointless if the results of a study were true only of the particular participants used, and the particular measures taken from them.

What is meant by 'generalisability' is not always clear, but it is usually taken to refer to the extent to which the results or findings of a study can be extrapolated to a wider context than that used in the implementation of the research design. There are many aspects of 'context', in this sense, but of particular importance are (1) the population the study participants are drawn from (and therefore represent), and (2) the operationalised measures of key study variables.

There are many ways in which the external validity of a research design can be bolstered, but it cannot be said that social scientists are vigilant in this respect. The reasons are twofold: In the first place, increasing external validity is a costly business, since research participant populations must be carefully defined and sampling strategies carefully used. In the second place, increasing the external validity of a study often leads to a commensurate diminishing of internal validity. Internal validity is strongest in situations where great control can be exercised over study conditions, but situations of this kind are somewhat artificial, and can rarely be said to adequately represent social conditions outside the laboratory.

A research study has external validity if its results are generalisable to other situations and/or representative of broader populations.

Both types of validity – internal and external – are important and desirable attributes of a research design. There is little point in having results that are coherent, and which are sustained completely by the research procedures one has utilised, if they are merely self-referring. Similarly, there is no point in conducting a piece of research that pays great attention to external validity if the design is flawed and leads to spurious results. It is a rare research design that secures both kinds of validity, though, and most researchers will be content with satisfactory internal validity and some degree of external validity. The notions of internal and external validity correspond directly to questions 1 and 2 outlined in

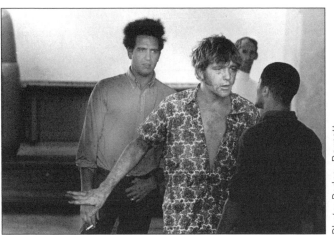

Do responses to a racism questionnaire generalise to racist behaviour?

Photo: Rodney Barnett

the introduction to this chapter. Used as interrogative guides, they constitute a general approach to the evaluation of research designs. At the very least, they are handy concepts, and you will find them of great assistance when reviewing particular pieces of research.

How do you judge validity?

Whereas internal validity rests on design logic and pertains to the validity of the conclusions, external validity is about representativeness, and pertains to how widely the results of the study apply.

Although many textbooks suggest formulaic approaches to judging the internal and external validity of research, it is better to keep general principles in mind when doing so. When you evaluate the internal validity of a study, the key consideration is whether the conclusions or findings follow from the data, and the procedures used. When judging external validity, the key consideration is the extent to which the results can be extrapolated beyond the study context.

Many potential threats to internal and external validity are well understood in relation to specific types of design, and we will review some commonly used designs in a later section of this chapter. At the end of the day, though, it is a question of rational deliberation, and applying a set of criteria in a formulaic way is no substitute for careful reasoning.

One way of approaching the question of internal validity is to consider as many alternative explanations of the results and conclusions as possible. Can the conclusions drawn by the researchers withstand the test of alternative explanations or plausible rival hypotheses? This is a strict test, since a single reasonable alternative explanation will bring the study to its knees. Indeed, there are few studies that escape the withering scrutiny of 'alternative explanation'! When we consider some sample designs later in this chapter, we will see how this approach works.

External validity is a little easier to evaluate than internal validity, and it usually suffices to question three aspects of the design:

1. Research participants

   From which population are the participants drawn? Is this population unique in some way, so that findings made in respect of them are not generalisable to other populations? Were appropriate sampling techniques used in selecting research participants, in order to ensure representativeness (see chapter 7)?

2. Independent variables, or manipulations

   Are these highly specific, or can a case be made for generalising them to other operationalisations?

3. Dependent variables, or outcomes

   Will findings on the dependent variable generalise to other, similar, variables?

The best way to acquire skill at evaluating internal and external validity is by getting practice; the final section of this chapter gives you an opportunity to do so.

Interrelationship of sound design and type of research

We argued earlier that asking questions about internal and external validity constitutes a general approach to evaluating research; that is, all empirical research can fruitfully be judged according to this scheme. This view has its opponents, particularly in some qualitative research traditions. Certainly, quantitative and qualitative researchers think about validity in different ways, and we will consider only quantitative research traditions in this chapter. This should not be taken to imply that qualitative research is immune from inspection for coherence (internal validity) and relevance (external validity), as you will see in chapter 16.

A useful simplification of quantitative research in the social sciences is as a three-unit typology consisting of descriptive research, relational research, and comparative (experimental and quasi-experimental) research. Each of these types of research has different goals and utilises different techniques, and these need to be borne in mind when evaluating specific instances of research.

Quantitative research can be descriptive, relational, or comparative.

Descriptive research

The key aim in descriptive research is to describe. The research might try to describe the distribution of attributes in a population, the social practices of a particular group, or simply a small-scale event such as a political demonstration. The studies conducted by Alfred Kinsey and his associates (Kinsey, Norton, & Pomeroy, 1948; Kinsey, 1953) provide good examples of descriptive research. The goal of this research was to describe the sexual behaviour of human males and females in considerable detail: the prevalence of certain behaviours (e.g., homosexual intercourse), the ages at which sexual interactions first started, the proportion of the population who were virgins when they married, and so on. This was motivated (in part) by Kinsey's conviction as a marriage counsellor that professional knowledge of sexual behaviour was highly inadequate.

To the extent that the key aim of descriptive research is accurate description, external validity becomes overwhelmingly important. Researchers will very rarely want to restrict findings to the study sample, and will usually select research participants from particular populations, thereby declaring an intention to generalise. The essential question that must be asked is whether the study has used any techniques that attempt to ensure generalisability. This can be spelled out in terms of two typical aspects of the design:

External validity is of key importance to research that aims to describe the social world.

1. Were appropriate sampling techniques used to ensure that research participants were representative of the target population? Was the target population defined (implicitly or explicitly)? Can we see such a lack of representativeness from the reported characteristics of the sample?

2. Were the measures taken by the researchers representative of the class of possible measures? For example, Kinsey sampled a great many different aspects of sexual behaviour, but it is not uncommon to find research articles where one aspect of sexual behaviour (e.g., intercourse) is taken to mean all sexual behaviour.

Although external validity is very important to descriptive research, internal validity is not irrelevant. One can ask questions about the internal validity of a descriptive research design in several ways, but most important is the set of measurement instruments and measurement methods used in the research (see chapter 22). If a measurement scale is used that purports to measure antisocial tendencies but has poor psychometric properties (reliability, validity), then it follows that any findings and conclusions made regarding antisocial tendencies are not sustained by the design. For example, an unreliable scale could give very different values for two individuals who are in fact equivalent on the criterion.

Kinsey's studies on male and female sexuality used carefully considered measurement methods, and have not been criticised for internal validity. However, they have been criticised vigorously for external validity – most of the research participants were selected opportunistically, and were university students. Kinsey suspected that Americans knew very little about homosexual behaviour(s), and deliberately recruited research participants who were practising homosexuals, often by their reputation. What effect do you think Kinsey's sampling had on his findings?

The sampling methods used in a piece of descriptive research are often crucial to the external validity of that research. Since the goal of

Because of the cost of drawing probability samples, it is rare for social scientists to use probability sampling methods, and most samples are best considered nonprobability samples. In nonprobability samples, however, the generalisability of the estimate is unknown, and the error of measurement is indeterminate.

Box 8.2

Causation in the social sciences – is experimental research sovereign?

Much discussion around research design may appear to suggest that experimentation is the logical endpoint of research, the most preferred route in the quest for social science knowledge. This view is held by many, and is not, to be fair, entirely nonsense. Experiments sustain conclusions about causes in a relatively effortless manner, and causes in turn naturally underpin explanations of phenomena. They appear to take us a lot further towards the goals of understanding and explaining than do other types of research study. There are major disquiets about experimental research, though, and many of these are based on analyses (and rejections) of the notions of 'causation' and 'causal explanation', which are central to the enterprise of experimental research. The customary understanding of a 'causal explanation' within the tradition of experimental research is that it satisfies three requirements (see Mouton & Marais, 1990, p. 45):

most descriptive quantitative research is to determine estimates of population parameters with a calculable amount of error, probability sampling methods are preferred (see chapter 7; see also Rosenthal & Rosnow, 1991).

Relational research

Many real-life situations involve interesting relationships. People who support gun control in South Africa also tend to oppose the death penalty. People who frequently have braais also tend to have cholesterol problems. Those who take Ecstasy also tend to be those who drink lots of water. For this reason, researchers frequently investigate relationships between things, and this tradition of research (the second in the typology referred to above) is known as relational research.

However, it is rarely enough to merely establish that there is a relationship between two (or more) things. We want to know *why* something happens, and *how* it happens. We want to know why cigarette smoking and heart attacks are related, not simply that they are related. We want to know how smoking cigarettes leads to heart attacks, not merely that it does. Is it because smoking narrows arteries, and this makes it more likely that a blood clot will block the artery, and stop the supply of blood to the heart? Would this explain another relationship we know about, namely that smokers with high cholesterol are more likely to suffer a heart attack than smokers who do not have high cholesterol? Even if we do not wish, or are unable, to get at an understanding of how and why something happens, we will

1. The independent and dependent variables co-vary.
2. There is a specific (temporal) sequence of cause and effect.
3. The independent variable is the real cause of the dependent variable.

What is meant by 'cause' in these requirements, though, is the subject of fierce debate in the social sciences. Most authors accept that causality in social contexts cannot mean the same thing as physical or natural causality. In the natural sciences, it is widely accepted that causality must be defined in terms of an underlying natural law. With one or two exceptions, nothing in the social sciences seems to qualify as a natural law. Some theorists maintain that there can be no laws in social and psychological contexts, while others maintain that 'mental causes' are the same things as 'reasons', and that explanations which posit reasons are causal explanations. The debate is beyond the scope of this chapter, and we recommend that those interested in these questions consult Simon (1982), and Bhaskar (1979), among others.

want to know the conditions that decrease or increase the association between it and other variables. This is the business of relational research: the description of how changes in one variable correspond to changes in another variable. The task is nonmanipulative, and observational: it requires coordinated observation of at least two variables.

Internal validity of relational designs

It is particularly difficult to attain high levels of internal validity in relational designs, but relatively easy to attain reasonably high levels of external validity.

We argued earlier that the aim of research is to know and understand the world as completely as possible. A statement of mere relationship is rarely enough no matter how precisely we render our description; the inclination, finally, is to seek a causal explanation. In this respect, relational research designs are always unsatisfactory. This is because they cannot sustain causal explanation, and are often difficult to interpret.

You have probably been alerted to this problem before, and may better recognise it as the warning that correlations are not causes. This is true, but we wish to add that the problem is one that is rooted in methodological, and not statistical considerations. It is quite possible that a correlation coefficient can reveal a causal relationship, provided that it is determined on data collected with the right methodological circumspection (namely, in a controlled experimental situation). However, a mere relationship between two variables (however it is quantified) tells us nothing about causes, unless we know (and have controlled) the conditions under which the observations of their relationship were made. Two substantial interpretive problems constantly undermine attempts to understand relationships: the 'third variable' problem and the problem of direction.

The 'third variable' or 'confounding variable' problem

We return to the relationship between cigarette smoking and heart attack rate. It is widely speculated that people who have heart attacks suffer from greater levels of stress in their lives. Similarly, it is also widely speculated that cigarette smokers have higher levels of stress than nonsmokers.

The variable of stress has not been isolated from our understanding of the causes of either heart attacks or smoking. It is quite possible that stress is responsible for the relationship between heart attacks and smoking – i.e., people who are more stressed tend to have heart attacks, and perhaps tend to

Photo: Rodney Barnett

How can we be certain that smoking causes heart disease?

smoke cigarettes to relieve stress. Stress is a so-called third variable in this research, which could be responsible for the observed relationship between cigarette smoking and heart attacks. To make matters worse, 'third variables' can affect relationships in complex ways. Two examples should suffice (see Huysamen, 1996).

Moderator variables

In some situations, 'third variables' moderate relationships. A moderator variable impacts on the strength of a relationship between two variables. Thus, cigarette smoking is known to increase the incidence of coronary heart disease by approximately seven times in high-cholesterol sufferers, but has less of an effect on smokers who do not have high cholesterol levels. In other words, cigarette smoking *moderates* the relationship between cholesterol level and coronary heart disease.

Mediator variables

Certain variables operate as the mechanism by which one variable affects another. For example, we might observe that stress and coronary heart disease are related, but, on closer examination, find that stress predisposes people to smoke cigarettes, and cigarette smoking, in turn, precipitates coronary heart disease. It is not stress per se that predisposes people to the disease, but the cigarette smoking that highly stressed people resort to. In other words, cigarette smoking *mediates* the relationship between stress and heart disease.

The problem of direction

Even if we could rule out stress, as well as any other 'third variable' that could cause both of the events we have observed, and conclude that there is a causal relationship between our measured variables, we could not conclude whether A caused B, or whether B caused A. Our research occurs after the fact, and we can say nothing about the direction of any relationship we have the good fortune to identify. At a basic level, the logic of a correlation does not support any causal claim – there is only measurement, no control or manipulation. Control and manipulation are the province of the experimental method.

There are two plausible rival hypotheses that undermine the ability of relational research to be used for causal explanation: third variables, and uncertainty about causal direction.

External validity of relational designs

Relational designs do not manipulate conditions, but instead make coordinated observations on unconstrained variables. For this reason, it is frequently easier to attain reasonably good levels of external validity with relational designs than with experimental designs. For instance, if we are interested in factors that make epileptic children susceptible to psychopathology, we will collect data on a number of factors (e.g., type of epilepsy, medication used) and on measures of psychopathology (e.g., Rutter's 'risk' scale), on a sample of epileptic children. It is very difficult to imagine an experimental design in which this question can be asked without being absurdly contrived and virtually bereft of external validity. However, this does not mean that external validity comes naturally to relational designs. We need to be vigilant about aspects of the research design that affect generalisability. These include, as before, (1) the selection of research participants, and (2) the selection of measures.

An important additional consideration, however, is that in relational research we are interested in generalising a relationship; that is, a bivariate attribute rather than a univariate attribute. This means that it is especially important to consider how carefully researchers have defined target populations, and how their sampling methods accommodate this. For example – to continue the case of the relationship between cigarette smoking and coronary heart disease – it is well established that rates of smoking and heart attack are related in some populations but not in others. Any further relational research needs to choose its research participants carefully if it wants to deepen its understanding of the relationship.

Where the logic of the correlation supports the construction of a picture depicting the nature (direction and strength) of a relationship between two variables, the logic of the experiment is geared toward conclusions concerning causation, and we now turn to such designs.

Comparative (experimental and quasi-experimental) research

The aspiration of the social sciences to become 'natural sciences of the social' has been tied up to a large extent with the final member of the typology of quantitative research, which we have called comparative research. This tradition of research includes true experiments, quasi-experiments and some marginal designs (often dismissed as 'pre-experimental').

The notions of internal and external validity were originally developed with this tradition of research in mind (see Campbell & Stanley, 1966), and it is not surprising that there is now a substantial literature on the kinds of threat to validity typically posed to different kinds of comparative designs. This section will summarise some of this literature, and show how it can be used to great effect for purposes of evaluating research. To do this, it is useful to identify the central goals of experimentation, and to distinguish **true experiments** from **quasi-experiments**.

The overarching aim behind experimentation – and perhaps any kind of comparative design – is to identify a cause–effect sequence. In operationalised terms, the aim is to show that changing the independent variable results in a change in the dependent variable, and to leave no doubt whatsoever that the observed change is due to the change in the independent variable and not to some other change. This is why testing for alternative explanations is such a powerful form of evaluation; if we identify a plausible rival explanation for the change in the dependent variable, it undermines the very foundation of the design.

How can we show that observed changes in the dependent variable are really due to changes in the independent variable and nothing

The unifying characteristic of experimental research is the attempt to compare two or more groups of research participants on one or more variable, after the application of some type of intervention or manipulation.

else? There are several strategies, but they all amount to the same thing. We can best see how this is the case by considering the definition of a true experiment with a single condition. In order to be a true experiment, the design must meet the following criteria:

1. The independent variable is an active variable. The experimenter is able to manipulate it – to turn it on or off at will.
2. The participants who receive one level of the independent variable are equivalent in all ways to those who receive other levels of the independent variable.

The second criterion is the really important one, and the one we have most problems with when we try to interpret experiments. Experimenters spend most of their time trying to ensure that this second criterion is met. We subsume efforts in this regard under the heading 'experimental control'.

Experiments are studies that seek to identify cause–effect relationships by manipulating the hypothesised causal variable (independent variable) in a controlled environment, and observing the effect of this manipulation on an outcome variable (dependent variable).

Different meanings of experimental control

There are several meanings of the term 'control' in experimental terminology, but these converge if approached in sufficiently general terms: Control is fundamental to all experiments in the sense that the purpose behind all forms is to isolate the independent variable from all other variables, and to show its effect on the dependent variable, if there is one.

Control of extraneous variables

The most characteristic use of the term 'control' is when we say that we control extraneous variables to ensure that they do not interfere with our experiment. By 'interfere' we mean two distinct things. First, the change we observe in the dependent variable is in fact due to a variable other than the independent variable. This is the worst case, and is very similar to the 'third variable problem' which plagues relational research. We say that the results of the experiment are confounded, or that we have overlooked a confounding variable. For example, we test a drug treatment on a group of hospital patients, but we forget to take into account other medications they might be taking. We run the risk of having our results confounded by interactions between multiple drugs; e.g., the patients get worse, but only because they are receiving incompatible medications! The other medications act here as a confounding variable.

Second, variables enter the experiment and cloud the results, but do not necessarily threaten the validity of the experiment. This is analogous to television interference – you can still see the picture, but it is masked by an extraneous signal. To continue the example above, imagine that we allow the group of hospital patients to administer the drugs themselves. Only a few of the patients take the correct dosage, if at all. We observe a very weak effect when we average over the patients, but the effect is weak only because the intervention has been greatly diffused.

A confounding variable is an uncontrolled 'extraneous variable' that co-varies with the experimental manipulation, thus undermining the internal validity of the experiment.

A control condition

Control is also used to describe a condition of the experiment that acts as a baseline against which the experimental manipulation will be assessed. The collection of research participants who make up this condition is known as the control group. A control group usually has nothing done to it – it serves as a baseline of no intervention – but researchers may also use several groups as benchmarks or baselines against which to measure the effect of the intervention, with each group receiving a different type or degree of intervention.

The ways in which the control (and experimental) conditions are created and maintained are of paramount importance for true experiments. The overriding consideration is that the control condition must differ in no way from the experimental condition other than the critical intervention administered by the experimenter. The groups must be equivalent in all possible ways bar those planned in the research design. This means, for example, that there should not be a greater number of males in one group, and that the groups should not differ with respect to age, even if these differences appear irrelevant.

When working with human subjects, it is difficult to form a control group that has 'nothing' done to it. This is discussed in greater detail in chapter 21.

This is perhaps the best way to characterise the difference between true experiments and quasi-experiments: In true experiments, complete equivalence is a requirement, but in quasi-experiments equivalence is only required in terms of relevant characteristics; that is, characteristics that could provide a plausible rival explanation of any observed effects. In true experiments, methods that guarantee group equivalence are supreme, and the most widely used in this respect are randomisation techniques. These are used in conjunction with an armoury of statistical methods, most of which assume that randomisation has been effected. Randomisation means the random assignment of participants to conditions or groups. This can be achieved in many ways, as long as the chosen method ensures that (1) each participant has an equal probability of being assigned to each of the conditions, and (2) participants are assigned independently of each other. In practice, researchers tend to use random number tables or computer algorithms to do random assignment.

Campbell's schema for evaluating internal and external validity

In the 1950s, the American psychologist Donald Campbell devised a schema for evaluating internal and external validity which has become very widely used in social science experimentation. This schema is constructed around a set of typical threats to internal and external validity, particularly in comparative designs. Although it is a very useful schema, the names Campbell assigned to the types of threat are somewhat cryptic, and we will alter them here, where necessary. In the discussion below, Campbell's original terms are given in parenthesis alongside the altered names.

A useful way to introduce this catalogue of threats is to describe an example study, and then to show how the threats apply. The study we use here is imaginary, but studies like it have been conducted on many occasions:

> A remedial teacher wants to explore the effectiveness of a new kind of reading intervention, called 'paired reading'. The idea behind the intervention is that parents of children in remedial classes are usually removed from the education of their children, but involving them directly will aid the learning process. The intervention is operationalised so that parents spend half an hour every day reading with their child. The teacher takes the 15 nine-year-old children in her class who score worst on a standardised measure of reading performance, and implements the intervention. She takes a reading proficiency measurement before the intervention and after the intervention, which continues for three months. She discovers that the children have gained six months' reading age as a result of this intervention.

Campbell suggested a notation for experimental design, which, in the present example, looks as follows:

$$O_1 \text{ --------- } X \text{ --------- } O_2 \quad \text{Design 1}$$

(O = observation; subscripts 1 and 2 indicate time; X indicates the presence of an intervention.)

You should be able to see that the imaginary study suffers from many problems. In fact, it probably suffers from each of the problems identified in Campbell's scheme. Let us contrast it simultaneously with an alternative experiment, as represented in the diagram below, which would have worked much better. In design 2, the teacher **randomly assigns** each child into either the control (which does not receive the intervention) or the experimental group (which engages in paired reading for three months). The reading abilities of both groups are measured before and after the intervention. The results of this study are analysed by judging whether the improvement in the experimental group exceeds that in the control group.

$$\begin{array}{l} O_{11} \text{ --------- } X \text{ --------- } O_{21} \quad \text{Design 2} \\ \hline O_{21} \text{ --------- } \quad\quad \text{ --------- } O_{22} \end{array}$$

(The blank space between the bottom observations indicates the absence of the intervention; the line separating the groups indicates random assignment.)

Threats to internal validity

1. The threat of co-varying events (history)
The study represented by design 1 suffers in the first instance from the fact that something could be happening alongside (co-varying), in the environment, during the three months that the intervention

Campbell's schema for evaluating the validity of experiments, originally published in 1957, has become part of methodological canon in the social sciences. Pick up any methodological textbook and you will see references to this schema. In his 40-year career, Campbell published landmark papers on many areas of measurement, experimental design, applied social experimentation, interpretive social science, epistemology, and the sociology of science.

Random assignment is a way of allocating subjects to experimental and control groups randomly, in an effort to make the groups equivalent.

continued. In other words, the improvement claimed by the teacher could be due to something else that happened at the same time. For example, the school syllabus could have been such that the children started a block which involved intensive reading, and it could be this additional practice and not the paired reading that produced the observed improvement. Of course, we do not know enough about the study to conclude this. In practice, we would carefully scrutinise the conditions under which the study was conducted for such possibilities. The point is that the design does not exclude any co-varying events.

Design 2 controls for this problem by assessing the effectiveness of a 'no intervention' condition: If there is a co-varying event, participants in this condition should also show (unexpected) change over the time interval.

2. The threat of independent natural change (maturation)

A second threat to the study is that children have a developmental trajectory for most cognitive abilities. The observed change may be due to this 'maturation' of ability quite independently of the intervention. In a three-month period, we would expect reading ability in young children to improve. However, the fact that the teacher has used a measure of 'reading age' controls for this threat to some extent, since she can compare the change in reading age to change in chronological age. The threat is well controlled in design 2, since natural improvement over time in reading ability will show itself in both groups, and the experimental group will have to improve more than the control group does in order to persuade us that there is real improvement going on.

3. Reactive effects to participating in a study (testing)

Human subjects are not usually inert. We react when studied, and changes that occur in our behaviour may be due to our reactions to being studied rather than to the intervention. Well-known demonstrations of this include the experimenter effect and the Hawthorne effect. Reactions present a severe threat in the present study. By identifying particular children and including them in a study, it is highly likely that singling them out will have an effect. The children, perhaps aided by their parents, will respond to the mere fact of being part of an experiment (which is supposed to have positive effects), and not only to the paired reading intervention. It is an effect of testing, because the first testing alerts the research participants to what is up, and they may change accordingly on the second testing.

Design 2 allows the teacher to assess whether repeat testing effects are present, since she takes two measures from a control group that receives no intervention. If the control group changes, she must conclude that something is amiss, or has to factor this into the comparison between the experimental and control groups.

4. Measurement unreliability (instrument decay)

In chapter 7 you were introduced to the concept of measurement reliability. Much of the data in the social sciences come from self-report inventories or other 'tests' that are constructed to measure theoretical constructs (e.g., intelligence, racism, altruism, conservatism). One of the axiomatic conditions of these scales is that they possess satisfactory measurement reliability and validity. In other words, a test that measures intelligence should give the same scores for persons x and y, if they have the same intelligence, or for person x at times a and b (provided a and b are sufficiently close in time).

A test that lacks measurement reliability can lead to completely erroneous conclusions, and can seriously jeopardise the internal validity of a piece of research. Imagine a weight scale that gives wildly different readings for the same individual. Imagine further that this individual happens to be somewhat obese, and on a new diet. Do you think that measuring this individual could reasonably assess the effect of the diet on weight loss?

In the case of the study devised by the teacher, she is likely to use a well-researched measure of reading ability, with good measurement properties. However, we would need to know what the measure is before we could conclude one way or the other.

Researchers sometimes become so involved in establishing carefully controlled experimental conditions that they forget that unreliable or invalid measuring instruments will jeopardise the validity of the entire experiment.

5. Statistical regression of extreme subjects (regression to the mean)

In the social sciences, we often choose to study people who are at the extremes of a criterion measure. In the present case, the remedial teacher has identified and recruited the 15 readers in her class who scored lowest on a criterion measure, because they are the ones who need assistance. While this seems like a reasonable thing to do from an intuitive point of view, it is an error. If you sample at the extremes on a single occasion and on a single criterion, you are likely to select participants who will change positively on the next measurement in the absence of any intervention. This is because all sets of scores exhibit random variability, and those scores at the bottom of such a set are there in part because this variability has not favoured them on this occasion.

This threat is a problem for design 1, but is controlled by design 2, in the sense that the groups are equivalent at the beginning of the design (due to random assignment). If regression occurs, it will affect both groups equally. The experimental group will have to show improvement greater than that shown by the control group if we are to believe that the intervention has any effect.

6. Participant dropout (subject mortality)

This threat should not be taken literally – rest assured that very few subjects die during social science research studies! However, it is true that human research participants often tend to withdraw from research studies, and this is often a threat to internal validity because the people who withdraw may share particular attributes.

The threat of participant dropout is applicable to design 1. If the ten children who are making no progress drop out, and the rest who are making some progress remain, the teacher's programme will seem to have worked, but it would be false to conclude this. Design 2 controls for the threat of dropout to some extent, but it cannot control for particular instances where properties of the intervention are responsible for the dropout. The reason for this is that it is precisely because of the intervention that the groups differ, by definition. For example, if a subsample of the remedial children suffers from concentration problems, and these children drop out of the experimental group (because the intervention is boring) but not out of the control group, then the two groups are no longer equivalent, and internal validity is compromised.

Threats to external validity

The list of typical threats identified by Campbell includes threats to external validity, although it must be said that he downplayed these in his original formulation.

1. Generalisability to participants, or subjects (subject selection)

Are there any aspects of the way in which subjects were selected that makes us think the observed results will not generalise? For example, an overwhelming number of social science studies use students as research participants, even though this is frequently a highly unrepresentative population. Worse still, many of these studies use volunteers, who can be expected to differ in many ways from nonvolunteers.

Is it possible to discover social laws that apply to everybody everywhere?

We noted earlier in the chapter that the social sciences have not paid much attention to this class of threat to validity. Part of the problem is that many of the social sciences have an implicit target population which is no less than the species *Homo sapiens* itself. The task of research is assumed to be the formulation of natural laws or, at least, universal truths, and it is assumed therefore that any human being will do as a sample member. Campbell did little to dispel this fundamental immodesty, but did suggest a more sophisticated approach to the quest for universal findings. He argued that it is usually implausible to set up representative sampling frames in the social sciences, and that the approach instead should be to sample for heterogeneity of participants (see Cook & Campbell, 1979). In order to secure external validity for our research, we must replicate the findings we obtain, with a different sample, or wait for someone else to replicate our findings. The history of successful and unsuccessful replications of the particular study will reveal the generality of the findings.

The problem, however, is that the social sciences are plagued by vast numbers of failed replications, part-successful replications, and flat contradictions. In order to solve this problem, quantitative researchers have turned in recent years to a technique of research accumulation known as meta-analysis (see Rosenthal & Rosnow, 1991, for more detail).

In the case of both design 1 and design 2, the teacher would have a hard time arguing for the generality of her findings. The sample is small, and probably exhibits little demographic variation (the children come from the same class, in the same school). A replication or two would provide useful information about generalisability with respect to participants.

2 Generalisability to other operationalisations of the intervention

A natural question to ask about an experiment is whether the results achieved by the intervention will generalise to other, similar, forms of intervention. In both designs 1 and 2, the intervention is the half hour of paired reading that happens daily. However, there are many ways in which this intervention can be delivered. Will three hours of daily paired reading produce the same results? Does it make a difference if both the father and the mother participate, or is one parent enough? Does it make a difference how the parent controls the reading practice? Are all parents equally effective, or are some personalities more facilitative than others?

This is an extremely important type of consideration in studies that involve intervention programmes. Research results are often reported in favour of such programmes, without careful attention to the conditions that affect generalisability.

3. Generalising to other operationalisations of the outcome measures

Just as the 'sampling' of the independent variable is important, so is the 'sampling' of the dependent variable(s). In much social science research, we measure only one operationalisation of an outcome variable, and it is not certain that the results will generalise to other operationalisations. In the case of the example study, the teacher measures reading ability in terms of performance on a standardised reading test, but it is not clear that the results obtained on the test will be reflective of performance in practical contexts – like the end-of-semester reading test, for example. This threat is countered to some extent by the use of a standardised reading test, which will have reasonable generality if its construct validity is high. However, this must be established rather than assumed.

Social science interventions are often treated as 'black boxes' in experimental research, but it is only by opening up the black box that we can discover which particular features of an intervention lead to its success or failure.

Advanced experimental designs

The introduction we give you in this chapter is of necessity relatively simple. However, it would be remiss of us not to mention that experimental design can get very complex, especially when coupled with statistical theory. More complex designs attempt in part to eliminate or ameliorate potential sources that can **confound** research findings, and we briefly discuss two such designs here to give you a glimpse of what is available.

The Solomon four-group design

Repeated-measures designs – where each participant is measured at more than one point in time – are typically very strong in terms of their statistical power, but they are particularly susceptible to reactive effects. Participants who are measured on attribute X at time 1, and then undergo an intervention which is clearly aimed at changing attribute X, and then at time 2 are measured again on attribute X, are likely to make the inference that the intervention was intended to produce change in attribute X. This inference could lead them to report scores that are in line with the experimenter's expectation, but which are not true reflections of any change in the attribute. The use of a control group can ameliorate this problem to some extent, but it cannot remove it, particularly as the control group does not receive the intervention, which is likely to differentially heighten the sensitivity of members of the experimental group to the experimenter's intention or hypothesis. For this reason, R. L. Solomon (1949) devised a simple (but expensive) addition to the standard two-group randomised repeated-measures design. He added two additional groups (hence the term 'four-group' design), which have the explicit purpose of detecting the presence of reactive effects. In terms of the design diagram elements introduced earlier, the four-group design can be represented as in design 3:

$$O_{11} -------- X --------- O_{12} \qquad \text{Design 3}$$
$$O_{21} --------\, \qquad --------- O_{22}$$
$$X --------- O_{32}$$
$$O_{42}$$

This clever design estimates reactivity effects in two ways. First, the control group that is measured at the end of the experiment (i.e., at the post-test) can be compared to the control group that was measured both at the beginning and at the end. Since participants are allocated to groups on a random basis, any difference between these groups is a reactive effect, and may be a consequence of a placebo treatment (if one was used), or of practice on the dependent measure, or of some other contingency. Second, the experimental group that receives the intervention but is only tested at the end of the experiment can be compared to the experimental group that is tested at both points in time. If the post-test scores of these groups differ, this can be attributed to a reactive effect of the pre-test, in the same way that it would be attributed if the two control groups differed on the post-test. More significantly, if the experimental groups show a difference on the post-test, but the control groups do not show such a difference, this can be interpreted to mean that the interaction of pre-test and intervention is producing a reactive effect.

Not only can the Solomon four-group design be used to estimate reactive effects, it can also be used to correct for reactive effects through appropriate statistical analysis. For further details in this respect, see Braver and Braver (1988).

Experiments can have more than two comparative groups. Each 'between group' comparison tells us more about the nature of the effect.

Reversal designs

Another problem often faced in the social and health sciences, especially in clinical applications (e.g., nursing, clinical psychology, health psychology, neuropsychology, and clinical social work), is that of low statistical power, or, in Campbell's validity phrasing, 'statistical conclusion validity'. In some studies, very few participants or patients are available, and, even though the experimental manipulation may be effective, it is not possible to detect the effect of the manipulation with standard statistical tests of significance. For instance, studies of brain damage are at the mercy of who is available, and precisely what brain damage occurred – a researcher interested in the effect of bilateral lesions in the medial parts of the hippocampus may be hard pressed to find a single patient in an entire city. Researchers who face problems of low participant numbers and statistical power have devised ingenious alternate designs, and we wish to bring your attention to one class of these, namely the 'reversal designs'.

The idea behind the reversal designs is that, if effects of interventions can be both 'turned on' and 'turned off' through controlled manipulations, it strengthens the inference that the intervention leads to the claimed effect. A simple reversal design is the ABA design, where an intervention (A) is introduced and shown to have a particular consequence, is then eliminated by removal (B), and is then re-introduced and shown to have the same consequence as it had initially (the second A). In our design terms, the ABA design can be represented as in design 4.

$$O_1 ---- A ---- O_2 ---- B ---- O_3 ---- A ---- O_4 \qquad \text{Design 4}$$

To make the nature of the design more apparent, consider the following example: We use a technique know as classical conditioning to get a dog to salivate when presented with a ringing bell (the bell is initially paired with the presentation of food, but becomes effective itself after enough paired presentations to induce the salivation). Now the question is whether the salivation was due to the classical conditioning or not. We therefore stop the conditioning, and observe the dog (i.e., the bell is presented without being paired with food). If the salivation declines or stops altogether, we are somewhat more certain that the conditioning is the 'active ingredient'. We then re-introduce the pairing of bell and food for a period, and, if the salivation increases after this with mere presentation of the bell, we are still more confident of the claimed link.

Experimental
observations can be
taken on one, two, or
more occasions.

The logic of this design is not that it increases the statistical conclusion validity of a study (although it can do that), but that it attempts rather to increase the validity of the claimed link between manipulation and effect by showing how it is 'under the will' of the experimenter. For further details on reversal designs, see Hersen and Barlow (1984).

Quasi-experimental designs

For many researchers, the randomised experiment is the benchmark method for ensuring the internal validity of research findings and conclusions. Indeed, for some methodological ideologues, it is the only way to true knowledge about causal relations, and the only way to truly test scientific theories. It is hard to deny the advantage that randomised experiments confer, at least in terms of the internal validity of a study. However, it is also clear that randomised experiments are often difficult to conduct, that it would be unethical in many cases to do so, and in some cases it is simply impossible. Most schools would refuse permission to randomly assign learners from two separate classes into two new classes, and people who have received varying levels of exposure to toxic substances can be studied after the fact, but it would be unethical to randomly expose a new group of subjects to varying levels of toxic chemicals.

Studies that cannot or do not use random assignment, but which resemble experiments in other respects (i.e., one or more of the independent variables is actively manipulated), especially in the attempt to ensure equivalence of conditions, are known as **quasi-experiments**. Donald Campbell and Thomas Cook (Cook & Campbell, 1979) extended the validity framework we outlined above to include quasi-experiments, and we will briefly give examples in this section to show how thinking in terms of the validity framework can bolster experimental designs that do not or cannot rely on randomisation techniques. The central idea is to construct the design so as to eliminate plausible rival explanations for a potential observed effect of the experimental manipulation. In a randomised multigroup experiment, the randomisation would ensure the equivalence of the groups, but in quasi-experiments there is no randomisation and the groups cannot be assumed equivalent. The groups will differ in many ways, and the experimenter's central task is thus to find manual ways of equating the groups, or eliminating these differences as explanations for any observed effects.

Matching designs

One class of quasi-experimental designs involves equating non-randomised groups by matching them on critical attributes. Thus, an experimenter who expects that men and women will respond differently to an intervention may attempt to ensure that equal numbers of men and women are enrolled in the groups. Any differences that then arise between the groups on the dependent variable cannot be due to gender differences, as there are no such differences. This method can be extended to multiple variables, but will become increasingly difficult to do as the number of variables increases. Software programs can help to achieve optimal matching, and to extend the range of variables on which participants are matched (Bergstralh, Kosanke, & Jacobsen, 1996), but matching can never ensure equivalence on variables that have not been taken into account, which is what randomisation is able to achieve.

Matching is a technique to attempt to make quasi-experimental groups equivalent.

Dosage designs

If an experimental manipulation can be made to vary in strength, then the presence of a systematic relationship between the strength of the manipulation and the outcome of the manipulation bolsters the internal validity of the experiment, particularly when randomisation has not been possible. Quasi-experimental designs that vary the strength of the central experimental manipulation(s) are known as *dosage designs*, by analogy to medical or pharmaceutical research, where the differential effects of varying drug dosages are often studied. The logic of dosage design quasi-experiments is that, although one or two statistically significant differences between an experimental and control group may be explicable as a consequence of a confounding variable, it is much less likely that a varying pattern of differences between experimental and control groups could be explained in the same way. For example, if the teacher we referred to earlier in the chapter administers 10, 20, or 30 hours of tuition per month to three nonequivalent groups of pupils, and notes steadily increasing performance across these groups, she will be more confident that the steadily increasing performance is due to the steady increase in tuition time than if she had simply compared a single experimental group to a single control group.

Interrupted time series designs

This class of quasi-experimental designs was first discussed by Campbell in 1969, and we alluded to this discussion in our earlier example of the Arrive Alive campaign in South Africa. The idea in this class of design is to observe an event over multiple instances or measurements (i.e., a time series) in order to assess its 'natural' variation in the absence of the experimental intervention. Data regarding the motor vehicle accident rate in a particular city can be collected for a period of several years prior to a major intervention (i.e., the 'interruption' in the time series), and the cyclical or seasonal trends identified from the data. If the intervention is launched in January of a particular year, and the accident rate for January is then compared to the accident rate for December, the comparison can be made much more informative by correcting for the seasonal trend. If the accident rate in December is usually higher than that in January, the observation of a reduction in the accident rate in the study at hand will not of itself indicate anything;

the amount of reduction will need to be compared to that which is normally present.

Some additional simple comparisons can increase the strength of inferences made about interventions, when observed in relation to a time series of measurements. The time series accident rate of a similar city, which did not mount an intervention at the same point in time as the target city, can be used as a point of comparison. If the comparison city shows regular seasonal reduction, but the target city shows an unusually large reduction, this will bolster the claim that the intervention worked to reduce the accident rate.

Conclusion

We started this chapter by pointing to the pervasiveness of research in modern life. It is a mistake to take a passive stance in relation to this glut of knowledge production: You will be better off adopting a critical approach, understanding particular pieces of research in terms of their limitations rather than their generalisations. We have here provided you with some of the tools that allow you to dissect research studies, and we hope that you will do this in your everyday life as well as in more formal academic settings.

You should now be in a position to start some 'hatchet work' of your own. Start by evaluating the sample designs given as exercises to end this chapter.

Exercises

Three sample research designs are briefly described below. Working on your own or in a group, evaluate each design and, if possible, recommend changes to improve the design. Remember that there are no set formulae for determining the adequacy of a design and nor is any design ever perfect, but by applying the general principles discussed in this chapter it is usually possible to improve a design. You may want to use the following steps to structure your thinking about each design:

- Decide what kind of research it is – descriptive, relational, or comparative. This should already provide you with some clues as to the likely weaknesses of the design.
- Evaluate the internal validity of the design by considering alternative explanations of the results that are likely to follow from the study.
- Evaluate the external validity of the design by asking about the sampling strategy used, the generalisability of the interventions (independent variables), and the generalisability of the outcome measures (dependent variables).
- Consider each of the known threats to validity discussed in this chapter and see if any applies to the study.

- For each weakness of the design you identified, try to suggest a way of improving it – but remember that sometimes improving a study in one way weakens it in another!

1. An occupational therapist devises a computer-based game for children that aids the rehabilitation of motor coordination after neurological injury. The game involves manoeuvring a small red ball through a maze. The therapist decides to test the efficacy of the game by comparing its effects when used as the sole form of therapy to the effects obtained by using the game in addition to a conventional rehabilitation programme. She is able to recruit only 12 suitable subjects, and decides to run a 'repeated measures' intervention experiment. There are two conditions: In condition A, all subjects are given three weeks of therapy in which the game is the only form of motor coordination rehabilitation. In condition B, six weeks later, all 12 subjects are given three weeks of therapy in which they are now given the game and a conventional rehabilitation programme as treatment.

   The occupational therapist uses scores on a widely known and well-standardised test of motor coordination as the dependent variable. Scores on this test range from 0 (poor motor coordination) to 100 (excellent motor coordination).

2. A cross-cultural researcher is interested in possible memory-recall differences between nonliterate and literate cultural groups: He thinks that nonliterate cultures may be better at recalling verbal information, since information characteristically survives in such groups by verbal transmission. The researcher chooses three groups of subjects: (1) a nonliterate rural group from Botswana, (2) a literate urban group from Botswana, and (3) a literate urban group from the USA.

   To obtain the 'memory score', the researcher identifies two European fairy tales and two African folk tales. These tales are translated into Setswana and English, respectively. Each subject is seen individually by the researcher, who reads them each of the stories. One day later, each subject is asked to verbally recall each of the stories, and this recall is tape-recorded. The researcher then transcribes each subject's recall into written text. An independent rater assesses each reproduced story for accuracy, giving a score of 1 to each object and event correctly recalled. The total possible score, summed over the four stories, is 100. The researcher compares the mean scores obtained by each of the three groups to test his hypothesis that nonliterate cultures may be better at recalling verbal information.

3. A psychologist has noticed that people who are the most depressed also seem to have the least social support. She asks her patients to complete the 'Perceived Social Support Scale' (measured on a scale of 1–20; 20 = high social support) and the Beck Depression Inventory (measured on a scale of 0–63; 0 = no depression). She

manages to get completed scales for 10 males and 10 females, all of whom are from the Cape Town area. The psychologist calculates the correlation between the level of social support and depth of depression.

Key readings

Campbell, D. T. (1988). *Methodology and epistemology for the social sciences*. Chicago: University of Chicago Press.
This is a collection of some of Donald Campbell's most influential writings. As you will have gathered from the chapter, Campbell is a major figure in research design and methodology in the social sciences, and this book will show you why he is held in such high regard.

Babbie, E., & Mouton, J. M. (2001). *The practice of social research*. Cape Town: Oxford University Press.
This is a South African edition of a classic research methodology text. It covers a broad range of design and methodological topics.

Rosenthal, R., & Rosnow, R. L. (1991). *Essentials of behavioral research*. (2nd edition). New York: McGraw-Hill.
A comprehensive survey of quantitative research methods in the social sciences, this book takes an innovative approach to statistical analysis.

Basic quantitative analysis

Kevin Durrheim

University of KwaZulu-Natal, Pietermaritzburg

Statistical methods are used to analyse quantitative data. Once the researcher has measured the relevant variables, the scores (observations) on these variables (i.e., the data) are usually transformed statistically to help the researcher (1) describe the data more succinctly and (2) make inferences about the characteristics of populations on the basis of data from samples. Statistical analysis has been much maligned as 'positivist' in recent years. Although it is true that statistical procedures are often rooted in positivist measurement techniques, and are sometimes believed to allow the researcher to describe populations accurately, using statistics does not make you a positivist, or vice versa. B. F. Skinner, arch-behaviourist and positivist, abjured the use of statistics because they encouraged 'squeezing significance out of ambiguous data [and discouraged] the more promising step of scrapping the experiment and starting again' (Skinner, 1988, p. 77).

Box 9.1

Tips on consulting with a statistician

- Have ready a list of your variables and the important relationships among them, together with information on the size of your data set.
- Negotiate the fees to be paid and the time frame up-front.
- Be sure that you know what kind of product you will be getting. For example, is it (a) statistical printouts only (difficult to interpret), (b) printouts together with consultation on what they mean, or (c) a full written report.
- Decide together who should enter the data on computer; if you are to do it, get precise instructions regarding the required format.
- If possible, clean the data set and calculate basic descriptive statistics yourself, or make sure that the statistician does this. Do not rush straight into advanced statistical techniques.
- Tell the statistician what kind of analysis you think would be appropriate, but be ready to consider other possibilities.
- Get her or him to explain the purpose and meaning of analyses performed. If any of the analyses are unusual, ask for a reference to the relevant literature.
- Make notes on computer printouts detailing what each part of the printout means.
- Write up a draft of how you expect to report on the results and ask the statistician to have a look at this.
- Unless it is a simple project, expect that there will be a number of false starts and changes in direction.
- Ask for an electronic copy of your data as well as a printout.

The position adopted in this book is that statistics are an extremely valuable tool in organising a useful argument from quantitative evidence (see Abelson, 1995). Statistics are a set of mathematical techniques that allow the researcher to make claims about the nature of the world using forms of principled statistical argument. No research can aspire to more than making principled claims, based on a symbolic system (numeric, binary, or linguistic) that is used to comprehend the world.

The purpose of this book is not to provide a comprehensive account of statistical procedures – there are hundreds – but to assist new researchers in using statistics thoughtfully in making principled arguments. Unfortunately, statistics are often taught cookbook-style as a set of (difficult) mathematical procedures that must be learned. Although computers have made tortuous mathematical computation a thing of the past, they have enabled researchers to analyse data without any understanding of statistics. We aim to provide an understanding of the use of statistics to make principled claims about the nature of the world comprehended in numeric terms. This involves making data analysis decisions by matching the type of data one has to the kinds of claim one wishes to make. This chapter concludes with some suggestions about making such analytic decisions. Its main aim is to introduce the reader to some basic descriptive statistical operations. The following two chapters consider more advanced statistics.

Preparing the data

Data are the raw materials of research. In quantitative research, data consist of lists of numbers that represent scores on variables. Quantitative data are obtained through measurement. The first stage of data analysis is a preparatory stage where the raw data are transformed into an electronic format using a computer spreadsheet. Raw data consist of a collection of unprocessed measurements such as a collection of completed questionnaires, a set of readings off an EEG machine (which records electrical activity in the brain), or strings of codes applied to written texts. Figure 9.1 provides an illustration of part of a questionnaire that was used by Slone, Kaminer, and Durrheim (2000) to investigate whether children who were exposed to stressful political events during the struggle in South Africa in the 1980s showed signs of psychopathological symptomatology. The real questionnaire contained four different scales. Section 1 below contains six items from the 53-item Brief Symptom Inventory, a measure of psychopathological symptomatology. Section 2 below contains five items from the 18-item Political Life Events scale, a measure of exposure to stressful political events and experiences.

Preparing data for analysis involves three steps: coding, entering, and cleaning.

The raw data for this study consisted of 570 completed questionnaires, each containing 150 items. Raw data are unordered, contain errors and missing values, and must be transformed into an ordered error-free data set before they can be analysed. Preparing the data involves three tasks: coding, entering, and cleaning.

Coding data

Coding involves applying a set of rules to the data to transform information from one form to another. It is often a straightforward clerical task that involves transforming the information provided on a questionnaire into meaningful numerical format. The computer does not understand what 'male' and 'female' are, so we transform this information into numbers by coding females '1' and males '2'.

Hi there! We are conducting a study with all Standard 8 pupils, and would like your help. Here are two questionnaires we would like you to fill in. There is no need to write your name on the questionnaire. All the information will be kept **confidential** and **anonymous**. Thank you.

Age: _____ **Sex**: Male ☐ Female ☐ (please tick the correct box)

Race: White ☐ Black ☐ Coloured ☐

Section 1

Below is a list of complaints that people often have. Read each item and put a cross (X) over the number (1, 2, 3, 4, 5) which describes how much you have suffered from the problem over the **past month** until today.

Possible answers: 1 = not at all; 2 = a little; 3 = sometimes; 4 = quite a lot; 5 = very much

1. Nervousness or shakiness inside	1	2	3	4	5
2. Faintness or dizziness	1	2	3	4	5
3. Trouble remembering things	1	2	3	4	5
4. Pains in heart or chest	1	2	3	4	5
5. Feeling sad	1	2	3	4	5
6. Your mind going blank	1	2	3	4	5

Section 2

Here is a list of events which you may have experienced in your life. Circle the 'YES' option if you have experienced the event **in your life**. If the event has not happened to you in your life, circle the 'NO' option.

1. A security drill at school	YES	NO
2. Presence in a situation where there is a suspected dangerous weapon	YES	NO
3. Harm to property as a result of political violence	YES	NO
4. Exposure to gunshot or the use of other weapons	YES	NO
5. Participation in a political demonstration	YES	NO

Figure 9.1 Questionnaire for the Political Life Events study

The data for the study in figure 9.1 were collected from two schools in the Western Cape during 1994: an affluent white school in Claremont and an impoverished black school in Khayelitsha. The variable 'Race' was transformed by coding white learners '1', black learners '2', and coloured learners '3'. Recall from the previous chapter that the variables Race and Sex are measured on a nominal scale of measurement, and that the numbers are merely labels for identifying categories. Responses to items in Section 1 were coded 1, 2, 3, 4, 5, and the items in Section 2 were coded by giving a score of 0 to a NO answer and a score of 1 to a YES answer. It often happens that some respondents do not complete the full questionnaire, giving missing values. Missing values are normally left blank in a spreadsheet or given a special code (e.g. –9999) that is recognised by a computer statistics program, and is different from all your other codes.

The scores for all the items of each scale are then added together to give a total scale score. Summed scores are useful because they provide a single, overall, and reliable measure of an individual score on the scale. Summed scores also have the advantage of producing a variable at a higher level of measurement than the constitutive items. Thus, although each of the items on the Brief Symptom Inventory (Section 1) and the Political Life Events scale (Section 2) in figure 9.1 is measured at an ordinal level of measurement, the summed scale is treated as an interval scale. This allows the researcher to use more powerful parametric statistical analyses for these measures.

Entering data

The numerical codes that are written on the questionnaires must then be entered into a computer in a format that can be used by a statistical computer package. Any spreadsheet can be used to enter the data for each subject or case in a row, while the columns represent scores on specific variables. The subjects or cases need not be individual people. Depending on the unit of analysis and research question, they could be municipalities, voting districts, national economies, and so on.

Figure 9.2 provides an illustration of the data for 10 subjects on the questionnaire in figure 9.1. The scores for each subject are recorded in rows. Subject 1 is female (code for Sex = 1), white (code for Race = 1), and it obtained a total score of 66 on the Brief Symptom Inventory (BSI), and a total score of 5 on the Political Life Events scale (PLE). The figure also shows scores for the first three items of the BSI. When entering data, it is important to label each questionnaire by consecutive numbers that are the same as the numbers in the 'Subject' column. This allows the researcher to go back to the original questionnaire for any subject, if necessary, at a later stage. Data sets are normally more detailed than that illustrated in figure 9.2. There are many more subjects, and frequently all the scores on each of the scale items on each scale (not just the summed scores) are entered.

Enter data so that each row represents a unique case and each column represents a unique variable.

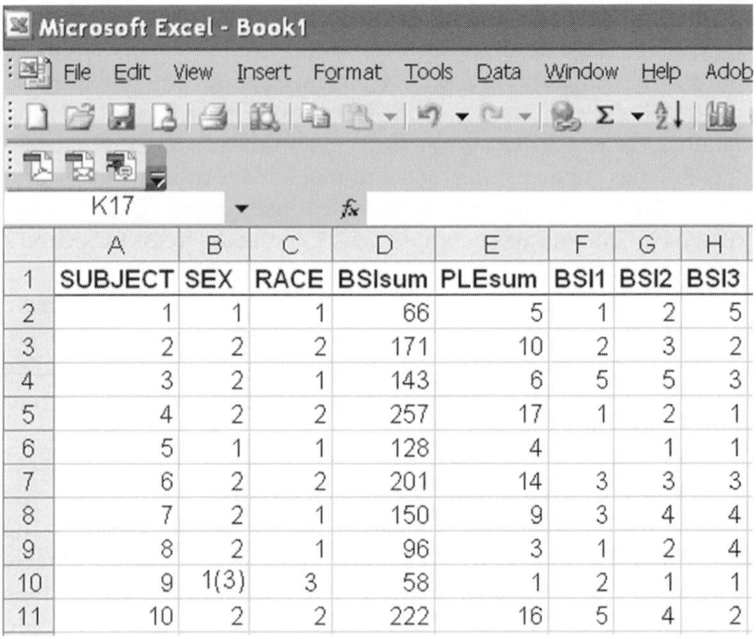

	A	B	C	D	E	F	G	H
1	SUBJECT	SEX	RACE	BSIsum	PLEsum	BSI1	BSI2	BSI3
2	1	1	1	66	5	1	2	5
3	2	2	2	171	10	2	3	2
4	3	2	1	143	6	5	5	3
5	4	2	2	257	17	1	2	1
6	5	1	1	128	4		1	1
7	6	2	2	201	14	3	3	3
8	7	2	1	150	9	3	4	4
9	8	2	1	96	3	1	2	4
10	9	1(3)	3	58	1	2	1	1
11	10	2	2	222	16	5	4	2

Figure 9.2 Data in Excel spreadsheet

Cleaning data

Errors invariably occur when coding and entering data, and it is therefore essential to clean the data before using them for statistical analysis.

The final stage in data preparation is cleaning the data. Coding and entering data are labour-intensive and boring tasks, and errors can easily occur. After all the trouble the researcher has taken to produce valid measures, errors at this stage must be eliminated. This cannot be emphasised too much. If the data set contains errors, the results of the study will be invalid.

Cleaning the data involves checking the data set for errors and then correcting these errors. There are two main ways of checking data. After coding, the researcher selects a random sample of 10 to 15% of cases and recodes the data. If there are many errors in this sample of the data, all the data must be re-entered. If there are no errors, the researcher then proceeds with the second check, which is to check all columns (variables) for impossible codes. This can normally be done with a 'summary' function of a statistical package, which gives frequency tables for each of the variables. While checking the data in figure 9.2, it was noted that subject 9 had a code of 3 for 'Sex'. Since there were only two 'Sex' codes, 1 and 2, this was deemed an entering error, and was rectified by going back to the questionnaire for subject 9 and determining her true 'Sex' code. It is usually necessary to generate a full set of descriptive data for each of the variables in the data set and to inspect these to identify any variables that appear to have errors. In addition, if computer functions are used to sum scales or manipulate or recode data in any way, it is a good idea to check a few cases manually to make sure that the computer has been given correct instructions.

Some researchers enter all the data twice and then compare the two spreadsheets to eliminate coding errors.

Once the researcher has a clean electronic database, the data may be analysed statistically. Two types of data analysis can be performed: descriptive analysis and inferential analysis. **Descriptive data analysis** aims to describe the data by investigating the distribution of scores on each variable, and by determining whether the scores on different variables are related to each other. Descriptive analysis is done first to help the researcher gain an initial impression of the data that were collected. Normally, researchers want to go beyond describing data from their samples. The purpose of most research is to determine whether relationships exist between variables in the real world – in the population in general – and not only in their sample. **Inferential data analysis** allows the researcher to draw conclusions about populations from sample data. We will introduce inferential data analysis in this chapter and explain it in more detail in chapters 10 and 11.

Popular software for statistical analysis

Box 9.2

SPSS (Statistical Programs for the Social Sciences) – This comprehensive set of programs is designed for use by social scientists. Easy-to-use pull-down menus make data analysis easy. Although the program provides a wide range of statistical options, software for a number of procedures (e.g., structural equation modelling and power analysis) needs to be purchased separately as 'add-ons'.

SAS – This is a comprehensive mainframe package. A friendlier personal computer version (JMP) is also available.

MiniTab – Although this package is good for training students in some basic statistics, it does not lend itself readily to social science applications.

Systat – This professional package is used widely by scientists and engineers. It is useful not only for analysis, but also for learning statistics. Users are drawn into thinking about their statistical needs, the assumptions underlying the methods they choose, and the interpretation of the results from the point of view of a statistician.

Epi-info – This package is aimed specifically at epidemiologists and other medical personnel. It thus contains some very specific statistical programs linked to medicine (e.g., risk ratios, age-to-weight ratios), as well as standard descriptive statistical programs. Epi-info is distributed as a free service by the Centers for Disease Control in the USA (find them at www.cdc.gov).

Statistica – One of the most comprehensive packages for the PC, Statistica contains a great variety of statistical techniques and a very large number of graphical possibilities. All of the latter can be customised. Data handling is by easy spreadsheet format, and there are excellent facilities for importing and exporting data and results.

Moonstats – This program provides a limited suite of programs that allow basic statistical analysis. It is designed for introductory users, and comes packaged with this book.

Describing variables

The first type of descriptive statistics aims to represent the scores or observations obtained on single variables in a summarised fashion. The best way of representing a set of scores to get a 'picture' of what they look like is to generate a frequency distribution. A **frequency distribution** is a graphical or tabular representation in which the values of a variable are plotted against the number of times (frequency) they occurred. Frequency distributions for categorical data (i.e., nominal and ordinal data) are easy to produce since the numbers represent categories, and all we have to do is count the number of people in each category and represent this graphically. Figure 9.3 shows two different kinds of frequency distribution that can be produced for the variable, 'Sex'. These data come from the study which is partly represented in figure 9.2. The bar graph and the pie chart are easy to interpret. The bars in the graph represent the frequency (i.e., the number) of cases falling in each category. We can see that there were just under 300 females in the sample, about 250 males, and about 50 subjects who did not specify their sex. The pie chart provides a simple representation of the proportion of cases in each category. It shows that there were proportionally more females than males in the sample, with quite a high proportion of missing values. Although this pie chart does not give the number of cases in each category, it is possible to ask computer programs to give numerical estimates of the frequency and proportion of cases in each category.

You may note already the value of statistical manipulations of data: Statistical representations depict real-world phenomena. From the graphs in figure 9.3, you can tell the number and proportion of male and female subjects that participated in the study. Statistics help the researcher to represent (on paper) exactly what occurred in practice in the real world. Thus, even though you had no previous contact with the study that was conducted in the Western Cape during 1994, you can tell the distribution of males and females among the subjects merely by looking at the graphs. The area represented on the bar graph and pie chart for males and females corresponds exactly with the proportion of males and females that actually took part in the study.

> *A frequency distribution is a graphical or tabular representation in which the values of a variable are plotted against their frequency of occurrence.*

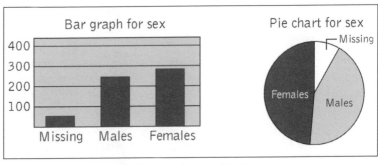

Figure 9.3 Frequency displays for the variable Sex

Frequency distributions can also be used to represent scores on variables measured on the interval and ratio scales. However, the scores must first be grouped into categories by the researcher. Figure 9.4 shows the distribution of PLE scores for the full sample of subjects in the Political Life Events study. Note that the scores are first tabulated in categories, and then this table is represented graphically. This computer-generated histogram has categories with a width of two. The first bar represents the number of subjects who scored 0 on the scale, while the second bar represents subjects who scored greater than or equal to 1 but less than 3, and so on. From the histogram you can see that the majority of the sample had experienced between 11 and 17 of the possible 18 stressful political events, with the highest proportion of subjects scoring about 14. Instead of using bars to represent the frequency of scores in a particular category, the middle points of the categories can also be joined by lines, to make what is known as a frequency polygon. Smoothed-frequency polygons (i.e., polygons where the midpoints are linked by curved lines) are frequently used to display the distribution of scores for large data sets or populations.

Interval and ratio variables can be displayed as frequency distributions, provided the variables are first broken down into categories.

Frequency distributions give the researcher a rough idea about what a distribution of scores looks like. In addition to this graphical representation of observations, researchers seek to describe the shape, variability, and central tendency of a distribution. Once we know these three features of a distribution, the researcher can calculate the most useful piece of descriptive information – that is, where an individual lies relative to others on a distribution of scores.

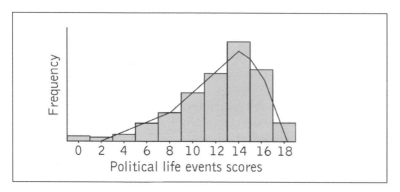

Figure 9.4 Histogram of political life events scores

The shape of frequency distributions is described in terms of their skewness; that is, the degree to which they deviate from symmetry. This is determined by inspecting the frequency distribution (see figure 9.5). A symmetrical distribution has its centremost point lying in the middle of the distribution, and the distributions to the top and the bottom of this centremost point are mirror images of each other. Asymmetrical distributions can be either positively or negatively skewed.

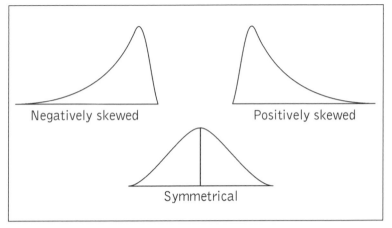

Figure 9.5   Describing the shape of the frequency distribution

Positively skewed distributions have the majority of the sample scoring low on the variable, and thus tail off to the right. Negatively skewed distributions have most of the sample scoring high on the variable, and tail off to the left. Skewness provides useful information about the sample and/or the measurement instrument. The histogram in figure 9.4 is negatively skewed, telling us something about the sample. The histogram indicates that the majority of the sample were exposed to many different stressful political life events. On the other hand, a negatively skewed distribution of examination results could indicate that the exam was too easy, and students who studied all scored high, while those few students who did not study scored low and fall in the tail.

Measures of central tendency

Measures of central tendency are estimates of the centremost score in a distribution. We use measures of central tendency as the single number to best represent the data collected for a variable. There are three different measures of central tendency – the mode, median, and mean – each of which is best suited to specific types of data. These will be illustrated with the following data set of the monthly income of a random sample of nine members of the provincial parliament. Measures of central tendency enable us to summarise a data set.

Table 9.1 Monthly salaries of nine provincial MPs

Radebe	Mkhize	Johns	Paulus	Adams	Dladla	Chonko	Smit	Dlamini
R14 000	R18 000	R21 000	R21 500	R25 000	R32 000	R32 000	R32 000	R56 000

The mode

The mode is the most commonly occurring score in a distribution, or the category with the highest frequency. In the above data set, the mode is R32 000 because this value occurs three times in the data set, whereas the other values occur less than three times. The mode is usually used as a measure of central tendency for nominal data, and is simply the value corresponding with the biggest area of the pie chart or the highest bar of the histogram. In the political life events study, the mode of Sex is female, and the modal category for PLE scores has the midpoint of 14.

The median

The median is the middlemost score in a data set which has been ranked from lowest to highest. In the above data set, the median is R25 000, because this value is in the middle of the ranked data set – that is, there are four values above and below the R25 000 entry in the ranked data set. The median is usually used as a measure of central tendency for ordinal data.

The median is particularly useful for ordinal data or when scores are strongly, positively, or negatively skewed.

The mean

The mean is the arithmetic average of all the values in the data set. It is calculated by summing all the values in the data set and dividing this sum by the number of values:

$$\bar{x} = \frac{\Sigma x}{n}$$

$$= \frac{14\,000 + 18\,000 + 21\,000 + 21\,500 + 25\,000 + 32\,000 + 32\,000 + 32\,000 + 56\,000}{9}$$

$$= \frac{251\,500}{9} = 27\,944.44$$

In the calculation, note that the mean is represented by $\bar{x}$ (pronounced 'x bar'), and the calculation is represented by $\Sigma x/n$ (pronounced 'the sum of x over n'), where x is the individual observations on the variable and n is the number of observations. In this case, the formula for the mean can be translated as 'sum (or add together) the parliamentarians' incomes and divide the total by the number of parliamentarians'. The mean or average income of these parliamentarians is thus R27 944.44 per month. The mean is the preferred measure of central tendency because it takes all the observed values into account in deriving an estimate. However, because it involves the arithmetic operation of adding, it should only be used with interval or ratio data. In practice, the mean is often used for ordinal and sometimes even nominal data, but the researcher should be wary in interpreting the results.

In data sets where there are a few very extreme scores, the median is a better estimate of central tendency than the mean. The median would be a better estimate of the 'typical' income of people in a country. The mean is bad for this, because in many countries there are a few super-rich people who have enormous amounts of money, and whose wealth makes the mean income in the country much higher than the typical income people in that country earn.

In data sets where there are a few very extreme scores, the median is a better estimate of central tendency than the mean.

Measures of variability

All data sets contain variability between the values of different observations. Measures of variability estimate the degree to which the observations for a variable are dissimilar to each other. They estimate the degree to which the scores spread out or vary from the measure of central tendency. The two most common estimates of variability are the range and the variance.

The range

The range is simply the difference between the value of the largest and smallest observation on a variable. The range of monthly salaries of MPs in the data set above is $56\,000 - 14\,000 = 42\,000$. This value gives us an estimate of the differences between the observations, which in the case of MPs' salaries, appears to be quite large. The range is often used for comparing the observed range (the range of actual scores obtained) to the possible range (the difference between the highest and lowest possible values on a measure). Consider, for example, the data for the first 10 subjects on the Political Life Events scale in Figure 9.2 (see the column PLEsum). The PLE scale has a potential range of 18, since the lowest possible score is zero (if the subject marked 'NO' = 0 for all 18 items), and the highest possible score is 18 (if the subject marked 'YES' = 1 for all 18 items). The observed range of the first 10 subjects is $17 - 1 = 16$. This shows that there was a lot of variability between subjects who scored along almost the full possible range.

The variance

The variance is an estimate of the average distance each score is away from the mean. It is the most important measure of variability because, just like the mean, every score in the data set contributes towards the estimate. Consider the data set consisting of the values $1, 3, 5, 7, 9$. The mean of this data set is 5. The degree to which each of the other values is different from the mean is illustrated in figure 9.6.

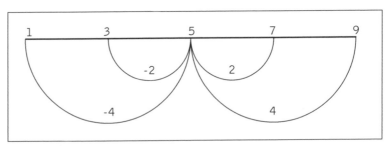

Figure 9.6 How 'far' scores lie from the mean

A simple calculation $(x - \bar{x})$ shows that the observations 3 and 7 differ from the mean by –2 and 2 respectively, and that observations 1 and 9 differ from the mean by –4 and 4 respectively. If we add up these differences, $\Sigma(x - \bar{x}) = -2 + 2 - 4 + 4 = 0$, we obtain a value of zero because, by definition, the mean lies in the middle of the distribution. One way of estimating the variation in the data set is to use the average deviation. All we do is ignore the negative signs and add up the numbers and then divide by 5 (i.e., the sample size). The average deviation is $12/5 = 2.4$. So we can say that 'on average' the observations are 2.4 away from the mean.

Another approach, more commonly used in statistics, is to calculate the variance. In calculating the variance, we do not ignore the negative numbers, but square them (i.e., multiply them with themselves) to get rid of the negative values. We then add these squared differences to obtain an estimate of the degree to which all the scores vary from the mean: $\Sigma(x - \bar{x})^2 = -2^2 + 2^2 - 4^2 + 4^2 = 4 + 4 + 16 + 16 = 40$. Now all we have to do is divide this sum of squared differences by an adjusted estimate of the number of observations in a sample to determine how much, on average, each observation differs from the mean: $40 \div 4 = 10$. This is the estimate of the sample variance, and all the steps we have performed can be summarised by the formula for s^2.

$$s^2 = \frac{\Sigma(x - \bar{x})^2}{n - 1} = \frac{40}{4} = 10$$

Squaring the values when we calculated the variance made the estimate of variation much bigger than it should be. To undo this, it is often useful to find the square root of the variance to give an intuitive understanding of the average degree of dispersion in a set of values. The square root of the variance is known as the **standard deviation**, or s.

$$s = \sqrt{s^2} = \sqrt{10} = 3.16$$

The mean, variance, and standard deviation are the most important descriptive statistics, as they form the basis of most advanced inferential statistical procedures discussed in the following two chapters. The first stage in any quantitative data analysis, after producing graphical displays of the data, is to calculate measures of variability and measures of central tendency for the data. Nowadays this is done on computer. Figure 9.7 is an extract of a computer output of descriptive statistics for the variable Political Life Events. This output provides a description of the data. First, we can see that we have 570 subjects in the data set. Given that the potential range of scores was 18 (from 0 to 18), we note that the obtained range was 17 because not one subject responded YES to all 18 items. Nonetheless, the results here confirm our interpretation of the histogram because we note that the mean of 12 is closer to the maximum score than the minimum score. The standard deviation of the scores was 3.4, suggesting that, while there was a large range, the average dispersion away from the mean was not very large.

Variable	Mean	Std Dev	Variance	Range	Minimum	Maximum	N
PLE	12.00	3.40	11.56	17.00	0.00	17.00	570

Figure 9.7   SPSS output of descriptive statistics for the PLE

The descriptive statistics discussed above all aim to summarise and represent features of scores (data) on a single variable. These are known as univariate statistics. **Univariate** statistics have two main purposes.

First, they allow the researcher to describe distributions of scores – one of the main results of the Political Life Events study was finding that South African youth had on average been exposed to a wide range of stressful political life events. The second purpose of univariate statistics is that they allow a researcher to determine where a particular individual scored relative to others on a measure. If you obtained a score of 4 on the PLE scale, by looking at the mean as well as the frequency distribution, you can conclude that you have been exposed to fewer political life events than most others. By converting your score into a z-score (as described in box 9.4), you can get an exact indication of how you compare with others. While univariate statistics provide useful information, the purpose of most research is to determine whether the scores on one variable are related to scores on another variable.

Box 9.3

Using calculator statistics functions

Many statistical operations can easily be performed on a common calculator. Some advanced calculators can do bivariate and multivariate statistics, but most inexpensive scientific calculators can be used to compute univariate statistics such as the mean or variance. The specific procedures to be followed differ across calculators of different makes or models, but the following three-stage approach is generic.

Stage 1 – Get the calculator into stats mode. Often you need to press the <2nd function> or <mode> key, followed by another key which switches the calculator into statistics mode.

Stage 2 – Enter the data. Univariate data are normally entered as a string of numbers. On most calculators you will find a <Data> key. To enter the data for your univariate variable, enter the first number and press <Data>, and so on, until all data are entered.

Stage 3 – Generate the required statistics. Once your data are entered, you can determine values for the mean and standard deviation simply by pressing the appropriate key. Most calculators allow you to determine the mean ($\bar{x}$), the standard deviation of samples (s) and populations (σ), and the sum of all scores (Σx), as well as the squared sum of all scores (Σx^2).

Play around with your own calculator to see exactly how it works.

Describing bivariate relationships

Most statistical procedures seek to identify relationships, either between two variables (i.e., bivariate statistics) or between many variables (multivariate statistics).

Is exposure to stressful political life events related to psychopathological symptomatology? Are developed countries more democratic than undeveloped countries? Is the incidence of tuberculosis related to poverty? These research questions seek to identify a relationship between two variables. In statistical language, a relationship between two variables involves a covariation between them. **Covariation** means that scores on measures vary in relation to (or together with) each other. For example, height and weight covary because taller people tend also to weigh more than shorter people. Poverty and malnutrition covary because poorer people tend to be more malnourished than wealthier people. Smoking and good health covary because smokers tend to have less good health than non-smokers. The opposite of covariance is independence. If two variables are unrelated to each other, they are said to be independent or orthogonal. Mayekiso and Bhana (1997), for example, found that the experience of some forms of sexual harassment (e.g., unwanted sexual jokes, unwanted sexual advances) was independent of gender among a sample of 827 UNITRA students. This means that male and female students had similar experiences of sexual harassment along these dimensions.

There are a number of ways in which researchers investigate the presence of covariation between variables. Graphical representations of two variables are a useful first step in showing patterns of relationship between variables. In addition, relationships between interval and ratio measures are computed mathematically by means of the correlation coefficient, and relationships between categorical variables can be represented in tabular form.

Scatterplots: graphical representations of covariance

A scatterplot is a graph in which each case is represented in two-dimensional space, with the score on one variable represented on the x-axis (i.e., horizontally), and the score on a second variable represented on the y-axis (i.e., vertically). Figure 9.8 presents a scatterplot of the relationship between the variables BSI and PLE in the Political Life Events study. Each dot on the graph represents a case (i.e., a research participant who completed both scales). The vertical position of the dot represents the score on the BSI scale, and the horizontal position represents the score on the PLE scale. Because this study had a sample size of 570, many dots are placed very close together, and tend to form lines. Scatterplots are interpreted by looking for patterns in the arrangement of dots. Usually, this involves attempts to draw a straight line through the middle of the dots. This line, which has been inserted into figure 9.8, is called the **regression line**, and summarises the distribution of cases along the two variables.

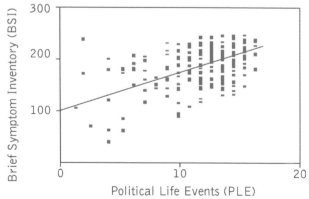

Figure 9.8 *Scatterplot of the relationship between BSI and PLE*

Box 9.4

Standardised or z-scores
(Lance Lachenicht, University of KwaZulu-Natal, Pietermaritzburg)

Remember being told at school not to compare apples and oranges? Of course your teacher was right. But there is a way in which apples and oranges may be meaningfully compared. You can say of a particular apple that it is a large apple, and of a particular orange that it is a large orange, so that the apple and the orange are similar in their relative largeness. Here we compare the relative position of the apple with respect to other apples to the relative position of the orange with respect to other oranges. Such comparison of relative positions on different scales is often crucial in quantitative research. For example, a quantitative researcher may want to know whether a person who scores above average on a introversion scale will also score above average on a scale of enjoyment of long-distance running.

There is a clever way to simplify such relative comparisons: the z-score. The z-score is a transformation of some measurement on a scale into a *standardised* form. The z-score is defined by the following formula:

$$z = \frac{x - \bar{x}}{s}$$

In the formula, x is the original untransformed score, $\bar{x}$ is the mean of the set of scores (measurements) and s is the standard deviation of the set of scores. The numerator of the above formula tells us whether the score is above or below the mean (because the mean is subtracted from the score), while the denominator (s) rescales the score in standard deviation units. A z-score of 0 means that the score was equal to the mean. A z-score of 2 means that the score fell two standard deviations above the mean. And a z-score of −1.4 means that that the score fell 1.4 standard deviations below the mean. Any scores that have been transformed into z-scores can be compared with any other scores that have been transformed into z-scores because they are all measured in terms of distance from the mean in standard deviation units.

Suppose four people obtained these class marks:

Student	Test score	Z-Score
Jabulani	48	+2
Margaret	36	−2
Lindiwe	45	+1
Johan	39	−1

The mean of these scores is 42 and the standard deviation is 3. Applying the z-score to Lindiwe's score:

$$z = \frac{x - \bar{x}}{s} = \frac{45 - 42}{3} = +1$$

Here we substituted Lindiwe's score (45) into the formula, but used the group mean (42) and the group standard deviation (3). From the z-score, we notice that Lindiwe scored one standard deviation above the group mean (a z-score of

+1). As practice, try to calculate the z-scores for the other students in the above table. Also try to make up a different data set (a set of four scores) where Lindiwe keeps the same score of 45 but now attains a higher z-score because her relative position in the group is higher.

Standard scores are particularly useful when we think about the normal distribution, a bell-shaped curve that is of great importance in statistical theory. Many naturally occurring frequency distributions are normal. The weights of male elephants, the heights of new recruits to the army, and the errors of measurements of astronomers are all normally distributed. However, each of these bell-shaped distributions cannot be compared with the others because they are expressed in different units (e.g., the weight is in kilograms, the height in centimetres, and the astronomers' measurement errors in milliseconds). The solution to this problem is to transform all these different scales into z-scores. Such a transformation will ensure that they all form a new bell-shaped curve, with the same units of measurement (standard deviation units) and a mean of 0. This new bell-shaped curve is called the **standard normal distribution**. By mapping different raw or untransformed scores onto the common standard normal distribution, it becomes possible to make direct comparisons between measurements that use different raw score scales.

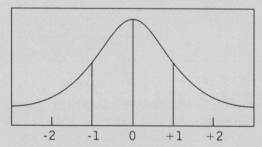

The standard normal distribution

The standard normal distribution is particularly useful when we think of the relative position of a score in terms of the number of scores it *exceeds* in the distribution. The mean of the distribution is exactly in the middle of the distribution, so any score that falls at the mean (i.e., z = 0) must exceed 50% of the scores in the distribution. Similarly, a z of 1.0 will exceed approximately 84% of the other scores in a standard normal distribution, and a z of 2.0 will exceed about 97.5% of the scores in a standard normal distribution. This notion of the number of scores exceeded can give us a measure of probability. How likely are we to find an army recruit 2.3 metres tall? We place our score of 2.3 in the distribution of the heights of army recruits; we transform the distribution to a standard normal distribution. We see that 2.3 metres yields a z-score greater than 2, so it would exceed 97.5% of the other scores, and would therefore only occur in 2.5% of the recruits (i.e., it is very unlikely that we will find a recruit 2.3 metres tall).

It is possible to construct detailed tables showing the percentage of a standard normal distribution exceeded by every possible z.

There are two features of the relationship between variables that are of interest to the researcher: the **direction** and the **strength** of the relationship (see figures 9.9 and 9.10). The direction of the relationship is indicated by the slope of the regression line. Positive relationships occur when high scores on one variable are associated with high scores on the other variable. In such cases, the regression line slopes upward from left to right. When high scores on one variable are associated with low scores on the second variable, a negative relationship occurs, and the regression line slopes downward from left to right. When the dots appear to be randomly distributed, and a horizontal straight line can be drawn through the dots, we conclude that there is no relationship between the variables. In such cases we say that the variables are orthogonal, which means that they do not correlate with each other (i.e., they are unrelated).

The relationship between two variables can be strong or weak and positive or negative.

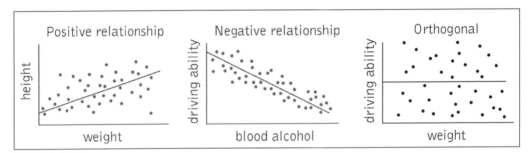

Figure 9.9   The direction of association

While the direction of the relationship is represented by the slope of the regression line, the strength of the relationship is indicated by the degree to which the dots cluster closely around the regression line. In orthogonal relationships, the dots do not cluster around the regression line at all, indicating no correlation between the variables. When the dots cluster closely around the regression line, the correlation between the variables is strong. Figure 9.10 shows two regression lines with exactly the same slope but with different degrees of cluster around the two lines.

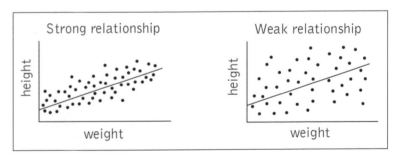

Figure 9.10   The strength of association

As you have seen from figure 9.8, the relationship between PLE and BSI is positive. This indicates that individuals who were exposed to more stressful political life events tended to show higher levels of psychopathological symptomatology than individuals who were exposed to less stressful political life events. This was expected. The scatterplot also shows that the strength of the relationship was rather weak. The dots do not cluster closely around the regression line, suggesting that, although high scores on the PLE were associated with high scores on the BSI, there were many cases where this did not occur. Consider the dot in the upper left-hand corner of the scatterplot. This individual scored very low on PLE, but scored very high on the BSI. This case does not fall in with the general pattern of scores and serves to weaken the strength of the relationship between the two variables. We call these uncharacteristic cases **outliers**. They are caused sometimes by coding errors as we have seen earlier, but are sometimes due to measurement or sampling anomalies. Extreme outliers can have a very strong impact on the strength of the correlation, making it unrepresentative of the sample in general.

Outliers can drastically weaken the apparent relationship between two variables.

In such cases, an argument could be made for removing outlying cases. However, be careful. Do not get rid of cases just because they do not fit your theory of how variables should be related.

The correlation coefficient

Although scatterplots are useful for giving a general picture of the association between variables, they are imprecise and often ambiguous to interpret. A more exact way of representing the relationship between variables is mathematically, by means of the correlation coefficient. The correlation coefficient is a numerical estimate of the degree to which the points on the scatterplot cluster around the regression line. It is a single number that summarises the dispersion of scores on a scatterplot. You will recall that the variance is the estimate of the degree to which scores cluster around the mean. The correlation coefficient is calculated in much the same way, by determining how far, on average, all the dots on the scatterplot are from the regression line. Figure 9.11 shows an enlarged view of a small section of the scatterplot. This illustrates what is meant by 'distance from the regression line'.

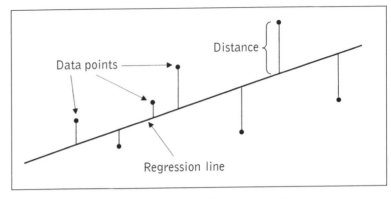

Data points

Distance

Regression line

Figure 9.11 The distance of cases from the regression line

A strong **correlation** between two variables means that they are related, but not necessarily that the one variable (e.g., race) causes the other (e.g., school marks). Among other possibilities, there could be a third variable (e.g., quality of schooling) that explains the relationship between the first two.

The correlation coefficient represents the strength of covariation between two variables by means of a number that can range from –1 to 1. If all the cases on the scatterplot fell exactly on the regression line, we would have a perfect relationship that would have a correlation coefficient r = 1 if the relationship was positive, or r = –1 if the relationship was negative. In Figure 9.10, the cases cluster more closely around the regression line for the strong relationship than for the weak relationship. The correlation coefficient for the strong relationship is approximately r = 0.90, while that for the weak relationship is in the region of r = 0.20. Since the cases do not cluster around a regression line in an orthogonal relationship, r = 0. The correlation between BSI and PLE in the Political Life Events scale was r = 0.24, suggesting a weak positive relationship. In most social science applications, we do not expect to find very strong relationships between naturally occurring variables, and correlations of between r = 0.25 and r = 0.75 are typical.

Although there are a number of different kinds of correlation coefficient, each tailored for use with variables measured on different measurement scales, Pearson's product-moment correlation coefficient is the most common. All computer statistics programs offer procedures to calculate this correlation coefficient, and it can be used for variables measured on ordinal, interval, and ratio scales.

Bivariate tables

When we are investigating the relationship between two categorical variables, the data are normally represented in the form of a bivariate frequency table. Bivariate frequency tables are constructed by cross-tabulating two variables, with the frequency of cases in categories of one variable recorded in columns, and the frequency of cases on

In addition to Pearson's r, there are several other correlation coefficients, each optimally suited for use with particular kinds of data and each calculated using a slightly different formula: Spearman's rho is sometimes used instead of Pearson's r when working with ordinal variables; the point biserial correlation is used when one variable is at an interval level and the other is dichotomous; and the phi coefficient is used when both variables are dichotomous.

another variable represented in rows. The bivariate table is then inspected to determine whether the observed frequency of cases in each cell is similar to the expected frequency of cases if the variables were independent.

Table 9.2 is a bivariate frequency table for a study that sought to determine whether smoking behaviour is related to sex. A random sample of 100 males and 100 females were selected. The numbers printed in bold in table 9.2 indicate how many of the males and females were smokers and how many were non-smokers. Looking for the moment only at the numbers printed in bold, you will see that there were 80 smokers and 120 non-smokers. The males were evenly divided between 50 smokers and 50 non-smokers. In contrast, only 30 females smoked, whereas 70 did not. Already we can see that the two variables are not independent. Proportionately more males than females smoke. Although half the total sample is male and half female, more than half the smokers are male, whereas less than half the non-smokers are male. Thus, just by 'eyeballing' the data, it is possible to see that the variables are related. However, just like scatterplots, it may be difficult to determine the nature of the relationship between the variables just by eyeballing.

Table 9.2 Frequency table of sex and smoking behaviour

	Smoker	Non-smoker	TOTAL
Male	**50** (40) $d = 10$	**50** (60) $d = -10$	100
Female	**30** (40) $d = -10$	**70** (60) $d = 10$	100
TOTAL	80	120	200

The relationship between two categorical variables is represented mathematically by the chi-square statistic (χ^2). The **chi-square statistic** is an estimate of the degree to which the observed frequencies in all the cells differ from the expected frequencies if the two variables were in fact independent. The frequencies in the column and row labelled 'TOTAL' tell us what the frequencies in the cells should be. Since there are 100 males and 100 females, the expected frequencies in the cells should be equally divided between males and females. Since there are 120 non-smokers, half (i.e. 60) should be males and half females. Similarly, if the two variables were independent, we should have 40 male and 40 female smokers. The expected frequencies are reported in parenthesis in the table. The difference between observed (i.e. actual) and expected frequency for each cell is also reported in the table (next to 'd ='). The cells with negative difference scores show groups that are under-represented in the sample, whereas cells with positive differences show groups that are over-represented in the sample. The chi-square statistic uses these differences between observed and

In addition to dichotomous variables like grades (male or female) and smoking (yes or no), the chi-square statistics can be used to investigate the relationship between categorical variables that have more than two categories each. For example, the relationship between music preference (rock, kwaito, or rap) and party membership (ANC, IFP, DA, or other).

expected frequencies as a basis for a mathematical estimate of association. Because table 9.2 contains cells with differences between expected and observed frequencies, we know that the χ^2 value will be greater than zero, indicating that smoking behaviour is related to sex, with proportionately more male than female smokers. How to calculate and interpret the χ^2 value is described in chapter 10.

Drawing inferences

The previous discussion has shown how useful statistics are for describing data. Statistics allow us to represent our observations of the real world in a manner that is easily interpretable. Mostly, however, researchers are not primarily interested in describing their samples. They have greater ambitions. They would like to draw conclusions about populations. No one is really interested that BSI and PLE were weakly related among a small group of 570 South African youth. However, if we could conclude more generally that people who are exposed to stressful political life events manifest symptoms of psychopathology, this would be useful information. Similarly, very few people would be interested in the fact that proportionately more of your male friends smoked than your female friends. However, if we knew that males in general smoked more, this would have major implications for health care and cigarette advertising.

Is it possible to draw conclusions about populations after making observations on samples? Can we make inferences about populations based on sample data? Statisticians answer 'Yes, under certain conditions'. The first set of conditions is methodological: The sample must be representative of the population. This is normally achieved by drawing a random sample. (The technique of random sampling is described in chapter 7). The second set of conditions is statistical: Certain assumptions about the sampling distribution must be satisfied to draw inferences about populations. (Chapters 10 and 11 consider these statistical assumptions and methodological conditions in detail.) The discussion here aims to introduce the reader to the concept of inferential statistics.

Inferential statistics allow us to use information obtained from samples to draw conclusions about populations.

Inferential statistics are used to draw conclusions about populations on the basis of data obtained from samples. If we want to know something about a large population (e.g. all people living in South Africa), the best way to answer this question is to select a representative sample of individuals from this population, and then use information about the sample to draw conclusions about the population. Although this is the best way of drawing inferences, there is always uncertainty involved in inferring facts about populations from observations on samples. There is always a chance that the inference will be incorrect. Inferential statistics are statistics of chance. They allow us to determine the chance that our inferences will be correct. Just as there is random variance between individuals on measures, so there will be random variance between different samples drawn from a population. Inferential statistics allow us to estimate how much this random variance will be, and thus allow us to estimate the amount of chance involved in drawing inferences.

Inferential statistics are used for two main purposes: to estimate population parameters, and to test hypotheses. A **parameter** is a population value. Most commonly, researchers wish to estimate the mean of the population. Since populations are usually too large to measure, the mean of a sample of subjects from the population is used to estimate the population parameter. If we wanted to estimate the number of sexual partners that South African university students have per year, we would draw a random sample of students from all South African universities, and use the mean of this sample as our estimate of the population parameter. If we found the sample mean to be 9, we could conclude that the parameter is around 9. When estimating population parameters, we cannot make conclusive estimates because there is always a possibility that, purely due to chance, our estimate could be wrong. Instead, we conclude that the parameter is approximately 9. The power of inferential statistics is that it allows us to estimate how much we mean by 'approximately'. They allow us to draw conclusions such as 'There is a 95% probability that the population parameter lies somewhere between 8 and 10'.

The second use of inferential statistics is to test hypotheses. **Hypotheses** are educated guesses or expectations about differences between groups in the population or about relationships among variables. If we claim that male professionals earn more money than female professionals, this is a hypothesis about differences between two populations (male and female professionals). This hypothesis is an educated guess, because we know that the ideology of patriarchy (see chapter 23) underlies a relationship between the variables 'sex' and 'income'. The best way to test our hypothesis is to draw random samples of male and female professionals from a population of all South African professionals, and calculate the mean income of these samples. If we find differences between the mean income of the male and female samples, this suggests that there may be a difference between the two populations. However, the difference may have occurred purely by chance, and if we were to draw a second set of samples we might not find a difference. Inferential statistics get around this problem by giving us an estimate, in addition to the means of the populations, of the probability that there is no difference between the populations. If this probability is very small – i.e., usually less than 0.05 (5%) – then we conclude that there is a significant difference between the populations. The term significance means that the differences between our samples is of such a magnitude that it is unlikely to have occurred by chance, and must be caused by differences between populations.

When you read journal articles, you will find many inferential statistics reported in the 'Results' section of the articles. Normally, you will find parameter estimates and inferential test statistics, as well as probability values (p-values). The parameter estimate is usually (but not always) the mean of the sample that is used to estimate the mean of

Certain statistics, such as the mean and correlation coefficient, can be used both as descriptive statistics to describe a sample, and as inferential statistics to estimate features of a population.

the population. The inferential test statistic is the outcome of a statistical test to determine the amount of chance involved in using information from the sample to estimate the population parameter. There are many different kinds of inferential test, each appropriate to a specific application (see box 9.5). The probability value is the chance that there is no relationship between variables in the population, or that there are no significant differences between groups. In Duckitt's (1991) study of subtle racism, for example, he reports that the Subtle Racism scale was correlated with the Anti-Black scale among a group of 210 white university students. The size of the correlation coefficient was r = 0.79. This is a strong correlation, but can it be concluded that there is a significant correlation in the population of white university students as a whole? Duckitt calculated that the chance of obtaining an r of 0.79 in a sample of 210 was less than one in a thousand (written as 'p < 0.001'). This means that the chance that the two scales are not related (i.e. the probability that they are independent) is less than 0.1%. Because this probability is very small (much less than 5%), he concluded that there is a significant association between the two scales in the population.

Inferential tests can be broken down into two broad categories: parametric tests and nonparametric tests. Nonparametric statistical techniques focus on the order or ranking of scores (or merely the classificatory function of numbers) and ignore the numerical properties of numbers at interval and ratio scales. For example, the nonparametric statistic for the measure of central tendency is the median, which is the score in the middle of a ranked data set. The mean, in contrast, is a parametric estimate of central tendency because it takes the numerical value of scores into consideration by using mathematical operations. Whereas the median is determined only by ordering scores, the mean is determined by adding scores and dividing by n. Since only interval and ratio scales of measurement allow mathematical operations, parametric statistics are only appropriate with this data.

Box 9.5

Some examples of inferential statistics
(Merridy Wilson, University of KwaZulu-Natal, Pietermaritzburg)

Statistic	Purpose	Example	Interpretation
t	To test for differences between the means of two groups.	Nel (1987) used t-tests to determine whether her programme for creative conflict handling in marriage was effective. She compared an experimental and a control group to test her intervention. Results: (for empathy scores) $t = 9.99$, $p < 0.05$. The p-value is smaller than 0.05.	This means that there is a significant difference between the control and experimental groups. An inspection of the means showed that the experimental group showed more empathy than the control group. Thus the programme was effective.
F	To test for an effect, i.e., differences between the means of more than two groups.	Sibaya and Sibaya (1997) made use of the F-statistic to test for the effect of the independent variable, age (divided into the three age groups), on mathematical performance. Results: $F = 2,39,442$, $p = 0.03$.	Since the p-value is less than 0.05, the F-value is significant, and it is concluded that age does affect mathematical ability. An inspection of the means showed that this effect was especially noticeable in the 20-year-old, and 15/16-year-old age groups.
r	To test for the strength of the relationship between two variables.	Strümpfer (1997) correlated scores on a test of job satisfaction with self-reported absenteeism among a sample of 149 farm workers in the Western Cape. Results: $r = 0.18$, $p < 0.05$	There is a very modest positive correlation between job satisfaction and absenteeism, which is statistically significant (p is less than 0.05).
Chi Sq (χ^2)	To test for the association between two nominal variables.	Mufune (1995) used the chi-square statistic to check for an association between gender and perceived chances of job promotion scaled nominally (e.g., very good, not good, I don't know). Results: chi-square $= 15.6$, $p < 0.05$	Since the p-value is reported as less than 0.05, the chi-square is significant. There is thus a significant association between gender and perceived chances of promotion. An inspection of the frequency cross-tabulations showed that males' self-assessment was significantly more positive than that of females.

In addition to requiring that variables are measured on interval or ratio scales, parametric tests make various assumptions about populations – for example, that the population from which the sample is drawn has a normal distribution, or that two populations have equal variances. There are occasions, therefore, when parametric tests are not appropriate. Although some authors argue that most measures in the behavioural sciences are ordinal, and that statistical analysis should be predominantly nonparametric (Siegel & Castellan, 1988), this is possibly an outdated opinion. Parametric and nonparametric statistics often yield very similar results (e.g. Howell, 1997), and since parametric techniques are more powerful, they should be preferred. Only when the researcher is working with categorical (nominal) data, or when distribution assumptions for parametric tests are seriously violated (see chapters 10 and 11), should parametric tests be employed. In box 9.5, all the tests except the χ^2 test are parametric tests. These are appropriate to use when we are working with ratio and interval variables, and sometimes with ordinal variables, and when the frequency distributions for the variables are roughly symmetrical. The χ^2 test is appropriate to use when we want to draw inferences about the relationship between categorical (nominal) variables.

Nonparametric tests are appropriate when using nominal or ordinal data or when assumptions about distributions that underlie parametric statistics are seriously violated.

Conclusion

The types of statistical procedure a researcher employs in analysing data depends on the purpose of the study and the kind of data the researcher has collected. In this chapter, we have considered descriptive statistics. These are appropriate when the sole aim of the research is to describe single variables or relationships between variables. The purpose of most research is to move beyond descriptive aims, and to determine whether relationships exist between variables in the population generally. Inferential statistical procedures that are designed to identify relationships between two variables (bivariate statistics) or between more than two variables (multivariate statistics) are discussed in greater detail in the following chapters. In addition to these research purposes, deciding on the appropriate statistics also involves reflection about the nature of the variables that are being used. In order to decide whether parametric or nonparametric statistics are appropriate, the researcher must (1) employ univariate descriptive statistics to determine whether the variable is roughly symmetrical, and (2) determine the scale of measurement of the variable. In most cases, parametric statistics will be appropriate, but if you have categorical data, or if any other inferential test assumptions are seriously violated, nonparametric procedures should be used.

Descriptive statistics help in arranging numerical data in an orderly and readable manner. Inferential statistics are used to estimate population parameters and to test hypotheses in order to decide whether variables are related to each other. In achieving these aims, both descriptive and inferential statistics have a role to play in making principled argument. They help researchers make decisions about the nature of reality, and are thus central to the positivist enterprise of science.

Exercises

1. The following data set consists of the annual inflation rates of 15 African countries:

   5%, 20%, 7%, 2%, 24%, 13%, 27%, 11%, 17%, 6%, 2%, 8%, 15%, 21%, 3%.

   (a) Draw a histogram of the data. First tabulate the frequencies in the following categories: 1% to 5%, 6% to 10%, 11% to 15%, 16% to 20%, 21% to 25%.

   (b) Describe the frequency distribution.

   (c) Use a scientific calculator to determine the mode, median, and mean of the data.

   (d) What is the best measure of central tendency for this data? Why?

   (e) Use a scientific calculator to determine the range and variance of the data.

2. The following table reports the inflation and unemployment rates for the same 15 African countries studied in question 1. The top row contains the inflation rates (in percentages) and the bottom row contains the unemployment rates (in percentages):

5	20	2	7	24	13	27	11	17	6	2	8	15	21	3
18	45	10	21	49	20	60	32	43	18	6	16	23	47	60

   (a) Construct a scatterplot for the data. Do this by placing inflation on the x-axis (horizontal axis) and unemployment on the y-axis (vertical axis). Then place a dot on the graph for each individual country.

   (b) Describe the scatterplot. Do you think there is a correlation between inflation and unemployment? If you think so, what is the strength and direction of the association?

   (c) Identify any outliers on the scatterplot. What impact do you think the outliers will have on the strength of the correlation coefficient?

3. Read through the results sections of articles in a current issue of one of the South African academic journals. Identify each of the inferential statistics discussed in box 9.5, and see if you can interpret what they mean.

Key readings

Abelson, R. P. (1995). *Statistics as principled argument*. Hillsdale, New Jersey: Erlbaum.

This is an up-to-date introductory overview of the use and application of statistical techniques. It is written in a reader-friendly style, and combines rigour with practical guidance for making statistical decisions.

Tredoux, C., & Durrheim, K. (Eds). (2002). *Numbers, hypotheses and conclusions*. Cape Town: UCT Press.

This is an easy-to-read book designed for new researchers. It provides step-by-step instructions on how to analyse and interpret many common descriptive and inferential statistics.

Siegel, S., & Castellan, N. J. (1988). *Nonparametric statistics for the behavioral sciences*. (2nd edition). New York: McGraw-Hill.

This book is the most thorough account of nonparametric statistical procedures available.

10

Jumping to conclusions:

an overview of inferential statistical methods

Colin Tredoux
University of Cape Town

Mario Smith
Stellenbosch University

This chapter assumes familiarity with basic quantitative concepts such as the mean and standard deviation. You may therefore want to re-read chapters 8 and 9 before embarking on this chapter.

In the previous chapter, you were introduced to data analysis, particularly the analysis of descriptive data. You were briefly alerted to the presence of a second kind of data analysis, known as statistical inference or inferential statistics. This is the focus of the present chapter. We will start by presenting some conceptual background, and then look at a number of commonly used statistical tests. The emphasis will be on conceptual rather than numerical understanding.

Analysis of research data is no different in some ways to ordinary argument. In both cases, the aim is to adduce evidence in favour of certain propositions or conclusions, and in both cases the way in which the evidence is pieced together into a 'chain of reasoning' is all-important. Hence, when we talk about 'statistical inference', we use the word 'inference' in a sense very close to its ordinary meaning. To make an inference is to draw a conclusion on the basis of evidence, to make a claim that is supported and follows from data or from premises. In inferential statistics, we are concerned with arriving at conclusions on the basis of data. What is most markedly different about statistical inference and ordinary argument, though, is that the justification for conclusions in statistical inference is bound up with the theory of probability and statistical distributions.

Probability and statistical inference

One of the most powerful statistical concepts is that of **probability**. Probability is particularly important to us in the social sciences because most of our statistical analyses work by identifying the likelihood or probability of obtaining the results that we did in a concrete study. The chief application of probability theory in the social sciences is **hypothesis testing** or **statistical inference**; which involves drawing conclusions about how the world works, or what the world looks like, on the basis of data from samples. Using samples to draw conclusions about populations is always open to error, and the purpose of statistical inference is to provide a reasonable way of making decisions about the meaning of data in a context of uncertainty.

Probability theory is immensely complex in its full manifestation, but it is possible to grasp some elementary aspects with relative ease. The key idea is that many natural (and social) events occur with calculable frequency, and the knowledge of this allows one a rich opportunity for decision making, prediction, and empirical inference. Many everyday events can be modelled with a suitable probability conceptualisation.

Imagine a game of dice on the street corner. Sipho is betting R10 that '5' will come up on the next throw and Malungisa will pay him R30 if it does. You should be able to see intuitively that the chance of the '5' coming up on the next throw is 1/6. If Malungisa and Sipho continue to play at these odds, Malungisa will become a rich man and Sipho poor. Can you see why? Malungisa understands the laws of probability and chance: If, on average '5' comes up once in every six throws, then, on average, over every six throws, Sipho will earn R30 while Malungisa will earn R50. The game of dice can be understood in terms of a probability model, and this model allows those who understand it considerable opportunity. Malungisa will be a rich man if he continues to entice players like Sipho into the game.

Many other phenomena can be conceptualised with suitable probability models. Take an example of a simple two-group experiment. We randomly assign participants to Groups A and B, give Group A one Ecstasy tablet, and compare them on rapidity of speech in number of words per minute. We find that Group A's average speech rate is 90 words, and Group B's average speech rate is 110 words per minute. This appears to show that Ecstasy slows one's rate of speech (among its other virtues). However, are these scores *really different*? If we repeat exactly the same experiment with different participants (or with the same participants at a later date), we might find that Group A gets 110 words per minute and Group B 90 words per minute. Probability theory allows us a way to conceptualise this situation, and to make decisions. It allows us to determine the likelihood that the difference we observe between two sample means reflects a real difference between two populations (i.e., all people who are on Ecstasy and all those who aren't), or if it was a chance event attributable to natural variations between samples. In other words, probability theory allows us to make statistical inferences about populations on the basis of observations with samples. To do this in practice, we need to have statistical models of probability, of which the normal distribution is the most important.

Statistical inference is certainly a powerful empirical method, but it has probably been bad in the long run for research in the social (and medical) sciences. This is because researchers seized on it as an easy analytic method, abusing it more often than not, and because it lends a cloak of scientific respectability to otherwise pedestrian pieces of research.

The normal distribution

The normal distribution is an ideal frequency distribution that is used as a model for the likelihood (probability) of observing a particular case from a population. In chapter 9 we considered how a frequency distribution could be constructed for a sample of data. Figure 9.4 shows the frequency distribution for a sample of scores on the Political Life Events scale. From this distribution you will see that the chance that a randomly selected individual from the sample would have a score of 2 is much smaller than the chance that the individual would have a score of 14. This is because there are more people who score 14 in the sample than people who score 2 (this is indicated by a big bar for 14 and a small bar for 2). In other words, by inspecting the area under a frequency distribution, we are able to determine the probability of an event occurring.

In inferential statistics, we use frequency distributions for populations rather than sample frequency distributions like that in figure 9.4. However, since we never construct population frequency distributions from actual data (because populations are usually too large), we have to rely on model frequency distributions. The **normal distribution** is a case in point: it is a common (and fairly reasonable) assumption that many naturally occurring variables are approximately normally distributed in the population. Height and weight are well-

If we can safely assume that 3rd-year Sociology marks are normally distributed and know the mean and standard deviation of marks, then it is easy to determine the probability of obtaining any particular mark.

known examples. Most people are of average height, and the proportion of people in the population who are taller or shorter than average gradually tapers off as they get much taller or shorter than average. This produces a bell-shaped normal distribution such as that represented in figure 10.1, with most individual cases clustering around the mean in the centre, and few extreme cases (very tall and short people) in the tails. The normal distribution acts as a model frequency distribution for many naturally occurring variables and, importantly, it allows us to determine the probability that a randomly selected individual from the population will score above or below a particular value (e.g., will be heavier than 105kg or shorter than 1.5m).

There are many ways to characterise the normal distribution. In the first place, it is not a single distribution as much as a family of distributions. There are different normal distributions for the height and weight of humans, human intelligence, and the height and weight of giraffes. All instances of the distribution have a particular and common 'bell' shape observable in the examples shown in figure 10.1. The only way in which normal distributions differ from each other is in terms of the parameters μ and σ (mean and standard deviation).

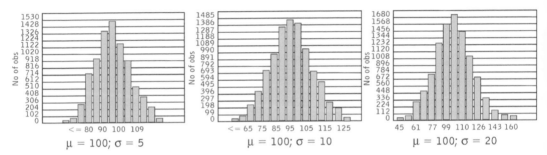

Figure 10.1 Three examples of normal distribution – the histograms represent the distribution of 10 000 scores

The normal distribution allows us to make fairly precise probability statements regarding variables, which is done by determining the size of areas under the curve. This is a straightforward task, since the mathematical properties of the normal distribution are well known. The only problem is that there are many different normal distributions (each with different mean and variance), and, to simplify things, statisticians have defined a standard normal distribution with a mean of 0 and standard deviation of 1, for which the full mathematical relation between scores and areas under the curve have been calculated, and which are available in tables of the normal distribution, or computed by statistical software packages. A simple transformation (the z-score transformation) reduces all normal distributions to the standard normal distribution. The z-score transformation is defined as:

$$z = \frac{x - \mu}{\sigma}$$

Thus, a person's z-score equals their score minus the mean, divided by the standard deviation.

A simple example of how we use the normal distribution to make probability statements will show the logic of transforming scores on a normal distribution (called x-scores) into scores on the standard normal distribution (called z-scores). Imagine that a paediatric nurse is examining a newborn infant, and suspects that it is seriously underweight – the baby weighs 1.7 kilograms. One way of answering this question is to locate the relative position of the infant's weight in the population of infants. She consults her manual, and discovers that infant birthweight is normally distributed with a mean μ = 3.2 kilograms, and standard deviation σ = 0.5 kilograms. She uses the z-score transformation to locate the particular infant's weight in the standard normal distribution, and looks up the probability (on tables of z-scores) of obtaining this score or a score lower than it. Thus,

$$z = \frac{x - \mu}{\sigma} = \frac{1.7 - 3.2}{0.5} = -3$$

The area under the curve of a frequency distribution represents the proportion of cases that score above or below a particular value in the real world.

The z-formula transforms an x-score of 1.7 on the normal distribution of infant birthweight to a z-score on a standard normal distribution. Once we have a z-score, we can use tables to determine that the proportion of area under the curve that lies below $z = -3$ is equal to .0013. This is precisely the same as the area under the curve of the birthweight distribution that lies below a score of 1.7 kilograms. The paediatric nurse can thus conclude that a proportion of only .0013 babies are born with a weight of 1.7 kilograms or less. In other words, there are only 13 babies in 10 000 that are this weight, or lower. The baby certainly is seriously underweight. In statistical notation, the convention is to say that p = .0013, with p standing for the probability.

In this example we applied the normal distribution to an individual score, but it is more usual in the social sciences to apply it to group data. In order to show how this is done, we need to introduce the concept of a **sampling distribution**.

Sampling distributions

You probably understand the notion of a 'distribution' to refer to the pattern of dispersion of a set of raw data around a mean. However, we can also use this notion to refer to the hypothetical dispersion of a set of sample statistics (say the mean). Suppose that samples of a certain size are drawn an infinite number of times from a population, and the mean of each sample is determined. The distribution of these sample means is known as the **sampling distribution of the mean**. We can use this distribution in the same way that we use the normal distribution: in other words we can calculate the probability that a sample mean will have a particular value. A key theorem that allows us to work statistically with the sampling distribution of the mean is the **Central Limit Theorem**, which states:

Box 10.1

Maths avoidance

An obstacle to learning. How do you feel as you read the material in this chapter? Many students feel anxious when working with mathematical symbols or statistical concepts and admit defeat before even trying to learn. In some extreme cases, students seem to switch off their minds and freeze up in the presence of maths symbols. If you feel comfortable with statistics, you can skip this box. However, if the labels 'math-anxious' and 'math-phobic' fit you, you should read on.

Maths anxiety appears as a continuum, with different people having varying levels of symptoms. Perhaps the most harmful symptom of maths anxiety is maths avoidance, the flight from settings that involve learning or showing maths skills. Escaping lecture situations in which lecturers ask hard questions may serve the short-term goal of blocking fear. Sadly, the long-term costs of maths avoidance are very high. The term **vocational filter** describes the process of people taking themselves out of contention for certain careers or job promotions by avoiding maths skills required for the best jobs. Do some of the following statements describe you?

- I have avoided or postponed taking courses that involve maths or statistics.
- Because I know that I cannot do maths, I am trying hard to find a major that does not require maths skills.
- When I read assignments that have statistics in them, I get bogged down and have to skip to other sections where the authors tell me what the statistics meant.

If these statements describe you, you probably are not looking forward to the parts of this text that use mathematical symbols. For more detail on this problem, consult extended works on the origin of maths anxiety (Tobias, 1978) and the treatment of maths avoidance (Hollander & Proschan, 1984; Tobias, 1987).

Coping with this chapter. This chapter was written with you in mind and includes only the minimum statistics necessary to understand research reports. In reading this chapter, keep four points in mind: First, you have already discovered that this chapter focuses on the common-sense meaning of statistics. This chapter should enable you to read rather than skip the results section in standard research reports. Second, guard against telling yourself that you cannot learn this material. This kind of prediction can become self-fulfilling and self-defeating. You have the right to flounder, fail initially, and try again. Third, you can learn the scant statistical material given here if you take it in small steps. Sometimes a statistic seems hard because it uses symbols. If you translate the symbols into verbal synonyms, you can decode even the most complex expression.

Finally, in order to relax with statistical expressions you need to work with them. Later in this chapter there are a number of exercises that you can complete. You should also practice by reading the result sections of actual reports.

If samples of size N are drawn from any population with mean
= μ, and standard deviation = σ, then the sampling distribution
will be normal, with mean = μ, and standard deviation = $\frac{\sigma}{\sqrt{n}}$

A practical example may convince you of the analytic importance of
this theorem. Figure 10.2 shows the hypothetical distribution of 'time
to pass out' (in minutes) amongst alcohol-consuming male university
students in residence at South African universities. The distributions
were constructed by drawing 1 000 samples of (1) N = 10 and another
1 000 samples of (2) N = 50 from this population of male students,
calculating the mean 'time to pass out' value for each sample, and
generating a frequency distribution for each set of 1 000 samples. These
two sampling distributions are shown in figure 10.2, along with the
parent population.

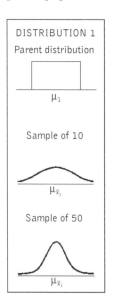 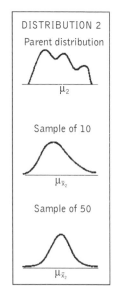 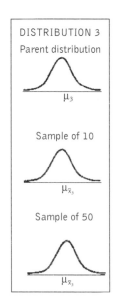

Figure 10.2 *Graphical depiction of the Central Limit Theorem 'at work'*

The figure shows very clearly how increasing sample size improves
the average approximation to the true mean value. Most estimates of
the mean for N = 50 cluster around the true value of 120, whereas they
are quite widely dispersed for samples of N = 10. In addition, the
means and standard deviations of the sampling distributions are very
close to the values predicted by the Central Limit Theorem.

Perhaps the most important result of the Central Limit Theorem is
that sampling distributions will be normal, regardless of the form of
the underlying parent population. This means that the normal
distribution can be used as a model for situations where the
distribution of the parent population is not normal, or where it is
not known. But, in addition, it should be noted that the Central
Limit Theorem applies not just to the sample mean, but to any sample
statistic.

*x-values appear along
the x-axis of a normal
frequency distribution,
z-values appear on the
x-axis of the standard
normal distribution,
and $\bar{x}$ (mean) scores
appear along the x-axis
of the sampling
distribution of the
mean.*

Hypothesis testing

The most important application in the social sciences of the statistical theory around sampling distributions has been significance testing or statistical **hypothesis testing**. Consider any situation in which we are interested in the outcome of a study or experiment: We may be interested in the difference between two groups, or the difference between a sample mean and a population mean, or some other measure. Let us say that it is the difference between two sample means that interests us. We can expect this difference score to be susceptible to random sampling variation: If we draw two means from the same population they may differ just by chance. The next step is for us to determine how likely it is (i.e., the probability) that this difference is due entirely to random variation between sample means drawn from a single population. If it is not very likely at all, then we conclude that the evidence favours the view that the difference is not merely due to chance, and that it is due to some real difference between the two groups. An example may make this clearer.

Clinical psychologists claim that anorexics have a distorted perception of their own bodies. We want to see whether this claim is valid – whether the hypothesis that anorexics have a distorted body perception is justified empirically. We recruit a sample of anorexics and a sample of control subjects (i.e., people with 'normal' body weights) and we administer a scale, which measures body perception, to both groups. We test the claim made by clinical psychologists as follows: We will conclude that anorexics have poor body perception if the difference between the mean body perception of the anorexic and control groups is larger than could be ascribed to chance. We proceed by calculating the probability that the difference is due to chance. If we find that there is only a very small probability that the difference between the anorexics and the controls is entirely due to random sampling variation, then we will accept the psychologists' claim.

The choice of the value 0.05 as the level of significance is in fact totally arbitrary, but has become enshrined as a standard in social science statistics. Rosnow and Rosenthal (1989) comment sardonically: 'Surely God loves the 0.06 level almost as much as the 0.05 level!'

What is a 'very small probability' in this context? Conventionally, a probability of 0.05 (5%) is used – we say that we use a 5% **significance level**. The idea is to choose a value (designated α) that makes an event very unlikely to occur just by random sampling variation. Of course, there is a small chance that we will draw the incorrect conclusion (which is exactly equal to α), and we acknowledge that, in the long run, $(100 \times \alpha)$ per cent of our conclusions will be incorrect.

Hypothesis testing dominates the social science application of probability theory to an overwhelming extent. It is applied to nominal, ordinal, interval, and ratio data (see chapter 7), in the form of statistical tests. We will review a number of the most commonly applied tests in the next section of the chapter.

Tests involving interval data

We start by considering research designs where there is at least one group of participants, and where we have measures for all of these participants on an interval scale of measurement (see chapter 7 for a discussion of scales of measurement). The unit of comparison in these cases, most of the time, is the sample mean. We could be comparing a sample mean to a normative or population value (a one-sample test), or we could be comparing two sample means (a two-sample test). We rarely do one-sample tests in the social sciences, but the nature of the test very clearly demonstrates the logic of statistical hypothesis testing introduced earlier in the chapter, and it is worth dwelling on these at some length.

One-sample tests

One-sample z-test

Imagine a situation in which we wish to compare the mean of a particular group of participants to a normative value or population mean. For instance, we might want to determine whether medical patients with typhoid fever can be characterised as having a higher body temperature than the population average µ (which is 36.6° Celsius, with a standard deviation, σ = 0.3°). We draw a random sample of 16 patients with typhoid fever from the records of a local hospital, and find that the mean body temperature for this group is 36.6° Celsius. The question, from a statistical point of view, is whether the difference of 0.6° Celsius can reasonably (i.e., with an acceptable level of probability) be ascribed to mere random sampling variation, or whether the difference is large enough to conclude that typhoid sufferers in fact have higher body temperatures than normal.

A one-sample z-test allows us to determine whether a sample mean is significantly different from a population mean, provided we also know the population standard deviation.

The logic underlying the test is very simple, and follows directly from the discussion of hypothesis testing and the Central Limit Theorem earlier in the chapter. We assume that the sample of 16 is, in fact, drawn from the population in question (i.e., with a mean of 36.6, and standard deviation of 0.3). Then, using the Central Limit Theorem, we can determine the properties of the sampling distribution formed by sampling 16 participants from this population. We know from the Central Limit Theorem that, although the mean of the sampling distribution is equal to the population mean (i.e., $\mu_{\text{sampling distribution}} = \mu$), the variance of the sampling distribution is different from the variance of the parent population (i.e., $\sigma^2_{\text{sampling distribution}} = \frac{\sigma^2}{n}$). We must change our z-formula accordingly:

$$z = \frac{\overline{X} - \mu}{\sigma_{\bar{x}}}; \text{ but } \sigma_{\bar{x}} = \sqrt{\frac{\sigma^2}{N}} = \frac{\sigma}{\sqrt{N}}; \text{ thus } z = \frac{\overline{X} - \mu}{\frac{\sigma}{\sqrt{N}}}$$

This formula allows us to transform mean values into z-scores, and thus allows us to determine probabilities and proportions relating to sample means. If we substitute our example values into this formula, we get a z-score of 9.33:

$$z = \frac{\overline{X} - \mu}{\frac{\sigma}{\sqrt{N}}} = \frac{37.3 - 36.6}{\frac{0.3}{\sqrt{16}}} = \frac{0.7}{0.075} = 9.333$$

We can determine the probability of this being a random chance event by determining the area under the curve of the standard normal distribution that lies above a z-value of 9.333. Using either tables or a computer, the value of this probability can be found to be $p < 0.00001$. Since the likelihood of obtaining an average temperature of 37.3° by randomly drawing a sample of 16 people is (much) smaller than 0.05, we conclude that patients with typhoid fever appear to have higher temperatures than normal body temperature. From a technical point of view, our conclusion is that the sample of 16 cases is likely to belong to another population than that assumed (i.e., the population of normal body temperatures), and the typhoid population has a higher mean body temperature.

If we think about the z-formula above, we will note that, on the right-hand side, the numerator is an index of 'difference', and the denominator is an index of sampling variability, or 'error' (it expresses the average error likely to occur in estimating the particular population mean with samples of size 16). The left-hand side is a statistic whose distribution we know, and which we can use to calculate probabilities. We can re-write the formula conceptually as:

$$\text{Statistic} = \frac{\text{Difference}}{\text{Sampling error of the difference}}$$

When rewritten in this way, the formula can be considered the basic conceptual apparatus of all the inferential statistical tests we will examine in this chapter. This formula shows that you cannot look at the absolute difference between means to determine whether they are significantly different, but you should consider the difference between means in the light of error variance. This is what was done in the z calculations above.

One-sample t-test

In the previous example, we assumed that both μ and σ are known. It should be obvious to you that this is very rarely the case in the social sciences. However, we do sometimes know μ, and we may wish to run a test on the hypothesis that an obtained sample mean is drawn from a population with mean $= \mu$, where σ is unknown. This is often the case where we are looking at social statistics like mean height of soldiers, or mean number of car hijackings per year, as recorded in archival documents like parliamentary reports.

Imagine that the mean estimated height of the earliest human inhabitants of South Africa is 162 cm, and that this was estimated from fossilised human skeletons no longer available for inspection. We unfortunately have no data regarding the standard deviation in height. We wish to compare the average height of the earliest inhabitants with the average height of present-day South African humans to determine whether South Africans have got taller or shorter with time. We therefore take a sample of 36 South African adults, measure their height, and find that the mean height is 170 cm, with a standard deviation of 15 cm.

We cannot use the one-sample z-test for this comparison, as that test requires knowledge of the standard deviation of the population (σ).

However, if we are prepared to make the assumption that the sample standard deviation (s) for contemporary South Africans is a good estimate of the population standard deviation for the earlier inhabitants (σ), then we can use a closely related test, the one-sample t-test. (We are assuming that, even if they are different populations, their standard deviations are equal). This test uses a probability distribution that is closely related to the normal distribution, namely the **student's t distribution**. The distribution is defined by the following formula, which, as you will note, looks very similar to the z-formula except that it uses s rather than σ:

$$t = \frac{\overline{X} - \mu}{s_{\overline{x}}}, \text{ where } s_{\overline{x}} = \frac{s}{\sqrt{N}}$$

This formula is used in much the same way as the z-formula to make probability calculations. There is one complication, though. The price of estimating σ from s is that we have to be more conservative in reaching conclusions that there are significant differences between means. In statistical jargon, this conservative approach is achieved by allowing for one less **degree of freedom** in estimating the probability (the total degrees of freedom, or df, are N – 1 rather than N in the case of z). In practice, this merely amounts to using a probability table in a particular way. Nowadays, degrees of freedom are not of much concern in practice to applied social scientists because computers are used to determine probabilities rather than having to look them up in a table.

For the running example, t = 3.2 (calculate this by substituting the data into the t-formula above), with 35 df, and the probability value is 0.003. In other words, since .003 is less than .05, it appears that earlier inhabitants of South Africa were shorter on average than present inhabitants.

Very few social scientists still calculate statistical tests by hand. Computer programs generate 'output' which includes all information that is required to interpret the results. In reporting the results for publication, it is conventional to specify, at least, the value of the statistic (e.g., z, t), the probability level (p), and the degrees of freedom (df).

One-sample t-test on related (or repeated) measures

A common type of research design in the social sciences involves administering a measure prior to some intervention, and again after the intervention. A design of this kind yields two sets of scores, even though there is only one group of research participants. The most common way to analyse this data is to create a single variable that reflects the difference between the first and the second scores for each subject, and then to apply the usual one-sample t-test, taking the population mean to be zero. We are testing here whether the difference between the first and second scores is zero (i.e., there was no change).

If five research participants score {3, 6, 8, 9, 11} on the pre-test, and {6, 5, 9, 10, 11} on the post-test, the difference variable is {3, -1, 1, 1, 0}. The mean of the difference variable is -0.8, with a standard deviation of 1.48. From the conceptual formula above, you should be able to work out the test statistic:

$$\text{Statistic} = \frac{\text{Difference}}{\text{Sampling error of the difference}}$$

$$\text{i.e. } t = \frac{\overline{D} - 0}{s_{\overline{D}}} = \frac{-0.8}{\frac{1.48}{\sqrt{5}}} = -1.21$$

If you had done this example using a computer program, you would have obtained the same value for the t-statistic. In addition, the output would have reported that you had 4 degrees of freedom (i.e., N – 1), and would have reported a p-value of 0.29. In other words, the difference score is not significantly different from 0.

T-test for Dependent Samples (new.sta)
Marked differences are significant at p < .05000

	Mean	Std. Dv	N	Diff.	S. Diff	t	df	p
PRE-TEST	7.400000	3.049590						
POST-TEST	8.200000	2.588436	5	–.800000	1.483240	–1.20605	4	.294256

Figure 10.3 STATISTICA output for dependent sample t-test

Two-sample tests

We come now to the case where we have two independent groups of research participants, and we wish to compare the mean of one group against the mean of the other group. Note, though, that we are not concerned simply to compare the sample means against each other – we can do that by simple visual inspection. What we really want to do is to treat each sample mean as an estimate of a population of scores, and decide whether it is reasonable to conclude that the samples are drawn from the same population (i.e., there is no difference between them), or whether we need to entertain the possibility that they are drawn from two different populations. There is no need to detail calculations here, and we simply report the formula for this test as follows:

$$\text{Statistic} = \frac{\text{Difference}}{\text{Sampling error of the difference}} ; \text{i.e. } t = \frac{\bar{X}_1 - \bar{X}_2}{S_{(\bar{X}_1 - \bar{X}_2)}}$$

Microsoft Excel can be used to calculate z, t, and p.

The degrees of freedom for this test are a combination of the two sample sizes, i.e. $(N_1 - 1) + (N_2 - 1)$, and the sampling (or standard) error of the difference depends on whether the sample sizes are equal or not.

From this point onward, we will give less detail about the formulae and statistical logic of the tests, since the complexity increases somewhat. The basis for all tests is closely related to the logic underlying those we have discussed here, though. We will instead report relevant result output from a widely used contemporary statistical software package, STATISTICA (StatSoft, Inc., 1995). For the two-sample t-test, consider again the data set given for the dependent t-test, and imagine that it represents the performance of two groups, and not one group at two points in time; i.e., Group A = {3, 6, 8, 9, 11} and Group B = {6, 5, 9, 10, 11}. When this is submitted to STATISTICA for analysis, the resultant output is as shown in figure 10.4.

Grouping: GROUP (texample.sta) Group 1: A Group 2: B								
	Mean A	Mean B	t-value	df	p	Valid N A	Valid N B	Std. Dev A	Std. Dev. B
DV	7.400000	8.200000	−.447214	8	.666581	5	5	3.049590	2.588436

Figure 10.4 STATISTICA output for independent sample t-test

Tests on more than two samples

The next level of complexity in tests on sample means is reached when we wish to compare more than two means on a dependent variable. In this situation, the method of choice is usually Analysis of Variance (ANOVA). The logic of ANOVA is similar to the inferential tests discussed previously, with one or two important differences.

Consider a situation in which there are three groups of three research participants, measured on a dependent variable, as shown in table 10.1

Table 10.1 Example data for a simple ANOVA design

Group 1	Group 2	Group 3	
3 5 7	7 9 11	11 13 15	$S_{\bar{x}} = 4$ $\sqrt{\bar{S}^2} = 2$
$\bar{X}_1 = 5$	$\bar{X}_2 = 9$	$\bar{X}_3 = 13$	
$S_1 = 2$	$S_2 = 2$	$S_3 = 2$	

What we want to evaluate is whether the variation between the three group means is greater than that which we would expect just by random sampling variation. What we need, following the conceptual formula outlined earlier, is an estimate of 'difference', and an estimate of sampling error. We cannot simply take the arithmetic difference of two means, as in the two-sample t-test, as there are three means. However, the variance or standard deviation of the three means, considered as individual data elements rather than aggregates, will provide the information we want. This is shown in table 10.1. Calculation (1) below shows how the 'difference' score in our conceptual formula is calculated by computing the variance between group means and multiplying this by the group sizes. Calculation (2) shows how the 'sampling error' estimate is calculated by determining the average variance within each of the groups.

(1) $nS_{\bar{x}}^2 = \text{cell } n \times (\text{variance of } (5, 9, 13)) = 3 \times 16 = 48$

(2) $\bar{S}^2 = \text{average of } (4, 4, 4) = 4$

We put these two estimates into the conceptual formula to calculate the F-statistic, and the ratio of the two estimates takes the form of the F-distribution. (Please note that the F-formula below is not technically accurate – we have simplified the logic for demonstration purposes).

$$F = \frac{nS_{\bar{x}}^2}{S^2}$$

STATISTICA output for the sample data is shown in figure 10.5. A number of terms in the figure may not be familiar to you.

	SS Effect	df Effect	MS Effect	SS Error	df Error	MS Error	F	p
VAR1	96	2	48	24	6	4	12	.008

Analysis of Variance (new.sta)

Figure 10.5 STATISTICA display of results for sample one-way ANOVA

1. The notation 'df' refers, as before, to 'degrees of freedom', but notice that there are two sets of degrees of freedom for One-way Analysis of Variance, one each for 'Error' and 'Effect'.

2. The term 'error' refers to the unexplained variance in the experiment, and is estimated by the average variability within cells (e.g., the average standard deviation) (formula (2) above).

3. The term 'effect' refers to the systematic or explained variance in the experiment, and is estimated by the average variability of cell means (e.g., the standard deviation of cell means) (formula (1) above).

4. The abbreviation 'SS' is short for 'Sums of Squares', which is a component in the calculation of variance, and refers to the summation of quantities that have been squared. For example, the sample variance can be expressed as Sums of Squares/df:

$$S^2 = \frac{\sum(X - \bar{X})^2}{N - 1} = \frac{SS}{df}$$

5. In ANOVA terminology, we use the abbreviation MS, short for Mean Square, to refer to the estimates of variance that make up the numerator and denominator in the F-formula. The Mean Square can be thought of as an 'average Sums of Squares'. Thus, in the example data,

$$MS_{effect} = \frac{SS_{effect}}{df_{effect}} = \frac{96}{2} = 48$$

and

$$MS_{error} = \frac{SS_{error}}{df_{error}} = \frac{26}{4} = 4$$

6. Thus, we now have a new way of expressing the F-formula:

$$\text{Statistic} = \frac{\text{Difference}}{\text{Sampling error of the difference}}$$

i.e. $F = \dfrac{MS_{Effect}}{MS_{Error}}$

Just as we use the t-distribution to make probabilistic decisions about whether two means differ by more than random sampling variation, so we use the F-distribution to make probabilistic decisions about whether three (or more than three) means differ by more than random sampling variation.

However, if we obtain a significant F-ratio, and conclude that it is unlikely that the variation between three means is due to mere random sampling variation, we are in a more complex position than we would be in with a t-test. This is because the observed variation between three means may stem from a number of patterns: For example, the variation shown by the following set of means {4, 6, 8} is quite different from the variation shown by {4, 4, 10}, even though the overall amount of variation is equivalent. It is typical, therefore, to conduct **post-hoc tests** on differences between individual means in an ANOVA design, but only when the overall F-ratio is significant. These post-hoc tests are similar to t-tests, but the way in which computer programs report them is quite different from usual t-tests. Figure 10.6 reports Fisher Least Significant Difference (LSD) tests (one of many different post-hoc tests available in the STATISTICA package) for the example data.

Post-hoc tests are statistical procedures, similar to t-tests, that detect a pattern of differences in a set of means.

LSD Test; Variable: VAR1 (new.sta)			
	{1} M = 5.0000	{2} M = 9.0000	{3} M = 13.000
{1}		.049825	.002714
{2}	.049825		.049825
{3}	.002714	.049825	

Figure 10.6 STATISTICA display of post-hoc Fisher's LSD tests for sample one-way ANOVA

In this figure, {1} refers to the first mean (its value is shown as M = 5), {2} to the second mean, and so on. The cell at the intersection of row {1} and column {2} records the probability value resulting from the comparison of the first and second means, and so on. Since all the p-values are less than 0.05, it is clear that means 1 and 2 differ significantly, as do means 1 and 3, and means 2 and 3. In other words, all means are significantly different from each other. Often, however, there are significant differences between certain pairs of means, but not others.

If a significant F-ratio is obtained in an analysis of variance, post-hoc tests should be performed to establish which pairs of means differ significantly.

Factorial ANOVA

The example we have given of an ANOVA design is for an ANOVA with a single independent variable and a single dependent variable. This is the simplest kind of ANOVA you are likely to meet in the literature. You are more likely to encounter research reporting factorial Analysis of Variance, which is an ANOVA with one dependent variable but more than one independent variable. Although Factorial ANOVA is technically a multivariate procedure, and somewhat more complex than those we have discussed thus far, we include a brief description of it here because it is so widely used in social science research.

In Factorial ANOVA, we are interested in the separate and simultaneous effects of more than one independent variable (known in ANOVA-speak as a 'factor') on a dependent variable. An example of a Factorial ANOVA can be found in a study reported by Dixon, Tredoux, Durrheim, and Foster (1994). Research participants listened to tape-recorded exchanges between a coloured, Cape-Afrikaans-speaking criminal suspect, and a white, English-speaking interrogator. The participants were asked to rate the suspect on a 7-point scale ranging from innocent (7) to guilty (1). The independent variables, or factors, were (a) type of language shift, and (b) type of crime. In the case of the language shift factor, participants heard one of three versions of the tape-recorded conversation: (i) the suspect 'converged' linguistically by speaking the same language as the interrogator, (ii) the suspect 'diverged partially' by inserting some phrases in Afrikaans, and (iii) the suspect 'diverged completely' by answering all questions (which were always put in English), in Afrikaans. In the case of the type of crime factor, the suspect was either accused of committing a 'blue-collar crime' (physical and verbal assault), or a 'white-collar crime' (cheque fraud). Figure 10.7 depicts this experimental design. Research participants were randomly assigned to the cells in the six-cell design, such that each participant had an equal chance of being assigned to any particular cell.

> *Factorial ANOVA is used to analyse experimental data containing more than one independent variable.*

Language shift			
Crime type	Convergence	Partial divergence	Complete divergence
Blue-collar			
White-collar			

Figure 10.7 ANOVA design used by Dixon, Tredoux, Durrheim, & Foster, 1994

The separate effects in a factorial design are known as **main effects**, and the simultaneous effects as **interaction effects**. Each effect is evaluated, as in the case of one-way Analysis of Variance, by an F-ratio, and its associated probability. The interpretation of significant F-ratios for main effects is that the means across the levels of that independent variable differ significantly. In figure 10.7, for example, a significant F-ratio for crime type means that, overall, blue-collar and white-collar crimes attract different ratings of suspect guilt. A significant F-ratio for the interaction effect leads to a somewhat more complicated interpretation. It means, in the case of the running example, that the rating of suspect guilt differs across crime type, but this difference depends on the kind of language shift exhibited in the tape recording. For example, it could be that blue-collar suspects are rated as 'more guilty' than white-collar suspects, but only when they exhibit complete language divergence. The two-way Analysis of Variance conducted by Dixon et al. (1994) identified a main effect for crime type (F = 5.62; df = 1, 110; p < 0.019), and a main effect for language shift (F = 5.96; df = 2, 110; p < 0.003), but the interaction effect was not significant (F = 0.63; df = 2, 110; p > 0.52).

Which statistical test?

Box 10.2

Beginning researchers often have difficulty knowing which statistical test to use for a particular problem. The diagram shown here attempts to assist you in making the decision for the tests discussed in this chapter.

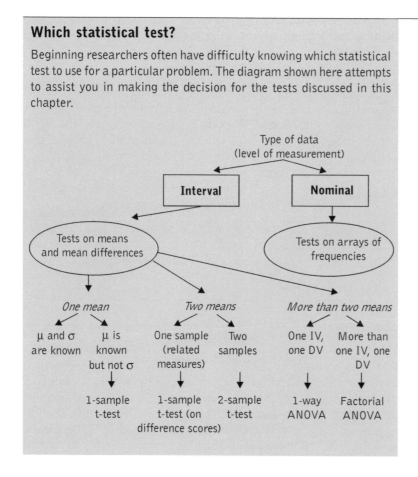

Tests for nominal data,
such as chi-square,
allow us to detect
trends in frequency
tabulations.

Tests involving nominal data

Although we have focused thus far on methods of inferential analysis that are applicable to interval-level data, this does not mean that nominal-level or ordinal-level data cannot sustain statistical hypothesis testing. There are many tests for use with nominal and ordinal data, and at one stage in the 1950s and 1960s some authors argued for the general use of these ('nonparametric') tests in social science research, on the premise that measurement practices in these disciplines did not meet the requirements for 'parametric' analyses (see Siegel & Castallan, 1988).

This argument has waned in popularity in recent years, and we will not attempt to introduce readers to the large number of tests devised as alternatives to those discussed earlier in the chapter. We will instead introduce an important test of the distribution of frequencies, known generically as the χ^2 (Chi-square) test, since it is widely used, and because it underlies many multivariate forms of categorical or nominal data analysis.

The Chi-square test

Consider the following study: We want to determine whether political stances on certain issues generalise in their inherent conservatism or liberalism to other issues. Thus, do people who support the death penalty in South Africa also oppose universal franchise? Imagine that we decide to test this hypothesis in a local shopping mall. We approach 119 people and ask them to indicate their support – separately – for the two issues in question. We can produce a bivariate table to represent the data (see chapter 9). The tabulation is shown in table 10.2

Table 10.2 Bivariate cross-tabulation of support for two social practices

Universal franchise	Death penalty	
	In favour	Not in favour
In favour	16	30
Not in favour	55	18

Just as we constantly asked earlier in the chapter whether observed patterns or differences were real or acceptable within the limits of random sampling variation, we need to do the same here. Although it appears that people who support the death penalty are more likely to oppose universal franchise, if we had sampled another 119 people, for example, we may have found a markedly different distribution of frequencies. In other words, we need to test the hypothesis that the unequal distribution of frequencies observed in the table is within acceptable limits of random sampling variation.

The statistical logic underlying the χ^2 test of bivariate cross-tabulations is so simple and elegant that it is worth spelling out here. In particular, it re-emphasises the dependency of statistical tests on the theory of probability. The bivariate tabulation shown in table 10.2 has a total of 71 people in favour of the death penalty (d.p.). It also has a total of 46 people in favour of universal franchise (u.f.). If support for these practices is independent of support for each practice, then we can apply the definition of joint probability to determine how many people we expect to support both the death penalty and universal franchise. We do this by determining the probability that someone supports both and multiplying this probability by the total number of people sampled. The probability will be the product of the individual probabilities:

$$p \text{ (support both d.p. and u.f.)} = \frac{71}{119} \times \frac{46}{119} = 0.23$$

When this probability is multiplied by 119, we get 27.4. In other words, if there really is no relationship between support for the two practices, we would expect 27.4 people to support both practices. Thus, for this cell, the observed frequency is 16 and the expected frequency is 27.4. There are fewer people in favour of both u.f. and d.p. than expected. The same logic can be used to calculate the expected frequencies for the remaining three cells in the table. Once we have done that, we can use the following statistic, which takes the form of the χ^2 distribution:

Chi-square works by comparing observed and expected frequencies.

$$\chi^2 = \sum \frac{(o - e)^2}{e}$$

where o = the observed frequencies, e = the expected frequencies, and sigma (Σ) means the sum of. Determining the χ^2 statistic involves calculating the difference between observed and expected frequencies for each cell in the table of frequencies, squaring the difference, and dividing it by the expected frequency for each cell, and finally summing (adding together) the results of the calculation for each cell.

The χ^2 distribution is used in a very similar manner to the other probability distributions introduced earlier. Like the t- and F-distributions, its use requires the determination of degrees of freedom. In the case of a bivariate tabulation, the calculation is simple: (number of rows – 1) × (number of columns – 1), which in the present case is 1. For the given example, $\chi^2 = 19.29$, df $=1$, p < 0.0001, and we conclude that it is very unlikely that the observed pattern of frequencies could have arisen just by random sampling variation. By way of example, figure 10.8 shows an example of output produced by the statistical software package STATISTICA.

	Chi-square	df	p
Pearson Chi-square	19.290	df = 1	p = .00001
M-L Chi-square	19.508	df = 1	p = .00001

Figure 10.8 STATISTICA output for Chi-square analysis of data in table 10.2

Although we have given an example of the use of Chi-square analysis for two-dimensional cross tabulations, the χ^2 distribution and χ^2 test statistic is used extensively in social science research, in applications ranging from tests of normality and complex modelling of nominal data, to simple tests of differences between proportions.

Box 10.3

Using inferential statistics

All inferential statistics share the same purpose, and you can read journal articles and computer printouts using these techniques even if certain of their symbols appear unfamiliar. The following steps will help you to interpret any statistic by focusing on the essential parts of their display. Skip the parts that are not crucial, and you can grasp the essence of the finding.

Identify the relationship at issue. Typically, the inferential statistic pertains to an association of two or more variables or the difference between two or more groups on some variable. Remind yourself which are the dependent and independent variables under study.

Identify the statistic(s) that describe(s) the relationship. For an association, you could look for a correlation coefficient such as the Pearson r. This measure would tell you the sign, positive or negative, of the association and whether it appeared large or small in size. For a difference between groups, you would look for a measure of central tendency of the two groups, such as their means. These measures tell which group did better and by how much.

Find the inferential statistic for the relationship and its p value. Did the inferential statistic reach significance at the level set by the author (usually .05)? In most cases you will find this information in an expression, such as $p < .05$, immediately after the inferential statistic. In other cases, you will see a footnote symbol such as * referring to the significance level at the bottom of a table.

Express this probability as the likelihood that the observed difference (or association) occurred by chance. For example, if $p < .01$, one might say that the risk of obtaining the observed effect by chance was less than 1 per cent.

Moving away from tests of difference

Statistical significance testing is far and away the most common application of probability theory in the social sciences – indeed, many people think that quantitative social science research is statistical significance testing. This is an unfortunate state of affairs, since the body of mathematical and statistical theory that social science research could draw on is vast, and not in the least circumscribed by statistical hypothesis testing. There are a number of recent attempts to de-sanctify significance testing in the social sciences, though it remains to be seen whether they will have much effect. In this section of the chapter we shall look at some of the arguments against significance testing, as well as some suggestions for better practice.

A major problem with significance testing is that it is at the mercy of sample size. On the one hand, studies in the social sciences often have too few research participants relative to the true size of the mean difference (and the true size of the population variance), and fail therefore to correctly reject false hypotheses. This is known as a lack of statistical power. Imagine a (fairly typical) situation in which $\mu_1 = 100$, $\mu_2 = 110$, $\sigma_1 = \sigma_2 = 27$, and a researcher has nine cases from each of two samples drawn from the corresponding populations. The probability of obtaining a significant difference here with a two-sample t-test is very small, even though the populations differ quite markedly. There are simply too few cases to sustain reliable estimates of parameters. On the other hand, if one is able to draw large samples, then it is easy to ensure statistically significant results even if the population differences are marginal. For example, if $\mu_1 = 100$, $\mu_2 = 100.1$, $\sigma_1 = \sigma_2 = 27$, a researcher can show this difference to be 'statistically significant' by using 1 200 000 cases in each sample. The problem is that the conclusion drawn from a statistical hypothesis test says nothing about the real size of the effect – we have no idea of what the 'practical significance' of the effect is.

Using a small sample size decreases the probability of obtaining a significant result; a large sample size increases the probability.

There are a number of ways in which these problems can be taken into account. In the case of the first problem discussed above, it is easy enough to take statistical power into consideration when planning a piece of research. There are standard methods for calculating power, particularly after the extremely useful simplificatory work by Jacob Cohen (Cohen, 1988) over the last thirty years. However, even though Cohen aimed his work at a social science audience, it has had little impact on general practice. In the case of the second problem, researchers can report useful descriptive statistics that make it easy to evaluate the *size* of the difference or effect, rather than merely reporting the result of a significance test. It is particularly useful to report a statistic known as *effect size*, which – in the case of the test on two means – expresses the observed difference in standard deviation units:

Statistical power is the ability (likelihood) that a study is sensitive enough to detect an hypothesised effect that does actually exist.

$$\text{Effect size} = \frac{\bar{X}_1 - \bar{X}_2}{S_p}$$

$$S_p = \text{the pooled standard deviation} = \sqrt{\frac{n_1 S_1^2 + n_2 S_2^2}{n_1 + n_2}}$$

Imagine a situation analogous to the example above, where two sample means are 100 and 100.1 respectively, and the pooled standard deviation is 27. With a sample size of 1 200 000, the difference between the means is statistically significant, but when we calculate effect size, we find that it is only 0.004. In other words, the difference between the two means is 0.004 of a standard deviation. This can be interpreted to suggest that there is a great degree of overlap between the population distributions from which the scores are drawn, or that the difference between the means is very small relative to the inherent variability in the sample.

Box 10.4

Inferential problems

Although inferential statistics appear in nearly all quantitative studies, when misused, they can mislead us. This section addresses the problems of confusing social and statistical significance, using the wrong statistics, increasing Type I error by using many tests, and confusing statistical significance with causation.

Sample size and social significance. The number of subjects in a study can help to decide whether or not the test statistic reaches significance. Small effects can reach significance if the study has a large enough sample. We ought to assess the size of the effect, not just whether it exists. We need to distinguish trivial but statistically significant findings from socially significant findings. Social significance depends on the importance of the variables and the practical size of the effect. The relative strength of an effect can often be judged from the data. The social importance of the variables derives from a subjective reading of personal and social values.

Inappropriate statistics. The improper use of tests or the choice of a poor test can produce false results. All inferential statistics derive from certain assumptions about the data. Such data assumptions require checks by the analyst that may or may not be reported to the reader. For example, the *t*-test assumes that the two samples come from normally distributed populations. Editors review papers sent to their journals to ensure, among other things, correct analyses. Sometimes authors may violate statistical protocol on purpose, trusting that the test is robust enough – that is, relatively immune to distortions by the violations of assumptions or relatively free of assumptions. However, you should pay close attention to the motivation provided for the appropriateness of a test use in a particular analysis.

The Alpha Problem. The Alpha problem appears when a researcher computes dozens of tests. If a few tests reach significance at the

Another very useful correction to the 'blind' procedure that typifies significance testing, but which retains the very valuable quantification of uncertainty implicit in it, is to report **confidence intervals** around estimates of parameters. Thus, when we report an estimate of a population mean, we do not report just the 'point estimate' – the sample mean – but instead express the estimate as an interval in which we have a certain (quantified) amount of probabilistic confidence. For example, instead of reporting the mean of the height data for our sample of 36 South Africans (refer to example of one-tailed t-test above) as 170cm, we report the 95% confidence interval around the estimate as {167.7; 172.3}. We can interpret this – albeit crudely – to mean that we are 95% confident that the true value of the population mean lies in this interval. This tells us what the margin of sampling error is, it keeps the original metric intact rather than replacing it with a 'z' or a 't' statistic, and it allows us to make probabilistic conclusions in the alpha level of .05, should we consider them to be good evidence for the hypothesis or just chance fluctuation? One approach to this problem estimates the number of significant findings expected by chance as a gauge for judging the number observed. If the number of significant findings does not exceed that expected by chance, the null hypothesis is accepted for all of the comparisons. Another approach sets alpha at a more stringent level, e.g., .001. The third method uses statistics that can combine many tests into a single overall test. The single test has to prove significant initially before you can proceed to analyse subtests.

The File Drawer Problem. The file drawer problem consists of the unknown risk that our publications report those studies that by chance rejected the null hypothesis. In other words, journals are filled with the 5% of studies that show Type I errors, while the file drawers are filled with the 95% of the studies that show non-significant results. At best, we can estimate the tolerance of the published literature to filed null results.

Replication. Sometimes a significant finding in one study seems to imply that a replication would yield the same results. Significant results can give a degree of confidence about the relationship but do not remove the need for replication.

Over-interpretation. Inferential statistics cannot by themselves prove a causal relationship. Statistics receive more weight in the overall interpretation of research than they deserve. Statistics appear elegant, precise, and decisive. Readers unfamiliar with statistics often skip past the baffling results section to the point where the authors conclude that the statistical analysis supported some causal link. Only careful analysis of the method section can support or reject the numerous rival hypotheses.

same fashion as significance tests. Thus, we can conclude that this interval does not include the value for the population of 'earliest inhabitants of South Africa (162 cm), and we can therefore say with 95% probability that the height of present inhabitants is greater than the height of earliest inhabitants. The general form of a confidence interval is:

Confidence interval = estimate ± (distribution statistic × standard error of the statistic)

For a sample mean, population variance unknown, the specific form is

$$\bar{X} \pm (t_{0.025} \times \frac{s}{\sqrt{N}})$$

Conclusion

Although the use of confidence intervals and effect sizes goes some way towards making the use of statistical significance testing in the social sciences less problematic, researchers in these disciplines remain wedded to the significance test, and do not commonly show any recognition of its limitations. The problem is that the significance test has become institutionalised, especially in quantitative psychology. Journals insist on its usage, and scores of students are trained in its blind application. We may speculate about the reason(s) for this state of affairs (see Danziger, 1986), but it is clear that it is highly problematic. One solution to the problem involves 'the flight from quantitative methods', but this is like fleeing from the syllogism because it is to be found in many perturbations of logical reasoning! A better solution to the problem may be to re-invent quantitative social science, and to use much more of the huge corpus of knowledge available in the disciplines of mathematics and statistics, and their applied derivatives. This may be a real alternative to the present reductionist dependence on the significance test.

Exercises

1. At a well-known hospital, researchers want to compare the efficacy of Insight and Behaviour modification therapies for the treatment of anorexia nervosa. Ten anorexic patients are recruited as subjects. For six months, the subjects are treated using Insight therapy, and their weight gain measured. For the next six months, the subjects are treated with a behaviour modification regimen and their weight gain measured. The data are as follows (in kg):

Patient No.	1	2	3	4	5	6	6	8	9	10
Insight:	3.4	2.3	4.5	1.7	1.4	−1.2	2.3	0.4	1.0	1.6
Beh. Mod:	4.2	2.8	4.9	1.8	1.4	−1.0	2.8	0.9	1.8	1.9

Do the data indicate a difference in the efficacy of the treatment procedures (let a = 0.05)? Check your answer against the STATISTICA output in figure 10.9

T-test for Dependent Samples (new2.sta)								
	Mean	Std. Dv.	N	Diff.	S. Diff.	t	df	p
Insight	1.74	1.57						
Beh. Mod.	2.15	1.67	10.00	−0.41	0.27	−4.83	9.00	0.0009

Figure 10.9 STATISTICA output for exercise 1

2. It is possible to use One-way Analysis of Variance in situations where one would typically use a two sample t-test. Thus, Rudenberg, Jansen, & Fridjohn (1998) conducted a study in which they compared (among other things) children in Gauteng from 'high-violence areas' (HV) to children from 'low-violence areas' (LV). The variables for comparison were 'stress signs' (SS) and 'emotional indicators' (EI), which were measured from the Draw-a-person test. They report that, for SS, $F(1, 19) = 4.42$, $p < 0.05$, and for EI, $F(1, 17) = 10.29$, $p < 0.01$. The means for SS were 4.05 (HV) and 2.38 (LV), and for EI the means were 3.09 (HV) and 1.05 (LV).

   Do their results show that there are statistically significant differences between children from high- and low-violence areas? If so, at what level of probability? Which group registered higher scores?

3. A researcher is interested in the relationship between 'population group' and perceptions that people have about South Africa's future. Five hundred and seventy-one matric pupils from white (W), black (B), and Indian (I) groups write an essay entitled 'What will happen in South Africa in the next 20 years?' Each essay is then analysed, and is classified as falling into one of the following categories:

   • Catastrophic (C): The essay writer envisages a violent and catastrophic 20 years.

   • Revolutionary (R): The essay writer envisages a revolution in which power is seized.

   • Liberal (L): The essay writer envisages a 'happy ending' in which present woes are banished to an unhappy past and power is shared amicably by all groups.

   The distribution of frequencies across 'population group' and 'perceptions of the future' is shown in table 10.3. Is there an association between population group and 'perception of South Africa's future'?

Table 10.3 Table of frequencies for Exercise 3

	W	B	I
C	63	60	60
R	11	69	75
L	67	78	68

Key readings

Tredoux, C., & Durrheim, K. (2002). *Numbers, hypotheses and conclusions.* Cape Town: UCT Press.
This introductory text is widely prescribed in South Africa. Concepts are clearly explained, and calculational methods concisely set out.

Rosenthal, R., & Rosnow, R. L. (1991). *Essentials of behavioral research.* (2nd edition). New York: McGraw-Hill.
This book provides a comprehensive survey of quantitative research methods in the social sciences, and takes an innovative approach to statistical analysis. The first author, Robert Rosenthal, is an authority on artefactual effects in research, and on meta-analysis.

Hays, W. (1994). *Statistics.* (5th edition). New York: Harcourt Brace.
This comprehensive tome is often recommended as 'The Bible' of social science statistics. It leaves little undiscussed, and is a good reference source.

chapter

11

Multivariate data analysis

Colin Tredoux
University of Cape Town

Tyrone Pretorius
Monash University

Henry Steele
Stellenbosch University

To illustrate the complexity of the social world to yourself, think of all the causes of crime and write them down in a list. Now, for each of the causes in this first list, make another list where you write down all the causes of each of the causes in the first list. Finally, using all the lists of causes that you have made, create a spider diagram by writing 'crime' at the bottom, and above write all the causes from your lists. Situate the causes that you think are the most important causal variables close to the word 'crime', and place the causes that are only weakly associated with crime near the top of the page. Finally, draw lines connecting all causal variables that you think are related to each other. You have just created a multivariate data display.

By now you will have at least a passing familiarity with some of the most popular methods of data analysis taught to students in the behavioural and social sciences (see chapters 8, 9, and 10 for a review). It may have struck you that the research examples used to illustrate these methods are somewhat simplistic and overlook the complexity of social and behavioural problems. How much can we say about the social world, after all, if all we have in our data arsenal is a two-group experiment and a t-test? This is like exploring a continent with a divining rod and a notepad!

The social world is enormously complex, and behavioural and social phenomena are determined by a great many factors, working in complex, interacting patterns. It is likely that this complexity is to some extent irreducible, and therefore simply undiscoverable by univariate statistical methods. Box 11.1 summarises some research on the determinants of anorexia nervosa and shows that we need to consider a multitude of factors if we are to shed any light on this important social problem.

Fortunately, there are some statistical methods that allow us to address complexity and inter-relatedness. These are known as multivariate methods, or data procedures. This chapter will introduce you to some of these methods. We cannot provide a detailed introduction, though, since the mathematical and statistical theory underlying multivariate statistics is itself quite complex. We will therefore simply describe the kinds of method available to researchers, and provide examples of how these methods can be applied. We will structure the discussion according to the overall aims of the methods: those which aim to simplify complexity or to identify hypothetical (or latent) constructs underlying complexity, and those which aim to explain or model phenomena.

First, we distinguish the terms univariate and multivariate. **Univariate statistics** or methods are those methods that study one variable at a time or, more precisely, that consider variables (their distributions, statistics, and other properties) independently of other variables. **Multivariate statistics** or methods are those methods that study several variables simultaneously or, more precisely, that consider variables in conjunction with other variables (their joint distributions, statistics, and other properties). Multivariate procedures study the relationship(s) of multiple variables to an outcome or dependent variable, usually simultaneously, but at least to some extent in terms of their interrelatedness.

Simplifying complexity and identifying underlying dimensions

Sometimes, all we want to do with a complex phenomenon is to reduce the complexity to a form where we can better grasp the phenomenon. For example, consider the research on police stress conducted by Spielberger, Westbury, Grier, and Greenfield (1981). These researchers

Multiple determinants of anorexia nervosa

Box 11.1

Human societies tend to have characteristic diseases at different historical times. Thus, the typical diseases of so-called first world countries in the nineteenth century were tuberculosis, syphilis, and polio, but are now cancer and cardiovascular disease. There are several peculiarly modern 'diseases' that are disorders of eating, the best known of which is probably anorexia nervosa. Although social (and historical) factors are undoubtedly important if we are to explain this disease, there are a host of other factors that need to be taken into account, particularly if we are to explain its manifestation in individual people. Some of these factors are intrapsychological, some are psychosocial, familial factors appear to be important, and physiological factors should undoubtedly also be taken into account. It is a good example of the way that complex social phenomena turn out to be when we try to explain them.

A systematic attempt was made by Slade (1982) to set out a model that takes this complexity into account. This model is shown here in diagrammatic form. The key propositions of the model are that (1) initial dieting behaviour is triggered by psychosocial stimuli, in the context of major setting conditions which predispose the individual towards self-control, and (2) successful dieting is powerfully reinforced by its consequences, rapidly leading to full-blown anorexia nervosa.

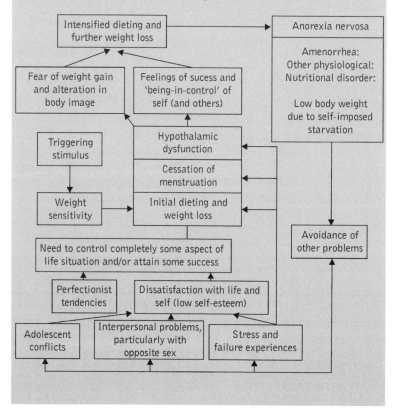

found that police officers find many aspects of their jobs stressful, including high-speed chases, excessive paperwork, disagreeable departmental regulations, and having to deliver death notifications. However, by using a multivariate simplifying procedure known as principal component analysis, the researchers were able to show that most stressors either derived from (1) police organisational culture, or (2) the inherent nature of policing work. This allowed them to simplify a list of 60 stressors to just two dimensions.

Police find many aspects of their work stressful. Using multivariate statistics such as factor analysis, we are able to reduce this complexity and better understand the main sources of the stress they experience.

Three multivariate procedures are typically used by researchers to simplify complex data sets. These are cluster analysis, factor analysis, and multidimensional scaling. All of these procedures identify patterns of relationship in a data set, but both factor analysis and multidimensional scaling go further, and attempt to identify dimensions which are hypothesised to underlie the patterns.

Central to these procedures – and indeed, all multivariate procedures – are covariance and correlation matrices. The notion of a matrix may require some explanation. A matrix is a collection of data points, ordered in dimensions. Thus, a 3x3 matrix is a collection of 9 data points, ordered in 3 rows and 3 columns. Table 11.1 shows a correlation matrix for the variables x, y, and z. The entries are the correlations between the variables. Please note that a covariance matrix is not the same thing as a correlation matrix, but it is closely related. Correlation matrices are conventionally shown as in table 11.1, but may also be shown in diagonal form, that is, only the top or bottom triangles of the matrix, since the top and bottom triangles of the correlation matrix contain the same information.

Table 11.1 An example of a correlation matrix

	x	y	z
x	1.0	0.3	0.4
y	0.3	1.0	0.8
z	0.4	0.8	1.0

The correlation matrix is the pivotal information for most multivariate procedures, and much can be understood about how these procedures work by examining an example of such a matrix. In table 11.2, we report a pattern of intercorrelations between nine items taken from Spielberger's Police Stress scale (for an article reporting the administration of this scale in South Africa, see Gulle, Tredoux, & Foster, 1998).

Items	1	2	3	4	5	6	7	8	9
Table 11.2 A matrix reporting correlations between nine items from Spielberger et al.'s Police Stress Questionnaire									
1: Inadequate or poor quality equipment	1								
2: Poor or inadequate supervision	0.64	1							
3: Fellow officers not doing their job	0.53	0.63	1						
4: Excessive paperwork	0.58	0.65	0.49	1					
5: Disagreeable departmental regulations	0.81	0.72	0.62	0.76	1				
6: High-speed chases	0.23	0.38	0.27	0.2	0.3	1			
7: Exposure to death of civilians	0.18	0.29	0.15	0.24	0.08	0.91	1		
8: Responding to crime in progress	0.32	0.17	0.3	0.29	0.15	0.73	0.67	1	
9: Exposure to dead or battered children	0.09	0.13	0.05	0.25	0.12	0.8	0.71	0.6	1

Examination of the matrix shows that there are distinct patterns of intercorrelation. There is a pattern of high intercorrelations between items 1 to 5, and a similar pattern between items 6 to 9. Intercorrelations across items in the range 1 to 5 and those in the range 6 to 9, however, are low. These results make sense in that the pattern of intercorrelations appears to correspond with item content: items 1 to 5 describe organisational sources of stress, whereas items 6 to 9 describe inherent sources of stress in police work.

Cluster analysis works by classifying all the items in a matrix of the type shown above into a (structured) set of such patterns, whereas factor analysis and multidimensional scaling treat such patterns as evidence of underlying variables or dimensions, and find the best way to represent the correlations (and therefore the variables) in terms of these dimensions.

Cluster analysis

The goal of cluster analysis can be stated very simply as the attempt to introduce a classification of elements or objects where none exists prior to the analysis. It is a method of meaningfully organising a set of objects according to their similarities. A complex set of interrelationships is reduced to a hierarchical classification or clustering system, and each variable (or alternatively, case) is given a location in this system.

Cluster analysis is appropriate when the research is descriptive in nature and many variables or objects are being explored. Research of this kind frequently leads to large, unruly amounts of data, and cluster analysis can be very useful in 'sifting' the data. If the cluster analysis is conducted with respect to variables, then the variables will be sorted into categories according to their similarity across cases. Similarly, if cluster analysis is conducted with respect to cases, the cases will be sorted into categories according to their similarity across variables.

Cluster analysis is most often used to classify cases on the basis of multivariate information about each of the cases. In marketing research, for example, cluster analysis is used to identify subgroups of consumers by looking for relationships between a number of variables, including age, gender, the motorcar one drives, the breakfast cereal one eats, the TV programmes one watches, and where one shops for clothes. Young people are quite different from old people on all these variables, and their responses tend to 'cluster together'. At another level of clustering, one might find one group of young people who enjoy outdoor pursuits, eat health foods, and aspire to owning a four-wheel-drive vehicle, and another cluster of young people who prefer shopping for smart clothes and clubbing, and who look forward to owning a sports car.

The way in which cluster analysis organises variables or cases into classification structures can be made to vary, as can the depth of the classification system. The most commonly used form of cluster analysis, though, is hierarchical cluster analysis, and we will restrict ourselves to this form. In hierarchical cluster analysis, the starting point for the analysis is a data set which records the measurements of a number of variables for each of a number of cases. For example, the data may record values for each of 20 psychiatric variables on 120 psychiatric patients (who are the cases). The first analytic step is to compute similarities or distances between each of the variables (or cases, if we prefer). This is typically done by computing Euclidean distances, but Pearson correlation coefficients can also be used. The matrix representing the distances between variables is then subjected to a step-by-step analysis of these distances.

Although we will be working mainly with correlation matrices in this chapter, it is useful to have some understanding of the concept of Euclidean distance, as it is an important concept in multivariate data analysis. It expresses the distance between a pair of n-tuples in n-dimensional space. Thus, it will tell us the distance between the tuples

{1,4,8} and {3,2,9} in three-dimensional space. It is easy to understand in two-dimensional graph space (for example, a space created by charting an x variable against a y variable) as the distance between two points. In figure 11.1, the absolute value of the length of the line connecting the points $\{x_1, y_1\}$ and $\{x_2, y_2\}$ is equivalent to the Euclidean distance.

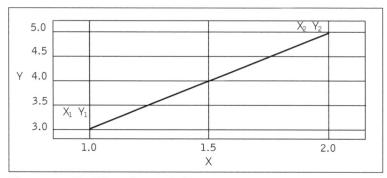

Figure 11.1 Euclidean distance in bivariate space

Imagine a classification system very similar to that used by biologists, with a horizontal axis (indicating degree of similarity) structuring the classification, as shown in figure 11.2, for a hypothetical cluster analysis of psychiatric symptoms. (Often, all we want from a cluster analysis is a classification diagram like this. For this reason, we omit examples of detailed computer printouts in favour of a 'dendrogram' similar to those produced by most software packages). On the left margin of the plot – the first step – each variable is entered in a class by itself. At the next step – moving from left to right – we create categories according to the distances between the variables, clustering variables that are proximal to each other in terms of the (changing) similarity criterion. The 'categories' are the rectangles created by joining or linking variables together. The categories are thus empirical, and emerge as a function of the joint similarities of variables or items. We continue to do this, progressively relaxing our criterion of distance between variables, creating categories at each of a number of steps in the process, until the criterion distance is so large that we have one large category containing all the variables. We are left with a diagram that allows us to identify as many clusters as we want, depending on the distance criterion that we choose. The closer to the left margin the criterion is, the greater the number of clusters (less data simplification), and the closer to the right margin the criterion is, the smaller the number of clusters (more data simplification). The choice of criterion must be made by the researcher. In the case of figure 11.2, there appear to be three readily identifiable clusters, which correspond to psychiatric diagnostic categories (schizophrenia, bipolar disorder, and anxiety disorder).

The dendrogram provides an ambiguous representation of clusters. The researcher must decide how many clusters are useful. Usually, fewer clusters are better than many, so the researcher begins at one side of the dendrogram and locates clusters at the first three or four places where the lines diverge.

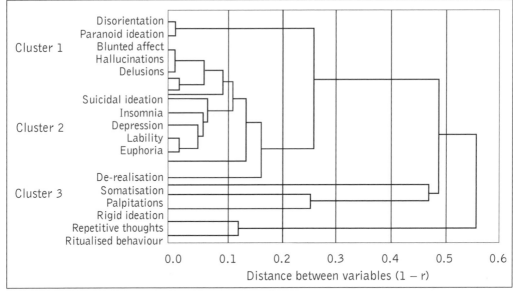

Figure 11.2 A hierarchical clustering diagram representing symptoms in a sample of psychiatric patients

Identifying clusters in this way can help us to detect patterns of relationship between variables (or cases). This may be a goal in its own right, or it may be an interim step prior to a more formal data-reductive procedure like factor analysis.

Factor analysis

Factor analysis is a statistical technique that is used to identify a relatively small number of factors in order to represent the relationship among sets of interrelated variables. For, example, one study found that a wide range of individual and environmental characteristics appeared to play a role in dealing with stress (see Pretorius, 1997, for a description of this study). The range of variables identified in this study and the intercorrelations between these variables are shown in table 11.3.

Given this wide range of variables, the researcher was interested to know whether these variables could be more meaningfully represented by a small number of underlying dimensions. Such dimensions could be more useful, both in future research and in planning interventions, than the vast range of variables indicated in the table.

Factor analysis usually involves three steps: (1) computing the intercorrelations between the variables, (2) extracting initial factors, and (3) rotating the factors to obtain a clearer picture of the factor content. The intercorrelations between the factors have already been computed and presented in table 11.3. Since factor analysis represents an attempt to account for the relationship between variables, the correlation matrix needs to be examined for evidence of such relationships.

Table 11.3 Intercorrelations between individual and environmental variables

	1	2	3	4	5	6	7	8	9	10	11	12
1. Self-esteem	1											
2. Problem-solving	-0.34	1										
3. Competence	0.47	-0.30	1									
4. Frequency of support from others	0.10	-0.09	0.08	1								
5. Satisfaction with support	0.19	-0.12	0.04	0.24	1							
6. Quantity of support	0.26	-0.24	0.18	0.20	0.33	1						
7. Support from friends	0.12	-0.11	0.07	0.27	0.41	0.35	1					
8. Support from family	0.42	-0.07	0.16	0.19	0.29	0.25	0.33	1				
9. Family cohesion	0.31	-0.09	0.11	0.12	0.14	0.23	0.11	0.68	1			
10. Expressiveness in family	0.26	-0.12	0.15	0.06	0.18	0.09	0.02	0.51	0.59	1		
11. Family conflict	-0.24	0.18	-0.24	0.00	-0.05	-0.10	0.11	-0.32	-0.41	-0.35	1	
12. Family organisation	0.19	-0.26	0.15	0.06	0.14	0.13	0.14	0.38	0.52	0.29	-0.43	1

The goal of factor extraction is to construct a set of new variables (or factors) based on the interrelationships between the starting set of variables. There are many methods of factor extraction, the most common being principal components analysis. Principal components analysis identifies the best combination of variables in the sense of accounting for most of the variance in the data as a whole. This best combination of variables represents the first principal component. The second principal component represents the second best combination of variables after the effect of the first component is removed. This process is repeated until there are as many components as there are variables. In the above example, there were 12 variables, and therefore a principal component analysis of this data set would result in a maximum of 12 principal components. Such a principal component analysis, as performed by computer software (SPSS), is shown in table 11.4.

Table 11.4 Computer printout of factor extraction (principal components)					
Variable	Communality	Factor	Eigenvalue	Pct of Var	Cum Pct of Var
Self	1	1	3.55792	29.6	29.6
Problem	1	2	1.71717	14.3	44.0
Competen	1	3	1.39922	11.7	55.6
Frequency	1	4	.89527	7.5	63.1
Satis	1	5	.81761	6.8	69.9
Quantity	1	6	.70649	5.9	75.8
Friend	1	7	.68152	5.7	81.5
Family	1	8	.65320	5.4	86.9
Cohesion	1	9	.53106	4.4	91.3
Expresiv	1	10	.46882	3.9	95.2
Conflict	1	11	.32765	2.7	98.0
Organis	1	12	.24407	2.0	100.0

An eigenvalue for a particular factor is the sum of the degree to which all the variables are associated (correlated) with the factor.

All the factors are standardised to have a mean of 0 and a standard deviation of 1. Since the variance is 1 for each variable (the square of the standard deviation), and there are 12 variables, the total variance for this data set equals 12. Eigenvalues represent the amount of variance explained by each factor. For example, Factor 1 explains 3.56 (column labelled 'Eigenvalue') of the total variance of 12, which represents 29.6% (column labelled 'Pct of Var' – percentage of variance) of the total variance. The first two factors together account for 44% (column labelled 'Cum Pct' – cumulative percentage) of the total variance.

Since there were originally 12 variables to start with, the principal components analysis produced 12 components or factors. The aim, however, is to reduce the 12 variables to a smaller number of meaningful dimensions, so we must decide which of these 12 components can meaningfully represent the data. The general convention is that only those factors with eigenvalues greater than 1 should be considered meaningful factors. It is also

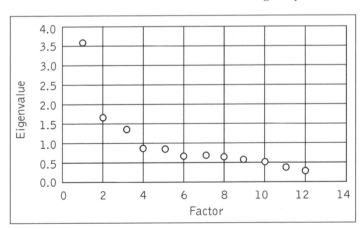

Figure 11.3 Scree plot of eigenvalues

highly recommended that the eigenvalues of the various factors be plotted by listing the eigenvalues on the Y axis and the components on the X axis. This is called a scree plot, which is shown in figure 11.3

It is suggested that in such a scree plot there is a distinct break between the significant factors and the rest of the factors. This break is said to resemble the slope of a mountain and the rubble (or scree) at the foot of the mountain. In the above plot, the break between the first three big factors representing the slope of the mountain and the other factors representing the rubble is quite noticeable. In our example, only the first three factors have eigenvalues greater than 1, and this is confirmed by the scree plot. These three factors account for 55.6% of the total variance, and are accepted as the summarising factors for which we have been looking.

The relationships between the variables and the factors are indicated by correlation coefficients called factor loadings. A table of factor loadings is shown in table 11.5. (The variable names have been shortened in the table; refer to table 11.3 for the full names.) This matrix of factor loadings (called a factor matrix) indicates, for example, that the correlation between family cohesion and Factor 1 is 0.76, Factor 2 is -0.31, and Factor 3 is 0.33. The ideal factor solution would be one where each variable would load on (correlate with) only one factor. The factor matrix is not that easily interpretable, as most variables correlate with more than one factor. The next step in the factor analytical procedure is therefore to rotate the factors to achieve a more interpretable structure. There are two main classes of rotation procedures, namely orthogonal and oblique. Orthogonal rotation methods ensure that factors are uncorrelated, while oblique methods allow factors to be correlated. A rotated factor matrix resulting from an orthogonal rotation is shown in table 11.6.

Table 11.5 Factor loadings for 12 variables

	Factor 1	Factor 2	Factor 3
Family	0.78	0.04	0.32
Cohesion	0.76	0.31	0.33
Expresiv	0.63	0.34	0.24
Self	0.61	0.02	0.45
Organis	0.60	0.25	0.09
Conflict	0.53	0.48	0.10
Friend	0.37	0.68	0.19
Satis	0.43	0.54	0.20
Frequency	0.29	0.47	0.12
Quantity	0.47	0.47	0.12
Competen	0.42	0.02	0.66
Problem	0.40	0.11	0.60

Table 11.6 Rotated factor matrix

	Factor 1	Factor 2	Factor 3
Cohesion	0.87138		
Expresiv	0.75189		
Family	0.75074	0.38403	
Organis	0.63071		
Conflict	0.62064		
Friend		0.79634	
Satis		0.70527	
Quantity		0.58340	
Frequency		0.56328	
Competen			0.78025
Problem			0.71538
Self			0.67674

To facilitate interpretation, factor matrix loadings of less than 0.35 have been omitted, which provides us with a much clearer indication of which variables load on the various factors. At this point, the researcher is faced with the task of deciding whether the factor analytic procedure produced any meaningful results, and whether a conceptually sound interpretation can be attached to the results. Each of the factors has to be identified and labelled. The variables that load on Factor 1 all relate to the family environment (family cohesion, expressiveness in the family, extent to which family members support each other, family organisation, and family conflict), while those that load on Factor 2 all relate to support received from others (support from friends, satisfaction with support, quantity of support, frequency of support). Also note that family support quite correctly loads on Factor 1 as well as Factor 2. The variables that load on Factor 3 appear to be personal characteristics, namely competence, problem-solving skills, and self-esteem. The names assigned to these three factors were therefore Family Appraisal, Support Appraisal, and Self-Appraisal. A substantive interpretation of the obtained results could therefore be that the person who manages stress well has a positive appraisal of the family environment, and is supported by significant others and the self.

Multidimensional scaling

There are many similarities between factor analysis and multi-dimensional scaling (MDS). Both procedures essentially try to reduce a large set of variables by finding dimensions that can be said, in a statistical sense, to underlie the variables. The original variables are then represented in terms of the underlying dimensions, which can make for great simplification of complexity. Both procedures require a similarity matrix, which summarises the relationships between all variables in the analysis. However, in factor analysis, this is a correlation (or covariance) matrix, whereas multidimensional scaling will work with any kind of similarity matrix. Measures of similarity commonly used in MDS are Euclidean distance and 'city block' distance, but any consistently applied metric will suffice, for example, subject ratings of item similarity on a scale from 1 to 7. There are other important differences between factor analysis and MDS: Data submitted to factor analysis should be drawn from a multivariate normal population, and relationships between variables in the data set must be linear, but neither of these is a requirement for MDS. In both procedures, a vitally important step is to interpret the meaning of the dimensions. In MDS, this is often the sole analytic purpose; that is, to find the dimensions that underlie human judgements of similarity of certain objects or entities.

Multidimensional scaling is similar to factor analysis, both in procedure and purpose, but makes fewer assumptions about populations and the nature of the data, and is thus particularly useful for analysing nonmetric data, e.g., respondents' judgement of preferences (towards different countries, motor vehicles, or TV programmes).

The mathematical logic underlying MDS is complex, so we will restrict ourselves to a few general remarks about the procedure, and an example. The aim in MDS is to represent a set of items or objects along a number of dimensions (specified by the analyst), according to the similarities given to each possible pairing of items or objects. The weighting of each of the items on the dimensions can be used to interpret and define the dimension. It is frequently difficult to know how many dimensions are needed to provide a satisfactory representational basis, and it is often useful to compare several bases of different dimensions for interpretability.

A well-known example that beautifully demonstrates the operation of MDS is that of finding a geographical representational basis for the distances between a number of cities. Consider 11 cities in Southern Africa – Pretoria/Tshwane (PTA), Johannesburg (JHB), Polokwane (PB), Pietermaritzburg (PMB), Cape Town (CT), Durban (DURB), East London (EL), Mthatha (UM), Bloemfontein (BM), Windhoek (WH), and Colesberg (CB) – and the distances by road between them. If a matrix representing these distances is submitted to multidimensional scaling, a two-dimensional solution will be as shown in figure 11.4 below (after rotation).

One interpretation of the dimensions is as north–south and west–east axes; the solution shown in figure 11.4 is

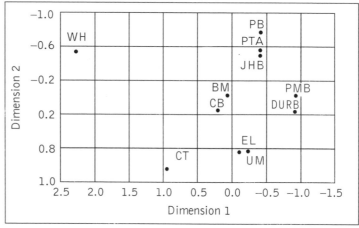

Figure 11.4 *Multidimensional scaling applied to distance between cities in South Africa*

much like a two-dimensional map of Southern Africa! MDS is widely used in the social sciences as a tool for investigating structures or dimensions that may underlie perceptions of similarity or difference. Box 11.2 discusses the application of MDS by Louw-Potgieter and Giles (1987) to intergroup perceptions of Afrikaner groups in South Africa. Since MDS makes no assumptions about linearity of relationships or the distributional nature of data, it is often useful, as an alternative to factor analysis, where it is difficult to sustain such assumptions.

Box 11.2

Multidimensional scaling and perceptions of social groups

Multidimensional scaling can be very useful when we wish to differentiate a number of social groups: The notion of a 'difference between groups' translates with ease into the spatial distance between groups on an axis-referential system. Louw-Potgieter and Giles (1987), for example, investigated the differentiation of own-group perceptions amongst Afrikaans-speaking white South Africans. They asked research participants to rate their similarity to each of the following:

Afrikaans speakers	Asp	White right-wing Afrikaners	wrA
Afrikaners	A	White left-wing Afrikaners	wlA
White Afrikaners	wA	*Ware* Afrikaners	WA
White NP Afrikaners	wNPA	*Bruin* Afrikaners	BA
South Africans	SA	Africans	Afr
English-speaking South Africans	E		

The matrix of similarities was then subjected to MDS, and spatial maps of the classification are shown below for NP and AWB members in the sample.

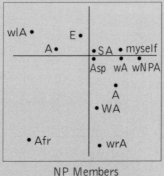

NP Members   AWB Members

Understanding complexity

We have seen that multivariate data analysis is very useful when our research design is essentially descriptive in nature, but it also plays an important role in explanatory and predictive research designs. This is particularly the case when explanatory research designs have a number of independent or predictor variables, and one or more dependent or response variables. Indeed, one can argue that most phenomena in the social and behavioural sciences are inherently complex, and that we will only understand relationships involving these phenomena if we use analytic techniques that enable us to examine multiple, complex relationships. Box 11.1 makes it clear, for example, that anorexia nervosa must be seen as the outcome of a number of interrelated factors.

There are a number of multivariate procedures that are useful for the purposes of modelling complex phenomena and relationships. The most important of these is **multiple regression**, and we will deal with it in some detail – most other multivariate procedures are derived from it, and are easier to understand in relation to it. We will briefly discuss two other procedures: path analysis (and its logical extension, structural equation modelling), and discriminant analysis.

Multiple linear regression

Multiple regression is a method of studying the separate and collective contributions of several independent variables to the variation of a dependent variable. As an example, consider a study of burnout in the teaching profession, where the researcher was interested in the role that student numbers and participation in decision making play in the experience of burnout (see Pretorius, 1994). Participation in decision making was measured using six, 6-point Likert scale items. Values for this variable therefore range between 6 and 36, with higher values indicating more participation in decision making. The variable 'student numbers' was operationalised as the number of students for which a teacher was responsible. Burnout was measured by nine 7-point Likert scale items, with higher values indicating higher levels of burnout. The relationship between these three variables is summarised in table 11.7.

Multiple regression analysis is one of the most commonly used multivariate procedures in the social sciences, and is used to build models for predicting scores on one variable (the dependent variable) from scores on a number of other variables (the independent variables).

Table 11.7 Correlation matrix for burnout (Burnout), number of students (Students), and participation in decision making (Decision)

	Students	Decision	Burnout
Students	1.000	.358	.418
Decision		1.000	.328
Burnout			1.000

Considering one predictor

If we have one dependent (Y) and one independent variable (X), the linear regression equation for predicting Y from X is $Y = a + b(X)$, where 'b' is the regression coefficient and 'a' is the intercept of the regression line. In the given example, if we were to predict burnout for a teacher who is responsible for 100 students, we would substitute 100 for X in the equation. We know that a and b are values that are associated with the regression line, as illustrated in figure 11.5.

The intercept a is the value of Y when X is equal to 0. From the graph, we can tell that if a teacher is responsible for no students (i.e., X = 0), burnout equals 14.03. The regression coefficient, or b, refers to the steepness of the line – that is, the degree to which Y increases for every unit increase in X. Since the value of b in our example equals 0.004, it means that every increase of one student would lead to a corresponding increase of 0.004 units in burnout. The regression equation for predicting burnout on the basis of number of students would therefore be: predicted burnout = 14.03 + 0.004(X) = 14.03 + 0.004(100) = 14.43.

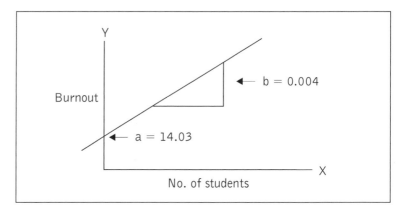

Figure 11.5 Regression line for predicting burnout on the basis of number of students

Considering more than one predictor

If, apart from number of students, we also wish to include the teacher's evaluation of the extent to which they participate in decision making, and then consider these two variables together to predict burnout, the multiple regression equation would take the form $Y = a + b_1(X_1) + b_2(X_2)$. In this equation, X_1 (the number of students) and X_2 (participation in decision making) are values on the two independent variables, 'a' refers to the intercept, and b_1 and b_2 refer to the regression coefficients for the two independent variables. The calculation of these coefficients uses matrix algebra and falls outside the scope of this chapter. The statistical package SPSS generated the printout in table 11.8 for our example.

This printout provides us with the following values:

- a (intercept or constant) = 7.98 (last line of the printout)

- b_1 (regression coefficient for Number of Students) = 0.003 (second last line)
- b_2 (regression coefficient for Participation in Decision Making) = 0.34 (third last line)

Table 11.8 Computer printout of the prediction of burnout on the basis of number of students and participation in decision making

Multiple Regression

Equation Number 1. Dependent Variable. BURNOUT
Block Number 1. Method: Enter STUDENTS DECISION
Variable(s) entered on Step Number
1. DECISION
2. STUDENTS

Multiple R	.46000
R Square	.21160
Adjusted R Square	.19214
Standard error	9.22692

Analysis of variance

	DF	Sum of Squares	Mean Square
Regression	2	1850.87430	925.43715
Residual	81	6896.01856	85.13603
F = 10.87010		Signif F = .0001	

Variables in the Equation

Variable	B	SE B	Beta	F	Sig F
DECISION	.339071	.174793	.204923	3.763	.0559
STUDENTS	.003377	.001095	.345041	10.668	.0016
(Constant)	7.975670	2.804977	8.085	.0056	

We can therefore write the multiple regression equation for this example as $Y = 7.98 + 0.003(X_1) + 0.34(X_2)$, and use this equation to obtain predicted Burnout scores for any specific set of values for Number of Students and Participation in Decision Making. For example, if a teacher indicated that she or he was responsible for 200 students and evaluated their level of Participation in Decision Making as 25 (on a scale of 6 to 36), the equation would be written as: $Y = 7.98 + 0.003(200) + 0.34(25) = 17.8$ (on a scale from 0 to 54).

Partial regression coefficients

When we have more than one independent or predictor variable, the regression coefficients, the b-values, are called partial regression coefficients. In multiple regression, b for any independent variable is the regression coefficient for that variable when the effects of any other independent variable are held constant. Note that, when we only had Number of Students in the equation, the regression coefficient for this variable was 0.004. When we added Participation in Decision Making, the partial regression coefficient for Number of Students became 0.003.

Standardised regression coefficients

The regression coefficient b is not an indication of the relative importance of the two variables. In other words, simply because the regression coefficient for Participation in Decision Making is larger than the regression coefficient for Number of Students, this does not imply that the former is a more important predictor than the latter. The magnitude of a regression coefficient is dependent on the variance (and scale) of the variables and should not be used in making judgements about the relative importance of predictors.

One way to make regression coefficients more comparable is by standardising all variables that are used in the multiple regression equation. This simply means that the means of all variables are set at 0 and the standard deviations set to 1 (see box 9.4). All variables would now have the same variance and are thus comparable. The regression coefficients based on these standardised variables are called beta coefficients, denoted by 'β'. These coefficients give us a rough indication of the relative contributions of each variable in the regression equation. Beta coefficients tell us how important each of the independent variables is. From the beta coefficients in our example, we could tentatively conclude that Number of Students, with a beta coefficient of 0.35, contributes more to the prediction of Burnout than Participation in Decision Making, with a beta coefficient of 0.20.

Multiple correlation coefficient

The multiple correlation coefficient (R) is simply the correlation between the criterion (or dependent variable, in our case Burnout) and the best linear combination of the predictors. In our example, the multiple correlation between Burnout and the combination composed from the two predictors simultaneously is 0.46. This value can be interpreted in exactly the same way as any other correlation coefficient, and can be understood as the correlation between the dependent variable and all the independent variables taken together. With multiple regression, we prefer dealing with R_2, which refers to the percentage of accountable variation. In this instance, $R_2 = 0.212$, indicating that, together, the two independent variables account for or explain 21.2% of the variance in Burnout.

Tests of statistical significance

When looking at the results of a multiple regression procedure, there are various kinds of significance test that can be applied, depending on the interest of the researcher. Two of the most common are (1) the significance of regression coefficients, and (2) the significance of R^2. When testing R^2, one is in fact testing whether the independent variables taken together are significant predictors of the criterion.

Testing the significance of the regression coefficients indicates whether each of the independent variables, separately, makes a significant contribution to the prediction of the dependent variable. Both of these significance tests use the F-distribution.

The F-test for R^2 is reported in the computer print-out under the Analysis of Variance table, and is 10.87 with a probability value of 0.0001. Since $p < 0.05$, we can conclude that the two independent variables together account for a statistically significant proportion of the variation in Burnout. The F-tests for the regression coefficients are indicated next to each variable. For Participation in Decision Making, $F = 3.76$, with $p = 0.06$, whereas, for Number of Students, $F = 10.67$, with $p = 0.002$. From these results, we can conclude that the effect of Number of Students on Burnout is statistically significant ($p < 0.05$), whereas the effect of Participation in Decision Making is not statistically significant ($p > 0.05$). Participation in Decision Making should thus be eliminated from the final regression model.

Multiple regression analysis can be used for hypothesis testing, much the same as factorial analysis of variance. A significant regression coefficient indicates that the independent variable is associated with the dependent variable at higher than chance levels.

Path analysis, causal modelling, and structural equation modelling

Although the aim of multiple regression is to develop models of the way variables relate to each other, many of its constituent procedures and concepts can be used to other ends. The concept of partialling variance is particularly useful, and is the basis of a procedure known as causal modelling (or sometimes as path analysis). The central idea in causal modelling is that (1) if we can safely make certain assumptions about the chronological order of variables in our research (along with some other assumptions), then (2) we can use partialling techniques to test complex causal (or quasi-causal) hypotheses or models about the interrelationships of these variables.

Imagine an investigation of income differences in an organisation. A preliminary analysis shows that both Age of Employee and Level of Technical Qualification are highly predictive of variation in Annual Income, when considered separately. This might lead a researcher to enter the variables simultaneously into a multiple regression equation, in order to arrive at the best prediction of income. However, a little thought about the variables that are being entered should convince you that this is probably not the best way to proceed. Age logically precedes Level of Technical Qualification, since some levels of qualification (e.g., doctoral degrees) take a long time to attain, and employees will therefore attain these when they are on average older than those starting out. A multiple regression equation will not take logical priority into account, and will treat the two variables equally, although we know that Age precedes Technical Qualification. Instead, we can think about the variables in a causal sequence (see figure 11.6).

One possibility is to see the relationship between Age and Income as solely mediated by level of Qualification. This is equivalent to proposing that the relationship between Age and Income is nil, once we have controlled for level of Qualification. This can be tested by

Although it is often said that 'correlation does not imply causation', path analysis uses theoretical assumptions and regression analytic techniques to enable researchers to build causal models from correlational data.

running several regression equations, in order, or by using one of the special statistics developed for testing causal models of this type. In the former case, we could run a hierarchical set of equations: (1) the equation containing just Level of Technical Qualification, and (2) an equation containing Level of Technical Qualification and Age. We could use the sequential F-test to determine whether Equation 2 resolves more variance than Equation 1. Specialised statistical programs would follow similar procedures to develop causal models, but would use statistics based on the fit between the proposed model and the observed pattern of correlations.

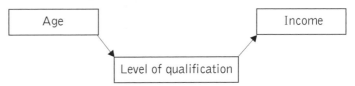

Figure 11.6 A causal or 'path' diagram linking three variables

---

Box 11.3

Job stress, burnout, and coping strategies in the South African Police Service
(Mostert & Joubert, 2005)

Police work is usually pictured as very stressful, with police officers showing high levels of work stress and burnout. Mostert and Joubert (2005) tested the hypotheses that job stress leads to burnout and that coping strategies moderate the relationship between job stress and burnout. They constructed a causal model of burnout, job stress, and coping, based on observed product–moment correlations and the consensus of findings from a review of the literature.

The path diagram represents the final model in which only statistically significant standardised path coefficients are shown.

In the model, the primary relationship investigated was between Job stress and Burnout, with the different coping mechanisms as possible mediating variables. Avoidance coping was a manifest variable on its own, while Approach coping was a latent variable measured by the indicators Active coping, Emotional support, and Turning to religion. The factor Job stress was indicated by Job demands and Lack of resources, while the factor Burnout was indicated by Exhaustion and Cynicism. As can be seen in the diagram, the hypothesis that job stress leads to burnout was confirmed. Partial support for the hypothesis that coping strategies moderate the relationship between job stress and burnout was also found (avoidance coping moderated the relationship). Although there was no relationship between job stress and the use of an approach coping strategy, there was a negative relationship between approach coping

We can also estimate the strength of the relationships indicated in the diagram – it is conventional to determine weights and to show these on the path diagram.

It should be clear that causal modelling is a tool of considerable potential in the analysis of multivariate relationships. However, highly restrictive assumptions must be made for all but the simplest causal models, and the train of reasoning behind causal models has several weak links. The problems that plague simple, bivariate regression are equally true for multivariate causal analysis: the variables may be linearly related for reasons which have little to do with causation, or they might be related in a nonlinear way. It should – at the very least – be undertaken with great circumspection, and interpreted with commensurate caution.

A much more elaborate approach to 'causal modelling', known as Structural Equation Modelling (SEM), has recently become widely

and burnout. Thus, when police officers use coping strategies like active coping, emotional support, and turning to religion, burnout levels are likely to decrease.

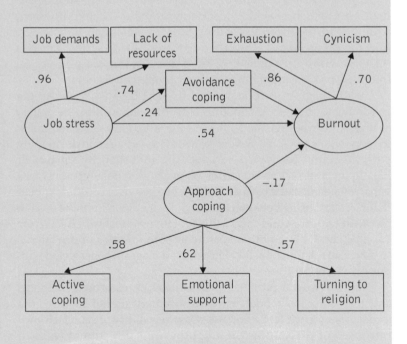

used. SEM is an umbrella or unifying approach for an entire family of models, among them multiple regression analysis, path analysis, factor analysis, and analysis of covariance structures, and is sometimes referred to as 'LISREL' analysis (LISREL is the name of a popular approach to SEM, as well as the name of a software package used for such analysis). SEM techniques can be considered a unified approach in that (1) they estimate multiple and interrelated dependence relationships, (2) they represent unobserved constructs (factors) in their models, and (3) they account for measurement error in the estimation process.

SEM is usually viewed as a confirmatory rather than exploratory procedure, in that models constructed by researchers using this approach are tested with measures of the degree to which the data fit the models. That is, the analysis determines if the pattern of variances and co-variances in the data (indicative of the relationships between variables) is consistent with a structural or path model specified by the researcher. As such, SEM can be used to investigate possible causal relationships between a clutch of independent and dependent variables. However, SEM cannot itself sustain causal conclusions in models, or resolve causal ambiguities. Causal inferences are a combination of theoretical insight and a researcher's judgement (i.e., quality of model specification), and SEM analysis.

The first step in SEM is to specify a model (by implementing a path diagram), which is simply a statement about the hypothesised relationships between variables. These variables can be manifest (measured) variables which can be directly measured, or latent variables (factors) which cannot be measured directly, but can be assessed indirectly by measuring other related variables (indicators).

A path diagram is fundamental to SEM because it allows the researcher to arrange the hypothesised set of relationships (the model) so that they can be translated into a series of structural equations (similar to regression equations). Several conventions are used in developing path diagrams. Measured variables are indicated by squares or rectangles and factors by circles or ovals. Relationships between variables are indicated by lines; lack of a line between variables implies that no relationship between the variables has been hypothesised. A line with one arrow indicates a directional relationship between two variables and a line with an arrow at both ends a nondirectional (reciprocal) relationship. Box 11.3 shows a diagram constructed with these conventions.

There are two components within a model: the measurement model and the structural model. The measurement model specifies the indicators for each factor and assesses the validity of each factor for purposes of estimating the hypothesised directional (causal) relationships. The structural model specifies the relationships between latent variables (factors). Factors can be placed into one of two classes: exogenous or endogenous. An exogenous factor is not predicted by any other variable in the model. In the path diagram there are no arrows pointing towards it. An endogenous factor is predicted by other variables in the model (arrows pointing towards it), but can also predict other endogenous factors. Note that the distinction between exogenous and endogenous factors is determined solely by the researcher.

The structural equation modelling process centres on two steps: (1) specifying and validating the measurement model, and (2) fitting the structural model. The former is accomplished primarily through confirmatory factor analysis, while the latter is accomplished primarily through path analysis with latent variables.

Once the parameters of the model have been estimated, the covariance matrix implied by the model can be compared to the observed (data-based) covariance matrix. If the two matrices are consistent with one another, then the structural equation model can be considered a plausible explanation for observed relations between manifest and latent variables. Several measures of goodness-of-fit, serving different purposes, can be used to assess the fit of the proposed model to the data, for example the Goodness-of-Fit Index (GFI), Normed Fit Index (NFI), Comparative Fit Index (CFI) and the Root Mean Square Error of Approximation (RMSEA).

Assuming the model is a good fit of the data, the next step is interpretation. The hypothesised relationships between variables can be quantified by calculating path coefficients (weights). These coefficients can be interpreted like standardised regression coefficients when the relationship is directional, and like correlation coefficients when they are nondirectional. The latent variables in SEM are similar to factors in factor analysis, and the indicator variables likewise have loadings on their respective latent variables. As in factor analysis, the loadings can be used to understand the meaning of the factors (latent variables).

A common misconception about SEM is that it provides statistical evidence of a causal link between variables. The estimated coefficients in SEM tell us nothing about causality per se. Causality can only be inferred from the hypothesised model originally constructed by the researcher, and not merely from the statistical test of that model.

In SEM, causality is hypothesised by the researcher. It is not founded upon experimental design.

Compared to regression and factor analysis, SEM is a relatively young technique, having its roots in papers that appeared in the late 1960s. As such, the methodology is still developing, and even fundamental concepts are subject to challenge and revision. This rapid change is a source of excitement for some researchers and a source of frustration for others.

Discriminant analysis

In multiple regression, we attempt to understand or predict the relationship between a set of predictor variables and a response (or dependent) variable. It is quite common in selecting suitable predictor variables to code membership of a group, and to use this as a variable. For example, the variable Sex (females = 1, males = 2) can be entered as

Discriminant analysis is used to build 'regression models' when the dependent variable is a categorical variable.

an independent variable into an equation that attempts to predict Salary Differences in an organisation. However, it is also possible to do just the reverse, namely to attempt to predict group membership (a categorical or nominal variable) from a number of independent variables.

The basic idea in discriminant analysis is to find the optimal (weighted) combination of a number of variables that best predicts or discriminates subjects of different group membership. When there are two groups to be discriminated (e.g., males and females), the procedure will generate one discriminant function, consisting of a linear combination of independent variables that predicts whether an individual will fall into one category or the other. When more than two groups make up the dependent variable (say, k groups), there will be k-1 orthogonal functions. Thus, if the dependent variable consisted of three groups – people with Aids, people who are HIV positive, and uninfected people – discriminant analysis would generate two equations, showing how the three groups differ from each other. We will not concern ourselves here with the computational procedure used to derive these so-called linear discriminant functions. The best way to understand discriminant analysis may be by analogy to multiple regression, in the context of an example.

Imagine that we are trying to discriminate adolescents who have been sexually abused from those who have not been sexually abused. A preliminary analysis of a number of predictor variables tells us that the variables most likely to be of use to us are (1) severity of Depression (on a scale from 0 to 30), (2) the presence/absence of Suicidal Ideation, (3) the presence/absence of familial history of Alcohol Abuse, (4) the number of previously Attempted Suicides, and (5) the presence/absence of Familial History of sexual abuse. In order to select from this list, we run a procedure analogous to stepwise multiple regression, known as stepwise discriminant analysis. This procedure tells us that (1) severity of Depression and (2) number of previously Attempted Suicides are the best variables to enter into the final discriminant analysis. When we do this, we find that the optimal combination of these variables is given (in standardised form) as:

$$-0.87 \text{ (Suicidality)} - 0.26 \text{ (Depression)} - 0.19 \text{ (Family History)}$$

In this function, Suicidality is a binary variable recording whether or not the adolescent has ever seriously attempted to commit suicide, Depression is a variable recording severity of depression on the Beck scale, and Family History is a binary variable recording whether the adolescent has a family history of abuse. The estimates in the equation were derived from a data set collected at a psychiatric treatment centre for adolescents in Cape Town.

The weights in this equation can be interpreted in the same manner as beta coefficients (β) in multiple regression; that is, as indicators of the importance of individual variables (in discriminating the groups). The values of the β coefficients, however, are often low and difficult to interpret, and the coefficients are highly unstable, and may change greatly from one sample to another. As in multiple regression analysis, an overall F-test is conducted to determine the significance of the discriminant functions. In the case of the present example, the overall F statistic is 4.29 (df = 3, 300; p < 0.006), suggesting that the three independent variables, taken together, are useful predictors of sexual abuse.

A feature of discriminant analysis which is not found in multiple regression, though, is the derivation of a classification function, and a classification accuracy matrix, which shows at a glance the success – or lack of success – of the analysis. Table 11.9 shows the matrix for the example we have just discussed.

Table 11.9 Classification matrix for discriminant analysis in sexual abuse study

Observed	Predicted	
	Not abused	Abused
Not abused	512	106
Abused	194	122

There are a number of considerations in interpreting a matrix like this, some of which are beyond the scope of this chapter. Perhaps the most important thing to bear in mind is the level of accuracy one can expect if the equation were no better than mere chance. Since there are exactly two groups, randomly guessing whether a person has been sexually abused or not will lead to an accuracy level of 50% in the long run. We can clearly see that the discriminant analysis has done a lot better than chance in predicting non-abused cases (512/706 = 73%), but it has done slightly worse than chance in predicting those who have been abused (106/228 = 46%). The overall prediction accuracy is 68% but, since the discriminant function is no good at predicting the group of interest, it is of little value.

Conclusion

Although we have taken a somewhat uncritical approach in this chapter to methods of multivariate data analysis, we wish to note in conclusion that there are many opponents of this kind of analysis in the social sciences. Two kinds of criticism are frequently lodged.

First, social scientists have long stood in awe of the natural sciences, and (perhaps mistakenly) believe that the success of these sciences stems from their mathematical and quantitative sophistication. The turn to multivariate analysis is an attempt to emulate this sophistication, but with measures and methods that cannot sustain the sophistication. Most social science measuring instruments have

There is a fast-growing class of multivariate techniques for analysing categorical or nominal level data. These include analogues to linear regression, like logistic regression, and loglinear analysis, as well as analogues to cluster and factor analysis like correspondence analysis. Agresti (1990) provides a comprehensive, if somewhat technical, introduction to these procedures.

A taskforce on statistical methods convened by the American Psychological Association recommends that researchers should use the most elementary design and analytic strategy possible to answer the question at hand. While complex statistics are sometimes necessary, the taskforce maintains that simpler approaches can provide elegant answers to important questions (Azar, 1997).

only moderate measurement reliability, and this is not usually taken into account at all when conducting complex multivariate analyses.

Second, some argue that it is a fallacy to assume that complex phenomena require complex forms of analysis. This is like mediaeval medicine, where cures had to mirror diseases (e.g., fox's lung was prescribed for diseases of the chest). In fact, many multivariate methods add unnecessary complexity to analyses, and are often just meaningless. Rosnow and Rosenthal (1989) give the example of the typical use of Multivariate Analysis of Variance in the social sciences, which tests a meaningless null hypothesis. Similarly, Cohen (1990) argues that simple forms of data analysis, particularly mere visual inspection of graphical and tabular representation, provide more useful information than many multivariate methods.

There are undoubtedly many researchers who are beguiled by the complexity of multivariate methods, and who think that greater complexity of analysis must make for better research. This is certainly not true, and it underscores the important point that methods (statistical or otherwise) are no substitute for hard (pre-quantitative) reasoning. This is as true for researchers who use multivariate statistics as it is for researchers who conduct textual analysis.

Exercises

Read each of the following research problems and suggest an appropriate multivariate statistical procedure for purposes of data analysis. Assume, where necessary, that appropriate measures exist.

1. Duckitt (1991) has constructed a 'subtle racism' scale, which attempts to measure less overt forms of race attitudes. The scale consists of 24 items, each of which is a proposition which requires the respondent to agree or disagree, on a seven-point scale. Duckitt claims that the scale is unidimensional, that is, it measures one latent or underlying trait, racism. You have some data from 100 respondents for the scale, and you want to check Duckitt's claim that the scale is unidimensional.

2. You are in charge of student admissions at a big university, and you want to evaluate the practice of basing student admissions on the joint performance of applicants on the Grade 12 subjects of Mathematics and English. You decide that you need a method that will allow you to predict the overall results of students in their first year of study from knowledge of the results students obtained in their matriculation subjects.

3. In a cancer treatment centre, the resident oncologist is interested in psychological determinants of successful treatment. In particular, he wonders if it is possible to differentiate a group of successful cases from a group of unsuccessful cases on the basis of (1) an introversion score, (2) their reported level of trait anxiety, and (3) their level of social support.

4. A sociologist wants to know if there are discernible subgroups of people within the voting caucus of a particular political party, based on demographic and attitudinal data. She measures a variety of demographic and attitudinal variables on 100 supporters of a right-wing party.

5. A researcher is investigating the possible relationships between race attitudes and some potential precursor variables, specifically (1) number of cross-race friendships, (2) amount of cross-race contact, and (3) strength of own-race or group identity. He assumes that (1) chronologically precedes (2) and (3) and (1), in turn, precedes (2). He uses several measures of (1)–(3), arguing that each set will estimate a latent variable.

Key readings

Cohen, J., Cohen, P., West, S. G., & Aiken, L. S. (2003). *Applied multiple regression/correlation analysis for the behavioral sciences*. 3rd edition. Hillsdale, New Jersey: Erlbaum.
This classic text by Jacob and Patricia Cohen, recently revised by West and Aiken, provides a highly readable, nonmathematical approach to multiple regression analysis, particularly as applied in the social sciences.

Flury, B., & Riedwyl, H. (1988). *Multivariate statistics: A practical approach*. London: Chapman & Hall.
This book takes a fascinating approach to multivariate analysis. One problem (the detection of counterfeit bank notes) is used to illustrate a range of multivariate procedures. However, it relies to some extent on mathematical exposition.

Tabachnick, B. G., & Fidell, L. S. (2001). *Using multivariate statistics*. 4th edition. Needham Heights, Massachusetts: Allyn and Bacon.
This book is perhaps the most commonly prescribed text in social science disciplines on multivariate statistics and methods. It provides a thorough treatment of most multivariate methods, with extensive examples.

Many of the volumes in the Sage series on quantitative methods (Sage Publications, Beverly Hills, California) are also useful reference sources on particular multivariate methods.

Qualitative research techniques

chapter

12

Why qualitative research?

Martin Terre Blanche
University of South Africa

Kevin Kelly
Rhodes University, CADRE

Kevin Durrheim
University of KwaZulu-Natal, Pietermaritzburg

It is estimated that 40% of South Africa's wealth is owned by only 7% of the population (Wilkins, 1988), but what does that mean for the people concerned? What is it like to be very rich? What kinds of lives do rich people live? Or, conversely, what is it like to be one of the many millions of South Africans who live below the poverty line? These are the kinds of question that can be addressed by qualitative research methods – methods that try to describe and interpret people's feelings and experiences in human terms rather than through quantification and measurement.

Whereas section 2 of this book introduced quantitative research design, in this section we will focus on techniques for doing good qualitative research. However, before diving straight into the practicalities, we first pause to ask exactly why doing qualitative research is a good idea.

A common-sense perspective

Quantitative research makes sense in situations where we know in advance what the important variables are, and are able to devise reasonable ways of controlling or measuring them. But what about situations in which it is difficult to say what the variables are, which ones are important, or how to measure them? In such cases, we need to engage in the kinds of open-ended, inductive exploration made possible by qualitative research.

Take, for example, a question such as why inappropriate types of medication are sometimes prescribed to elderly hospitalised patients. If we have good reason to suspect that certain variables (say, for example, doctors' lack of knowledge, or faulty communication between doctors and nurses) play a role, we could try to measure these variables in a carefully controlled quantitative study. However, when Anne Spinewine and her colleagues (Spinewine et al., 2005) became interested in the problem of inappropriate prescriptions to elderly patients, they decided that measuring variables in this way would be premature. They simply did not know enough about the issue to warrant doing a focused quantitative study. Instead, they embarked on more open-ended, inductive, qualitative exploration. They interviewed doctors, nurses, pharmacists, and elderly patients, and spent a month at a hospital ward for elderly people, observing what happened when medicines were prescribed.

By carefully considering the material collected in this way, Spinewine and her colleagues were able to conclude that the main reasons for inappropriate prescription are that doctors do not take sufficient notice of the medications their elderly patients are already on when they arrive in hospital, that they do not make enough of an effort to keep up to date with good prescription practices, and that they have a paternalistic attitude toward their patients.

Of course, this is not a properly controlled study. Although Spinewine et al. were as systematic and careful as possible in the way in which they collected and analysed material, they cannot in any sense be said to have proven that the factors they identify really are the main reasons for improper prescriptions. They may have been inaccurate in their observations, inconsistent in the way they interviewed people, and biased in the way they analysed and interpreted their material – and it would be much harder to try to replicate their work than if they had done a quantitative study. However, their findings are certainly interesting and suggestive of possible future lines of enquiry. One could well imagine follow-up studies that subject Spinewine et al.'s tentative conclusions to more rigorous quantitative testing.

Photo: Ashley Clements

Qualitative research is now commonly used in many different contexts, including medical research where it is often seen as an adjunct to more carefully controlled clinical trials.

This common-sense perspective on qualitative research is now accepted in most social science and medical research settings. While quantitative experimental studies are seen as the 'most scientific' way of doing research, and the only way of answering questions such as 'does the HIV virus cause Aids?', qualitative research is accepted as a useful adjunct to quantitative science. It can be used to identify potentially important variables and to generate hypotheses about possible relationships among variables, and it can add some 'human drama' to the impersonal world of scientific research.

The common-sense perspective on qualitative research is essentially a positivist perspective (see chapter 1 for a brief introduction to positivism). In this view, qualitative research should be judged by the same standards of reliability and validity as quantitative research. Qualitative researchers should therefore strive to eliminate or control sources of subjective bias in the same way as quantitative researchers do, and, to the extent that qualitative research by its very nature is less susceptible to control than quantitative research is, it should be classified as less scientific. A large body of very valuable qualitative research has been done in contexts where people implicitly or explicitly accept these positivist premises. However, it is important to realise that qualitative research is often based on a very different set of assumptions, which do not see qualitative research as the poor relation of, or help-mate to, quantitative research. In the rest of this chapter we will consider these perspectives.

Beyond common sense: qualitative research from an interpretive perspective

You may recall from chapter 1 that the interpretive paradigm involves taking people's subjective experiences seriously as the essence of what

The one hotel room drifts into the other. The one breakfast buffet provides the same as the other. The one sorrow-filled room flows into the other. The one rental car smells like the other ... but the language, the detail, the individual tone ... it stays. 'I heard shots ... I ran ... slipped and fell ... I crawled out at the front door ... On the steps my son sat ... with his father's face in his hands ... He was covered in blood ... He cried over and over: Daddy talk to me ... Today he is 11 years old. I am still woken at night by his cries. When I reach his bedside, he cries: "Wipe the blood ... wipe the blood from my father's face."'
(Krog, 1996)

is real for them (ontology), making sense of people's experiences by interacting with them and listening carefully to what they tell us (epistemology), and making use of qualitative research techniques to collect and analyse information (methodology). Thus the interpretive approach does not focus on isolating and controlling variables, but on harnessing and extending the power of ordinary language and expression to help us understand the social world we live in.

Arguably some of the best interpretive work has been done by people who would never describe themselves as social science researchers. Think for instance of Antjie Krog's (1998) account of the Truth and Reconciliation Commission, or Frank McCourt's (1996) autobiographical novel about his childhood in Ireland, or Steve Biko, who, in an article entitled 'We blacks', showed how reflection on his own experience contributed to his interpretation of the broader context in which he lived: 'My friendships, my love, my education and every other facet of my life have been carved and shaped within the context of separate development. In stages in my life I managed to outgrow some of the things the system taught me' (1978, p. 47).

Biko's analysis of how he and those around him 'outgrew' what the system taught them informed his understanding of society and, particularly, black consciousness. Biko, while not an interpretive researcher in any formal sense, was in effect constantly engaged in interpreting his observations of life into ideas. Interpretive research, like the work of the authors mentioned above, relies on first-hand accounts, tries to describe what it sees in rich detail, and presents its 'findings' in engaging and sometimes evocative language. A novice interpretive researcher could therefore do worse than to study works of personalised or investigative journalism, biography, autobiography, and social history.

However, to be accepted as a competent interpretive researcher, it is equally important to become familiar with the principles, skills, and techniques developed by social scientists working in this tradition. A good starting point is provided by two key principles of interpretive research, namely that it involves **understanding in context**, and that it positions the researcher as the **primary 'instrument'** by means of which information is collected and analysed.

Understanding in context

Dilthey's early work on interpretation suggested that there is a strong affinity between textual interpretation and the epistemology of the social sciences. He proposed that a method of understanding, termed *verstehen* (understanding), is shared by social researchers and interpreters of texts (Bleicher, 1980).

Following the model of *verstehen*, the meaning of a written text would be established through piecing together the context of the text's creation and thereby recreating the meaning of the author's words. In order to do this, Dilthey suggested that not only is it necessary to understand the author's specific communicative intentions, but also to include in the operation of *verstehen* a knowledge of the socio-historical and linguistic context in which the author worked. Thus we need to know not only what the author specifically intended to mean, but we also need to understand the context in which the author writes. In the social sciences, this has translated into the idea that the meaning of human creations, words, actions, and experiences can only be ascertained in relation to the contexts in which they occur. This includes both personal and societal contexts (Bleicher, 1980). Faced with texts (be they recorded words, graffiti scribbled on toilet walls, or old photographs), social scientists – whether psychologists, anthropologists, sociologists, historians, or any other – usually deem the task of understanding to involve 'recontextualisation'; that is, the text is placed back in its context and there understood. *Verstehen*, the method used for this, is sometimes referred to as 'empathic reliving' or simply 'empathy', which in general means to imagine and try to understand texts in their context.

An example of contextual understanding of this sort is the use of interview transcripts to imaginatively recreate a prisoner's life in Pretoria Central Prison (Vogelman, Lewis, & Segal, 1994). By reading Vogelman et al.'s account, one is able to form a vivid impression of such things as a typical day on 'death row', a prisoner's interactions with other prisoners and the prison authorities, and his tremendous relief when the death penalty was abolished. In a similar vein, Coetzee and Wood (1995) examined the biographies of political activists detained during the 1980s to reconstruct for the reader the political and emotional 'journeys' undertaken by such individuals.

What we here call the interpretive paradigm is also sometimes referred to as the phenomenological paradigm.

The principle of understanding in context (or, to put it more simply, empathy) has had a strong influence in the social sciences, and particularly in the development of qualitative methodologies. The idea of 'telling it like it is, is telling it in context' has been formulated in many ways. We have anthropologist Clifford Geertz saying that, in

Photo: Centre for Peace Action

Thinking of this photograph from the 1950s as a text, how could one go about understanding it empathically, within its context?

studying other cultures, one has to understand from the 'native's point of view' (Geertz, 1979), while Mishler (1986) claims that meaning is always contextually grounded – inherently and irremediably – and one only has to learn how to gain access to the context to grasp meaning. There are various ways in which this has been expressed: 'to reflect the specific rationalities of everyday life', 'to access local knowledge', 'the understanding of everyday subjectivity', and so on.

The commitment to understanding human phenomena in context, as they are lived, using context-derived terms and categories, is at the heart of interpretive research, and the development of methodologies for understanding human phenomena 'in context' is arguably the central achievement of qualitative methodology. In the following chapters we will see what this means in practice.

Everybody has the skills required to do interpretive research, but to do it well one needs to turn these into specialised research skills.

The self as instrument

Researchers opting to do interpretive research may have reason to think that they are taking an easier route. Interacting with people in an empathic manner in naturalistic, everyday settings is, after all, only an extension of what we do all the time. Doing interpretive research may thus at first glance seem to come easily and naturally. To an extent this is true, and the special skills – including mathematical skills – that are required to do positivist, quantitative research are by comparison quite alien to everyday human capacities, in other words, what we naturally know as human beings by virtue of being able to look, listen, and speak. As you will see in this section of the book, however, interpretive research also requires special skills, which, while derived from everyday skills, need to be developed in particular ways in order to become research skills.

Whereas in quantitative research one can rely on tried and tested assessment instruments to collect data, and on proven statistical techniques to analyse the data, in interpretive research it is the researcher who is the primary instrument for both collecting and analysing the data. To do better interpretive research, you therefore have to undergo some personal change. It may be possible to do quantitative research simply by following instructions, but one has to *become* an interpretive researcher.

Skills such as listening and interpreting are in some ways much more difficult to describe than quantitative skills, and certainly more difficult to develop. Anyone can pick up a chisel and use it to make an arbitrary impact on the physical world, but one has to learn to use it if one wants to make something specific with it. In the same way, we need to learn to listen, to look, to question, and to interpret, although we do these things anyway, almost all of the time. Consider, for example, the skill of learning to listen better. What specific skills make up good listening? Perhaps you might pause and list for yourself five skills which are essential to good listening and see if you can imagine how you might teach a person to develop these skills. Not easy, is it?

Another difficult skill required of interpretive researchers is to describe and interpret their own presence appropriately in any research project. In positivist research, the challenge is to design a study in such a way as to exclude any possible subjective biasing effects that the researcher might have on the results. In interpretive research, subjectivity is not considered the enemy of truth, but the very thing that makes it possible for us to understand personal and social realities empathically. In reporting on qualitative research, the challenge then becomes to show how one *used* one's subjective capacities, and where one may have lacked the necessary empathic understanding to make proper sense of the phenomena being studied.

In the following chapters, we will consider the actual concrete skills required in actions such as self-reflection and empathic listening in more detail. But before doing that, let us first consider another paradigm that goes beyond common-sense understandings of what qualitative research is about.

Qualitative research within a social constructionist paradigm

When Diana Spencer, the Princess of Wales, died in a car crash in August 1997, there was an outpouring of public grief, faithfully recorded by the television cameras over a period of several weeks. Even now, long after the event, one can still buy Princess Di coffee mugs at airport gift shops in London, Johannesburg, or New York, or visit the hundreds of Princess Di memorial sites that litter the internet. Remarkably, most of the people who were moved to tears by Diana's death, and who perhaps still feel a deep sense of personal sadness and loss at her departure, knew her only from the media. News footage of Diana on a skiing holiday or visiting landmine victims in Africa, interviews in which she spoke about her psychological problems, magazine articles speculating on the reasons for the break-up of her marriage – these are the materials from which people constructed their grief.

It would be possible to approach the death of Diana from an empathic perspective, perhaps interviewing people most deeply moved by the event in an attempt to come to an inter-subjective understanding of their sense of loss. But clearly there is a need for another kind of understanding as well – a more distant and sceptical understanding that would take into account the social images, signs, and meanings

'She was the people's princess, that's how she will stay, how she will remain in our hearts forever ...' (Tony Blair, British Prime Minister)

that came before any real or imagined experience of the event. Although people did have an emotional bond with Diana, and did experience feelings of loss with her passing, most got to know her and to build a 'relationship' with her only through images, signs, and meanings that were circulating in the media and society (e.g., on TV, and in conversations), and which had the effect of structuring their experiences of and beliefs about Diana. We can say that something underlies our experiences and beliefs, and this is a reality that is 'always already' meaningful to the degree that it is discussed and debated, reproduced in language, and transformed into slogan and cliché. The research approach that seeks to analyse how signs and images have powers to create particular representations of people and objects – representations that underlie our experience of these people and objects – is called social constructionism.

Positivist researchers often understand qualitative research as a less carefully controlled variety of quantitative research, and consider it useful for 'exploratory' purposes. They find it more difficult to come to terms with qualitative research done from an interpretive perspective or a constructionist perspective.

Social constructionist methods, like their interpretive counterparts, are qualitative, interpretive, and concerned with meaning. But where those working within the interpretive tradition focus on the subjective understandings and experiences of individuals or groups, social constructionist researchers want to show how such understandings and experiences are derived from (and feed into) larger discourses. Interpretive approaches (sometimes referred to as 'romantic hermeneutics') treat people as though they were the origin of their thoughts, feelings, and experiences. Social constructionist approaches (sometimes referred to as 'critical hermeneutics') treat people as though their thoughts, feelings, and experiences were the products of systems of meaning that exist at a social rather than an individual level. Thus the most obvious difference between the interpretive approach and social constructionism is ontological – they have different assumptions about the nature of the reality that is to be understood. At the level of epistemology (assumptions about how things can be known) and methodology (the practical procedures that give effect to this), constructionism and the interpretive approach would at first appear to be identical as both assume that we can only understand the social world by accounting for meaning, and both draw on qualitative methods. However, these apparent similarities conceal some profound differences, and we highlight some of these below.

Social constructionist research: the language machine

'The reality that any individual inhabits is a vast inverted pyramid of discourse poised on a tiny apex of experience.' (Tallis, 1989, p. 13)

Social constructionism takes language seriously, but it does so from a radically different perspective to the interpretive approach. Both positivism and interpretive research work by privileging what is outside language (either objective facts or subjective experiences) over language itself – using language as a window onto some other reality. Constructionism, by contrast, holds that the human life-world is fundamentally constituted *in* language and that language itself should therefore be the object of study. Thus constructionism does not treat language as if it were neutral and transparent (as both positivism and interpretive research may assume), or as a route to underlying realities; rather, language helps to *construct* reality.

Imagine a research project on stress. A quantitatively oriented, positivist researcher might interview people or get them to fill in questionnaires so as to find out how independent variables such as age, gender, and 'cognitive overload' impact on stress level (dependent variable). A qualitative, interpretive researcher would also conduct interviews, although probably in a more open-ended and in-depth manner, with a view to understanding how people experience stress and what it means for them. A constructionist researcher would use interviews and other kinds of text to trace the ways in which 'stress discourse' – a widespread socially shared way in which people talk about stress – functions to construct a world in which failure to 'cope' with 'life events', and a lack of 'social support', leads to physical or mental 'breakdown'. Stress is here treated neither as an objective fact, nor as a subjective experience, but as a set of linguistic possibilities within which social life comes to be organised. The stress discourse that circulates in many societies enjoins us to understand stress as a psychological disorder (mental breakdown) which we as individuals should monitor in ourselves by evaluating how we are coping with ongoing life events. We could imagine different forms of discourse, each with different linguistic possibilities, such as a discourse that emphasises political rather than psychological constructions of social problems, and communal rather than individual solutions.

In attending to language as object of study, rather than as pointing to other more real objects beyond language, constructionism should not be confused with linguistics, much of which is concerned with highly technical aspects of language use and structure. Constructionism is concerned with broader patterns of social meaning encoded in language. The origins of social constructionism can nevertheless be traced, amongst others, to Ferdinand de Saussure, a key figure in modern linguistics. Saussure introduced a fundamental distinction between *langue* (the system of language) and *parole* (its use in actual situations). Although we can use language (*parole*) to mean particular things, we are always constrained in what we say by the universe of possible meanings made available to us by language (*langue*), just as the possible moves at any point in a chess game are constrained by the rules of chess. When we decide to play chess, however, we consciously submit to the rules of the game, whereas with the rules of language we have no choice – we have already submitted to them by the time we are able to conceive of things such as 'language', 'rules', or 'submission'. Or, as Harland (1987, p. 18) puts it, 'In Saussure's theory, language is constantly and secretly slipping into our minds a whole universe of assumptions that will never come to judgement'.

Accepting that language constrains what we are able to experience and perceive, we might think to overcome these limitations by compiling a long list of all the concepts available to us in language

Have a look at the articles by Young (1980), Pollock (1988), and Yardley & Beech (1998) in the reference list at the end of this book as examples of how one could study stress from a constructionist perspective.

wife
home
marriage kiss
love hurt
romance happy
promise beautiful
together family
handsome sex
sorry
us
faithful
husband
sex
forever
children

and simply adding to it where we find gaps or hitherto 'unsayable' things. English, for example, has only a single word for snow, so we may want to borrow additional words from Eskimo to help us differentiate among different colours and consistencies of the substance. Or, we could coin neologisms (such as 'conflibbulate') to describe newly identified concepts ('the act of trying to explain constructionism with reference to Saussure'). However, as Saussure pointed out, language is not a collection of signs each pointing to a particular concept, but a system of meanings – more particularly, *a system of differences without any positive terms*. Thus, a sign such as 'woman' does not have a positive meaning in that it points to some definite idea. It has meaning by virtue of standing in a certain relationship to other signs, such as 'girl', 'man', 'mother', 'whore', 'lady', 'marriage', 'feminist', 'son', 'daughter', 'motor car mechanic', 'family', 'beautician', 'warm', and so on. Every time we invoke the sign 'mother' we therefore not only implicitly draw on these related meanings, but in a very real sense find ourselves 'up against' them.

Constructionist researchers most often focus on language – for instance, the language used by white male students in a bar to show that they are 'real men' (Kaminer & Dixon, 1995), the stories township residents tell to try to explain why they were violently attacked (Butchart, Lerer, & Terre Blanche, 1994), or the subtle racist strategies South African newspapers use when reporting about public violence (Duncan, 1996). However, constructionist research is not in the first place about language *per se*, but about interpreting the social world as a *kind of language*; that is, as a system of meanings and practices that construct reality. Just as our everyday talk helps to create and maintain the world we live in, so too with everyday actions (e.g., a doctor placing a stethoscope on a patient's chest, or a lecturer marking an exam) or images (e.g., a cellphone advertisement).

Think, for example, of a hospital building read as a kind of language. While the immediate function of the hospital is simply to provide a space for treating sick people, it is also telling us certain things about the world of illness and disease. By looking at the way in which hospital space is divided and utilised, we can reflect on the world of

What kinds of text, image, and practice helped to construct Africa as a dark and mysterious continent?

Box 12.1

Beyond langue and parole

Saussure's theory was formed in the context of the technical issues that concern linguists, and can thus be read as reflecting purely on the relationship between the formal rules of grammar and the way in which people use these to construct actual meaningful sentences. However, it is now frequently referred to in the social sciences and humanities as an analogy of the way that transindividual structures of meaning are present in and shape what appear to be individual articulations.

There are many theorists who have suggested ways of extending or moving beyond Saussure's formulations. Bakhtin (1981; 1986), for example, rejects the distinction between purely individual acts and formal (grammatical) systems implicit in Saussure's categories of parole and langue. Instead, he proposes the terms *utterance* and *speech genre*. Like parole, utterances have to do with the actual use of language in particular situations, but such use is seen as social rather than individual, in that they occur as part of dialogical interaction with other people. Thus, an utterance is enabled and constrained both by the materials available in the system of language (what Bakhtin would call speech genres), and by what other people (real or imagined) are saying during the interaction of which the utterance is a part. As Bakhtin (1986) puts it: 'Each utterance refutes, affirms, supplements, and relies on the others, presupposes them, and somehow takes them into account' (p. 91).

Where utterances are like *parole*, speech genres are like *langue* in that they are normative forms of language usage that organise what it is possible to say. However, they are more flexible than *langue* and more clearly seen as historical products – in fact, a slow sedimentation of utterances, sometimes formed over the course of centuries. Speech genres provide 'forms for conceptualizing the world in words, specific world views, each characterised by its own objects, meanings and values' (Bakhtin, 1981, p. 291), and help to make particular utterances meaningful.

Another set of terms now often used instead of *langue* and *parole* is *discourse* and *text*. Discourses are broad systems of meaning; texts are particular bits of speech or writing which draw on such discourses to make themselves appear plausible.

medicine and observe a world that treats different illnesses separately (the oncology ward here, psychiatry over there), a world in which individual privacy is at issue (single rooms for those who can afford them) and a world where sick people are expected to remain in bed (there is very little provision for other activities).

Social constructionists want to flag the idea that representations of reality (e.g., scientific accounts, news stories, and maps of the world), practices (e.g., marriage proposals, school attendance, and breast inspection), and physical arrangements (e.g., hospital buildings, family sleeping arrangements, and magistrate's courts) are structured like a language, or a system of signs. As such, they construct particular versions of the world by providing a framework or system through which we can understand objects and practices, as well as understand who we are and what we should do in relation to these systems. The manner in which people engage with the world – e.g., what you can and cannot do – is thus structured by the way in which the world is constructed. When we act, what we achieve is to reproduce the ruling discourses of our time and re-enact established relational patterns. Think, for example, of a man asking a woman, 'Will you marry me?' This re-enactment has proper subjects (heterosexual male and female adults), a proper manner (loving, caring), and a proper context (private, candlelight dinner). This re-enactment would indeed be strange if the act of proposing marriage was done under the assumption that the world was otherwise constructed – for instance, a woman getting on her knee and proposing to a man (or another woman), a man proposing to a young child, the proposal being done in an aggressive and demanding manner, or the proposal being made in an odd context (e.g., at a funeral, or in a supermarket).

Social constructionist research: so what is really real?

'Last but not least, the major enemy, the strategic adversary is fascism ... And not only historical fascism, the fascism of Hitler and Mussolini – which was able to mobilise and use the desire of the masses so effectively – but also the fascism in us all, in our heads and in our everyday behavior, the fascism that causes us to love power, to desire the very thing that dominates and exploits us.' (Foucault, 1977, xiii)

There are numerous debates about exactly how far constructionism should go in claiming that language constructs reality. For example, does it leave space for objective reality and individual agency? (See Parker, 1998.) These debates are often quite sterile, so we shall not pursue the question further than to say that it can be strategically useful to put such questions to one side and to proceed as if there were no other reality than that constructed through Saussure's 'system of differences without any positive terms'.

Social constructionism is an attempt to introduce an explicitly critical element to social science research, and constructionist researchers sometimes present positivist or interpretive research as naively playing into the hands of the political status quo. It is true that there are certain inherent political dangers in these approaches. Positivism, for example, presents itself as value-neutral, and it can therefore provide a convenient tool for social groups who are interested in domination and control. Similarly, interpretive research, by foregrounding the subjective aspects of experience, can provide a means to avoid having to confront the political dimensions of human action. However, constructionism also has certain inherent dangers, two important ones being idealism and relativism.

Idealism refers to the tendency of constructionist work to reduce everything to language, and therefore to the world of ideas. This tends either to trivialise the real world of human oppression and suffering as just another text or to leave it beyond the reach of our research. Parker (1989), for example, acknowledges that there are certain real, concrete things that require a different kind of political analysis – but one which he unfortunately never fully articulates. This critique is often made by Marxist scholars, who argue that the social world is governed by economic realities and that these are constantly being disguised by false ideologies (including theories that prioritise ideas and language over material) that have been superimposed on top of them.

Relativism refers to the idea that there are many truths, an idea that some see promoted by the social constructionist assertion that all descriptions of reality are merely accounts and constructions. If we argue that all texts do things and that we cannot evaluate their doings by the criterion of truth, we are left with no way of distinguishing good from bad texts, or malign from benign effects. Not only does relativism render all texts morally equivalent in this way, but our interpretations of all these texts also become equally valid. Thus, when Hitler issued a proclamation for the internment of Jews, and when Nazi scientists interpreted this as a rational necessity, constructionism would have been hard pressed to explain the reasons why these constituted abhorrent actions.

Social science research is today still largely enchanted by the twin ideas of objective facts (positivism) and subjective feelings (interpretive research), and, in this context, social constructionist research can indeed be critical and progressive. We should not imagine, however, that it provides a recipe for doing progressive work in all contexts. Of all research paradigms, constructionism is perhaps the most attuned to the real-world political consequences of texts, including the texts produced by social science researchers. It is therefore ironic that it should also be the most prone to styling itself as a form of armchair critique. According to Parker (1992), constructionist research should become a variety of **action research**, and, even as we work to develop the constructionist paradigm in that direction, we should be careful not to claim for it any exclusive ability to bring about progressive consequences.

Conclusion

In this chapter we have considered what qualitative research looks like when viewed from a common-sense (positivist) perspective, as well as from the perspective of interpretive and constructionist research paradigms. In doing this, we have highlighted differences between these three paradigms. However, it is worth considering that the boundaries between paradigms are not as clear-cut as we have thus far presented them. In particular, interpretive and constructionist approaches frequently transmute into each other. In the following chapters, we will maintain the distinction between different paradigms where it seems useful (e.g., in describing how to do qualitative data analysis), but in other cases we will speak about qualitative research more broadly to include work done in any paradigm.

Exercises

1. Skim through a few editions of an academic journal such as *Psychology in Society* or the *South African Journal of Sociology*, and identify the articles appearing to make use of qualitative methods. For each such article, try and decide whether the article appears to be working from a positivist, interpretive, or constructionist perspective (or some combination of the three). Is the perspective explicitly stated in the article, or is it implicit?

2. Speak to two people you know about their experiences during the past year. Choose one person whom you consider to be quite like yourself, and one whom you consider to be very different. Listen empathically to each person – in other words, don't evaluate or judge what they have to say, but rather try to imagine what it must be like to be them. Afterwards, think about your attempts at empathic understanding. What about yourself helped you to understand each person's life situation? What about yourself made it more difficult to imagine their lives? Which one of the two people were you best able to empathise with? Which one did you learn most from? Why?

3. Choose two texts that you find interesting (this could include images) – one that you think is particularly clever and with which you agree, and one that you find stupid, disgusting, or wrong. For each text, try to describe how the text becomes meaningful and persuasive by drawing on certain ready-made cultural ideas. Which of the two texts did you find easier to make sense of? Which one turned out to be the more interesting? Why?

Key readings

Bannister, P., Burman, E., Parker, L., Taylor, M., & Tindall, C. (1994). *Qualitative methods in psychology: A research guide*. Buckingham: Open University Press.
The introductory chapters in this book provide a good starting place for understanding why many social scientists are no longer satisfied with positivist approaches. The other chapters are a bit thin on practical details on how to do qualitative research, but provide a good theoretical grounding.

Denzin, N. K., & Lincoln, Y. S. (Eds.). (2000). *The SAGE handbook of qualitative research*. Thousand Oaks, California: Sage.

Miles, M. B., & Huberman, A. M. (1994). *Qualitative data analysis: An expanded sourcebook of new methods*. Beverly Hills, California: Sage.
These two texts are considered by many to be the 'bibles' of qualitative research methods, and each is packed with useful advice. Miles and Huberman call themselves 'soft-nosed positivists' and tend to advocate more structured techniques, while Denzin and Lincoln have a more interpretive flavour.

Durrheim, K. (1997). Social constructionism, discourse and psychology. *South African Journal of Psychology*, 27, 175–182.
This is a useful eight-page introduction to the main theoretical principles of constructionism, especially as they apply to psychology.

chapter

13

From encounter to text:

collecting data in qualitative research

Kevin Kelly

Rhodes University, CADRE

Photo: Rodney Barnett

A text is a record of life held over after the moment of its production.

In this chapter we consider the processes a researcher engages in while gathering material and creating the texts that form the information base of a qualitative study. A text is any record of life held over after the moment of its production for later comprehension and interpretation. This may refer to visual material, but could also be artefacts or any remnant of a context which it is the researcher's job to interpret. For example, Finn (1997) studied political murals in Northern Ireland to understand justifications for political violence, while Butchart, Lerer, and Terre Blanche (1994) studied the pattern of injuries found on cadavers in the Cape Town morgue to better understand the process of violent interaction that precedes homicide. In these examples, graffiti walls and dead bodies were understood and read as texts. But, more often than not, the texts that qualitative researchers work with are written texts, frequently in the form of the transcribed voice. We will see in the following chapters why the term 'text' is so appropriate and central to the social sciences. But for now we will busy ourselves with better understanding some of the practical decisions involved in generating texts, including decisions about who the participants will be, what kind of relationship to the context of study will be entered into, and how the data will be gathered.

The first thing to know about data collection in qualitative research is that the word 'data' is not universally popular. **Data** represents bits of discrete information that can be extracted from their context and analysed as numbers, whereas qualitative researchers typically work with material that is richly related to its context and would lose its meaning if broken into discrete bits. Additionally, the word 'data' conjures up images of some kind of knowledge factory, where raw materials (data) are processed (analysed) to manufacture products (results). Qualitative researchers do not make such clear-cut distinctions between the different phases of research, but may reformulate their research questions as a result of new material they have collected, or change their sampling strategy in response to new findings. For ease of explanation, however, we do sometimes use the term 'data' in this chapter (in addition to more neutral terms such as 'research material'), and we treat data collection and analysis as two more-or-less distinct phases of research (with analysis covered in the next chapter). But we will also emphasise the importance of considering qualitative research as a process rather than as a set of distinct procedures.

Qualitative research adopts an iterative approach to the research process, and qualitative research designs act as flexible guides to the implementation of the research.

Collecting data in context

Qualitative researchers want to make sense of feelings, experiences, social situations, or phenomena as they occur in the real world, and therefore want to study them in their natural setting. This is particularly true for those who approach qualitative research from an interpretive perspective. Concepts such as 'the real world' and 'natural setting' are not always as straightforward as one might think, but the principle of wanting to study individuals and groups as they go about their lives, rather than under artificially created conditions, should be clear. A central axiom of qualitative research is therefore to work with data in context. Simply by becoming interested in a particular phenomenon or situation (e.g., child prostitution), we are in a sense already isolating it from its surroundings, and a large part of what qualitative research is about is (ironically) to try to place the phenomenon back into its proper context. So the question is: How can we collect data in such a way as to make it easier to get to know the phenomenon in its real context?

The answer typically given by interpretive researchers is that one should not disturb the context unduly, but attempt to become a natural part of the context in which the phenomenon occurs. This can be achieved by entering the research setting with the necessary care and engaging with research participants in an open and empathic manner.

Social constructionist qualitative researchers, just like their interpretive counterparts, value data collected in context and with minimal disturbance to the natural setting. However, as the focus in constructionist analysis is precisely to uncover the ways in which the social world is constructed to appear real and natural, recognising a setting as 'natural' and knowing when it has been unduly 'disturbed' becomes a lot more problematic. While social constructionist researchers are opposed to imposing preconceived categories and measuring instruments on phenomena being researched, they are also sceptical of claims that some kinds of data are necessarily more authentic than others. Thus, interpretive research might privilege first-

---

Triangulation   *Box 13.1*

Triangulation entails collecting material in as many different ways and from as many diverse sources as possible. This can help researchers to 'home in' on a better understanding of a phenomenon by approaching it from several different angles. For example, if we want to understand why many small businesses fail within the first year, we could interview new and established entrepreneurs, spend some time with an entrepreneur, collect newspaper articles and other documents on small businesses, and so on. Apart from data triangulation, we could also engage in method triangulation, for example, by analysing our data both quantitatively and qualitatively. However, triangulation is labour intensive and often not feasible for smaller research projects. (See chapter 16 for a more detailed discussion of triangulation.)

hand accounts of actual experiences, as for example in Cleaver's (1988) research on the experiences of township residents whose houses had been attacked, while constructionist research would make use of such sources as well as 'inauthentic' second-hand opinions, as in Wilbraham's (1996) study of constructions of women's bodies in magazine advice columns.

Sampling

In section 2 of this book, we learnt about the various sampling strategies used in quantitative research to ensure that cases are selected in such a way as to be representative of a larger population. The temptation is to apply these same principles to qualitative research, and then to judge qualitative studies (which usually have smaller, less randomly selected samples than quantitative studies) as being less scientifically rigorous. If one approaches qualitative research from a strictly positivist perspective, this would be a reasonable judgement. However, as soon as one considers qualitative research from an interpretive or social constructionist perspective, different sampling concerns and procedures become operative.

For example, when qualitative researchers are researching a rare phenomenon such as spontaneous remission from a supposedly incurable condition, or near-death experiences, the challenge becomes one of finding appropriate cases, and in such circumstances it is reasonable simply to take every 'case' that one can find. Taking cases on the basis of their availability is referred to as 'convenience' or 'opportunistic' sampling. Researchers might advertise on notice boards or in magazines to get hold of participants, and, if they are lucky enough to get a response, they may have to travel great distances to interview the respondent, whom they regard as 'a find'.

But, more often than not, the researcher will be able to find more respondents than are needed, and then decisions will have to be made about which cases to use. Such decisions need to be carefully thought about. In this section, we will consider criteria for making such decisions. Let us begin with the quantity of material that is going to be needed.

Quantity of material required

A question that often crops up is 'How many cases is enough?' The experienced researcher will have a good intuitive sense of when there has been a comprehensive and in-depth coverage of the main issues at stake. Let us try to break down the components that lie behind the perception of the researcher having 'enough' material.

The idea of theoretical saturation, taken from **Grounded Theory** (Strauss & Corbin, 1990), is useful here. Recall that, in qualitative research, data collection and analysis are often not seen as two distinct phases, but may occur simultaneously. Theoretical saturation marks the point when one stops collecting new material because it no longer adds anything to one's unfolding analysis. At the point of theoretical saturation, additional cases no longer provide new information that challenges or adds to the emerging interpretive account, and there is a sense that the theoretical account is nearing a complete and adequate form. This is sometimes termed 'sampling to redundancy', because further information becomes increasingly redundant, to the extent that it becomes repetitive.

Theoretical saturation is an elegant concept, but in practice we are often required to present research proposals to obtain research funding or to get approval to do the research, and it is usually expected that we will be more specific and outline how many cases we are going to look at.

One way of judging the likely number of cases required is to consider the degree of theoretical development in the field being studied. In a field where there is a strong body of existing theory, one is usually expected to have fairly specific research questions, and one may look for particular cases to verify or challenge certain ideas – in which instance a few cases may suffice. We may even settle for a single-case study design when we wish to test a theory in an exceptional context. Durrheim (1997), for example, used a single 30-minute television interview with the South African fascist leader, Koos Vermeulen, to contribute theoretically to an understanding of authoritarian cognition. On the other hand, if we are conducting exploratory research into a new phenomenon, we are in all likelihood going to need to look at a range of cases to ensure that what we are describing covers the field, at least in a preliminary way. The activity of doing qualitative research always involves a circular movement between the general and the specific. The outcome is usually presented in general and theoretical terms, but is at the same time an account of particular experiences. In thinking about sampling, we might say that it is necessary to have enough material to begin to talk 'in general' on the basis of the specific instances we look at.

How many cases to include in a qualitative study depends, among other things, on whether we have general or specific questions and the sample is homogeneous or not.

The decision about 'how many cases is enough' also depends in part on how much detail one is likely to gather in each case. Using Seidman's (1991) three-interview research format, we might end up gathering as much as four hours of interview material per case, in which case we are going to have a great deal of detail. This will allow for an in-depth understanding of a phenomenon. On the other hand, if we are planning to conduct relatively brief, semi-structured interviews on, say, attitudes, we would probably be interested in the range of opinions that exist across a larger number of cases. We would then need enough cases to ensure that we have covered the range of attitudes that we are likely to encounter in the population. Experience has shown that six to eight data sources or sampling units will often suffice for a homogeneous sample – that is, where there is not much variation in the sample, or when the protocols are based on several hours of interviewing. Shorter interviews require a larger sample of perhaps 10 to 20, while about the same number is needed when looking for disconfirming evidence, or when one is seeking maximum variation. But there are certainly no hard-and-fast rules, and decisions about the number of cases are also determined by constraints imposed on the researcher by budgets and deadlines. Furthermore, it makes a difference whether the project is an exploratory, pilot project or whether it plans to be a definitive study in an area. If the research is exploratory – in other words, it sets out to explore what the important issues are, as a basis for doing further research – the researcher will call it a day when there is sufficient material to know more or less what issues are going to be paramount in a larger study. In the latter case, the researcher will call it a day only once a fairly robust theory has been built or tested.

'All cases are unique and very similar to others.' (T.S. Eliot)

Tracing cases

We use the term 'case' to refer to the idea of a case study, and in this section we are concerned with criteria that are useful in tracking down

---

Box 13.2

Useful sampling strategies

The following are some useful sampling strategies to consider in planning a qualitative study:

Maximum variation sampling. This is employed when one seeks to obtain the broadest range of information and perspectives on the subject of study, resulting in looking for participants who have had different experiences or think differently about the topic.

Critical case sampling. Here we look for data that is particularly information-rich or enlightening. This may involve looking for the exceptional case because, if our interpretive account can be shown to be true for an apparent exception, then it is probably true more generally.

Confirming and disconfirming cases. Here we elaborate and deepen analysis by seeking to confirm or disconfirm the emerging analytic account. We build a stronger case for an emerging account and make it more robust by trying to falsify it. When we try but fail to falsify an account, the truth value of the account is enhanced. However, if we have found a new tendency, we might not initially try to disconfirm it but rather try actively to find support for the case by looking for cases that serve to confirm this tendency.

Theoretical sampling. Theoretical sampling is a hallmark of Grounded Theory (Strauss & Corbin, 1990), and involves the process of data collection specifically for the purposes of generating or building theory. In the grounded theory approach, the processes of data collection and analysis are interconnected. Decisions about what data to collect next and where to find them are made according to the researcher's theory-development needs. The process of data collection is determined by the emerging theory, and one looks for material that assists in addressing particular theoretical issues at any given moment.

---

and selecting cases. A case can also be a group, a context, or an event. In building theory or understanding, we are concerned with talking in a 'general' way about phenomena, while, in finding 'cases' of the phenomenon, we are concerned with the particular or specific manifestations of the phenomenon in the world.

For various reasons, people who have similar life experiences tend to seek each other out, or at least they are often

How many is enough?

aware of others who have similar experiences. You might try to think of some reasons why people tend to be aware of others who have had similar experiences. Why for example, are hearing-disabled people usually able to refer you to other hearing-disabled people? More often than not, when we find an appropriate case, that person is able to lead us to others. This process is called 'snowballing', referring to the way in which a rolling snowball gets larger and larger as it rolls down a hill. So, for instance, if I am interested in studying the use of a particular illicit drug, and I manage to find one person who is involved, the contact may lead to a whole network of users, dealers, law enforcement officers, and so on. The same may be said for many domains of human experience. Word of mouth, or what may be called 'the friend-of-a-friend approach', is often very successful. If you let it be known that you are looking for a particular kind of respondent, you may find that in no time at all you are in a position to choose between potential respondents.

However, people are sometimes not in contact with others who have had similar experiences. In such instances, one sometimes gets the response 'Oh, I thought I was the only one!' You might try to imagine what conditions are likely to lead to the isolation of people from others who share similar experiences, such that contact with one will not usually lead to snowballing contact with others. There are a number of routes that the researcher might follow in such circumstances and in other circumstances where participants are difficult to trace.

It is not uncommon for researchers to use community notice boards, the press, specialist and popular magazines, and newsletters to gather together a sample of respondents. An example might be the use of letters in popular magazines to find participants for a study of near-death experiences. In this way you are likely to receive a range of responses from which you might select a few who fulfil your selection criteria. Another way of making contact with potential participants is through support or advocacy groups who represent people who have particular kinds of life experience. Such groups are often willing to put the researcher in touch with potential participants.

Another very fruitful channel to follow is the internet. The internet enables people to rally together across distance and to form interest groups in an unprecedented way. Choose the field – open adoption (where the adoptee has ongoing contact with the biological parents), sexual deviations, specific medical conditions such as tinnitus (ringing in the ears), you name it – and there are sure to be related internet sites, weblogs, and discussion forums. Not only does one often find sites that summarise the key arguments and issues in the area and answer frequently asked questions, but individuals who have had particular experiences of, for example, a debilitating medical condition often publish their personal experiences via the internet. This is of great help to the qualitative researcher in planning a study. But, if we are studying something more local and context specific, we will need to use other means, and find access to participants through local channels of communication. Also, the internet may attract specific types of people, and may not be a mode of communication available to the kind of respondent we wish to trace.

Having identified potential respondents or sites of study, the next step is physically making contact with participants and gaining their cooperation. In making contact, it is important to set up a process whereby you are able first to evaluate whether the potential respondent is really suitable or not before you set up an expectation that you are going to include them in the study. Sometimes researchers will ask the respondent to write a short account in response to a particular question, such as 'Please describe in a page an experience you may have had of not having your feelings of ill-health accepted as legitimate by others'. Based on this response, the researcher can predict whether the respondent is likely to be able to provide further illuminating material, and thus whether the person is worth interviewing.

The politics of consent

In section 1 of this book we included a chapter on the ethics of research, which dealt, among other issues, with the question of informed consent. Because this is such an important issue, we'll briefly return to it here.

For more on the practicalities and politics of gaining entry to a research setting, have a look at the section further on in this chapter on 'participant observation' and at Nolwazi Gasa's box on 'community entry for research' in chapter 21 (see Gasa, 1998).

Having found potential research participants, one then has to negotiate consent. It often happens that consent is negotiated with a gatekeeper, and this is regarded by the gatekeeper as sufficient. For example, the gatekeeper (a school principal) sets up the meeting between the researcher and a class of students, and they have little choice but to attend. In one instance, however, an employer set up a meeting between a researcher and his workforce, and assured the researcher: 'Don't worry, they will be there!' This is not good enough. One has to establish **informed consent** with the participants themselves.

Besides the matter of informed consent, problems often arise when researchers are introduced into a research context by a gatekeeper, and the participants associate the researcher with the vested interests of the gatekeeper. So, for instance, if a school principal introduces a group of pupils to the researcher, the pupils will associate the researcher with the principal, and their mode of engagement with the researcher will have this backdrop. You can imagine some of the consequences of this.

In addition to 'micropolitics' of this kind, one also often encounters political issues of a larger scale in research contexts. In South Africa, where there is hardly an area of social life that has not been a site of debate and contestation, this is the rule rather than the exception. Establishing trust requires a keen political sensibility and an understanding of the way in which power relationships are structured in the context, so that one does not, for example, appoint a research assistant who is known to have an interest in the research having a particular outcome. It is advisable to conduct an informal 'scoping' of the context, whereby one gets a sense of the major stakeholders, the main interest groups with respect to the issue at hand, the likely obstacles to the research, and the best way to 'market' the research. It is also useful if an 'authority' acceptable to respondents has commissioned the research and that the parameters, objectives, and methods of the research are agreed at the start.

Box 13.3

Respondent characteristics

Ideal respondent characteristics differ according to the purposes of the study. If the study is to describe personal experiences of a phenomenon, the following are important:

- personal experience of what is being researched,
- good communicative skills (ability to describe experience in detail),
- openness and undefensiveness, and
- interest in participating, as well as the perception that it may, in some way, be of value to participate.

However, if one is concerned with understanding how a phenomenon is socially constructed, one does not necessarily have to find people who have a rich personal history of the phenomenon. The reality of HIV infection, for example, is not only constructed by, and through, people who have direct personal experience and knowledge of HIV infection. Indeed, anyone who is HIV positive will tell you that their reality is very much constructed by people who are ignorant of the facts and have little experience of contact with HIV-infected persons. Furthermore, these people may have thought very little about the issue, may have an inability to describe their experience in great detail, may be closed and defensive, and may be reluctant to talk. The themes that can be extricated from their defensiveness, prejudice, and lack of engagement with the subject might be just what the researcher needs to get hold of.

Researching sensitive topics

Informed consent is an ethical requirement for all research studies. However, sometimes the topic of the research is such that it requires a special sort of ethical caution, because in some way the material being covered is of interest to outside parties and its disclosure may be threatening to the participants concerned.

Box 13.4

Power and dialogue in participatory research

Habermas's (1984) 'theory of communicative action' outlines the 'speech conditions' that are likely to lead to open dialogue. These conditions refer to communication contexts where there is no domination of the dialogue by one of the participants in the dialogue, or by one of the perspectives represented. Often, it seems that people have equal opportunities to participate in a joint research process, but there are deep structural reasons why their respective capacities for engagement are in fact not equal. Such reasons may include greater legitimacy in the context enjoyed by certain ways of speaking. So, language which seems more educated, more ordered, or more in keeping with professional, academic, and scientific standards may overshadow other ways of speaking that do not enjoy the same kind of influence. This means that certain voices remain marginalised unless these people get someone to speak for them. These problems are particularly acute when one is researching intersubjective experience; that is, experience shared by a group. This typically results in the over-weighting of certain influential people's experiences and disregarding the experiences of those who are marginal with respect to access to leadership, decision-making capacity, and general social dominance. Schrijvers (1991), in an article entitled 'Dialectics of a dialogical ideal', is somewhat pessimistic about the possibility of conducting research in contexts where power is strongly contested or where strong forces of domination prevail. She suggests that dialogical forms of communication can be established most easily if there are only small power differentials in the research situation, a condition she describes as 'studying sideways' as opposed to 'studying down' or 'studying up'.

Research may pose not only a personal risk for participants, but also a 'contextual' risk. For example, in a high-school context, openness about drug use on the part of respondents is likely to lead to a clampdown on drug use in the school. Where the research report gives details of the way that students obtain drugs, when and where they use them, and so on, disclosure of the research results is likely to have a significant impact on the situation being researched in a way that is not necessarily invited by those who agree to participate. Whatever we may think of drug use, it is unethical to ask participants to participate without fully informing them of what will be done with the results of the study and giving them an opportunity to consider possible ramifications. All illicit activities are similarly classed, especially when there are forces of social control strongly pitted against the activity.

Sensitive research also includes research into issues where there are strong social alignments and tensions, such as relationships between the staff of a school and the principal. In a piece of evaluation research conducted on an Aids education programme (Kelly, 1996), it was found that communication between principal and teachers in a particular school was problematic and seemed to have had an impact on the reception of the programme. The final report dealt with the issue at a general level. This was easy to do because the evaluation was done across three different schools, so there were no direct references to the particular actors involved. However, a co-researcher naively provided a teacher at the school mentioned above with an interim document drawn up for the researchers' use only, in which specific findings about that school's communication problems were detailed in no uncertain terms. All hell broke loose when this was disseminated, and the relationship with the school was severely compromised.

Not only in writing reports, but also in the process of asking questions, researchers can easily shift a situation from a state of uneasy calm to one of conflagration. In Participatory Action Research (see chapter 19), the researcher's presence is designed to lead to social action, but when one merely wants to assess a situation and the assessment leads to a change in the situation (an outcome known as 'reflexivity'), then one is in ethically problematic territory.

We need to be especially cautious in areas of deep personal experience. Although we may have established an agreement that the interview is going to be on a personal topic, it may happen, and often does, that the interview takes on a life of its own, and becomes almost like a psychotherapy session where the respondent discloses thoughts and feelings that she or he may not have previously admitted to having, even to her- or himself. In such circumstances, the interviewer may feel that the exercise has been extremely successful, but the interviewee may walk away with a bad feeling, perhaps that they had been intruded upon, or had something taken away from them. The interviewer needs to ensure, at all times, that the interviewee is comfortable with the level of exploration and discussion. In researching open adoption (where the child has an

Photo: Rodney Barnett

What is considered normal, desirable behaviour by some may be severely censured by others, or even illegal, so be careful to respect your research participants' rights to confidentiality.

ongoing relationship with one or both of the biological parents as well as the adoptive parents), Euvrard (1996) had to feel her way forward. She wanted to ask potentially sensitive questions such as 'I wonder if you ever feel a little bit jealous of the relationship between the biological mother and your adopted child, because of her biological link to the child?' But she had to avoid forcing the respondent (the adoptive mother) to directly address issues that she may have been avoiding by way of coping with the social and psychological pressures around open adoption. As it happens, such issues were not taboo for the mother, but the point is that the interviewer could not have known this beforehand and had to approach with care. In such circumstances, we need to back off when we realise that we have transgressed the bounds of comfort. Another approach is to preface sensitive questions as follows: 'I am going to ask you a question which you don't have to answer if you don't want to, if it makes you uncomfortable. If you don't want to answer, please say so and I will move on. Here is the question: ...'

When your research interviews start feeling like a counselling session, you know you're in sensitive territory.

Box 13.5

You know you are researching a sensitive topic when

- you have to negotiate with numerous gatekeepers in making contact with the participants in the study,
- participants want to know who you work for,
- participants want to know what is going to be done with the results and what motivates the study,
- the media take an interest in your study,
- institutions of social regulation (e.g., the police, the church) take, or might take, an interest in the results of your study,
- you are researching an area which is not often spoken about in its context,
- you are researching the following: children, confidential relationships, sexuality and other deeply personal experiences, illicit activities, psychiatric institutions, or prisons.

Possibly the best approach is to prepare your respondents beforehand for the types of question you are going to ask them. Moeketsi (1998) let his respondents know from the outset that he would be asking them to talk about the intimate details of how they actually negotiate condom use in their sexual lives, and this seems to have led to a favourable degree of directness on the part of respondents, who knew from the start what they were in for.

Data-gathering techniques in qualitative research

Having considered some of the general principles of how to gain access to and sample qualitative research material, we now turn to some of the practicalities of actual qualitative data collection. Below we shall consider how to conduct qualitative research interviews with individuals and with groups, how to engage in observation (including participant observation), and how to collect documentary material.

Interviewing

Conducting an interview is a more natural form of interacting with people than making them fill out a questionnaire, do a test, or perform some experimental task, and therefore it fits well with the interpretive approach to research. It gives us an opportunity to get to know people quite intimately, so that we can really understand how they think and feel. At one level, interviews are simply conversations, similar to the hundreds of short and long conversations we have all the time, but at the same time they are also highly skilled performances.

Interviews are skilled performances.

Interviewing is probably also the most commonly used source of data for constructionist research, and the various techniques and principles described below apply equally to interpretive and constructionist research. The difference lies in the way that the interview (or any other similar linguistic event) is seen. Interpretive approaches see it as a means to an end (namely, to try to find out how people really feel about or experience particular things), and will therefore try to create an environment of openness and trust within which the interviewee is able to express herself or himself authentically. Constructionist approaches see the interview as an arena within which particular linguistic patterns (such as typical phrases, metaphors, arguments, or stories) can come to the fore. Constructionist researchers are also sceptical of the idea that an interviewer, however skilful, can ever play a purely facilitative role in allowing the interviewee to give expression to her or his feelings and experiences. Instead, whatever meanings are created in the interview are treated as co-constructed between the interviewer and interviewee. These meanings are, moreover, not only constructed by the two people involved in the interview but are products of a larger social system for which these individuals act as relays.

Planning for the interview

Before you get started, you need to ask yourself what kind of interview you need to be conducting. Just as there are many different kinds of everyday conversation, from a short informal chat to a long political argument, there are many kinds of interview. A useful way of thinking about this is in terms of how structured the interview should be. If all you need from somebody is some straightforward information, a very structured interview – essentially just a list of standard questions – would do fine. This kind of interview is really more like a questionnaire used in quantitative research projects. On the other hand, if you want people to talk to you in some depth about their feelings or experiences, you will do better to plan for an unstructured interview. In the latter case, at least have a sense of what kinds of feeling and experience you want to find out about, and maybe jot down some questions in advance. The most popular kinds of interview are semistructured interviews, where you develop an 'interview schedule' (or list of key topics and perhaps subtopics) in advance. Whatever type of interview you choose, be sure to pilot it a couple of times to ensure that you are asking useful questions and asking them in the right way.

Just as there are many types of conversation, there are many different kinds of interview.

Setting up the interview

Ensure that you are not going to be unduly disturbed in the interview context (an adequate degree of privacy), and, if you are recording, ensure that the sound environment is not going to drown out your recordings. Ensure that the interviewee has planned to put aside the required amount of time so that she or he is able to give the interview undivided attention.

The ins and outs of recording

Most people don't mind if you tape-record or video an interview, but be sure to get their consent first. The advantages of recording are obvious: It allows you to keep a full record of the interview without having to be distracted by detailed note-keeping. It also shows the interviewee that you take what they say seriously. On the negative side, it could detract from the intimacy of the encounter, with both interviewee and interviewer in part performing for the camera or tape recorder rather than really talking to each other. If you decide to record, don't feel that you have to go out and buy an expensive tape recorder – rather spend money on getting a good microphone. Placing the tape recorder on a soft surface (such as a cushion) can also help to improve the sound quality of the recording. Ensure that your recording equipment works and that you know exactly how to use it. Know whether you are going to be able to plug it in, if you don't have batteries. Take along some extra blank tapes – sometimes interviews go on longer than you expect.

Starting the interview

It can be a good idea to start with a summary of what the interview is about – but make this very short. You could follow this with a non-threatening open-ended question that gets the interviewee talking and helps to put them at ease. Remember that an interview is a process of getting to know one another better. At the start of the interview, you and the interviewee may not know each other at all well and still need to establish (or re-establish) trust, so do not rush in with difficult or sensitive questions right at the start.

The interview itself

Even though you may be recording the interview, it is a good idea to scribble down questions or thoughts that occur to you while the interviewee is speaking. Know your interview schedule sufficiently well not to have to refer continually to the interview format and thus interrupt the contact and flow that are characteristic of a good interview. Keep reminding yourself why you are doing the interview, for example, that you are interviewing the person because you want to learn more about the way that people experience sexual fantasy (Evans, 1998), spouse abuse (Hay, 1998), or soap-opera viewing (Moodley, 1998). Draw the interviewee into becoming a co-enquirer rather than a research subject (you know you are blowing it when the respondent has glassy eyes and a bored expression). In short, have a conversation, not a question and answer session. Seidman (1991) says that, as an interviewer, one should do the following:

Be aware of your own and the interviewee's 'body language' – not just what the two of you are saying verbally.

- listen more, talk less,
- follow up on what the participant says,
- ask questions when you do not understand,
- ask to hear more about a subject,
- explore, don't probe,
- avoid leading questions,
- ask open-ended questions which do not presume an answer,
- follow up and do not interrupt,
- keep participants focused and ask for concrete details,
- ask participants to rephrase or reconstruct,
- do not reinforce the participant's response, and
- tolerate silence and allow the interviewee to be thoughtful.

It is also a good idea to keep 'process notes' during an interview – in other words, quickly jotting down things that happen that may not be obvious from listening to the tape recorder. Unfortunately, however, while these words of experience are valuable as guidelines, what you really need is interviewing practice. Exercise 1 at the end of this chapter will give you some experience of this and will alert you to some of the difficulties involved in interviewing.

Interviewees have ways of letting you know that you're not getting through to them.

Ending the interview

Interviews typically last from 20 minutes to an hour and a half – people find it difficult to concentrate much beyond that! Do not be driven by time limits, but ensure that you do not get caught up in details that are extraneous to the study so that you run out of time for the important questions. Ask the person towards the end of the interview if there is anything more that they have to say. Be aware of what the person says after the recorder is switched off – sometimes the most interesting understandings only emerge then. If you will be conducting further interviews with the same person, make arrangements for the next interview. Store the tape recording in a safe place. Stories abound of people having their research tapes stolen or damaged. It is also a good idea to make notes about the interview as soon as possible after it is over. These are your 'process notes'. Write down anything that you think might not be obvious from the recording, such as how you were feeling at the time, interesting things that were discussed while the recorder was switched off, ideas that occurred to you in the course of the interview, and additional questions you would have liked to ask but did not get round to. If you do not do this soon after the interview, it is very likely that you will forget most of it.

Sometimes you will 'click' with an interviewee and get on brilliantly; at other times the interaction will feel forced and stilted. Concentrate on getting better at it rather than worrying whether a particular interview was a complete success.

Box 13.6

Common questioning errors

Too many questions. Interviewees will often answer questions before we ask them if we allow the interview to be more like a conversation. We can create a less defensive and more open attitude by prompting people to 'say more' or by leading them into discussing an issue without asking questions. The use of 'minimal encouragers', such as nodding your head and using expressions like 'uh-huh', reassures the interviewee that you are listening and encourages them to keep talking. The interviewee should be a co-enquirer rather than an answerer of questions.

Closed questions. 'Were you scared when it happened?' is a closed question which can be answered with a simple 'yes' or 'no'. Questions like this tend to lead to a question–answer format, with little contribution from the participant. We might say 'I wonder if it made you feel scared ...', which is more likely to lead to an open-ended exploratory discussion. Ideally, we invite interviewees to tell extended stories about their experiences.

Leading questions. Leading questions put pressure on the interviewee to answer in a specific way. The less directive and leading the question, the more likely the person is to explore an experience from her or his own point of view.

Excessively probing questions. Probing questions should only be asked when there is an indication that the person has become comfortable with the interview situation and is not likely to be threatened by the question. Otherwise, the person feels intruded upon, and this diminishes the likelihood that she or he will be willing to enter into a deeper exploration of the issues.

Poorly timed questions. Questions relating to more personal or intimate experiences, or questions that might be threatening, need to be asked in the context of ongoing exploration of an issue rather than be unexpected – they should flow naturally out of the conversation.

'Why' questions. We should not assume that people are able to account for 'why' they did or felt or thought something. Whereas we can usually describe our own experiences accurately, our motivations are not always evident to ourselves. Speculation about motivations can lead an interview into ungrounded abstraction. The question 'Why did you decide at that point to join the Movement?' should rather be phrased 'Tell me about what was going on in your thoughts at the time you decided to join the Movement'. The response to the latter question will give the researcher the answer to the 'why' question and will avoid the possibility of the interview getting lost in 'after the fact' speculation about motives.

Transcribing the interview

It is easier to refer back and forth to different parts of an interview if we have it on paper in front of us than it is to find our way around an audio cassette. A practical tip is to use a tape recorder with a foot pedal, which frees up your hands to type or write, but be warned that it can take six or more hours to transcribe a one-hour interview. Transcription is best done directly onto a word processor to facilitate the moving around of data and searching for particular words later on. It is usually important to transcribe everything rather than try to decide which data are relevant and which not. The meaning of what is being said in an interview can usually be interpreted only in the context of the sentences which surround it and the conversation as a whole, so beware of the temptation to skip over 'filler' chat that may seem to be of little value. Make 'analytical notes' to yourself if any good ideas about interpretation come to mind while transcribing. You should then check the reliability of the transcription by reading it through while listening to the recording. This is not simply a technical exercise. By doing this you will get an increasingly clear image of the interview as a whole. At the same time, it is of value to annotate the text with notes on nonlinguistic expressions such as sighs, laughs, and silences, which you may have missed in the transcription, and to add information from your 'process notes'.

You could consider returning transcriptions of interviews to interviewees to have them confirm whether you reliably recorded their views.

Box 13.7

Interview ideas

Specific examples. Ask interviewees to tell you about specific experiences when they say things in general terms such as 'I get so angry with my father when he throws the money away on gambling'. As an interviewer, one might respond by saying: 'Tell me about a time when that actually happened?' Be curious about the details and context of the story, and ensure that you can picture exactly what happened. Thus, we might ask 'Where exactly were you standing in the room?' or 'What had you been doing before it happened?'

Role play. Invite participants to role-play, for example, 'If I were your boss, I wonder what you would like to say to me?' After they have responded, continue as if you were the boss and thus enter into an imaginary conversation between the interviewee and the boss (yourself). This kind of request is going to tell you a lot more about the way that the person experiences the boss than 'Tell me about your feelings towards your boss'.

Self-disclosure. Sometimes we help people feel comfortable in talking about what they have experienced by sharing our own experiences. The interview is obviously about them, and must focus on their experience, but it can get them going to talk about oneself a little, provided one does not assume a greater degree of intimacy than actually exists between oneself and the interviewee.

There are a number of conventions for indicating interruptions, speakers talking at the same time, pauses, raised voices, and so on. A useful summary of such symbols is contained in the appendix of Potter and Wetherell (1987), but, unless one is doing a close conversational analysis (a rather specialised method), bracketed notes will suffice.

Different kinds of interview

Apart from the degree to which they are structured or not, interviews can also vary in terms of several other dimensions, so none of the guidelines given here is cast in stone. For example, phenomenologically oriented researchers sometimes prefer a single open-ended question right at the start of an interview (such as 'Please tell me about your experience when your house was broken into'), providing very little further structuring during the rest of the interview. If you want to find out about something quite specific and superficial (such as how people feel about a particular brand of washing powder), you may want to conduct short, structured interviews with a fairly large number of people. If you want to know about something more weighty, such as trying to understand why people sometimes find it difficult to withdraw from situations of abuse, you could opt for a series of in-depth interviews with a single person, in which trust is established over an extended period.

Not just words

Box 13.8

Here is a sample interview transcript. Think about what the bracketed insertions tell us of the respondent's relation to the experience, which would have been lost had only the words been transcribed. Imagine, from the sample, why it is helpful to transcribe the interview while it is still fresh in your mind and you can still remember unclear expressions and contextual details.

Interviewer. Tell me more about what you thought when you first heard about the accident.

Respondent (sighs). Shew, I dunno. It was just like, kinda (10 sec. silence) ... I felt like numb. Sort of blank. I just, you know, couldn't believe it, it couldn't be true. It was like everything just went dead, (tears in eyes, 10 sec. silence). I'm sorry.

Interviewer. It's OK. Would you like to leave it alone?

Respondent. No it's OK, I'm used to it. (little laugh)

Interviewer. Just like totally shocked?

Respondent (little laugh), (five-second silence). Ja, it took a few days to sink in; still hasn't. Can I get some water. (Leaves room for three minutes and returns) That's better, OK go on.

Interviewer. Right, we were talking about when you first heard. Is there anything else that you might add to give me an idea of what it was like for you?

Respondent. I dunno really ...

Interviewing groups

Whereas, in interviewing an individual, we develop an understanding of subjective experience, when we work with groups we can gain access to intersubjective experience. Intersubjective experience is experience shared by a community of people. In accessing **intersubjective** experience through group interviewing, we also gain access to understanding differences between people whom we might previously have thought of as an homogeneous group – in other words, the ways in which they do not share a common base of experience. In working with groups, one should be constantly aware of commonality and difference, looking for the boundaries of commonality and the cultural dimensions of apparent individuality.

Focus group is a general term given to a research interview conducted with a group. A focus group is typically a group of people who share a similar type of experience, but a group that is not 'naturally' constituted as an existing social group. Thus, for example, a focus group could consist of people who are affected by a proposed change in pension payout points, but who do not know each other in the normal course of their lives.

The researcher would usually identify a set of criteria for selecting respondents and then, usually by an informal 'scoping' process (getting to know the situation by speaking to people involved and spending time there), and in liaison with people knowledgeable about the context, identify participants fitting the criteria. Focus groups are often selected so as to reflect a heterogeneous cross-section of interests and attitudes within the parameters of whatever main criterion qualifies them for membership. For example, you might decide to use only pensioners who use a particular payout point as your main selection criterion, and then sample for heterogeneity within that group by selecting male and female pensioners, younger and older pensioners, and so on. Thus, sampling is often purposive in that one is looking for particular types of participant, according to what one already knows about the field, so as to include a range of perspectives. The researcher will then go about asking targeted individuals to participate, if necessary providing some kind of incentive. As often as not, people are motivated to participate because the issues at hand are important to them, but it is sometimes necessary to pay people to participate, or to provide refreshments to show them that their participation is appreciated, and thus further build on whatever motivation might have led them to agree to participate in the first place. People should also be told what is going to be required of them, both in terms of the content and process of the group, and the amount of time they are being asked to set aside. Although this can differ, one should bear in mind that most people cannot concentrate for more than about one and a half hours. Most focus groups are composed of between 6 and 12 people. There are four basic components to a focus group: procedure, interaction, content, and recording.

Procedure

This refers to the 'rules of play' that give structure to and set the limits on the group process. These are usually established by together discussing group 'norms' or expectations, which might include (depending on the sensitivity of the topic) the commitment to not talking about what was said in the group afterwards to others (confidentiality), no smoking, respect for the views of others, giving everyone a chance to speak, and so on.

Interaction

The facilitator needs to be aware of the personal and interpersonal dynamics at work within the group. This includes the marginalisation of certain people, the avoidance of particular topics, and the concentration span and comfort level of the group from beginning to end. The facilitator needs to devise ways of getting people to introduce themselves, and needs to introduce the topic in a way that engenders active, lively participation. It is also important to plan beforehand how one will draw the group to a conclusion.

When we work with groups we can gain access to intersubjective experience.

Photo: Centre for Peace Action

The *Community Workers' Handbook* (Hope & Timmel, 1984), based on the work of Paulo Freire, is packed with 'ice-breaking exercises' (for getting a group to relax and introduce themselves), group games for exploration of relational dynamics, and guidelines for facilitators of group research processes. Augusto Boal's (1992) *Games for Actors and Non-Actors* is also a rich source of exercises for groups that have met for the purpose of exploring and describing the realities structuring their everyday experience. There are many other resources on this, and a search on the internet for 'icebreaker games' will yield many results.

Group facilitation is an art. One of the best ways of learning about it is by watching and emulating an experienced facilitator.

Content

This refers to what is spoken about or done, and usually follows a semi-structured interview format. It gives the group an opportunity to talk about what is most pressing for them by allowing a degree of meandering discussion. The content may include structured group exercises like role playing and using 'codes' (see chapter 19 on Participatory Action Research). The facilitator constantly listens for commonalities and differences of opinion, and gets the group to reflect on the extent to which their understanding or experience is homogeneous or diverse. Good facilitation involves interpretation and thematising to deepen reflection on experiences, and the facilitator should frequently summarise with statements such as: 'Now let me see if I have got that right. It sounds like you are saying that ...'

Good facilitation works in a tensional relationship between 'zooming in' or 'focusing', to concentrate the group on an issue of interest to the researcher, and 'pulling back' to look at what issues are most compelling to the group. In this sense, it may also be said that facilitation requires a balance between initiating (leading) and listening.

Box 13.9

Attending to the nonverbal environment

More often than not, qualitative researchers find themselves talking to people rather than observing them. Yet, there are other domains of meaning besides that which is accessed through listening to words, and they employ other senses. We see people, and through seeing we can understand the body's movements and the ways that bodies interact in the social environment. We feel within our own bodies, and this gives us a sense of what is happening in the world. So, too, does smell tell us about the world (think of the wine taster's 'nose'), and there are disciplines of enquiry that employ the sense of taste (think of the interpretive skills of the chef and the herbalist).

Speaking is more than the production of words. Bodies speak, and they can be seen to speak through the complex gestural language which is part of speaking. Yet we seldom come across interview transcripts that are accompanied by systematic notes on gesture. It might be argued that, by limiting ourselves to the study of verbal descriptions of experiences, we limit ourselves to understanding that which has already been filtered through the conscious cognition of a person. We well know that we can say one thing and feel another. Indeed, words can be most deceptive, and often people do not account openly and honestly for their spontaneous feelings and thoughts. The reasons why people might be motivated to give deceptive accounts of aspects of their experience are legion, and range from conscious intentions to make a positive impression on the researcher to being unconsciously inclined to shield themselves from the reality of their own emotion or confusion. For example, a person suffering from a serious illness might be motivated to avoid recognising her or his own fear of dying, and would avoid being aware of and describing vulnerable feelings.

It is useful to provide participants with a stimulus to respond to as a way of initiating discussion. To initiate discussion about sexual harassment in the academic environment, one might ask a focus group the following: 'What do you think a female student should do when her tutor privately slips her a note saying that she is beautiful and maybe it would be a good idea for them to get together for an "extra lesson" sometime?' The group could then be assisted to explore possible responses on the part of the student. This process is likely to provide a much richer understanding of prevailing discourses around sexual harassment than abstract questions such as 'What do you think about the issue of sexual harassment in the tutoring system?'

Recording

Focus groups are usually recorded by note-taking. While audio and video recording are sometimes used, this can be problematic because background noise often makes recordings incomprehensible. It is helpful to work with a co-researcher, with one researcher doing the main facilitation and the other recording the proceedings. The researcher may find that it works better for the recorder to sit outside the main circle, so that people are not constantly made aware of the writing activity which detracts from the spontaneity of the discussion. A useful tip is to mentally number the participants and try to record the main points made by participants in the order that they are made. Finally, it is very important to set aside a 'debriefing' time immediately after the focus group, for the researchers to go through the notes between themselves to try to re-create the session while it is still fresh in their minds. By doing this, especially if one has recorded the session, it is usually possible to reconstruct the content and process of the session in a fairly reliable way. Video recordings are valuable because they provide information about the way in which people said things, which often says as much as the content of their words.

Observing experience

Students of psychology would probably have come across studies in the field of social psychology that employed the visual sense as a way of understanding. The well-known studies on bystander apathy and queuing behaviour are examples. Sociologists have also been interested in the study of the body, and this has been popularised through the work of Desmond Morris (1985; 1992), whose books *Manwatching* and *Bodywatching* provide fascinating sociological insights into the meaning of gestures and bodily interactions. Anthropology students would have encountered studies of dance, ritual, adornment, and gait from a cultural perspective. 'Kinesics' (the study of body movements), 'proxemics' (the study of the use of space when people interact), and various approaches to the study of 'body language' have also emerged as disciplines for the study of social life through the body. Numerous conventions have been developed for documenting human movements so that they may be represented in two-dimensional format on paper.

Here we will first discuss some of the general principles of observation, followed by an outline of the phases in a typical participant observation study. While talking to people is a good, direct way of getting to know about their feelings and experiences, it usually comes 'after the fact' in the sense of relying on the interviewee's recollection of an experience. Observation, on the other hand, takes place while things are actually happening, and thus gets you even

Photo: Neil Lightfoot

closer to the action. Because the interpretive approach emphasises studying pheno-mena in a naturalistic way, observation most often takes the form of participant observation, where you as researcher become fully involved in the setting being studied. Participant observation is less frequently used by constructionist researchers, but the tech-niques and principles described below can be applied to constructionist research projects, provided a

By observing experience, we reflexively become a part of the experience.

Box 13.10

Audience watching

A study of audience response to a play provides some insight into the value of observation as a method. This piece of research was conceived as part of a programme evaluation of a comprehensive HIV/Aids intervention in Eastern Cape high schools (Kelly, 1996). The play was a piece of educational theatre presented to a standing audience. Focus groups and interviews conducted after the play had led to some understanding of the meaning of the play to the audience. However, when videotapes of the audience watching the play were studied, a whole new world of understanding opened up to the researcher.

Observation revealed that engagement with the play did not only take place between play and audience, but also involved each spectator in an ongoing interaction with other members of the audience and especially those in their immediate surroundings (usually friends). The focus groups and interviews had revealed nothing of this experience, and had mainly involved reflections on the play (e.g., 'I thought it was unfair that Condom Girl was treated like that').

Let us look at some of what was revealed through observing, using the example of audience laughter. Through observation, laughter was shown up as a process whereby the audience communicated with each other about events in the play. The role of this form of communication in the process of engagement with the play was seen by the researcher as crucial to answering research questions relating to the impact of the play. Laughter would typically start at points in the audience (not always the same points, and this seemed to differ according to the issue at stake in the play) and then spread like wildfire, until it reached a crescendo encompassing almost the entire more sceptical distance is maintained with regard to what is seen as 'authentic' and who is considered to be the originator of meaning.

One of the hallmarks of observation is the need for non-intrusiveness (Adler & Adler, 1994). In general, systematic observation conducted in the public domain is highly reflexive. People being observed usually start behaving very differently. So systematic observation is often conducted from hidden vantage points. For example, if you were to study driving behaviour and position yourself with a camera and notebook at a stop-street, it is highly unlikely that drivers would behave 'naturalistically'. In all likelihood, they would dutifully stop at stop signs that they would otherwise ignore. Thus, in doing such research we often need to 'hide ourselves'. There are obvious ethical implications in doing this, which are well addressed by Adler and Adler (1994).

It is useful, following Spradley (1980), to distinguish between descriptive observations, focused observations, and selective

audience. Then, almost by consensus and on cue, it subsided like a retreating wave. Closer observation of sectors of the audience revealed a process whereby groups of friends were nonverbally communicating with each other about their perceptions of the play. Among other responses, this involved touching, back-slapping, finger-pointing, and feigned aggression. In this way, they commented on and moderated each other's responses within their social groups. Such responses also appeared to be used as ways of negotiating new responses to the funny yet emotionally unsettling material presented in the play (including shame, embarrassment, horror, gender inequality, sexual harassment, interpersonal humiliation, and abuse).

Much more could be said about the conclusions that could be drawn from these and similar observations about the impact of the play. The point of the example is to illustrate that a whole new world of meaning and understanding was opened up when the researcher observed, rather than simply interviewed. Through observation, it was possible to understand what the play meant to the audience in ways which participants themselves were not subjectively (inter-views) or intersub-jectively (focus groups) well positioned to describe.

Photo: Rodney Barnett

observations. **Descriptive observation** is where you only have general questions such as 'What is going on here?' It will usually lead to a descriptive account, where the observer merely describes in detail everything that she or he witnessed, usually in sequence (e.g., how people find their way around a library). This is an exploratory or scoping approach, usually done as a first step by way of generating ideas, before the researcher knows which more focused questions are the most useful ones to be asking. **Focused observation** involves asking more particular or well-honed questions about general events and looking out for particular kinds of interaction (e.g., help-seeking behaviour at the library's enquiry desk). **Selective observations** involve the selection of particular events that we have specific questions about (e.g., hesitation or reluctance in asking for help).

As with interviews, observation can be more or less structured. At the more structured end, one finds essentially positivist studies, for example, studies making use of standardised rating scales to record samples of children's classroom behaviour, or job applicants' behaviour in 'assessment centres'. Highly structured methods may include the following: the use of time samples (observing for two minutes every ten minutes as a sampling strategy), checklists for particular kinds of behaviour, and independent observers who observe different facets of what is going on (or independent observers noting the same thing as a reliability check).

However, the kinds of observational study conducted by interpretive researchers tend to be very much more naturalistic than this. A typical example is Schurink & Schurink's (1988) study of a gay club in Johannesburg, which entailed regular visits to the club and informal interaction with club members and management, rather than any kind of structured observation. Unstructured approaches to observation are impressionistic, in the sense of noting down what one sees as one sees it; they use continuous time sampling (the entire sequence of events), and they are naturalistic (interacting and then afterwards noting down what one has observed). Sometimes a pilot observation study will use a relatively unstructured approach in preparation for a more structured approach to be taken in the main study.

Many observational studies take the form of participant observation, often used by anthropologists to study other cultures. The practice of **ethnography** entails the study of cultures, and initially this typically meant the study of 'exotic' cultures – meaning cultures other than white European. Perhaps the most famous example is Margaret Mead's (1943) study which entailed spending many years living with Samoan villagers. Ethnography has since come to encompass a study of culture more generally, often the study of subcultures – e.g., geographic communities such as rural settlements, professional groups such as policemen or doctors, or marginalised groups such as drug users. We will use the word 'culture' to mean the particular ways of living together that such groups have developed, rather than just the kind of culture associated with ethnic differences among people.

In recording observations, one needs to make notes not only on what one is directly observing, but also on the peripheral context in which the observation occurs. The time of day, or storm clouds on the horizon, for example, might provide central clues in understanding crowd behaviour at the interpretation stage of the research. Details of participants such as age, dress, and so on may also be important, and one has to decide beforehand what kinds of data are likely to be useful and hence worth recording. If one is not using a checklist, it is important to think carefully about how one is going to record one's observations.

Box 13.11

Useful tips for recording observations

- 'Speak' your observations into a mini tape recorder rather than try to write and observe simultaneously.
- It is sometimes useful to draw a map of how people are positioned in the situation or a flow diagram of their movements.
- Use a video recorder (but it is important to realise that it makes you more conspicuous and forces you to be more selective in your observations than the 'roving eye' would be).
- Get ample practice using whatever recording system you decide on, before you set out to do your observations.

Some studies have used cameras to get people to record their own environments, but more often qualitative researchers will use the cameras themselves and introduce them in a way that does not create an undue disturbance of the naturalistic setting. For example, letting people experiment with the video camera and letting them see themselves played back usually helps to create a sense of ease.

Phases in participant observation

Because observational studies are often unstructured, it can be useful to think about the process as unfolding through a number of typical phases, which are outlined below.

Preparation

Participant observation can be a particularly time-consuming way of collecting data, and before embarking on such an enterprise you need to decide what the limits of your commitment are. To really immerse oneself in a culture one ideally needs to spend years living as a part of it, but this is not always practical or necessary. Ask yourself how much time you have available for the study and how much is needed. Then try to arrive at a compromise. One possibility is to engage in intermittent observation over a longer period. For example, when studying how passengers behave at an airport, you hardly need to live there, but could plan for a series of observations of several hours at a time, stretched out over a month or two.

Getting in

Once you know what you want to study, in what setting, and roughly how much time you can afford to spend on it, you have to find a way of gaining access to the setting. Some settings, such as taxi ranks, streets, shops, public meetings, music concerts, soccer matches, and the like, are relatively open and you can enter the setting and proceed with observation without any difficulty and without causing much or any disturbance. Other settings are more difficult to get into. For example, if you wish to conduct a participatory observational study of 'The Network', an elite group of black businesspeople and decision makers (Haffajee, 1998), you had better buy some smart clothes and find somebody who is a member of The Network to introduce you. In ethnographic research, the technical term for this person is your **sponsor** – that is, somebody who is accepted in the group or culture you want to study and who helps you to gain initial acceptance.

It is more difficult to gain entry to some cultures than to others.

Sometimes a sponsor is also a gatekeeper, and, if not, he or she is usually on good terms with some of the gatekeepers. **Gatekeepers** are people who have a say over who is let in and who is not. These are usually parties who have vested interests either in the issue at stake or in the wellbeing of the potential respondents. In medical settings, this is often the superintendent of a clinic or hospital, a senior medical specialist in charge of a ward, or a matron or nursing services manager, while at schools researchers usually have to contend with education authorities, principals, and senior teachers before gaining access to pupils. In the police service, it may be a station commander. In informal settlements, there are usually elected or self-appointed leaders whose permission for conducting a study needs to be obtained.

There is often a whole series of gatekeepers, and if you want to be sure that your study does not get sabotaged along the way it is a good idea to get on good terms with both senior and junior ones. In many settings there are informal as well as formal gatekeepers, and you need to persuade both kinds that your study is acceptable. For example, even though the minister of a church may have given you permission to do participant observation, you will not get anywhere if prominent and respected members of the congregation do not trust you.

Dealing with gatekeepers

Box 13.12

Gatekeepers have a habit of referring one to other authorities. In primary schools and many high schools, consent of parents is often deemed to be necessary. This can be very frustrating to a researcher when, for example, parents are difficult to contact. There are similar frustrations when working in medical settings. In such contexts, one has to strike a balance between practicality and obtaining the consent of all stakeholders in the research. If we are too rigorous about obtaining permission, we will eventually find recalcitrant gatekeepers who prevent us from starting the research, but, if we are not rigorous enough, we risk being turned back by gatekeepers once the research is already underway.

Considering that researchers need, in any case, to negotiate consent with the participants themselves, we should not get too caught up in obtaining permission from gatekeepers, and should follow a path of practical expedience. Experienced researchers learn to be wily. They know that the order of consultation is important. For example, in school settings, letters of authority or permission from education authorities usually help in getting principals to agree to the research being conducted. Or, when one is doing research in work settings, one has to be careful not to alienate either management or labour unions through the order in which one seeks permission. One has to find an appropriate forum in which to propose the research, and this forum should be one in which they are both represented.

Getting on

Once you are past the first hurdle, the difficult work begins of becoming part of the setting so that you can understand it 'from the inside out'. You will need a good cover story – that is, a plausible explanation of who you are and what you are doing there. Do not assume that you have to lie; in many settings (such as on the street, in nightclubs, or in public buildings), you do not have to go about explaining yourself. In other cases, it is best to be up-front about what you are doing (i.e., research), and people will soon get used to your presence or find ways of fitting you into the scene. Think, for example, of Jacques Pauw (1997), the journalist who exposed many of the sinister acts committed by the apartheid government's Civil Cooperation Bureau (CCB). Pauw did not lie about being a journalist, but he built up relationships with former CCB operatives over a long period and so they came to treat him as a legitimate part of their circle and to reveal the truth to him.

Your best bet is simply to act the role of the interested but not overly inquisitive researcher. Sometimes, however, it may be necessary to deceive people about who you are and what you are after, but do not even think about doing this without discussing the ethical implications with the ethics committee at your institution, and perhaps with the gatekeepers whom you encounter while gaining access to the situation you are researching. Also, do not lose sight of the roles assigned to you by society by virtue of your skin colour, accent, gender, and age. If you are a young white woman, it would be no use to pretend to be a member of The Network.

What to look for

As in an interview, it is important to keep thinking about what you are after in doing the study. Maybe you have quite specific questions (such as why people always complain about the Post Office), or maybe you want to describe more broadly the culture of a group of people (such as Kaizer Chiefs supporters). Remain focused on your research question, but be open to unexpected information. Never take anything for granted. Keep asking yourself questions about what is going on – who, what, when, where, why, how? Look for unusual things (e.g., a Chiefs supporter wearing a Pirates t-shirt), but also look for what seems unremarkable and obvious (e.g., people queuing in the Post Office). One useful technique is to 'funnel' the questions you are trying to answer: Start with general questions, and then start homing in on specific things that you would like to understand better. For example, Swartz (1989) was interested in discovering more about race and culture in psychiatry in quite a general way, but, in the course of participant observation at psychiatric ward rounds, came to focus on more specific issues such as the politics of English–Xhosa translation.

Observation is more than being a passive spectator – it entails actively seeking out answers to your questions.

Some participant observation studies incorporate long interviews, although more typically you are likely to get involved in short, informal discussions. Researchers not infrequently find that they rely quite heavily on a number of key informants. A key informant is somebody you get on with, who is part of and knows the culture you're studying, and who likes talking about it. Such people often operate as links between different cultures – even though they are fully part of a culture (e.g., they are part of a group of street vendors), they are also sufficiently able to stand outside that culture to explain to outsiders what is going on. Just as key informants are in an ambiguous position – half insider, half outsider – so too, you as a researcher will increasingly find yourself in the same position. If you are not careful, you could 'go native', a derogatory term from colonial times now sometimes jokingly used to refer to ethnographers who identify so closely with the culture they are studying that they lose all perspective. If you are studying a group of Zen Buddhists, the worst that may happen is that you will start meditating a lot and that your research report will read like an advertisement for Zen Buddhism rather than a proper analysis. If you are studying a group of drug addicts, however, the consequences could be worse. The opposite danger is to remain entirely aloof, in which case you will probably learn little new about the phenomenon you are studying, produce a trivial report, and entirely miss the point of doing participant observation.

Kinds of participant observation

Observational studies vary a lot in terms of how structured the observation is, whether deception is used or not, the degree of participation involved, and whether the study relies entirely on observation or is supplemented with other data sources such as formal interviews or documentary material. There are also different traditions with varying conventions regarding such practicalities as how to take notes and the use of single or multiple observers. After working through this chapter, you may want to study some of the many books on participant observation (see key readings at the end of the chapter), but the best way of learning is to try it out for yourself – with an experienced researcher, if possible.

There are two pitfalls that participant observers should avoid: getting too close to the participants (losing perspective), and staying too distant from the participants (losing empathy).

Keeping records

While it is relatively straightforward to record an interview, walking around with a tape recorder or camera can be perceived as very intrusive, and is rarely done in participant observation studies. It is therefore doubly important that you should make copious notes, often referred to as field notes. In some situations it is easy to take notes without attracting much attention at all – for instance, if you are conducting a study of what students do during lectures at your university. In other cases it will be very distracting, and should rather be done as soon as you get a moment of privacy. Do not put off doing this, though; the longer you delay, the less you will be able to remember the finer details of what happened.

Participant observation (where the researcher participates in the setting being studied) should be distinguished from participatory research (where people from the setting being studied become active participants in the research project). You can read more about participatory research in chapter 19.

Notes are essentially of two kinds. First, you will want to describe as fully as possible what people did and said. In the beginning, you will probably want to get everything that happens to you down on paper. Later on, you may become more selective, but try not to be too selective, as seemingly unimportant events could turn out to be very important. Try to get down as many verbatim quotes as possible; they can be very helpful in conveying the 'flavour' of a particular culture. If you are sure about the exact words somebody used, put them in double quotation marks; if you think you have got what somebody said basically right, but you are not so sure of the exact words, put them in single quotation marks.

Notes of the second kind that you should keep are concerned with your unfolding analysis. These are for recording ideas you may be developing about the phenomenon you are studying, for your reflections on theoretical, method, and ethical issues, and for recording points of uncertainty that you still need to clarify.

One way of keeping notes is to divide each page of a notebook into two columns: a wide one for descriptions and a narrower one for analytic comments. You could also have a column for recording your personal reactions to what you are describing. Some people prefer to keep descriptive and analytic data in separate notebooks, or to have a notebook for notes written in the heat of the moment (or soon after), and a diary for more carefully edited analysis and description. Whatever note-taking strategy you use, be sure to record basic information such as the date, time, and place, and a list of the people present, for every event described.

Documentary sources

'Among the multiple realities there is one that presents itself as the reality par excellence. This is the reality of everyday life [which] always appears as a zone of lucidity behind which there is a background of darkness.' (Berger & Luckmann, 1976, p. 35)

Documentary sources such as letters, newspaper articles, official documents, and books can be useful in all forms of qualitative research. Such materials are also particularly suitable for constructionist analysis, as they have an obviously 'constructed' nature and are a means by which ideas and discourses are circulated in our society. Interpretive analysis tends to treat such material as if it were of somewhat less worth than direct 'first-hand' experience, and it typically focuses on trying to reconstruct the author's motives and intentions by seeking to understand what the author really meant when she or he wrote the document. For constructionist analysis, by contrast, a document carries meaning independently of what its author's intentions were: It is simply a point of intersection for social meanings (or discourses) and is no more distant from what 'really happened' or what somebody 'really felt' than an interview.

In practical terms, using documentary sources is in some ways easier than doing interviews or participant observation. This is because one does not have to 'think on one's feet' as in an interview, nor engage in the tedious process of transcribing everything. The advent of the internet has made collecting documentary material even easier. Internet discussion groups of various sorts, as used for example by Thatcher and Feldman (1998) in their study of cybersex, are a rich source of already-transcribed material. However, documentary material is by no means always easy to come by, and some research projects, particularly those concerned with historical issues, require painstaking and time-consuming archival searches. South African examples include Swartz's (1995; 1996) work on the historical role of case histories and diagnosis in psychiatric hospitals, and Butchart's (1998) analysis of colonial constructions of black bodies, both of which required intensive searches through archival sources. If you plan on doing a study of this sort, we strongly recommend that you first consult texts dealing with methodological issues in historical research.

Some examples of material readily available from the internet are white papers, Bills and Acts of Parliament (www.info.gov.za/documents), press releases by local and international politicians, and back copies of newspapers.

Documentary material can be even more extensive than interview transcripts and field notes, and requires very careful management if you are not to become swamped by the sheer volume of material. You should make a point of recording the origin of each bit of material as soon as you collect it (e.g., title, date, and page number of the newspaper, the internet address, or the file number in the archive), as it is often very difficult to trace the source of a particular extract at a later stage. Working out a proper filing system, and sticking to it, is also a very good idea. You may want to have another look at section I of this book, as many of the techniques for dealing with published sources discussed there can equally well be applied to the management of documentary data sources.

Conclusion

In this chapter, we have considered qualitative data-gathering techniques. It should be apparent that there are no hard-and-fast rules in data gathering, and that many of the necessary skills, being so close to our everyday capacities for interacting with the world and others, are not easily learned. The ability to find and gather good quality data requires you to be alert and perceptive and to be able to 'think on your feet'. Astute researchers are able to talk and look, listen, and think. They are also able to combine openness and curiosity with an ability to distinguish what is significant from that which is superfluous. Becoming a good qualitative researcher also requires the development of one's interpersonal skills, especially the abilities to build and maintain rapport, to make others feel relaxed and unguarded, to be open and forthright, to tolerate ambiguity and contradiction, and not to be thrown by confusion and apparent chaos. Furthermore, the qualitative researcher is often in the position of being a facilitator, and the fruitfulness of the enquiry is a product of the skill of the researcher in engaging creatively with participants and contexts.

Exercises

1. In a tutorial context, you might pair off, work out a topic for an interview in pairs, and conduct an interview including the following stages:

    (a) Negotiate the terms of the interview, including agreement about what you are researching, what is going to be done with the findings, and other matters relating to informed consent.

    (b) Conduct a half-hour interview and end it in an appropriate way, asking the interviewee if there is anything further that she or he wants to say.

    (c) Reflect on the interview together and discuss the type of rapport established, the type of questioning and following-up, and the sense of whether the interviewee felt she or he was heard and understood by the interviewer.

    Ensure that your interview is based on description and exploration of the interviewee's own experience rather than simply reflecting their attitudes towards the experience. Ask the person for examples and assist them to go fully into the experience by asking fruitful and penetrating questions. Try also to provide a comfortable and relaxed interpersonal situation through which to explore the thoughts, feelings, and actions involved in the experience.

    Some suggested topics are

    - the experience of being a newcomer to a situation,
    - the experience of putting off important tasks (procrastination),

- the experience of being jealous of someone else's achievements.

You might choose your own topic, ensuring that it is a narrow enough topic to be adequately covered in the time you have available.

2. This exercise is suitable for a tutorial group. Imagine that you are a research team that has been asked by the general manager to investigate a particular factory where there is a substantially higher rate of absenteeism than the industry average. Your brief is to offer recommendations to reduce the level of absenteeism amongst factory floor workers. The factory has a trade union and an employee assistance programme. Assume that it is to be a qualitative project and, using the following questions, decide as a group how you would go about setting up the project. Consider the following:

   (a) what background information you would need to have before you proceed to plan a study.

   (b) possible ways of introducing the project to employees, and

   (c) possible sampling and data-gathering strategies.

   If you need to have further details before making decisions about some issues, make these up among yourselves (e.g., to make decisions about sampling you need to know what types of group make up the workforce).

3. This exercise is suitable for a tutorial group. Each group member is required to decide on a public context of study where social interaction can be studied and where observation would not reflexively alter the situation being observed. A taxi rank, a traffic light, the entrance to a shop, or a bank queue would be suitable. Group members are required to do no more than position themselves in the situation in such a way that they are not conspicuous, and simply observe what is going on. The point of this exercise is to explore the achievements and limits of the method of observation. Do not interact with people in the situation. Do this for about half an hour and then re-convene as a group. Briefly describe to each other the situations you observed and then choose an interesting one to discuss in greater depth. Address the following questions:

   (a) What could you tell about what was happening in the situation simply by observing? Did any themes or patterns emerge through your observations?

   (b) What could you only guess at because you did not have enough data?

   (c) How did you feel as an observer?

   (d) What additional material could have been gathered by talking to or otherwise interacting with others in the context?

Key readings

Denzin, N. K. (1989). *The research act*. Englewood Cliffs, New Jersey: Prentice Hall.

This is a comprehensive book on research methods for studying social interaction, including observation methods.

Hope, A., & Timmel, S. (1984). *Community workers' handbook (1, 2, 3)*. Zimbabwe: Mambo Press.

These three books, based on the work of Paulo Freire, are brimming with ideas about how to collect data in community settings, and how to run research groups. Here you will find 'ice-breaking' exercises (getting a group to relax and introduce themselves), exercises for developing listening skills, and group games for exploration of social realities and group dynamics.

Kvale, S. (1996). *Interviews: An introduction to qualitative research interviewing*. London: Sage.

This is a very useful resource book on interviewing as a research method. It covers all areas in a reader-friendly and thoughtful manner.

Pattern, M. Q. (1990). *Qualitative evaluation and research methods*. Newbury Park, California: Sage.

As well as being a good overview of the entire field of qualitative methods, this book provides a fine summary of approaches to sampling.

Renzetti, C. M., & Lee, R. M. (1993). *Researching sensitive topics*. London: Sage.

A useful resource book on the subject of researching sensitive topics.

Stewart, D. W., & Shamdasani, P. N. (1990). *Focus groups: Theory and practice*. Applied Social Research Methods Series 20. London: Sage.

This is a useful and comprehensive text on using focus groups. The book takes the reader through the various decision-making processes that are involved in setting up and running focus group research. Many of the examples are from marketing research in an American context, but the book is sufficiently general to be of help to African researchers in different fields.

First steps in qualitative data analysis

Martin Terre Blanche

University of South Africa

Kevin Durrheim

University of KwaZulu-Natal, Pietermaritzburg

Kevin Kelly

Rhodes University, CADRE

In a qualitative study, there is no clear point at which data collection stops and analysis begins. Rather, there is a gradual fading out of the one and a fading in of the other, so that at first you are mainly collecting data and towards the end you are mainly analysing what you have collected. In this chapter, we will focus on how to proceed when that point is reached where data collection has faded into the background and data analysis has become your main concern.

We will present two basic 'patterns' for doing qualitative data analysis – one based on interpretive assumptions, and the other on social constructionism. Our purpose is to provide you with straightforward, practical guidelines so that you can get on with your analysis immediately. However, once you have started to get your hands dirty and gained some practical experience, we suggest you read carefully the following two more advanced chapters, which tackle some of the fundamental conceptual challenges inherent in all qualitative data analysis.

Interpretive analysis

The key to doing a good interpretive analysis is to stay close to the data, to interpret it from a position of empathic understanding. The anthropologist Clifford Geertz (1973) said the purpose of interpretive analysis is to provide 'thick description', which means a thorough description of the characteristics, processes, transactions, and contexts that constitute the phenomenon being studied, couched in language not alien to the phenomenon, as well as an account of the researcher's role in constructing this description. Clearly this would be impossible if you kept the data at arm's length. At the same time, however, such description is more than a mere copy of the original phenomenon being studied. The purpose is not to collect bits and pieces of 'real life', but to place real-life events and phenomena into some kind of perspective. A useful aphorism associated with interpretive research, and indeed all forms of qualitative research, is 'to make the strange familiar and the familiar strange'. Margaret Mead, living in a tent among tribespeople, was engaged in a process of trying to make the strange familiar, as are modern-day researchers studying unusual religious sects or fringe phenomena such as paedophilia (see Ivey & Simpson, 1998). However, researchers as often as not do not need to go to out-of-the-way places to find material for interpretation. Apparently unremarkable and everyday South African events, such as riding in a lift (Dawson & Scott, 1996) or consulting an indigenous healer (Sodi, 1996), can prove to be far more nuanced and involved than casual observation would suggest. This is what is meant by 'making the familiar strange'.

Qualitative research aims to make the strange familiar and the familiar strange.

Box 14.1

Bracketing

The term 'bracketing' comes from phenomenology, a qualitative research tradition that has enjoyed some popularity in South African social science. Dreyer Kruger, one of the pioneers of phenomenology in South Africa, said: 'It is necessary to give up manipulation of the phenomenon in favour of allowing this to show itself by an intimate communion with it' (1990, p. 404). Our preconceived notions and prejudices often get in the way of such 'intimate communion', and we should therefore try to 'bracket' them. This means temporarily 'forgetting' about everything we know and feel about the phenomenon, and simply listening to what the phenomenon is telling us now.

Data analysis involves reading through your data repeatedly, and engaging in activities of breaking the data down (thematising and categorising) and building it up again in novel ways (elaborating and interpreting).

Interpretive analysis can be seen as a back-and-forth movement between the strange and the familiar, as well as between a number of other dimensions – description and interpretation, foreground and background, part and whole. What you want to come out with at the other end is a compelling account of the phenomenon being studied – close enough to the context so that other people familiar with the context would recognise it as true, but far enough away so that it would help them to see the phenomenon in a new perspective. More will be said in the next chapter about the tension between these two poles of analysis.

Steps in interpretive data analysis

There are many different qualitative analytic traditions that come under the umbrella of interpretive analysis, for example, phenomenology (Kruger, 1979), grounded theory (Strauss & Corbin, 1990), and thematic content analysis (Smith, 1992). Miller and Crabtree (1992) argue that interpretive analytic styles vary along a continuum from quasi-statistical styles to immersion/crystallisation styles. Quasi-statistical styles involve using predetermined categories and codes that are applied to the data in a mechanistic way to yield quantifiable indices. Immersion/crystallisation styles, on the other hand, involve becoming thoroughly familiar with a phenomenon, carefully reflecting on it, and then writing an interpretation by relying on one's intuitive grasp of what is going on rather than on any particular analytic techniques.

The analytic steps we present here fall somewhere between these two extremes. We present this not as a fixed recipe that has to be applied to the data, but rather to 'unpack' some of the processes involved in immersing oneself in and reflecting on the data. In reality, interpretive analysis rarely proceeds in as orderly a manner as may be suggested by our step-wise presentation, but it can be a helpful starting point.

Step 1: Familiarisation and immersion

By the time you have completed collecting data, your analysis should already be well under way. As should be clear from the previous chapter, data gathering in interpretive research is not just a mindless technical exercise, but involves development of ideas and theories about the phenomenon being studied, even as the researcher makes contact with gatekeepers and sets up interviews. So, by the time you come to data analysis, you should already have a preliminary understanding of the meaning of your data. What you need to do now in the data analysis stage is to take all your material and immerse yourself in it again – this time working with texts (field notes, interview transcripts) rather than with lived reality. Read through your texts many times over. Make notes, draw diagrams, brainstorm. By the time you have finished you should know your data well enough to know more or less what kinds of things can be found where, as well as what kinds of interpretation are likely to be supported by the data and what are not.

Step 2: Inducing themes

Induction means inferring general rules or classes from specific instances. It is thus a bottom-up approach: You look at your material and try to work out what the organising principles are that 'naturally' underlie the material. This is the opposite of a top-down approach, where you would use ready-made categories and simply look for instances fitting the categories. Of course, there are no hard-and-fast rules about what sorts of theme or category are best, nor is there one best way of organising any given collection of raw data. Here are some pointers, though.

Themes should ideally arise naturally from the data, but at the same time they should also have a bearing on your research question.

First, try using the language of your interviewees or informants, rather than abstract theoretical language, to label your categories. So, if you're doing a study on racial tensions at a Northern Cape school and people keep talking about 'political agitators', consider using that as a label rather than some obscure expression such as 'fears of outside interference in educational matters'.

Second, try to move beyond merely summarising content. Think in terms of processes, functions, tensions, and contradictions. So, when studying commuter behaviour in taxis, you could find it useful to organise the material in terms of events that function to assert a community of interests between driver and passengers versus events that threaten to break up this community. To give you some idea of the range of themes that one could come up with, here are three examples of interpretive research conducted by South African researchers in medical settings. Berger (1990) researched women's experiences of breast cancer, and one of the thematic schemes she used was implicit explanatory models of the disease (e.g., it is caused by not having babies, hereditary factors, and so on). In their study of diabetes, Cleaver and Pallourios (1994) organised their material in terms of different stages of living with the disease, such as the appearance of the first symptoms, initial reactions to the diagnosis, and changes in people's long-term views of the future. Ferreira (1988), in her study of medical encounters at an outpatient centre, also used chronological themes such as 'prior to consultation', 'during consultation', and 'after consultation'.

Box 14.2

Managing qualitative data using computers

The use of computer programs for processing and managing qualitative material is becoming increasingly common (see Weitzman & Miles, 1995). These allow you to assign very complicated systems of codes to bits of text, and are particularly useful if you have large amounts of data, a complex coding system, or want to be able to ask complex questions of your data. Imagine, for instance, that you are doing a study (as Wright, 1997, has done) on ways in which South African students react to health warnings on cigarette packets. If you have many interviews and you want to know such things as whether women react differently from men, or whether they talk about the way that smoking can affect unborn babies, or whether those women who mention the effects of smoking on unborn babies are also those who are concerned about passive smoking, you could save yourself a lot of trouble by using a computer program for qualitative analysis. Two of the most powerful and popular qualitative analysis programs are Atlas.ti and Nud-Ist. Below are a number of ways in which such programs can be useful in interpretive research:

- They provide a means for efficiently storing textual data in a systematic and ordered fashion.
- They make unnecessary the 'cutting and pasting' of physical text in the process of grouping and regrouping your material. We can label segments of text with code headings, and instantly retrieve as a batch all of the text under a particular code heading. Should

Third, try to find an optimal level of complexity. Just having two or three themes is probably not enough to do anything interesting with the data. On the other hand, if you have ten or fifteen themes, you should probably rearrange them so that there are a smaller number of main themes, with several subthemes under each.

Fourth, do not settle for one system too quickly. Play around and see what happens when you try different kinds of theme.

Finally, do not lose focus on what your study is about. If you want to provide a 'thick description' of a beauty competition, you may need many themes covering a broad array of issues, but, if the study is specifically about the way participants feel about being seen as sexual objects, most of your themes should relate directly to this.

Step 3: Coding

Coding means breaking up the data in analytically relevant ways.

During the activity of developing themes, you should also be coding your data. This entails marking different sections of the data as being instances of, or relevant to, one or more of your themes. You might code a phrase, a line, a sentence, or a paragraph, identifying these textual 'bits' by virtue of their containing material that pertains to the themes under consideration. The content of the text might refer to a discrete idea, explanation, or event, and any textual 'bit' might be we need to, we can then take this collection of text and recode it, or code it into further categories.

- They make it possible to attach notes or comments to a text. It is also possible to attach bits of recorded speech or video footage to a document.
- Some programs allow for connections between categories to develop higher order conceptual structures – sometimes referred to as theory building – and can also be used for theory testing.

As useful as such technology is, does it not seem a huge distance away from Dilthey's suggestion that empathy is the foundation of epistemological practice in the human sciences? We need to be circumspect about what computers can do. It is absurd to imagine that they can know and summarise in words what it might mean to have suffered a personal tragedy, for example. And a computer cannot know how to search creatively for associations between different aspects of an account. A computer also cannot formulate and reformulate research questions for us. In Kvale's (1996) words, 'The current emphasis on coding may lead to analysis of isolated variables abstracted from their context in live interpersonal interactions' (p.174).

Software for qualitative data analysis is not a magic wand which can hide or eradicate the flaws inevitably present in any project, it can merely aid the rigorous and honest researcher to better manage vast amounts of data in ways which can best do justice to the project. (Payze, 1997, p. 172)

labelled with more than one code if it refers to more than one theme. There are different ways of doing this. Some people like to use coloured marker pens to highlight pieces of text, so that, for example, in a study on Aids prevention, all text relating to condom use is marked in blue. Others prefer making several photocopies of each page of their data and then physically cutting these into smaller sections which are grouped together. This was the method used by Sehlapelo and Terre Blanche (1996) in their interpretive study of public perceptions of psychometric testing. Some of the categories they used were 'doubts about testing organisations', 'doubts about tests', 'the trauma of testing' and 'suggested alternatives'. The advantage of this procedure is that you can easily change which sections should go under which categories, or even do away with some categories and add new ones. Just be sure to mark each cut-out slip of paper carefully, so that you know where it comes from (e.g., which interview), and that you have a large, open (and wind-free!) space to work in.

A similar and more efficient method is to use the cut-and-paste function in a word processor to move bits of text around. Alternatively, you can use one of a variety of software programs that aid qualitative analysis. In coding, we break down a body of data (text domain) into labelled, meaningful pieces, with a view to later clustering the 'bits' of coded material together under the code heading and further analysing them both as a cluster and in relation to other clusters. In practice, thematising and coding blend into each other, because the themes which we are using tend to change in the process of coding as we develop a better understanding of them and how they relate to other themes. Frequently, we will realise that a particular theme contains subthemes and begin to analyse these as well. Thus, codes should never be regarded as final and unchanging.

Step 4: Elaboration

When collecting material for interpretive analysis, one experiences events or the things people say in a linear, chronological order. When one then immerses oneself in field notes or transcripts (see step 1 above), the material is again viewed in a linear sequence. What the induction of themes and coding (steps 2 and 3) achieves is to break up this sequence, so that events or remarks that were far away from one another are now brought close together. This gives you a fresh view on the data and allows you carefully to compare sections of text that appear to belong together. At this stage, you are likely to find that there are all sorts of ways in which extracts that you grouped together under a single theme actually differ, or that there are all kinds of subissues and themes that come to light. Exploring themes more closely in this way is called elaboration. The purpose is to capture the finer nuances of meaning not captured by your original, possibly quite crude, coding system. This is also an opportunity to revise the coding system – either in small ways or drastically – and to go back to step 3. This is not a sign of failure, but of a thorough analysis. The purpose is not to come up with the one correct way of structuring the material, but to keep playing around with ways of structuring it until you feel that you can give a good account of what is going on in your data. In the previous chapter we used the term 'sampling to redundancy'. The same principle applies to analysis: Keep on coding, elaborating, and recoding until no further significant new insights appear to emerge.

Step 5: Interpretation and checking

One way of checking your interpretation is to discuss it with other people. Be sure to talk to people who know a lot about the topic, as well as those who don't, but who are able to consider it from a fresh perspective.

The final step is when you put together your interpretation. This is a written account of the phenomenon you studied, most probably (but not necessarily) using thematic categories from your analysis as sub-headings. Now go through the interpretation with a fine-tooth comb and try to fix weak points. See if you can find examples that contradict some point or another in the interpretation. Are there parts of the interpretation that are just summaries and nothing more? Are there instances of over-interpretation where you made a great deal out of something quite trivial? Are there instances where you got carried away by your prejudices? This is also a good opportunity to reflect on your own role in collecting the data and creating the interpretation. Nobody expects you to be perfectly objective, but it is expected that you should give some indication of how your personal involvement in the phenomenon may have coloured the way you collected and analysed the data.

Being there

Box 14.3

The poststructuralist philosopher Jacques Derrida claims that Western philosophy has, since ancient Greece, been characterised by two fundamental biases, which he terms logocentrism and phonocentrism. **Logocentrism** has to do with the idea that actual, physical presence in the moment (as opposed to being distanced from it by time or space) allows for more valid observation of what is really happening. **Phonocentrism** has to do with believing that speech, because it supposedly happens spontaneously, is more authentic and true than writing. Thus we are inclined to believe somebody who tells us 'in their own words' about an event which they have personally experienced, rather than a second-hand account, or some theorist's written speculations about it. What these biases disguise is the way in which our experiences are 'always already' constructed in language – there is no 'pure' experience that we merely communicate in language. To experience something is already to have interpreted it. Your experience of meeting a guerrilla depends on whether you have already understood the guerrilla to be a terrorist or a freedom fighter – terms that have a complex history, but which provide us with frameworks for experience. To counter phonocentric and logocentric

A guerrilla

biases, it is therefore strategically useful to treat speech as a form of writing, and to 'read' spontaneous, first-hand accounts as carefully crafted attempts at persuasion, in the same way that one might read a philosophical treatise. Now read the transcript of the following advertisement for CNN (an international television news company) and see if you can identify how phonocentrism and logocentrism operate in it.

> [Transcript of CNN advertisement, spoken by Peter Arnett while images are shown of him reporting from various parts of the world] 'My philosophy is to go where the facts are, wherever they may be, on the frontline, behind the frontline and to report back what I see ... I joined CNN because going live from any location meant that you were first, that what you saw you can share with the audience. [Image of Arnett arguing with Iraqi officials] 'Are you saying we can't broadcast anymore? Are you closing us down?' The more information we get from a crisis, the better ... live coverage, and what CNN does is to assemble building blocks of facts so that public opinion and government policies can be based on those facts'.

Social constructionist analysis

Where interpretive research is interested in the experiences, feelings, and meanings that people talk about, social constructionist researchers are interested in ways in which talk is used to manufacture experiences, feelings, meanings, and other social facts in the first place.

As with interpretive analysis, constructionist analysis should not be seen as a separate phase that starts only after all the data has been collected; rather, the different phases shade into one another. We discuss it separately here purely for the sake of conceptual clarity.

There are many forms of constructionist analysis, but all share the aim of revealing the cultural materials from which particular utterances, texts, or events have been constructed. One of the most popular approaches is discourse analysis, and we shall base our discussion largely on this approach.

Discourse analysis can be defined as the act of showing how certain discourses are deployed to achieve particular effects in specific contexts. Different analyses emphasise different aspects of this definition. Some may be most concerned with identifying the discourses that operate in a text, others may focus more on how particular effects are achieved in the text, while yet others may be most concerned with explicating the broader context within which the text operates. Below we discuss each of these three elements in turn.

Discourses

The term 'discourse' is used in many different senses, and, although this can be confusing, the openness of the term is also useful in signalling the fluid quality of what is being analysed. Discourse analysts cannot rely on hard-and-fast definitions of what constitutes a discourse. As with interpretive research, the researcher is the principal instrument of the analysis, and can never fall back on a set of technical procedures or definitions. It is important, however, to draw a distinction between how the term 'discourse' is used in discourse analysis and how it is used more commonly in everyday talk as a synonym for speech or conversation. For discourse analysts, discourses are broad patterns of talk – systems of statements – that are taken up in particular speeches and conversations, not the speeches or conversations themselves. The latter are most often termed 'texts' (which, when written up or transcribed, are the materials we read closely when doing the analysis). Thus, one would say that certain discourses operate in a particular text, or that the text draws on, or is informed by, these discourses. Text is used here to refer to written and spoken language, as well as to images (Parker, 1992).

> Twenty-nine-year-old unmarried female, no children, staying with parents in X, presenting in a psychotic state with tactile hallucinations, sexual delusions, and delusions of misinterpretation, delusions of influence, that started 1 m ago and got progressively worse over last week. Delusions are directed towards father. Father is transmitting his 'lust' to her. Hypomanic features. Marked conduct disorder with substance abuse as child. 4 previous admissions. Defaulted meds.

A field guide to discourses?

Box 14.4

It is sometimes tempting to think of discourse analysis as a kind of bird-spotting exercise, so that all we have to do is identify known discourses operating in particular texts. However, discourses are not discrete entities like bird species, but are intertwined with one another and constantly changing. To complicate matters further, discourses vary greatly in scope, with analysts sometimes referring to quite insignificant local patterns of talk (such as the slang used by a particular football team) as a 'discourse', while at other times using the term to indicate large-scale phenomena, such as 'colonial discourse', 'sexist discourse', or 'racist discourse'. Although there is little to be gained from simply 'spotting' such discourses in whatever texts you are working with, you may well find that your analyses can be improved by referring to previous work similar to your own. For example, if you are interested in racist language, you may find similar rhetorical strategies as those identified by Van Dijk (1987) in his work on subtle racist talk in Holland and the USA, or Wetherell and Potter (1992) in their investigation of white New Zealanders' talk about race. Examples include avoiding unacceptable ethnic terms (such as 'Negro') while nevertheless indicating social distance from the speaker (e.g., by using 'they', 'them', 'those people'), conceding that people of other races have some positive qualities (e.g., 'they are very musical, but ...'); and pre-emptively denying racism (e.g., 'I am not a racist, but ...'). South African authors who show how similar patterns of talk operate locally include Duncan (1996) and Dixon, Foster, Durrheim, and Wilbraham (1994).

So there is no 'field guide to discourses'. There are, however, at least three kinds of publication that can provide clues as to the kinds of discourse you might want to be on the lookout for:

1. **Philosophical, cultural, and political critiques of South African and global society**. One starting point would be to read the chapters in the final section of this book and to move from there to areas that are of particular interest to you, such as feminist theory or the work of Foucault.
2. **Methodology textbooks**. These increasingly contain sections on discourse analysis (see the key readings at the end of this chapter), often with illustrative examples of particular discourses.
3. **Discourse analytic studies**. Look through back issues of the *South African Journal of Psychology*, which now contains a good number of local empirical studies using discourse analysis. There is also a published volume of local studies edited by Levett, Kottler, Burman, and Parker (1997). In addition, many articles published in South African journals of, *inter alia*, gender studies and anthropology, although not always termed 'discourse analysis', operate from similar principles. Good overseas sources of discourse analytic studies in the social sciences include the journals *Discourse & Society* and *Text*.

The text on page 328 (taken from Terre Blanche, 1997) is part of a short case history written by a psychiatrist. At first it appears to be purely informational, but, like all texts, it is also 'doing things', such as starting to 'make a case' for various possible diagnoses, and showing that the psychiatrist is a competent medical professional. In accomplishing these tasks, the text draws on a variety of discourses, such as scientific discourse (which represents the world as a collection of objective facts), medical discourse (which organises speech around signs, symptoms, and possible diagnoses), and psychiatric discourse (which incorporates various stereotypical ways of talking about aberrant behaviour in terms of various disease entities). Within these, one could point to various smaller-grained discourses, such as the 'old maid discourse' (having violated the 'normal' developmental path for a woman – getting married and having children – the patient is now sexually frustrated and projects her frustration onto the nearest male figure), the 'noncompliance discourse' (people who stop taking their medication can be expected to relapse), and the 'recidivism discourse' (once somebody has been admitted to a psychiatric hospital a few times, there is every reason to expect that they will be admitted again). The latter two are frequently appealed to in psychiatric texts when clear-cut diagnoses prove difficult to make.

You may be wondering how a discourse analyst goes about identifying discourses. How, for instance, did we find a medical discourse or an 'old maid' discourse in the text on page 328? There are no hard-and-fast methods for identifying discourses and analysing texts. To a large extent, discourse analysis involves a way of reading that is made possible by our immersion in a particular culture, which provides us with a rich tapestry of 'ways of speaking' that we can recognise, 'read', and dialogue with. In the family, for example, there are ways in which children can (and cannot) speak to adults and ways in which adults should (and should not) reply. These ways of speaking are structured by discourses that, as members of a particular culture, we can recognise. During the 1960s, the child-rearing advice of Benjamin Spock was adopted by numerous parents in Western countries. Spock advocated a nonpunitive form of child rearing – known as 'permissive' child-rearing – in which parents should always be kind, loving, and affirming to children. If we were to overhear a father respond to his child who had just started a large fire in his room in the following manner, 'You are a very good child, son, and you know your mom and I love you very much, but fires are dangerous, and should be kept out of doors', we could say that the father has adopted a way of speaking, a manner of address, that is permissive. We would know this only because of our familiarity with different ways of speaking within that particular culture.

We can identify discourses because we are part of a culture and because we are able to strike a critical distance from that culture.

Although cultural background – something everyone already has – is a prerequisite to doing a discourse analysis, doing an analysis requires something more. As discourse analysts, we need to extract ourselves (to a degree) from living in culture to reflecting on culture.

Parker (1992) calls this 'striking a critical distance from the text'. When the father in the above example addresses his son, he does not first say to himself: 'I will speak in a permissive register'. The father is *acting within* a discursive frame. But we, as discourse analysts, must *reflect on* the text in an effort to identify the discourse that the father is drawing on in his 'way of speaking'.

There are a number of little tricks that can help us reflect on textual activities. First, we should look for **binary oppositions** – for instance, love–hate, sick–healthy, clever–stupid, true–false, good–bad – in a text. These alert us to the kinds of discourse at play in the text. In the psychiatric text above, there is an opposition at play between being normal and insane, and this alerts us to the fact that the author of the text is drawing on a psychomedical discourse. Often, binary oppositions are implicit in texts, as only one side of the opposition is explicitly mentioned. This is the case when the father says only that the child is good and loved very much. The second term, a bad child, is silenced, and in fact it is this silencing of badness in children and feelings of hate in parents that alerts us to the permissive discourse.

A second trick is to identify recurrent **terms**, **phrases**, and **metaphors** that are present in the text (see Potter & Wetherell, 1987). Each discourse has a particular way of speaking that includes the content of what is said as well as how it is said. The permissive child-rearing discourse speaks in loving and affirming tones to children, and says such things as 'you are a good child' and 'we love you very much'. These phrases signal, for the analyst, that a permissive discourse may inhabit the text. Similarly, as members of contemporary culture, we recognise terms such as 'psychotic state', 'tactile hallucinations', 'sexual delusions', 'disorder', 'hypomanic', and 'delusions of misinterpretation' to be psychomedical, and their recurrent use in a piece of text will suggest that things are being framed within a psychiatric way of speaking. We can also recognise ways of speaking in the text that are typical of scientific discourse, for example, expressing facts in terms of numbers (1 month, 29 years, 4 previous admissions).

The third trick that can be used to identify discourses is to consider the **human subjects** that are spoken about in the text. At one level, this is a straightforward task. The permissive child-rearing discourse speaks about good children who are to be affirmed for all their positive qualities, and the psychomedical discourse talks about 'patients' and 'the mentally ill', so, if we encounter such subjects in a text, we know that these discourses are probably at work. However, a closer look often reveals that there are more subjects present than are at the centre of the text. In the case of the psychiatric text, for example, we find children, parents, a father, and so on, alerting us to the fact that family discourses also operate in this text. Indeed, the psychomedical discourse (think of Freudian sexual repression) and the family discourse (think of the expectation to set up one's own nuclear family) articulate with one another in creating a pathological subject: the sexually frustrated 'old maid'.

By identifying what binary oppositions, recurrent terms, phrases, and metaphors are present in a text, we begin to see how the text is the product of particular discourses.

Finally, there are two shadowy, but omnipresent, subjects in most texts: the 'author' and the 'listener'. We put author and listener in quote marks to signal that these are not the actual people who may have created and listened to the text, but are effects of the text. To do its work, the text 'imagines' an author and a listener, and, as analysts, we have to imagine what kinds of people these have to be. The author of our psychiatric text is an expert who speaks with authority through medical and scientific discourses as an objective assessor of behaviour. At the same time, there is a second authorial voice, more subdued than the former – possibly a fatherly figure who understands the ethical regime of family life. The kind of language used (i.e., technical terms) suggests that the listener is a colleague who is being enjoined to agree that a correct and factual assessment is being made. There is always some form of collusion between author and listener in a text; in this case, they are 'on the same side', working together to make the world of psychiatry seem dependable and real. However, even when author and listener are on different sides of an argument, they are still in collusion in that together they set up a world that can be understood in terms of their argument.

Other terms that you may come across that have meanings similar to 'discourse' are 'interpretive repertoire', 'narrative' (or 'grand narrative'), 'speech genre', 'cultural resource', and sometimes even 'ideology'.

Box 14.5

Reality effects

There is a science fiction story about an alien ship that arrived one day from outer space and began orbiting earth. The military were all for shooting it down, but when it was discovered that there were no life forms on board and that it did not appear to have any offensive capacity, people began to relax. What the space ship did have was a large computer database, containing writings in an unknown language, presumably giving more information about the star system from where it originated. The database was downloaded onto computers on earth and cryptologists, linguists, and ordinary people all over the world immediately set to work trying to decipher the alien language – a very difficult task, which took many years of hard work and intellectual discipline. However, eventually the code was broken and the texts could be read.

What people did not realise was that, in the act of coming to understand the alien language and way of thinking, they had been utterly transformed, and, although outwardly still appearing to be human, they were in fact themselves now aliens. Soon after, the ship quietly disengaged from earth's orbit and set out to colonise other planets.

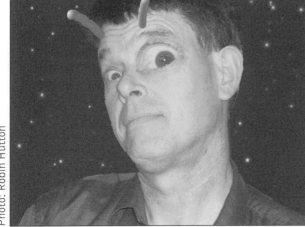

Effects

The first stage in doing a discourse analysis is striking a critical distance from the text in order to identify discourses. The second step (often conducted simultaneously with the first) is to see what these discourses do. As we have seen, what distinguishes constructionism is its lack of interest in identifying some truth behind the text; it does not ask questions about which version of events is more accurate or more meaningful. Instead, constructionist analysis aims to link accounts to actions. In discourse analysis, texts are examined for their effects rather than their veracity; the question is 'what do texts do?', not 'what do they say?' Parker's (1992) definition of discourse – 'a system of statements which constructs an object' – gives us one indication of what discourses do: they construct particular realities. Collins's (1997) definition – 'narratives that organise meaning so as to produce what then show up as facts' – gives a related indication of what discourses do: they construct particular truths. In fact, texts often want to do a number of things (simultaneously): Convince the reader that the author of the text is a good person (e.g., a reliable witness in a court of law), advance a particular ideology (e.g., in parliamentary debate), tell the truth (e.g., a scientist giving a conference paper) or motivate the reader to act in a particular way (e.g., to donate blood).

> 'Discourses are practices that systematically form the objects of which they speak.' (Foucault, 1972, p. 39)

Sometimes these aims are quite explicit in texts, and people can 'see through' them. For instance, when a salesperson tells us that we must purchase a particular product because it will make our lives so much easier, we know the profits will make the salesperson's life easier. In many cases of public debate, people conduct a form of discourse analysis when they undermine opposing accounts, pointing to what the texts are trying to achieve (e.g., advertisements).

Discourse analysts can use the three tricks considered earlier as tools to orientate a critical reading of action in text and to show the kinds of effect they try to achieve. This involves a sceptical reading of texts, in which the researcher asks (1) why these particular binary oppositions, why these terms, phrases and metaphors, why these subjects? and (2) what other language(s) could have been used, and then (3) provides a detailed reading of the way in which these features of a text work to achieve certain effects.

Oppositions within a text set up particular problematics by framing issues in particular ways. Oppositions between the 'normal' and the 'mentally ill' in the psychiatric text first alert us to a 'problem', and then frame the 'problem' as a psychomedical one. Of course, a different set of oppositions could have been used, for example, between the woman as a victim and the father as an aggressor, and this would construct the 'problem' in a completely new way. Such an opposition might have resulted in the situation being framed as a legal problem – leading to judicial rather than psychomedical intervention.

Thus, rather than reading texts for truth – asking whether the woman is really mad – discourse analysts read for effects – asking what happens when the text raises the question of the woman's madness. Reading

Box 14.6

Knowledge and power

Social constructionism in the social sciences follows in the wake of developments in social and cultural theory and is in some ways a pale reflection of these. Particularly influential has been a group of mainly French theorists associated with structuralist and post-structuralist philosophy who have been active since the mid 1960s. Included among these are Barthes, Lyotard, Derrida, Lacan, Baudrillard, and Foucault. Today, a large proportion of critical work on cultural and social issues in some way refers to ideas drawn from poststructuralist philosophy, and it is therefore a good idea to get to know at least some of the basics of this work. There are many books offering introductions to poststructuralism and to individual theorists, but it is important also to read these authors in the original.

Of all the poststructuralists, Michel Foucault has possibly been the most influential, and his work on the history of criminality, medicine, psychiatry, and sexuality has revolutionised the way these fields are now viewed. According to Foucault, the modern world is characterised by a particular relationship between power and knowledge. In pre-modern times, power was exercised in a '**sovereign**' manner – that is, it was in the hands of powerful individuals, groups, or institutions and could be used to suppress others. For sovereign power to operate effectively, it was important that the might of (for example) the king should be constantly on display through military parades, public executions, and the like. This has now largely been replaced by '**disciplinary**' power, where it is no longer the king or the might of the state that needs to be made known, but the characteristics of individuals who are continually observed, recorded, and calibrated

for truth draws people into siding with one side or the other of an opposition (identifying whether the woman is really mad or normal), whereas reading for effects makes us consider how the opposition produces a particular type of world.

Recurrent terms, phrases, and metaphors lend a particular kind of meaning to the events or objects that are spoken about in a text. Consider these words: '29-year-old unmarried female, no children, staying with parents'. Why were these particular terms and phrases used to describe the woman? Why not 'good looking, unattached, loves sport and reading, looking for a steady relationship'? The terms used in the text function to pathologise the woman; that is, they position her as a person who is in some way ill, whereas an alternate set of terms, metaphors, and phrases could position her as a normal, healthy individual (if somewhat eccentric), or as a victim of an abusive family (imagine the woman explaining to a friend or potential employer why she was institutionalised).

Subjects are contained in discourse. As we have now considered in some detail, the psychiatric text constructs a pathological individual by institutions like education, medicine, and psychology. In addition to disciplinary power operating through such surveillance, it also functions through individuals themselves who are engaged in acts of '**confession**', in other words, constantly talking about themselves – their likes, dislikes, fears, and aspirations, and how they are different from everybody else.

Disciplinary power thus does not flow from a powerful centre, but seeps back from a myriad small acts of knowledge making that take place in the everyday lives of everybody. It also does not suppress and destroy, but is creative – always constructing new objects of knowledge, new ways of being a unique individual. However, this kind of power does not advertise itself for what it is. Instead, we are encouraged to believe that creating knowledge has to do with discovering the truth about ourselves and the world, rather than about constructing certain kinds of selves and social worlds. We are also encouraged to believe that power is exercised upon us from the outside, suppressing our individuality, rather than to believe that it helps to create us as manageable and calculable individuals in the first place.

Now have another look at the CNN advertisement in box 14.3 and see whether you can identify how it presents power as sovereign and repressive rather than disciplinary and creative.

> The individual is an effect of power, and at the same time, or precisely to the extent to which it is that effect, it is the element of its articulation. The individual which power has constituted is at the same time its vehicle. (Foucault, 1980, p. 98)

by drawing on a psychomedical discourse. We have also tried to show how this construction of the woman is always potentially under contestation, and different discourses could be employed to construct her in new ways. Discourses, however, have powers, and cannot just be discarded and replaced by other discourses. One of the effects of the psychomedical discourse is to bolster and preserve itself, and one way in which it does this is by constructing subjects who have no 'voice' – that is, no powers to speak. Mad people have no powers to speak through the psychomedical discourse. Being mad, they have no authority over medical terminology, and no right to use a scientific language (and be believed). Although the 'mentally ill' are encouraged to speak about themselves in psychiatric contexts (e.g., in therapy), they speak differently from psychologists and psychiatrists. In short, mad people are unqualified to speak the language of reason, and, as such, the woman in the extract is voiceless and has no power to challenge or oppose the manner in which she is spoken about. Psycho-medical discourses such as those used in psychiatric case reports produce effects of disempowering subjects and bolstering and preserving the profession.

Discourses have the effect of both limiting and enabling certain kinds of action and subjectivity.

Identifying the effects of discourse is an essential part of doing discourse analysis, for these effects limit the opportunities for certain kinds of action, certain forms of subjectivity, while enabling others, and it is this that becomes the focus of a critical discourse analysis. To achieve a critical reading of a text, however, we must investigate how discursive actions are rooted in context.

Contexts

We have used a single, short, and, at first sight, quite mundane text to illustrate some of the approaches and tactics that discourse analysts use. Our reading has been a layered and multifaceted one, in which we have examined the text repeatedly, using different tactics of interpretation. We have tried to illustrate the *detail* with which discourse analysts read texts. Although a researcher may want to engage in a detailed reading of a single piece of text, most often the aim is to provide a reading of a larger body of material. The aim of analysis is then to examine how discourses operate in a body of text, and this aim is achieved by showing how discourses relate to other discourses, and how they function on different occasions. In other words, in addition to engaging in detailed readings of pieces of text, we should read many different texts to show patterns of variation and consistency in discourse. To do this, we need to be sensitised to context.

> Texts do not operate in isolation, but through being embedded in contexts.

We have said that the third element in doing a discourse analysis involves explicating the broader context within which a text operates. However, speaking about a text as existing 'within' a context is a lot more problematic than one might at first anticipate. This is because it is seldom easy to say where the boundaries of a text are; that is, where the text ends and its context begins. In positivist research, it is possible to decide on categories of objects to study in terms of their attributes on certain variables (e.g., white male racists in their early twenties). In constructionist research, however, we have to accept that everything is part of everything else, so that isolating a text from its surroundings is of necessity already to misunderstand it.

Nevertheless, to get on with the practical task of doing an analysis, to understand what a text is doing, we have to situate the text in context.

Photo: Rodney Barnett

Consider the photograph of the two men in the bar, and imagine the conversation they may have been having:

Phil: That reminds me of the movie with the lekker chick hey, um um, what's her name ... You know the one man, the one ... the one with the legs.

Kobus: They should've had me in that movie, I would've made her happy.

We could analyse this text in detail by considering binary oppositions, the terms, phrases, and metaphors used, and the kinds of subject that are spoken about. It should be apparent to you that a discourse that constructs men as macho sexual conquerors and women as the objects of male desire – what Wendy Hollway (1989) calls the 'male sex drive discourse' – is at work in this text. Doing a discourse analysis, however, involves more than simply identifying discourses, and we should proceed with understanding what the text is doing. Although we have considered how one would begin reading a text for its effects, we need to interpret the context of the text to know what actions are being performed.

At a broad level, discursive research can heuristically be divided into two categories: one that contextualises the text in a microcontext of conversation and debate (e.g., Edwards & Potter, 1992), and another that contextualises text in a macrocontext of institutions and ideologies (e.g., Parker, 1992). At the micro level of interaction, the researcher attends to the way in which each participant in a conversation talks into spaces opened up by the flow of conversation. Context in this sense is the conversational (or dialogical) context, and we should understand the meaning of an utterance in terms of where the conversation has led, what opportunities it has opened up (what it has made possible to do), and what it has closed down (what it has made impossible). In the bar conversation, Phil opens up a space for action by introducing the topic of movies and women. Kobus seizes the moment by claiming that if he were in the movie, he would have made the actress happy. How are we to understand Kobus's making the actress happy? What is Kobus doing? He is not showing what a kind person he is, nor is he claiming that he wants to be an actor. We can read this text as a 'way of speaking', a particularly masculine way which objectifies women in order to affirm one's own manhood.

Although we can understand a lot from considering interactional contexts, this is not sufficient, since conversations themselves are structured in the sense that only certain kinds of conversation are possible in particular contexts. We could not imagine Kobus and Phil having the same conversation around the dinner table with their families, or in the boardroom at work. The bar provides an institutional context that makes possible particularly crude forms of sexist interaction among males. The bar provides a world of male camaraderie from which women are excluded. Sexist conversations thus serve not only to affirm individual masculinity, but also to preserve 'male' institutions such as 'the bar', and thus operate on a broader level to preserve social spaces wherein sexist practices proliferate. Discourses, such as the 'male sex drive discourse', serve ideological functions. At this broad level, discourses transcend particular institutional contexts. Sexualised constructions of men as macho conquerors, for example, would be deployed differently in bars, in boardrooms, and in the family, but, nonetheless, the discourse seems to have a life across specific contexts. Thus, discourses are inflected with nuances of the

Box 14.7

Common analytic errors

Just as there are many ways to do a good analysis, there are many ways of getting it wrong. Here are some common mistakes made by novice analysts.

1. **Summarising.** Doing well in exams unfortunately often depends on reproducing the content of lectures and textbooks, sometimes thinly disguised as some sort of critical evaluation. Many social science students are therefore in the habit of summarising material, and resort to this tactic when asked to analyse a text. Your analysis should show what the text does and how it does this, not repeat the text in condensed form.

2. **Thematising.** Another way of summarising a text is to thematise it. This is done by reading through a body of material and identifying recurrent themes or categories. These themes are then presented as discourses. Although some forms of qualitative analysis aim to code text for themes, and it can be a useful way for discourse analysts to orientate themselves toward the text, the aim of a discourse analysis is not simply to present themes, but to show how subjects and objects are constructed in the text, and to interrogate the effects of these constructions.

3. **Contesting.** In trying to do a critical analysis, students sometimes get sucked into an argument with the text. If a text claims that Aids is an American conspiracy, your task is not to present empirical evidence to prove this wrong, but to ask what cultural materials the text draws on in making this claim. We don't want to know whether texts are true or not, but how they achieve (or fail to achieve) their 'truth effects'. Constructionist methods, like all qualitative research, draw on your subjective capacity to make sense of the social world. However, using your subjectivity is not

'In contemporary western society human subjectivity (the individual) is shaped and given reality in particular ways in medical, psychiatric, legal, educational, political, and psychological discourses. These reverberate in ... discourse related to gender, race, nationality, age, class and so on.' (Levett, 1988, p. 184)

particular institution in which they are being used, and the analyst may find it necessary to study the way in which discourses work differently across different institutions.

Another context that frames the meaning of a text and the discourses that work in the text are the other discourses with which the text dialogues. We introduce a further text to illustrate the way in which discourses refer to other discourses, taken from a booklet sent to young, white men called up for national service during the late 1980s:

The onslaught against the Republic of South Africa is a continuing onslaught which the enemies of South Africa are waging with every means at their disposal. These methods are applied in every conceivable field, against all possible targets, military as well as civilian, wherever and whenever the enemy believes he can score a mark. In your formative years this onslaught was also aimed at you. Knowingly or unknowingly, you were subjected to a systematic, subtle process which has the same as stating subjective (or even objective) opinions. Rather, it is about being able to explain why a text makes (a certain amount of) sense even though you may not agree with what it is saying.

4. **Methodolatry.** Students sometimes think that by slavishly following methodological instructions (such as those contained in this chapter and in the list of key readings) they are guaranteed a successful analysis. Their analyses are therefore cluttered with technical details 'proving' that they have executed each analytic step correctly, but without ever pulling it all together. It is fine to explain what steps you followed in coming to an understanding of a text, but your main focus should be on presenting that understanding in an interesting and pithy manner.

5. **Psychologising.** Texts often have explicitly stated authors (e.g., the writer of a letter, or the architect who designed a building) and even when they don't it is tempting to start analysing the author behind a text rather than the text itself. We are interested in the discourses that speak through a text, rather than in knowing what the author really meant. In fact, it can often be a useful strategy to think of the author as just another one of the objects constructed in the text, and to ask how the text is organised to implicitly create the author in a particular way.

6. **Stating the obvious.** This is one step up from summarising, but unfortunately not a big enough step. It is better to make a smaller number of incisive comments than laboriously to spell out everything that is (obviously) happening in a text.

7. **Flights of fancy.** In trying not to be obvious, students sometimes resort to very far-fetched claims, without being able to present any evidence of this from the text. Try to be interesting, but not *too* interesting.

possibly given you a distorted view of certain principles and institutions – including the Defence Force. Soon, however, you will gain first-hand knowledge about the SADF and the role you play in defending our heritage. (Geldenhuys, 1989, pp. 2–3)

By this stage, you should be able to recognise certain discourses at work here. See if you can identify (1) the way in which what one might call a 'total onslaught' discourse is reproduced, (2) what the shift from a factual speech genre to a more intimate personal tone achieves, and (3) how logocentric tactics are used. To extend such an analysis, one would have to explore the context of the utterance so as to include, first, the dialogical context between the Defence Force (addressor) and the national servicemen (addressee) and, second, the broader context of the South African state, apartheid, and the liberation struggle. Here we want to introduce a third way of looking at context, namely the way in which discourses refer to one another and thereby provide contexts for one another. Just as there is a dialogue between

Discourses operate across different contexts and in interaction with other discourses.

the Defence Force leadership and the national servicemen (as there was a dialogue between the two men in the bar), there is also an implicit dialogue at a higher level between 'total onslaught' and liberation discourses. As an illustration of this, imagine a parallel text written by the leadership of MK during the 1980s. In these two texts, discourses (of apartheid, Afrikaner nationalism, militarism, socialism, African liberation) would be 'arguing' with one another, much like two people who dislike each other but know each other well and in some sense are dependent on each other.

The major difference between these dialogical contexts of a micro and macro level of analysis is that conversations and arguments between people take place in short periods of time, whereas struggle and collusion between discourses unfold over long periods of history. Discourses continue to exert effects long after they first came into being, and to 'place' the text we would need to trace this process as well. For example, we could investigate how the discourses of socialism and capitalism have changed in relation to one another as South Africa has moved politically from an apartheid to a post-apartheid state, and embraced both capitalism (GEAR) and socialism (reconstruction).

Finally, the analyst is also a part of the text's context, and has to account for her or his role relative to the text. We have presented a number of short texts in this chapter as though they existed as texts before we picked them up, but, by delimiting each text (e.g., reproducing just one paragraph from the booklet on military service), and by presenting them as instructional aids on 'how to do discourse analysis', we have re-created them in certain ways. What we have done, among other things, is to make it look as if these texts are no more than little puzzles to be solved using a set of analytic techniques. We have done this to convey something of the flavour of what a discourse analysis could involve. It is important to realise, however, that constructionist research is more than an intellectual game: Analysts choose certain texts, how to delimit the texts, and how to analyse them because they want to achieve certain effects. In the same way that your analysis should refer to the effects of the texts and discourses being analysed, so too should it refer to the effects of the new text brought into being by your analysis. Some of these effects are intentional, but invariably others seem to infiltrate themselves despite your best efforts to make your analysis say something different. In the next chapter we will discuss some ways of making sense when you have to start talking about your own talk as if it were produced by somebody else.

'Discourse analysis should bring about an understanding of the way things were, not the way things are ... When we strike a critical distance from a discourse we, in a sense, put it behind us, consign it to the past.'
(Parker, 1992, p. 21)

What texts would you choose to analyse and what effects might your analysis have?

Conclusion

In this chapter we have outlined two general patterns of qualitative data analysis – from the interpretive and constructionist perspectives. By its very nature, qualitative data analysis is an exciting and energising activity, which is probably why people are attracted to it in the first place. However, after having read this chapter, you may now feel that so many obstacles have been placed in your way (steps to follow, mistakes to watch out for, skills to learn), that the whole enterprise no longer seems like fun.

Talking about qualitative analysis as a technique, as we have done in this chapter, is useful, but can easily make it seem like a highly technical matter. As an antidote to this, we suggest you consolidate what you have learnt in this chapter by reading a number of journal articles based on qualitative research and deciding for yourself which ones are really good. In our experience, 'really good' qualitative research is only in part characterised by methodological excellence. Just as important are factors such as the author's intuitive 'feel' for the subject matter and her or his ability to tell a good story.

If you are already involved in qualitative research, we trust that you have found material in this chapter to enhance your practice. If you are new to this kind of research, we encourage you to give it a try. As with all research, real learning starts when you put theory into practice.

Box 14.8

Looking at sexual abuse in advice columns
(Lindy Wilbraham, University of KwaZulu-Natal, Durban)

You don't have to be a discourse analyst to see that sexual abuse is socially constructed:

> I am a 17-year-old girl. I have a happy life, do well at school and have lots of friends. My problem is that I get the creeps whenever my stepfather comes near me. Whenever he hugs or kisses me, I get scared that he is going to touch me somewhere else. I am sure my stepfather would never actually do that as he has never even hit me. But I have these strange feelings towards him and am scared he will notice. Please help as I really love my step-dad. (Janet Harding's Lifeline: *You*, 19 November 1992, p. 176)

My abiding fascination with advice columns is partly that, week after week, they manage to churn out, in spine-chilling 100-word synopses, the cultural scripts by which we live our lives. The various editing processes between the original (troubled) author – whether s/he be real or fictive – and the published version labour as distilling devices, and we are left with the bare, taken-for-granted rules that govern the 'normal' operation of bodies, psyches, relationships, sex, wellbeing, identities. And, by default, we are informed of the heinous effects of the derailment of that vulnerable normality. In the way of

➔

Box 14.8 continued

postmodernism, then, the confessions and pleas for help by the unhappy letter writers are eclipsed, first by the experts who patrol the boundaries of normality (e.g., psychologists, doctors, sexologists) and second, by the readers, who, in their own bedrooms, bathrooms, and classrooms, are impelled to act in particular ways. Advice texts reproduce the discourses and discursive practices that organise our health-obsessed, self-reflective, and expert-reliant subjectivities in late modernity.

The above 'problem' from an advice text was selected to explore the discursive machinery that polices the sexual abuse of children. Our embeddedness in these discourses is such that we might, for example, easily imagine the 'expert advice' that would be routinely issued in response to this problem. This does not offer certainty – far from it. The reader flounders amidst the uneasy contradictions between, on the one hand, a potentially 'dangerous' (or ambiguous) situation, unwanted (sexual) feelings and the promised damages of sexual abuse, and, on the other hand, innocent affection and the healthy development of a young woman's identity, self-esteem, body, and sexuality. My intention in this small space is to signpost the major goals of a critical/Foucauldian discourse analysis (e.g., Parker, 1992; Fairclough & Wodak, 1997) through briefly exploring the operations of the discourses surrounding sexual abuse that impact on the above advice text.

Why does the sexual abuse of children press our buttons? The overarching discourses that have 'constructed' sexual abuse of children as an 'abnormal' activity/object are institutional, namely psychological, educational, legal, religious, and so on. It is defined through relational opposites: it is 'other' to the ubiquitous 'normal childhood' (e.g., protected by custodial relations with adults, non-sexual, developing skills/knowledges at culturally appropriate ages), or 'other' to the even more ubiquitous 'normal sex' (e.g., heterosexual, penetrative sex between consenting adults in a monogamous relationship). Within these discourses, transgression of cultural normalities produces competing lists of dire consequences, danger signs, and symptoms of damage. Here, metaphors labour to emphasise ruination of entire lives – for instance, children are 'victims', trust is 'broken', self-esteem is 'eroded', schoolwork 'fails', bodies become 'ugly/dirty/promiscuous/frigid', intimacy is 'wrecked', and so on. According to psychological truths, unless the 'inner wounds' inflicted by sexual abuse are professionally repaired (through 'talking about it'), they will return throughout life to wreak ongoing emotional devastation. These discursive constructions pivot on fear, and thus instil a sense of anticipation of abuse (Levett, 1988), and hyper-vigilance. In the above advice text, the young woman is not only 'scared' of being touched, but also scared of her fear being noticed by her stepfather, as in being blamed, or making a false accusation. The media have been eager champions of the moral-panic construction of sexual abuse as an 'epidemic'. This is not a reading of the media's informative function as conspiratorial, but a recognition of this function as one category of action (or subject position), which implicates ideas about intervention into the macro/micro power relations which endure when texts stop (Parker & Burman, 1993). The site of the sexually abusive (power) relationship for children is often domestic: 'the family'. Within the litany of 'broken families' in advice texts dealing with sexual abuse emerge various subject positions, such as children, mothers, uncles, stepfathers, teachers. Perhaps the most ominous of these – or most recognisable cultural script – is 'the wicked stepfather', but the space is also fraught with 'disbelieving mothers', 'colluding mothers', 'silent victims', and so on.

Each of these subject positions presupposes sets of responsibilities, actions, rights, and rules. For example, while children may be positioned within legal discourses as 'innocent victims' in need of protection and care, advice texts also articulate children's responsibilities to assert their rights within psychological discourses: to know enough to be able to recognise, anticipate, or avoid abusive situations; to be assertive about their bodies and say 'no'; to talk about the experience with other adults (e.g., mother, teacher, counsellor). Similarly, school teachers are positioned as watchdogs with responsibilities to 'see' signs that mothers may have missed or ignored, to listen, to educate. In this textual version of the socio-sexual world, then, expectations are laid down: Rational behaviour is expected, as are 'normal' developmental paths, and 'good' parents give children a safe, caring environment, and are willing to consult with experts and follow their prescriptions. In this textual world, too, the blurry lines between a growing awareness of sexual feelings/needs (e.g., feeling 'strange' towards a stepfather), sexual experimentation (e.g., with same-age peers) and 'sexual abuse' (e.g., as something adults do to children) are clearly demarcated.

A critical/Foucauldian discourse analytic approach would explore the ways in which these psychological, educational, or legal discourses (and others) operate to 'naturalise' children, sex, families, and rights in particular ways, and the ideological effects and power relations that such institutional, social, and subjective structuring reproduces. This endeavour would not be aimed at undermining the necessary support for individual survivors of sexually abusive experiences, but would seek to explore the contradictory implications for us all of the massive mobilisation of surveillance/vigilance of sex, sexuality, bodies, and wellbeing in our times. However, this would resist the monolithic truths of Western psychological discourses that reproduce sexual abuse as 'a unilateral crisis' and a lucrative opportunity for psychotherapeutic colonisation (Rose, 1990), This might forge a (small) space for the exploration of other meanings of sexuality in the development of subjectivities, and alternative forms of empowerment and healing.

Exercises

1. Work with other students to conduct and transcribe a few short interviews on the way that people experience visiting a shopping mall. Ask each student to produce an analysis of the interviews using the steps for doing an interpretive analysis outlined in this chapter. Now compare the different analyses. How much do they overlap? What differences are there? Which are the better analyses? Why?

2. Find 10 or so journal articles using qualitative analysis that appear to operate from a social constructionist perspective. For each article, try to identify (a) what terms it uses in the place of 'discourse' (e.g. 'cultural scripts', 'speech genres'), (b) whether its approach to discourse tends towards the political or the neutral/technical end of the spectrum, and (c) whether it tends to focus on small- or large-scale contexts.

3. Consider the following quotation and then have a class discussion about the way in which both sovereign and disciplinary power operated in the work of the Truth and Reconciliation Commission:

    > We are subjected to the production of truth through power and we cannot exercise power except through the production of truth ... we must speak the truth; we are constrained or condemned to confess or to discover the truth. Power never ceases its interrogation, its inquisition, its registration of truth: it institutionalises, professionalises and rewards its pursuit. In the last analysis we must produce truth as we must produce wealth. (Foucault, 1980, p. 93)

Key readings

Miles, M. B., & Huberman, A. M. (1994). *Qualitative data analysis: An expanded sourcebook of new methods*. Beverly Hills, California: Sage.

Levett, A., Kottler, A., Burman, E., & Parker, I. (1997). *Culture, power and difference: Discourse analysis in South Africa*. Cape Town: UCT Press.
This is a useful volume of constructionist studies by South African researchers.

Parker, I. (1992). *Discourse dynamics: Critical analysis for social and individual psychology*. London: Routledge.
In this book, Parker sets out the philosophical background to his brand of discourse analysis and provides a step-by-step approach to doing an analysis. Chapter 2 is particularly useful for beginning researchers.

Potter, J., & Wetherell, M. (1987). *Discourse and social psychology: Beyond attitudes and behaviour*. London: Sage.
This is a classic text, which has influenced many constructionist researchers, especially in psychology. In addition to an accessible introduction to constructionist research, it also provides structured guidelines to performing an analysis.

Lived experience and interpretation:
the balancing act in qualitative analysis

Kevin Kelly

Rhodes University, CADRE

Qualitative methodology has emerged as part of a broad movement that Rabinow and Sullivan (1979) call an 'interpretive turn' in social science epistemology. In practical terms, this refers to a turn towards 'contextual' research which is less immediately concerned with discovering universal, law-like patterns of human behaviour (e.g., theories of cognitive and moral development that apply to all people in all contexts), and is more concerned with making sense of human experience from within the context and perspective of human experience. This approach has as a starting point the belief that we cannot apprehend human experience without understanding the social, linguistic, and historical features that give it shape.

There can be little doubt that this 'turn' has had a pervasive influence, and qualitative research has become much more widely accepted as a valid approach within the social sciences. Mainstream academic journals, which previously focused exclusively on statistically based studies, have increasingly become open to publishing research reports based on interpretive work. This new-found status has been a spur to qualitative researchers and methodologists, and the past few years have witnessed a surge in the number of academic conferences, journals, and books in the field. It is of significance that this development has been referred to as an 'interpretive' turn. One of the central theoretical concerns in the qualitative research literature (Schwandt, 1994), and the central theme of this chapter, is that of 'interpretation'. In addressing the topic of interpretation, we will look more closely at philosophical issues that are raised when we think about interpretation in social research. Specifically, we will look at the 'model of the text' which has, for over a century, been central to epistemological debate in the social sciences. Building on the foundations of our understanding of the 'model of the text' and its implications, we will then go on to develop an understanding of the underlying principles, and the practical steps, involved in interpretive practice in qualitative research.

In this chapter we deal with interpretive and social constructionist research together, and simply label both 'interpretive research'.

In this book you have been introduced to three paradigms which were understood to be more or less distinct, namely positivism, the interpretive approach, and social constructionism. The interpretive approach was presented as understanding phenomena from within their context, in an empathic manner, while social constructionism was said to involve a more distanced, sceptical understanding. In this chapter, we deal with interpretive and constructionist research together, and simply label both 'interpretive research'. We thus present a generic approach to the interpretation of qualitative material, which is sceptical or empathic depending on which side of a fundamental interpretive continuum it tends towards. We focus on understanding the act of interpretation as contrasted with lived experience. We create a distinction between life as it is lived in psychological experience and life as it is represented through interpretation.

On the one side of this continuum, we have what are termed 'insider' or 'first-person' perspectives, derived through empathic, context-bound research.

Box 15.1

'Witch' killing at a distance

A good example of interpretive research that shows the tension between contextual and distanciated understanding can be found in Delius (1996). In 1986, youthful 'comrades' in Sekhukhuneland set out to rid their communities of oppression and misfortune and in so doing, among other things, they turned to killing 'witches'. While belief in witchcraft was pervasive amongst the people of Sekhukhuneland, and provided a powerful and often-used repertoire of explanations for a wide range of natural and social events, formal accusations of witchcraft and direct action against witches were far from commonplace prior to the mid 1970s. From late 1976, the patterns for identifying witches and the ways in which they were treated changed, and there was a dramatic increase in the number of 'witch' killings. Delius understands this change as coming about in the context of the youth revolt which escalated in South Africa in 1976, and relates the phenomenon to wider cultural, economic, and political exchanges and the process of negotiation of the terms of participation in a common society. In doing this, he explores witch killing as part of the rural anti-apartheid struggle and the struggle to redefine the structure of Pedi society (the average age of those killed was over 60, two thirds were women, and most of the killing was done by young men who were known to the 'witches', with an average age of 19 years). He extracts many other themes, including conflict over legitimacy of chieftaincies, the intersection of domestic and communal struggles, the viability of a market economy, and the meaning of democracy. This part of the study (the study was not limited to post-1976 events) was largely based on 180 interviews conducted in Sekhukhuneland between 1987 and 1992. While the words of respondents are strongly present in the book which Delius has written on the subject, they are there as part of an overarching account which exceeds the understanding of any one of the voices. Indeed, had those responsible for the witch burning been able to account for the surrounding context in the way that the researcher was able to, using a sociohistorical perspective, they may not have burned witches. At least their justifications for doing so would have had to be different, because he understands their motivation in terms that are quite different to the kinds of reason they were inclined to give. Those who did the killing evidently 'believed in witchcraft', and their actions were justified in terms of this belief. The researcher accounts for this belief (at least partially), and to this extent his account surpasses the voices, and particularly the self-understanding, of those involved in the killings.

This involves adopting and representing the perspective of the person or group having the experience. On the other side, we have 'outsider' or 'third-person' perspectives, which are more 'experience-distant'. Such analyses are not necessarily immediately recognisable by the people whose experience is being researched as 'true' representations of their experience. The cooperation of these two orientations – 'lived experience' and 'interpretation' – is at the heart of qualitative practice.

The model of the text

In chapter 12, we presented an approach to interpretive research based on the notion of *verstehen* (often simply translated as 'empathy'), which basically means to understand a human phenomenon as it is lived in its context. It was suggested that this process is akin to the way we approach a written text when we attempt to understand the author's intention and the context in which the author was writing. We also presented a social constructionist approach to analysis, which goes beyond the idea of empathy to argue for a more distant and critical form of interpretation. Let us now consider in more detail the tension between empathic and distant models of interpretation.

Without contesting the value of *verstehen*, let us follow Ricoeur (1979) who, in an essay entitled 'Model of the text: Meaningful action considered as a text', suggests that there is more to the understanding of an experience than can be ascertained from within the context of the experience. He uses the term 'distanciation' to talk about the process of understanding a context from outside of that context. **Distanciation** adds to meaning not by imposition, but by pointing to the subjective and contextual *limits* of understanding. No matter how thoroughly we understand a context from within, there are certain things about the context that are only going to become evident when we look at it from the outside.

A 'model' provides us with guidelines for engaging in a task. Here, the task concerns the interpretation of human action and environments.

When a text is read, the context of the reading brings to light new questions and new concerns, and this allows us to read meaning into the author's words in new ways. At this point, the meaning of the text and the original intention of the author within the context of writing cease to coincide. Simply put, the text can mean more than the author meant it to mean. Thus, Ricoeur says: 'The letters of Saint Paul are no less addressed to me than to the Romans, the Galatians, the Corinthians, etc.' (Ricoeur, 1981a, p. 192). What the text says now is not necessarily what the author meant it to say, and the meaning of an inscribed (written) event surpasses the meaning contextualised in a situated event. This 'excess' or 'surplus of meaning' is a crucial feature of the text. It transposes directly to the understanding of human events. Our motivations as people in a particular context may well be differently interpreted by others, either now or in the future. The point is that, when we view an experience from a distance, we can say things about it that we could not say from within the situation.

It can be inferred from this that the apparent distancing from experience which occurs when, for example, we look back on an experience is not something to be overcome, but is essentially productive in the disclosure of meaning. Ricoeur (1981b) suggests that understanding of a situation needs to be developed both from the perspective of being in the context (empathy) *and* from the perspective of distanciation, using interpretation.

It all boils down to an appreciation that understanding can legitimately use the range of resources at the researcher's disposal, including an understanding of history, theory, society, language, politics, and so on, in understanding experience. This is not secondary interpretation applied to experience in an add-on fashion, but fundamental to an understanding of the very context of the experience, as it is revealed from outside of the experience, from the perspective of the types of question, experience, information, and concern which we as 'readers' have. The 'reader' is drawn into the apprehension of meaning, which is now no longer the 'writer's' domain. The central point in this argument is that distanciation is not only an epistemological necessity (because of the absence of the author), but it allows us to say *more* than can be known purely from within the author's context.

Before reading on, you might try some of the exercises on distance and understanding at the end of this chapter.

First- and third-person accounts

There are many ways of talking about the distinction between the type of understanding of the world that is lived by the experiencing subject and the understanding of this experience from the outside. There are, broadly speaking, two extended families of interpretive perspectives which can and should be distinguished. Pair-wise, they are variously referred to as follows:

- imposed and derived perspectives,
- emic and etic perspectives,
- first- and third-person perspectives,
- insider and outsider perspectives,
- intensional and extensional perspectives,
- understanding and explanation,
- description and interpretation, and
- local knowledge and expert knowledge.

In each pair, the first term refers to the way in which experience is lived from the perspective of the subjects who have the experience, and the second term to perspectives which are, to different degrees, alien to the form of life being described, and to the meanings immediately associated therewith.

We will now look at the process of understanding experience from outside of the context of the experience. We will term this process **distanciation**, which will be contrasted with **empathy**. Everyday life is lived in an attitude of understanding, to the extent that we understand the reasons for our actions. There is a rationality behind our actions (some would say even in madness), and in that sense we act intentionally. Of course, much of what we do is not *directly* intentional because much everyday action is done in a rote kind of way, without much reflection. Nevertheless, if asked to account for ordinary actions such as polite behaviour, we are able to account for ourselves. Schutz (1967) refers to the understanding by which we live as the 'stock of knowledge'. This stock of knowledge is subjective or, in the case of groups, 'intersubjective'. In distanciated interpretation, we are not only interested in understanding subjective understanding, but in revealing its contextuality. So we might say that we are interested in understanding 'understanding', or interested in interpreting understanding. Thus there are two movements, the first being the description of understanding, and the second involving the interpretation of understanding in its context. The first corresponds to the kind of orientation we have thus far called 'interpretive research', and the second to that which we have called 'social constructionist research'. We would argue that a really good research project should encompass both of these orientations. Thus, the project would want (1) to develop an understanding of subjective experience, and (2) to provide an interpretation of (1). In developing good interpretive accounts of this sort, we can employ four generic interpretive processes: playing the tension between insider and outsider accounts, balancing context and theory, integrating the reading of parts of the text into a coherent (whole) account, and the perceptual and cognitive processes of immersion, unpacking, and associating.

Playing the tension between insider and outsider accounts

Before proceeding, it should be said that the general direction we are about to take needs to be approached cautiously. Qualitative methods have provided a promising response to the need for contextual social science that speaks from the perspective of those being researched, and they constitute an effective antidote against hegemonic discourses which have tended to swallow up the voices of the excluded and marginalised in the quest for universal explanations.

As qualitative researchers we want to understand the world from the 'inside out' and from the 'outside in'.

Qualitative researchers in general are wary of the risk of overriding people's self-accounts. However, understanding does not go very far if it stops at summarising the way that people already understand their own realities. It has been said that one of the important strengths of qualitative research is that it is generative – that is, it constructs new ways of understanding, or new intelligibilities (Gergen, 1985). These may or may not be immediately recognisable as valid accounts of their experience by the people who are the subject of study. It may well happen that qualitative accounts describe people's actions in ways which are unfamiliar to them or which even seem incorrect to them. In such instances, the tension between description (insider perspective) and interpretation (outsider) is accented.

A good interpretive account shows what the world is like from a particular perspective, while at the same time drawing attention to its status as a perspective.

Sometimes it is possible to involve those 'being researched' in the analysis, and to explore understanding in a dialogue with them. More often, we play out an 'insider–outsider' dialogue in our own minds as researchers, trying to be true to the voices of the researched, but yet trying to answer our research questions. Our research questions may be extrinsic to the context, in the sense of not being the same questions that people in the context are currently addressing or able to answer. We need to hold their perspectives in mind and address, with our questions, what we thereby know.

The following are some practical conclusions we may draw from the above:

- Insightful accounts represent both insider and outsider perspectives – that is, we need not only to *understand*, but actively to *interpret* the voices of respondents.

- Well-crafted accounts are aware of their own interpretive strategies and make it clear when descriptive and when interpretive hermeneutic functions are being employed.

- We need to realise that our own speaking as researchers is also subject to interpretation by others. As far as is possible, we should write with this in mind.

- While those who are the subject of our research may not be able to confirm our interpretations, they are well positioned to confirm our descriptions of their understandings.

Box 15.2

Interpretation in participatory research (PR)

Participatory research is somewhat unique amongst qualitative approaches in that, following the textual model described earlier, accountability of the understanding to the author is not abandoned but maintained. Participatory research is equivalent to interpreting a text with the author. Enquiry is conducted in the presence of, and in dialogue with, the person (or group) being researched. This does not mean simply that the researcher defers to the author's interpretation of her or his own work, but that they enter into a dialogue where the researcher's questions and perspectives unlock previously unthought perspectives in the work. The intended outcome is that what emerges should be considered as 'their own' account, in spite of it having partly been crafted in conjunction with an outside researcher. Thus, 'inclusion of the self-understanding of the subject in the interpretive account' is a first, broad parameter to take into account in evaluating a participatory interpretive account.

There are a number of systems of participatory research that are characteristically innovative. One of the better known of these is Participatory Rural Appraisal (PRA), which consists of a process of engaging rural communities in reflecting on their own reality through exercises based on a 'mapping' of their reality. By creating images of their history, the structure of their community, the resources they have available to them, and so on, the community is brought through the epistemological function of distanciation to see their reality in different ways, which may represent previously unrecognised perspectives and needs.

Paulo Freire (1970) popularised the word 'conscientisation' to represent the awakening of critical awareness or consciousness. Critical consciousness is characterised by the development of a critical awareness of an issue, which exceeds everyday understanding of problems in the sense that it understands the expression of everyday understanding in a new or more critical light. Unfortunately, in participatory research this is the exception rather than the common case, and most PR work is nothing more than consultation. In this sense, it involves representation of a community's needs in such a way that it is a 'representative', rather than a 'critical', reflection on the community's experience.

Look at exercise 3 at the end of this chapter, which throws up some important questions in the understanding of participatory research interpretation.

Balancing context and theory

If qualitative research knowledge is contextually grounded, we might ask: 'What is the place of theory?' Theories are not to be found waiting to be discovered in the 'field'; they are *constructed* through a dialogue between questions and data, and with a view to achieving certain ends. To understand interpretation, we need to comprehend the relation between theory construction and contextual understanding.

The term '**emic**' was used by Pike (1967) to signify an approach to understanding from within a cultural system, one that provides insight into indigenous phenomena, and in which meaning derives from understanding phenomena in their own terms. An emic perspective involves a commitment to the forms of rationality that guide our everyday actions and the type of explanations that arise from the thinking that accompanies everyday action. Pike uses the term '**etic**' to refer to outside perspectives, and specifically the use of theory in understanding phenomena. '**Derived etics**' result from attempts to pull together knowledge from both etic and emic approaches. Emic understanding follows an inductive process, building general accounts from pieces of experience. This process usually begins with 'bracketing', which means suspending one's own framework and letting the data 'talk for itself'. The extent to which this is possible is a matter of debate, because we are usually led in our enquiries by specific questions which involve a particular approach to listening to the data. So bracketing is more like an orientation than an absolute position, whereby the intrinsic meanings which lie within the description of experiences are concentrated on.

As appealing as a 'homespun' approach to epistemology may be – whereby the context 'speaks' its meaning which we reliably record and describe – it is restrictive. The idea that meaning is 'indexical' – in other words, embedded in situations and events – restricts our ability to think about that which is trans-situational or general in nature. Using the example of Delius's (1996) research about 'witch' killing, it was the commonalities between discrete events – such as the finding, when looking at different situations, that they had in common the killing of older women by young men – that made it possible for the researcher to talk about generational and gender dimensions of the meaning of these events. A purely situated account, at least in most instances, would have ended with justifications for killing based on supernatural beliefs such as the belief that witches cause drought, lightning, and misfortune.

The degree to which we rely on the disclosive power of theory, or deductive thinking, to reveal aspects of a context which are not (and possibly cannot be) known in that context, varies. It varies according to the purposes of the research, and there is no *best* approach. Depending on where we place our qualitative accounts on a continuum, from experience-near (contextually derived) to experience-distant (theoretically led), the account will have different achievements and different shortcomings. Broadly speaking, experience-near accounts reveal the intricacies of the subjective experience of contexts, and tend to be inadequate for understanding patterns of experience across time and situation. More theoretical accounts, on the other hand, tend to be better at understanding the relation between experiences that occur across time and situation.

Good interpretive research should neither impose theoretical understandings on phenomena nor simply reproduce the phenomena uncritically.

Following a more phenomenological (experience-near) orientation, there is a concerted effort to reveal the 'structure of experience' using the terms of reference of the participants themselves. On the other hand, social constructionist researchers, being interested in interpreting as well as understanding the 'voices' of respondents, are more likely to draw on theoretical frameworks for making sense of situated events. Spanning contextual and theoretical orientations is the grounded theory approach (Strauss & Corbin, 1990), which has been elaborated as a system for developing theoretical accounts while keeping close to the phenomenological 'ground'. This matches Pike's (1967) notion of derived etics: The researcher endeavours to ensure that the theory is grounded to the extent that at all stages the original 'raw material' is brought back to the emerging account, to be accounted for, and to validate the theory. The researcher returns to the field to gather more material when existing material seems not to answer outstanding theoretical questions.

There is a close circular relationship between ground and theory. The degree to which one has successfully developed theory in a grounded way depends on the following:

- the degree to which the researcher has been led and surprised by the data,
- the extent to which the theory has been inductively generated,
- the degree to which 'prior' general accounts have given way to what the data suggest,
- the degree to which one has relied on prior (preconceived) and axiomatic (accepted as fact) frameworks of understanding in the development of the interpretive account, and
- the degree to which one has avoided or used technical language.

It is difficult to be prescriptive in this area, and possibly the closest that we should come to suggesting a particular generic approach is to say that theory which is not grounded, and description which is not theorised, stand in danger of being alienated from the advantages of the opposite perspective. Furthermore, research that maintains a tensional balance between them is most likely to draw on the advantages of both perspectives without suffering the disadvantages of adopting either one or the other.

Part and whole: working through the hermeneutical circle

The term 'hermeneutics' is sometimes used to refer to a particular kind of method, but we use it here in a more general sense to refer to the practice of interpretation in all of its forms – including work done from a social constructionist perspective.

Have you ever been frustrated when trying to discuss something at a level of the 'principle of the thing', and someone insists on getting bogged down in the detail of a particular example, or in telling a story that relates to the matter under discussion? Or have you ever been in a discussion so abstract that what one is talking about seems fuzzy and unclear? These instances demonstrate the qualities of a discourse that loses touch with the constructive tension between the particular and the general, or between detail and abstract understanding. This tension should be assiduously maintained at all stages of qualitative research.

Interpretive accounts should never be completely denuded of context, and details should never be presented without being positioned in relation to the overall structure of understanding. From listening and observation, through thematising, coding, and writing the final report, interpretation should keep one eye on the development of the whole and the other on the parts which are integrated therein. The idea of the **hermeneutical circle** prescribes that, in the interpretation of a text, the meaning of the parts should be considered in relation to the meaning of the whole, which itself can only be understood in respect of its constituent parts. This is usually conceived of as a circular movement between part and whole.

Proximity and distance provide different vistas of understanding, each with its own limitations and achievements.

Imagine a mosaic viewed from close up; in detail, it consists of so many pieces juxtaposed against each other. From a greater distance, the separate pieces begin to cohere or cluster into patterns of colour and form, configured in relation to each other and in their relation to the whole. Then the meaning of the whole becomes apparent. On the other hand, if it is viewed only from a distance, the mosaic loses the details and intensities that are apparent from up close. In the interpretation of texts, these are the feelings, the anecdotes, the isolated beliefs, and so on. The relation between the meanings of particular experiences and the meanings of themes that reflect a coherent clustering or ordering of themes of experience represents the operation of the hermeneutical circle. This process is important in all phases of interpretation in qualitative research. It begins with listening and observing, and gathers centrality in the entire process as the researcher moves through thematising, coding, and writing a final interpretive account.

The question of where to stand – how close, how far – is one that is close to the centre of qualitative research.

The intuitive thing to do when one is trying to say something in general is to look for commonalities across the material, but this is not enough. Sometimes one has to proceed indirectly to get to where one wants to go. In qualitative research, this may mean looking for differences, and giving this the same priority as the search for commonalities. In as much as we ask 'What can be said in general?', we must ask what must be retained of contextual detail that resists incorporation into a general account. By this means, we come to an understanding of what is distinctive about individual cases or contexts, or of events within a context. We should be reluctant to let go of contextual details, lest we lose something, even while realising that contextual detail and abstraction tend to exclude each other.

Immersing, unpacking, associating

In the previous chapter we spoke of immersing ourselves in our research material and of inductively discovering themes or discourses in it. Here we return to this most central aspect of interpretive work to discuss in a generic manner how we can analyse texts in a way that incorporates both experience-near and distanciated perspectives. We start with a consideration of the concept of 'over-determination'.

Dream images are appropriately spoken about as 'over-determined', which means that their meaning is not simple, and much has been 'condensed' into them. So, a 'raging bull' in a dream may refer simultaneously to an experience of being chased by a bull, a feeling of fear and panic which you generally have in your life, and an incident yesterday in which a colleague lost his temper with you. As in a thoughtful work of art, the images stand for many things, and there is no one-to-one correspondence between the image and a specific meaning. This is sometimes referred to as the 'polysemic' (many meanings) nature of images, and it applies as much to the interpretation of language as it does to visual images.

This quality of language is exemplified in metaphor, but it can also safely be said that, in everyday talk, discourses other than intended ones are present most of the time. Metaphors are forms of language that use words out of their usual literal context to impart meaning in another context. For example, the term 'babes' is sometimes used to describe beautiful young women. In such cases, and especially where this is systematically done, we need to reach an understanding of what meaning is being transposed to the context of the description through use of the metaphor 'babes'. What might it mean that we use the term 'babes'? How did that come about? Why 'babes'? Some would say it means nothing, and that it is 'just a way of speaking'. Others, and among them qualitative researchers, would recognise that in using conventional metaphors we participate in worlds of meaning that are implicitly invoked in the forms of speech that we use. In the previous chapter we called these 'worlds of meaning' discourses, interpretive repertoires, or speech genres. In using a way of speaking, we associate ourselves with, and participate in, the forms of social relations and understanding which it perpetuates. The use of 'babes' probably refers to a specifically male perspective on beautiful young women, which describes them as something to be taken hold of and looked after, as in 'my baby'. 'My baby' is something to be possessed and treasured, as in 'baby you're mine'. 'Babes' connotes 'baby-like', and the attendant actions of 'caring for' and 'looking after', and images of a relationship which position the male as the active provider and women as the

Interpretive research is motivated by the need to explain particular instances in terms of broad principles, but it also respects what is distinctive and unique about particular social phenomena.

Texts are 'over-determined' and 'polysemic' so that entire worlds of meaning are condensed into even the shortest of texts.

beautiful baby who needs simultaneously to be looked after and doted on. And so we might proceed as interpreters, 'immersing' ourselves in the world of meaning of 'babes', 'unpacking' its many meanings, and freely 'associating' on what it stands for. Let us now turn to these three processes of immersion, unpacking, and associating, which may be used to interpret the meanings of visual images and words.

Immersion

This refers to familiarising ourselves with images much as Beloff (1997) did when she put the images of artist Cindy Sherman on her walls so that she could interact with them in everyday life. Thus we get a feel for them and begin to know their details and nuances. In relation to written or spoken texts, this means becoming very familiar with the text, to the point of knowing where particular quotations occur in it, and getting a feel for the overall meaning and the different types of meaning in the text. In the case of interview transcripts, it is particularly important to develop a sense of the respondents' characteristic language usage. What metaphors are often used? Is there a family of metaphors used? We may notice, for example, that a person uses predominantly military metaphors to describe Aids (invasion, attack, 'battle against Aids'). At this point, we are still at the empathic, experience-near end of the interpretive continuum, but are starting to move towards a more distanced understanding.

Unpacking

The expression 'to unpack' is used to refer to the way in which we lay out the meanings of words and images, much as we would lay out the contents of a suitcase into different piles – these are socks, this is underwear, and so on. Apart from reflecting instances that show a thematic similarity, this is also a stock-taking activity. The suitcase contains many things, and each layer we take out reveals other layers, until the image or text seems to have had its contents revealed and we know what is there.

A good way of beginning this process is to list everything that has a bearing or comes to mind when thinking about the texts we are studying. Lists of themes help us to generate an overall idea of what we have got. We might then go on to develop maps showing how themes relate to other themes or subthemes, and showing ideas about which

Photo: Rodney Barnett

To unpack the symbolic meanings of certain images and texts, we need to understand the history of their creation.

themes are the more predominant in the images or stories we are faced with. Researchers develop their own ways of doing this, which might include simple graphic maps detailing which themes are predominant and which can be subsumed as subcategories of other themes. Miles and Huberman (1994) provide many examples of ways in which data might be graphically organised. Perhaps the most useful of these at this level of analysis is the simple dendrogram, which, like a branching tree, shows how a particular cluster of objects can split into a number of smaller ones, which in turn can be split into smaller ones, and so on, with the net result that one has many smaller objects all related to a central trunk through a network of branches. Thus, what was packed with condensed meaning has its contents and meanings revealed, and it is revealed as having a structure in terms of a network of themes. We are now starting to look at the material 'from the outside', although still remaining within the confines of what our research participants have told us, and without yet introducing much in the way of critical theory.

Associating

Returning to the dream analogy, we find that not only are meanings condensed into one another so that one thing can be unpacked into many smaller things, but we also find that one thing can *stand for* another (displacement of meaning). Something is *symbolic* if it stands for something else. In this way, the Voortrekker Monument in Pretoria is more than a building, it is a building that carries symbolic associations, which collectively may be said to be what it stands for.

In relation to dreams, Freud emphasised the value of 'free associating' on images, believing that by so doing the meanings of the associations would be revealed. This process involves speaking freely and spontaneously about whatever comes to mind when one thinks of an image. But images such as the Voortrekker Monument, while they require association to understand their meaning, tend to require resources beyond those which the imagination of the architect could possibly provide. As qualitative researchers, we need to refer to the contexts in which images and texts were created, and the history in which they were employed, to understand the fullness of their meaning. Finn (1997) did this in studying murals in Northern Ireland, as a way of understanding ideological dimensions to political violence in that context. A similar process can be undertaken using linguistic images (e.g., the use of the term 'settlers' to refer to 'white people'). Research participants often supply us with linguistic images that need to be thought about as reflecting a particular historical reference, having a sociocultural and political framework, and achieving something in the context of speaking.

Associating involves interpreting material in relation to a broader theoretical, historical, cultural, or political framework.

Notice how, in the 'babes' example earlier, associating with the term and the different contexts in which it might be used allowed some possible meanings to unfold. At the end of the chapter, there is an exercise that should assist in further understanding how we might go about developing an understanding of the meanings that lie behind our systematic use of metaphors. The process of associating with images is often led by, but also confined by, the dominant theoretical framework in our study If we are attempting to study everyday cognition or experience, we are likely to limit our associations to the kinds of meaning that are recognisable as meanings to the person involved. In cultural studies, we would typically stray much further away from intended meanings, and use resources other than the person's intended meanings. The field of transpersonal psychology, following the work of the psychologist Carl Jung, provides an example of a form of interpretation that exceeds personal or cultural experience. In interpreting symbolism at a level that transcends the psychology and sociology of the person, Jungian analysts find meaning in relation to a 'universal' and supposedly collective stratum of human consciousness. The question of validity rears its head here, and you may well be asking, 'Can I use any system to interpret the meaning of symbols?' The answer is yes, as long as you exercise the kinds of constraint that are discussed in the next chapter, and as long as you are aware that the understanding which you are thereby creating is a perspectival understanding in terms of a particular theoretical framework and your particular questions, rather than the final word on the matter.

In the previous chapter, we presented you with two possible sets of steps to follow when doing a qualitative data analysis. We are now ready to revisit some of these steps, which we will consider now in terms of the creative tensions between empathy and distanciation introduced in this chapter.

Themes, discourses, and the centrality of the research question

In the previous chapter, we saw that a central goal of analysis and interpretation is to discover regular patterns in our data – broadly termed 'themes' or ' discourses' in that chapter. In doing this, we should take care not to find only what we look for. It is easy to overlook the way in which the data do not quite fit the theme or discourse. One *can* get a square peg into a round hole if one tries hard enough, but qualitative researchers tend to change the categories to fit the data rather than to squeeze data into them. This is exemplified by the open coding process in **grounded theory**, according to which we develop new ways of coding if the codes that we are working with turn out not to accommodate the data. It also finds expression in the 'reading guide' method (Brown, Tappan, Gilligan, Miller, & Agyris, 1989), by which we are encouraged to formulate new questions as we proceed, and to condense these into a list of questions through which we read the material. In this sense, research is about asking and refining questions. It may even be said that research leads not so much to findings but to further questions. Some researchers dispense with the idea of identifying the questions that they are asking and proceed intuitively

Themes and discourses are both ways of apprehending aspects of a situation which connect it to other situations by virtue of inherent commonalities that bind them together, in spite of their contextual distinctiveness.

Box 15.3

Interpreting visual representations

Our everyday lives are crammed with visual representations that have been designed to persuade and enculturate us in different ways. In the area of media and cultural studies, and the social sciences in general for that matter, there has been a widespread recognition of the need to understand the impact of the images that surround us. Yet there has, to date, been very little development of clear methodologies in this area.

Ball and Smith (1992) summarise the analysis of visual data in qualitative research from a sociological and anthropological perspective. Photography has played an important part in anthropology from the 1920s onwards. But, for many years, photographs were included in studies for evidential rather than analytical purposes. They illustrated anthropological texts rather than provided a focus for sustained analysis. Obviously, in the study of visual cultural artefacts such as architecture and masks, they have played a more significant role, but in general Ball and Smith (1992) conclude that there has not been enough serious consideration of the use of visual images in anthropology. Goffman's (1979) work on 'Gender advertisements' might be regarded as part of a new generation of work in this area, where the visual domain is the primary textual domain. It uses photographs from illustrated newspaper and magazine advertisements to analyse 'gender displays' which Goffman interpreted as affirming basic 'engendered' social arrangements. This was one of the first of a wave of critical works to use 'found' images of contemporary culture to develop an understanding of society. At about the same time, Williamson's (1978) work entitled *Decoding Advertisements* and Berger's (1978) *Ways of Seeing* provided an important impetus towards the study of art and advertising in the social construction of reality.

The interpretation of visual representations or cultural objects is most often done in an 'open' investigative way, which is not prescribed by discrete methodological steps. It seems more akin to journalistic 'following of leads' than 'scientific' methodology. As an example, we might consider the work of Finn (1997), who undertook qualitative analysis of murals in Northern Ireland as a way of researching paramilitary justifications for political violence. He appears to have

to develop themes or identify discourses. However, it seems a good idea to be self-conscious about the questions we are asking, because it brings a degree of order into what can otherwise be an amorphous and muddling affair. It is also consistent with the generic model of understanding in interpretive and social constructionist research, which requires us to recognise that we are not entirely indifferent to the outcomes of the research and that we bring pre-understanding to the research process. Interpretive researchers do not try to assume 'the conducted a free-ranging exploration of the history of the images presented, the context of the creation of the images, the origins and context of the symbolism employed, and the supposed purpose of the murals. Using themes derived from his exploration, and keenly aware of contrasting themes, he developed an account of the ideological dimensions of the conflict in Northern Ireland. The account seems convincing, but how he got there is not something that one could easily describe in steps.

In a study of the work of feminist artist Cindy Sherman, Beloff (1997) provides some general guidelines for interpreting visual material, which is possibly as close as we would want to get to prescription in this young and evolving discipline. She suggests the following:

- Live with the material (Beloff pinned up Sherman's images in her room).
- Examine each image studiously and meticulously, and develop written descriptions of what is there.
- Reproduce the images and get a feel for them.
- Ask what metaphors, images are at play.
- Ask what the images were made for.
- Ask what the images achieve.
- Try out your interpretations on others.
- Read about and view relevant and related visual artefacts in order to understand the iconic and symbolic aspect of the visual data you obtain.
- Use other sources of information to help you identify other social representations on which the visual representations are based.
- Look for the contrary themes and the dilemmas represented by these.
- Write about the images as a way of opening up an interpretive account.

It could probably safely be said that qualitative researchers have a long way to go before they have achieved the same levels of competence in studying visual texts as in interpreting the written or spoken word. Almost any work in this area in South Africa is regarded as innovation, evidence that this is an undeveloped field deserving of greater attention.

view from nowhere', and thoroughly acknowledge the contextuality of their own engagement. This does not mean that their accounts need be relativistic – a most important point, and one that is often misunderstood. Because we ask particular questions does not mean that the account could be 'any account'; we ask our own questions, but we cannot make up the answers. The answers must devolve from the field or be evident in the data, and it follows that evolving understanding implies the evolution of questions.

Qualitative research is as much about asking and refining questions as it is about finding answers.

Thematic development is a kind of pattern-finding process, in which we identify a 'type' of occurrence by virtue of its being perceived as an underlying 'common form' found in different contexts. Thus, a theme or discourse can be said to exist both within a situation and also in other situations – that is, *within* and *across* situations. We do not apprehend a theme until we begin to look between situations, and the trans-situational character of themes is fundamental to understanding them. Therefore Delius (1996) can speak of the theme of gender in relation to witch killing because this can be recognised as a pattern which occurs in different situations. If there had been only one event to go by, it would have been much more difficult to identify gender as a feature of the event, especially if it was a theme that would not overtly be recognised and spoken about by those involved.

In deriving themes, we tend intuitively to look for generality and, in so doing, we necessarily overlook certain contextual differences in the things we are comparing. In doing this, we can bind together events in such a way as to override their uniqueness. By being careful to let both movements of the hermeneutic circle (particular to general and general to particular) have an influence, we are most likely to arrive at an interpretation that accounts both *for* contexts and *across* contexts.

One's interpretive framework may be preformulated, in which case thematising would mean no more than filling out the details of the theme or discourse using the contextual material one has gathered. Or one may be interested in conducting a more phenomenological study, and discover what themes can be extracted from within the context itself in the form of the subjective understanding of a phenomenon by a subject, or the intersubjective experience of a group (a shared 'local' understanding of a phenomenon). In forms of study that are oriented towards developing theory out of contextual research – most notably grounded theory – one would ideally find a medium between using established themes in the form of emerging theoretical structures which the researcher is becoming committed to and an openness to new themes emerging.

Themes as patterns and sequences

White (1980) says we tell life stories both 'at once' and 'in order'. Telling 'at once' refers to the thematic identification of past and present in the form of, say, a typical way of responding to a situation, which existed then and exists now. For example, the way in which a person responds to authority figures may have persisted from childhood to adulthood. Telling 'in order' is the **temporal**, sequential ordering of life events, where one event is recognised as being sequentially related to another event, much as procrastination can be related to depression. Let us look at these two types of 'telling' under the headings of pattern finding and temporal linking.

Pattern finding

Central to the idea of pattern finding is the notion of repetition. We notice that a given structure is a pattern by virtue of the fact that it re-occurs. The search for 'repeatable regularities' is central to qualitative enquiry. In a phenomenological study, patterns are the regularities in the way the respondent relates to the world in different situations and at different times. In a discourse analytic study, patterns are regularities in the way language is used to achieve certain effects. A simple way of talking about this is to talk of 'characteristics'. That which is characteristic is by definition not linked to a particular context or borne of a particular situation, and, in the same way that a person's character is more or less fixed across context, it endures across situations and times.

Temporal linking

When we identify a theme that exists across time and situation, it is not necessarily based on repetition, but can be based on an inferred link between two moments in time, such that one is assumed to cause the other. The facts of a person's life – such as the fact that a person's parents divorced when she was seven years old, or that she attempted suicide at the age of 20, or that she is feeling desperately lonely – do not in themselves mean anything. They imply something about this person's life because they are bound together in a sequence. We call this kind of linking together of moments in time 'temporal linking'. The construction of temporal links involves two processes: (1) inferring that two temporally distinct events are related, and (2) exploration of the conditions of that relationship. The same kind of linking is possible on a broader social level. In the previous chapter, for example, we saw how discourses from the apartheid era live on in present-day South Africa.

Integration: the final product

The rise to prominence of qualitative research methodologies has been accompanied by a suspicion of grand, all-encompassing theories of social life and human experience. The shift has been away from the universal and general towards the local and the particular. We have learned through the works of the Frankfurt School, the post-structuralists, and others that knowledge which attempts to 'cover' the world may serve interests of domination. In this context, we have learned to be very cautious about extending our knowledge claims to other contexts, and saying things 'in general'. Given this, it is important to think carefully about what kind of general account we settle with.

Earlier, we discussed the idea of the hermeneutical circle. We will now continue this discussion at the level of developing a final, overarching account. Our concern remains the need to craft accounts that have a satisfactory balance of particularity (context) and generality. Finn (1997) ended up talking about ideological dimensions in the conflict in Northern Ireland, having started with analysis of specific

The Frankfurt School was a group of critical theorists (including Adorno, Horkheimer, and Habermas) active before and after the Second World War. They predicted the rise of fascism in Germany and, in the post-war years, warned against authoritarian tendencies in the liberal Western democracies.

murals painted on walls. At this more general level, the account is still about the murals, but at a greater level of abstraction, and in relation to broader theoretical questions.

Having broken down texts into 'bits' and derived themes, the challenge facing the qualitative researcher is to put it all together again, or to tie the themes together into some form of general account. Let us now turn our attention to the question of how general or contextual the final account should be.

Situated and general accounts

If we are doing a phenomenological analysis, writing a situated account is the process whereby we reassemble the account of experience after it has been broken down into 'meaning units' and themes (Giorgi, 1985). If we are doing a more theory-led or category-led piece of research, a similar process is involved, although the account will tend to be more strongly thematised by extrinsic categories. But, in either case, the extent to which the account is given in terms of the contextual details which surround the events of interest is the degree to which it is 'situated'.

A situated account is the researcher's retelling of what research participants told her or him.

If I ask you to tell me about yourself, there is only so much that you can say about your thoughts and feelings at a general level, before you will begin to contextualise what you mean. You will in all likelihood begin to talk about your experience by telling stories about 'what happened'. The generation of 'narrative' accounts has emerged as one way of tying together the 'bits' of a case study, or the little stories, into a coherent, whole, unified story that could be likened to a biography. One might say that a narrative is a way of providing an account that communicates what happens in a context, and even explains why things happen as they do, without resorting to general, theoretical, or etic terms. In this sense, we may say that narratives are akin to 'emic theories'.

A situated account is reconstructive in that it begins by reconstructing the words of the respondents, or, in the case of observation, reconstructing what is observed from the perspective of the first-person account. However, this is usually written in the third person, although it represents the experience or phenomenon as it is seen by the first person. So, for example, a researcher writes:

> When the doctor told her that her symptoms matched a known disease syndrome, she was 'so relieved', because for the first time someone had recognised that she had what she termed 'a real disease' and that she was not just 'shamming' (malingering). She immediately thought of her husband and hoped that he would now accept that she was really ill.

Notice how this account is a mixture of description of what she experienced, her actual words ('so relieved') and the researcher's notes (italic emphasis on 'so' in 'so relieved' and explanation of the colloquial term 'shamming'). Note also that many contextual details have been stripped from the account because they are thematically irrelevant at this point. For instance, the time of day and the gender of the doctor are considered superfluous to the sick-role legitimisation theme which, at this point, is structuring the story.

The art of writing a situated account involves providing readers with enough contextual detail to allow them to imagine the situation as it was experienced within the parameters of the relevant theme. Quotations are very useful in this respect, but overuse of quotation should be cautioned against, as it often substitutes for thematic analysis. As a rule, it is advisable to quote only when the person said it better than the researcher could possibly say it, and only when the quotation fits in with the general thematic development. Quotations are over-determined, and putting them into the situated account can sometimes confuse the reader because the quotation leads in a few different directions, whereas the account is trying narratively to relate a particular 'theme of experience'.

Quotations enliven situated accounts, but can cause the account to lose focus.

It often happens that, when qualitative researchers write up their studies, they give an adequate account of the ways in which they interpreted the individual accounts, but the 'audit' (see the next chapter) is devoid of any reflection on the way that the individual accounts were integrated into a general account. This takes place as a distinctive interpretive process that involves examination of the commonalities and differences between the separate cases in the form of situated accounts and writing up of the processes involved without recourse to specific contexts. A general structure in a single case study is the account of the experience stripped of contextual detail. Given the example used above, one might write as follows:

> The recognition by a medical professional that the patient's malady corresponds to a known disease syndrome is accompanied by a sense of relief in the patient and a sense of the patient's experience being affirmed, in the context of there having been some doubt about whether the patient was malingering.

Notice that this is written without referring to a particular patient or situation, without particular details pertaining to one instance, and as a description of a general rather than an historical process (written in the present tense). This level of analysis is particularly appropriate at the level of providing an account across cases.

Conclusion

In this chapter, we have looked more closely at qualitative data analysis; in other words, how to get from text to interpretation. We have explored some aspects of the philosophy of interpretation in the social sciences, and from this we have extracted principles that can be used in interpreting texts. We have again stressed the view that in developing an interpretive strategy one has to think on one's feet. Qualitative research offers little comfort for those who need to be instructed as to what to do, or who need a recipe with fixed rules to follow. Qualitative data analysis is not a mechanical process, but an open process of engaging with a text in an attitude of enquiry. Even the recipes that do exist are no more than guidelines.

We have borne in mind, throughout this chapter, the distinction between two families of perspectives, and have concluded that the process of interpretation draws on both perspectives and ideally maintains a balance between them. It is the researcher's choice to decide which of the two is in ascendancy (like a see-saw) at any moment in the research process and in completing the research. For example, research goes through theoretical stages, where the researcher immerses herself or himself in theory; at other times, the researcher immerses herself or himself in the text or situation. Interpretation that moves more to one side of the tensional relationship between these opposing tendencies loses the achievements of the other perspective as its own achievements come to the fore. The optimisation of the balance depends on the reasons for doing the research and what one wants to achieve with the research. In participatory, action-oriented, and phenomenological approaches, one would ensure (as a matter of process regulation in participatory research) that the local, emic, contextual perspective comes to the fore, and there would be a graded and cautious development of general, etic, and critical perspectives. In discourse analysis and semiotics, the account would tend to adopt theoretical and distanciated perspectives as a more primary mode of interpretation, while striving to remain respectful towards local, emic perspectives. Accounts that stray to either end of this dialectical relationship suffer credibility problems, as the standards of confirmation or proof offered within each perspective recede along with the achievements of the perspective. In the following chapter, we will look more closely at what these standards of proof entail.

Exercises

1. Sometimes a bit of distance helps us to see things more clearly. There is benefit to hindsight. Can you look back on a period of your life and say, for example, 'I was really unsettled then, but did not realise it'? Think of a situation in the past which you have now come to feel very differently about. In other words, think of a situation about which you have changed your interpretation. You might imagine a kind of person you previously found unpleasant and who you now quite like, or perhaps a practice (drug taking, cigarette smoking), or a particular event might come to mind. It need not be a personal experience and might be a social perception about people from a background dissimilar to your own. First, in small groups, discuss examples of this kind of experience which show how we sometimes get to know a context or a situation differently after it has passed, or when we are removed from it. Second, consider whether knowing a situation as it *really* is means knowing it only from the perspective of being in the situation, or

whether distance offers equally legitimate understanding of the context, albeit from outside. Third, using your own examples, discuss which perspective enables more awareness of the details of the context, more awareness of the feelings which were experienced then (and the reasons for feeling that way), and more critical analysis.

2. Friend 1: 'Don't tell me what I feel. I know how I feel!'

   Friend 2: 'Well, you look angry to me!'

   Friend 1: 'Well, I'm not.'

   Is it possible to have an emotion and not know it? In discussing this, look at some possible reasons why people might either not be aware of, or might deny their own emotions, fantasies, and thoughts. What does this mean for qualitative researchers?

3. 'Some women say that they are happy in their marriages even though they are dominated by their husbands. They are deceiving themselves. One day they will realise how oppressed they are.' Can we be oppressed without knowing it? What does this mean for qualitative researchers?

4. Consider the following statements about Aids:

   - Aids is a dangerous invader and we must protect our innocent children.
   - Aids is a killer disease that knows no boundaries.
   - Aids is the new struggle.
   - Aids is the leprosy of our times.

   (a) For each of the above statements, identify the metaphors that are used. Remember that metaphor is used when a term is borrowed from another context to impart meaning in the present context.

   (b) Select one metaphor from each statement and elaborate on the meanings that are imparted to Aids by the use of this metaphor. In each case, discuss what the effects of the use of the metaphor might be.

   (c) Discuss whether it might be possible to discuss Aids without recourse to metaphors.

5. As a stimulus for group discussion, consider the following passage:

   Take the ideas of the masses (scattered and unsystematic ideas) and concentrate them (through study turn them into concentrated and systematic ideas), then go to the masses and propagate and explain these ideas until the masses embrace them as their own, hold fast to them and translate them into action, and test the correctness of these ideas in such action. Then once again concentrate ideas from the masses and once again go to the masses ... And so on, over and over again in an endless spiral, with the ideas becoming more correct, more vital and richer each time. Such is the Marxist theory of knowledge. (Mao Tse-tung, 1943, pp. 287–294)

(a) What might be meant by 'turn them into concentrated and systematic ideas', and specifically what might it mean that they are not already 'concentrated and systematic ideas'? What are they if they are not this?

(b) Why should we need our own ideas explained to us? What does this imply about understanding in general?

(c) When the quotation refers to ideas becoming 'more correct' every time, it presumably means that the ideas become more correct by virtue of translating into actions which somehow prove the understanding to be correct. How can the outcomes of actions based on a particular understanding prove the understanding which lay behind the desire to perform the action to be correct? You might find it helpful to think of practical examples such as being polite to your lecturer on the understanding that this will benefit you, or putting an alarm in your car to deter thieves. Consider how we might evaluate the correctness of possible underlying assumptions, according to whether the actions we take on the basis of them have the intended outcomes.

6. Take a group of 30 freely chosen objects, ensuring a diversity in the types of object, and spread these out on a work surface.

(a) A team of four should spend about ten minutes sorting the objects into piles. They should do this silently. The rest of the group should take note of how they go about sorting the piles and try to imagine what kinds of categories they are applying. After they have finished, the whole group should conduct a discussion based on the decision-making processes that took place during the course of the exercise. Discuss conflicts that may have arisen between the sorters about the categories being applied.

(b) About four of the former observers should now take a turn to sort the objects silently, but this time with the following instruction: 'Place the objects along a line (continuum) representing how useful or not the object would possibly be to someone going to university for the first time'. Alternatively, you might make up your own criterion for sorting. Note what they do and discuss it afterwards.

(c) Questions for general discussion after the above exercises: What difference did the categories make to the process? What happens when there are no questions? Can category or sorting decisions be made without questions? Are there natural relationships amongst objects that exist, apart from the questions we impose? For example, are a soccer ball and a rugby ball naturally more alike than, say, jeans and a tie? What lessons can we draw from this about thematising, coding, and research questions?

Key readings

Bleicher, J. (1980). *Contemporary hermeneutics: Hermeneutics as method, philosophy and critique*. London: Routledge.
This book provides an excellent introduction to hermeneutics, and is highly recommended for anyone wanting to come to grips with the complex history of thinking about interpretation in the Western philosophical tradition. It provides a good overview of the different positions that exist and helps to order one's understanding of what might otherwise seem a very difficult field.

Bogdan, R., & Taylor, S. J. (1975). *Introduction to research methods: A phenomenological approach to the social sciences*. New York: Wiley.
This book provides a fairly comprehensive and readily understandable overview of all stages of the qualitative research process.

Dey, I. (1993). *Qualitative data analysis: A user friendly guide for social scientists*. London: Routledge & Kegan Paul.
As the title implies, this book provides a handy introductory guide to the analysis of qualitative data and contains detailed descriptions of categorising and coding procedures.

Ricoeur, P. (1979). The model of the text: Meaningful action considered as a text. In P. Rabinow & W. M. Sullivan (Eds), *Interpretive social science: A reader*. Berkeley: University of California Press.
This is a very important paper in the field of interpretive social science. Although difficult to comprehend in all of its complexity, any time spent engaging with it will be rewarding.

Calling it a day:

reaching conclusions in qualitative research

Kevin Kelly

Rhodes University, CADRE

There comes a point in every research project where pressures of time and limited resources lead researchers to have to draw to a conclusion. In one sense, one can never say enough. It has been pointed out in previous chapters that enquiry is potentially open-ended, and, to the extent that research leads to new questions, which in turn need to be further researched and answered, we might say that research is never-ending. Yet, practically, we do need to draw research projects and programmes to an end, recognising that we embark on research to ask specific questions, and accordingly it is necessary to have a sense of when they have been answered. In this chapter, we will be looking closely at issues that need to be addressed in thinking about conclusions in qualitative research. However, we will see that some of these issues are not only relevant in wrapping up the research. While they come to a head at this point, they are important at all stages.

Intrinsic to our research efforts is the belief that our interpretations are somehow correct. It is hard to imagine research that is not in some way accompanied by a belief in the truth value of the emerging account. The issue of truth and correctness has been extensively discussed in the history of qualitative methodologies. In the social sciences, the emergence of qualitative methodologies has been accompanied by a 'crisis of legitimation' (Lincoln & Denzin, 1994). This means that qualitative researchers have not simply been able to rely on standards of verification and proof, or standards of rigour, from positivist epistemology. They have had to develop, and are still in the process of developing, their own standards, based on interpretive and social constructionist epistemologies. It may be said that the crisis is not over, and there is still little concordance about what constitutes scientifically adequate practice and proof.

An issue that confounds our thinking about evaluating qualitative research is that 'findings' are not only descriptions of that which is already 'there' in the context. Through the processes involved in developing themes and determining codes and integrating these into general accounts, knowledge is *created* (i.e., a 'construction'). These two aspects might be referred to respectively as **discovery** and **creation** (or invention). The former might be evaluated by checking out whether it matches with what it purports to describe; the latter has to be evaluated for its value and its consequences (i.e., what the account achieves). We will bear this distinction in mind throughout this chapter. It corresponds approximately with the insider–outsider and description–interpretation distinctions and related distinctions discussed in the previous chapter.

Qualitative research can be evaluated in terms of how well it accounts for the phenomenon studied, and in terms of the consequences that flow from the research.

Exhaustion/saturation

The term 'exhaustion' has its most literal manifestation in the state of mind that a qualitative researcher attains before what is left undone is 'let go of' and the project rushes hastily to a conclusion, frequently in pursuit of a deadline. As often as not, there is much, much more to be said, and the material that has been collected for the project could be further mined for meaning. If we are fortunate, however, a project draws to a conclusion not because we have run out of time and resources, but because our account has reached a point of 'saturation'. **Saturation** refers to the condition of an interpretive account where the account is richly fed by the material that has been collected, at least to the point where the researcher can intuitively say: 'I have thoroughly explored the data and have acquired a satisfactory sense of what is going on'.

It should be said that the process of analysis and interpretation continues and even accelerates as one writes up the research report. Writing, collecting data, reading theoretical work, analysing data, and so on often happen more or less simultaneously. This is especially so in grounded theory, but is also a general feature of all qualitative research. The writing-up of a research project, and especially the discussion section, engages the researcher in continuing analytic work as she or he begins to understand the material in relation to theoretical questions and literature in the field. This should really be thought of as a stage in the interpretive process, so significant is it at the level of generating understanding. Interpretation proceeds until the last word is written, and it is a pity that more time is not given to the final stages of research projects, where recommendations and indications are given and executive summaries drawn up. Even giving your project a title is part of this process. As one student said: 'At a fairly late stage I decided to change the title [of the project]. Through this I recognised that my research had taken a turn, which became central to the whole thing'. Using the title as an anchoring point, the student was able to work towards the new focus and to reach a conclusion.

Students are well advised to realise that the discussion, while it comes at the tail-end of a research document, is the centre of the whole endeavour.

Box 16.1

When have I done enough?

- When the new thoughts I am having about the material are not adding anything new to the understanding I have already developed.
- When it seems that my account answers the question that I set out to answer and adequately represents the material I have collected.
- When I have thrown a barrage of critical questions at the interpretation and it is still standing.
- When new material and new questions seem to confirm the account rather than break it down.
- When I have shared my opinions with other researchers or my supervisor, and the account has provided responses to their questions.

The need for standards of confirmation

In addition to knowing when we have done enough, we also need to know whether what we have done is *good enough*. As members of scientific communities and of societies with interests at stake in the degree of rigour with which research is conducted, we are interested in finding standards for good research. This is a challenging area of debate. Issues at stake range from whether the outcomes of the research warrant expenditure of funds, and whether the research rests on satisfactory ethical foundations, to technical issues about whether the data were reliably collected and processed. Traditionally, the latter has been the focus in establishing standards.

Although some qualitative research is positivist or quasi-positivist in nature, in many respects qualitative research emerged *in reaction* to positivism, and there has thus been a rejection of positivist notions of reliability and validity, without much agreement about what standards of proof should replace these. By their very nature, qualitative research systems are resistant to the imposition of uniform standards of good practice. They stand for understandings that are contextual and for tailor-made methods rather than canonical designs, and they accept the role of the researcher in changing the context of the research. The rest of this chapter will concentrate on how we might start to develop standards that are credible and rigorous without contradicting the fundamentals of interpretive and social constructionist epistemologies. We will look at the need to monitor and reflect on research processes, the qualities of defensible knowledge claims, and the characteristics of compelling narrative accounts. One often reads desperate attempts at damage control in the closing pages of theses, where researchers severely criticise their own work as a way of defending themselves against outside criticisms. But by then it is too late, a case of shutting the stable door after the horse has bolted. So we need to look not only at how we evaluate our own interpretive accounts at the end of the day, but how we do it in a 'housekeeping' way throughout the research process.

> 'Hermeneutic consciousness remains incomplete as long as it does not include a reflection upon the limits of hermeneutic understanding.' (Habermas, 1980, p. 90)

Steps toward critical enquiry

It is easy to find confirmation for an idea if we are selective enough in choosing evidence to prove it. It is only when we consciously set out to disprove our accounts that we can start to talk about accuracy. In a form of enquiry based on selecting, cleaning, sifting through, coding, and organising data, it is all too easy to embark on a self-fulfilling quest; that is, to find what you set out to find and find convincing reasons to convince others of the veracity (truthfulness) of these findings. Unfortunately, this often happens. Qualitative researchers take their questions to the material (which has been carefully selected) and begin, in a step-wise manner, to find corroboration for their ideas. This amounts to no more than using the guise of 'science and method' to make our pre-formed ideas appear more convincing. Packer and Addison (1989) call this process of projecting our own beliefs and prejudices onto the world and then rediscovering them as 'findings' the **vicious circularity of understanding**.

Whether or not understanding inevitably has a tendency to become no more than a self-fulfilling prophesy has been a major, if not the major, area of debate in the literature on hermeneutics. Despite this controversy there is general agreement that, without a 'backward arc', which involves looking back on our own progress and retracing our

> *Pause and think about the context of the vicious circularity of understanding. What might it do to your understanding to think of the concept as itself reflecting a particular interpretive framework or interpretive bias?*

steps in a critical way, our prejudices remain unrehabilitated. This process is also referred to as 'the critical moment' or the 'critical instance' in the process of interpretation. So how do we interrupt vicious circles of understanding? Habermas (1991) calls attention to the need for a critical process of reflection on the interpretive process and the effects that this has on the emerging interpretive account. He talks of interpretation as a dialogue, which in participatory research takes place between researcher and participant, but in other forms of qualitative research takes place between researcher and text.

Dialogical interpretive processes readily collapse into premature foreclosure, especially when there are pressures to reach a conclusion. You might have noticed that participants sometimes tend to agree on matters towards the end of a meeting, and sometimes important tensions get glossed over in this process, only to emerge later, like a stone in the shoe, to bedevil the dialogical process. One way of guarding against dialogical imbalances (e.g., domination of the 'dialogue' by one party or perspective) and correcting the same is constantly to reflect on or evaluate the process of the dialogue; that is, to reflect on the research process itself. It helps to look at the interpretive effort through other eyes, and discussion of one's interpretations with colleagues is an important corrective. Another way is to review one's own work after a bout of theoretical reading. New ideas help us to develop a 'distanciated' perspective, which is like 'the eyes of the other'. Here, we might recall the discussion of 'distanciation' in the previous chapter.

There is a wealth of reading on how we might attain critical perspectives on our own work. Apart from the work of Habermas referred to above, you might look at the critical theorists of the Frankfurt School of the 1930s and the poststructuralist philosophers such as Derrida and Foucault. The final chapters in this book provide further pointers on how one might attain a critical theoretical perspective on one's work.

The following seven questions, derived in part from Comstock (1994), will help to steer you away from research that simply finds evidence for what the researcher already believes, and towards more open and critical processes of enquiry:

- Are there possible exceptions to what has been found, but which the data simply have not shown up or which have not been included at the level of sampling?

Could the negotiations which led to the establishment of democracy in South Africa be seen as an example of 'dialogical imbalances' and 'premature foreclosure'?

Photo: Rodney Barnett

- What unquestioned assumptions, ideological positions, and unreflected-upon points of view lie behind the emerging account?
- Has the emerging account become rigid, so that it is no longer responsive to being changed by the emerging material, or is it 'porous' (permeable), where the meaning of terms is mutable and open to reinterpretation?
- Are terms used in an over-general or technical way such that their contextual meaning is not apparent?
- Is the emerging account based on often-repeated metaphors which are a screen for a lack of understanding?
- Is the account becoming self-referential – the meaning of term A defined by term B, which is defined by term A in a circular fashion?
- Has the researcher learned anything from the data or simply used the data to illustrate and 'flesh out' a theory?

Box 16.2

The seductions of narrative

Spence (1983) expresses reservations about an overly easy narrative rendering of experience that may lead the researcher to assume more order and more coherence in social life than actually exists. Narrative accounts of experience are very compelling, and we are easily persuaded to accept them as truthful. There are four reasons for this. First, if we explain something that has never been explained before, the story will carry conviction because almost any account is better than no account. Second, we are influenced by the range and scope of the narrative account, so that if a relatively compact account can be shown to account for a great range of happenings it is naturally considered more persuasive.

> If I can show that your life can be reduced to a limited number of significant themes, variously repeated and transformed, then it follows that this account will tend to be more persuasive than a formulation which must invent a new reason for each new happening. The rule of limited reasons (extended scope) draws some of its appeal from a mistaken analogy with the natural sciences. It is as if I have found a basic law that can be applied to a wide range of situations. (Spence, 1983, pp. 461–462)

A third ground of narrative persuasion lies in the aesthetic appeal or satisfaction that derives from finding that one theme continues to appear and reappear in a person's life, and which is more compelling than the difficult-to-grasp complexity of experience. Finally, there is a persuasiveness to accounts that have a 'here and now' sense of consistency. The current feelings experienced in a context add a persuasiveness to those accounts that are consistent with current feelings, so that we overlook that which is not consistent with current sentiment.

We may conclude that we need to be very cautious about the apparently convincing qualities of well-rendered narratives of experience.

Leaving a research trail and conducting an audit

As readers of research reports, we need to be able to form a second opinion, or to disconfirm the conclusions reached by the researcher. However, aspects of the study that appear arbitrary, puzzling, contradictory, or unsupported by the evidence are all too often 'left behind' as the final account is presented as smooth and seamless. It hardly needs to be said that this kind of scenario is less than satisfactory.

Qualitative research reports are usually amply peppered with illustrative quotes or anecdotes, chosen because they make particular points dramatically or very clearly. This makes such accounts seem convincing. However, as the adage goes: 'An example is not proof'. Examples assist us to make points, and possibly provide 'supporting evidence', but they are not convincing when we realise that they have been selectively chosen for their heuristic or illustrative value.

One corrective to this problem is the suggestion that writers of qualitative research reports should include interview and other 'raw material' in an appendix. This is of some assistance to people wanting to understand and evaluate the research, but because of the quantity of text involved it is usually not possible to include all of the 'raw' material, especially not when research is being published in the form of a journal article.

If it is impossible to provide all of the 'raw material' as an appendix to a research report, you should give the reader an opportunity to appraise at least some of the material in a 'raw state'.

There is another limitation in the extent to which one can give the reader access to the 'raw data'. By the time the researcher has 'the text' in hand, layers of selective questioning, recording, transcription, and exclusion have already occurred, which stand between the text and the 'uninterpreted' field. In addition to providing as much of the raw material as possible, the researcher should give an account of how the evidence emerged (in relation to what sort of questioning and prompting, and in what context) and how it was processed by the researcher in terms of cleaning, summarising, and organising.

Miles and Huberman (1984), together with other writers on methodology, recommend that readers of a research report should be provided with an **audit trail**. Unless the researcher leaves a trail and describes in detail what is done, the reader is left at the mercy of the researcher's ability to smooth over the cracks. Audit trails vary greatly in detail and complexity. Some researchers find it useful to document every step of the data-gathering and analysis process meticulously, even to the point of using special codes to identify what they have done. Others prefer to keep an 'analytic diary' or 'reflexive journal', which accounts for what is done and why it is done at all phases of the research process – such as initial concerns and how these have changed.

Whatever form of audit trail you use, it is important that it should not stop when you start writing up the research, and that it should find its way into the final report. While it is impractical, for example, to include an entire analytic diary in the report, writers will often give brief examples of each stage of data reduction and interpretation, and will account for issues that became relevant at each stage of interpretation. Ideally, the reader should be in a position to replicate the research method, and should have a sense of the interpretive lenses that have been applied to the analysis of the field. We should let the reader into our confidence and report not only the final resolution, but also the route we followed on the way there.

At the broadest level, leaving an 'audit trail' involves writing in such a way as not only to make a statement, but at the same time to reveal the statement's perspectivity. By perspectivity, we refer to a view being a particular kind of outlook (or interpretive framework) which is one of many possible outlooks. How do we make a convincing statement and at the same time put this statement in a way that it shows itself as appreciating itself as a particular position or standpoint?

Here is a thought puzzle that presents us with this conundrum: 'Can we believe in God and know our belief as a belief?' If my conviction were to be based only on belief, you would agree that my conviction stands on shaky ground. As it happens, 'believing' brings about circumstances and experiences which seem to provide proper evidence that the belief is more than just a belief; so my belief becomes an apparently 'evidenced' conviction. (See Elster, 1986, if these kinds of question interest you.) This is an example of how an initial understanding (taken uncritically or 'on faith') 'sets up' the circumstances which it purports to describe. Our question now is: 'Is it possible to use language in a way that is appreciative of itself as doing this?' This would mean using language in a way that understands its own effects, appreciative of the possibility, as Austin (1975) says, that words 'do things'.

Qualitative researchers sometimes 'feel' their way to their conclusions and rely on their imaginations, spontaneous impressions, personal experiences, and background knowledge of the field. Accounts of their research, if they are to be true, should explain how the more important of these personal motivations and experiences operated in the process of research.

One way of doing this is through a process of 'ironising'. Irony refers to expressing one's meaning in a way that is self-conscious, through adopting language of opposite tendency. It often involves the inversion of the typical use of a term to achieve other effects. For example, the self-conscious adoption of the term 'queer' in gay discourse, or the use of the term 'nigger' by black Americans, are both powerful ways of undoing dominant marginalising discourses. The relevance in this context is to show that the method of irony can lead us to avoid the trap of saying

Photo: Rodney Barnett

Is it possible to speak with conviction while maintaining an ironic distance from what we say?

things in a positive way, and then having to rescue the statement by applying critical and relativising perspectives. Irony is part of the process of leaving a research trail, but is arguably more deeply embedded in the language in which we report our research than the techniques described earlier. We are talking about a form of auditing that needs to take place in the act of writing, so that ideally every sentence of the report has built into itself a consciousness of the effects of its own saying.

Qualities of defensible knowledge claims

'The quest for absolute, certain knowledge is replaced by a conception of defensible knowledge claims.'
(Kvale, 1996, p. 242)

In the previous chapter we spoke about two types of meaning, which we could label 'intended meaning' (the writer's meaning) and 'interpretive meaning' (the reader's interpretation). It was established that we can posit the veracity of intended meaning by asking the speaker to verify or confirm whether the researcher has 'got it right'. This is 'descriptive' research which uses the methodology of empathy. The position with regard to establishing the truth value of interpretive accounts becomes less clear when we go beyond 'giving voice' to the respondent's perspective; that is, when we move from empathy to interpretation. For the most part, what follows is concerned with trying to think our way around how to establish standards for 'better interpretation'. We hope that it has been appreciated that the standards for descriptive research are self-evident – simply check with the respondent that you have understood correctly, something that supposedly happens in the context of the interview. It may also involve returning the narrative or summarised rendering of their experience to respondents. Here the term 'reliability' is not inappropriate and translates into the question, 'Have I reliably given voice to your experience?' Standards for distanciated interpretation are less definitive, and we will address these below.

Miller (1989) states that if a child asks about the difference between a man and a woman, and is told that a man has larger feet and hands than a woman, the answer is not false but evades central, more discriminating distinctions. Something may be true, but its truth value needs to be seen in the context of such questions as 'But how exclusively true is it?', or 'Does it identify the features that make this case distinctive from other cases?'

Within the qualitative research literature, the term 'validity' has come under critical scrutiny (Altheide & Johnson, 1994). Scheurich (in Lincoln & Denzin, 1994) says that validity is a boundary line that 'divides good research from bad, separates acceptable (to a particular research community) research from unacceptable research ... it is the name for inclusion and exclusion' (p. 578). One finds similar views expressed by Lather (1986), who suggests that validity is the researcher's mask of authority, which gives legitimacy to a particular regime of truth to have its way in the world and with the reader.

In the final chapters of this book you will find a discussion of what might replace notions of validity if we renounced the desire to produce an authoritative (valid) account (Lincoln & Denzin, 1994). In the following discussion, we are not going to immerse ourselves in debates about the status of reliability and validity in qualitative research any further, but attempt to establish some standards for evaluating research without falling back on simple notions of correspondence between truth claims and a determinate world. We will look at the following for our standards: good qualitative practice, triangulation, generalisability and transferability, communicative validity, and pragmatic proof through action.

Good qualitative practice

The family of qualitative research methods involves a great diversity of approaches, and it might sound unlikely that there could be general standards of good practice. Yet there are some generic considerations that most would agree should be found in almost all qualitative research. Lincoln and Denzin (1994) point to the common denominator of all good qualitative research in the closing sentence of their monumental collection of essays on the subject: 'The commitment to study human experience from the ground up' (p. 584).

Good interpretive accounts work not only with data that is vivid and compelling, but also with what at first appear to be everyday, unremarkable events.

Photo: Rodney Barnett

Good qualitative practice should

Box 16.3

- keep close to the data when labelling phenomena, and at all stages of the generation of interpretive understanding,
- seek disconfirming cases or rival explanations through comparative 'negative case' (the exceptional instance or case) analysis, realising that absence of negative evidence in a specific sample of data can never be a decisive 'check' or confirmation of an explanation, because the next case might be an exception,
- take into account the researcher's impact on the context of study and on the development of the interpretive account, and
- keep alive several possibilities or rival explanations.

At the level of interpretation, we could debate endlessly about how to establish standards of correctness, and never reach conclusions. However, without having recourse to ultimate standards of correctness, it may in certain circumstances still be possible to argue that certain truth claims are more correct than others. We can do this, for example, because some conclusions have been carelessly constructed or are not as properly thought through as other claims. Some tactics for checking the rigour of a qualitative study are peer examination (checking with fellow researchers), reasoned consensus (achievement of agreement between researchers on the basis of open discussion based on argumentation), satisfactory selection and training of researchers, observers, interviewers, encoders, and so on, and an audit trail, with independent auditors examining the process of the research.

Triangulation

The term 'triangulation' was briefly discussed in previous chapters, and we will now expand upon it. The term was originally used by land surveyors to describe a particular position in relation to two other positions (coordinates). But triangulation has come to refer more generally to the use of multiple perspectives against which to check one's own position. This process may be applied both within a single case (e.g., checking whether your findings about a person's perceptions coincide with your findings about their feelings) or across cases (e.g., checking your claims about the way a political party responded to the outcome of an election by seeing whether various people in the party responded to the outcome in the same way). Denzin (1970) identifies four basic types of triangulation:

1. **Data triangulation**. This refers to the use of a variety of data sources in a study. It is important to be circumspect about particular kinds of data, such as the following: data that are vivid and have been given emphasis in an account because they are all that was remembered, but are not necessarily the whole story; personal experience which has filtered out important features of the context, and is presented in a compelling way purely because it is currently relevant in the person's life; 'data' which are presented in an already-reflected-on and thematised way, leading us to interpret the situations as more patterned than they really are, and data from particular informants whose accounts can seem more compelling, charming, or illuminating than the data gathered from others.

2. **Investigator triangulation**. This refers to the use of several different researchers or evaluators, which is useful in drawing our attention to previously unnoticed researcher effects (i.e., the effects of the researcher on the research context).

3. **Theory triangulation**. This refers to the use of multiple perspectives to interpret a single set of data, and this also means finding that the research findings can be incorporated into a more macro-analytical level of inference.

4. **Methodological triangulation**. This refers to the use of multiple methods to study a single problem, looking for convergent evidence from different sources, such as interviewing, participant observation, surveying, and a review of documentary resources.

Following Janesick (1994), we might add a fifth type: **interdisciplinary triangulation**. By using the findings of other disciplines, we can triangulate to check out the effects of the disciplinary perspective that we have adopted – for example, we might compare the findings of medical sociologists, epidemiologists, and health psychologists on sociocultural factors affecting HIV transmission.

Generalisability and transferability

Generalisability relates to the extent to which the interpretive account can be applied to other contexts than the one being researched. If we are talking about the psychological consequences of being criminally victimised, for example, generalisability involves our findings being true of people other than the few who may have been part of a particular study, and being true in other places or in relation to other types of crime. Because of the contextual nature of qualitative research, there are usually strong limits on the generalisability of findings.

One of the more commonly heard objections to qualitative research concerns the issue of representativeness. It is often said 'But how can you draw conclusions from so few subjects?' This relates to what Smaling (1992) calls 'transferential validity', and refers to the ability of the account to provide answers in other contexts, and to the transferability of findings to other contexts. To create a foundation for transferability and allow other researchers to use the findings in making comparisons with their own work, a research report must contain an 'accurate description of the research process, and secondly an explication of the arguments for the different choices of the methods ... and thirdly a detailed description (thick description) of the research situation and context' (Smaling, 1992, p. 318).

Providing detailed information on the research procedures used in a qualitative research project helps to establish the extent to which findings can be generalised to other settings.

Communicative validity

This involves testing the veracity (truthfulness) of knowledge claims in a dialogue with either the respondents or the general public or the scientific community of scholars possessing the requisite theoretical and methodological competence to evaluate the research. In this sense, the index of validity is the recognition or criticism that the work attracts. 'If we are no longer able to rely upon correspondence with the empirical world as the ultimate arbiter of truth, a more pragmatic argument can be made that the outcome of research will tend to be evaluated in terms of [its] persuasiveness and ability to inspire an audience' (Pidgeon & Henwood, 1997, p. 271). Hence we find researchers putting their findings to the test of professional audiences through conferences and academic writing, and to 'lay' audiences through media and professional practice.

Pragmatic proof

For Kvale (1996), 'truth is whatever assists us to take actions that produce the desired results' (p. 250). If we are deliberately looking to achieve an end, and we are looking via our research to find ways to do it, the extent to which the actions indicated by the research bring about the desired results is a measure of the truth value of the research.

The theme of this book, 'research in action', reflects a contemporary interest in the way in which research, intentionally or unintentionally, brings about changes in the world. Patti Lather (1986) speaks of 'catalytic validity', referring to the degree to which the research process reorients, focuses, and energises participants towards transforming reality. By this, she also refers to the extent to which a given research project empowers and emancipates a research community. To evaluate catalytic validity, we would need to have a sense of the way in which the research 'catalysed' or instigated a movement towards social transformation.

In action-oriented research, the research is specifically aimed at bringing about practical achievements rather than merely aimed at developing understanding. When social transformation is the desired outcome, we might say, following Gergen (1985), that 'to tell it like it is' is to 'tell it as it may become'. Thus, good research should have the power to reorient and change practice. Incorporation of such considerations in evaluation of research does not come without its problems. For a start, adoption of presumptions of value neutrality and the canon of objectivity, which have been standards of the positivist approach, are fundamentally challenged if we adopt a 'change imperative' in evaluating social research. We know that research can have practical social consequences, and researchers have possibly always hoped that their research will be of some practical significance, but this is not the same as doing research specifically to bring about a desired outcome. There is an understandable concern about research that endeavours to do this – that it might depart from standards of reliability and neutrality in collecting and interpreting data. Research that sets out to support a particular kind of action is not likely to be impartial. However, the whole idea of partiality can be raised as a problem, and many qualitative researchers say that research is never and cannot be impartial or value neutral, and it is best that we declare our allegiances. Consciously acting from a particular standpoint (see chapter 23) does not mean that we are not genuinely and rigorously 'enquiring'.

Most, possibly all, research has a socio-political agenda, and one way of judging research quality is in terms of how effectively it advances that agenda.

The qualities of a satisfactory narrative account

Having suggested that one should give the reader an opportunity to retrace one's steps in the research process, and having offered some suggestions about what makes for more defensible interpretive claims, let us turn to the qualities of an adequate narrative. This will provide us with a few more indicators to add to our ways of evaluating satisfactory interpretive accounts. Your attention is also drawn to box 16.2, 'The seductions of narrative', which gives reasons to treat narrative accounts with suspicion. The idea of an interpretive account as a narrative was discussed in the previous chapter when we looked at the process of putting one's interpretations together into an overarching general account. We call this a narrative account because it has the qualities of a story, in the sense that it weaves all of the parts together into a single account. While it may still have different facets, the account stands out as having a kind of unity or integrity.

At the risk of over-simplifying complex philo-sophical arguments, we might say that debates around questions concer-ning the truth value of qualitative accounts are usually aligned with one or the other of two broad, competing theories of truth. These are sometimes termed 'correspondence' and 'narrative' theories. The former, also sometimes referred to as the 'copy' theory of truth, portrays the good account as accurately corresponding to an under-

He-said-she-said ... What, practically speaking, do we expect of a satisfactory narrative account?

Photo: Rodney Barnett

lying reality. The latter is concerned to establish the truth value of the account in terms of the qualities of the account itself, rather than through matching the account to an external source of reference. Kvale (1996) considers that the debates around criteria for judging social science research tend to have been limited to categories suggested by the traditional concepts of reliability, validity, and generality: 'leftovers from a modernist correspondence theory of truth' (p. 231). What then, if we are not to be reduced to 'scraping together leftovers', do we have as a way of ascertaining that our narrative accounts are truthful? What, practically speaking, might be the elements of a narrative theory of truth? What do we expect of a satisfactory narrative account?

In some ways qualitative research accounts are just stories and can therefore be judged by the same criteria as fictional stories.

Ricoeur (1976) speaks of two principles that one would expect to find in an adequate narrative account. The first of these is the principle of 'congruence', which consists of (a) **internal consistency** – one part of the narrative does not contradict another part, and the account is internally consistent, and (b) **coherence** – the ability to accommodate the answers to the questions of interest within a narrative and make them intelligible therein. A satisfactory narrative has an enstructuring or configuring quality, through which events are related to one another and the experiences contained in them are given a context in terms of their place in the overall story.

The second principle is the principle of 'plenitude'. This refers to comprehensiveness, or the degree to which the explanation is complete and incorporates the totality of the individual's or group's life, history, psychodynamics, social context, and so on.

To this we might add that a satisfactory research narrative should balance generality and contextual detail. An abstract general account that gives no sense of the contexts from which it is derived is unlikely to be convincing. Understanding of general phenomena, even within the context of a single life or single event, necessarily overarches the details of the world from which it is extracted. The text should be sufficiently related to such context if it is to be regarded as a satisfactory account of the same. On the other hand, an overly descriptive account which is 'all detail' fails thematically, to the extent that there is not enough 'linking' holding it into a whole.

There are also a few subjective criteria that are sometimes considered as aspects of a satisfactory narrative account. When we say that something is well argued, we mean more than that it is devoid of obvious errors of logic. Gadamer (1975) argues for a 'compelling' presentation, and a binding quality that imposes itself on the reader in an immediate way. A good narrative account also presents the meaning of a constellation of events in the manner of a satisfying and intelligible story; that is, by lending coherence and 'shape' (structure) to the events described therein (Woolfolk & Messer, 1988). Another criterion that comes up in the literature is that a better account is aesthetically pleasing in its structure, as opposed to being contorted and convoluted. These qualities are difficult to operationalise, in the sense that it would be difficult to develop hard-and-fast checklists about what exact features are expected in a 'compelling' or 'satisfying' account. It relies more on intuitive judgement, of the order of 'it sounds convincing', or 'it seems quite plausible', or even 'it works' – much like the kinds of response one hears in response to a work of art. Of course, these are not sufficient criteria, but they are criteria that we would nonetheless expect to find and which add to the general picture. Nevertheless, we should be cautious because, as pointed out earlier, narratives may be appealing at the expense of critical thinking. They may seem persuasive by virtue of glossing over inconsistencies and incoherences that are part of what is being studied. Human beings and their social arrangements are not necessarily ordered and neat, and accounts which present them as such should be approached with circumspection.

Conclusion

In concluding, let us consider the words of Gadamer (1975): 'The harmony of all the details with the whole is the criterion of correct understanding. The failure to achieve this harmony means that understanding has failed' (p. 259). These words might bring to mind the idea of the hermeneutical circle discussed in chapter 15. In this context, 'facts' are facts by virtue of being meaningfully linked to other facts, which are themselves facts by virtue of being meaningfully linked to other facts. It is the meaningful linking of parts into a network of meaning, and ultimately into a landscape of meaningful action, that gives interpretations status.

Checklist of criteria for evaluating a qualitative research account

- A thorough account of *how* findings were reached?
- Coherent and logically consistent?
- Weaves together the totality of the phenomena in question?
- Parts related to the whole?
- Able to incorporate new or parallel textual material (e.g., texts by the same author, or previously undisclosed events of a person's life)?
- Generalisable (applicable to other individuals or populations)?
- Consistency, scope, fruitfulness, simplicity, accuracy?
- External evidence?
- A search for disconfirming evidence or cases has not undermined the account?
- Consensus amongst researchers?
- Prediction of future events?
- Fits with other interpretations?
- Gives rise to problem-solving action?
- Opens up further areas of understanding?
- Covers a broad range of experience?

Exercises

1. Consider the following quotation:

   > If one succeeds in arranging the confused heap of fragments, each of which bears upon it an unintelligible piece of drawing, so that the picture acquires a meaning, so that there is no gap anywhere in the design and so that the whole fits into the frame – if all these conditions are fulfilled, then one knows that one has solved the puzzle and that there is no alternative solution. (Freud, 1923, p. 116)

   Keeping Freud's 'jigsaw analogy' in mind, discuss the following in small groups:

   (a) Describe the methodology involved in building a jigsaw puzzle (i.e., how you would go about it) when you don't have the picture to copy. What will your main criterion of certainty be here?

   (b) Describe the methodology involved when you don't have the picture and you are building a giant puzzle, with many pieces missing and no edge pieces. How would you proceed and when would you know that you have done as much as you can?

   (c) Extrapolating from the jigsaw analogy, what do you think of the idea that in human affairs 'the truth of the matter' lies waiting to be put together, implying a final, determinate meaning – that is, an underlying pattern waiting to be discovered and reconstructed? Discuss this question in relation to the following different 'types' of event and compare the answers for the various events: the attack on the World Trade Center Towers in New York on 11 September 2001, Eugene de Kock's motives for murder, someone's hopes for the future, and the reasons for a child's fear of the dark.

2. Listen to a news item on the radio, or a tape recording of the same. After listening to the item, write a half-page summary of the item from memory. Ask yourself the following questions, and write a written response to each. Discuss your response with someone or with a group who have also done the exercise.

   (a) What attitude to the material did you detect on the part of the reporter, and what leads you to these conclusions?

   (b) What alternative interpretations or accounts of the reported events might there be, and how would you confirm or disconfirm the alternative interpretations?

   (c) If there is material missing from the reporter's account which prevents you from reaching your own conclusions to (b), what material would you need to be supplied with in order to think through the material for yourself? Now consider how you would implement data, investigation, theory, and methodological triangulation in addressing the problems of interpretation and confirmation which you identified above.

3. Work through the three activities below and then discuss the questions that follow.

   (a) Write down on a piece of paper the sequence of the main events (about 5–10 events will be enough) in your life yesterday, in the order in which they occurred.

   (b) Write down the main events that occurred between any two of these events. These events will probably be at the level of fairly minor interactions with people or engagement in discrete but not very memorable activities.

   (c) Write down five events that happened between any two of the events given under (b) above. This time, you might be having to think of thoughts and feelings as events.

Now, as a group, discuss the problem of deciding what one should account for in a research audit trail, and the problem of being able to reflect on subtle thoughts which may have passed by without our even noticing them. How can we distinguish between peripheral perceptions and critical turning points in our understanding of a context? Is an audit trail important? Why?

Key readings

Banister, P., Buraian, E., Parker, I, Taylor, M., & Tindall, C. (1994). *Qualitative methods in psychology: A research guide*. Buckingham: Open University Press.
This book contains a chapter on 'Issues of evaluation', which provides an engaging introduction to the topics of triangulation, writing 'reflexively', and being accountable for one's research results.

Lather, P. (1995). Adventures with Angels. *Qualitative Inquiry*, 1(1), 13–24.
This article on women with HIV/Aids, and the iconography of angels, introduces a range of fascinating new ways of looking at the problem of validity in interpretive research. These include 'ironic validity', 'paralogical validity', 'rhizomatic validity', and 'voluptuous validity'.

Packer, M. J., & Addison, R. B. (1989). Evaluating an interpretive account. In M. J. Packer & R. B. Addison (Eds), *Entering the circle: Hermeneutic investigations in psychology*. Albany, New York: State University of New York Press.
This very accessible chapter addresses some of the key issues involved in thinking about how to evaluate interpretive accounts. It draws largely on literature in the field of hermeneutics.

Research in applied contexts

17

Jobs and careers in social science research

Linda Richter

University of KwaZulu-Natal, Pietermaritzburg

Sheila Tyeku

Council, University of the Western Cape

We were unsure how to write this chapter. Jobs and careers in research are not like accountancy, medicine, or engineering. There are few, if any, prescribed entry requirements, route maps, accrediting bodies, or certificates on the wall to distinguish researchers from anyone else. There are also no textbooks that lay out 'how to become a social science researcher', although there are books, including this one, that enable students to learn how to do research, as well as publications to help students, researchers, and academics to identify funders and write proposals to get money to finance their research (e.g., Haag & Van Vuuren, 1991; Ries & Leukefeld, 1998).

We asked ourselves how we could communicate something useful about jobs and careers in research to students who are beginning to think about possible areas for work and career development. Upon reflection, we came to realise that we have both made careers in research, and many of the people we know – as friends, colleagues, and by reputation – are researchers or have jobs in which research is a core element. So we adopted an investigative stance to writing this chapter, and began where all social science enquiry begins: with experience – our own and that of other people (Clandinin & Connelly, 1994).

Box 17.1

About the authors

Sheila Tyeku has an undergraduate degree in Mathematics, Mathematical Statistics, and Computer Science. In her formative career years, while doing an Honours degree in Statistics at Unisa, Sheila was part of a group of political and feminist activists who conducted a large study among female factory workers outside Pinetown, which was published by Madiba Press under the title *Factory and Family: The Divided Lives of South Africa's Women Workers* (Meer, 1984). Despite the fact that her children playfully chide her that she could have been a real scientist (meaning a mathematician!), this experience aroused in her an interest in researching complex human and social phenomena. After completing a Master's degree in Educational Policy, Planning and Management at Bristol University, she worked at the University of Durban-Westville. She then joined the Centre for Science Development (CSD) at the Human Sciences Research Council (HSRC) as Head of Research Capacity Development. Following this, she became Director of Quality Auditing and Quality Development at the Council on Higher Education.

We thought about our own careers, and collected information about researchers we know, or interviewed them especially for this book, to elicit important dimensions about jobs and careers in social science research. We acknowledge that this involves selective and constructive decisions on our part. We chose to interview certain people, not by objective or absolute measures of their prominence or influence, but because we knew or admired them. We asked them certain questions, not because we comprehended what would constitute a full and adequate inquiry on careers in social science research, but because our own experiences foregrounded some issues and not others. Our questions, in turn, influenced and shaped our informants' accounts of their careers. We acknowledge this personal view – what Geertz (1988) would call 'our signature' in the text – and through this we have tried to draw a rich picture of current jobs and opportunities in social research.

We have tried to give students a feel of the world of research – because working in research is a bit like working in advertising or on the stock market. Jobs in these and other similar environments do not involve the simple application of what was learned in a particular discipline, such as in consumer psychology, media and cultural studies, or economics.

Linda Richter is a clinical and research psychologist who has conducted and managed research in the fields of health, social welfare, and early education through her positions at the Institute for Behavioural Sciences at Unisa, the Department of Paediatrics and Child Health at the University of the Witwatersrand, and the Medical Research Council. Linda edited the *South African Journal of Psychology* for many years. She has worked on two large longitudinal cohort studies: *Birth to Ten*, a study of Soweto–Johannesburg children born in 1990, and a prospective study of teen maturation and health in the Africa Centre for Population Studies and Reproductive Health. She chairs the Technical Advisory Group of the Division of Child Health and Development at the World Health Organisation, which annually prioritises child health and development research issues for United Nations organisations and participating governments.

Research in a knowledge-driven world

'A single example can serve to put the technological revolution in perspective: in 1996, a new car in the BMW 7 series had more computer capacity than [South Africa's] total computer capacity at the beginning of the sixties!' (Marais, 1996, p. 82)

Countries in advanced states of development trade in knowledge. It is estimated that about 80% of the value of world trade in 1990 was made up of knowledge-intensive products – products with high techno-logical content (Pouris, quoted in Nel, 1996). For this reason, every country values scientific activities and the conversion of scientific progress into technological advances. With globalisation, all countries in the world strive to participate in the new **economies of knowledge**. Knowledge and know-how are the raw materials of the modern world. As a result, science and technology, or the 'S&T system', have become universal features of modern societies. The S&T system supports and influences all aspects of our lives – the economy, agricultural and manufacturing production, health, government, education, and so on.

These are critical issues for developing countries. First, as the key products for exchange move from raw materials and manufacturing to consumer and service items developed from ideas and inventions, the existing international divisions between rich and poor and powerful and powerless will increase, locking developing countries into new spirals of debt and dependency. Second, for many developing countries, including South Africa, science and technology, judiciously directed and applied, hold the key to social development. Democratisation, equity, and redress, the cornerstones of post-apartheid South Africa, rely on higher educational levels, science and technology development, increased wealth, and better understanding of the human and social factors involved in technological applications and advances. Research, both natural and social, basic and applied, is central to the processes needed to achieve our national goals.

It is important for students of the social sciences to understand that technology is not limited to science and engineering. Human science technologies include, *inter alia*, tools to aid decision making (such as the Delphi technique), geographic information systems to track diseases and community access to facilities, techniques for monitoring and analysing parliamentary questions or media trends, economic forecasting, psychological assessments for career selection, and environmental impact assessments. For example, in 1998 the Council for Scientific and Industrial Research (CSIR) put out a tender inviting social scientists to submit proposals to research human technologies to assist in crime prevention – including the role of better street lighting, the importance of preventing environmental degradation, the role of community policing, and many other aspects of social life that intersect with crime. Human science technologies originate in any effort to address social problems, from policy development to specific technical applications. In the mid 1990s, South Africa spent approximately 14% of the total S&T budget on the human sciences, and 86% on the physical sciences and engineering (Garbers, 1996). However, there is a growing appreciation of the imperative to tailor technological developments and environmental change to human and social needs. In line with the expressed people-centred values of a democratised South Africa, spending on the human and social sciences is anticipated to increase substantially, and research opportunities in this area are expected to grow correspondingly.

Research in the national and international context

As indicated before, there is in each country an S&T system that is linked with the S&T systems of other countries sharing bilateral or multilateral agreements, and internationally with global systems of S&T coordination. The latter include, for example, the World Bank and the United Nations organisations such as the United Nations Children's Fund (UNICEF). The systems are also linked through the networks of scientists and researchers working in cooperation with one another, or sharing membership of subject and disciplinary societies. So large, distinct, and interconnected is this system that Michael Polanyi (1962) referred to it as 'the republic of science'.

A country's participation in the international S&T system is usually measured in a number of ways, such as the following:

- The amount of money spent on research in the country relative to the gross national product – in South Africa this proportion in 1990/1991 was about 0.3%, compared to the highest world allocation, 3.1% in Japan (UNESCO, 1993).

- The number of scientists per 1 000 of the population – in South Africa in 1990/1991 it was about 0.1 compared to a high of 4.4 in Israel (UNESCO, 1993).

- The percentage of the world's research publications emanating from any particular country – in the mid 1990s South Africa produced 0.42% of all publications, compared to the United States' high at 31% (Gibbs, 1995).

South Africa leads on the African continent in all these areas. There is, however, an urgent need for South Africa to increase its participation in the global S&T system, and an important goal of the government is to create an environment conducive to scientific activities and technological innovation. This is being done in a number of ways, including the establishment of the **National Research Foundation** (NRF), which aims to coordinate research across the humanities, social sciences, health, and the natural sciences. Efforts are also being made to stimulate partnerships between researchers and the private sector through focused funding mechanisms. The Foresight project has been launched as a specific effort to seek out areas for potential technological development based on South Africa's unique resources and circumstances. Considerable effort is being put into research capacity development in order to achieve human resource equity in scientific work and achievement, as well as to ensure that the full spectrum of talent in the country, including previously disadvantaged groups, is brought to bear on the country's social and economic development.

This means that, since the late 1990s, there has been an unprecedented growth in the number of opportunities to use the research skills acquired in both undergraduate and postgraduate study to find employment in the broad research field, and to develop a career in research and research management. In 1998, we published the results of an extensive newspaper survey of job opportunities for

'In developed countries it is estimated that there are approximately 25 full-time equivalent researchers per 10 000 people. In the mid 1980s South Africa had 3.6, and work opportunities in this sector are expected to grow at about 6% per annum.' (Prinsloo, 1995)

graduates in psychology and the social sciences. In this study, we found that *more than a third* of the jobs targeted at social science graduates stipulated that research and data analysis skills were required (Richter, Griesel, Durrheim, Wilson, Surendorff, & Asafo-Agyei, 1998). This does not mean that all these jobs involve high science activities and advanced statistical analyses. Employers want social scientists with a capacity to understand and conduct research, including the ability to review and summarise existing knowledge, activities, and conditions, the ability to explore numerical or text data, to synthesise findings, to report concisely on outcomes, to offer plausible explanations for results, and the ability to apply the knowledge gained to a human or social problem.

Environments for social research

At a national level, research occurs in four main domains, which are similar in some ways and very different in others. These are the state (in the form of the science councils and government departments), universities and technikons, **nongovernmental organisations** (NGOs), and the private sector.

The state: science councils and government departments

South Africa has nine science councils, including the Human Science Research Council (HSRC) and the Medical Research Council (MRC). The HSRC was established by an Act of Parliament (No 23 of 1968), according to which it, like other science councils, receives baseline funding from a parliamentary grant. In 1994, this was just over R55 million. The HSRC also earns money – about a third of its total income, in fact – through commissioned research for government departments and large grants and contracts from local and overseas funders to conduct particular pieces of research. Since the late 1970s, the HSRC has gone through several rounds of restructuring and transformation (Cloete & Muller, 1991).

The National Research Foundation (NRF) promotes high-quality research in both the natural and the social sciences by supporting the development of individual and institutional research capacity, especially in those sectors of the educational and S&T system that have been historically disadvantaged. The NRF contributes to research capacity development, international scientific collaboration, and the dissemination of research information. The NRF offers a broad range of grants and bursaries for individuals and institutions, including grants for overseas study and conference attendance, and support for visits from international scholars.

Most government departments conduct or commission policy and operational research, as well as evaluation studies, to assist them with planning and implementation of their goals. For example, the Department of Water Affairs and Forestry might conduct research on the environmental and social impact of a planned dam. There are

Before becoming Corporate Affairs Director of South African Breweries, **Vincent Maphai** was the executive director of one of the main subdivisions within the HSRC, called Social Dynamics. He obtained his first degree in Politics and Philosophy at the University of South Africa, his master's at the University of Leuven in Belgium, and his PhD at the University of the Western Cape. He claims his career unfolded opportunistically, although  some key milestones stand out. He was strongly influenced in his young adult years by the black consciousness movement and by intellectuals in the Catholic Bishop's Conference, where he worked. He says one of his best moments, and a great spur in adopting a research career, was seeing his first peer-reviewed article printed in a journal.

In his experience, the social milieu of a researcher is critical. Like many black academics in the country, he was attracted to work in an historically advantaged white university. In retrospect, he thinks this was as damaging for him as it has been for other black intellectuals. During his six-year tenure at Wits he produced only one article. When he moved to the University of the Western Cape, his productivity blossomed. Despite being the head of a large department and teaching a heavy undergraduate load, in three years he completed his PhD and published six articles in accredited journals. Professor Maphai realises that knowledge is power, and he has made a deliberate career choice to stay in research, driven by the conviction that black people have to cease to be the subjects of study by others. Apart from being clever and technologically competent, the characteristics of good researchers he identifies are intellectual daring, open-mindedness, patience and endurance, an ability to tolerate uncertainty, self-confidence, and a capacity to bear criticism. In addition, the ability to communicate in a variety of ways, with a wide range of constituencies, is important; in social science research occupations, it is necessary to be able to write popularly as well as to compose policy documents and academic arguments for publication in scholarly journals.

several mechanisms by which government departments can do research, including the employment of full- or part-time researchers and consultants. However, large projects are put out to tender through publication in the *Government Gazette* and sometimes in the national newspapers. Interested research groups respond by submitting proposals for the advertised projects, and their proposals are evaluated by appointed expert panels. The group that wins the tender then enters into a legal contract with the government department, with stipulated responsibilities and obligations on both sides.

Box 17.3

Mala Singh is Executive Director of the Higher Education Quality Committee of the Council on Higher Education, having previously directed the Centre for Science Development at the HSRC, and lectured in the Department of Philosophy at the University of Durban-Westville. Professor Singh remembers always having a love of reading – reading by lamplight at night during her childhood and all day in the library after her husband left for work!

Her family was strongly supportive of her intellectual development and, although she won a place in medical school, she was strongly attracted to the world of ideas. After a few undergraduate courses in politics, she switched to philosophy, which was for her a restless attempt to apply ideas to human and social problems. She was the first postgraduate student in the department at UDW, and was surprised at the offer of a junior lectureship when most of the university's staff was still white. Through teaching came her attraction to research, and through philosophy she entered the terrain of politics. She sees the role of the intellectual activist as critical, with a strong moral responsibility. One of her greatest experiences was the award of a postdoctoral scholarship to study at the University of Cologne in Germany. She had a liberating mentor who advised her to 'go and do everything else she wanted to do as philosophy was what she had to do for the rest of her life'. For her, she says, this broke down the boundaries of knowledge. She later became involved in the issues of tertiary education, and was elected to the presidency of UDUSA, the United Democratic Universities' Staff Association. It was a time for strategic alliances, new insights into the higher education system, consultation with the ANC in exile, and a fellowship at Yale University, which gave her an opportunity to reflect on the role of intellectuals in a society undergoing major political change.

Many government departments also have in-house research units; for example, the Department of Posts, Telecommunications, and Broadcasting has a Broadcasting Research Unit, the South African Defence Force has a Military Psychology Institute, and the South African Protection Services has an Institute for Behavioural Sciences and a Centre for the Analysis and Interpretation of Crime Information. Statistics South Africa (Stats SA) is one of the largest government research units. Its main task is the production and maintenance of basic census and household data on the South African population. You can visit Stats SA on the internet at www.statssa.gov.za.

Government departments and science councils provide opportunities for lifelong careers in research. Researchers normally work in teams with colleagues from other disciplines, and, because of the variety in the work they have to do, they normally become 'expert-generalists' – people who know or can find out a lot about a wide variety of subjects, without losing expertise in a specific discipline or field. The research questions they address are not conceived by themselves, but are mostly conducted under commission, and usually in a hurry – because the government and other institutions that commission research need information and results so that they can initiate and respond to priority issues in good time.

Tertiary education institutions

Research is part of the 'core business' of academics, and at the University of Natal, for example, lecturers are expected to spend about 30% of their time doing research. In the past, there was a stereotypic view that pure, basic, or 'blue skies' research was done at universities, and applied and policy research was done in the commercial sector, by nongovernmental organisations, and in government departments. In one sense, this is true: Sustained and in-depth theoretical, methodological, and content-oriented research is encouraged in the university environment, and universities are generally the places where disciplinary innovations originate and where new discoveries are made. However, many academics have been drawn into the post-apartheid government, both directly and indirectly, and there is wide participation in national research and policy initiatives by staff members at tertiary educational institutions. Universities also encourage academics to take on government and private sector contracts and obtain grants to do applied research, both to supplement the income of universities and to create an environment of applied research to host the socialisation of postgraduate students. In fact, so extensive is the entry of scholars into the contract domain that Lawrence Soley (1995) refers to it as the corporate co-optation of academic research.

Sometimes a group of university researchers, usually under the direction of an outstanding academic, forms a unit or centre which attains recognition by the administration as a separate entity and begins to attract national and international funds for its research programme.

The research of academics is judged in several ways, the most important of which is publication of their work in peer-reviewed journals. In some sense, academics only accord credibility to views and analyses that have gone through the rigorous process of peer-review (Fisher, Friedman, & Strauss, 1994). Ratings of individual research accomplishments do not just depend on the number of papers they have published, but also on the status of the journals in which the papers appeared. There are several ways to evaluate scholarly journals (Kim, 1992), but the most widely used index is the Impact Factor. Basically, this is compiled from the number of instances in which articles in that journal have been quoted, or cited, in other journals over a fixed time period. Young scholars who are trying to make an international name for themselves in a particular field carefully monitor the prestige of the journals in which they try to publish their articles.

Universities also take into account other outputs from the research of academics, including policy papers, books, presentations at national and international conferences, works of art, and the number of postgraduate students who successfully complete their degrees. Increasingly, as money becomes a fulcrum for research activities, the number and the financial value of grants awarded to researchers have become important entries in the curriculum vitae of individuals who see research as a major part of their academic career.

The private sector

Around the world, most research and most research money is to be found in the private sector. In a global economy of knowledge, inventions, and products, commercial organisations are forced to make enormous investments in research and technology. Commercial contractors for major construction projects are also obliged to undertake a variety of impact assessments in fields requiring social and psychological research expertise – for example, the effect of dams on the livelihood, cohesion, and health status of people living in the affected and catchment areas.

One area in which social scientists are in great demand in the private sector is in the field of ergonomics, or human factors research. All technologies have consequences for the way in which human beings live, work, and relate to each other, from the seemingly simple matter of the height of a hospital bed best suited to reduce stress on nurses' backs, to the size and visibility of instrument panels on rocket ships. To work efficiently and safely, all these technologies need to be designed to best fit human physical, cognitive, and social capacities. Options for design need to be researched.

Other key private sector research activities involving human and social scientists are those built around market research and consumer behaviour. There are several major market research companies in South Africa, as well as countless smaller businesses breaking into this dynamic market. Although traditional market research focuses on questions relating to product, price, and promotion (Martins, Loubser, & Van Wyk, 1996), market research companies in South Africa have entered into the full domain of social research. Many companies employ consultants with specialised knowledge, and they use the company's field work infrastructure and expertise to tender successfully for government contracts in health, education, agriculture, and so on.

Private sector research careers are for those who enjoy working in a constantly changing environment and meeting very tight deadlines.

A considerable amount of research in the private sector is conducted and supported by consultants working in contractual ways with different groups and on different projects. There is a worldwide trend for individuals who have expertise to 'sell' to become what Charles Handy (1994) calls 'portfolio people'. These people are the quintessential **knowledge workers** – they maintain high levels of knowledge and technical skill to enable them to pick up opportunities as they arise and to negotiate lucrative and personally rewarding work conditions with employers for varying durations. For the first six months of a year, they might be contracted to assist the Department of Health to evaluate the Primary School Nutrition Programme. For the next 18 months, they might be employed by a consortium of private game reserves to collect the data necessary to support decisions about the volume of cars that should be allowed to enter the park on any one day without spoiling everyone's sense of being in the wild!

Nongovernmental organisations, including trade unions

Nongovernmental organisations (NGOs) boomed in South Africa during the 'struggle years'. It has been estimated that there are around 54 000 NGOs operating in South Africa across a large number of sectors – environment, education, gender, health, human rights, housing, economics, land and water affairs, religion and culture, and so on. Research was one of the things that NGOs (more than a third of them, according to Jennings, Mulaudzi, Everatt, & Orkin, 1995) were tasked to do. In order to move political and developmental programmes forward, progressive organisations found it necessary to establish basic demographic, social, occupational, health, educational, and other data on the majority of the population, who were previously ignored within the official construction of South African reality. They also needed to evaluate their programmes and account to donors for funds. Trade unions, too, found they needed to have data. If union representatives wanted to negotiate higher wages or better conditions of service, say for night-shift workers, they had to acquire and bring in the expertise needed to find and summarise information to support their cause.

In this way, a strong research capacity developed in NGOs and trade unions, such as the Community Agency for Social Enquiry (CASE), the Urban Foundation, the South African Institute for Race Relations (SAIRR), the Careers Research and Information Resource Centre (CRIC), the Black Sash, and the Institute for Democracy in South Africa (IDASA). The political and activist agendas that many of these organisations pursued forced them deeply to consider issues of knowledge, power, expertise, and the like. They also began to use 'newer' research approaches, particularly participatory action research (see chapter 19), and they trained many young aspirant researchers. More often than not, they used secondary research methods (research using available documents and historical-comparative analyses) rather than primary data collection. They also brought in a commitment to make research relevant, meaningful, and accessible to the people who needed it, and research was more frequently value-driven than directed by theory or disciplinary consistency (Jennings, Mulaudzi, Everatt, & Orkin, 1995).

Since the democratic elections in 1994, many NGOs have entered into competition with the private sector and universities for research grants and contracts. In 1993, Johan Garbers, then president of the HSRC, commented on the emergence of a free market in research and research funding (Prinsloo, Marais, & Maree-Snijders, 1996). Research is no longer the purview of universities or any other group.

Young researchers now have to learn many skills apart from the specialised research techniques of their discipline. They have to learn how to write attractive research proposals, and they have to learn how to budget for studies and how to work in and manage complex, multisite studies conducted by teams of researchers in different stages of the project.

> The applied research conducted by NGOs during the apartheid years invigorated social research in South Africa.

> One study found that the 53 most published researchers in the world on the topic of 'mass communication' (between them they published 292 scholarly articles in five years) had only written a total of three popular magazine articles in ten years! (Soley, 1995)

Team research and research communities

Large applied projects can normally not be done by one expert in a narrow field of specialisation. Very often, there are historical, ethical, managerial, methodological, and educational dimensions that go beyond a single discipline or a single researcher. This complexity reflects the interrelationships and multidimensionality of many human and social problems.

To do justice to these problems frequently requires human and social scientists to work with natural scientists. For instance, infant deaths from pneumonia are not merely the result of organisms and drug resistance but also concern, among other things, people's access to health services, household food security, and adult carers' knowledge about the significance of infant signs and symptoms and their sense of confidence to act on their observations.

Box 17.5

Debbie Budlender is a principal researcher with the Community Agency for Social Enquiry (CASE) in Cape Town. She is the editor and author of several books on gender economics, including *The Women's Budget* (1996), *The Second Women's Budget* (1997), *The Third Women's Budget* (1998) and (with K. Hurt) *Money Matters: Women and the Government Budget* (1998). Debbie first trained in economics, and then industrial sociology, computer science, mathematics, and Xhosa (during six years of a political banning). She has worked for and with trade unions and other progressive organisations as an activist and researcher, mainly on topics of poverty, sanctions and disinvestment, law, and gender.

Debbie says that curiosity, inquisitiveness, and a desire for social justice are what drive her, together with the pleasure of constantly learning new skills and working with new groups of people. She also likes the fact that in her work at CASE she does not generate the research questions; the questions come to her from people and groups with real-life problems to be solved. This makes her feel that her research is needed, wanted, and relevant.

Despite the good sense of it, it is not always easy for social and natural scientists to work together. Snow (1965) first described what he called two separate cultures: the science culture (meaning the natural sciences) and the intellectual culture (covering the humanities and the social sciences). He argued that the gap between the two is brought about by the lack of emphasis in the natural sciences on human and social issues and, on the other hand, the low level of technical literacy among human and social scientists. Natural and social scientists differ in a number of ways: Their epistemologies and methodologies are different, they are socialised in different ways, and there is an enduring view that they may actually be of different personality types ('hard-minded' versus 'soft-minded'), although there is not much evidence for this (Garbers, 1996).

Also, there are strong inhibitions to researchers cooperating with one another across disciplines. After all, many young researchers are schooled on tightly insulated, and sometimes competitive, disciplinary turf. There is also currently not much reward for working in multidisciplinary ways because there are very few multidisciplinary journals, conferences, and scholarly societies – and a great deal of research funding is still determined by discipline. Nonetheless, the need to address complex human and social problems is driving a new kind of fusion and hybridisation among disciplines. Many of the researchers we spoke to had criss-crossed the natural and social sciences; most found it invigorating to expand their disciplinary dimensions but scary to work in areas where they had little foundational knowledge.

Research communities, like other social structures, function best if they are neither too homogeneous (resulting in insular and uninteresting work) nor too heterogeneous (resulting in a lack of focus).

Research is done by individuals and by groups, and the research enterprise is held together as a series of networks and communities. A **research programme** consists of groups of researchers working on different parts of large national and international research projects. Research networks are loosely linked connections between researchers that enable them to work together while still retaining their independence (Lipnack & Stamps, 1993). Research associations are interest groups, both within and across disciplines (e.g., the Consortium of Human and Social Sciences in South Africa). Groups with similar interests meet during workshops and conferences and communicate with one another through the internet, newsletters, and journals. These interlinked groups and networks have been called 'invisible colleges' and 'thought collectives' because the connections between them are ideas, methods, and new findings from their research. In order to access information about networks, several organisations maintain databases of network nodes and connections.

Becoming a researcher

Many established or career researchers would probably say something like 'I didn't begin my career as a social researcher ...' For example, Sheila Tyeku graduated in mathematics and statistics; Sue Grant, Managing Director of Markinor, obtained her first degree in chemistry; the social and political analyst, Lawrence Schlemmer, started his career as a probation officer. Often, career researchers are led to opportunities for research by their intellectual curiosity and their conviction that ideas can influence social conditions.

Researchers typically love research for research's sake; they enjoy the process of seeking evidence and solving problems. They like the variety and challenge of the unexpected, and they thrive on opportunities to learn and master new ideas and new skills. Researchers have to be practical and resourceful people, and they need to know where to find material (such as data, technologies, and expert opinion) when they need it. Researchers need to have broad practical experience and to be socially and politically aware. Despite very high levels of stress occasioned by deadlines, external demands, and internalised self-expectations, most career researchers love their jobs. The majority of us would probably agree with Roediger's observation that 'It is rare in the world of work to be permitted to decide what you want to do and then have someone pay you to do it' (1997, p. 23).

Many people use research or do research, sometimes without being especially aware that it is research. A nurse in charge of a clinic who counts the number of patients who arrive before lunch, so that she or he can efficiently allocate staff and plan shifts, is doing research. This level of research is pervasive in the world of work, and competence in basic research skills is therefore invaluable in almost any career. However, professional research jobs and careers begin with advanced academic study. Most students do not get personally involved in research or do a research project until their senior undergraduate or postgraduate years. For many students, it is an intimidating experience, and some students back off from research because they are anxious about technical components of research investigations, including statistics and computer use. It often takes a special social milieu to engage students' interest in research and to foster the development of their competence – such as a department in which approachable staff are actively engaged in research, or the special interest and guidance of a mentor and the opportunity to get personally involved in a research project. Barriers to students' entry into the research field have led to a concentrated effort to build research capacity generally in South Africa, and particularly in the human and social sciences. We hope that this chapter will go some way towards encouraging students to embark on a research career.

Research capacity building is a complex but essential activity. One definition of capacity development is to produce and foster the intellectual talent needed, among all sectors of the population, to fill the highest scientific and technical jobs in the public and private sector (Namuddu, 1997). While Africa has been expanding its higher education system, there is concern that the majority of graduates, regardless of where their training takes place, do not have adequate proficiency in research. Katherine Namuddu ascribes the nadir in research competence, at least in part, to an over-expansion in training institutions, which have spewed out 'generations of graduates with few or no research skills whatsoever, who have gone out to head various faculties and departments where production of high-quality research is expected to be the main criterion for academic leadership and promotion' (1997, p. 11).

Research capacity development is not just about providing training in a particular subject or in a particular methodology. As Namuddu says, it is about creating a social and cultural environment in which personal creativity can be promoted, at the same time as the technical, social, and critical skills needed to conduct research are imparted and fostered. It is about 'becoming part of the culture' through one's own interests and through collegial relationships with established researchers.

A good way of getting started on a research career is by working as a paid or volunteer assistant for an established researcher at your university.

In their analysis of employment opportunities for postgraduates in research psychology, Bedell and Phayane (1998) found that prospective employers want not only technical competence, but also skills in areas such as project management, internet searches, report writing and presentation, and client liaison.

Box 17.6

Jonathan Jansen is Dean of the Faculty of Education at the University of Pretoria. Among many other publications, he is the editor of *Knowledge and Power in South Africa: Critical Perspectives across Disciplines* (1991) in which he expressed two concerns about power and knowledge as South Africa enters a post-apartheid century. The first of these concerns is the largely unchanged status in knowledge/power relationships in the academy. Instead of providing new grounds for the interrogation of knowledge and power in the university curriculum, a series of  policy papers has imprinted on the higher education system a rigid, mechanical, accountancy model of change, which is concerned more with efficiency and accountability than deep transformation in the means by which knowledge is generated within the academy.

Jansen's second concern is the growing intolerance of social and academic criticism by external political authority in South Africa. This extends from the harassment of journalists to editing a commissioned paper by the Centre for Policy Studies on the grounds that its analysis of a centralist and authoritarian Mbeki presidency could threaten bilateral relationships between South Africa and the United States. But a much more effective process of intolerance is the political and intellectual marginalisation of academics who fail to serve as unquestioning agents of state policy. Their isolation takes many forms, such as exclusion from commissions and councils, and even subtle intervention in their careers. Jansen predicted that, as the state failed to deliver on its promises in the economy, such intolerance of criticism will increase with direct consequences for the future of knowledge/power relationships in South Africa.

Jansen argued that, not unexpectedly, new forms of control and authority are emerging within the academy under the guise of democratic discourses. Our challenge in the twenty-first century is not so much in dealing with explicit forms of racist knowledge or authoritarian control but with institutionalised patterns of racialised thinking and the regulation of academic authority in the name of accountability, which constitute new terrain for engaging the knowledge/power complex.

Conclusion: knowledge and power

In this chapter we have attempted to create an image of the world of work of researchers in the social sciences by taking a broad view of the research context in South Africa, and by describing the personal experiences and views of some exemplary social scientists.

The social significance or meaning of research – its potential to affect the wellbeing of individuals and society – appears as a recurring theme in the motivations of individual researchers and the broader societal quests for competition and control. Knowledge generated by research inquiry is powerful, both in instrumental ways that directly affect people, and by the impact of ideas on society. Research is frequently conducted by elite groups of people who are highly educated, and requires funding and support by organisations and institutions. This means that research occurs at the intersection of interests and resources, and of knowledge and power. The relationship between knowledge and power, universally and in South Africa in particular, has important implications for the way in which research is done and by whom, as well as the way that research is financed and used. It highlights the need for critical self-examination among researchers and a keen sense of moral and ethical responsibility for the way in which research can be used.

Research occurs at the intersection of interests and resources, and of knowledge and power.

Not only is research a viable and interesting career option for students in the social sciences and humanities, it also provides an opportunity to remain actively involved in critical philosophical and political debates, even after leaving the university environment. There are few firmly established training requirements for becoming a researcher, and there is now such variety in the kind of work researchers do that we have been able to give no more than a foretaste of the many possibilities. While this can be bewildering, it also means that prospective social science researchers are able, to a surprising extent, to invent for themselves the kinds of career that best suit their needs and interests. The remaining chapters of this section of the book describe some of the contexts within which such a career could unfold.

Exercises

1. Scan through the appointments section of the national newspapers, especially the *Sunday Times* and the *Mail & Guardian*, and look at jobs for which research skills are a requirement, or in which incumbents are required to do research. How do the activities, organisational setting, salary, conditions of service, and opportunities for development compare with other jobs you have considered?

2. Go to the library and scan through copies of the *Government Gazette* published over the last few months to see what tenders were published requesting social research. You can also do this on the internet. Try and find the site. How could your knowledge and interests contribute to these projects?

3. Enquire at your university about the institution's research policy. Find out which staff in your department are publishing in what fields and through which outlets. Ask what departmental or interdepartmental research programmes are currently underway, and investigate the opportunities for students to get involved in

staff or departmental research either in a voluntary capacity or as paid research assistants.

4. Read Jansen's (1991) introductory chapter, and then investigate what Jansen calls the 'ethnicisation of research' at the institution where you are enrolled. Find out what kinds of research are being done by whom. Go through the annual research reports of the institutions, as well as of the departments in which you are studying. Generally these are available from departments, the library, the research office, or the public relations and communications departments. What can you conclude from your findings?

Key readings

Garbers, J. (Ed.). (1996). *Effective research in the human sciences: Research management for researchers, supervisors and master's and doctoral candidates.* Pretoria: Van Schaik.

This is a compendium of pragmatic advice on managing your own research, research teams, and student research. It also contains information on conducting research in the South African context.

Hugo, P. (Ed.). (1990). *Truth be in the field: Social science research in Southern Africa.* Pretoria: UNISA.

This book is an interesting read, full of experienced researchers' accounts of work in the field, with an autobiographical flavour.

Jansen, J. (Ed.). (1991). *Knowledge and power in South Africa: Critical perspectives across disciplines.* Johannesburg: Skotaville.

This is a hard-hitting critique of the politics of knowledge production across a number of disciplines, focusing on research practices, research institutions, and the organisation of academic knowledge in South Africa.

18

Programme evaluation

Charles Potter

University of the Witwatersrand

Programme evaluation research is concerned with establishing whether social programmes are needed, effective, and likely to be used. In South Africa, a growing number of programme evaluations are being conducted, but this is still relatively small in comparison to the number of social programmes that exist. It has been estimated that over R6 billion of overseas and local funding has been spent since the 1970s in supporting the various nongovernmental organisations (NGOs) that have worked to promote innovation and change in various sectors of South African society, but only a limited number of these programmes have been evaluated.

In the absence of evaluation research, it is not possible to make informed decisions about social programmes, based on evidence that they have been effective. This is not the case in many other countries, where programme evaluation has a long tradition, based on both donors' and the public's right to know whether interventions undertaken to promote social change are successful. In North America, particularly, evaluation has been an integral part of the development of most social programmes since the 1960s, when a wide variety of programmes were developed as a result of the Kennedy and Johnson administrations' 'War on Poverty' (Atkin, 1979). Similar developments demanding accountability took place in Britain in the 1970s, carrying with them increasing demands for evaluation (McCormick & James, 1983). Since the 1980s, programme evaluation has been a fast-growing frontier of social science research, reflecting the growth of investment by both government and corporate sponsors in social programmes (Cronbach, 1982; Weiss, 1998), as well as the internationalisation of evaluation approaches and methodologies (Chelimsky, 1997).

Since the early 1990s, there has been growing recognition in South Africa that evaluative evidence is necessary for accountability purposes, and that the process of evaluation is an essential part of the development of social programmes. With this change in perception has come a growing demand for programme evaluations and an increasing number of evaluations commissioned and completed, as well as progress in the training of evaluators (Meyer & Hofmeyr, 1994; Potter, 1996).

Programme evaluation research arises from the need for social accountability.

What is evaluation research?

Evaluation research tracks the efficacy of social programmes – not financially (that is done by auditors), but in human and social terms (Shadish, 1990; Royse, Thyer, Padgett, & Logan, 2006). The term 'social programme' is understood to mean any kind of organised endeavour, ranging from an industrial company to a political movement, but the kinds of programme most commonly evaluated are those aimed at educational or social development (Worthen, Sanders, & Fitzpatrick, 1997; Potter & Kruger, 2001), often initiated by NGOs. It is important to distinguish programme evaluation from individual evaluation or assessment, which is discussed in chapter 22. Although programmes are sometimes evaluated by means of the psychological assessment of individuals who are involved in the programme, there are also many other ways by which researchers can tell whether a programme is effective or not. In fact, nearly all the research methods that you can read about in this book have been applied to the evaluation of social programmes.

Programme evaluation also draws on many different theories of social development. One purpose of evaluation research is to focus on the theories of change implicit in social programmes, and to analyse the ways in which those involved in social programmes go about their work, the issues they deal with, and the manner in which they confront these issues. The central goal of programme evaluation, however, is not theoretical but is focused on answering specific practical questions about social programmes and their development. These questions normally focus on programme implementation and outcomes, as well as on the quality of service provided.

The position adopted in this chapter is that there is no one 'correct' way either to define or to conduct a programme evaluation. The evaluator will normally use a set of assumptions and a methodology that suits the particular context of the programme and the requirements of those commissioning the evaluation. In common with other forms of social science research, particular evaluation practices reflect different methodological, epistemological, and ideological assumptions (House, 1983; Scriven, 1983; Potter, 1988). Reflecting broader trends in the field of social science research as a whole (Neuman, 1997), there are three traditions of evaluation research that can be distinguished, namely positivist, interpretive, and critical–emancipatory.

Positivist approaches to evaluation research

Positivist evaluation research is based on the belief that the scope of programme evaluation is limited to those aspects of social programmes that can be objectively observed and tested. This is accomplished using a variety of methodologies and procedures (Weiss, 1998; Posavac & Carey, 2003). These are usually applied within a systematic framework, which means that different forms of evaluation are conducted depending on the phase of development of a programme (Rossi, Freeman, & Lipsey, 1999). The following forms of evaluation are commonly used as part of the positivist approach:

Needs assessment – This is usually conducted by means of surveys or situational analyses undertaken by using questionnaires, interviews, and observation, to determine a particular area of need requiring intervention. It frequently incorporates analyses of documents or archival data, as well as analyses of previous research or evaluations of the work of other programmes in the area in which intervention is likely to take place.

Programme planning – This focuses on the process of programme conceptualisation and on the feasibility of programme plans. It usually

Imagine being asked to conduct a needs assessment in your neighbourhood. Who would you ask about what is needed in the neighbourhood, and exactly how would you go about asking them?

examines the aims and purposes of a programme to determine whether these relate to needs and to programme policy, and whether the intervention as planned is feasible.

Formative evaluation – This focuses on the process of programme implementation. It usually incorporates a process of programme monitoring to establish whether the intervention is being implemented as planned.

In formative evaluation, the evaluator attempts to identify aspects of the programme that are working well, aspects of the programme that are problematic, and aspects of the programme requiring modification or improvement.

Summative evaluation – This form of evaluation has a retrospective focus, and involves an attempt to establish the outcomes, effects, or impact of the programme by observation or measurement. Summative evaluations examine evidence relating to indicators of programme effectiveness, and, for this reason, they often incorporate quasi-experimental or *ex post facto* research, as well as some form of cost effectiveness or cost–benefit analysis.

In practice, these different forms of evaluation research are often combined in a single evaluation design directed at quality improvement (Unrau, Gabor, & Grinnell, 2001). Despite having different emphases, they share a common conceptual basis, namely that evaluation is a systematic activity, and that programme development and programme evaluation are closely linked.

Box 18.1

Definitions of programme evaluation: from the 60s to the present

- Cronbach (1963) – providing information for decision making;
- Joint Committee on Standards for Educational Evaluation (1981) – the systematic investigation of the worth or merit of some object;
- Heiman (1995) – a variety of procedures for developing and evaluating social programmes;
- Posavac & Carey (2003) – a collection of methods, skills, and sensitivities necessary to determine whether a human service is needed and likely to be used, whether it is sufficiently intense to meet the unmet needs identified, whether the service is offered as planned, and whether the human service actually does help people in need at a reasonable cost without undesirable side effects;
- Royse, Thyer, Padgett, & Logan (2006) – applied research used as part of the managerial process.

How positivist approaches to evaluation are applied in practice

In practice, the majority of programme evaluations are conducted on contract, being commissioned either directly by donors (the people who provide the funds to run a programme) or in response to donor requirements for information about programme effectiveness. The evaluation brief often includes a specific request for quantitative evidence concerning outcomes, and, for this reason, the majority of published evaluations have been based on positivist assumptions (Lipsey et al., 1985). Such evaluations focus on a programme's aims, and examine evidence concerning programme implementation and outcomes to establish whether these aims have been met.

Positivist approaches to programme evaluation typically make use of quantitative data and may take the form of experiments or quasi-experiments.

An example of such an evaluation is Potter's (1991a; 1991b) longitudinal evaluation of a pre-university project preparing black matriculants for university studies in engineering. In this evaluation, the assumptions and aims of the programme developers were examined against forms of instruction utilised as the project developed, and performance of successive cohorts of project students, as reflected in university pass rates over a ten-year period. Forms of instruction associated with high pass rates were identified and contrasted with those that were less effective. A series of analyses were conducted using nonexperimental and quasi-experimental designs (see chapter 8) together with multivariate statistics (see chapter 11) to provide evidence of the predictive relationship between forms of instruction and pass rates in different engineering courses. Different forms of evaluation were also used in combination to monitor ongoing programme effectiveness (Potter & Van der Merwe, 2003; Potter et al., in press).

An example of a nonexperimental evaluation is Reekie's (1997) evaluation of an Aids education programme conducted in Soweto high schools. Another is Kantor, Schomer, and Louw's (1997) evaluation of a stress-management programme in Cape Town. In the former, Reekie used a questionnaire based on items used in previous evaluations of Aids programmes in an *ex post facto* design, to establish significant differences between both factual knowledge about Aids and intentions

Photo: Centre for Peace Action

Education has been one of the most fertile areas for programme evaluation research, but there are nevertheless thousands of education programmes in South Africa that have not been formally evaluated.

to practise safe sex in pupils who had watched an Aids education play as compared to those who had not. He used age, gender, and educational levels as covariates affecting the receptivity of pupils to the message of the play. Kantor, Schomer, and Louw used a single-group, repeated-measures design based on pre-testing, post-testing, and subsequent follow-up of participants in a stress-management course, and established significant differences on a number of lifestyle measures. These indicated that both short- and long-term changes had occurred in the health beliefs and behaviour of programme participants.

Interpretive approaches to evaluation research

Interpretive approaches to evaluation value insider perspectives on programmes.

In contrast to the assumptions of positivist science, Guba and Lincoln (1981, 1983) have suggested that there is an alternative set of interpretive assumptions from which many programme evaluators work. These are fundamentally different from positivist assumptions, which Guba and Lincoln term the 'traditional' view of science. Until the 1960s, the majority of programme evaluations were objective and measurement based. This implied doing evaluation research from an outsider, as opposed to an insider, perspective on the programme's work, objectivity being necessary for credible and valid knowledge to emerge from the evaluation.

During the 1960s and 1970s, this paradigm was criticised as being too narrow in focus and unsuited to yielding relevant information on the development of programmes. This was accompanied by the rejection of evaluation designs based on positivist principles as being too limited in focus to be useful for the purposes of decision making (Stufflebeam et al., 1971; Patton, 1980). The argument was advanced that the outsider position adopted by positivist researchers worked against the aims of evaluation, which required methodologies sensitive to the values underpinning a programme's work. Understanding of values required access to the knowledge and understanding of programme insiders, as well as qualitative and subjective interpretation.

The critics of the dominant positivist tradition looked to social anthropology and clinical psychology for alternative methodologies based on interpretive premises (Stake, 1974). A number of alternative evaluation approaches were suggested, focusing on analysis of the perceptions of stakeholders involved in a programme, analysis of the transactions between different stakeholders, and analysis of the context of a programme.

Interpretive evaluation designs drew on the research traditions of participant observation (Denzin, 1970), case studies (Simons, 1980), qualitative interviewing and analysis (Patton, 1987), ethnography (Fetterman,1998), and multimethod approaches involving triangulation between different investigators, methodologies, data sources, time frames, and levels of human interaction (Cronbach et al., 1980; Cook, 1985). It was argued that both subjectivity and reflexivity were necessary for valid interpretation. Without being personally involved and drawn into the world of others, it would be impossible to develop an understanding of social life and discover how people create meaning in natural settings. And without this type of understanding, it would be impossible to evaluate a programme.

The strengths of interpretive approaches lie in the prolonged engagement of the evaluator with a programme, the breadth of data that is considered to be relevant to the evaluation, the ability of the evaluator to focus progressively on a variety of issues relevant to the development of the programme, as well as the flexibility to incorporate issues into the evaluation design that emerge from the contact between the evaluator and various programme stakeholders.

Some evaluation researchers (e.g. Guba & Lincoln, 1989) have argued that interpretive evaluation designs are based on criteria of scientific rigour that are so fundamentally different from those of traditional science that they are incompatible. Others (e.g. Cook, 1985; Smith, 1986) suggest that all science has the same aims, that all research approaches have strengths and weaknesses, that there is virtue in utilising both qualitative and quantitative data to evaluate social programmes, and that there is value in combining the best in different methodological approaches in multi-method evaluation designs.

How interpretive approaches to evaluation are applied in practice

There is no single best way to conduct an interpretive evaluation. However, the majority of interpretive evaluation designs are based on the assumption that different programme stakeholders are likely to have different perspectives on the programme and its development, that these differences may be indicative of different value positions and ideologies, and that understanding of stakeholder perspectives is essential to understanding the programme.

For this reason, the departure point in interpretive evaluation design often involves contact between the evaluator and the various stakeholders involved in the programme's development. This usually takes the form of an initial visit or series of visits to the programme, followed by interviews with the various stakeholders. In certain cases, group meetings or focus groups are conducted, the purpose being to inform various stakeholders about the possibility of an evaluation taking place, and to consult with them concerning the evaluation design. The design is often posed as an open question, enabling various stakeholder groups to become involved in posing the type of research question they would like answered, and to suggest possible issues or sources of data that should be included in the design.

The aim of a responsive evaluation is to create an evaluative agenda and a climate in which issues relevant to a programme's development can be analysed and discussed by all those involved. This is often as important as any report which emerges from the evaluation.

The evaluation design that emerges is thus conceptualised as responsive to the needs of various programme stakeholders, rather than being preordinate and inflexible in character – this approach is therefore often referred to as 'responsive evaluation' (Stake, 1974; 1983) or 'stakeholder evaluation' (Weiss, 1983a; 1983b; 1998). The position of

Box 18.2

Evaluation of a community-based childhood injury prevention programme

(Lu-Anne Swart, Unisa Institute for Social and Health Sciences & Unisa-MRC Crime, Violence and Injury Lead Programme)

The Unisa Institute for Social and Health Sciences (ISHS) has been active for many years in violence and injury prevention work, and co-directs the Crime, Violence and Injury Lead Programme with the Medical Research Council (MRC). Part of the Institute's work focuses on the development and evaluation of community-based injury prevention programmes for replication in low-income contexts. An example is the Home Visitation Programme (HVP), which aims to reduce unintentional home injuries among young children. This programme uses local community workers, who receive extensive training, to visit households and provide caregivers with education and counselling about injury prevention to create a safer home environment for children.

To evaluate the effectiveness of the HVP, we implemented the programme in two informal settlements, one near Johannesburg and one near Cape Town. A cluster, randomised, controlled study design was used with pre-assessment and post-assessment. Volunteers from the study sites drew up maps demarcating all the stands, stand numbers, roads, and facilities in the areas. To limit potential contamination by families talking to their neighbours about the programme we decided not to randomise individual households but rather to cluster the households into blocks. Data collectors, trained community volunteers, were given lists of all houses in each block, sorted in random order, and instructed to select houses from the top down until a total of 200 houses were recruited from each of the sites. Houses eligible for the study were those with children aged 10 or younger. Data collectors approached the households to

the evaluator is as an outsider to events in the programme, but also as a person with the mandate to collect information concerning the development of the programme, to interpret this information, and to share the information and the interpretations with all programme stakeholders. This is typically done in a series of report-back meetings held with various stakeholder groups, or as an integral part of a series obtain informed consent for participation and to gather baseline data using the injury risk assessment questionnaire. This instrument was designed to collect information on household demographics, attitudes to injury prevention, safety hazards, and injuries sustained by children over the past year.

After the pre-assessment, the blocks were randomly allocated to the intervention and control groups. There were approximately 100 intervention households and 100 control households for each site. Home visitors called on the intervention households four times over a period of four months. Families in the control group were not visited. Visits focused on child development, the prevention of burns, poisoning, and falls. During each visit, home visitors provided parents with information on safety practices, completed an injury hazard checklist with the parent, and discussed changes to improve home safety. Parents were also given safety devices, such as a child-proof lock and paraffin container safety caps.

Two weeks after the final visit, data collectors followed up both the intervention and control households and re-administered the injury risk assessment questionnaire. We evaluated the effectiveness of the HVP on the reduction of home hazards for poison ingestion, burns, and fall-related injuries by comparing the data at follow-up to the baseline data, and by comparing intervention with control households. In all areas of injury risk, namely electrical burns, paraffin burns, burn safety practices, poisoning, and falls, a decline was noted in the intervention households, with significant reductions for burns safety practices and poisoning risks. Although these results suggest that the HVP has potential as a strategy for child injury reduction, further follow-up is required at a later stage to evaluate whether the initial improvements are sustained over time. At this stage we would also compare injury data with the baseline data to determine the effectiveness of the HVP on injury reduction among children. While this evaluation is essentially positivist in nature, being systematic and measurement based, we have also collected data on the implementation process and conducted focus groups and interviews with study participants and home visitors to obtain their views of the HVP. We will use this data to modify and improve future implementation of the HVP.

of focus groups in which interpretations are shared and further information or clarification sought.

The process involved is essentially a consultative one, providing both a means by which the evaluator can come to understand insider perspectives on the programme, as well as a means of establishing whether his or her interpretations are valid.

Box 18.3

What is a stakeholder?

The term 'stakeholder' was coined by Robert Stake (1974), and refers to persons with a vested interest in a particular programme. This includes those who fund programmes, those who plan and implement programmes, programme participants and users, and those whose interests are affected by the work of programmes. Stakeholder approaches to evaluation are those which attempt to develop an evaluation design sensitive to the interests of various stakeholder groups, and which implement the evaluation in a way that reflects these interests.

A major issue in interpretive evaluation is whether the evaluator's role is to judge the merit or worth of the programme, or whether such judgements emerge naturally from the process of information sharing in which stakeholders become engaged in the course of the evaluation. Another issue is how the process of negotiation, interpretation, and discussion can be reconciled with criteria of scientific rigour. If the evaluator's role becomes one of facilitator of an evaluative process, what is the rigour of the understandings generated? How do these relate to the data, and to the evidence? Are the understandings an outcome or conclusion, or are they themselves data and evidence? How should these understandings be captured, and how should they be reflected in any evaluation report? What is the evaluator's role in this process?

Photo: Rodney Barnett

Stakeholder approaches to evaluation ensure that not only the interests of management will be served.

A variety of evaluation models have been suggested that provide different applied frameworks for conducting evaluations based on interpretive principles. A number of authors (e.g., Simons, 1987) have utilised case study methodology in conducting evaluations, in which the various events and transactions involved in developing a particular programme have been described and analysed. Scriven (1973) has suggested the value of a goal-free evaluation approach, in which programmes are judged on the evidence of what they actually do, and consumer interpretations of the value of what they do. Eisner (1975; 1977) has proposed use of a connoisseurship model based on the use of expert judges in evaluating the quality of work done in programmes, while Wolf (1974; 1983) has suggested use of an evaluation process similar to that used in the judicial system, in which evidence for and against the programme's value is led and argued. Guba and Lincoln (1989) have suggested a methodology of responsive constructivist evaluation, in which the evaluator progressively interviews those involved in the programme, sharing information and interpretations in an attempt to achieve consensus on issues. Another common approach is to use ethnography as a way of developing an understanding of the programme through the eyes of those who participate in its development (Fetterman, 1989). As Stufflebeam (2001) suggests, programme evaluations are designed to assist an audience to assess a programme's merit or worth, and a wide variety of approaches to programme evaluation is available.

Interpretive evaluation designs have been widely utilised, both internationally and locally. In South Africa, interpretive approaches have been applied in a number of evaluations of educational programmes (e.g., Ashley et al., 1996; Basson, 1992; Davies & Terre Blanche, 1997; Holderness & Altman, 1992; MacDonald, 1993; Morphet et al., 1986; Mouton, 1995; Ntshoe, 1999; Potter & Moodie, 1992; Silva, 2003). They have also been applied in evaluations of community development programmes (e.g., Ballen et al. 1991; Graham & Zungu, 1987; Kelly, 2001; Mazibuko, 1990a; 1990b; Potter & Kruger, 2001; Siwani, 1986a; 1986b; Siwani et al., 1990; Silva, forthcoming), and in social responsibility programmes mounted by industry (Cole, 1987; Meyer & Pinto, 1982). While different methodologies are applied in these evaluations, they share a commitment to examining the work of those involved in the programme in context, analysing the perspectives of the various participants or stakeholders, and attempting to understand the various events and transactions involved in developing the programme.

Critical–emancipatory approaches to evaluation research

Critical social science differs from positivist and interpretive research approaches in its emphasis on the social concerns and agendas of those involved as participants in social science research. While there are a number of critical perspectives and approaches, critical science offers a radical and emancipatory perspective which is diametrically opposed to the objectivity and the bracketing-out of personal values implied by positivist science.

Box 18.4

An 'insider' perspective on programmes of instruction
(Ray Basson, University of the Witwatersrand)

Our evaluation of Integrated Studies (developed since the early 1970s at Riverside, a nonracial private secondary school north of Johannesburg) was based on ethnographic assumptions, namely that in-depth descriptive data, gathered on site over an extended period of time, could assist one to better understand the programme, and that understanding is a necessary and prior step to adjudicating a programme's worth.

The evaluation design was based on a series of interviews conducted with teachers and pupils at the school over a six-month period (Basson, 1992). A transcript of each interview was made, which was then analysed with a view to understanding how the Integrated Studies programme was perceived by those involved. Emerging themes were noted, and the respondents were then re-interviewed to clarify the researcher's interpretations. This process of transcription, analysis, and re-interview was continued until the researcher was able to account for all themes raised by the respondents.

From this process, Integrated Studies came to be understood as a programme that initiates pupils into forms of communication and allows them to experience a measure of empowerment through language in classrooms. This differed sharply from mainstream programmes where language is used to convey knowledge content and is linked to testing and examination. Integrated Studies reflected a transformative approach to curriculum, orienting classroom teaching to fostering a 'positive self-concept', to seeing 'connections and relationships between themselves and the world around them', and to bringing into society pupils 'who feel a deep sense of responsibility to their ecological and social environment'.

Integrated studies encouraged critique and the reformulation of meanings through activities such as whole-class discussion, research, small-group work, assignment writing, dramatisation, and plenary report-back.

Thus, the evaluation approach used was interpretive, with the evaluator gathering information concerning the programme through repeated engagement with the same respondents in a series of interviews, which were transcribed, analysed, and interpreted. As the research unfolded through the interview process, the evaluator was able to move progressively from the text of the interviews to the interpretations of those interviewed, and ultimately to emerge with a holistic understanding of the programme. Clearly, such understanding needs to precede adjudication if a programme is to be evaluated for what it is, rather than for what an evaluator may presume it to be.

Evaluation researchers from the critical school have chiefly criticised positivist thinking as being narrow, anti-democratic, and non-humanist. In addition, however, they also criticise interpretive approaches for their lack of involvement in social issues. Critical social science is based on activist assumptions about knowledge and human interests (Habermas, 1971), with researchers being seen as either conscious or unconscious agents of the operation of wider social forces that act to reinforce or reproduce the existing social order.

In terms of their view that both positivist and interpretive research is undertaken uncritically, and used to reinforce the status quo and existing power relations in society, critical evaluation researchers undertake research to transform social relations. This is done by a process of analysis of the underlying forces that keep oppressive relations in place, and the development of empowerment strategies (Freire, 1972a; 1972b). The critical evaluation researcher is action oriented, working to change the world and transform the social order (Fay, 1987).

A key issue in critical–emancipatory evaluation is how the evaluator's own values relate to the programme and its work. Another is whether the evaluator can remain uninvolved, or should adopt an activist position relative to the issues dealt with by the programme. Also at issue is whether the evaluator should remain an outsider to the programme, or should attempt to take an insider position and become fully involved in the programme. There are thus a number of different critical approaches to programme evaluation research, which vary in the degree to which the evaluator becomes directly and practically involved in the programme's development, and the degree to which the evaluator's own ideologies and social activism influence the programme's participants.

Critical approaches to evaluation are usually based on action research, undertaken for the purposes of improvement and involvement (Grundy & Kemmis, 1982). One form of evaluative action research is the approach of research-based teaching and self-evaluation suggested by Stenhouse (1975; 1983), in which emphasis is placed on developing the practical skills and understandings necessary for those involved in programmes to conduct research into and to evaluate their own practices. Another is the democratic approach of Simons (1987). This approach is based on the assumption that the impetus for evaluation, as well as the issues, questions, and foci of the evaluation, should arise from the understandings and interests of those working within the programme, rather than from bureaucratic interests or the interests of the evaluator as an external agent.

Contrasted to these pragmatically orientated approaches to participatory evaluation are those with a more ideological purpose. Approaches to evaluation based on critical action research have been proposed by Carr and Kemmis (1982) and Grundy (1987), who suggest that the role of a researcher should be one of a social activist. They suggest that the purpose of evaluation is to develop the critical

Critical evaluation research is about challenging the status quo.

Paulo Freire was a radical Brazilian educator who used everyday concepts (such as 'land' and 'hunger') to teach illiterate people to read – and to be critical of the political status quo. His 1970 book Pedagogy of the Oppressed brought him international fame and, after being banned from Brazil, he continued to advocate education for 'critical consciousness' and 'pedagogy of liberation' worldwide until his death in 1997.

awareness of those involved in programmes – not only about their own practices, but also about social issues and the power relationships implicit in the social contexts in which they work.

Similar assumptions underpin the empowerment evaluation approach developed by David Fetterman and his colleagues (1993; 1994; 1996), who ascribe to the evaluator roles in capacity-building as well as advocacy for the programme's work. These aim at increasing the ability of those in the programme to identify and deal with their problems, and are accomplished through an educative process which involves learning to 'speak the language of power'.

How critical–emancipatory approaches to evaluation are applied in practice

There are a number of methodological issues that confront evaluators conducting participatory, empowerment, and critical evaluations. A central issue concerns the purposes of participation in the programme, and why the evaluator considers this to be desirable and necessary. Another issue concerns the optimising of the developmental and educative value of evaluation, as a means to enable persons involved in social programmes to further their work, enhance their power through gaining access to skills and knowledge, and to overcome the problems they face.

According to Paulo Freire (1972a; 1972b), the development of critical awareness involves a process of conscientisation, undertaken experientially through an ongoing reflective process termed 'praxis', which occurs both individually and collectively in groups. You can read more about Freire's approach to conscientisation in chapter 19.

Photo: Rodney Barnett

Critical evaluation research involves understanding forms of structural oppression (e.g., relating to race, gender, and socio-economic status) and empowering programme participants to mobilise against them.

Critical–emancipatory approaches to evaluation differ not only with respect to the way in which evaluators conceptualise their roles vis-à-vis participation in a particular programme and their relationships with those involved in programme development, but also how they view the work of those involved in the programme in the context of broader social structures. Empowerment evaluation, for example, focuses on the educative potential of evaluation, with knowledge providing avenues for power and emancipation of the individual and of groups. The evaluator plays a collaborative and facilitative role that includes advocacy for the work undertaken by the programme (Fetterman, 2001).

Critical programme evaluation often turns into a form of social activism.

Critical action research, in contrast, is based on a more structural view of society. Given the power relationships implicit in society, the aim of the evaluator is to develop critical theory, as embedded in the understandings and actions of those involved in social programmes. The development of critical theory is achieved through the critiques of individuals and of groups, and in active engagement and struggle with social issues and with oppressive practices. The assumption is that a critical theory has the capacity to grow and become effective in shared understandings.

The different ways in which these issues have been addressed in practice can best be illustrated by practical examples. These reflect different methodologies by which the process of reflection, or praxis, is facilitated by the evaluator, and different ways in which the evaluator is involved in the programme. Participatory, empowerment, and critical approaches to evaluation have been associated with work in developing countries (Hall, 1976; 1978; Choudhary & Tandon, 1988), in countries where there is opposition to totalitarian or oppressive governments, and in those undergoing rapid transformation or social change. In South Africa, there is an emerging tradition in this area (e.g., Davidoff & Van den Berg, 1990; Kelly, 1998; McNaught & Raubenheimer, 1991; Van Vlaenderen & Gilbert, 1993; Walters & Manicom, 1996; Walker, 1990; 1991; 1994).

The Primary Science Programme evaluation (Potter & Moodie, 1991) was based on the work of six separate evaluation teams over an eighteen-month period. Four of the teams utilised interpretive designs based on questionnaires, interviews, and observation, while two teams used participatory designs, one of which will be described here. In the Western Cape region, the project team focused on developing awareness of the issues involved in the in-service training of primary school science teachers. The process of critical reflection was facilitated by an internal evaluator who worked as a member of the project team, as well as an external evaluator who provided an outsider perspective. Team members were encouraged to reflect continually on their work, with the aim of interrogating the nature of their aims and their practices. Reflection was undertaken collaboratively, based on classroom teaching and classroom observation, the process being developed over a series of sessions, both individually and in groups. The evaluator's aim was to stimulate ongoing questioning, so that those involved could reach increased insight and shared understanding of the issues, and agree on strategies for intervention. Understandings of the project team of past implementation thus formed the basis for future implementation, which was then, in its turn, subjected to critical scrutiny.

Kelly (1998) describes an evaluation of the National Training Project in Theatre for Development undertaken in the Eastern Cape. This evaluation was not only based on a critical approach, but took place in the context of a programme which in itself was aimed at developing critical awareness. The central focus of the programme was a ten-day residential training workshop run by Augusto Boal, the originator of the tradition of Theatre of the Oppressed. The workshop was experiential, involving direct involvement of the participants in a variety of theatre exercises and games that engaged them in questioning their taken-for-granted understanding of themselves and the

Box 18.5

Issues-based multimethod evaluation – using ethnography to develop capacity for self-evaluation

The Open Learning Systems Education Trust develops interactive radio learning programmes for use by teachers in schools, and commissioned an evaluation design for its 'English in Action' programme in 1993. When the evaluation commenced, the programme was being implemented using audio tapes in 289 classrooms. The number rose to 532 in 1994.

The evaluation has taken place longitudinally, in three stages. The first stage used an issues-based multimethod approach, focused on a series of evaluation questions posed by the project team and external evaluators. These were answered through a series of analyses by the evaluators, based on data from interviews, observation, questionnaires, achievement tests, focus groups, and personal accounts and case studies provided by teachers (Potter, 1995; Potter & Leigh, 1995).

The second stage was implementation focused, using an ethnographic approach from 1995 to the end of 2000. This was developed through ongoing formative contact involving repeated engagement with the programme, followed by a series of process studies and two summative reviews in 1998 and 1999. The programme grew substantially, implemented nationally in approximately 1 200 schools, with the numbers of participating teachers and pupils rising rapidly. Given the scale of the programme and the wide area covered by its radio broadcasts, central issues during the second stage concerned programme quality in relation to rapidly changing scale, response to changing teacher needs and national curricula, and how the evaluation process could be used to build self-evaluative capacity in the programme (Potter, 2003; Potter & Naidoo, 2005, in press).

The third stage involved use of self-evaluation data to meet external donor requirements (DfID, 2003; 2004). The methodology for self-evaluation was relationships that they had with others. The evaluator's role was as active participant, both in the programme as well as in a Development Support Committee set up to plan and monitor the programme, in which programme participants also became increasingly involved. An evaluation report was written, reflecting the process as well as the longer-term effects and carry-over from the workshop. The report was based on the perceptions of those involved in the workshop, as well as follow-up work in the communities from which the participants were drawn. Due to the participatory nature of the programme and of the evaluation, and to the increasing involvement of programme participants at the planning and monitoring level, the distinction between programme development and evaluation became increasingly blurred, while the evaluator's role became increasingly one of active participant and programme insider.

---

participatory and collaborative, based on the development of regional materials and case studies to document the process of development at school and community (Potter & Silva, 2002; Potter et al., 2003).

Documents, stories, teaching materials, and examples of classroom work were collected by the project team, supplemented by photographs. Workshops on writing and on self-evaluation were also held with the project team, teachers, and parents. In addition, a database was developed of quantitative indicators reflecting teacher participation and involvement, supplemented by analysis of data (Silva, 2003; forthcoming). Owing to the impossibility of obtaining matched comparison groups of teachers and pupils who were not working with or influenced by the programme's radio broadcasts, these indicators were utilised for trend analyses (DfID, 2003; 2004), as well as nonexperimental studies of the relationship between database variables and indices of teacher involvement, self-efficacy, and learner performance (Masuku, 2000; Jacobson, 2001).

The evaluation has been ongoing since 1993, sharing many of the epistemological and methodological assumptions of responsive evaluation, responsive constructivist evaluation, and empowerment evaluation. It has focused on programmatic issues to effect developmental improvement, with the evaluator acting as a catalyst to developing a self-evaluation process. Of interest is the movement from outsider to insider evaluation roles and the ethnographic focus on developing programme theory based on understanding of the programme's culture. This has emerged progressively, through use of a participatory and collaborative evaluation approach focusing on individual, organisational, contextual and instructional issues. While quantitative and measurement-based data have provided focused indicators of the impact of involvement and learning, qualitative data and personal accounts have provided breadth of interpretation and scope for self-evaluation.

If you were to become a programme evaluation researcher, what kinds of programme do you think would you enjoy evaluating, and what kinds of programme would fit your style of doing evaluation research?

Conclusion: putting it all together

This chapter has outlined a number of models of programme evaluation, reflecting different theories of evaluation and different approaches to the practice of evaluation. There are commonalities between these models, as well as epistemological, methodological, and ideological differences. The approach taken in this chapter has been to attempt to cluster different evaluation models in terms of three broad paradigms, namely positivist, interpretive, and critical–emancipatory.

There is no single correct approach to programme evaluation, and evaluators typically choose an appropriate methodology to fit the pragmatic requirements of each programme, rather than being guided by one particular model or approach. There is also evidence that the process of choosing an evaluator involves a process of matching the style and values of the evaluator and the style and values of the programme (Becher, 1974). A process of negotiation normally takes place as the evaluator considers the evaluation brief and establishes whether what is required is feasible and 'do-able'. In establishing which approach is likely to fit the needs of the programme being evaluated, an attempt is made to establish who wants the evaluation and why, the types of questions that are being asked, and by whom.

The process of evaluation design thus normally commences with an evaluability assessment based on a series of visits to the programme, and on meetings between the evaluator and different programme stakeholders.

These establish the nature of the work of the programme, the reasons why the evaluation is being requested, the time framework involved, and the vested interests likely to be supported or threatened by an evaluation. The evaluator then negotiates with those commissioning the evaluation and the various programme stakeholders the particular evaluation approach which is likely to best fit the circumstances and lead to maximum benefit.

Due to the variety of possible approaches that can be used in conducting a programme evaluation, a number of definitions of evaluation have been considered in this chapter. While there is no consensus as to how evaluation should be defined or how it should be conducted, there is consensus that there needs to be a set of standards governing acceptable practice (Joint Committee on Standards for Educational Evaluation, 1981). Many universities in North America and Britain have taught postgraduate courses in programme evaluation for the past thirty years, either as dedicated courses in the field, or as an integral part of more general courses on research methodology. Reflecting the high level of interest, there are large numbers of publications about evaluation, as well as a number of dedicated journals in the field.

Programme evaluation is an area of applied social science research that has grown rapidly over the past thirty years, and holds great promise for those social scientists who wish to conduct research with high social relevance. In South Africa, the development of the field of evaluation has been a comparatively recent phenomenon. Evaluation research was relatively unknown until the early 1980s, and it was only in the 1990s that local social scientists started demonstrating increased interest in the area.

During the last ten years, there have been signs of widespread interest in the field, as evidenced by the number of programme evaluations being commissioned, and by the number of courses in which programme evaluation is taught at South African universities. There are also several short courses in programme evaluation that have been organised nationally by agencies such as the University of the Witwatersrand's Centre for Continuing Education, and the South African Association for Academic Development, as well as those run locally by nongovernmental organisations. Finally, there is evidence subsequent to South Africa's first democratic elections in 1994 that the Association for the Study of Educational Evaluation in Southern Africa (ASEESA) has become more active, organising an international conference every two years, and publishing a journal and a bulletin dedicated to assessment and evaluation issues. There has also been the emergence of a national evaluation network of professional evaluators in South Africa, linked to the emergence of an African evaluation association and the internationalisation of programme evaluation as a field.

You can find out more about the journals and conferences of the Association for the Study of Educational Evaluation in Southern Africa (ASEESA) by visiting their website at www.aseesa-edu.co.za or by writing to them at PO Box 650, Bedfordview 2008.

Programme evaluation research is in many ways typical of the kinds of professional, applied career now open to researchers in the social sciences (Potter, in press). It involves practical hands-on work, dealing with real-life situations, yet requiring high levels of conceptual abstraction and technical skill. It involves working not only with quantitative and qualitative data but also with people – negotiating the parameters of each evaluation, interviewing stakeholders, and facilitating the development of skills and new understandings. Although programme evaluation is not the sort of activity that one can ever get exactly 'right', it is exhilarating to know that this is not just research for its own sake, but research that makes a difference.

Exercises

1. While the field of evaluation was described in the early 1980s as the fastest growing frontier of social science research, it has only recently achieved prominence in South Africa. List ten social programmes in South Africa that, in your opinion, could most benefit from programme evaluation. Now compare your list with those of other students in your class and try to draw up a 'core' list of ten programmes agreed upon by everybody. Finally, have a class discussion on ways in which greater public awareness of the potential benefits of evaluating these programmes could be achieved.

2. A social worker is interested in reducing the amount of prejudice expressed by members of the community with which she works. She has designed what she believes will be an effective programme

for changing prejudicial attitudes. The programme will be implemented on a pilot level in a community centre with a view to being more widely implemented. A corporate sponsor has agreed to support the development and implementation costs over a two-year period, provided that the programme is properly evaluated. The sponsor has stipulated that hard (quantitative) evidence is needed from the evaluation, as well as evidence of support from the programme's various stakeholders. Describe how you would go about evaluating this programme so as to meet the needs and vested interests of the programme planners and the users of the programme, as well as those of the corporate sponsors.

3. Design a programme to encourage safe-sex practices among students on your university campus. Also provide a detailed account of how you would evaluate the programme.

Key readings

Fetterman, D. M. (2001). *Foundations of empowerment evaluation*. Thousand Oaks, California: Sage.

Feuerstein, M. (1986). *Partners in evaluation: Evaluating development and community programmes with participants*. London: Macmillan.
Useful ideas for planning and implementing participatory evaluations.

Guba, E. G., & Lincoln, Y. S. (1989). *Fourth generation evaluation*. Newbury Park, California: Sage.
Outlines the principles of responsive-constructivist evaluation.

Rossi, P. H., Freeman, H. E., & Lipsey, M. W. (1999). *Evaluation: A systematic approach*. (6th edition). Beverly Hills, California: Sage.
This describes forms of programme evaluation and evaluation designs.

Stufflebeam, D. L. (2001). *Evaluation models. New Directions in Program Evaluation, No. 89*. San Francisco: Jossey-Bass.
An overview and analysis of 22 models of programme evaluation.

Weiss, C. H. (1998). *Evaluation: Methods for studying programs and policies*. (2nd edition). Upper Saddle River, New Jersey: Prentice Hall.
This links programme theory and the types of evaluation for assessing the operation and outcomes of a programme or policy.

Participatory action research:

a practical guide for realistic radicals

Arvin Bhana

Human Sciences Research Council

In the early 1980s, a number of health professionals – including nurses, social workers, psychologists, doctors, and dentists – initiated an alternative health-care organisation called the Organisation for Appropriate Social Services in South Africa (OASSSA). The organisation was set up in direct response to the apartheid government's social and health services, which mainly benefited the white urban population. While the government preferred to ascribe the ill-health of South Africa's mostly black population to unhealthy and unhygienic lifestyles, OASSSA focused on poverty and deprivation as causal factors. Not only did OASSSA challenge the state regarding its differential treatment of the various population groups, it also embarked on a programme of providing health care to those whom the state deemed to be its enemies. The focus was on caring for oppressed groups such as student and political activists, township communities, and political detainees and their families. In addition, OASSSA established an extensive training programme to help victims of violence and torture deal with psychological and medical problems. Workshops were organised, and training manuals for primary health care were written in both English and the first language of trainees. At the same time, members of OASSSA collected information about the human rights abuses of the apartheid regime and used this to engage in subversive activities against the state.

The work of OASSSA, being community based and combining information gathering with activism, is an example of **participatory action research** (PAR). PAR aims to produce knowledge in an active partnership with those affected by that knowledge, for the express purpose of improving their social, educational, and material conditions. Unlike many other models of research in the social sciences, PAR arose in and from the developing countries (notably South America), from where the work – especially that of Paul Freire in establishing 'education for liberation' (Hall, 1981) – has spread across the world. Participatory action research has been influential not only in education but also in fields such as agriculture, rural development, and community health (Tandon, 1996).

It should be obvious that PAR exists in a tensional relationship with regard to positivism, which values objectivity, distance, and precision of measurement over active engagement. PAR also presents a challenge to the interpretive research paradigm. Interpretive research, like PAR, emphasises intersubjective engagement and the fostering of democratic research relationships, but PAR goes further in locating this in a community rather than an individual context and in emphasising the action consequences rather than the reflective truths of research. Table 19.1 lists some of the differences between participatory action research and its traditional (positivist and interpretive) counterparts.

While PAR is a distinct research approach with its own history, principles, and methods, in recent years there has been a growing consensus among researchers of all persuasions regarding the value of participatory action-oriented work. Indeed, the title of this book, *Research in Practice*, reflects the extent to which most social science

Unlike many other research approaches, PAR is not a Euro-American import.

researchers have come to understand their work as pragmatic and contextual rather than aimed at producing value-free knowledge. Thus, you will have noticed that many of the research fields described in this section of the book rely on standard scientific methodologies but frequently apply these in a democratic setting and for emancipatory purposes. In chapter 16, you will note that one criterion used in evaluating interpretive research is precisely the nature and extent of its action consequences.

A distinction is sometimes made between **action research** (AR) and **participatory research** (PR). The former arose in the context of the need to change the way industrial companies and other companies are managed, while the latter first became popular in the fields of education and community development. The signs of this difference in history are still visible in slight differences in emphasis between the two approaches (Brown, 1993). However, these differences have become increasingly inconsequential, and current usage favours the term 'participatory action research' for any kind of research with an action and/or participatory consideration.

We turn now to a more in-depth theoretical consideration of the main principles of participatory action research, following which we will go on to illustrate the theory with some real-life examples and with a practical exposition of three phases in the design and execution of a PAR study. Finally, we will return to theoretical issues in a discussion of empowerment as the central goal of PAR.

Table 19.1 Values and ideologies in traditional research and participatory action research

	Traditional approaches	**PAR**
Values	Promotes self-determination of individuals but neglects distributive justice. Helps individuals not communities.	Promotes balance between self-determination and distributive justice. High degree of concern for wellbeing of individuals and communities.
Assumptions	Based on scientific or interpretive assumptions about knowledge. Good life and good society are based on value-free liberalism, individualism, and meritocracy.	Promotes grounded knowledge through collaborative relationships which emphasise mutuality, obligations, and the removal of oppression.
Practices	Problems defined in asocial and deficit-oriented terms. Interactions are reactive.	Problems defined in terms of interpersonal and social oppression. Interventions seek to change individuals as well as social systems.
Benefits	Preserves values of individuality and freedom.	Promotes sense of community and emancipation of every member of society.
Risks	Victim blaming and tacit support for unjust social structures. Solutions may have little relation to real-world experience.	Denial of individuality and sacrifice of personal uniqueness for good of the community. Solutions may not generalise beyond immediate contexts.

What is participatory action research?

PAR can be understood as straddling a series of three tensions. First, PAR draws on the tension between science and practice. Where traditional approaches may divorce the discovery of scientific truths from their application, PAR researchers argue that authentic knowledge of the human and social world can only be gained in the process of attempting to change that world, and that authentic change can only happen when it is accompanied by shifts in the knowledge base of those involved (Hoshmand & O'Byrne, 1996). Thus, PAR attempts to contribute both to the practical concerns of people in an immediate problematic situation and to the larger goals of social science, and emphasises both rigour and relevance (Rapaport, 1970). After all, a key reason for community participation is the promise of change. Of what benefit would it be to the participants otherwise? This becomes even more critical in communities where major issues are crying out for change and there is little prospect of such change from existing structures.

PAR is about democratising the knowledge-making process.

Second, PAR attempts to mediate between individual and collective needs. Traditional research, when it does become concerned with action, operates from a purely 'instrumental' perspective; that is, it aims to find the most efficient solutions to applied problems. In a society dominated by capitalist ideologies of individual success, this most often translates into the development of social technologies for individual betterment or the optimal management of capitalist enterprises. PAR, by contrast, insists on communal participation in the process of knowledge creation, so that knowledge can never become the property of individuals or small interest groups (Brown & Tandon, 1983). While there is a danger that individual needs will become secondary to those of an all-powerful collective, in practice PAR emphasises the empowerment of the least powerful groups and individuals in society.

Third, PAR addresses the tension that exists in the relationship between researcher and researched. PAR researchers try to know *with* others, rather than *about* them, and to reconceptualise and foster knowledge as something that exists among people, rather than as some sort of barrier between them.

To this end, PAR encourages egalitarian research relationships and the full involvement of those being researched in every aspect of a research project – from initial conceptualisation to final implementation (Whyte, Greenwood, & Lazes, 1989). Where citizens participate in research, they do not remain merely objects of a study but become full partners in the research process and committed to its success.

The tensions that characterise PAR as a form of social science enquiry all revolve around a commitment to work with knowledge from the bottom up, rather than from the top down. Thus there is an attempt to champion the everyday world of social give-and-take over rational scientific discourse, the interests of research participants over those of the researcher, and the needs of disempowered groups over those of powerful elites. The difficulty, however, is that the impetus for PAR frequently comes from academics and researchers who, by virtue of their social position and expertise, cannot but operate in a top-down manner. We will return to this question later, when we discuss the concept of empowerment more fully.

Let us now see what a PAR project might look like in practice. Small (1996) describes a project undertaken in collaboration with an inner-city community to address the social problems of adolescents. Adolescents are exposed to many dangers as they start becoming sexually active, and begin experimenting with drugs (Small, 1996). In South Africa, both alcohol and marijuana are serious public health problems among young people (Parry, Bhana, & Bayley, 1998). The project, called TAP (Teen Assessment Project), was developed to provide the community with research-based knowledge to support local adolescents through various adjustment difficulties. In such a context, a traditional research project might have used standardised questionnaires and randomised sampling techniques to obtain information about the adolescents, and then used the findings to recommend a series of specialist interventions. Instead, Small set up and consulted with a number of 'steering committees' in the community. These committees helped to frame the research questions and the manner in which these were operationalised in questionnaires and interview schedules. The committees also nominated young people from the community to actually conduct the survey. At each step along the way, Small gave expert advice (e.g., on the technicalities of sampling) and provided community members with training in interviewing skills. The results of the survey were used by the steering committees to decide on policy changes in local schools and other institutions, and to inform the next round of community-based knowledge generation. The major advantage of using the PAR model was that the community felt that they were part of the research process, and were thus happy to act on the basis of the research findings. If an external consultant had come into the community, conducted research, and then formulated policy, the community would have felt that the initiatives were being imposed on them from outside, and in all likelihood would have resisted the interventions.

In PAR projects, communities are typically involved in all aspects of the research process.

Developing and executing a PAR study

Participatory action research is by its very nature a cyclical process. Traditionally, a research project is designed in the researcher's office and implemented in the field, and the findings are then taken back to the researcher's office for analysis. In PAR, by contrast, design, implementation, and analysis are combined in a single cyclical process that happens in the community. However, for purposes of exposition, it is useful to distinguish three phases in developing and executing a PAR study.

Box 19.1

Creative participatory enquiry
(Kevin Kelly, Rhodes University, CADRE)

There is a wide range of facilitation methods for fostering community involvement in processes of enquiry into their own conditions and development needs. These methods range from general techniques for facilitating communication and interaction within focus groups to self-surveys and more comprehensive methods for conducting community audits, such as Participatory Rural Appraisal (PRA). One interesting approach is the use of Freirian codes, which can be creatively adapted to suit different settings.

Freire's epistemological framework is dialogical and participatory, meaning that research is conceived of as the joint effort of a facilitator (or animator) and a group of people aspiring to understand their own circumstances better in order to change them. The first stage of a typical Freirian intervention begins with researching people's *thematic universe*, usually together with a group of people from the community, coopted as co-researchers. The themes are the ideas, values, hopes, and concepts that are important to people in relation to a particular issue. These can be elicited through interviews or focus-group discussions.

These themes are then condensed into some form of representation or 'code', which depicts some of the central constituent elements of a community's thematic universe. One can either create a code or use existing materials that are deemed suitable to the task at hand. Existing materials that have been used include photographs, poems, posters, and plays, but it is usually better to create a custom-made code to capture the particular tensions and problem areas which are central to the thematic universe of the group in question. A simple method is to use a group of four or five co-researchers to model a scene so as to form a still-life representation of the issues at stake. The representation or code (whether it is a photograph or play) is then used to elicit discussion relating to the issues being researched.

The code is then presented back to the community in a group discussion context conducted by a facilitator. People are required to describe what is happening in the context of the scene depicted by the code and imaginatively to develop the story of the code. Codes are typically

Photo: Rodney Barnett

A 'code' for a study on community policing

structured so as to present ambiguous images that evoke rich material as the group discusses their different interpretations and tries to come to a common understanding.

Having begun to 'unpack' their understanding of what is happening in the context of the images presented by the code, and having discussed the dominant issues, contradictions, and tensions which are evoked in that situation, the facilitator then asks them if the kind of situation depicted in the code occurs in their own community. Having already spontaneously entered into talking about the code from the perspective of their thematic universe, the group is usually easily able to talk about their everyday reality in terms of the themes which have been evoked. Thus the method begins with projecting the participants' understanding onto the code context, and then uses the momentum of the discussion and the prevailing themes to discuss their own everyday reality.

Why is the use of codes necessary? Why not just begin talking directly about people's own reality? It is not always easy for a group freely to discuss issues that are most deeply important to them. Real life is often 'too close' to understand, and it helps to project one's own understanding onto an external image before turning to understand one's own situation. The code enables us to step back a couple of paces and look at the problem from a distance – to think about the range of interpretations that exist – without running aground on the rocks of community conflict or falling back on failed problem-solving strategies.

One thereby creates a context involving 'discussion about', before addressing at first hand what to do about hotly contested and sensitive community issues. It is a method for developing understanding of the community's existing ways of understanding itself, and for developing new ways of understanding and new strategies of problem solving based on this knowledge.

The following questioning sequence, adapted from Hope and Timmel (1984), gives an idea of the process of interacting around a code:

Stage 1

Description: What do (did) you see happening in the poster/play/photograph?

First analysis: Why is it happening?

Stage 2

Real life: Does this happen in your lives?

Related problems: What problems does it lead to?

Root causes: What are the root causes of these problems?

Stage 3

Action planning: What can we do about it?

Phase 1: definition of problems

The way in which a problem is defined will shape and constrain the results of an enquiry. For example, if South Africa's crime rate is considered in relation to criminal justice and policing, then the questions one could ask would focus on issues such as the relationship between capital punishment, arrest rates, and crime.

If crime were to be considered in relation to social factors such as unemployment, poverty, crowded housing, and poor educational opportunities, very different questions would be asked. The range of questions that can be asked about any particular problem is theoretically infinite, and, although questions do not determine what the answers will be, they do constrain the kinds of answer that can potentially be given. If a researcher asks questions about the criminal justice system, she or he will not uncover information relating crime rates to educational opportunities. By concentrating on the technical aspects of research design, and de-emphasising the manner in which research questions arise in the first place, traditional researchers disguise the *political* nature of enquiry. As a consequence, many questions in the social sciences are constructed in such a way as to 'blame the victim' (Ryan, 1976). Evidence for this may be seen, for example, in the literature on the personality and other characteristics of abused women. Not only may social science researchers 'unconsciously' side with the powerful against the powerless, but they are also subject to overt and covert pressure from powerful political and economic groups who want to discourage the investigation of certain types of problem to prevent them from becoming a part of public knowledge.

PAR attempts to overcome these difficulties, first by acknowledging the interdependence of science and politics and, second, by framing research questions through a process of participation with less powerful groups and communities. Where traditional research in industry would, for instance, frame questions from a management perspective (e.g., 'How can productivity be increased by eliminating time-wasting on the shop floor?'), PAR would frame questions in collaboration with workers (e.g., 'How can we make our work more meaningful so that we don't feel we're wasting our time on the shop floor?'). This kind of approach is more than merely siding with 'the oppressed', but represents a commitment to the idea that those most directly affected are also most likely to be able to provide solutions to their own problems. As Hall (1981, p. 7) puts it, 'the problem originates in the community or workplace itself,' not in the manager's office or the social science textbook.

Phase 2: data collection and analysis

Traditional social science research emphasises data collection and analysis methodologies such as experiments and surveys. These usually require trained researchers and individuals with access to data-processing facilities.

Box 19.2

Some key steps in PAR

Identifying the issue. This can be something researchers believe is worth pursuing, or it can emerge from NGOs or CBOs working in local community contexts. For example, the issue could be domestic violence. It is important to identify the groups and organisations in the local community who are involved in working with issues of domestic violence. So, invite everyone who has an interest, which could include the church and the police, to a meeting to discuss domestic violence issues.

Identifying roles and responsibilities. This meeting could be used to indicate who would be willing to help run the project and in what capacity. It is important to include not only individuals who have research skills but also those who wish to participate in the project and have few or no research skills. Usually a formal structure needs to be established. In addition, formal mechanisms need to be established for the way in which this group works in relation to developing the project and delivering on its objectives. The group must also have mechanisms by which it can provide feedback on developments about domestic violence to the wider community.

Conducting the research. Everybody knows something. Some know more about research enquiry, while others know more about domestic violence and yet others know more about what is likely to help in addressing the problem of domestic violence. In other words, everyone has something to bring to the table but everyone also has something to learn. A researcher may know a lot about the use of focus groups in gathering information, and this would be something that others could learn. A community activist may know a lot about the cultural contexts of domestic violence which could be used to help others understand the problem better.

Mutuality of purpose. Through the process described above, it is evident that PAR as research enquiry has the potential to create awareness beyond the immediate objectives of the research project, to skill individuals, and to increase belief in their own abilities to promote social change and thereby empower individuals and groups to act in their own best interests.

PAR seeks to establish 'joint collaboration within an ethical framework' (Rapaport, 1970, p. 499) with a view to engaging participants directly in the data collection and analysis. The emphasis is on open relationships with participants (Argyris & Schon, 1996), so that they have a direct say in the way in which data are collected and interpreted. If participants decide that technical procedures such as sampling or skilled tasks such as interviewing should be part of the data collection and analysis process, they could draw on expert advice and training supplied by researchers. For example, Comer (1998) recognised that

Suppose you want to examine the question of poverty from a Marxist perspective. What are your chances of being able to get a research grant from the Department of Finance or your university?

many children living in poor neighbourhoods were placed at risk for failure of school drop-out. He relied upon parents and teachers to gather extensive data about children in their schools whom they deemed to be at risk. The data were analysed at joint meetings between the psychologist, parent-helpers, and teachers, and provided solutions appropriate to that particular context.

Phase 3: utilisation of results

Experience has taught many communities to be suspicious of academic researchers, who frequently publish their findings in academic journals but do not provide any feedback to those from whom the data were collected.

The PAR approach, which involves a partnership in all phases of research, ensures that community members have access to and control over the findings, and participate in decisions about dissemination and the choice of how to link results to implementation.

In a good PAR study, the term 'researcher' could therefore refer both to the community and to those with expert knowledge. Outside researchers become committed participants and learners in a process that leads to militancy rather than detachment (Alinsky, 1971; Hall, 1981). While the researcher seeks to advance knowledge, in PAR she or he has a primary obligation to enable communities to act on their own behalf. Some of the ramifications of this are discussed in box 19.2.

Conclusion: PAR and the ideal of empowerment

You have probably gathered from the examples of participatory research projects presented so far that the goals of PAR extend beyond solving particular problems such as drug abuse or violence in a community. The ultimate goal of a collaborative relationship between researchers and participants is **structured transformation** and the improvement over a broad front of the lives of those involved. The outcome of a successful PAR project is not merely a better understanding of a problem, nor even successful action to eliminate the problem, but raised awareness in people of their own abilities and resources to mobilise for social action. This is known as **empowerment**.

Faced with conditions of oppression and inequality, individuals and communities often experience a sense of hopelessness, apathy, and powerlessness. In Freire's (1970; 1973) conception of powerlessness, people become powerless in assuming the role of 'object' acted upon by the environment, rather than 'subject' acting in and on the world. Powerlessness arises from passive acceptance of oppressive cultural 'givens', or surrender to a 'culture of silence'. One community activist described her sense of powerlessness as follows:

> It would never have occurred to me to have expressed an opinion on anything ... It was *inconceivable* that my opinion had any value

Some communities are targeted so often by social science researchers, who contribute little to the betterment of the community, that they become 'over researched' and reluctant to cooperate with researchers. Do you know of a community like that in your area?

... that's lower than powerlessness ... You don't even know the word 'power' exists. It applies to *them* ... I didn't question that's the way the world was ... It was *their* world ... And I was an intruder, you know? (Kieffer, 1984, p. 14)

Empowerment thus operates, in the first instance, at the individual level, helping people to start seeing themselves as being able to make a difference and being worthy of voicing opinions. Psychological empowerment of this sort is a long and difficult process. Researchers do not instantly turn their research collaborators into empowered individuals simply by allowing them a say in the research process. There are real power differentials between (professional) researchers and (often unschooled) community members, as well as among community members (such as between husbands and wives).

For this reason, it is important to realise that empowerment is more than a psychological process; it has to do with structural changes within a community and between a community and the rest of society. Shifts in the balance of power can, and should, occur in two related domains: knowledge and economic resources. The initial focus in PAR is often on finding practical, workable solutions to problems, and, at the very least, knowledge should be generated that addresses these applied concerns. However, empowerment also entails more fundamental changes to the ecology of knowledge. For example, people may learn new skills, and individuals and groups whose opinions were previously not valued may now be regularly consulted. In the economic domain, the participatory action research process could result in previously marginalised groups gaining access to self-employment opportunities, jobs, bank loans, and other resources. Obviously, such shifts in who has access to knowledge and resources will not be to the benefit of parties with vested interests within and beyond a community, and any effective PAR project will of necessity provoke opposition and controversy.

Successful PAR projects result not only in solutions to immediate problems but also in more far-reaching changes to the balance of power.

Empowerment is a grand and seductive concept, and it is easy for researchers to start thinking of themselves as rescuers sent to reconfigure communities along more psychologically and socially 'healthy' lines. This is sometimes fed by the inflated expectations people have about the ability of researchers (as representatives of the world of wealth, opportunity, and power) to change local conditions. This kind of patronising and victim-blaming relationship is, ironically, exactly what the PAR approach sets out to counter.

Box 19.3

Working for change in a Tanzanian village

Rahman (1991) describes a Tanzanian government project to identify the planning and implementation needs of villagers in order to help them develop their own resources and become self-reliant. The government employed a multidisciplinary team of researchers to study villages in three districts, but this soon degenerated into an academic exercise, with many papers and seminars produced but little change to the lives of the villagers.

The project was given over to an organisation promoting participatory rural development. They recruited field staff with the following characteristics: a sense of commitment and a desire to live and work among villagers; innovativeness in work and willingness to experiment with new approaches; communication skills, especially the ability to discuss and listen to others; flexibility and a readiness to learn from one's own and others' experiences; and intellectual ability and emotional maturity.

These individuals were given six days to stimulate people's self-reliant collective action. The field staff ran workshops emphasising self-deliberation and initiatives arising from the villagers themselves. The trainees then drew up a programme of action to immerse themselves in specific village situations, to understand these situations in detail, to identify the basic concerns of the villagers, and to analyse these issues with the people in order to explore possibilities of collective action.

Some of the outcomes were the improvement of agricultural production and incomes, without depending on state handouts, through securing land and establishing group farms on this land. Apart from agriculture, a range of other activities were started. These included brick-making, timber and carpentry, pottery, basket- and mat-weaving, tailoring, and consumer shops. At a local level, a 24-member group in a village called Ukwamami each gave one head of cattle for sale to half-finance the cost of a tractor. The remainder of the cost was financed by a village bank. This group cultivated a collective farm of 69 acres using the tractor, and assisted another group of 15 members to cultivate a 41-acre group farm.

In addition to the direct economic effects of this PAR project, other initiatives have emerged on a similar basis, having taken note of this example. Thus, information about the process, which only existed among the trainers, now becomes part of the expertise of the villagers themselves. No doubt some of this information will be coloured by local experience and may not always work in new settings. Nevertheless, it signifies an important departure from the way in which information is disseminated and used in traditional forms of research.

There are no fail-safe ways of preventing the ideals of empowerment from degenerating in this way, apart from researchers maintaining a critical awareness of the politically fraught nature of their enterprise. If we enter communities in a respectful way, and are as eager to learn as we are to impart knowledge, we may eventually be able to disseminate the results of our research endeavours in ways that are equally accessible to community members and our academic peers (Weinstein et al., 1991).

The PAR model of research can potentially have a far greater social impact than the conventional professional-expert role that has dominated the social sciences. PAR provides researchers committed to social change with an important tool, not only for promoting such change but also for advancing social theory.

Exercises

1. Consider the community or current context in which you live. What is considered to be the most common problem impacting on this community?

    (a) Identify key individuals, groups, and organisations who you know are involved in trying to deal with this problem. Gather as much information as possible and solicit support for undertaking research into the problem.

    (b) In collaboration with this group, advertise and initiate meetings to further discuss the problem. One way to ensure participation is to get the individuals, groups, and organisations to help you organise a meeting with the broader community.

    (c) Following the key steps described above, initiate research into the problem through collaborative definition of the problem and mapping of roles and responsibilities. What would be the mutuality of purpose in carrying out such research?

2. Read the following quote and then discuss how participatory research can have a positive and a negative impact on the way that power is distributed in a community: 'The need to have "community participation" ... has encouraged and often sanctioned the emergence of "community leaders" who may have dubious qualifications other than concern for their own personal and family interests' (Thornton & Ramphele, 1988, p. 31).

3. To be effective, PAR should focus not only on individuals but on community and social structures that tend to perpetuate social problems. For example, what would you say are the structural causes of educational problems in township schools?

Key readings

De Koning, K., & Martin, M. (Eds.). (1996). *Participatory research in health: Issues and experiences*. Johannesburg: NPPHCN.
This South African book represents the experiences and reflections of academics and participatory action research participants in developing and developed countries. The concern is with health rather than agriculture or rural development.

Fals-Borda, O., & Rhaman, M. A. (Eds.). (1991). *Action and knowledge: Breaking the monopoly with participatory action-research*. New York: The Apex Press.
This edited book brings together social scientists active in participatory action research from various parts of the world to reflect on examples of PAR within local settings. The book critically examines the essential ingredients of PAR, followed by programmes of PAR in South America, North America, Asia, and Africa.

Freire, P. (1970). *Pedagogy of the oppressed*. Harmmondsworth: Penguin.
This is Freire's classic text in which he explains his approach to education for critical consciousness and the empowerment of the poor.

Tolan, P., Keys, C., Chertok, R., & Jason, L. (1990). *Researching community psychology: Issues of theory and methods*. Washington, DC: APA.
An excellent reference for current debates on epistemology and research methods in community psychology. It describes the thinking and practice of leading community psychologists in their fields of expertise.

Weinstein, R. S., Soule, C. R., Collins, F., Cone, J., Mehlhorn, M., & Simontacchi, K. (1991). Expectations and high school change: Teacher–researcher collaboration to prevent school failure. *American Journal of Community Psychology*, *19*, 333–364.
A description of participatory research in a school setting that is unique not only for its methodological innovations, but also for its reporting style. The authors detail the collaborative nature of their work, reporting both their successes and failures. This reporting style helps the reader better understand the negotiated nature of participatory research.

Researching public policy

Yogan Pillay

Department of Health

This chapter will explain the relationship between research and the policy-making process. In addition, methods that are used to analyse policies are mentioned, so that when you read a policy document you will be able to tell if it is a good policy or not. We will also consider creative ways of inserting research findings into the politics of policy making, because policy making is a political process that is influenced by a variety of factors besides research and empirical evidence.

By now, you should have a pretty good idea of what research is and of some of the methods that can be used to conduct research, as well as some of the statistical tools that can be used to analyse data to test hypotheses. However, what policies are and who makes them might be unclear. The *Concise Oxford Dictionary* (9th edition) defines a policy as 'a course or principle of action adopted or proposed by a government, party, business, or individual' (p. 1057). A **policy** can be as simple as a student deciding to study from 5:30 am to 6:30 pm every day, a policy for the opening and closing times of the local supermarket, or a policy on who may receive health care at the local public hospital.

These examples illustrate two defining features of policy: (1) that policy is developed to influence or shape behaviour, and (2) that policies are the result or outcome of some need. The need of the student may be to get better grades or not to fail the examinations, and the need of the public health sector may be to ensure that it has sufficient resources to enable the hospitals to provide an effective service. Universities make policies about various issues, such as student admission policies, and the type, form, and duration of examinations.

It should also be clear from the above examples that policy is not only made by government. Everyone can and does make policies. However, government policies are usually more important than those made by individuals because they affect large numbers of people.

The policy-making process followed by the South African government has changed since 1994. Prior to the election of the first democratic government, policy making was a closed affair with very little public participation. This is not surprising, since the government was not open to persuasion by the general public but based its policies on the grand policy of apartheid (see Pillay, 1995, for more details on the way that apartheid shaped health policy until 1990).

Since 1994, the South African government has created new 'grand' policy, as well as structures and processes for policy making. All policies of the current government are shaped, to a greater or lesser extent, by two policy documents: the Reconstruction and Development Programme (RDP), which was published in 1994 and used as the primary election platform of the African National Congress (ANC), and the Growth, Employment and Redistribution policy (GEAR), which was developed as a macroeconomic strategy in 1996. South Africa also has a new Constitution and a constitutional court that interprets the Constitution. The Constitution contains a Bill of Rights which sets out the rights of all citizens, and the actions of Parliament and other bodies are shaped by the provisions of the Constitution. The parliamentary process in policy making is structured

Most policies are framed within the context of 'grand policies' such as apartheid or national reconciliation, so it is important to understand the broad political context within which policy research operates.

to allow for both policy and laws to be made. Policies are typically in the form of **white papers**, while laws are in the form of acts of Parliament. White papers are governmental policy position papers. So, if you want to know what the government's policy on social development is, you should get a copy of the white paper for social development prepared by the Department of Social Development. Likewise, if you wish to know what the government's policy for the transformation of local government is, you should read the white paper on local government issued by the Department of Provincial and Local Government.

White papers are preceded by **green papers**, which are discussion documents. They are circulated widely; many are available on the internet and are open for comment. The relevant portfolio committee (these are parliamentary committees tasked with ensuring that policies and bills are thoroughly discussed before being debated by Parliament) may hold hearings on the green paper at which individuals and institutions are invited to make oral or written representations. The portfolio committee may make changes to policy documents or bills. Typically, there is a long consultative process to be followed in finalising a policy document.

You can find details of green papers, white papers, and other government policies at the government website: www.gov.za.

The development of a white paper on health

Box 20.1

- Specialist committees created by the Minister in 1994/5.
- Ministerial committees consulted widely in developing recommendations (1995).
- Draft document drawn up that integrates recommendations of the ministerial committees: 'Towards a National Health System' (1996).
- Draft document published for consultation.
- Revised document published as 'White paper on the transformation of the health system in South Africa' (1996/7).
- Portfolio committee holds hearings on the white paper in March 1998.

How are research and policy related?

A policy is usually created in response to some need. However, the need may have to be clearly understood before any action is taken. For example, a policy on termination of pregnancy was developed and passed by Parliament as a law and implemented in 1996 (*The Choice on Termination of Pregnancy Act*, 1996). This policy and the act were considered necessary to reduce the number of so-called backstreet abortions, to decrease the pain and suffering caused as well as the number of deaths from unsafe terminations, and to decrease the cost to the health sector of repairing the damages caused by such interventions. The identification of these factors and their effects on individuals and the health system resulted, in part, from research.

Research conducted by the Medical Research Council and testimony by the Women's Health Project assisted in supporting the issue of termination of pregnancy. One of the sources used was the historical research by Bradford, who investigated the issue over a 150-year period, and showed that all races and classes in South Africa made use of illegal abortion services (Stevens, 1998).

It may be argued that these things were known for a long time without a policy on terminations being adopted. This raises the issue of who influences policy. According to Walt (1994), there are two schools of thought: the pluralist view and the elitist view. The former believes that power to influence decision making is not concentrated in a few people, whereas the latter considers it to be concentrated in the hands of the elite in a society. The elite may be politicians, business people, the military, or a combination of these groupings. An alternate set of theories suggests that it depends on the type of policy. A resolution of this issue is, however, beyond the scope of this chapter.

While some policy decisions reflect political priorities, different types of research and analysis are important for different stages of the policy-making process. According to Hogwood and Gunn (in Walt, 1994) and Porter (1995), the process of policy making includes the following steps:

- issue search and agenda setting,
- issue definition,
- setting objectives and priorities,
- analysis of the policy options and selection of the best option,
- policy implementation, monitoring, and evaluation, and
- policy review.

One should add the concept of pilot studies to the above list. Often, one wishes to test out the policy under controlled conditions before making it applicable throughout an organisation or country. For example, because of the complexities involved, a Department of Social Development policy on the financing of nongovernmental organisations by government was piloted before it became government policy. Pilot sites should be selected with care to ensure that, at minimum, they represent the population to which you wish to generalise the results, and that the resources required for replication and the cost of the resources are available.

To illustrate the steps mentioned above, let us take access to primary health care as an example. Say we are asked by the Minister of Health to draft a policy on primary health care. In this instance, the issue search and agenda setting have already been done by the Minister, who wishes to increase access to health care in the country. She or he may have decided on this issue for a number of reasons – for example, it is common knowledge that one way to improve the health status of the population is to increase access to health services. It may also be nearing election time and the political party in power wants to deliver on its previous election promises to increase its chances of getting re-elected. In addition, powerful constituencies (such as organised labour) may be demanding increased access to public health services. As a researcher supporting the development of policy, it is useful to fully understand the motivation behind the request or the agenda.

Drug master plan – dealing with substance abuse
(Melvyn Freeman, Department of Health)

Box 20.2

Policies are often not the exclusive domain of any one government department. For example, dealing with substance abuse involves the departments of Safety and Security, Justice, Correctional Services, Social Development, and Health. To coordinate policy and ensure the attainment of a unified goal, a drug advisory board was established, made up of representatives of key stakeholders both inside and outside government.

Based on recently conducted South African and international research on the extent of the drug problem, its consequences, and effective ways to reduce supply and demand, the board developed an inter-sectoral 'Drug Master Plan'. This plan was subjected to public hearings and approved by Cabinet in 1999. It now forms the framework for more detailed policies in each of the departments named above, as well as in nongovernmental organisations.

Photo: Rodney Barnett

The next step is to define the issue more precisely. Access to primary health care is a broad issue. At this point, a literature search may be indicated to explore what strategies other countries have used to increase access to primary health care and what the effect of these strategies was. One would document the various policy options at one's disposal and attempt to analyse each. The analysis might demand further research. For example, if one of the options was to make health care free of charge, the obvious questions would be 'Can we afford it?' and 'What would be the impact of increased volumes of patients on health personnel, facilities, and quality of care?'

Research can occur at each step of the policy formulation process. Even if research is only conducted at the problem identification (agenda-setting) stage, it is still considered policy research. This issue is highlighted by De la Rey and Eagle (1997) with respect to putting gender issues on the policy agenda. They argue that the

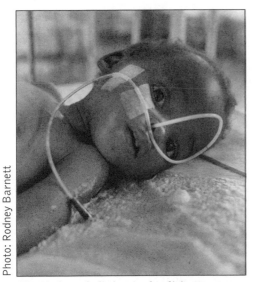

Photo: Rodney Barnett

Hospitals and clinics need policies to ensure that their services reach those who need them most.

availability of documented research will help to create policy that is informed:

'... State mental institutions and clinics should be instructed to keep statistics of the number of women and men in admissions, nature of pathology and treatment. These statistics should be collated annually by the national directorate of mental health and included as part of their annual report' (pp. 162–163).

In fact, it may be argued that research at this stage is crucial if it is used to convince decision makers about the importance of a particular issue.

Various types of method may be used in the different phases of the policy process. These are indicated in table 20.1. As already suggested, a literature search may be useful in the problem definition stage.

Table 20.1 Methods to be used at the different stages of policy making

Policy-making stages	Methods
Problem definition	Literature search Interviews with key stakeholders Needs assessment
Evaluating policy options	Political feasibility analysis (e.g., political mapping force-field analysis) Economic analysis Implementation analysis
Monitoring policy implementation	Before-and-after comparisons Actual versus planned performance comparisons Programme evaluation (see chapter 18) Quasi- and true-experimental methods (see chapter 8)

By contrast, a '**force-field analysis**' may be useful at the policy option evaluation stage, while a before-and-after comparison is useful in the monitoring of policy implementation. Examples of such analyses are described below.

Table 20.2 is an example of the use of force-field analysis to evaluate policy options to increase access to primary health care. Force-field analyses attempt to depict diagrammatically the forces that may support or oppose a particular issue or policy. These forces may be political, social, or economic, and part of the exercise is to judge their relative strengths with respect to the issue being analysed. The options that are tested in table 20.2 include providing free primary health care at clinics, building more public sector clinics, and issuing vouchers to the needy to purchase private health care. In table 20.2, we have mapped out a range of powerful constituencies that will support or oppose the introduction of free primary health care.

Table 20.2 Force-field analysis: free PHC services

Oppose	Neutral	Favour
Private sector (taxes may increase) Private health sector (loss of patients)	Middle and upper classes (provided taxes do not increase)	Labour unions Unemployed Small and medium employers

The usefulness of this type of analysis lies in the need to conduct a risk assessment with regard to implementation. It is possible that a required policy will not be implemented, as the forces opposed to it may be more powerful than those that support it. It is therefore important to identify opponents and supporters clearly, as different research findings may be used either to convince the opponents or to strengthen the resolve of the supporters. For example, it is highly likely that issues of affordability will be relevant to those who think that they will have to pay additional taxes to fund the new policy.

Policy research is about supplying useful information at each phase of policy development.

Some government departments conduct policy research, but the majority of research that has implications for policy is conducted by institutes and organisations outside of government. Besides universities and technikons, other institutes and organisations that conduct research informing policy development include the Human Sciences Research Council (HSRC), the Medical Research Council (MRC), the Health Systems Trust, Education Policy Units at various universities, the Centre for Health Policy, and the Centre for Policy Studies.

Analysing policies: steps in policy analysis

One is often not involved in the policy-making process but is asked to analyse an existing policy. Part of the analysis may include original research to determine whether the policy objectives have been met or can be met. In analysing a policy to determine whether it can meet or has met the needs that it seeks to address, the following questions may be asked:

- Who initiated the policy and why?
- What does the policy do?
- What is the desired impact?
- What are the benefits, who will benefit, and who will lose?
- Can the policy be implemented?
- Who will implement the policy?
- Are the systems in place to implement the policy and are the required skills available?

- What are the costs of the policy and who will bear them?
- Are the costs sustainable?

Let us take an example of a policy decision and analyse it using the questions posed above. The policy is free primary health care at the point of delivery. It was initiated by the Department of Health in order to fulfil two of the obligations listed in the RDP, namely provision of free health care to children under six and to pregnant and lactating women. The aim of the policy was to increase the access to health care for children and pregnant mothers. The impact was to make care available on the basis of need rather than ability to pay for services. It is also possible that illness could be treated earlier as a result, leading to better treatment outcomes. An analysis of who benefits and who does not must, in this case, focus on both the users and the health care providers. Health care providers may complain about the increased workload if more resources are not made available. Users, on the other hand, may complain about long waiting times, overcrowding, impolite nurses and doctors, and inability to afford transport costs.

In analysing a policy such as free health care, one therefore has to consider resource requirements such as the following: Are there sufficient clinics, nurses, and doctors? Do we have sufficient supplies (e.g., drugs)? And would users abuse the system if care was provided free? In addition to resource requirements, the cost of implementation must be calculated and a determination made with regard to affordability and sustainability. It is possible that it is affordable in the short term but not in the medium to long term.

The free health care policy was evaluated by McCoy (1996). He looked specifically at three areas of the policy: (1) the effect of the policy on the utilisation of health services, (2) the cost of the policy in terms of additional costs and loss of revenue (fees lost that would otherwise have been collected), and (3) perceptions, attitudes, and opinions of health care users and providers. The method used was as follows: twelve sites in four provinces were chosen (the report does not say whether these were randomly selected) and data reflecting utilisation patterns collected for 17 months prior to the implementation of the policy and 14 months thereafter. Information was solicited from the nine provincial health departments, and data from health workers and users were collected by means of structured interviews and focus groups.

Instead of focusing on the research results, it is more useful for the purposes of this chapter to focus on the limitations of the study. First, as is often the case in real-world policy research, the data were unreliable in the sense that the sampling strategy was less than ideal. In addition, nonstandardised definitions or classifications were used. For example, classification of children ranged from under 5 years, under 6, under 11, to under 12, or whether the child was still attending school. This meant that it was impossible to determine from aggregate records whether one was dealing with children under 6 – the target of the policy – or not. Second, the study was retrospective, which meant that the researcher had to make do with routinely collected data to obtain the baseline. It also meant that she did not have data on many variables that she would have liked to measure, for example, severity of illness and socioeconomic status.

Notwithstanding the limitations of the study, the above example illustrates a few important points: (1) it is possible to evaluate a policy even when practical constraints result in one having to work with inadequate data, (2) it is important to have a good information system so that baseline rates are readily available, and (3) it is better to set up a monitoring and evaluation system while developing the policy rather than conduct the research retrospectively.

If asked to participate in research that is evaluative, such as the study described above, how should one proceed? While there is no single correct approach, the following is suggested:

- Become involved as early as possible.
- Determine the focus of the evaluation or the policy objectives to be evaluated or what change will be measured.
- Decide what data to collect, who will collect it, and how.
- Use multiple methods of measurement.
- Design the evaluation to take into consideration any changes to the policy that may have been introduced during its implementation.
- Provide clear recommendations based on rigorous analysis.

Policy researchers often have to work with inadequate existing data, but this can sometimes be supplemented by collecting good-quality additional data.

Some ways of facilitating the use of research in policy development

While it appears to make good sense to use research in the policy-making process, this does not always happen. How then can one ensure that policy making is guided by good-quality research?

Even in developed countries, research is not always used as the basis for policy changes. The reasons for this are numerous, with both researchers and policymakers contributing to the problem. Policymakers often do not take research seriously, and researchers do not always share their results or market their research effectively.

Uses of research in the NHS reforms

Box 20.3

A study of the use of research results in the UK National Health Service reforms found the following:

- Despite the fact that there was a lot of research available, not much was actually used by policymakers.
- There was a lack of interest in taking research seriously.
- Policy was driven ideologically, not by sound research.
- Policy research was seen as threatening because it held up a mirror to policymakers.
- There was a lack of effective dissemination of research results.
- Researchers were not good at getting their message across.

The International Health Policy Programme (1996) provides the following guidelines to ensure an increased role for research in policy making:

- Research is more likely to be used if commissioned by policymakers to provide answers to specific questions.
- Research must take into account the political factors that impact on policy – it is not sufficient to include only empirical considerations in a research report for use by policymakers.
- Research findings do not have to identify specific courses of action to be useful – policymakers may find it helpful to be alerted to problems and issues.
- Researchers are as important as their research – as advisors to policymakers they can alert the latter to questions that need to be asked and answered.
- In commissioning research, it is vital that policymakers and researchers have the same understanding of the questions being asked and the nature of the problems that need to be solved.
- Researchers need to provide models and solutions that can be flexibly applied, as the conditions for which solutions are sought are rarely uniform.
- Research can influence policy indirectly through its influence over public opinion.

Robertson et al. (1997) also note the importance of translating research findings into mental health policy. They suggest the following strategies to achieve this:

> training researchers (including university departments) to do relevant research, and to formulate their findings in a way which is more accessible to policy makers; [and] training health and social policy makers to be more knowledgeable about mental health issues and how to use research findings (p. 90).

Research is most likely to be used when it is commissioned by policymakers. This means that policymakers have to be knowledgeable about what research can offer the policy process at its different stages, placing an onus on researchers to make this information available to policymakers.

Policymakers usually need 'ready-made' answers; that is, they need answers as soon as the question is posed. For example, it is unlikely that a policymaker will give a researcher sufficient time to conduct a thorough experiment before she or he makes a policy decision. There is therefore a lack of synchrony between the policy process and the research process – the former is typically significantly faster than the latter. It may be argued that if researchers are 'ahead of the game' they will be able to provide results to questions that are about to be asked. One way of achieving this type of insight may be for researchers to follow the policy-making and political process more closely and to

Policy researchers work against tight deadlines and have to be able to anticipate requests for research.

work more intimately with policymakers. Examples of policy areas that require research in the health sector are noted by Parry (1997) and Pillay, Freeman, & Foster (1997). The danger of working too closely with policymakers, however, is that it may dim one's objectivity as a researcher.

Writing research reports for policymakers

Researchers must learn to present research findings clearly and succinctly. Policymakers usually do not have the time or skills to understand elaborate experimental design issues or complex statistical methods. They usually want to know the bottom line, for example, 'Will this policy work?' or 'How much will it cost?' Researchers should also avoid the temptation to suggest the need for further research as there is usually no time for additional work, and such suggestions are often construed as attempts to create more work for the researcher!

Policymakers don't care much about research methods, but they do want to know that the findings you present to them are accurate and reliable.

There is no single correct way of writing research reports for policymakers. You may want to read again the section on policy publication in chapter 6. Here are a few additional guidelines:

- Ensure that the question being asked is clearly defined.
- Set out the research methods as simply as possible.
- Tabulate the research findings for easy reading.
- Set out the policy options and their pros and cons, as policymakers often wish to be guided but not told what to do.
- Write as concisely and simply as possible, since policymakers, usually politicians, do not have much time to read lengthy reports and do not always understand technical jargon.

Research findings that have policy implications should therefore be communicated to the relevant policymaker in clear, nontechnical terms that specify the policy implications unambiguously. While the focus of the report should not be on the technical details of the research design or the statistical tools used, the research itself must be rigorous.

Conclusion

In changing societies such as South Africa, policies are continually being revised and replaced. Universities, for example, are rethinking admission and learning/teaching policies, employers are re-engineering their systems to be more competitive in the global market, and the government is transforming the delivery of public services such as health, education, welfare, communications, and transport. Good-quality research is essential to guide policy making. However, it is not always the case that policymakers utilise research. To strengthen the role of research in policymaking, various strategies may be used. Critical issues include the following: how knowledgeable policymakers are about the value of research; the ability of researchers to conduct relevant, rigorous, and timely research; and the ability of researchers to present their findings in succinct, user-friendly form. Researchers have a critical role to play to ensure that policies that can make society better are implemented.

Exercises

1. Select a policy about which you have some knowledge, or use a policy document from any government department obtainable from the internet. Explain how you would go about evaluating the implementation of that policy.

2. Select an issue that requires the development of a policy. Design a force-field analysis illustrating who would support the policy options and who is likely to oppose them.

4. Use a piece of research that you have conducted, or choose an article published in an academic journal. Now draft a policy report making use of the research findings. The intention is to convey the results and their policy implications in clear, nontechnical terms.

Key readings

Foster, D., Freeman, M., & Pillay, Y. (Eds). (1997). *Mental health policy issues for South Africa*. Cape Town: MASA Press.
This publication analyses mental health policy in South Africa in general, and explores policy and research issues related to specific topics like education, substance abuse, and gender.

Putt, A. D. (1989). *Policy research: Concepts, methods, and applications*. Englewood Cliffs, New Jersey: Prentice Hall.
This is a good introduction to and an overview of the field of policy research.

Walt, G. W. (1994). *Health policy: An introduction to process and power*. Johannesburg: Witwatersrand University Press.
This book explores the way in which policy is made, who makes it, and what should be taken into consideration in making policies.

Research methods in clinical research

Graham Lindegger

University of KwaZulu-Natal, Pietermaritzburg

Clinical research broadly refers to research in areas pertaining to health, and may include epidemiology, prevention, treatment, and rehabilitation, as well as the evaluation of various parts of the health-care system. The concept of **clinical research** is also applied to social science and behavioural science disciplines that have contributed to various aspects of health. It includes areas of research and practice such as clinical and health psychology, clinical social work, and medical sociology. While clinical research overlaps with public health research, the latter tends to have a population rather than an individual focus, and to be more concerned with prevention and policy development rather than treatment.

Among the many areas of involvement of social scientists in health care are:

- the development of indices and measures of quality of life for patients with chronic illness such as arthritis,
- evaluations of the relative efficacy and effectiveness of different clinical interventions, for example, in the treatment of chronic pain, arthritis, or depression,
- examining variables associated with noncompliance with medical intervention such as antiretroviral treatment of HIV/Aids,
- styles of coping with chronic conditions such as HIV/Aids,
- identification of the effect of coping styles on outcome of diseases, and
- identification of risk behaviours or personality factors associated with common diseases such as heart disease and respiratory diseases.

With the advent of the HIV/Aids pandemic, social scientists have truly come of age in clinical research. Journals such as *Social Science and Medicine* and the South African journal *Critical Health* reflect the extensive contribution of sociologists, psychologists, anthropologists, and other social scientists to HIV/Aids research through examining the patterns of risk behaviours, attitudes to HIV/Aids, community responses and interventions, impact on health-care systems, individual and family coping mechanisms, interventions to change patterns of sexual risk behaviours, social policy around HIV/Aids, and a host of other areas.

Methods used in clinically applied research

Clinical research applies virtually all the research methods described in this book. In fact, many of these methods have been pioneered and perfected in clinical research settings. Clinical research involves the full spectrum of quantitative research methods and designs (especially survey methods, and correlational, experimental, and quasi-experimental designs), as well as a broad range of qualitative methods and designs. There are two broad epistemologies for studying health-related phenomena. They are the natural science approach, which searches for 'a single, "true", account of reality' (Marks, Murray, Evans,

& Willig, 2000, p. 5), such as the cause of disease, and the human science approach, which aims to understand 'meanings and the texture of human experience'.

This chapter will concentrate on a sample of the more specialised research methods traditionally associated with clinical research, as well as some emerging alternative methods. We will examine double-blind studies, case studies, single-case experimental designs, phenomenological methods, and narrative analysis. In order to compare these methods, we will take the example of the condition called chronic fatigue syndrome (CFS), which has been of interest to both medical and social science researchers.

CFS facts and figures

Box 21.1

Chronic fatigue syndrome is a chronic benign condition with both physical and psychological features, most centrally a profound fatigue of more than six months' duration that causes a reduction in the capacity to perform daily activities. Available evidence suggests that CFS involves immune system processes, physiology, and psychological processes. Prevalence figures for CFS range from 3 to 1 400 cases per 100 000 (the range reflecting the diagnostic uncertainty of the condition), with the condition tending primarily to affect females, whites, and more highly educated people. The exact prevalence in South Africa is unknown, although there is a specialised treatment unit for CFS at Groote Schuur Hospital in Cape Town.

CFS is a medical condition characterised by extreme and chronic fatigue, difficulty in concentration and, frequently, depression. It is a debilitating condition that affects an individual's ability to work, and is resistant to treatment.

Attributional style and illness behaviour in CFS

Box 21.2

Hewlett and Lindegger (1996) conducted a between-groups quasi-experimental study to investigate whether CFS patients showed distinctive attributional styles and illness behaviour, and whether these were partially a function of CFS being a chronic illness or of being a variant of depression. Three groups of subjects were obtained: patients with CFS, patients being treated for major depression, and patients with chronic illnesses other than CFS. Subjects were matched on gender, age, and education level. An F-test showed that the CFS group and the chronic illness control group had similar, positive attributional styles, whereas the depressed group had a negative attributional style. On illness behaviour measures, the CFS group had similar scores to the depressive group in hypochondriasis, irritability, and denial. These findings confirm that CFS patients have high levels of depression, as reported in previous studies, but show that these depressive features are not a function of a negative attributional style typically associated with depression.

Clinical trials: randomised controlled experimental studies

The most rigorous methods for evaluating new forms of clinical intervention in medicine, especially new drugs, are experimental randomised controlled studies (known as clinical trials). Clinical trials use two groups in the research design: the experimental group (that undergoes the new treatment being tested) and the control group (that does not undergo treatment). Subjects are allocated to one group or the other on a strictly random basis.

Randomisation is used to ensure that the two groups are equivalent before the treatment begins, and has the advantage of reducing experimenter effects and biases (e.g., deliberately giving certain treatments to certain groups). Randomisation also introduces an ethical dimension to the research by allowing each subject an equal chance of participating in the new treatment (which might be beneficial or hazardous). See Germond, Schomer, Meyers, and Weight's (1993) study of pain management for an example of a randomised experimental design.

The ideal form of the randomised control trial is the **double-blind study**. Suppose a medical researcher develops a new drug that is believed to be a treatment for CFS, and claims that this drug is more effective than other treatments. In order to substantiate these claims, the researcher will need to test them in a well-controlled, randomised clinical trial. There are two major threats to validity in such studies, however. First is the **placebo effect**, which refers to the possibility that other factors such as the patient's expectancy or the doctor's expectancy that the drug is effective may account for the outcome. Second are **expectancy effects**, which refer to the researcher's expectations about the drug's efficacy. The researcher may expect or 'know' that this drug is so powerful that she or he influences the patient's expectations when taking the drug, or the researcher's evaluation of the drug's effects may be biased when examining the patient. In either case, we have no way of knowing the extent to which the outcome of the study is the result of the patient's or the researcher's expectancy of the effect of the drug versus the effect of the drug itself. These effects must be controlled in order to evaluate the true effect of the drug. The double-blind study is used to control for these effects.

You can read more about experimental designs in chapter 8.

In the typical double-blind study of a new drug, a '**placebo**' (usually made of some inert substance such as starch) is produced, which looks identical to the experimental drug in every respect (e.g., in appearance and wrapping) and which is prescribed in the identical way to the real drug (dose, time, and frequency). Patients are randomly assigned to one of two groups – the experimental group receives the treatment (the real drug), and the control group receives the placebo. Neither the medical staff administering the study nor the patients know which patient belongs to which group. Hence the 'double-blind' study – both the people running the study and the subjects are unaware of who receives the real drug. Often this decision has been randomly

Preventative HIV vaccine trials in South Africa

Box 21.3

Given the very high prevalence of HIV/Aids in South Africa, and its devastating impact on all aspects of life, it is imperative that methods be found of limiting the spread of HIV/Aids. Extensive research has been done on various behavioural interventions to reduce HIV transmission. However, it has been argued that the most effective intervention to reduce the rate of HIV transmission would be the development of a safe, effective, and affordable vaccine for HIV. The South African Aids Vaccine Initiative (SAAVI) was established by the South African Government in 1999, and was tasked with the development of a suitable and effective vaccine for South Africa. SAAVI works in close collaboration with many international partners such as the International Aids Vaccine Initiative (IAVI) in its quest to find a suitable vaccine for South Africa. There are many different subtypes or 'clades' of HIV in different parts of the world, with Clade C as the dominant subtype found in South Africa. There is still considerable debate as to whether an effective vaccine developed for one subtype would be effective to protect against infection from other subtypes. In the absence of an answer to this question, particular attention is being focused on the development of a Clade C vaccine for South Africa.

Clinical trials, such as HIV vaccine trials, go through a series of distinct stages in researching the drug or vaccine in question. Before the vaccine ever enters human trials, its safety and its capacity to evoke the desired immune response are tested in primates. Once human trials of particular vaccines commence, they go through three distinct phases. Phase I trials largely research the safety of the vaccine, and are conducted on a small sample of healthy participants. Phase II trials primarily investigate the capacity of the vaccine to evoke the desired immune response. If the vaccine is found acceptable in phase I and II trials, then phase III trials, using many thousands of people, assess the effectiveness of the vaccine in impacting on HIV transmission. The original hope of vaccinologists was that a successful HIV vaccine would have 'sterilising immunity', meaning that it would completely prevent the transmission of the virus. However, the findings of research conducted to date make this seem unlikely, and the hope is now to develop an HIV vaccine which substantially slows the rate of transmission.

Psychologists play a key role in the design and implementation of HIV vaccine trials both in South Africa and internationally. The issues that involve psychologists in HIV vaccine trials include how to increase the willingness of people to participate in these trials, how to monitor and reduce risk behaviour while participating in trials, how to reduce the negative effects or psychosocial harms that may arise from participation, and the development of appropriate methods of informed consent for trial participation.

The efficacy of many
common medications
such as aspirin has
been established
through repeated
double-blind evaluation.

made by a computer. In this way, the biasing effects of expectancy are controlled or eliminated. The double-blind study is seen as the litmus test for the evaluation of any new intervention, whether in conventional medicine (e.g., drug therapy or surgery) or complementary medicine (e.g., reflexology or psychotherapy).

There are times, however, when neither doctor nor patient can be 'blind' to the treatment. In addition, many complex ethical issues arise in the application of controlled, randomised trials and double-blind studies. For example, does a doctor have the ethical right (in the interests of research) to withhold treatment that is thought to be effective from someone who is severely ill? The practical and ethical problems with clinical trials have meant that, although they are the most scientifically rigorous clinical methods, they are often rejected in favour of other methods.

Table 21.1 Single-blind and double-blind studies

	Experimenter *is* aware of who is in experimental or control group.	Experimenter is *not* aware of who is in experimental or control group.
Subject *is* aware of group membership	**Non-blind study** Both patient and doctor are aware that the patient is being tried on a new drug. No control of doctor or patient expectancy.	**Single-blind study** Patient is aware that she or he is on a new drug, but doctor is unaware. Involves experimental control of doctor's expectancy.
Subject is *not* aware of group membership	**Single-blind study** Doctor knows whether the patient is getting the real drug or a placebo, but patient is unaware. Involves experimental control of patient's expectancies of outcome.	**Double-blind study** Neither doctor nor patient knows whether patient is on new drug or placebo. Only the researcher knows this. Involves experimental control of both doctor's and patient's expectancy of outcome.

Case study research

Case studies are intensive investigations of particular individuals. They may also be studies of single families, units (e.g., hospital wards), organisations (e.g., NGOs dealing with HIV/Aids), communities (e.g., an informal settlement), or social policies. Case studies are defined as ideographic research methods; that is, methods that study individuals as individuals rather than as members of a population. Freud's famous case studies, which involved intensive study of particular patients (such as the 'Rat Man'), are good examples of this method.

Case studies are usually descriptive in nature and provide rich longitudinal information about individuals or particular situations. Case studies have the advantage of allowing new ideas and hypotheses to emerge from careful and detailed observation. Rich ideographic information about cases has been the start of many grand theories in the social sciences, and has also been used to promote critical reflection on existing theories.

Freud's Rat Man

Box 21.4

'"The Rat Man" ... was one of Freud's most interesting and most successful cases. The "Rat Man" was a lawyer aged 29 ... He complained of obsessional thoughts; that is, of unwanted ideas and phantasies that came into his mind spontaneously, of which he could not rid himself ... The worst obsessional preoccupation concerned an Eastern punishment of which he had been told while serving in the army. This consisted of tying a pot containing rats to the buttocks of a criminal with the intention that they should bore their way into the man via the anus ... Freud's long, but necessarily incomplete, account of this case comprises the second half of Volume X of the *Standard Edition*. It displays Freud at his most brilliant and convincing. Freud ... succeeded in ridding the "Rat Man" of his tormenting, horrifying thought ...' (Storr, 1989, 103–104)

But case studies do have limitations: there may be problems with the validity of information, causal links are difficult to test, and generalisations cannot be made from single case studies. However, case studies often generate hypotheses that may be more rigorously tested by other research methods. Because of the importance of checking the original data from which the case study is drawn, contemporary case studies often use methods such as video or audio tapes, which provide data that can be re-analysed by other researchers.

The *SA Journal of Psychology* and the *SA Medical Journal* provide a range of interesting examples of different uses of case studies for clinical research. Suffla's (1997) study of the experience of induced abortion is a good example of individually focused case study research. This paper reports a detailed study of five women through intensive interviews which were thematically analysed. The results of this study showed that the experience of abortion had many dimensions, although most respondents had ambivalent responses to abortions. Abortion was commonly perceived as a way of avoiding unwanted child-bearing for women of different ages and of different social classes. Ultimately, the response to abortion was a function of the interaction of the psychological state of the woman and the social environment in which the abortion was performed.

While experimental studies establish the efficacy of treatments, case studies allow researchers to understand syndromes and situations 'in depth'.

Single-case experimental designs

The single-case experimental design (SCED) is a specific form of case study, but based on more rigorous elements of design (including control and manipulation), and more careful specification and operationalisation of dependent and independent variables. SCED studies usually start with baseline measurement of variables, and consist of a longitudinal follow-up of intervention with a particular person (or family, group, institution, community) in order to study the effect of the intervention on the subject at various points in time. Single-case designs are often used by clinicians to evaluate the efficacy of their interventions with single patients. Suppose that a researcher is interested in studying the effect of meditation (intervention A) and exercise (intervention B) on chronic fatigue syndrome (CFS). The interventions represent the independent variables.

Single-case experimental studies involve rigorous measurement of the impact of interventions on a single person.

Initially, the researcher will decide on a couple of good indices of CFS status (i.e., dependent variables), for example, depression, level of activity, and pain. On commencement of the study, the subject is assessed on each of these measures in order to obtain pre-treatment baseline scores. The subject is then taught a meditation practice (intervention A) and encouraged to implement this practice on a daily basis, while keeping everything else (e.g., medication use) constant. (Ideally, the subject will be required to keep a detailed log of when, where, and how long he or she does the meditation, as well as a record of other variables such as medication use.) At a predetermined time after the onset of meditation (e.g., 30 days), all the (dependent) measures are repeated in order to assess the effect of meditation. Then intervention B (exercise) is implemented, records kept, and follow-up measurement repeated at the fixed intervals.

The aim of such research is to determine which intervention is the most effective. Visual data analysis (e.g., graphical displays) is the most common form of analysis. Such single-subject experimental designs, while using the methods of case studies, allow for rigorous observation and more careful control of extraneous variables. Numerous variations of design are available for single-case experiments, allowing great flexibility for the implementation of this methodology in various settings (Kazdin, 1998).

Qualitative research methods

Research on clinical populations has tended to be strongly influenced by research methods dominant in medicine, including and especially those deriving from positivist, quantitative research methods. However, over time, there has been increasing recognition of the important role of qualitative methods in clinical research. There is even a dedicated journal called *Qualitative Health Research*. While these qualitative research methods derive from very different paradigms, they are all characterised by a reaction against quantitative, positivist research as the only criterion of good clinical research. Among the qualitative methods used in clinical research are phenomenological methods, systems analysis, discourse analysis, and narrative analysis. In this section we will examine phenomenological and narrative analysis in more detail as illustrations of such qualitative research methods.

Phenomenological analysis

Phenomenology was probably the earliest qualitative method used in psychology. It has been extensively used especially in the field of clinical psychology, investigating issues in psychiatry and psychotherapy, but has also been used in health psychology. Phenomenology derives from the existential-phenomenological approach in philosophy which is (and was) concerned about human existence and experience, rather than metaphysical reality, and the way in which phenomena are experienced by human beings. Phenomenologists urge researchers to return to 'the phenomena themselves' as they are revealed in consciousness and lived experience, rather than to impose previously derived theories in the search to understand human behaviour.

One of the best-known contemporary phenomenologists is Amadeo Giorgi from Duquesne University in the USA. Giorgi has argued that, in its quest to attain the status of the natural sciences, psychology was historically dominated by experimental research methods derived from natural sciences such as physics. As a result of this, human beings were treated in the same way as inanimate objects which might be the focus of natural science research. This is seen in psychology's preoccupation with objectivity in research, and the requirement that the researcher be careful of contaminating the behaviour that is the object of research. This implies a clear distinction between the researcher and the subject or behaviour that is the object of research. But phenomenologists like Giorgi argue that, as a human science, psychology cannot directly apply the methods of natural science. He has written extensively on the distinction between natural and human science and the implications of this distinction for research on human behaviour and experience.

Phenomenology is especially interested in what it terms the self–world relationship. All people exist in a dialectical relationship with their lived world of experience, and there can be no clear separation of self and world, or subject and object. The lived world is in no way the same as the physical environment, but is rather the world of personal experience within which each person lives. This world can only be understood by accessing the consciousness of the person. Much clinical research has been concerned with understanding the lived experience of people with particular psychiatric conditions such as depression or schizophrenia. Careful description based on suspension of all preconceptions is the key element of phenomenological research. The challenge for researchers using the phenomenological method is to describe the lived world and its temporal, spatial, and interpersonal characteristics.

Phenomenology, sometimes called interpretive phenomenological analysis, has been used as a research method to arrive at a better understanding of chronic illnesses, in particular for understanding how individuals make sense of the experience of chronic illness and attempt to find meaning in chronic illness. It has also been used to study the lived experience of people on long-term dialysis treatment for kidney failure (Smith, Flowers, & Osborn, 1997). In contrast to more quantitative studies of sexual risk behaviour for HIV infection, phenomenology has also been used to understand the personal experience of sexual decision making as a way of understanding how and why it is that people who understand the importance of safe sex fail to apply this understanding in their behaviour. Reporting on such studies, Smith, Flowers, and Osborn (1997, p. 85) say 'Decisions relating to penetration and condom use appear to be based around the meaning of sexual acts, and these meanings are to do with the status accorded to particular acts within a particular context and especially point to the relational significance of sex.'

Narrative analysis methods

Narrative methods in clinical research have provided a novel set of procedures for understanding various aspects of health and disease. These methods are based on the assumption that all people construct and live a narrative for their lives that is often dramatically challenged by the onset of major health changes accompanying disease. Researchers using these methods are interested in discovering the unique personal narratives by which people live, as well as in discovering shared narratives (sometimes called 'canonical narratives'). Using tape recordings of intensive interviews (and to some extent case studies), narrative approaches seek to understand and reveal the

Photo: Rodney Barnett

People often experience their lives as an unfolding story. Narrative methods in clinical research are interested in the unexpected twists and turns in that story brought about by the onset of illness.

subjective meanings of health and disease, and how people use public (including cultural) and private constructions for making sense of health-related experiences. Armed with a couple of carefully defined qualitative questions (often starting with a simple invitation, such as 'tell me the story of your illness'), researchers invite subjects to discuss and reveal their implicit narratives of health that intersect with other life narratives.

Methods of **narrative analysis** range from more traditional content analysis, through thematic analysis, to discourse analysis. Some researchers also make use of computerised qualitative analysis packages such as NUD*IST or Atlas-ti as part of the process. Stevens and Tighe Doerr's (1997) study of the narratives of HIV-positive women provides an excellent example of qualitative methods of data collection and analysis, as well as the application and implementation of their findings in the health-care system.

The World Health Organisation (WHO) has recommended the use of narrative methods in studies of adolescent health. WHO argues that, in comparison with traditional epidemiological research methods, narrative research can 'realistically describe patterns of adolescent behaviour'. (WHO, 1993, p. 88)

Psychotherapy outcome research

An active domain of clinical research focuses on the efficacy of psychotherapy. A widely cited study by Eysenck (1952) reported that psychotherapy was no more effective at removal of psychological symptoms than 'spontaneous remission'. With the development of many diverse forms of therapeutic intervention, a debate emerged over which therapies were the more effective. With the growing financial crisis of the health-care industry in many countries, questions about therapeutic efficacy have moved to centre stage.

A broad range of research designs have been employed to investigate the efficacy of psychotherapy: double-blind randomised designs, single-case experimental designs, correlational designs, repeated measures designs, and many others.

While these designs work effectively when applied to medical research, numerous complications arise when they are applied to psychotherapy research. Three examples will demonstrate the possible complications. First, medical research may be able to control for the placebo effect, but it is far more difficult to separate the active ingredients of psychotherapy from placebo. In fact, many would argue that psychotherapy operates largely by the mobilisation of hope or expectancy. Second, double-blind studies are nearly impossible to design because therapists are usually aware of themselves providing the therapeutic intervention. Third, there is the possible contamination of therapist and procedure. How can one be sure that the outcome of treatment is not the result of the therapist's skills (or lack of them) rather than the particular technique of intervention?

One of the most difficult issues in psychotherapy research concerns the outcome criterion. What should be taken as the criterion against which to evaluate the effectiveness of psychotherapy, and who should do the evaluation? The history of psychotherapy is littered with examples of criteria and methods for evaluating therapy outcome, with very little agreement among proponents of different approaches.

Box 21.5

The effectiveness vs. the efficacy of psychotherapy

Seligman (1995) has argued that traditional efficacy studies of psychotherapy are not the best for evaluating psychotherapy, and that effectiveness studies should also be employed. He reports the results of a Consumer Report Survey done in the USA, asking 26 questions about mental health (MH) services used by the subjects, alongside other market survey questions about appliances and services. Subjects were questioned on whether they use MH services, for what problems, what type of therapy, whether therapy helped, degree of satisfaction, and reasons for termination. A multivariate measure of therapy effectiveness was created from the questionnaire. Among the findings were the following: treatment by MH professionals usually worked; long-term therapy produced better results than short-term therapy; there was no difference between psychotherapy alone and psychotherapy plus medication; Alcoholics Anonymous did

Most contemporary researchers would be highly suspicious of outcomes based on subjective therapist or patient evaluations. In some respects, the most reliable criteria for outcomes are 'hard' objective measures such as actual behaviour. But even these measures are often dependent on subjective verbal reports. Further, many psychotherapists would be unhappy with observable behaviour as the only, or the most highly valued, outcome criterion.

The psychotherapy research literature has seen the recent development and use of a number of novel research strategies and methods to answer some of the questions above. We shall look at four examples.

First, **therapy manuals** have been employed to standardise the therapeutic procedure offered, and to control for the effect of therapist skill. While this has had some positive benefits, it is an interesting example of the debate over effectiveness versus efficacy. Most studies on psychotherapy have been rigorously designed (often laboratory-based) efficacy studies. Valuable as these are, they have been criticised for not being representative of conditions outside the laboratory. **Effectiveness studies** are those which examine the effects of psychotherapy in less well-controlled, but more real-world, community conditions. Is the demonstrated efficacy of a laboratory-based procedure sufficient to draw conclusions about therapeutic effectiveness in the field? Second, the use of **dismantling** to evaluate the relative importance of different subcomponents of a therapeutic intervention involves the careful operationalisation of a therapeutic procedure, and the gradual removal of certain components in order to determine which components are necessary and sufficient for therapeutic change. Third, Martin Seligman (1995), president of the American Psychological Association, has argued that market research methods (relying on reported personal opinion) are perfectly valid complementary methods for assessing psychotherapy's effectiveness.

especially well; no particular form of psychotherapy did any better than any other form. While numerous criticisms have been launched against the use of this methodology for assessing the effectiveness of psychotherapy, Seligman argues that the main methodological virtue of the study is its realism – it assessed the effectiveness of psychotherapy as it is actually practised in the field; the sample was extensive, unbiased, and representative; it sampled a full range of treatment durations; the sample reported multiple problems rather than the single problems of laboratory studies, and outcomes were concerned with general personal functioning in various domains of life. While Seligman admits that this study has limitations, such as lack of control groups, he sees it as an important prototype of the kind of research method that should complement more traditional efficacy research.

Fourth, there has been a move away from outcome to process research. Many psychotherapy researchers are as concerned with the process of therapeutic change as with the outcome of therapeutic treatment. Methods such as specialised video-tape technology allow for careful, qualitative investigation of in-therapy processes contributing to outcome.

Psychotherapy outcome research is a good example of research based on principles of accountability. In so far as the cost of psychotherapy is borne either by the public health sector (state funded) or by private medical schemes, practitioners are accountable for what they do. With

Difficulties in applying traditional double blind designs have led to the development of novel techniques such as therapy manuals, 'dismantling', market research, and process research.

Photo: Rodney Barnett

Some 75 to 80% of people around the globe rely on traditional medicine for their health care. There are around 250 000 traditional healers in South Africa alone, compared to only 30 000 doctors and 200 000 nurses (Lee, 1988). What would you consider the best way of evaluating the efficacy and effectiveness of traditional treatments?

the South African public health system facing an enormous financial crisis, many private medical schemes on the brink of financial collapse, and so-called managed health-care companies cornering the health market, the efficacy and incremental value of psychological intervention – in comparison with medical treatments, alternate health care and traditional healing – needs to be evaluated in order to decide on the most cost-effective and clinically effective service to offer and fund.

<table>
<tr><td>Box 21.6</td><td>

Evidence-based psychological intervention

There has been a growing international trend in clinical treatment to mandate the exclusive use of intervention or treatment methods that have been empirically validated. This is referred to as evidence-based medicine. An interesting example from medicine has been the use of hormone replacement therapy (HRT). It was assumed that HRT had significant health protective benefits, such as prevention of coronary heart disease. However, research based on randomised trials has shown that not only does HRT not lead to these benefits, but that women on HRT are at increased risk of disorders such as breast cancer. As a result of such research findings, there has been a marked decline in the use of HRT.

While there has been a similar argument for the use of evidence-based psychological intervention, there has also been substantial controversy over such evidence-based care. Much of the argument has focused on the issue of internal versus external validity. Internal validity, as employed in clinical trials, derives from subjects with conditions being studied meeting rigorous diagnostic criteria. For example, in researching treatment of obsessive-compulsive disorder, it is necessary to ensure that the research subjects meet the rigorous diagnostic criteria for OCD and that they only have OCD. External validity refers to the validity of diagnosis in community-based rather than research samples. It is argued that community samples seldom meet these rigorous diagnostic criteria, and often have additional, so-called co-morbid, conditions. Therefore, the argument goes, it is highly debatable whether the findings from clinical trials are applicable to community samples.

Westen, Novotny, and Thompson-Brenner (2004), in their review of evidence-based psychological intervention, argue that most psychological interventions are unvalidated, rather than invalidated. This means that most psychological intervention methods have not been subjected to empirical investigation, rather than being found ineffective in empirical investigation. One of the major reasons for this is that it is very difficult for psychologists to find the necessary funding to conduct such clinical trials. A large portion of the investigation of medical treatments is funded by pharmaceutical companies that have vested interests in such research. By comparison, it is very difficult to find equivalent funding for research into psychological treatments, which leaves many psychological treatments unresearched.

</td></tr>
</table>

Initiating clinical research: practical considerations

Samples

One of the problems with much clinical research is the difficulty in obtaining representative samples. The unavailability of subjects often means that researchers are forced to settle for **convenience samples**; that is, any subjects who are available to participate in the study. These are often 'clinic samples', consisting of samples of people attending clinics for treatment. Often these convenience samples are biased samples. For example, in studying psychological aspects of depression, it would be easiest to take samples of people attending clinics for treatment of depression. It is both possible and likely that this clinical sample is not representative of the population of depressives as a whole. Can you think of reasons why? However, people who are depressed but not undergoing treatment are difficult to identify or to motivate to participate in such a study, and can thus not be included in the sample.

Ethical issues

While it may once have been thought that an ethical dimension was an attractive addition to good research, today it is recognised that all good research is, of necessity, ethical research. The need for ethical considerations in research is most apparent in clinical research. We have already referred to the use of randomised controlled trials and the ethical problems of withholding apparently effective treatment from needy subjects. One of the essential components of all research is that of 'informed consent' from participants. This condition requires that prospective participants be fully informed about the nature and steps of the research and explicitly consent to participate in the research.

Action/intervention research

In clinical research contexts, there is frequently the double agenda of treatment and research. Clinical samples are usually made up of subjects with particular conditions – for example, chronic fatigue syndrome – from which these subjects are seeking relief. Participation in research projects is usually motivated by a desire to derive some personal benefit from the study through the amelioration of their condition. Medical researchers are well aware of the double agenda, and their ethical concern is to address the patient's need. Social scientists are likely to be at a greater advantage in clinical research contexts if they are also trained and effective in a range of clinical skills that can be applied to subjects participating in the project for personal reasons. First, the ability to offer a clinical service alongside the research often opens up greater access to clinical populations. Second, clinical knowledge and experience often equip researchers better to understand both patients and clinical contexts, such as hospitals, in a way that facilitates the research. Third, clinical intervention of some kind offers the patient some form of service in return for participation in a research project.

Research and intervention are often hard to separate in clinical research.

Box 21.7

Informed consent in clinical research: questions to be asked

1. What information should be given to prospective subjects, and how should it be explained? For example, how will concepts like placebos and randomisation be explained?
2. How can the researcher be sure that all subjects have understood the information in ways that are meaningful to them?
3. How can the researcher be sure that the interests of the participants are protected? For example, do the subjects fully understand that they have the right to withdraw at any time without prejudice?
4. How can the researcher be sure that subjects are freely participating without manifest or subtle pressure?

Clinical research is not confined to the laboratory or consulting room, but is strongly influenced by real-world concerns.

Community-based clinical research

Much contemporary clinical research takes place in community settings. Such research has to take seriously the community context within which it operates, as well as the needs and perceptions of the community members. Increasingly, researchers are becoming aware

Box 21.8

Community entry for research
(Nolwazi Gasa, Medical Research Council)

Community entry is one of the most challenging tasks for the researcher who is about to embark on a research project in a community context. If not properly handled, it may destroy the project before it has even started, but may determine its success if well handled. The following hands-on guidelines have emerged from experience over six months of setting up a clinical research project in a rural area of KwaZulu-Natal:

1. It is important to read up or enquire about the target community before you meet it. Keep an open mind as you note relevant issues such as current problems, controversies, and successes within the community. The implications of past research conducted in an area may have triggered community anger and suspicion about researchers. Listening to community members' perceptions regarding the effects of research – without taking sides – and asking them how the research could have been better handled often facilitates the rapport-building process.
2. It is most useful to have contacts in the area who could introduce you to key members of the community who may be most helpful to your research project. The most important group is the leadership structure, as will be discussed below. Your contacts are likely to give you an indication of how best to behave with community members (e.g., the accepted dress code for females in meeting with traditional leaders). You might also learn about the accepted ways of addressing leaders, men, women, and so on.
3. It is also useful to enquire about the 'culture' of the target community, e.g., is it a rural or urban area? Is it under traditional

that they need to establish a relationship with the community and a base of credibility within the community, and that they are as accountable to community members as they are to the research funders or principals. Many researchers have suggested that community-based clinical research needs to treat the community and its members as an integral part of the research team from the outset.

Box 21.9

Public health research
(Alexander Butchart, World Health Organisation)

Preoccupied with preventing disease and illness before they occur, public health operates beyond the institutional settings usually associated with clinical research. Instead, it applies itself to those spaces where matter, energy, and information are exchanged between people and their human, social, and physical environments, for it is through such exchange that the health status of individuals and groups is determined. Public health is therefore a profoundly social activity, as conveyed by Last's definition of it as '... the combination of science, skills and beliefs ... directed to the maintenance and improvement of the health of all the people through collective or social action. The programmes, services, and institutions involved emphasise the prevention of disease and the health needs of the population as a whole. Public health activities change with changing technology and social values, but the goals remain the same: to reduce the amount of disease, premature death and disease-produced discomfort and disability in the population' (Last, 1988, p. 107).

Public health works at the aggregate level with emergent phenomena (such as society, culture, and demography) that do not exist at the individual or small-group level. Its research demands are therefore somewhat different from those of the clinical sciences. For one, the identification of social pathologies and risk factors requires observational techniques that can monitor entire societies, regions, and even global processes. Hence, much public health research is expressly quantitative in nature, for only by establishing numeric proxies for qualities such as life quality, social capital, corruption, or civil society status can such factors be made visible and therefore potentially manipulable. Second, because public health interventions frequently target processes beyond the ability of a single community or discipline to alter (such as poverty, violence, substance abuse, and sexual practices), public health research is oriented, in both design and dissemination, to incorporating the perspectives and resources of multiple disciplines (e.g., psychology, building science, economics, and medicine), and many social

Photo: Centre for Peace Action

The public health approach has long been concerned with preventing disease through mechanisms such as the provision of clean drinking water, adequate nutrition, and inoculation.

sectors (e.g., professionals, church groups, and community residents). Third, public health is always action orientated, and its first aim is to effect positive change at the social level.

Reflecting these and other differences from clinical research are some of the more prominent public health research concepts and tools. The most fundamental is **epidemiology**, referring to research that studies the distribution and determinants of health-related conditions and events in populations, and the application of this information to the control of health problems. **Descriptive epidemiology** describes the occurrence of disease and health-related characteristics in terms of person (the who: age, sex, social class), place (the where: geographic location) and time (the when: season, day of week, time of day, day of month). **Analytic epidemiology** analyses causal and protective factors to explain why health-related outcomes occur and whether interventions work. **Social epidemiology** uses qualitative and quantitative techniques to connect the individual, culture, society, and economy in order to establish how problems (e.g., tuberculosis or coronary disease) at the micro-level of individual activity are related to macro-level socioeconomic determinants. While specialisation in epidemiological research requires postgraduate study, these and many more core concepts can be accessed through introductory texts such as *Epidemiology: A manual for South Africa* (Katzenellenbogen, Joubert, & Abdool Karim, 1997).

From the 1930s, until suppressed by the apartheid government in the 1960s on the grounds that it was inciting communist revolt, South African public health was globally renowned for its research and innovation. Social scientists such as the anthropologist Hilda Kuper (1947) and the psychologist Guy Steuart (1962) were prominent participants alongside practitioners like Kark (1944) and Gale (1938) who had moved to public health from clinical medicine. This period produced such classic studies as Kark's *The social pathology of syphilis*, the many works that emanated from the Polela Native Health Unit (e.g. Kark & Steuart, 1957) and Kark and Steuart's (1962) *A practice of social medicine*. In the late 1990s, public health schools have again been re-established in the Western Cape and Gauteng, and the existence of a number of World Health Organisation collaborating centres for public health research (e.g., urban health and development, women's health, reproductive health, and injury and violence prevention) suggests that South African public health research is beginning to take up where it left off in the 1960s.

Public health and the complex interplay of forces shaping it can never belong to a single discipline or social sector. The place of social science in public health research is thus to be part of this synergy by contributing its positive powers to make visible such things as subjectivity and society, while seeing itself as neither slave nor master to other public health disciplines descended from medicine.

Regulation of clinical research

While carefully designed research is a necessity in clinical contexts, the implementation of such research often requires the explicit permission of public regulators for the research to be implemented. Most human research today requires the clearance of ethics committees (sometimes called Institutional Review Boards in medicine) in order to be implemented. This is especially strict in medicine. Clinical trials of biological substances also require the authorisation of the Medicines Control Council in order to take place in South Africa. These requirements are part of a broad national and international process of protecting human subjects of clinical research.

Conclusion

In this chapter, we have discussed the application of a variety of research methods in clinical contexts, as well as some of the difficulties associated with applied clinical research. A final question might be asked about where this clinical research takes place. As we noted in the introduction to this chapter, research is no longer considered an add-on or superfluous luxury in applied clinical contexts, but rather an integral part of all work in clinical settings (Belar, 1998). Today, social scientists working in a variety of clinical contexts are required to design and implement a range of research projects, from epidemiological surveys in particular communities, to programme/treatment evaluation and clinical trials in hospitals, clinics, and specialised agencies such as HIV/Aids treatment centres, to the investigation of various aspects of the health-care system and the training of others in the basic skills of applied research. While all social science professionals in health-care settings are involved in some clinical research, there are others who are specialised researchers in health-care contexts. In South Africa, such specialised social scientists are most likely to be found in organisations like the Medical Research Council or the Aids directorate of the Department of Health.

Finally, there can be little doubt that clinical research is likely to play an ever-growing role in the South African health-care system.

Exercises

1. Design a study to investigate the benefits of regular aerobic exercise at a gym. Show how you would control for placebo and expectancy effects, as well as for other extraneous variables that would undermine the validity of the study.

2. Consider some of the possible ways of studying the variables that may impact on adherence to antiretroviral treatment by HIV-positive people.

3. A managed health-care company asks you to design a study to evaluate the cost-effectiveness of three different treatments for depression. Describe the possible elements of an appropriate study,

and some of the issues to be considered in beginning to plan such research.

Key readings

Kazdin, A. (1998). *Methodological issues and strategies in clinical research.* (2nd edition). Washington, DC: APA.
This text is one of the classical works on clinical research, with chapters covering many of the major topics in clinical research.

Marks, D. F., Murray, M., Evans, B., & Willig, C. (2000). *Health psychology: Theory, research and practice.* London: Sage.
Chapter one of this textbook provides a good overview of different research paradigms and methods used in health research.

Seligman, M. E. (1995). The effectiveness of psychotherapy: The consumer reports study. *American Psychologist*, 50, 965–974.
This article describes the consumer report on psychotherapy. Apart from giving details of the report, it examines many of the critical issues in psychotherapy outcome research design.

Smith, J. A., Flowers, P., & Osborn, M. (1997). Interpretative phenomenological analysis and the psychology of health and illness. In L. Yardley (Ed.), *Material discourses of health and illness*. London: Routledge.
This chapter provides a good description of phenomenology as applied to health research, and gives a number of interesting health research studies using phenomenology as the research method.

Stevens, R. E., & Tighe Doerr, B. (1997). Trauma of discovery: Women's narratives of being informed that they are HIV-infected. *AIDS Care*, 9, 523–538.
This article is a good example of a contemporary clinical research project using qualitative methods that are very rigorously applied.

Westen, D., Novotny, C., & Thompson-Brenner, H. (2004). The empirical status of empirically supported psychotherapies: Assumptions, findings and reporting in controlled clinical trials. *Psychological Bulletin*, 130, 631–663.
This article is an excellent review of the application of the findings of clinical trials in mental health care, and the associated problems and challenges.

Assessment research

Anil Kanjee
Human Sciences Research Council

Assessment involves collecting information from individuals, groups, and organisations with a view to practical issues of problem solving. Assessment is used in a variety of situations to facilitate decision making around diverse problems. Consider the following two examples.

In the past, the University of Cape Town used matric examination results as the main criterion for student admission to university, and as a predictor of a student's academic success. With changing demographics of the student population, it was soon recognised that this was a poor index of student success – especially in the case of students from disadvantaged schools – as matric results were not a true reflection of a student's ability or potential. To address this problem, the university felt that another criterion should be used in deciding who should be accepted for university study. What do you think they should do to address this dilemma?

One of the fundamental ways in which the South African education system is changing is with regard to examining and testing procedures that are used in schools. However, to ensure that the new testing procedures will be properly implemented, it is important that teachers support the new procedures and implement them properly. A lecturer at a teacher training college has recently developed a curriculum for training teachers in new testing procedures. To gauge the degree to which teachers support the new procedures, the lecturer decides to ascertain the attitudes of teachers to classroom assessment and to determine what testing skills these teachers feel they require to make the new system work. How could the lecturer obtain this information?

The two situations described above illustrate common problems where information is required to facilitate decision making. This can range from information about individual ability, potential, or attitudes, to group aspirations and organisational beliefs. In all cases, the information should be sound if it is to be useful in guiding decision making. Research with a strong assessment focus will be required to obtain this information.

There are many definitions of assessment, most of which explicitly link assessment to measurement. Broadfoot (1996), for example, defines assessment as 'the deliberate and overt measurement of performance in order to obtain information for purposes beyond the immediate interactive situation' (p. 6). There are two defining features of assessment. First, assessment involves measurement of one form or another, and this chapter should therefore be read in conjunction with chapter 7. Assessment, however, is a broader concept than measurement or testing, as it encompasses the collection and use of information in addition to measurement. Also, testing and measurement are usually associated with the use of standardised tests, while assessment includes the use of structured and semi-structured questionnaires and interviews.

Assessment is a broader concept than measurement or testing.

The second defining feature of assessment pertains to where the information comes from, and the use to which the information is put.

The primary purpose of conducting any assessment is to obtain additional information – i.e., information beyond the immediate interactive situation – about characteristics of an individual or group, in order to facilitate decisions. For example, when matric results are used to decide how an individual will perform at university, the matric results are assessment data that come from outside the university context, but which help in making decisions within the university context. Usually, assessment involves the use of a questionnaire or test to measure some attribute of a person, group, or organisation (such as their ability, aptitude, attitude, opinions, interests, knowledge, personality), and then using this data as additional information to make decisions about the performance of the person, group, or organisation in a specific context.

Assessment in South Africa

Assessment practices have adversely affected the lives of many thousands of South Africans, and assessment thus remains a highly contentious and controversial activity. Nzimande (1995), for example, has shown how assessment practices in South Africa were used to support the racist policies of the apartheid state. Assessment instruments were used to justify the exploitation of black labour and to deny blacks access to education and economic resources (Apple, 1989; Bulhan, 1993; Mathonsi, 1988; Nzimande, 1995). In addition, psychological testing, specifically IQ tests, was also used to promote the belief of the superiority of whites over blacks (Apple, 1989).

Photo: Alex Butchart

Miners being subjected to a heat tolerance test, circa 1935 (from Butchart, 1998).

In the mining sector, tests that constituted violations of basic human and civil rights of workers were conducted by the now defunct National Institute for Personnel Research (NIPR). Bulhan (1993) describes one such test in which 'a heavy weight is carried up a flight of five steps and dropped down one of three chutes ... In combination with pulse rate, this yields a score which gives a reasonable prediction of above or below average performance in shovelling rock' (p. 35). Another instrument developed by the NIPR is the 'Leaderless Group Test' which was used to identify Africans with high 'cooperative qualities' so as to fill positions that were then known as 'boss boys' (foremen) (Bulhan, 1993).

Assessment has been a highly controversial practice in South Africa, and has often been accused of being racist.

Arguing for the immediate transformation of assessment practices in South Africa, Sehlapelo and Terre Blanche (1996) note that:

> Tests are used on a large scale to determine who gains access to economic and educational opportunities, and if psychology as a profession is truly interested in empowerment, the reform of testing practices should be one of its priorities. (p. 50)

This is true of all professions that use assessment instruments. However, the specific nature and content of the required reform is yet to be specified. This is certainly one area in which a great deal more research is required, for although it has sometimes been used for exclusionary and oppressive purposes, assessment is vital to decision making in contemporary society.

Assessment is especially relevant in a changing South Africa, where decisions about best practice are vital. For example, a critical aspect of current concern in the education and training sector – the introduction of the National Qualifications Framework and Outcomes Based Education – is developing valid and reliable assessment instruments to grade learners.

Research applications

What do researchers in the area of assessment actually do? What types of research do they conduct? What can I expect if I were to conduct a research study in the area of assessment? These are some of the questions that will be addressed in this section.

Focus of research

Typically, two scenarios are encountered in assessment research. In the first scenario, the research focuses specifically on assessment issues, while, in the second scenario, assessment forms only an aspect of the research study. For example, to address the University of Cape Town admissions dilemma considered in the introduction to this chapter, researchers developed new instruments to assess academic potential. In developing these instruments, academic potential had to be defined, specific indicators of potential had to be identified, and test questions written. These questions were then tested and administration procedures finalised. The focus of the research was on the development and testing of an assessment instrument. The research focused on the definition of academic potential, the predictive validity of the test, the

Cross-cultural research on psychological measuring instruments

(René van Eeden, University of South Africa)

Recent socio-political developments have placed increasing pressure on test developers to provide culturally appropriate assessment instruments and practices. However, test development in a multicultural, multilingual society in transition is a complex process (Foxcroft, 1997). Numerous moderators of test performance have been identified, including language proficiency, culture, education, socioeconomic status, home environment, urbanisation, and test-wiseness (Nell, 1997; Owen, 1996). These variables have to be considered when delineating norm groups and interpreting test results (Bedell, Van Eeden, & Van Staden, 1999). Environmental deprivation and language in particular have been identified as possible sources of bias in research on cognitive tests (e.g., Claassen & Hugo, 1993; Claassen, Krynauw, Holtzhausen, & wa ga Mathe, 2001; Claassen & Schepers, 1990; Van Eeden & Van Tonder, 1995; Van Eeden & Visser, 1992). Research on personality tests has also shown that the role of language proficiency needs to be considered to enhance fair testing practice (Maree, 2002; Prinsloo, 1998; Van Eeden, Taylor, & Du Toit, 1996).

Owen (1996) specifies methods for determining score comparability (or item bias), construct comparability, and predictive comparability. Bedell et al. (1999) provide an overview of research on cognitive and personality tests in which comparison across different groups was done in terms of one or more of these categories. Cognitive research includes studies on, inter alia, the General Scholastic

length of the test, the time it took to complete the test, and whether any language or cultural bias was evident in the test (Tshwete, 1998).

In the second example given in the introduction, that of the lecturer from the teachers' training college, assessment formed only one aspect of the study. To address the dilemma of how to determine the assessment skill levels and needs of teachers, Malaka (1995) decided to use a questionnaire. He had two options: either to find an existing questionnaire that would enable him to obtain the information he required, or to develop a new questionnaire. Either way, the assessment instrument (questionnaire) was only used to obtain information from teachers for use in developing the new curriculum. Here, the focus of the study was the development of the curriculum and not the assessment instrument. However, in both the cases noted above, the same rigorous process for developing instruments was followed.

Assessment instruments

Different contexts of assessment research may be distinguished with reference to what is being assessed. Traditionally, instruments are

Aptitude Test (GSAT) (e.g., Claassen & Hugo, 1993), the Senior South African Individual Scale – Revised (SSAIS-R) (e.g., Van Eeden & Visser, 1992) and the Wechsler Adult Intelligence Scale – III (WAIS-III) (e.g., Claassen et al., 2001). Results on the item functioning, reliability, and validity varied, but differences between groups in terms of the mean score performance were common. The tests that have been mentioned are measures of crystallised ability, and Taylor (1994) suggests that measures of learning potential are more suitable in a context of diverse backgrounds.

Personality research includes a number of studies to determine the cultural appropriateness of the various forms of the Sixteen Personality Factor Questionnaire (16PF) (e.g., Abrahams & Mauer, 1999a; 1999b; Prinsloo, 1998; Van Eeden & Prinsloo, 1997) while work has also been done on, inter alia, the 15FQ+ (e.g., Meiring, Van de Vijver, & Rothmann, 2003), the Occupational Personality Questionnaire (OPQ) (e.g., Swanevelder, 2003) and the NEO Personality Inventory – Revised (NEO PI-R) (e.g., Heuchert, Parker, Stumpf, & Myburgh, 2000; Taylor, 2000). Results in terms of item bias and construct comparability varied, while numerically lower reliability estimates were generally found for second-language speakers. Differences in response patterns on personality tests could be a reflection of real differences in the manifestation of constructs (Prinsloo & Ebersohn, 2002), and as such they can be used in developing personality tests that at a conceptual level provide for different cultures. Regardless of the statistical properties of a test, it should be used fairly for all groups and only as part of the assessment process in combination with other relevant information.

categorised according to what they measure. The main areas within which assessment research is conducted can accordingly be categorised as the assessment of (1) abilities, (2) personality, and (3) interests and attitudes (Murphy & Davidshofer, 1998; Nunnally, 1978).

Ability assessment refers to the assessment of intellectual abilities or physical and artistic abilities. Measures of general cognitive functioning include individual and group tests of intelligence, while measures of specific abilities refer to aptitude tests and measures of specific cognitive functions such as verbal or perceptual functions. These tests are used for the assessment of infant and preschool development, and, in the case of school-going children, to predict subsequent performance in the selection of school subjects or a course for further study, or for diagnostic and prognostic purposes. For example, the UCT admissions instrument was developed to assess the academic potential and ability of students, and has been used as an admissions criterion. Cognitive testing in an organisational context includes the assessment of general ability and specific aptitudes such as mechanical aptitude or clerical aptitude. Scholastic tests (proficiency tests, achievement tests, and diagnostic tests) also measure abilities, but these are more focused in terms of school subjects. Scholastic tests are used, inter alia, to measure the effects of a specific programme of instruction, to evaluate and improve teaching, and for remedial purposes.

Personality assessment aims to determine what people are like (e.g., introverted or extroverted). Personality instruments thus provide a general description of the person being tested along one or several dimensions – depending on the way in which personality is defined – that are thought to be relevant for the understanding of a person's behaviour in everyday situations (Murphy & Davidshofer, 1998). Many personality tests provide a comprehensive personality profile, but there are also tests available that deal with specific traits such as anxiety or depression, or that focus on particular behavioural patterns such as coping styles and relationship styles. These tests are used in an organisational context as part of selection, placement, and training, as well as for individual counselling. They sometimes also form part of psychodiagnostic assessment, an in-depth assessment of an individual that is characterised by the use of multiple sources of data in order to make a diagnosis and to recommend treatment. Currently, personality instruments used in South Africa are mainly imported from the USA. A great deal of research still needs to be undertaken to ensure that these instruments are relevant to South African conditions. Kanjee and Van Eeden (1998), for example, have conducted research on the use of the Sixteen Personality Factor Inventory in a South African context.

What does the assessment instrument measure: abilities, personality, or attitudes?

The assessment of **interests** is concerned primarily with preferences for particular activities, while **attitudes** focus on feelings about particular social and physical 'objects', including persons and groups. Typically, attitudes and interests are assessed by means of a questionnaire which respondents are asked to complete by providing a response to one or more questions or statements according to their feelings, preferences, or experiences. Malaka's (1995) questionnaire, for example, ascertained teacher attitudes towards classroom assessment by asking teachers to record their opinions towards a number of specific assessment practices (e.g., examinations, oral tests). Interest questionnaires and value scales are used in career counselling, while opinion surveys and attitude scales have a wide variety of application areas.

In addition to formal assessment instruments, biographical data, interviews, and observer reports are frequently used as part of organisational assessment. Other forms of assessment that are sometimes used include work samples and situational tests. In these tests, people are evaluated by means of tasks that are identical to, or simulate, tasks they will have to perform if selected for a particular position.

Box 22.2

Some popular assessment instruments

Career Preference Inventory (CPI). The CPI is a self-administered questionnaire designed by the Human Sciences Research Council (HSRC) to assist in career planning for South Africans. This questionnaire measures respondents' occupational interests, and these are then linked to specific occupations. This instrument is suitable for use by all South Africans aged 15 (Grade 9) and upward. The CPI consists of 126 items divided into 18 subscales that include career preferences in human service and crafts, mathematical and computer sciences, medical and related fields, education, social and personal services, and nursing and caring. The CPI can be administered individually or in groups, and takes approximately 15 to 20 minutes to complete.

NEO Personality Inventory – Revised (NEO PI-R). The NEO PI-R is a personality assessment instrument based on the five-factor model of personality. The five traits measured by the subscales of the NEO are neuroticism, extraversion, openness to experience, agreeableness, and conscientiousness. The instrument consists of 240 items, rated on five-point Likert-type scales, and takes approximately thirty minutes to complete.

Senior South African Intelligence Scale – Revised (SSAIS-R). The SSAIS-R is the revised version of the Senior South African Intelligence Scale that was first released in 1964. The SSAIS-R is a battery of tests developed by the Human Sciences Research Council to measure intelligence of English- and Afrikaans-speaking South African children between the ages of 7 and 17 (Van Eeden, 1996). The test consists of 11 subtests divided into two scales: Verbal (vocabulary, comprehension, number problems, story memory) and Nonverbal (pattern completion, block designs). This instrument must be administered individually, and it takes about 90 minutes to complete the full battery.

The Ability, Processing, and Learning Battery (APIL-B). The APIL-B is a test battery based on the dynamic assessment model, and is designed to measure the core cognitive capacities and potential of an individual. The instrument is suitable for individuals with a minimum of 10 years of formal education. The battery provides a profile of eight scores (e.g., abstract thinking, speed of information processing, accuracy of information processing, cognitive flexibility, performance gain in a learning task). The test battery can be administered to a maximum of 12 persons for every administrator and takes approximately two and a half hours to complete.

Research practice

In practice, assessment research often follows a circular path, repeatedly moving from the practical to the theoretical level, and back again. To identify bias in the use of the Sixteen Personality Factor

Inventory (i.e., ways in which it might discriminate against one or another race group), Kanjee and Van Eeden (1998), for example, first identified an appropriate bias-detection technique. This was a theoretical exercise that involved defining and operationalising bias in the context of personality measurement. They then applied this technique to data from a South African sample. Any biased items detected were either removed or revised. To ascertain whether the new bias-detection technique did indeed work, the instrument was administered to another South African sample and bias analysis was conducted once again. The procedure of devising new items and administering the scale to test for bias was repeated over and over again until no bias was detected. Once this stage had been achieved, the research confirmed both the theoretical perspective of the researchers – i.e., that the bias identification technique was plausible – and the practical value of the revised personality measure – i.e., that the instrument could be regarded as valid for a South African sample.

Box 22.3

Bias in clinical assessment: An ideological issue
(Rashied Ahmed, University of the Western Cape)

Clinical assessment is a complex, multifaceted process aimed at understanding the difficulties that clients present with, and deciding on a suitable intervention strategy (most commonly some form of psychotherapy). The clinician uses interviews and/or psychometric tests to gain information about aspects of an individual's intellectual and personality functioning.

In South Africa, two main criticisms have been raised about clinical assessment. First, the tests have mainly been standardised and normed on samples of white respondents, and this raises questions about the generalisability and utility of the test with other groups. Second, cultural and linguistic differences make interpretation difficult. Some have argued that clinical assessment is an ideological issue. Clinical practice takes place in a broad political, social, and historical context, and the clinician's role in identifying pathology plays a part in reproducing unequal power relations that lead to discrimination and the exploitation of economically and politically marginalised groups.

Questionnaire development

A questionnaire can be defined as a group of written questions used to gather information from respondents, and it is regarded as one of the most common tools for gathering data in the social sciences (Vogt, 1993). A questionnaire usually consists of a number of measurement scales, open-ended items for qualitative responses, and other questions that elicit demographic information from respondents. In this section, the process followed by Malaka (1995) in his study on teachers is used to demonstrate the basic steps to follow and the issues to consider when developing questionnaires.

Identify the purpose of the questionnaire

The first steps Malaka (1995) undertook were (1) to clarify the reason for the study, (2) determine the information he required from the respondents (in this case, teachers), (3) list the research questions he wanted to answer with the questionnaire, and (4) identify any additional (demographic) information required to address the research questions. These four initial tasks should be undertaken by anyone planning to develop a questionnaire. The purpose of Malaka's study was to develop an appropriate curriculum to train teachers in new forms of learner assessment which were introduced with the adoption of outcomes-based education in South Africa. The information he required and the research questions he wanted to answer were the following: What do teachers know about assessment and what are their attitudes towards assessment? What kinds of assessment do classroom teachers carry out? What is the nature and extent of assessment training of teachers? He also wanted to collect demographic information – age, sex, subjects taught, socioeconomic status, educational qualifications, and teaching experience – to determine whether these variables were related to teachers' classroom practices and attitudes towards assessment.

Some questionnaires contain a small number of items which together measure the same thing (e.g., depression). Malaka's questionnaire contained several subscales (i.e., groups of items), with each scale measuring a different thing.

Draft questions

The drafting of questions is a crucial aspect of developing any assessment instrument, since 'what you ask for is what you get'. Questions are usually developed by researchers with the assistance of people knowledgeable in the subject area. With regard to the development of standardised tests, subject area specialists can be enlisted to assist with drafting questions. Questions should be short and concise, and relevant to your research purposes.

Some tough decisions must be made regarding the length of the questionnaire. On the one hand, the researcher wants to collect as much information as possible, but, on the other hand, the questionnaire should not take too long to complete. Although the researcher aims to keep the questionnaire as short as possible, questionnaires can be quite long when the study has a broad scope and a wide variety of content must be included in the questionnaire. The subscales included in a questionnaire can also vary in length. Some scales include many items, as the reliability of multi-item scales is stronger than the reliability of measures with few items. If you are measuring a clear-cut construct (such as support for the death penalty), it is possible to compile a reliable scale containing only a few items, whereas more widely defined constructs (such as 'community-mindedness') may require many more items. Typically, scales contain around 12 to 15 items, but some are very much shorter or longer. It is a good idea to write at least 30% more questions than required, since some questions inevitably have to be rejected after data have been collected (see the section on item analysis on page 491).

Box 22.4

Asking the right questions

Van Vuuren, Maree, and De Beer (1998) provide the following checklist of errors to avoid when drawing up questions:

- Are the words used simple, direct, and familiar to all respondents? It is vital that respondents understand exactly what is meant by each question.
- Are any items double-barrelled? Double-barrelled questions ask two different things with one question. For example, a positive answer to the question 'Do you like tea and cake?' could mean that the respondent likes only tea, only cake, or both tea and cake.
- Are the questions leading or loaded? Leading questions are phrased in such a way that they encourage respondents to answer in a particular way. For example, the question 'Doctors tell us that smoking is bad for you, do you agree?', encourages respondents to agree because of the weight of authority (if doctors believe it, it must be true).
- Is the question applicable to all the respondents? Don't ask male respondents if they have ever been pregnant.
- Will the answers be influenced by response styles? If you have a list of items, it is important to phrase some positively (e.g., 'Being pregnant was the best time of my life') and others negatively (e.g., 'I felt depressed while pregnant') to ensure that respondents do not develop a particular response style by noting, for instance, that the first few items are positive and then responding in the same manner to all items on the questionnaire.
- Are any of the questions vague? A vague question will be interpreted differently by different people, and the question will elicit inappropriate and meaningless responses. Vague questions are often either too short or too long. If an item can be shortened without loss of meaning, do so.

Choose a response format

There are a number of different response formats that can be used to gather information from respondents. Slightly different kinds of information will be obtained for the same item, depending on the type of response format used. At the broadest level, questions can elicit quantitative or qualitative data, depending on the response format. **Open-ended questions** allow respondents to communicate their experiences or opinions about a specific issue in their own words, without any restriction. Responses can vary from a couple of lines to an essay of one or more pages. For example, to assess teachers' attitudes towards a particular form of learner assessment, Malaka used an open-ended question ('What are your views about the value of teacher-made tests?') to which respondents were expected to give a short written response.

An example of an open-ended item yielding qualitative data. How does this picture make you feel? Please write down your first impressions in a short paragraph.

Closed questions do not allow respondents to provide answers in their own words, but force respondents to select one or more choices from a fixed list of answers provided. Closed questions have the advantage of eliciting a standardised set of responses from all the respondents, and thus allow for easier comparative data analysis. There are a number of different closed-question response formats, each of which is illustrated below with an example from different parts of the questionnaire used by Malaka (1995).

Checklists

A checklist consists of a list of all possible answers to a question, and the respondent is usually allowed to choose (or 'check') more than one alternative. This format is most useful when the researcher wants to survey responses to a full domain of activities. In a study of sexual fantasy, for example, the researcher would provide a comprehensive list of all sexual fantasies found in the literature, and ask the respondent to check off any fantasies that she or he has had in the past month.

An item similar to a checklist item used by Malaka

How many minutes in a typical week do you spend on the assessment activities below? Indicate your answers by writing in the minutes beside the activities.

Assessment activities	Minutes
a. Reviewing and selecting assessments	_____
b. Developing own assessments	_____
c. Administering tests	_____

In the example above, the use of the 'other' category allowed respondents to specify topics that the researcher might have omitted. Instead of asking the respondents to state the number of minutes they spend on the list of activities, respondents could also be instructed to 'Tick those activities that you use' or 'Rank the assessment activities in order of importance'.

Dichotomous questions

Dichotomous questions present only two alternatives for respondents to choose from. This format is used when there are clear yes–no answers to a question, and is appropriate for obtaining factual information from the respondents (e.g., 'Are you a smoker?'). Dichotomous items should not be used to determine opinions (e.g., 'Do you think smoking is bad?') because they cannot capture the more subtle differences in opinion.

Scaled questions

Scaled questions consist of statements or questions, followed by a rating scale where respondents indicate the degree to which they agree or disagree with the item. Scaled questions are useful for measuring attitudes and personality as they can capture subtle gradations of opinion or perception. There are a number of different kinds of rating scale format, of which the Likert scale format is the most commonly used.

Multiple choice questions

Multiple choice questions consist of a stem (i.e., a question or statement) and a series of options or alternatives. Usually the respondent is allowed to select only one alternative. Multiple choice questions are commonly used for measuring knowledge, but can also be used for gathering factual or attitudinal information.

A multiple choice item

What is another name for the average score of a set of test scores? (Circle **one** choice)

a. z-score   b. standard deviation   c. mean   d. alpha value

True–false questions

True–false questions are similar to multiple choice questions, but the respondent is only given two possible response options.

A true–false item

T   F   When you prepare a test, the test directions should explain how the test will be scored.

Assemble the questionnaire

Questionnaires typically consist of a number of different subparts or scales, each consisting of a number of items. These must be arranged into a well-ordered and easy-to-read final questionnaire. Assembling a questionnaire involves finalising the layout and the questionnaire format, as well as the instructions for completing the questionnaire. The format used by Malaka (1995) was as follows:

Part one

The first section of the questionnaire consisted of a paragraph that provided background information for respondents. Respondents were informed of the purpose of the study in a paragraph that briefly stated why the information was collected and how it would be used. Respondents were also guaranteed confidentiality and given general instructions about how to complete the questionnaire.

Part two

The main body of the questionnaire consisted of the actual questions. Malaka included four different scales in his questionnaire. These scales related to (1) teachers' previous training in assessment, (2) techniques of classroom assessment that teachers practised, (3) teachers' attitudes towards classroom assessment, and (4) teachers' assessment skills. Each scale consisted of a number of items, and part 2 of the questionnaire consisted of a total of 44 items.

Part three

Finally, the questionnaire included a section that elicited demographic information from the respondents. Various response formats were used

Box 22.5

The use and value of a pilot study
(Catriona Macleod, University of Fort Hare)

Pilot studies are used to identify possible problems with proposed research, using a small sample of respondents before the main study is conducted. Pilot studies are conducted with either a subsample of the proposed sample or a small sample representative of the proposed sample. Pilot studies may take on two distinct forms, depending on the nature of the research. The first type is more 'free range', in which open-ended questions are asked and participants' opinions about the study are used to improve the research. This type of pilot study is useful in exploring the potential issues pertinent to the study prior to a more structured format being put into place. The second type reflects the proposed collection of data more closely, and is thus more structured. The actual questionnaire, interview schedule, or observation schedule is administered and the data analysed for inconsistencies, gaps, repetitions, or flaws in the data collection instrument. Structured pilot studies help the researcher (1) to ensure that no offensive language is contained in the questionnaire, (2) check the clarity of instructions and questions, administration time, layout, coding of questionnaires, and data input, and (3) conduct preliminary data analysis. Sometimes it may be necessary to interview respondents for further clarification regarding their responses. The value of both forms of pilot study is enhanced if participants are asked to comment on the questions and the manner in which they were posed.

The following are some evaluative questions that can be asked concerning the various aspects of the research:

to determine the respondents' age, gender, race, qualifications, and teaching experience. Although the demographic section was included last in Malaka's questionnaire, this section of a questionnaire is often included first.

Evaluate measures included in the questionnaire

Once the questionnaire has been developed, it is administered to a sample of respondents. The questions are then scored and analysed to determine how good the questionnaire is. It is recommended that a pilot study be conducted to check the questionnaire before it is administered to the final sample. The first thing to do once you get the completed questionnaires back from the respondents is to code the data, enter the data into a computer, and clean up the data. Before any investigatory analyses are conducted, researchers should evaluate each of the scales that are included in the questionnaire. Certain questions, particularly those using checklists and open-ended response formats,

- **Instrument design and evaluation** – Does the instrument render the depth of data needed? Is the theoretical question posed in the study being answered? Is the order of questions correct (avoid asking sensitive questions near the beginning of a questionnaire)? Is the language understandable to the participants, and are there no ambiguities? Is there equivalence of translation? Is the time taken to complete the data collection too long/short?
- **Research explanation** – Is the explanation of the purpose of the research clear and acceptable to the participants?
- **Method of data collection** – Is this adequate, or could the data be more effectively elicited via another source (e.g., group rather than individual)?
- **Logistical/practical issues** – How well did the venue, the recording, and gaining access to the participants work?
- **Researcher/research assistant issues** – How has conducting the pilot helped the researcher's understanding of the context of the research? Were there any errors in the administration of the research instrument? What further training is required?
- **Political issues** – What are the political issues surrounding the research, including aspects such as the problem being posed, sensitivity of topic, gaining entrance into the community, method of data collection, person doing the data collection, and participants used in the research?

The rationale of a pilot is to save time and money in the main study. It allows space for revision, reworking, complete overhaul, or, potentially, abandonment of the project. Pilots are not, however, without their ethical difficulties. The following question needs to be asked: What do the participants of the pilot study gain from their participation?

are best evaluated on the basis of the pilot sample's comments. Respondents in a pilot study could recommend that other items be included in the checklist, or that the open-ended question be rephrased. Scales and measures consisting of dichotomous questions and scaled items, as well as multiple choice and true–false questions, can be evaluated using standard quantitative methods. This evaluation has two primary aims: to identify poor items that should be eliminated, and to evaluate the reliability and validity of the full scale as a whole.

Item analysis
Item analysis is a procedure for identifying poor items in a measure or scale.

Poor items in this context are items that prove to be meaningless (e.g., everybody responds to the item in the same way) or that elicit responses that are different from the kinds of response elicited by the other items in the scale. These items thus do not measure the same thing as the rest of the scale.

Item analysis gets rid of bad items.

The most commonly used form of item analysis involves calculating item–total correlations. A simple two-step procedure can be adopted to do this: (1) sum the scores for each item of the scale, thereby creating a summed scale score; (2) correlate the scores for each item with the summed scale score. If any of the items correlate weakly with the summed scale score, the researcher can conclude that those items do not measure the same thing as the rest of the scale and the items can be eliminated.

Consider Malaka's (1995) four-item Likert scale reported earlier (i.e., the Classroom Testing Attitude Scale, CTAS). If we score the scale in such a manner that high scores on the scale indicate positive attitudes towards classroom testing, we will have to score the positively and negatively phrased items differently. Responses to the positively phrased items (i.e., a and d) are scored by the following coding scheme: $SD = 0, D = 1, U = 2, A = 3,$ and $SA = 4$, whereas responses to the negatively phrased items (i.e., b and c) are scored in the reverse: $SD = 4, D = 3, U = 2, A = 1,$ and $SA = 0$. Can you see why?

You will notice that we have indicated how one teacher responded to the scale by circling her or his responses. The teacher's scores for each item on the scale are as follows: $a = 3, b = 4, c = 2, d = 4$. Scores on all the items are then added to create the summed scale score. The teacher's summed scale score is thus 13. (This would appear to be quite a high score because the potential range for the four-item scale is between 0 and 16, but it could be that most teachers score highly on the scale.) The next stage in running item–total correlations is to correlate – across all respondents – the scores on each of the items with the summed scale scores. Strong item–total correlations indicate that these items tend to measure the same thing as the whole scale. These items should be retained. Low item–total correlations indicate poor items that should be eliminated. Individuals who scored high on the whole scale do not tend to score high on these items, suggesting that the items do not measure the same thing as the rest of the scale. The results of a pilot study with Malaka's scale (n = 40) produced the following item–total correlations for the four-item Likert scale: $a = 0.78, b = 0.21, c = 0.59, d = 0.65$. It appears as though item b does not measure the same thing as the rest of the scale and should be eliminated.

Item–total correlations can be conducted for dichotomous items, true–false items, and multiple choice items. All the correct answers on the true–false and multiple choice scales, or the yes responses to dichotomous scales, are added up to form the summed scale score. Scores on each item of the scale – which will be either 1 (correct, yes) or 0 (incorrect, no) – are then correlated with the summed scale score. Again, items with low item–total correlations do not measure the same thing as the rest of the scale and should be eliminated.

Other kinds of item analysis

In addition to item–total correlations, there are many other ways of evaluating the quality of items. For example, in a test with right and wrong answers, it is important to include a good spread of easy and

Assessment instruments should be thoroughly investigated before they are used in research or for decision making.

difficult items, with most of the items of average difficulty. By looking at the proportion of respondents who get each item right (also known as the 'item difficulty'), one can ensure that there are not too many overly easy or overly difficult items in one's test. One may also want to discard items that are 'biased' against particular groups of respondents. Test developers in South Africa and elsewhere increasingly make a point of calculating item bias statistics to ensure that the items included in their questionnaires operate in comparable ways in black and white samples. It is not necessary that the same proportion of people from different race groups endorse a particular item (there may be real differences between the race groups), but the item should relate to other items in the questionnaire in a similar way for both groups. Although we will not discuss the details of how to calculate item bias statistics here, you should know that such analysis will become increasingly important to questionnaire construction in the South African context.

There are many highly sophisticated statistical procedures for determining if an item is biased against a particular race group.

Depending on the outcome of the pilot test, the questionnaire should be revised to address any problems identified – e.g., unclear instructions, biased items, sexist language, and so on. After this, the instrument is ready to be administered to the sample or population identified.

Evaluating the scale as a whole

Once the researcher is satisfied with the quality of each of the items of each scale in a questionnaire, the reliability and validity of the scales can be determined. Reliability and validity are discussed in detail in chapter 9, and we recommend that you have another look at that chapter now.

Although test–retest reliability information is very useful in judging a scale, the inconvenience involved in having to administer a scale to the same group of people twice means that test–retest reliability information is rarely obtained. The most commonly calculated reliability information relates to the internal consistency of a scale; that is, the degree to which the items of a scale all belong together or cohere. (You can see that by eliminating items that do not correlate well with the scale total during the item analysis phase discussed above, we have helped to ensure that our scale will be internally consistent.) Many statistics programs make provision for the calculation of internal consistency statistics, the most commonly used being Cronbach's alpha statistic for scaled items and one of several different Kuder-Richardson statistics for dichotomous items. Reliability statistics range from 0 to 1, and, as a rule of thumb, the internal consistency coefficient for personality or attitude scales should be 0.70 or greater, and the coefficient for scales measuring ability should be 0.90 or greater.

Validity statistics are generated by correlating scores on a newly developed scale with scores on other criterion or concurrent measures. Although there are no perfectly valid and reliable measures in the social sciences, a newly developed scale should only be used for research and applied purposes if there is evidence that it is both valid and reliable.

Development of norms

Raw score	Percentile rank	
Spatial 2 D test	**Female**	**Male**
30		99
29	99	97
28	98	95
27	97	91
26	96	88
25	94	84
24	91	80
23	88	74
22	85	69
21	80	62
20	76	56
.	.	.
.	.	.
.	.	.
2	1	1
1	1	0
0	0	0

Table 22.1 Percentile norms for Grade 12 learners on the Spatial 2-D test

If the intention is to compare an individual's score to that of a population, then norm tables need to be developed. Norm tables provide a frame of reference for interpreting the scores of individuals in comparison to a particular 'norm group' (Murphy & Davidshofer, 1998). If you know that the mean score of a group of Gauteng teachers on the Classroom Testing Attitude Scale was 9 and your score is 7, you know that you have a less favourable attitude to testing than most Gauteng teachers. This is a crude form of comparing yourself to a norm group. Norm tables allow for such comparisons, but in a more fine-grained way. They are constructed by calculating the standard scores that correspond to each possible raw score on a scale.

You could therefore look up your raw score on the norm table, see what the corresponding standard score is, and thus know exactly where you are placed relative to Gauteng teachers.

Standard scores are ways of expressing individuals' scores in terms of where they stand relative to other individuals in a sample or population. One type of standard score comprises z-scores, which show how many standard deviations above or below the mean an individual lies. However, norm tables can also make use of various other ways of expressing the relative standing of an individual vis-à-vis a group. For example, T-scores are like z-scores, but rather than a mean of 0 and a standard deviation of 1, they have a mean of 50 and a standard deviation of 10, and IQ scores have a mean of 100 and a standard deviation of 15. **Percentiles** are also often used in norm tables. They indicate the percentage of individuals in the group who received the same or lower score as each possible raw score. Table 22.1 is an example of a norm table containing percentile norms for both male and female testees on the Spatial 2-D Test (total marks 30). From the table, it is clear that 96% of female testees scored 26 or below, while only 88% of male testees scored 26 or below.

Scales often have many different norm tables, allowing one to compare an individual's score with different norm groups. In most cases, one should compare a person to a norm group that most closely resembles that person. So, if you are a newly qualified teacher who lives in Gauteng, you should look up your standard score for the CTAS scale on a norm table for young Gauteng teachers rather than on a norm table for American university lecturers.

New trends in assessment

Computerised applications in assessment

The introduction of computer technology has had a significant impact on assessment practices in the social sciences. In most situations, computers provide greater security and improved accuracy, and save a great deal of time, for example, in providing automated interpretation of test scores in terms of population norms. Computers also allow for greater flexibility in the administration of assessment instruments, make scoring easier, and allow for the use of innovative item formats (e.g., animated displays).

An interesting way in which computers are used to administer tests is computerised adaptive testing or CAT (De Beer, 1998). In CAT, testing is conducted in stages as the test adapts to the level of the respondent. The process begins at stage 1, with the respondent answering a question of average difficulty. If the answer is correct, a score is awarded and the next question that the computer selects (in stage 2) is more difficult. If the answer is incorrect, the computer then selects an easier question. In stage 3, a similar process occurs, and continues until the respondent can no longer answer any questions correctly or the test is complete. See figure 22.1 for a diagram of the stages in CAT testing.

In computerised adaptive testing, each testee in effect completes a different test, custom-made to fit with their unique abilities.

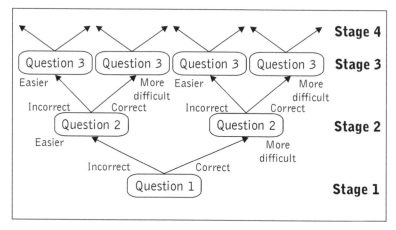

Figure 22.1 Stages in CAT testing

Box 22.6

Making your questionnaire available to others

If you have gone to the trouble of constructing a reliable and valid questionnaire, even if it is quite a simple instrument, it is a good idea to 'package' it in such a way that others can use it as well. The best way to do this is to compile a short manual that you can photocopy and give to other researchers. The manual could contain the following:

- A copy of the questionnaire itself.
- A brief explanation of the theoretical background that its development was based on, perhaps giving some references from the literature.
- Instructions on how to administer the questionnaire, e.g., can a group of people do it at the same time, and what should they be told before starting?
- Instructions on scoring the questionnaire, e.g., which items are reverse-scored, and are there subscales in the questionnaire?
- Statistical information on each item in the questionnaire, e.g., how strongly it correlates with the scale total.
- Information on the reliability and validity of each of the scales in the questionnaire.
- Norm tables.
- Instructions on how to interpret scores on the questionnaire, together with any warnings about how to avoid misuse or misinterpretation of the scores.

The computer is able to select appropriate items according to the examinee's response by using an assessment theory called Item Response Theory, which also enables the results of the test to be provided immediately after the test is completed (Wainer, 1990). CAT systems are useful as they can establish a person's ability level quickly without the need to administer a large number of items, and can provide detailed and immediate feedback on how the individual has performed. Test security is also increased as no two persons take exactly the same test (each sees only those items needed to establish her or his ability level), and tests can be taken at any time when the individual is ready.

Dynamic assessment

The dynamic assessment approach is used to determine the learning potential of individuals and is based on the test–teach–retest model of assessment. Rather than assessing knowledge, dynamic assessment aims to assess modifiability (also sometimes termed 'learning potential'), which is the change in the cognitive functioning of the learner given relevant support and assistance (Lidz, 1987). First, a pre-test is administered to all examinees; they are then exposed to some training, and finally a post-test is administered. Scores from the pre-test reflect the individuals' current level of functioning, while scores from the post-test reflect their future level of functioning. The difference between pre-test and post-test scores reflects the amount of potential that can be developed with relevant support and assistance. Dynamic assessment may prove especially useful for trainers and teachers in the South African context, since dynamic assessment holds promise for identifying learners who were denied access to education and training but have demonstrated potential (De Beer, 1998; Haeck & Yeld, 1993). The University of Cape Town has, for example, used the dynamic assessment approach to select applicants for admissions (Haeck & Yeld, 1993).

The **Human Sciences Research Council** has also used this approach in developing an instrument to assist teachers to assess learning difficulties among 6- to 8-year-old South Africans (De Beer, 1998). While available standardised instruments such as the SSAIS could be adapted to serve this purpose, Sabate (1997) argues that these instruments have been developed using traditional assessment approaches, and may lead to misdiagnoses and prejudice against South African learners who have had a disadvantaged educational background.

Where to obtain information on assessment instruments

Box 22.7

Usually, information about commercially available testing instruments can be obtained from the test publishers. In South Africa there is a range of companies and organisations who publish tests, including the Human Sciences Research Council (HSRC). A useful regularly updated source for international tests (mainly American) is the *Mental Measurements Yearbook* published by the Buros Institute of Mental Measurement (Buros, 1988). A copy of this yearbook can be found in most university libraries. A useful source of personality and attitude tests is Robinson, Shaver, Wrightman, and Andrews (1991). Journal articles and textbooks are also useful sources. Finally, the internet can be used to obtain access to test publishers as well as additional information on the various testing instruments.

Conclusion

Assessment practices are certain to have a significant impact on the continuing transformation of South African society. How assessment instruments are developed and applied will determine to a large extent how valuable resources – especially human resources – are utilised. In this context, interesting challenges are likely to be confronted in the assessment arena, and the need for more competent and creative assessment practitioners and researchers is certain to increase.

Exercises

1. For each of the standardised measures presented in box 22.2, design a study where the measure is the principal dependent variable. Repeat the procedure, but now design studies where the variable is the independent variable.

2. Draw up a list of 10 bad assessment instrument items or questions. Be sure to include vague, double-barrelled, ambiguous, leading, and loaded questions. State why each question would be a poor indicator of the construct being measured, and consider what type of information the question would elicit from a sample.

3. Develop a questionnaire to determine (a) the attitudes of high-school students to the matric examinations, or (b) the experiences and attitudes of first-year students to the use of the internet as an educational tool. Working together as a group, follow the procedures set out in this chapter. During the question-writing stage, each group member should write about ten questions on her or his own, before rejoining the group to assemble the instrument. Each group member should then administer the full questionnaire to about five respondents as part of the pilot study. Next, ask somebody with experience in doing item analysis to help you use a statistics program to decide which items to discard. Finally, calculate reliability statistics, compile a norm table, and write a short manual for your new questionnaire.

Key readings

Broadfoot, P. (1996). *Education, assessment and society*. Buckingham: Open University Press.
This text provides an excellent analysis of the use and role of assessment in modern societies. Although it has an education focus, it is a useful introduction to a variety of applied assessment practices.

Crocker, L., & Algina, J. (1986). *Introduction to classical and modern test theory*. Orlando, Florida: Holt, Rinehart and Winston.
This comprehensive book covers all aspects of assessment theory and is one of the best books on this topic. It is not an entry-level text.

Lidz, C. S. (Ed.). (1987). *Dynamic assessment: An interactional approach to evaluating learning potential*. New York: Guilford Press.
This edited collection includes papers by some of the best-known researchers in the area of dynamic assessment, and provides a comprehensive overview of the field in an accessible and easy-to-read volume.

Foxcroft, C., & Roodt, G. (Eds). (2006). *Introduction to psychological assessment in a South African context*. (2nd edition). Cape Town: Oxford University Press.
This is the leading South African text on psychological assessment and provides a comprehensive introduction to the subject. Essential reading if you plan on doing research about, or making use of, psychological assessment instruments.

23

Standpoint methodologies:

Marxist, feminist, and black scholarship perspectives

Gill Eagle
University of the Witwatersrand

Grahame Hayes
University of KwaZulu-Natal, Durban

Thabani Sibanda
University of the Witwatersrand

This chapter is designed to introduce you to the three theoretical research positions of Marxism, feminism, and black scholarship, and to this end is divided into three subsections. Thus far, the book has covered material relating to the philosophical foundations of research, key applications of research in social science, and a range of methods to conduct research. Here, we introduce an alternative perspective, in some senses a more overtly political examination of research approaches. Although the three standpoints have different historical origins, and are geared towards different agendas, each seeks to challenge entrenched interests and practices within the research domain; it is in this sense that they are political. Feminist, Marxist, and black scholarship positions represent both a critique of prevailing (or **hegemonic**) social science research assumptions and an attempt to offer guidelines for alternative practice.

Feminist, Marxist, and black scholarship positions represent both a critique of prevailing social science research assumptions and an attempt to offer guidelines for alternative practice.

Strictly speaking, these approaches to conducting research cannot be termed methods or even methodologies, although they may sometimes be referred to in these terms, as in a researcher talking about using 'a feminist methodology'. Rather, these approaches should be viewed as positions, allegiances, or standpoints which researchers may embrace in conducting research. The term 'standpoint', which is adopted from feminist literature (Harding, in Henwood & Pidgeon, 1995), is used to indicate that the researcher takes a critical stance which is made explicit and defended throughout the research process.

Standpoint methodologies argue that no research study can be entirely value-free, and that research always carries vested power interests and serves to perpetuate dominant frameworks of thinking. The research approach that is the primary target of attack is positivism, since it claims to be free of subjective bias, and requires that the researcher retains distance from the subjects.

Standpoint methodologies argue that no research study can be entirely value-free.

It is not coincidental that research approaches that have been marginalised by the domination of positivism have been associated with marginalised groups in society, such as women, blacks, Marxists, socialists, the poor, and rural communities. Critical social research seeks to give voice to the concerns of such groups and to broaden the scope of research. In addition to criticising the positivist approach, standpoint theorists are also critical of interpretive approaches (e.g., phenomenology, hermeneutics, and constructionism) to the extent that they lack overt political commitment and fail to do justice to real (e.g., economic) aspects of people's lives. Interpretive approaches may afford the same weight to a right-wing, racist interpretation of affirmative action policies as they would to the interpretation of such policy by a disadvantaged person. By emphasising subjective experience, interpretive approaches are also viewed as guilty of ignoring the historical and social location of subjects in material reality. Thus, for critical theorists, positivist approaches are viewed as largely conservative, and interpretive approaches as not going far enough in incorporating a commitment to a set of emancipatory values in undertaking research.

Three central premises place standpoint methodologies apart from other social science research approaches. First, such approaches seek to uncover hidden or disguised relationships, ideas, and concepts, and in this sense aim to conduct research at a deep rather than surface level. Second, such understanding is directed towards change in an emancipatory or liberatory direction. Third, such research is generally focused on neglected, disempowered, or 'voiceless' populations or issues. Standpoint research is thus directed towards challenging vested power interests, and becomes a moral and political endeavour. Research is viewed as a tool through which to effect change.

Critical researchers maintain that it is more dangerous to conduct research pretending to be neutral or ignoring issues of power than it is to make one's position as researcher transparent and explicit. It may be useful to link the first aim of standpoint methodology to the concept of **ideology**. The project of uncovering hidden or deeper meaning and exposing the operation of power could be considered an exercise in ideology critique. As Abercrombie, Hill, and Turner (1980, p. 187) and many others have noted, the term 'ideology' has taken on a range of meanings and evoked much debate, but a common understanding of the term is that it refers to 'false beliefs' that disguise and support dominant power relations. Ideology can be viewed as the production and dissemination of beliefs or values that have material effects: they shape discourses and social practices, and confer power on dominant groups to control and exploit others (Walby, 1990).

The second characteristic of standpoint methods of research is that they are generally aimed at producing change. The research agenda is usually tied to some form of activism. In this respect, standpoint approaches often demonstrate similarities to action-orientated, participatory, and community-based forms of research. The aim is to transform some aspect of society, usually to the benefit of the powerless and disenfranchised. For example, a book produced by Foster, Davis, and Sandier (1987), drawing on the work of the anti-apartheid Organisation for Appropriate Social Services in South Africa (OASSSA), documented the physical and psychological effects of torture and detention on political activists during the 1980s. The aim of this research was not merely to describe such effects, but also to guide the work of counsellors working with ex-detainees, and more

'To the degree that a positivist theory of scientific knowledge has become the criterion for all knowledge, moral insights and political commitments have been de-legitimised as irrational or reduced to mere subjective inclination. Ethical judgements are now thought of as personal opinion.' (Brown, quoted in Neuman, 1997, p. 67)

Standpoint research is focused on neglected, disempowered, or 'voiceless' communities.

Photo: Rodney Barnett

particularly to use the findings to place pressure upon the apartheid government. The study was conducted with the explicit intention of exposing abuses and attracting international and national attention to political detention, in order to lobby against solitary confinement and torture.

The third dimension of standpoint research, the commitment to working primarily in the interests of oppressed and disadvantaged groups of people, will best be highlighted in relation to the three focus areas that we will examine below.

Feminist research

Feminist research emerged during the 1980s as feminist thinking became established in the academic community. Feminist research continues to be the subject of debate and is open to constant modification (see Burman, 1998).

Underlying principles

Feminist research addresses itself to several principal interconnected goals. These will be discussed first, following which their implication for research practice will be elaborated. Feminist theorists are concerned with the lack of research directed specifically towards understanding women's experience. Up until the 1980s, much social science theory had been developed from research with male subjects, in most cases conducted by male researchers (Squire, 1989). For example, many grand theories in psychology, such as Freud's description of the Oedipus complex and Kohlberg's (1966) theory of moral development, were derived from observations of male subjects. Where women's experience was taken into account, this tended to be in comparison to the male norm or to be limited to the domain of female affairs such as child bearing and rearing.

Women researchers are not necessarily feminist in outlook, and many women are coopted into 'malestream' social science practices.

Feminists reject the implication that universal theories of human functioning can be derived from research with men. A primary aim of feminist research is to put women's issues on the agenda. This involves advancing women's careers as social scientists and researching issues that do justice to women's experience. For example, the work of Carol Gilligan (1982) has expanded Kohlberg's theory to incorporate such factors as the role that women's closer interpersonal connections play in their moral evaluations. However, it is important to recognise that women researchers are not necessarily feminist in outlook, and many women are coopted into 'malestream' social science practices.

In addition to putting women's experiences in the forefront, feminist researchers are invested in tackling discrimination and oppression of women. They believe theory should be tied to action, and tend to design research projects with this end in mind. For example, in a project conducted in Newlands East township outside Durban, Louise Mina (1986) researched adolescent boys' and girls' ideas about rape causation. Her analysis of the attitudes and beliefs of these students was then shared with teachers to assist them in developing a rape awareness and prevention programme for adolescents. A large proportion of feminist research has similarly been directed at issues relating to sexism and oppression, such as violence against women, women's sex-role position and status (including domestic and occupational roles), women's representation in the media, and sexual and reproductive issues. More recently, feminist research has increasingly focused on differences in the experiences of oppression of subgroups of women, such as lesbian, black, and working-class women. In South Africa, the life conditions of rural women have been highlighted. The popular South African feminist journal, *Agenda*, has featured a number of special issues illustrating the kinds of action concerns that feminist research may tackle. These include women's health, rural women's social and economic positions, debates on abortion policy, women's education and literacy levels, and wife battery. In most cases, the knowledge developed around these issues is used to inform policy developments and anti-sexist lobbies.

Ilse Pauw (1995) interviewed sex workers in the Western Cape about Aids risks they encountered in the course of their work. She found that street workers were at greater risk of coercion and violence from clients than escort agency-based workers, and made recommendations about education and health-care policy for such sex workers.

A further dimension of feminist research is its opposition to positivist assumptions. For feminist researchers, distinctions between the researcher and the research subjects perpetuate power relations in which subjects become the object of investigation of a detached, knowledgeable researcher. Additionally, positivist methods are seen as **patriarchal** as they attempt to understand the world in order to control and exploit resources. Positivism is seen as being '... consistent with a male point of view; it is objective, logical, task-oriented, and instrumental. It reflects a male emphasis on individual competition, on dominating and controlling the environment, and on hard facts and forces that act on the world' (Neuman, 1997, p. 80). In contrast, feminist researchers are committed to eradicating power imbalances between researcher and subjects. Research interaction is construed as an open dialogue rather than an opportunity to 'mine' information.

Photo: Rodney Barnett

Patriarchy can be seen in every aspect of our lives.

Motsei (1993) studied undisclosed battery-related injuries among women attending a health clinic in Alexandra. The study has lent momentum to a men's anti-violence project in the community. It has also encouraged medical staff to be sensitive to the possibility of such injuries and alerted them to the need for follow-up and counselling.

Feminist research is defined by its focus on women's (or gender) concerns, its action orientation, its recognition of the subjective role of the researcher, and its critique of the artificial distinction between the personal and the political. These features of feminist research reflect both epistemological and ontological concerns. In simple terms, feminist research is concerned both with the *content* and the *process* of research. In more sophisticated language, Banister et al. (1994) write:

> What identifies feminist research is a commitment to a specific, feminist, epistemology, that is a theoretical and political analysis that critiques dominant conceptions of knowledge, and poses questions about the gendered orientation of, and criteria for, knowledge. It is this assertion of the connection between being and knowing, between ontology and epistemology, that defines feminist research. (p. 124)

An example of the interrelatedness of ontology and epistemology comes from a set of debates about heterosexual penetrative sex and oppression, published in the 1995 issue of *Feminism and Psychology*. Discussants debated whether arguments could be validated by either theory or personal experience. Hollway (1995) suggests that some of the attacks against her positive outlook on aspects of heterosexual sex stemmed from an adherence to a 'politically correct' feminist position and a concern with her own choice to be heterosexual. In defending her position, she writes:

> Thompson [another discussant] asserts that 'I want radical feminist theory to validate (my) own choice of heterosexuality' ... What I want is for any feminist theory to be capable of understanding political reality in a sufficiently complex way that, first, it can relate to people's lived reality; second theorise change; and third it does not leave a wide open space in which a backlash can become established. It is also important that feminist voices attempting to break a silence about heterosexuality are not simply written off as part of that backlash. (p. 129)

In this response, Hollway is arguing for both ontological and epistemological principles. In asserting that the subject matter of feminist research should not be constrained by political correctness and should relate to people's lived experience, including their possible pleasure in heterosexual relationships, Hollway is illustrating concern about the ontology of research, or the *'what'* that should be examined. In addition, she also points to the *'how'* of examination, or her epistemological stance, in claiming that her own and other women's direct experiences of heterosexual sex are a valid basis from which to develop theory. These kinds of debate represent the commitment to flexibility and self-examination or reflexivity that characterises much feminist research. They also represent a refusal to create artificial distinctions between the private and public, or between the personal and political domains. It is difficult to imagine conventional researchers discussing the possible role of their own sexual preferences in debating whether the development of their theoretical position is biased or valid.

Methods and practice

Feminist research has been associated primarily with qualitative research methods. However, this is not an exclusive position, and there is some debate about the methodological direction of feminist studies. Feminist researchers are open to employing multiple methods, and Henwood and Pidgeon (1995) acknowledge that feminists have become more open to using quantitative research methods, sometimes for strategic reasons.

Although feminist research has been associated primarily with qualitative research methods, this is not an exclusive position.

How do all the issues raised thus far guide a person wanting to undertake feminist research? In the first place, the research question will obviously be determined by feminist concerns. Once the question has been posed, various practices are suggested for conducting the research in accordance with the principles identified previously. Some of these practices are described below.

Subjects versus informants or participants

The researcher is particularly conscious of reducing the hierarchical difference in the researcher-to-subject relationship. To this end, feminist researchers are at pains to inform subjects about the goals of the research and to ensure that participation is truly willing and voluntary. In many instances, the subjects are viewed as co-participants in the research, and may well be referred to as 'informants' or 'participants' rather than subjects. Much feminist research is initiated and planned collaboratively with women's organisations or potential beneficiaries of the research.

Feminist researchers are concerned with the political dimensions of what are sometimes considered personal or psychological issues. Feminist research often involves asking participants to talk about deeply-felt personal concerns, and therefore raises difficult ethical issues.

Participatory action orientation

Some feminist research has much in common with participatory action research (see chapter 19). In such models, the research may aim to convey and transfer research skills to participants in the course of its execution. For example, community members may be trained in questionnaire design and interview skills. Participants may also become co-authors of research reports. In most instances, in any case, participants are given feedback about the implications of the data and encouraged to join in dialogue around the findings.

Depth of engagement

Feminist researchers invest considerable effort in obtaining the trust of informants. Since feminist social scientists are often interested in hidden or what are conventionally considered personal or private aspects of people's lives, they often use interviewing, focus groups, or open-ended information-seeking methods. Eliciting meaningful data in these contexts requires a considerable level of trust. For example, in workshops held by The Women's Health Project (attached to the Health Policy Unit of the University of the Witwatersrand) around Aids prevention and condom usage amongst couples, it was considered important that women felt free to describe their actual experiences rather than what professionals might want to hear. In some workshops around the country, women have begun to discuss sensitive topics such as 'dry sex' (Morar & Abdool-Karim, 1998), infidelity, and condom usage.

There has been a fair amount of writing about the relationship between interviewer and interviewee in feminist research (Finch, 1984). Some researchers have suggested that interviewing may become the basis of establishing closer relationships, such as friendships (Oakley, 1981). Others have cautioned that women may over-disclose to other women and feel exposed by the experience (Banister et al., 1994). Thus it is important to be aware that there are pitfalls to greater intimacy in research, and that feminist researchers need to be particularly sensitive to the ethics of the researcher–subject relationship.

Reflexivity

Feminist researchers are self-conscious of the role their identification or dis-identification with subjects might play in the research process. This is referred to as 'reflexivity'.

Since feminist social scientists insist upon recognising the shared human attributes of researcher and subject, they are self-conscious of the role their identification or disidentification with subjects might play in the research process. In addition, as emphasised in some forms of discourse-analytic research (Potter & Wetherell, 1987), feminist social scientists are of the opinion that the researcher's demographic and personal characteristics play some part in the eliciting of research data. Thus, in writing up research reports, feminist researchers will almost invariably provide some commentary on their subjective response to the research process. In some instances, feminist researchers will use the counter-convention of referring to the researcher in the first person, referring to the fact that '*I* observed this', or 'in *my* analysis', explicitly acknowledging their role in the research process.

Sex-related terminology

Researchers are careful about the use of sexist language and avoid writing in this way. You may already have come across feminist writing in which the author is self-conscious about using the pronouns 'he', 'his', and 'him' to describe generic experiences and either substitutes 'she/he' forms, or more challengingly 'she', 'hers', and 'her' instead, or alternatively 'their', even when referring to the singular. Such non-sexist writing styles have become the preferred style in social science texts since the 1990s, but there is still evidence of the traditional use of the male pronoun in many texts. Feminist writers may choose to use the feminine pronoun in certain instances in order to highlight the political power of language usage and challenge the dominance of the masculine in academia.

Accessibility of findings

Finally, feminist researchers are interested in disseminating their findings in popular as well as academic forums. The Women's Health Project writes up most of their research in a widely distributed newsletter as well as more formal reports. They also share research material in workshop forums. The journal *Agenda*, unlike most academic journals, combines popular and academic content (for example, poetry and letters), and is committed to writing articles in easily accessible English, primarily because of the need to ensure that knowledge is more widely disseminated amongst South African women.

Box 23.1

Journals that publish feminist research in the social sciences

Agenda (South African)

Anthropological Forum

Feminism and Psychology

Feminist Issues

Feminist Review

Feminist Studies

Gender and History

Gender, Place and Culture

International Journal of Women's Studies

PINS (Psychology in Society) (South African)

Psychology of Women Quarterly

Signs

Social Text

The European Journal of Women's Studies

Woman's Review

Women and Therapy

Women: A Journal of Liberation

Women's Politics

Women's Studies International Forum

Women's Studies Journal

Black/African scholarship

Black/African standpoint methodology refers to a range of agendas, including anti-racism, black consciousness, Africanism, and valuing African cosmology. This lack of uniformity in perspective may reflect the recency of the introduction of such scholarship into social science disciplines.

History and foundations of black scholarship

Prior to the 1970s, most social science writing was dominated by colonial assumptions of superiority and entitlement. Black people's views were seldom reflected in theoretical formulations or the analysis of research findings. Research that was applied to the study of black and African populations tended to be driven by colonial and neo-colonial agendas, and tended to compare these populations unproblematically to the assumed norm of white standards. For example, early cross-cultural research contrasted black and white subjects' understanding of time, their depth perception, and their models of illness causation, and concluded that the black subjects' functioning was primitive or 'behind' that of their white counterparts.

Some of the original distinction between Eurocentric and Africanist perspectives on human functioning stemmed out of polygenesis theory (Franklin, 1991). Orlando Patterson (1979) observes that the scientific movement of the early nineteenth century generated data to prove that subgroups within the human race had evolved separately as distinct and unequal species. Race differences were seen as clear examples of these 'genetically distinct' evolutionary strands. The Darwinian, Thomas Huxley, wrote:

> No rational man, cognizant of the facts, could deny that the Negro was inherently inferior. Consequently, it is simply incredible 'to believe that' he will be able to compete successfully with his bigger-brained and smaller-jawed rival, in a context which is to be carried on by thoughts and not by bites. (Quoted in Franklin, 1991, p. 45)

While such views are now discredited, pseudo-scientific theories had considerable influence in the developing social sciences.

Racial discrimination rested upon ideological premises of difference and superiority. Blackness was understood as inferior, often described in terms such as 'primitive', 'uncivilised' and 'pre-literate'. Under apartheid, Bantu Education provided few black students with the intellectual tools to progress to tertiary education and was aimed at maintaining an image of a pre-literate African (Foster, 1991). Where African people entering academia became conscious of these kinds of interpretation, it became difficult to be black while maintaining a positive image of oneself (Manganyi, 1973). Teffo (1996) writes: 'Being-black-in-the-world is to experience oneself as a problem, a non-being in the eyes of the non-black. Blackness is a way of being, a mode of comportment in a world ruptured by alienation, hate, indifference and confusion' (p. 102).

Black scholars increasingly identified with broad-based black protest movements against colonialism and racism (Bulhan, 1977; Fanon, 1963), including the black consciousness movement of the 1960s

The colonial gaze constructed black people as different and inferior.

which sought to redefine black existence and identity. Leading figures in the movement were Malcolm X and Martin Luther King in the USA, and Biko and Manganyi in South Africa. Black consciousness provided a positive base (Pityana & Ramphele, 1991) from which to challenge Eurocentrism and apartheid, and thus created a foundation for the pursuit of black scholarship. In South Africa, the concept of 'black is beautiful' was adopted to reinforce a positive reformulation of identity, while in East Africa Ngugi Wa' Thiongo talked of 'decolonising the mind', highlighting the disempowering effects of using English as a medium of communication (Wa' Thiongo, 1986). Much progressive scholarly work in the social sciences, not only that associated with black scholarship, gained impetus from such political developments and has the flavour of these kinds of liberatory discourse.

Although broad political change has provided a base from which to affirm the rights of black people in South Africa and elsewhere, the consequences of discrimination can still be seen in many domains, including universities and research institutes. Black scholars entering academia have become acutely aware of the uneven ground on which they are expected to perform, and a strong sense of anger and resentment has became identifiable in some black writing. One view is that white scholars cannot research the lives of black people, since their interpretations will necessarily represent their structural position as oppressors. In this view, white researchers are culturally insensitive and intent on colonising black experience. However, black scholarship is more than a critique of white scholarship, and has developed a set of positive principles of its own.

'For if the last shall be first, this will only come to pass after a murderous and decisive struggle between two protagonists. That affirmed intention to place the last at the head of things, and to make them climb at a pace (too quickly, some say) the well-known steps which characterise an organised society, can only triumph if we use all means to turn the scales, including, of course, that of violence.' (Fanon, 1963, p. 37)

Principles of black scholarship

Central to black scholarship is the project to create a liberatory social science. Seedat (1997) identifies four phases in this project: disillusionment, reactive engagement, constructive self-definition, and the development of emancipatory discourse. Black standpoint research may fall within different categories along this continuum. Some theorists focus primarily on criticising 'white' research assumptions (reactive engagement), and others on propounding an 'African World View' in undertaking research (constructive self-definition). Although Seedat (1997) does not claim that individual black scholars have to pass through each of these phases in succession, there is a sense in which later phases are dependent on the successful negotiation of prior ones.

At the level of disillusionment and reactive engagement, most black scholarship shares in common the contestation of the colonisation of black experience by white researchers. It is argued that black researchers may need to be more clearly recognised as carrying potentially privileged knowledge in relation to groups with whom they can identify. It is also argued that the incorporation of more black scholars into social science research would serve the dual purpose of placing race concerns on the map as well as tackling race and gender inequities in disciplines which have been dominated by white, male academics.

At the level of constructive self-definition and the development of emancipatory discourse, many black scholars have been involved in the preservation of cultural forms and African traditions. Research methodologies that promote and respect cultural values and norms associated with Africanness engage researchers with such an agenda. However, black scholarship standpoint methodology needs to acknowledge that culture is not unitary (Thornton, 1988) and that black scholars have differing understandings of what constitutes culture. For example, black scholars may argue for the recognition of traditional healing practices as an important knowledge base, yet the influence of Christianity and exposure to Western medical models of healing have altered the degree to which traditional healers are viewed as carrying authority and expertise. The resilience and transformation of cultural practices is illustrated by the fact that many township residents make use of the dual treatment services of traditional healers and Western practitioners (Korber, 1990). In some colonial impressions of Africa, culture has been idealised as quaint and exotic. Contemporary appeals to tradition need to be careful of not falling into the trap of romanticising culture, including its oppressive aspects. In this respect, the not uncommon practice of witch hunting in some rural communities represents the negative potential of appeals to culture (Minnaar & Wentzel, 1997).

Another example of constructive self-definition is the Forum for Black Research and Authorship Development, created in 1995 (Duncan et al., 1997). Part of the project of this forum is to stimulate research in the interest of oppressed groups of people, particularly black populations. Under apartheid, most social science research ignored the plight of African people (Durrheim & Mokeki, 1997), and in some instances researchers were actively involved in supporting apartheid and racism (Nicholas & Cooper, 1990). Research funded and undertaken by the Human Sciences Research Council (HSRC) placed priority on studies tending to support apartheid capitalism. Since 1994, there has been a transformation in such statutory bodies and increasing emphasis on research which has application for policy development and the South African agenda of transformation. For example, there has been an increased focus on the interests of people in rural areas. The Centre for Health Policy undertook several studies into the possibility of integrating traditional healers into mainstream mental and physical health-care delivery (Freeman, 1989). The Centre for Peace Action (a project of Unisa's Institute for Social and Health Sciences) has been involved in violence reduction in the coloured community of Eldorado Park for several years. Problems such as gang-related violence and rape have been tackled through research-based interventions incorporating members from the community (Seedat et al., 1992).

Box 23.2

'Race' research in the SAJP

Historically, three kinds of study can be identified in the *South African Journal of Psychology (SAJP)*: *scientific studies* that focus on race, racism, or racial issues but treat these as unproblematic descriptive variables; *political studies* that investigate race in ways intended to challenge apartheid and social inequality; and *studies that do not mention race at all*. There has been a proportional decrease in 'scientific' studies of race, corresponding with an increase in 'political' studies. Three periods can be identified: the scientific study of race during the 1970s, the lack of concern with race during the early 1980s, and the political consideration of race during the 1990s (Durrheim & Mokeki, 1997).

Methods and practice

African humanity versus objectification

Black scholarship is unapologetic about African humanism and its opposition to 'scientific objectivity' and determinism. For example, understanding causal relations and the prediction of behaviour are not necessarily primary objectives in research. Causality may be understood in everyday terms or in the light of African cosmology (belief systems), and does not demand laboratory proof. The methodology of scientific experimentation is viewed as overlooking levels of human experience which may facilitate transcendent forms of existence, such as spiritual and ritualistic dimensions of human life.

Research based on an appreciation of African tradition is concerned with human values that are broadly recognised as part of African culture, such as a sense of identity as inseparable from one's community and a strong sense of collective being and consciousness. In this context, a person's merit is 'judged in terms of his kindness and good character, generosity, hard work, discipline, honour and respect, and living in harmony' (Teffo, 1996, p. 103).

These valued qualities represent community-enhancing or even altruistic behaviours, in contrast to more individualised attributes, such as high achievement, which may be more valued in Western capitalist societies. Given the objectification, outside scrutiny, and judgement that colonial practices brought to Africa, it is particularly important that researchers are sensitive to the implications of their approach to disempowered research subjects. A common feature of black/African standpoint methods is represented in counteracting racial oppression by relating to subjects with respect for their identity and culture. Such respect may be understood within the framework of '**ubuntu**' or African humanism.

It is important to note that respect for collective identity and tradition does not require that the researcher should be uncritical of social formations. Aspects of community and tradition have been

Yvonna Lincoln (1995), a well-known American research methods expert, argues that respect for the 'sacred' and 'spiritual' character of the world should be a criterion for judging quality in social science research. African cosmology may provide one means of translating this into practice.

Black scholarship emphasises African humanism.

invoked for political ends, and it may be the role of social science researchers to explore and challenge these without losing respect for their subjects of study. Appiah notes that 'Pan-Africanism, black solidarity, can be an important force with real political benefits, but it doesn't work without its attendant mystifications' (1996, p.106). The uncovering of these mystifications, as well as the exploration of the benefits of such social formations, should be the role of a critically engaged social science researcher.

Individualism versus commonality

The primary objective of research in academic circles would appear to have become the pursuit of personal promotion. Research has become a commodity produced through competitive activity, and has become so 'careerised' that the concept of beneficiaries is often ignored. Historically, African life has been abundant with a sense of sharing and partaking, and social science researchers should be cognisant that, within such a world view, it is understood as their responsibility to share the knowledge they accumulate with the communities that they subject to scrutiny.

In illiterate communities, sharing knowledge may require verbal rather than written dissemination of research findings. For example, during a spate of adolescent suicides in the largely African community of St Wendolin's outside Durban, researchers from the Organisation for Appropriate Social Services in South Africa (OASSSA) were asked to investigate the problem.

Following initial interviews with the youth, the researchers were expected to attend a large community meeting at which the problem was discussed. A number of issues were raised, including tensions with elders, and the researchers were asked to assist with input in coming to a communal solution that appeared satisfactory to the entire community represented (Eagle & Pillay, 1988). It was clear that, although the researchers could perform a useful role as expert consultants, their input was weighed in the context of community understanding, and intervention planning was considered a communal responsibility.

Alienation versus relevance and familiarity

Black scholars also assert the need to employ concepts that are familiar and relevant, arguably making the subject matter of research more accessible and engaging, particularly for black students. Seedat (1997, p. 261) describes his experiences of alienation as follows:

> When I entered the discipline as a masters' student, I felt estranged from the arsenal of psychological concepts that held the false promise of explaining familiar psychological experience. In dialogue with other black students and psychologists, I discovered that they shared my scepticism in the ability of Euro-American psychological concepts to explain the psychological world of black and female South Africans and those other than Euro-American the world over.

Attempts to engage with one's social origins may require employing introspection and self-reflection. Within African tradition, knowledge generation was usually dependent on oral transmission, and answers would be found through a consultative process that took into account 'common knowledge' and respected the input of elders. Such traditional practices for deriving knowledge may still be respected by African-sensitive researchers, for example by utilising elders as key informants.

Addressing topics of social relevance

Black scholarship is invested in promoting socially relevant research. Most research into race in South Africa has failed to problematise the construction of race and the relationship of race to economic and discriminatory practices.

In the past, for example, much of the research on depth perception (reviewed in Rasekoai, 1993) has failed to problematise race. In Rasekoai's own research, he did not use race as an unproblematic variable, but investigated differences between black children exposed to different forms of schooling, including urban/rural and multiracial/single-race schooling environments. His results indicated that both urbanisation and multicultural schooling appeared to improve capacity for depth perception, a necessary skill in engaging with engineering and architecture-related training.

Further projects dealing with issues of social relevance include research into black adolescent development (Stevens & Lockhat, 1997), the role of traditional healers (Hopa, Simbayi, & du Toit, 1998) and the testing of theoretical models in terms of their applicability to African populations (Stead & Watson, 1998). In some instances, socially relevant research is concerned with addressing issues that reflect the confluence of financial and racial oppression, e.g., education, health, and housing policy development. In the next section we will consider the issue of economic oppression more closely. Like feminism and black

Box 23.3

Bereavement and mourning in Zulu culture
(Mpfariseni Nembahe, University of the Witwatersrand)

In a study of mourning practices of Zulu-speaking women (Nembahe, 1998), I tried to bring an African world view into Western psychological frameworks on bereavement.

Communality. From a Western psychological perspective, grieving tends to be regarded as an individual process. In contrast, death in an African context appears to be viewed as a communal loss and hence dealt with collectively. The findings emphasised that researchers should bear in mind that an African person is an integral part of her or his community and that identity is tied to the collective.

Humanity versus objectivity. It was of great importance to show respect for the interviewees during the interview process. This involved having initially to discuss issues unrelated to the research in order to establish a polite and respectful relationship between researcher and participant. Being too goal-focused initially would have been alienating, and I had to be flexible about time, sometimes extending the time originally stipulated for an interview. Interviewees often expected me to respond to personal questions, such as from where I originated, which it would have been considered disrespectful not to answer. The observance of such traditional African patterns of communication reflects some of the differences between African-sensitive research and conventional practices.

Race. As a black researcher conducting research in a black community, there was a degree of identification between the researcher and the participants. This facilitated access to information as there was familiarity with the language of the participants, and I could draw on my own understanding of the concepts discussed. Whilst it is conceivable that a researcher from another race group could have conducted the research, it is important to recognise that at times there are advantages to such areas of familiarity between researcher and participants.

scholarship, Marxism is a reaction to oppressive practices – in this case class oppression. It also provides a sophisticated analysis of the way in which theory relates to methodology.

Marxist research perspectives

Marxism is not usually associated with methodology, and especially not the *practicalities* of research methods. Marxism is more usually associated with abstract and *theoretical* analysis, and these days, since the fall of communism in Europe in 1989, with the moribund political theory of state socialism or communism. In short, Marxism has most often been identified as a theory of politics, or a theory of political change (revolution). At one level, this overly theoretical view of Marxism is odd, given that it has regularly been accused of having subversive practical effects (one need only recall the apartheid government's banning of many Marxist works during the 1970s and 1980s), and that Marxism itself has always stressed the intricate link between theory and practice. Yet, at another level, Marxism has championed a form of theoretical critique, from Marx right through to the present. These two strands of theory and practice live unevenly within Marxism, and their waxing and waning can be charted in relation to the demands and exigencies of different historical moments.

The practice that we are talking about in Marxism is one that is connected primarily with politics and economics, often at quite broad levels of analysis, and very rarely the micro-analysis of research methodology. However, the methodological implications of most Marxist theory are not far below the surface. An obvious reason for this is that, as a system of theoretical *critique*, the practical or political implications of Marxist theoretical analyses bear quite directly on real concrete issues or problems. This is evident in Marx's (1978; 1979; 1981) wide-ranging study of nineteenth-century capitalism contained within the three volumes of *Capital*. This is simultaneously a work of (abstract) theory – the abstract categories of capitalist political economy, a work of political criticism – a moral attack on the social relations under capitalism, and a work about method – *Capital* contains detailed accounts of the practical analyses of the interstices of capitalist social and economic relations. Leaping from Marx's work of the 1860s to the self-consciously abstract work of the Marxist philosopher Louis Althusser during the 1960s and 1970s, we find yet again a Marxist concern with practical analysis amidst the most recondite theoretical arguments. We are thinking of the enormous practical and *methodological* impact of Althusser's famous (1971) paper on ideology and ideological state apparatuses (ISAs). Regardless of whether or not one agrees with Althusser's particular formulations concerning ideology, his essay re-invigorated debates concerning the theory of ideology, and stimulated a range of practical studies on the operations of ideological practices.

The import of the discussion thus far has been to identify one of the central claims of Marxism to methodology; that is, methodology is nothing if not intricately linked with theory. In other words, Marxism's challenge and contribution to methodology is the insistence of the practical or research implications of theory. It is in this sense that Marxism can be understood as *theoretical critique*.

The identification of Marxism as a system of theoretical critique hinges on the core methodological concept of **dialectics**. Dialectics is often described as Marxist method (see Bottomore, 1983). In general, dialectics refers to the fact that processes and relations are reciprocal, interwoven, and co-determining. Dialectics is a way (method) of looking at how things, ideas, and social relations are constituted, maintained, and changed. This perspectival understanding of dialectics is captured by Ollman (1993) when he writes:

Like feminism and black scholarship, Marxism is a reaction to oppressive practices – in this case class oppression. It also provides a sophisticated analysis of the way theory relates to methodology.

'Ideology represents the imaginary relationship of individuals to their real conditions of existence.' (Althusser, 1971 p. 153)

Dialectics restructures our thinking about reality by replacing the common sense notion of 'thing', as something that *has* a history and *has* external connections with other things, with notions of 'process', which *contains* its history and possible futures, and 'relation', which *contains* as part of what it is its ties with other relations. Nothing that didn't already exist has been added here. Rather, it is a matter of where and how one draws boundaries and establishes units (the dialectical term is 'abstract') in which to think about the world. (p. 11) (Emphases in the original)

Ollman (1993, p. 10) suggests that '... dialectic, as such, explains nothing, proves nothing, predicts nothing, and causes nothing to happen. Rather, *dialectics is a way of thinking that brings into focus the full range of changes and interactions* that occur in the world' (emphasis added).

Dialectics, therefore, is not a method in the pragmatic sense of suggesting what steps we should embark upon in our research. Instead, dialectics suggests an attitude towards the world, and requires that we pose certain research questions. For example, one of the most undialectical areas of research in psychology at the moment is the area of multiple personality disorder (MPD). Much of this work is dominated by a very linear and quantitative conception of the problem. The following kinds of question are being asked: Has there been a *real* increase in multiple personality (disorder)? What *are* the different prevalence rates? Is there a consensus in the definition or identification of multiple personality disorder? Do MPD 'sufferers' present with more 'personalities' than previously? How do we explain MPD, as an organic condition or as psychological in origin? It is not to suggest that these questions have no bearing on clinical and psychological considerations, but they are startling in their avoidance of critical and dialectical considerations. For example, a dialectical attitude might produce the following set of research questions: What is the link between the seeming increase of multiple personality with the postmodern championing of multiple identities? If the normal position is that we are plural, multiple in our identity formation, how should we then best understand multiple personality *disorder*? What are the contradictions – social and clinical – between multiple personality as lifestyle as opposed to psychopathology? Is there anything in the historical moment that can explain the rise (of the identification) of multiple personality? And so on. The second set of questions tries to insert the issue under discussion (multiple personality) into the *processes* and *relations* with which it is bound. This might make for more complex and 'messier' (less distinct) research questions, but it at least holds the possibility of closer connections with the reality under investigation.

While dialectics attempts to ground research questions within the materialism of processes and relations, there is also the grounding of questions *in time* that is an essential part of the Marxist project. Marxism, as a *materialist* theory is said to comprise two strands of materialism:

Marxist analysis focuses on economic realities, their historical origins, and the dialectical interplay among competing social forces that bring them into being.

dialectical materialism, or in this instance, dialectics; and historical materialism. Historical materialism asserts the importance of *empirically* determining the way things are, and how they have come to be this way (over time). The technicalities of historical materialism involve such concepts as the forces of production, the relations of production, and consequent class relations and struggles. For Marxism, history is the history of class struggles. However, as a research programme in the social sciences, a more general conception of historical materialism is justified, one that is less class-political than is usually the case in more classical variants of Marxism. Historical analysis requires searching for clues within the material conditions of social life for the reasons how things are or have come to be. For example, much of the current research on gender is less feminist than it was, say, 10 years ago. Gender was often a code for women, with an unashamed feminist focus on issues affecting women's lives. Now gender studies are much more 'representative', in that both women's and men's lives are subjected to investigation.

Given the fact that there is still a significant gender bias in society in favour of men, is this 'gender-neutral' swing in research studies considered progress? Marxism would want to suggest that this question cannot simply be answered as a substantive concern of gender research. One would at least want to ask what historical conditions have given rise to gender studies, to sociological analyses of men and masculinity, and to the decline of *feminist* thinking. As the advent of feminist issues and subsequent feminist research can be located in terms of quite precise *historical* forces, so it is with the 'new' gender and masculinity research. Marxism asserts that these historical factors are not merely 'external' or contextual to our understanding, in this case of gender, but are *dialectically* enmeshed within these changing categorisations themselves.

The three dimensions of Marxist theoretical practice are theoretical critique, dialectics, and historical (materialist) analysis.

In sum, then, it could be argued that the three dimensions of Marxist theoretical practice discussed above, namely theoretical critique, dialectics, and historical (materialist) analysis, form the cornerstones of the Marxist approach to research. We have further suggested that these dimensions have profound methodological implications, albeit not straightforward method implications; that is, they suggest a way of approaching research, and are less oriented towards the steps of practically doing research.

However, over the last 20 years, Marxism has turned its attention to some of the specific considerations of methodology in terms of developing empirical research method competences. This came about as a result of Marxism gaining respectability and a modicum of acceptance within the universities. In the 1960s, many social and political changes were attributed, directly and indirectly, to the influence of Marxist theory – for example, revolutions in many third-world countries, anti-imperialist and independence struggles, and the student revolts of May 1968. One of the consequences of these political shifts was the increasing esteem that Marxism achieved as a theory of society and revolution. Marxist theory, therefore, held sway for many years in certain academic disciplines, namely sociology, development studies, economics, and politics.

Marxism could no longer only rest on its laurels as a powerful theory of society and change; it also had to develop means (methods) of 'testing' its theories. There is now a proliferation of empirical studies, wholly or in part influenced by Marxism. And still, in its research maturity, Marxism operates as primarily a (theoretical) approach to empirical questions, rather than as a set of procedures of method. In this, it is very similar to discourse analysis.

Implications for practice

The Marxist approach to research entails two dialectically related objectives. First, it is imperative to understand the Marxist theoretical approach to any particular problem under investigation. Second, as a researcher, one should attempt to concretise and operationalise as many of the cluster of concepts that pertain to the area of investigation as is possible. The theory will suggest what concepts are available and appropriate to be operationalised. In the process of trying to operationalise certain (theoretical) concepts, the concepts themselves might be modified or changed, and hence dialectically impact back on the theory. By way of illustration, we'll briefly discuss two central concepts of Marxist theory – class and contradiction – and demonstrate how we might *prepare* them for the process of operationalisation, which is so essential to empirical research. The same process could be extended to other Marxist concepts, such as alienation, hegemony, base and superstructure, and ideology.

Although it is primarily a general theoretical orientation, specific methods have been developed for conducting empirical investigations from a Marxist perspective.

Class

For Marxism, class is primarily a concept that refers to the *structural* dynamic of capitalist societies. In other words, the logic of capitalism is such that it structurally locates two distinct classes in terms of opposing economic identifications. The two main classes of capitalism are the **bourgeoisie** and the proletariat, or, more simply put, the factory owners and the workers. Because capitalist social relations structurally determine the relations between the classes, the interests of the two classes are in conflict. Class conflict thus refers to a fundamental problem (contradiction) of capitalism, which can only be properly overcome with the overthrow of the whole system (class struggle). So much for the class structure of capitalism, though there is much more that could be added concerning the empirical investigation of structural causality (see Wright, 1979, pp. 9–29, for a detailed discussion of these issues). However, what Marxism has tended to neglect are the less structural determinants of class.

The fundamental contradiction of capitalism concerns the opposing interests of the bourgeoisie and the proletariat.

Marx distinguished between the objective (structural) dimension of class membership, and the subjective awareness of this class membership. This subjective dimension he referred to as *class consciousness*. Class consciousness refers to our awareness of our class membership. It also refers to the way we perceive our class location, and the membership of a particular class. While class might be structurally determined and hence limiting, this does not mean that we necessarily perceive our class position accurately or objectively. Class consciousness can therefore also refer to our misperception of our class position. Not misperception in the sense that we think we are part of the bourgeoisie, when in fact we work as a shop assistant, but misperception in being aware of only part of our class-determined reality. Furthermore, class consciousness needs to be expanded (or operationalised) to include the experiential dimension of class lives. How do people experience their class-determined lives? In the language of phenomenology, how do we understand the lived-experience of a particular class membership? How do we actually live our class lives? Seeing as there is more to social relations and social life than class awareness, how are we able to distinguish class consciousness from other forms of social consciousness? For example, how do gender, 'race', and ethnicity intersect with class consciousness? By posing some of these questions – and there are many others – we start to derive questions about class consciousness which lead us to more concrete formulations that in turn lend themselves to empirical investigations. These questions, at the same time, seem to expand our understanding of class consciousness, and therefore present challenges to the theoretical conception of class and class consciousness.

Contradiction

There are four main senses in which Marx understands the complex notion of contradiction. We intend to focus here on only one of these, and at the same time to change or extend this meaning of contradiction. Marx says that contradiction can be used to designate structural or systemic dialectical contradictions. In this sense, class would be an instance of a structural contradiction (see above). This idea of structural or systemic contradiction can usefully be referred to as 'social contradiction'. What this means, and this is consistent with a Marxist interpretation, is that there are contradictions 'out there' in the real world. The nature of social reality, and especially under capitalism, is contradictory, so the systemic (or structural) nature of society 'produces' social contradictions. In other words, the social relations within which we live, and

Photo: Rodney Barnett

Race, gender, and class identities are the result of social processes over which we have little control.

are 'forced' to live, produce contrary, dissonant, and, in many instances, irreconcilable experiences and obstacles.

This is particularly evident if we take the example of identity. The forces of socialisation and identity formation are various and often at variance. Our identity as a Christian might at times conflict with our identity as a democrat committed to the South African Constitution, if the issues around abortion are anything to go by. Our identity as a black man committed to traditional African systems of belief might conflict with our identity as a feminist when it comes to certain practices pertaining to marriage. Our identity as a Marxist activist might be at variance with our identity as an intellectual living a life of middle-class privilege. The point of these examples is to show that each identity is formed within a particular set of social (and structurally determined) relations. While identity sounds like something we 'have', or something we 'choose', it is in fact more aloof and less under our control than this. This is not to suggest that we are passive, and merely 'receive' our many identities, but rather that identity formation is a *social* process that happens behind our backs. We do give shape to our particular identities, but this is mostly so *within* particular identity configurations, rather than being able to resist some of the identities foisted upon us. It is in this sense that our conflicting identities are understood as social contradictions under which we are forced to live.

What are some of the possible questions that we could ask about the lived-experience of social contradictions? For instance, how do people in fact live these social contradictions (or contradictory identities)? How do people experience the conflict between certain identities? How is it that people (often) do not notice the conflict between certain identities? When people are aware of the social contradictions of their lives, how do they explain these? Some of these questions are potentially quite disruptive of the theory of social contradictions. The theoretical understanding of social contradiction seems so clear and relatively easy to determine, and yet the practicalities of living in socially contradictory worlds are anything but clear and precise. Again, there seems to be a dialectical loop between theory and practice in this instance.

To sum up, the intention in briefly discussing class and contradiction was to expose the process of how we might go about developing empirical research ideas or programmes generated through the use of Marxist concepts. Marxism's value as a rigorous theoretical system can, and indeed must be, extended to incorporate an equally rigorous approach to methodology and research methods (Morrow, 1994). The strength of Marxism's contribution to the field of research remains its relentless commitment to the dialectical cohesion of theory and practice.

'If then the social agents experience capitalist society as something other than it really is, this is fundamentally because capitalist society presents itself as something other than it really is ... It is not the subject that deceives himself, but reality which deceives him.' (Geras, 1989, p. 79)

'The philosophers have only interpreted the world, in various ways; the point is to change it.' (Marx, 1975)

Conclusion

In concluding this chapter on standpoint methods of research, it is important to reiterate that such approaches represent a value orientation to research rather than a specific set of methods. It should be clear by now that the choice of research styles and techniques in such cases is based upon the principles to which the researcher is committed in conducting the research. This may sometimes require the transformation or modification of existing research practices. As in most good research, method is informed by the aims of the project, and the goals of standpoint research are overtly political in nature. Embarking on a feminist, Marxist, anti-racist, or Africanist research project thus entails a moral or political choice on the part of the researcher. Since this way of talking about research falls outside the mainstream of social science, students need to recognise that doing such research entails risk and may have to be more strongly defended than conventional approaches. Banister et al. (1994) point out that, because feminist research often engages with new territory, with no body of pre-existing theory to back it up, it may well be considered illegitimate against conventional academic standards. This is equally true of the other approaches discussed. Standpoint researchers need to develop a community of supportive colleagues and to be aware of the pitfalls of their choices before they adopt such approaches. On the other hand, for many standpoint researchers, the moral or political commitment of their work provides them with a sense of purpose and integrity. It can also be very satisfying to conduct research in a manner that allows one's personal and professional life to be in closer communion. Thus, the rewards of standpoint research often outweigh the risks.

Exercises

1. Type or write out a couple of paragraphs chosen at random from this book. Now make a second copy of the same paragraphs, but with all gender-neutral pronouns (she/he or their) changed to the masculine form (he). Hand out gender-neutral and masculine copies to people at random and ask them to rate the quality of scholarship. Using a t-test (see chapter 10), determine whether people rate masculine academic writing more or less highly than gender-neutral academic writing. How would you explain the difference (or lack of difference) between the two groups? Now repeat the experiment using feminine pronouns.

2. Design a research study to investigate newspaper reports that unemployed African teenagers in KwaZulu-Natal are deliberately engaging in unprotected sex in order to spread HIV infection. The claim is that this behaviour is driven by feelings of alienation and demotivation. Your goals as researcher(s) are to understand the phenomenon and to attempt to alter harmful behaviour.

3. As a way of trying to give practical expression to the notion of contradiction, ask a friend, or anonymous research subject(s), to describe two of their roles or identities that are often are variance with each other – for example, a 20-year-old woman who is a practising Christian, and yet wants to have (pre-marital) sex with her boyfriend, or a young practising Muslim man, who enjoys drinking alcohol and partying occasionally. Get them to discuss how they *live* these contradictions between two or more identities, and at the same time try to understand what the social and material conditions are that support these roles and identities.

Key readings

Althusser, L. (1971). Ideology and ideological state apparatuses. In L. Althusser, *Lenin and philosophy and other essays*. London: Verso.
This famous essay of Althusser's is a classic in the Marxist literature on ideology. While it is in many respects a theoretical paper, Althusser presents some very concrete ideas about the way ideology works in practice.

Appiah, K. A. (1996). African identities. In L. Nicholson & S. Seidman (Eds), *Social Postmodernism: Beyond identity politics*. London: Cambridge University Press.
This chapter deals with some of the debates and difficulties in outlining the territory that might be occupied by black scholarship in discussing the notion of African identity.

Banister, P., Burman, E., Parker, I, Taylor, M., & Tindall, C. (1994). *Qualitative methods in psychology*. Buckingham: Open University Press.
Chapter 8 on 'Feminist methodology' provides an overview of aspects of feminist research principles with practical examples and some discussion of the politics of doing research.

Hayes, G. (1996). The psychology of everyday life: Some Marxist reflections. In I. Parker & R. Spears (Eds), *Psychology and society: Radical theory and practice*. London: Pluto Press.
This chapter shows how contradictory 'everyday life experiences' are, and how and why we should study them.

South African Journal of Psychology.
A special edition of this journal published in 1997 (volume 27, number 4) focuses specifically on black scholarship in South Africa. The editorial and articles deal with the underdevelopment of such scholarship, difficulties facing black scholars, the manner in which racial issues have been researched, and examples of research in this area.

Wright, E. O. (1979). *Class, crisis and the state*. London: Verso.
The first chapter very systematically presents six basic modes of methodologically (or empirically) understanding the process of determination in Marxism.

Postmodernism:
a critical practice?

James Sey

Independent researcher, Wits School of the Arts

Postmodernism is a
broad term for many
different approaches
that set themselves up
in opposition to the
coherence and
rationality of the
modern world.
Postmodernity is the
cultural setting within
which postmodernism
has been able to
flourish.

This chapter introduces some of the main currents of postmodernist thought that have had an impact on the way in which knowledge and critical enquiry in the social sciences have taken shape in the past thirty years. More than this, it will call into question some of the assumptions and thinking about postmodernism made in contemporary intellectual contexts, and attempt to sketch some of the ways in which postmodernism can be used as a mode of enquiry in the humanities and social sciences in the twenty-first century.

The chapter makes some prior assumptions of which you should be aware. First, the term 'postmodernism' has a very involved conceptual, disciplinary, and critical history which will not be exhaustively dealt with in this discussion. Should you wish to find out more about this background, you should consult the list of key readings. Instead, this discussion is intended to take issue with the present understanding and uses of postmodernism as a critical practice. Thus, the discussion will inevitably be somewhat selective in addressing issues from what is a convoluted and contested intellectual history. Second, the discussion will be guilty of conflating, predominantly in the first section, some of the major concerns and paradigms of poststructuralism with those of postmodernism.

Ultimately, this chapter wishes to address one important question: has postmodernist social science thinking of the last few decades of the twentieth century led to a critical intellectual practice? The tension between conservative and critical tendencies in postmodernism is discussed in relation to three central questions of postmodern enquiry: the role of discourse and text in 'constructing' social reality, the nature of the postmodern subject, and the ways in which technology has refashioned this subject. The chapter concludes with suggestions on ways in which postmodern theory can inform social science practice in South Africa today.

Box 24.1

Postmodernism and ideology

A common line of critique against postmodernism is that it is not an ethical or politically responsible intellectual paradigm, but that, as Fredric Jameson's famous position (1991) has it, postmodernism is a cultural symptom of late capitalism, and is therefore ideologically complicit and by implication non-critical. In his view, we have moved from an era of high industrial capitalism, corresponding to modernism in the arts, to the era of 'late capitalism', a term he used to distinguish his understanding from those who see our historical era as being a 'post-capitalist' one. According to these theorists, we are in a post-capitalist era because the world is now based on a service and information economy rather than the commodification of workers' bodies and goods. Jameson argued that such a formulation misses the fact that the locus of the production of commodities has simply moved from the first to the third world. In

Discourse, textuality, and constructionism

Perhaps the most pervasive impact that postmodernism has had on the social sciences derives from its use of analytic methodologies based on the model of language and discourse (see chapter 14). The so-called 'linguistic turn' of French philosophy in the 1960s especially brought theories of reference and meaning sharply into focus once more in a Western intellectual world that had been dominated for over a century by positivism and materialism in the social sciences, and by empirical theories of reference in the human sciences, emblematised by the dominance of realism in literary studies. Under the impact of a rediscovery of the theories of 'structural linguistics' of Ferdinand de Saussure, many intellectuals in widely disparate disciplines undertook a revision of theories of reference and meaning, based on the central insight that apparently objective reality, individual consciousness, and thought itself were all profoundly mediated by linguistic structure.

A good example of this would be the shift in the production and interpretation of literature from the late nineteenth to the mid-twentieth century. The dominant literary form in English literature in the nineteenth and early twentieth centuries was that of the social realist novel, such as those of Dickens, Eliot, and Hardy, or the 'naturalist' fiction of Balzac in France or Mark Twain in America. Critical understanding of literature followed the realist lead of such fiction in evaluating the work as a more or less successful picture of actual social conditions.

Later in the twentieth century, literature and criticism began to shift away from such 'reflectionist' models of social realism towards a more self-consciously experimental mode where the role of language in the production of meaning became of interest in the literature itself, as well as in new critical approaches. Examples of this shift include the so-called 'new novel' in France, and the early 'postmodern' fiction of Thomas Pynchon, Kurt Vonnegut, and others.

the third world, exploitive conditions are maintained by the multinational companies, emblematised by the global symbolism of brand names like Coca-Cola and Nike. Postmodernism's 'collusion' with late capitalism, in Jameson's view, was that it contributed to the appearance that culture has reached the end of history, since it is no longer teleological and now recycles itself — and the rest of history — in ironic variations and pastiches.

The kind of critique of postmodernism developed by Jameson persists in the form of the sometimes entirely justified rejection of 'relativist' or 'constructionist' postmodern social science approaches. Such ideological attacks on postmodernism focus not only on the charges of ethical and political irresponsibility raised by Jameson, but also on the supposed division between theory and practice in the social sciences — the idea that empirical verification is necessary to justify an epistemological method.

The same shift from realist to reflexive modes, as occurred in literature, can also be seen in the social sciences, although in a delayed and less thorough fashion. To rehearse very briefly the critical shift away from realist and empirical theories of reference, Saussure's theory held that there is no natural or necessary connection between objects in the world – referents – and the linguistic signs which refer to them and give them meaning. The idea that the connection between signs and meanings was a conventional one rather than a natural or necessary one had the profound epistemological consequence for the social sciences of inverting the hierarchical relationship between interpretation and its objects, thus prioritising interpretation. In other words, where interpretation in the empirical model was a transparent method of understanding phenomena in the world, it became in the postmodern conception an end in itself rather than a means.

A further influence in more recent times on such a concept of interpretation has been that of so-called 'chaos physics', derived from a range of post-classical physics hypotheses about the nature of space-time and the physical universe. Many of the concepts originated in such post-classical physics – such as four-dimensionality, the concept of temporal recursivity, and especially the Heisenberg Uncertainty Principle – have been adopted by humanities academies as a mode of cultural and aesthetic interpretation – and also as a means of gaining some form of institutional legitimacy for disciplines likely to be overlooked for university funding in favour of scientific research. Heisenberg's principle formulates the subatomic phenomenon that particles accelerate at different rates depending on where, in relation to the nucleus of the particle, they are observed. Unfortunately, this has been mostly mangled by its analogous interpretation in the humanities, to mean that meaning itself is partly dependent on who makes the interpretation, that the position of truth in epistemology is relative.

It has been said that the postmodern era started in 1972, the year when the first giant skyscraper was imploded in New York. Postmodernity represents a breaking up of the heroic projects of modernity: the rational individual, scientific progress, liberal democracy.

As a consequence, interpretive strategies began to develop which operated from the premise that cultures and their objects, products, and practices were all equally interpretable, or 'readable', on the model of the interpretation of texts, or, more generally, narratives. This perhaps goes some way towards explaining the privileged and influential position enjoyed by literary theory in the post-linguistic-turn social sciences.

The proliferation and dominance of interpretation also had other important methodological consequences. Generally speaking, in the post-1960s era of '**postmodernity**', it became possible to reconstrue the social sciences as a range of disciplinary enquiries into the 'constructedness' of culture. The notion that cultures are constructed by interest groups or forces within them, rather than being embodiments of natural forces or expressions of universal truths, emerges logically from the notion that it is possible to interpret cultural phenomena on the model of a text. Perhaps the most influential statement of this position comes from Lyotard's (1984) defence of

The Duchamp of South African Social Science? Neil Lightfoot (1997) published a series of photographs of car exhaust pipes in the South African Journal of Psychology.

postmodernism as an attack on the universalised and transcendental nature of truth claims inherent in the older realist or dialectical models of critique, models which Lyotard termed 'metanarratives'. To this end, Lyotard emphasised the connection between postmodernity and the avant-garde project of high modernity, the 'defamiliarisation' of the fantasy of realist representation in art and truth claims in philosophy. Among the avant garde, perhaps the best-known example of such 'defamiliarisation' is the famous case of Marcel Duchamp's urinal at an exhibition of modern art in Paris in the 1920s. Duchamp took a urinal from a public toilet, signed it, and placed it on exhibition at the gallery. The gesture both demystifies the 'aura' of the work of art and suggests that any object might be interpretable as having aesthetic value.

The constructionist approaches in the social sciences, which arose in the wake of the linguistic turn and the rise of postmodernist thinking, invested much in their ability to expose the self-interested truth claims of '**metanarrative**' approaches to history and culture. These include, perhaps most significantly, the metanarratives of history and post-enlightenment rationality themselves. A good example of this in the discourses of history would be the rewriting of South African history in school textbooks after the fall of the Nationalist apartheid government. The Nationalists had produced a written history which presented the very partial and ideologically loaded history of Afrikaner nationalism as the history of South Africa. More generally, the discourse of scientific rationality of the nineteenth century presented certain models of knowledge, those of the apparently empiricist natural and human sciences, as being the culmination and high point of knowledge and 'civilisation' themselves. This ideology lay behind the colonial project of nineteenth-century Western European cultures. The self-reflexive and critical epistemology of postmodernism was given added coherence by the contemporary interest in reinterpreting psychological subjectivity after Freudian psychoanalysis – an approach most influentially associated with Jacques Lacan, and dealt with in more detail in the next section – and the revision of Marxist ideological critique shaped by Louis Althusser.

The constructionist character of 'postmodernist' critique was methodologically strengthened by the still potent idea that all cultures and cultural phenomena are analysable through their 'discourses'. The idea of socio-cultural forces taking a discursive shape was most convincingly broached by Foucault, the philosopher who has perhaps been most co-opted by postmodernist thought, though he himself strongly denied the association.

Foucault's notions of the function of discourse, and what he called 'discursive networks', were outlined in the methodological work *The Archaeology of Knowledge* (1972). For Foucault, a discourse network was a nexus of the possibilities existing for a given culture at a given point in history to conceptualise and articulate its own existence – bearing in mind that such a conceptualisation and articulation was possible only in terms of the relations existing between power and knowledge at that time in that culture. A particular discourse would thus be one such articulation, of whatever form (not necessarily textual or narrative). Foucault analysed these discursive articulations as a series of 'genealogical' investigations, which took the form of analyses of the conditions under which certain arrangements of power and knowledge become manifest as epistemologies and institutions in socio-cultural reality.

Photo: Alex Butchart

A 'fan compound' in the shape of a panopticon, used to house South African mine workers.

The best-known and most influential of such analyses is the book *Discipline and Punish* (1977). The ostensible aim of the book is to demonstrate the shift in socio-political attitudes towards crime and punishment between premodernity and a modernity ushered in by the eighteenth century. In practice, the book is much more ambitious than this, for it analyses the shift from public punishment on the body of the offender in the premodern era to the psychologised self-regulation of the modern citizen, achieved through an astonishingly wide-ranging set of discursive means. These range from medico-legal documentation to new ways of organising time and utilising the body in the military and educational spheres.

This is expressed emblematically by the eighteenth-century plans of the British political economist Jeremy Bentham for a 'panopticon', a prison organised in such a way that the inmates would never know when they were being observed in their cells and would therefore impose normative behaviours on themselves for fear of observation and discovery. The influence of this epistemology, characteristic of what Foucault termed modernity rather than an alleged postmodernity, is still very much with us, as shown by plans to turn Johannesburg's Ponte City block of flats into a humanitarian, Benthamite panoptical prison. These plans would turn the block into a self-enclosed community, with ordered work regimes and plentiful recreational facilities, which the prisoners would be responsible for maintaining.

What is important to remember about Foucault's understanding of the knowledge/power relationship is that it is responsible for the production of the subjects and institutions which reproduce the effects of knowledge and power in a more or less willing and positive normative mode. In the example of the plans for turning Ponte City into a prison, it is crucial that such an institution is seen as humane and reformist rather than punitive, and that the prisoners take responsibility for their own conduct, as a basic prerequisite for their reintegration into society. We can thus see how discursive operations (the plans for a prison) both reflect and condition what is expected from the citizens of a society, in order for them to be properly integrated and normative.

Go to images.google. com and search for 'panopticon' to see some images of panoptical buildings.

The constructionist approach to the human and social sciences – derived from the epistemological impact of postmodernist thought, particularly the attack on universalist truth claims – has become by and large a contemporary orthodoxy. Although Foucault was at pains to draw a distinction between his genealogical method and constructionist ideological analyses, his genealogical work has often been associated with a constructionist analysis of culture which prizes a kind of epistemological relativism, as an attempt to expose the operation of ideology and standpoint in the construction of objects of knowledge and methods of analysis. An exemplary and influential instance of such relativised noninterventionist knowledge formation is the collection of essays on the process of constructing anthropological knowledge entitled *Writing Culture*, edited by Clifford and Marcus

(1986). A similar example from psychology is Shotter and Gergen's (1989) volume, *Texts of Identity*.

This relativist tendency within postmodernist epistemology has indeed been so influential that it has strongly inflected the development of entire intellectual currents within and across human and social science disciplines – for example, the privileging of the local, marginal, and dispossessed in the interdisciplines of cultural studies and postcolonial theory. The next two sections of this chapter will investigate some of these assumptions and how they are used as a way of reading culture.

The subject in postmodernity

We may identify two major influences on thinking about the subject in postmodern human and social science, best exemplified by some of the theoretical positions of Foucault and Jacques Lacan.

A useful corrective to the kind of reading of Lacan with which I take issue here is Malcolm Bowie's (1991) introductory volume, Lacan.

It is in the domestication of Lacan's revision of Freudian psychoanalysis by some versions of postmodernist thought that we may begin to see a divergence between the critical possibilities of postmodernism and the noncritical uses to which it has been put. In these versions, Lacan's work is reduced to a restatement of a fundamental Freudian proposition – that identification and desire cannot exist in the same place. The Lacanian subject is thus a split one, impelled by the desire to recover the original ego identification between child and mother.

Cultural studies and postcolonial theory – two important interdisciplines with a postmodern modus operandi within the human and social sciences – have both made much of the idea of a fundamentally split subject, erecting upon it the notion that much in contemporary history and culture is produced by the necessity for a person, group, nation, or culture to be put into a negative position of 'otherness' – a 'subaltern' position – vis-à-vis the subject, the latter usually being identified with a position of cultural power.

Dominant instances of such a subject–other dichotomy would be the sex and gender differences that concern feminism and queer theory, and the racial and cultural differences between the colonising West and its colonised others with which postcolonialism is concerned. In these cases, a psychological account of the structuring nature of the self–other dichotomy for the subject is given as the ground for a critical investigation of the 'problem of difference'. What ostensibly motivates such postmodern investigations is the obvious wish to react politically and ethically to a historical situation of the abuse of power and the flouting of human rights. Much commendable work has been done in elaborating a new approach to knowledge which takes cognisance of the situation of the 'other' and attempts to expose the sociocultural processes whereby the ideologically loaded dichotomy between hegemonic subject and dispossessed other is established.

However, there remains a problem in this approach for a postmodern epistemology that wishes to be critical. In elaborating this problem of the subject for much postmodern social science focusing on the issue of cultural difference, we must return once more to Foucault. Throughout Foucault's work there is a consistent refusal to distinguish between institutions and practices of knowledge formation and those of any other sort. Only in the instances of psychoanalysis and ethnology, in the book *The Order of Things* (1970), is a special case made for the particular kinds of knowledge emerging from these disciplines. This is because both of these disciplines have as their motivation the investigation of the subjective grounds of knowledge itself – that is, the limits of what can be known – since both psychoanalysis and ethnology are concerned with the very difference between culture and nature which constitutes our sense of subjectivity, our power relations, and our knowledge formations. Both disciplines, Foucault points out, consider it axiomatic that the subject cannot know itself either as a being driven by instinct or as a member of a particular culture, since this would involve the paradox of adopting a nonsubjective, or transcendental, position. Foucault then goes on to argue that culture in modernity has ignored the lesson these disciplines offer in favour of the illusion that both the subjective and the 'meta' position on culture can be known. Thus, psychoanalysis comes to be replaced by humanist psychologies, or the 'psy-industries', as Foucault witheringly called them, which foster this illusion of a recoverable and knowable subject – a subject which supposedly 'heals' its split condition. In the idea that psychoanalysis and ethnology might be taken as disciplines which investigate the limits of knowledge/power itself, Foucault makes it possible to employ a postmodern method for critiquing the conservative and normative uses to which the constructionist methodologies of postmodernism have themselves been put.

Foucault's early work, especially his doctoral thesis, published as *Madness and Civilisation*, concerned the constitution and institutionalisation of a distinction between the normal and the pathological, which continued to inform much of his later work. Ultimately, and this is what distances his work from the later postmodern theorists influenced by it, Foucault was concerned with the network of power and knowledge relations which produced the classificatory systems and institutional understandings of the subject that constitute culture in modernity, rather than with those systems and subjects as such. Of course, the strand of postmodern thought inaugurated by Foucault may be seen to have an ethical dimension (e.g., the types of subject which concern his work and that of later postcolonial or cultural studies theorists tend to be similar – the marginalised, fugitive, and subaltern), but certainly this ethics cannot be understood as a politically correct reconstitution of a particular type of subject.

The question must be asked: Is it possible then to produce a critique of the 'metanarrative' role of knowledge and power in modern (and postmodern) subject constitution without becoming representative

What kinds of subjectivities are created by the photographs included in this book? What other kinds of technologies of subject creation are deployed in the book, and what are their effects?

of a position within such a metanarrative? Ultimately, this question captures the chief methodological significance of postmodernism for the social sciences – i.e., it potentially provides a means of asking questions about the construction of knowledge and power, the forms they take and the role played by them in social phenomena, and ways in which those phenomena are understood.

Foucault would have answered the question in the affirmative, and his later work focused on the twin notions of a new conception of ethics and responsibility for and of the subject, and a new conception of the role of technology and life practices in modern subjectivity. Think for example of the DSM method of psychiatric classification, an apparently descriptive cornerstone of diagnosis that, nevertheless, participates in and helps to produce a particular arrangement of power and knowledge in modern science. In the next section we will examine the ways in which recent thinking about the relationship between power, knowledge, subjectivity, and technology has perhaps pushed postmodern social science into the role of sustained critique.

Technology, the body, and image politics

We have spoken of the interpretive imperative in postmodernism, the tendency to believe that all cultural objects and practices might be read on the model of a textual analysis. As the twentieth century has progressed, and the twenty-first century continued to fulfil and confirm its prognoses, the textual model of interpretation has moved away from textual objects (e.g., a documented medical discourse) to, it might be argued, the analysis of visual images. Culture has moved from a print base to an image base, in forms like television, video, and home computing.

Such a shift in the form of culture, which is basically a technological shift, was first coherently analysed by the leftist Frankfurt School of

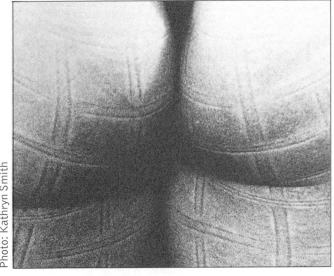

Photo: Kathryn Smith

social theorists, including Theodor Adorno and Max Horkheimer, in the early part of the twentieth century. Their critique of capitalist culture focused on the propensity of capital to produce culture as commodity and to render art a consumable product. They were most concerned about the collapse of the distinction between high and low culture, considering the massification of culture to be the final alienation of the proletariat from the potentially liberatory function of great art.

In the postmodern era, the critique of capitalism has been advanced with some success by postmodern theorists, and perhaps even more successfully by postmodern artists (since they are in a position to utilise the subversive potential of new visual technologies), specifically when connected to an analysis of the cultural impact of the great proliferation of image technologies in the last two decades.

The critique of capitalism mounted by many contemporary postmodern theorists and artists devolves on the relationship between the body and new technologies of culture, such as video and computer technology. It is no accident that the postmodern era has seen a spectacular renewal of aesthetic and theoretical interest in the body. The late twentieth century has seen a movement away from the modernist culture of industrial production, which laid emphasis on the subjection of the body to factory machines in the regimes of mass industrial labour, to the contemporary emphasis on technologies of leisure at the service of the consumer and tailored to their bodies and environments. What such a shift offers postmodernist theorists and artists is the opportunity to see the effects of the move from production to consumption in terms of its impact on the body in culture (subjectivity once more) and in terms of its global cultural impact.

Jameson, as we have seen, has argued that postmodernism was a theoretical justification for the globalisation of late capitalism. But this standpoint is not one that necessarily excludes the possibility of a postmodern critique. As we mentioned at the outset, postmodernism is often accused of first-world elitism and ethical and political irresponsibility with the suggestion that power, knowledge, and the constructedness of discourse are responsible for the postmodern subject, thus apparently removing the possibility of political intervention and human agency. This would seem to be the major upshot of Jameson's analysis. However, this denies the possibility of a political or ethical intervention based on purely epistemological or aesthetic grounds and rooted in a kind of postsituationist subversion of images and political and cultural discourse.

Jean Baudrillard, the French media philosopher who now spends much of his time in the USA, is usually caricatured as most representative of the irresponsibility of postmodern cultural analysis. Baudrillard began his career as an analyst of the philosophical conditions of political economy, but has subsequently become interested in the effects of the new media on human subjectivity. His position emerges as a kind of theoretical science fiction, whereby the world is headed out of postmodernism and into a 'posthuman' era of a culture dominated by self-regulating and perpetuating technologies. His most famous statement of the fragile position of the human being in postmodern culture comes in the 1983 book *Simulations*, in which he argues that no subject is unique, and that cultures are effects of the predominantly visual technologies that apparently serve them – a culture of what Baudrillard called 'hyperreality' and 'simulation'. The idea that a culture is simulated, a rerun version of its own elements

Some critics have argued that postmodernism was a theoretical justification for the globalisation of late capitalism.

and history, has since become quintessentially postmodern. Baudrillard has extended the idea that representations of bodies in culture are in fact more real than the bodies themselves, producing a notorious text called 'The Gulf War did not take place', in which he argued that entire political events need only have a media reality in order to have effects. The idea that representations replace real events is of course a polemical one, a form of ironic provocation and therefore of political activism, as we can see in the following quotation:

> Go and organise a fake hold-up. Be sure to check that your weapons are harmless, and take the most trustworthy hostage, so that no life is in danger (otherwise you risk committing an offence). Demand ransom, and arrange it so that the operation creates the greatest commotion possible – in brief, stay close to the 'truth', so as to test the reaction of the apparatus to a perfect simulation. But you won't succeed: the web of artificial signs will be inextricably mixed up with real elements (a police officer will really shoot on sight; a bank customer will faint and die of a heart attack; they will really turn the phoney ransom over to you). In brief, you will unwittingly find yourself immediately in the real, one of whose functions is precisely to devour every attempt at simulation, to reduce everything to some reality – that's exactly how the established order is, well before institutions and justice come into play. (Baudrillard, 1983, p. 39)

Box 24.2

Postmodernism and image politics
(Derek Hook, London School of Economics)

Given the characteristic crisis engendered by postmodernism – the emergence of a certain distrust and vigilance regarding the power of texts, discursive regimes, and the autocracy of the signifier – and a corresponding reaction which attempts to recuperate postmodern epistemologies to hegemonic norms, we can trace in recent years one field for a critical political strategy – that which falls under the rubric of a kind of 'image politics'. By this we mean the image understood. That is, the image in a state of (relative) critical grace, as Eco's 'image of the layman', as the form of representation that through its very 'democracy of access', through its massive proliferation and consumption, would seem to preclude the prospect of being owned by any secure and stable meaning. This should be the 'textual' site of choice for a postmodern activism. Such an image politics may take two possible routes:

1. A campaign of the mass distribution of obscenity, blasphemy, and abjection – the subjection of others, the leprous, the syphilitic, those afflicted with Aids, the seriously sexually aberrant, the dying, the debilitated, and geriatric to the liberty of prime-time-exposure

In contrast to Baudrillard's contested position, other postmodern social theorists have analysed the impact of technologies on bodies in culture in markedly different ways. Donna Haraway (1990), an American historian of science, has produced a seminal reading of the inevitability of human bodies interacting ever more intimately with technologies – medical, recreational, and labour – and how this 'cyborg identity' might provide a model for a more productive and engaged postmodern culture. The text is called 'A Manifesto for Cyborgs', and has been widely reprinted.

In Europe, a growing sociology of technology movement, led by sociologists Michel Gallon and Bruno Latour, has carefully applied Foucault's insights regarding discourse networks and human agency to an analysis of contemporary technologies of transport and labour organisation, and, in Latour's case, to the problem of historicisation for postmodernity.

These examples show differently inflected social engagements and politically responsible roles for the insights of postmodernism in theoretical and scientific fields. Outside of the academy, too, the human body as an actor in culture is being reclaimed by art in different and surprising ways, as a response of the abject, taboo, or transgressive body to the disciplinary and normative character of late capitalist culture.

The subversive possibilities of the postmodern use of images of bodies has been explored in both the fine art and mass media contexts

'What surfaces is the anxiety-producing erosion of the distinction between living and mechanical processes, their mutual absorption into the flows of information.'
(Seltzer, 1995, p. 136)

---

ad flightings, massive highway billboards, and glossy centre-spreads. The taking of multiple otherness to that private place, that zenith of representational reification – not to exercise any maleficent power upon the world, but to call attention to the increasingly homogenised and normalised structures of meaning required by hegemonic representational regimes and the extent to which this dominant media order exercises power upon the world. An imagery whose job is political displacement; perverse, subversive – not of people, morality, or minds, but of a particular scheme of image construction, a particular representational order.

2. An over-determination, a saturation of the number of narratives springing from a single representation – not only to re-enter old representational conventions with new objects (as is the case with pastiche) but also to proliferate by a kind of scattershot range of recontextualisations and critical reinventions the explanatory narratives of otherwise neglected or reviled icons. As, for instance, the three obese and drunken women porno 'actresses' of Lynch's *Wild at Heart* suddenly re-produced as the Three Graces.

Finally, the attempt to restore to images the power of possible resistance and possible meaning.

Want to create your own postmodern text? It's easy – visit the postmodern generator at www.elsewhere.org/cgi-bin/postmodern. Simply click on your browser's refresh button to create another text.

(e.g., the art of Damien Hirst or Cindy Sherman and the so-called 'indie cinema' and self-aware ethos of films such as *Being John Malkovich* and *Kill Bill*). This may represent both a politically aware comment on the role of media technologies in postmodern culture, and a celebration of the elements of human experience, which both Foucault (in *The Order of Things*) and Lyotard (in the 1988 collection of essays entitled *The Inhuman*) have referred to as 'the Unthought' – those unconscious, invisible 'knowledges' which perhaps define our sense of our own humanity. In South Africa, examples of the unsettling and taboo-breaking possibilities of postmodern image politics include the parliamentary controversy aroused in the late 1990s by the award-winning 'black ashtray vagina' sculpture of artist Kaolin Thompson, the radical homoerotic performance art of Steven Cohen, and some of the exhibition work of artists Marc Hipper and Terry Kurgan, which deals with child subjects and has attracted accusations of child pornography.

Conclusion

The end of the twentieth century and the beginning of the twenty-first has seen something of a backlash against the more extreme forms of postmodern constructionist critique, with calls for renewed attention in the social sciences to be paid to real socioeconomic and political conditions. This is true particularly in the Western academic context, where forms of constructionism have been the norm for the past thirty years. In a newly constituted and developing national context such as South Africa's, however, there may be a role for such theoretical constructions, particularly in providing a self-reflexive check on the ongoing relationship between theory and cultural practice, and in providing a space for the consideration of the effects of power and knowledge in the application of policy and in the lives of people.

In addition, this chapter has suggested some ways in which the tendency to relativise in postmodernism might be differently understood – that is, as representing the possibility of politically progressive critique. We have mentioned the examples of postmodernism reflecting on the operations of power and knowledge in the production of social structures and subjects, and the avant-gardist role that postmodernist images play in unsettling received ideas and re-evaluating social taboos and the limits of thought and experience.

Until such time that postmodernism ceases to play this critical role – that is, until it becomes entirely a constructionist orthodoxy within social science research methods and thought – we would do well to grasp the nettle of its sometimes utopian and even irresponsible – but always intriguing – example.

Exercises

1. Take a 'postmodern' text (such as this chapter) and have two groups of students each draw up a list: one of ways in which ideas in the text could be used to further conservative political agendas, and the other of how ideas in the text could be used for progressive purposes. Let each group present their list. Then discuss together the implicit or explicit definitions of conservatism and progressiveness used in drawing up the lists.

2. Create something in bad taste (such as a nasty story, a joke that pokes fun at something that's actually sad, or a sexually explicit sculpture or drawing). Hide your creation away for a week or so and then look at it again. Are you shocked?

3. Go to a social gathering (such as a party) and pretend to have a doctorate in philosophy. See if you get caught out.

4. Working together as a group, draw up an outline of a one-semester university course on 'image politics'. When you have finished this, discuss the group processes that occurred. Did people's class and gender positions appear to affect their willingness to participate in the task and the seriousness with which other group members took their contributions?

Key readings

Baudrillard, J. (1983). *Simulations*. New York: Semiotext(e).
This is a good introduction to Baudrillard's postmodernist approach to mass media.

Foucault, M. (1977). *Discipline and punish: The birth of the prison*. Harmondsworth: Penguin.
Foucault's most famous and accessible work in English, and a useful analysis of power and knowledge in modern society.

Haraway, D. (1990). A manifesto for cyborgs. In L. Nicholson (Ed.), *Feminism/ postmodernism*. London: Routledge.
Feminist historian of science Haraway argues for a politically aware response to the increasing role of technology in postmodern culture.

Lyotard, J-F. (1984). *The postmodern condition: A report on knowledge*. Manchester: Manchester University Press.
This is one of the first and most influential theorisations of postmodernism as a philosophy of culture to appear in English.

Postcolonial African methods and interpretation

Kopano Ratele

University of the Western Cape

Introduction

There are two main goals to this chapter and three minor objectives that elaborate the principal goals. The first main goal is to sketch the basic form of what could be called an hypothesis on ghosts in social science. The second is to deal with the question of researching 'others', looking at what and how it is possible to approach and interpret ghosts.

Who are the 'others', you might ask right away? In a way, 'others' are ghosts, but waking-day ones. More commonly, though, 'others' is a term that is employed in the **Hegelian** sense of that which contradicts the self. The full elaboration of this contradiction, negation, or differencing is found in a number of theoretical movements, including feminism, anti- and postcolonialist, and postmodernist work.

In this chapter, concepts such as African are used. Yet I must admit to a deep-seated prejudice myself, or at least a suspicion about its referents. Terms such as indigenous, black, community, and African, especially as adjectives, as in the seemingly transparent *African social science* or *indigenous methods*, at times obscure and mystify instead of clarifying what they seek to describe. For this reason, putting African before methods and interpretation is done with trepidation. It is true that an article that uses indigenous, black, community, or African in the way I am cautioning against does make me jittery. And where I am not immediately nervous, I remain sceptical. This chapter explains why – this being the first of three ancillary objectives.

Where black and African tend to come with massive baggage, in particular with an identity-ossifying project, the notion of postcolonial, even though contested too, can be used in ways that evade some of the dispiriting aspects of the other terms. **Postcolonial** is employed here to indicate the following two understandings: (1) a specifiable period, when former colonies won their freedom, and (2) a transdisciplinary form of thinking, a critical modality of engagement.

The second minor aim of the chapter is to show the evasions and pretension that characterise much human science research method and analysis. It may of course be said that researchers do not evade the questions their studies put before them, or that they do not pretend at all – that, given the constraints of resources and time, they will always be unable to respond to them fully. I argue, though, that what with the colonial past and its effect on how we look upon others, there has always been little chance that many of us could not pretend when confronted with questions posed by our objects of study. Pretension is indeed a key part of the moving spirit and effect of doing research in the way that most researchers are taught.

The final set of aims is to argue that there are abiding questions that social science researchers have generally refrained from asking about others – to ask a few of these questions, as well as to offer a particular approach to objects of study that are preceded by adjectives such as indigenous, black, community, or African. The chapter is structured in the following way. It will first look at the question of research

The nineteenth-century German philosopher, G.W.F. Hegel, saw ideas and history as progressing from thesis to antithesis and thence to a synthesis. This feature of Hegelian thinking – dialectics – impacted also on Marxist ideas of history and class consciousness (see chapter 23) and on postmodernist ideas of difference and alterity (see chapter 24).

The term 'postcolonial' can be used descriptively to refer to the period after former colonies achieved independence, but also to refer to a transdisciplinary, critical, theoretical stance.

questions. It then outlines three preparatory steps I see researchers needing to engage in if their intention is to approach 'others'. This is followed by an outline of an hypothesis on ghosts. Finally, the chapter sketches what I call a methodology to ghosts, or a methodology to 'others'.

Research questions
What are they and where do they come from?

In simple terms, a research question refers to the question that the study wants answered. It is the phenomenon investigated. It tends to be thought of as a question because it is often put in the form of a query. For example:

- What has been the impact and result of apartheid urban planning on natural resources?
- What is the role of the media in anti-Nigerian xenophobia in South Africa?
- How central is geographical location and class in girls' under-participation in mathematics?
- What are the prevailing discourses on social integration among Muslims in South Africa?

A research problem can also be put as a statement of relationship, of course. But the statement obviously implies a question to be answered or already answered:

- The relationship between stranger crime, household quality of life, and the use of methamphetamine ('tik').
- The perception and experiences of teacher and students of the abolition of corporal punishment in a rural school in Harding.
- Cape Town as a gay city and its relationship to the history of jazz.
- The relationship between drop-out rates of boys from school and birth order.
- The relationship between household size, income level, and recycling among residents in Mangaung.

It is usual to think of a research question as sourced from one of the following:

- Extant literature on the problem, including theoretical concerns about the problem – this is the main source from which postgraduate students are required to identify their questions.
- An exploratory investigation on what to study – this is where there is little previous research or a clearly undocumented aspect of social life, on, for instance, a subject such as the history and role of virgins as rainmakers among the Batswana.
- A needs analysis.
- Personal speculation and experience.

- Commissioned or contracted research, such as that which arises from a set of priorities of a body dedicated to fund research such as the National Research Foundation and the South Africa–Netherlands Programme for Alternatives in Development, or contracting companies with specific needs for certain types of information.

A good question

What is not immediately clear above is that not all research questions are good questions. What then is a good question? There are two answers to this question. The one answer is that a good research question must be one that can be answered. This condition for a good question has also been formulated as referring to the fact that what exists must be measurable. In this case, as usually happens, it is misleading to interpret measurability as referring only to putting a number on something, although this may be regarded as the best way to measure something (see chapter 7). Neither does measurability refer necessarily to experiments, clinical trials, surveys, and statistics.

Measurability

In fact, measurability incorporates any model or technology used to read human reality in the human sciences. Indeed, the interview, that form of it that might be referred to as the unstructured or phenomenological interview, has attained an almost consecrated place as the tool used to read human lives. It is employed in Oprah, Hard Talk, and inserts of experts during television and radio news, for features on Posh Spice, the poor, and Mandoza. It is employed to get a post-match description of the game by Ronaldinho, on SAFM's After 8 Debate, on Asikhulume, and by Noleen Maholwane-Sanqu. It is used for job interviews, in respect of the lives of fat housewives who lost 300 lbs, and to find out why 'cheaters' do it. That is to say, the non-standardised interview outstrips by far any other alternative mode in producing knowledge about others and the world.

Interviews are no longer the sole preserve of the social sciences. As a means to produce knowledge about others and the world, interviewing is an almost inescapable feature of contemporary culture.

In the sense that a research question must be a question that can be answered or measurable, therefore, the goodness of the research question is conditional on the robustness and level of development of methodological tools and techniques. In other words, a good question is one that is fit for the available methods of the discipline. But ultimately, to say that a good research question is one that can be answered is an unsatisfying answer.

Importance

The second answer is that a good research question should be important enough to investigate. This condition is elaborated here along the lines followed by Kalat (1996) in his textbook, *Introduction to Psychology*. Kalat tells the story of the development of the discipline of psychology. I shall cite the story at some length, as it illustrates fundamental elements about research questions as well as methods – besides other issues relevant to the aims of this chapter which will become clearer below

Box 25.1

An important question may not be a good start

The textbook is an object of endless fascination and horrors. Due to their place in education all over the world, one cannot avoid textbooks. One had to read them as a student. I now read them as a teacher and a potential 'prescriber'. I also read textbooks because they are one more site where imperial and colonial histories, cultures of disciplines, their subjects, methods, and other tools can and must be resisted and interrupted. Indeed, one writes in a textbook such as this one in order to rewrite the subject, history, and culture, including the culture that social sciences and their methodologies are.

I find those textbooks that come bearing the sign, 'for international students', immediately fascinating and horrifying – for international here stands for foreigners, strangers, others. However, textbooks do not have to be intended for 'other' students in order to engage in 'othering' their readers. It is hard in fact to find a department of psychology in South Africa (and I refer to psychology as the discipline I am trained in and train others in, but examples can be made of other social science disciplines) that does not use one or another textbook.

One hidden lesson from prescribing one or another North American or British textbook is that, on the whole, South African psychology departments are still learners (in contradistinction to North American or British departments who see themselves as teachers) of what psychology is. It also suggests that non-adjectivalised (without adjectives such as 'International' or 'South African') and thus real psychology is that made in the West. Postcolonial theory articulates this as a problem of the periphery to the centre, or, in Stuart Hall's formulation, the West and the rest.

At the University of the Western Cape, as one example, students are in effect introduced to their 'psyches' by way of Boston, the United States of America: Three of the four first-year modules, 'Introduction to psychology', 'Introduction to research methods', and 'Brain and behaviour', prescribe and use only *Fundamentals of Psychology: The Brain, the Person, the World* by Kosslyn and Rosenberg (2005). Both writers are teachers in universities in the United States of America, one of them at the university ranked in the latest rankings as the best in the world. Rather than belabouring it, let me make my criticism of *Fundamentals of Psychology* brashly: I suspect both teachers will need lots of help to make any sense of Ricky's person and world.

Ricky was a marketing manager in an international company when I approached him to be part of an investigation intended to find out what meanings males like Ricky attach to the self and their world as gendered African subjects. In its approach, the study was explicit in evading interpretations that tend forcefully to fit the experiences of African male subjects into pre-existing frameworks, but without overlooking theoretical resources that might be helpful in fully 'getting' a situation like Ricky's. In other words, by letting Ricky tell it in his own way, investigators are enabled to evade the trap of measuring what the participants are up against in a world that is supposed to pre-exist them. Participants in such a case are able to show more easily how they feel, think, and live, to give their perception of the world and of themselves from where they are, in their language. However, this study on the social psychology of men and masculinities never let up in critically examining what the subjects said – did not skirt the sensitive area, whether it is supposed to be decreed by tradition, custom, or practical exigencies. That is to say, approaching the subjects with critical empathy was urged by the need to guard against xenophobic, sexist, uncritical attitudes even while we seek to recapture the truth of postcolonial existence. In attempting to understand men as *males*, the methodological and analytical tools were thus levelled at showing up practices that are constructed as 'real' in opposition to some other 'unreal' ones, and, in this, challenging the domination of one group over another and an oppressive masculinity.

At this juncture, though, all I am wondering is whether Kosslyn and Rosenberg would manage *on their own* to say much about the fundamental makeup of this manager's hybrid, street-language articulated brain, person, and world: 'Amabra amadala, hei baba,' Ricky said at one point during the interview, 'they rough you up, they send you anywhere. So, you got no control eloksion. It was even worse ke mina ekhaya, because enext door yasekhaya kwa kuyispoti, itavern. It was one of the hottest taverns zaseMlazi'. (Extract taken from an interview with a male subject, Ricky, then 28, born in Umlazi, and living and working in Cape Town after completing a degree at the University of Cape Town. See Ratele, 2001.)

My money is on 'no, they won't'. What they would need is a good research partner or assistant who knows how to understand such street talk. On the other hand, as anyone knows who has enjoyed an English DVD movie bought on a street in China or Malaysia, the subtitling is another drama on its own. But, at other times, even where navigating between two languages is fairly ordinary, subtitles can still do a disservice to many viewers. Consider for instance a television series such as *Zone 14*. Because the subtitles often miss the play, rhythm, idiom, and figures of speech of the language, I venture that listeners other than those young urban-based males in the case of *Zone 14* do not appreciate the full range of discourses, and indeed psyches and world, being portrayed. This is principally because translation is not a side issue, but needs long training and deep expertise on its own. Hence, I suspect that authors like Kosslyn and Rosenberg can *only* pretend that a psyche is a psyche is a psyche, and, of course, from their textbook they have little to say to colonial power.

(such as the idea of 'blind alleys'). 'Throughout the discussions of the early history of psychology', Kalat writes,

> I have shown that many psychologists went down some blind alleys, devoting enormous efforts to projects that produced disappointing results ... Still, if psychologists of the past have spent countless person-years on fashionable projects, only to decide later that those efforts were misguided, how do we know that some psychologists are on the wrong track right now?
>
> Well, we don't. Thousands of psychologists are doing various kinds of research, and chances are, some of them are working on projects that will never accomplish much ... Maybe some psychologists' questions are not so simple – or their answers not so solid – as they seem; perhaps you can think of a better way to approach certain topics.
>
> In short, psychologists do not have all the answers. But that is not a cause for despair. Much like the rats in the mazes, psychologists make progress by trial and error. They pose a question, try a particular research method, and find out what happens. Sometimes the results turn out to be fascinating and rich in practical consequences. Sometimes they turn out to be puzzling or inconclusive. If one study after another proves to be disappointing, psychologists either look for a new method or change the questions. By abandoning enough unsuccessful approaches, they eventually find their way to better questions and better answers. (Kalat, 1996, p. 28)

In these paragraphs, James Kalat actually ends up not simply answering the question 'What is a good research question?' but the more fundamental question of 'What is psychology?' That this response about the nature of psychology comes in answer to the question of what is a good research question alerts us to the entwinement of subjects and their tools, disciplines, and method – of what we know and how we get to know what we know. Little need be said about the notions of cumulative knowledge and scientific progress in psychology contained in this story. It is all too easy to see through these notions: The idea of a coherent science and the related plug for scientific progress in social sciences has been thoroughly challenged, although Kalat does at least concede that 'we cannot promise that we are not going down some blind alleys, like many psychologists before us'.

Anyhow, Kalat will also pose the question before us, giving it a fine historical context: What might a good question for a young scholar in a young discipline like psychology (in 1880) have been? One of the answers offered is of course that 'a good research question is both important and answerable.' Kalat then goes on to trace the changing questions and dominant answers that have characterised the discipline over the ages. It would be disingenuous to say I really expected a satisfactory answer to the question of what to study, once and for all. However, the response offered is not merely unhelpful, it indulges in the sort of cons and shirking games that students get schooled into at the beginning of their studies in the human sciences (and of course in the wider culture) that only the greatest unlearning efforts will rid them of.

Banished questions

Contrary to the belief of Kalat and others that disciplines progress by backing out of blind alleys to pursue more fruitful avenues of enquiry, blind alleys are exactly where we must go to learn about the expelled of social science. It is to dark alleys that researchers informed by postcolonial critique go to find that which is human yet banished or forgotten from disciplined inquiry by colonialists.

Critical postcolonial African methodology and interpretive work indeed requires that a researcher takes on, for instance, Native Yard 1 in Gugulethu or in Kgabalatsane as part of his or her project. The point is that learning the language of, living with, eating with, sharing with, and in general relating with 'others' in as unaffected a manner as possible, using methods and analytic resources informed by postcolonial critique, is by far the best way to get to the reality of 'others'.

Critical postcolonial scholarship seeks to illuminate lives and realities that have been 'expelled' from mainstream social science – rendered silent, not worthy of study, or described in terms foreign to their own experiences and conditions.

The context of answering a question with a nod

At the end of that long quote above, we have very little. What is an important and answerable research question indeed? Is an important question an important question to all – all researchers, all research students, or all research in sociology, or to all researchers in developmental psychology, or to all researchers in developmental psychology who work in universities in the Western Cape Province? Would the Clarks (Clark & Clark, 1947), the African American psychological researchers who did the society-shifting racial identification and preference studies, agree that what Kalat (1996) thinks is an important question is indeed a question of any importance?

I doubt whether there is one question in all of these that can be answered in the affirmative. One might have hoped that, at least, Kalat would have given us some idea about what the majority of North American researchers believe is an important and answerable research question. Actually, he may have – it is simply what many mainstream social scientists in the United States of America would say is important. In that case, we are forced to – and it is long overdue that we must – think about what *we* on this continent might regard as important and answerable research questions.

Surely what we are likely to perceive as a good question cannot be extricated from its context. This includes not only the disciplinary context but, vitally, the broader social context in which the research question, the methodological lenses, and social science disciplines more generally are nested. Such a context is one where nodding, or deceiving the researcher, or loud laughter, or different ways of greeting, and the questions asked about them are seen as acts which emerge out of a field of power – a field of power that is itself made of disciplines.

Box 25.2

A religious-like conversion

Saul Zuratas was ugly, likable, and entered San Marco University as a law student to please his father, Don Salomon Zuratas. Because of a dark birthmark, the colour of wine dregs, that covered the right side of his face, people called him Mascarita. Having saved up some money from his grocery store, Don Salomon wanted the family to make its mark though his son — saw him in, say, the diplomatic corps. Making his mark as a lawyer did not appeal to Saul, though. At first he was not sure what interested him, but sometime around General Odria's dictatorship over Peruvians and the return to democratic rule, Mascarita discovers, not suddenly or with the conviction that would come later, but 'the extraordinary machinery had already been set in motion and little by little was pushing him one day here, another there, outlining the maze he eventually would enter, never to leave again' (Llosa, 1987, p. 12). By then, in his third year, he had added ethnology to his law studies, had visited Quillabamba in the Amazon, and with even a little break at University he would head to the jungle. 'Was that ardent fellow feeling, sprung from the darkest depths of his personality, already burning within him for those compatriots of ours who from time immemorial had lived there, harassed and grievously harmed, between the wide, slow rivers, dressed in loincloths and marked with tattoos, worshipping the spirits of trees, snakes, clouds, and lightning? Yes, all that had already begun' (pp.12–13). He already knew a great deal about the Machiguengas, of whom it had been written that

To be sure, this field of power where disciplines develop and are practiced is made up also of other social facts or actors: the larger education system and its programmes, government policies and laws, industry, and churches, for a start. In other words, there is nowhere in the world where a nod, a white lie, a laugh, and a handshake is not already imbricated in the interpretative background, where each of these actions is not already informed by power.

In search of a good question: Into the alley of ghosts

The fact is there are very many blind alleys in the history of the social sciences. The fact is that there have been many research questions in the social sciences that have been perfect for nobody else but researchers and, in truth, have been very bad for those the researchers made conclusions about.

There are one or two questions researchers have not dared ask and a few affidavits missing from the archive of social science research conclusions. Some alleys are not only blind but appear to be regarded as dangerously dark. Very few are darker than the social science researcher's view of Africa and its peoples. Therefore, what needs they were savages, childish, and believed in sorcery. However, the feeling for the gods, customs, love of stories, and myths of the tribe aroused in him the respect and admiration that others reserve for Marx, Weber, Fanon, Diop, Foucault and Freud. While he still read Kafka's *Metamorphosis*, which he knew almost by heart, all his reading was in anthropology. What Saul was experiencing was a conversion, beyond the cultural sense to a religious one. You could say '"he was touched by grace"... From his first contact with the Amazon jungle Mascarita was caught in a spiritual trap that made a different person of him. Not just because he lost all interest in law and began working for a degree in ethnology, or because of the new direction his reading took, leaving precisely one surviving literary character, Gregor Samsa, but because from that moment on he began to be preoccupied, obsessed, by two concerns which in the years to come would be his only subjects of conversation: the plight of the Amazonian cultures and the death throes of the forests that sheltered them' (p. 20). Mascarita never finished his doctorate. What happened was that he went beyond intellectual curiosity, beyond studying the Machiguenga, learning their language, history, and way of life, to finding a justification for life: he became a storyteller. 'Talking the way a storyteller talks means being able to feel alive in the very heart of that culture, means having penetrated its essence, reached the marrow of its history and mythology, given body to its taboos, images, ancestral desires, and terrors' (p. 244). (Adapted from Mario Varga Llosa, 1987, *The storyteller*, London: Faber and Faber)

doing is to walk into some of these dark alleys, if you will. This is what I shall do more of now.

I will do two other things too: The second is in the form of a question. The first is to elaborate on the method and hypothesis of studying ghosts. I suspect that this is a preferable method to those which human scientists have learned to use in their studies, and I believe it is one which 'others' would use to study themselves.

An hypothesis on ghosts

A meta-hypothesis of others tells us that, in researching human subjects, especially if parts of their lives are in the dark, especially if the subjects are like ghosts, one must begin with intricate lived cultural politics.

To begin with the complex lived **cultural politics** of postcolonial existence is to reject many of the formalistic pre-existing questions or frameworks about their reality. It is when one begins with lived cultural politics that a researcher soon finds what can be regarded as a good research problematic. Naturally, we cannot but do away with pre-existing questions and interpretive frames because of those deep prejudicial suppositions that characterise the very questions and frameworks used to study subjects who believe in wrong types of ghosts.

The psychoanalytic notion of 'repression' can be used to talk about the way certain topics are rendered invisible, through various forms of systematic exclusion, by the social sciences.

What am I talking of? Of what is expelled from the culture and mind of social science? In the language of psychoanalysis, what is repressed? Let me use an example to illustrate. I have used different examples elsewhere, but the argument stays. And it runs along these lines: There are males and females in this country who, when asked why they dropped out of university or never have success in their relationships, might attribute it to evil magic cast by an envious neighbour. These people will also relate their good achievements, getting the boss's vote for promotion at work, to good magic, say a fortifying potion given to them by a *ngaka* (medicine man or woman) or something revealed by a *sangoma* (diviner).

I put this last onto-epistemological theory alongside two others. First, many people around the world and in this country will maintain without hesitation that some of the things they are and do, their loves or failures in relationships, their achievements at work, were caused by God or Allah. These two theories of reality and the world are well known, referred to respectively as Christianity and Islam.

Second, consider the position put forward by Sigmund Freud and his colleagues and students. While there are many people in this country and on this continent who will attribute their fear to come out as homosexual or to stay in the closet to unconscious processes, the number is miniscule compared to those in the last two categories of believers. Indeed, the people who believe in the invisible essence of the unconscious tend to be for the most part from a certain class, usually with a higher education.

In the classes I teach, and in professional circles, the latter two explanations, that which the majority of people around the continent and elsewhere in the world use, the theory of God or Allah, and that which might be found when talking to a certain class of people, find no resistance and are easily accepted. They are often articulated in public and without any shame whatsoever. God, someone might say, did not make males to have sex with other males because it is not natural.

In the classes I teach, the first set of explanations does not fly, not in the class. It largely stays underground, as it were. It stays hidden, because to bear a gay son and to believe that your success is because of such invisible causes as something that a sangoma said or something a ngaka did, to actually speak in this manner, makes you suspect, weird.

Why is this so? Because it is indigenous, African, black, or cultural. The problem is, it is indigenous, African, black, and cultural in a bad way. All these terms – indigenous, African, black, and cultural – in this instance are not very well-veiled codes for primitive. This is the first reason they have to be avoided. This is what could make a person prejudiced, or nervous, critical against these adjectives.

An important and complicating matter which needs to be kept in mind when regarding the hypothesis of ghosts people live by is this: A person who speaks about a ngaka as responsible for her fortune may be the same person who speaks of God and may at other times speak of her unconscious as having led her to omit doing something. This simultaneity, or **in-betweenity** (Bulhan, 1980) arises out of the violent meeting of African and European methods and interpretive repertoires, from different theories of life or cultures.

To give it its proper name, then, the reason you find individuals who can hold divergent and at times aggressively opposed theories about causality is the fact that they are part of cultures that have been colonised and have come out from under colonialism.

The reason you find a man who can believe in a God of the Bible and Gods who lived in the same yard, is that there are parts of their lives that need to be kept separate from each other, some in the light and others in the dark. Now what is in the light may sometimes be moved to the dark, and what is in the dark at other times is given light and air, the different parts in a moving, changing relationship.

The reason you find a woman who works with *The Interpretation of Dreams* (Freud, 1901/2001) for her Master's dissertation but holds that her grandfather visited her in her dreams and said she has to *thwasa* (become a sangoma) implies she has a difficult time of it trying to reconcile such two opposed understandings of dreams.

All of this means that, for certain women and men, the need to deal with the psychic and social residues of the systematic disrespect for the way in which their root cultures view phenomena and people is one of the first and most difficult arenas they have to make sense of when they encounter what they read, what they research, with their sense of the world.

And so this is the ultimate reason why indigenous, African, black, or cultural cannot be evaded. This is why a good researcher in the postcolony is one who has unlearned her or his prejudices, dealt with her or his nervous condition, yet remains critical about these adjectives.

Reading ghosts: A methodology to others
The first three preparatory steps

1. A postcolonial approach to a nod
The fact that a nod to the interviewer's question has a past, a culture, politics, and psychology has been noted. To be clearer: a nod, as a 'cha' when a 'yes' seems the patently obvious answer to a questionnaire item, as the loud laugh at the beginning of a focus group, and a desire to do the three-fold handshake at the end of the interview, each of these has a place, a time, a value, and a trajectory.

A 'cha' is part of a specific context – a geographic and symbolic place, a time, a culture. It can only be fully apprehended if the context itself is studied. This idea of context is something that anyone with more than a passing mercenary interest in the study of what is African now cannot fail to miss. In talking of doing discourse and constructionist analyses, Terre Blanche, Durrheim, and Kelly (chapter

Under colonial and postcolonial conditions, people often find themselves living in and in-between two or more cultures, languages, idioms, and identities at the same time; straddling dominant as well as dominated ones. Postcolonial theory studies both the problems and possibilities of such positions.

Tsitsi Dangaremba's 1988 novel, Nervous Conditions, is a classic of postcolonial African literature. It was the first novel by a female Zimbabwean author to be published in English. The title was borrowed from an introduction to Fanon by Jean-Paul Sartre, and refers to the psychosomatic effects of colonial domination on individuals.

14 in this book) avow the necessity to 'explicate the broader context within which a text operates', indicating at once that this is not as easy as it may seem at first blush. Approaching our objects informed by African postcolonial thought, we get assisted in understanding how to understand lived cultural politics of what is regarded as African now (e.g., Ashcroft, Griffiths, & Tiffin, 1995; Fanon, 1968, 1970; Hook, 2004), including how to interpret a 'cha', nod, and handshake.

With a postcolonial approach, we therefore take up radical understanding of such things as nodding, shaking hands, answering 'yebo' or 'no', an approach that interrupts the colonial history which infects how these acts are misread in the human sciences.

None of the acts, indeed, with their cultural, political, and economic history, have received any reading whatsoever in the methods and analysis sections of published studies that speak about African subjects. Hence, only when methodology and analysis sections in theses and journal articles cease pretending to tell us anything of worth about how to study will we get to the beginning, will we start to listen.

This is the first act a researcher would do then: physically and psychically immerse oneself in the others' culture, supplemented by reading on how to read like a dominated or formerly subject person.

2. Showing up the firm handshake

It is of course possible to speak about being dominated, for example about Africa in relation to the West, without saying, 'there, this place is called Nobody; they shake hands like this' (see Ratele, 2005). This, in fact, is usually unnecessary. It is only in those moments when one way of greeting, for instance, or one way of telling a story, or one way of saying no, is confronted with another way of greeting – especially when misunderstanding occurs – that the temporal, cultural, or geographic coordinates of the terms of encountering each other are articulated. Only then, when a boy remains mute or says 'cha' when it is clear that the answer is 'yebo' – 'yes' – that another might explain that in some places a boy is not encouraged to contradict his elders.

Yet even then (where the time, place, and codes of the terms of reference when 'two others' meet are spelled out), those whose terms rule the way in which those who find it necessary to mention that in their culture boys cannot say adults lie, never find it necessary to name their acts. For the rulers, who may include researchers, a 'no' tends to be taken as a definite no (which may tell us something about rulers' lack of sense of irony), just as a handshake is a firm handshake, and that's how you say no or shake hands.

The second step one should take then is to show up a firm handshake. One must show that a handshake is part of the context with a method into and an interpretation of the world, as well as reveal what it hides and what its effects are. One way to show up a firm handshake, as camp culture does, is to meet it with a limp wrist, to offer one's queenly wrist to be kissed.

That does not mean the three-point gentle handshake is better. There are questions that one has for the three-point gentle hand-shakers too. Also, when the answers received are not satisfactory, we have to encourage losing this form of greeting.

3. A manifold refusal

Postcoloniality is a revolt, a search for independence. Of course, this has been clear since African countries, from Ghana to South Africa, moved against their colonisers, settlers, and dominators, against their laws, politics, and cultures.

Even in the early years of the anti-colonial struggles, around and even before the first country got its independence, critical thinkers have argued that a vague African unity will not wash. They have been proven right over and over again: in the form of one military dictator after another in Nigeria, in ethnic genocide in Rwanda, in a pseudo but still brutal tyranny in Zimbabwe and ex-Bophuthatswana, in the rule of graft in many places. These cases show that it is not such a bad idea to refuse to shake hands at all, whether once or three times.

However, why would anyone turn against their culture? Individuals need culture – that much is clear. Individuals need others as much as they need sex, and maybe even as much as to satisfy hunger. If this is the case, turning against culture would be tantamount to committing a kind of suicide.

Breaking rank is a quality that characterises some but still way too few social scientific investigators' work today. Be ready to say no, many times over, to power.

Notwithstanding this, supposing a person wished to do so, what are the options available without rendering himself culturally dead? One option is to go on what amounts to a discursive hunger strike. By this it is meant to refuse to be coopted. For example, when one witnesses a man verbally abusing or pulling a gun on a woman, whether of the culture or of another, one must break rank. Breaking rank is not a quality that many social researchers used to display when white folks had black people under their thumb. Breaking rank is a quality that characterises some but still way too few social scientific investigators' work today. This is the third step then: be ready to say no, many times over, to power.

Identification

From the other chapters in this volume, and from the sketch on the hypothesis on ghosts, we know that there are a variety of ways to understanding whatever it is we seek to understand. Some of these ways may bring us more quickly to where we wish to be, and it has nothing to do with a good or bad question. Quickness to the goal, which obviously harks back to answerability, often may be seen as a good reason to follow them.

Other ways might take us a little while. Some ways require that we use many subjects, and others require only a few. From one way, we get answers to questions such as 'how many'. From another way, we learn about what this or that other thing means. Let us also call these ways techniques and methods of research. In the language game of research these are discrete bits in the logic of the operation of research.

Box 25.3

Making practicable methodological and analytical refusal

One of the things which may not be an explicit objective of this chapter, but which is as vital as the ostensible aims, a basic goal of postcolonial methodological and analytic interventions, is disruption, insurgency, the development of critique of all forms of colonisation. This manifold 'no' that man says is, to use Frantz Fanon (1955), a refusal at once theoretical and practical. This refusal, however, ultimately means being, in a democratic nation, the equivalent of what Albert Memmi (1965) in respect to the colonial situation proper, might have called the coloniser who goes all the way in his refusal. What Memmi was saying was that 'there are so few of those colonisers, even of extreme good will, who seriously consider following this path [to becoming turncoats], that the actual problem is rather theoretical' (p. 22).

In order to get beyond only talking postcolonial shop, the refusal must be made practicable. The practicalisation of insurgency has five acts:

The first act is concerned with culture, here used to indicate those implicit technologies of doing or being. What must be refused are the ruling traditional cultures:

- the traditional culture of data gathering,
- the traditional culture of analysis, and
- the traditional culture in which we live.

Act two is the rejection of the culture that tends to be stealthily and at other times forcefully passed on in social science methodology classes and consequently what undergirds social scientific knowledge generally.

A third act is to refuse to be part of uncritical African theory, methods, and analysis.

Fourth is to quit pretending that existing research methodological and analytical frameworks tell us anything about African people worth knowing.

The last act is about refusing, if one is part of dissenting scholarly voices, to lie down and die quietly.

The idea around this implicit objective of the chapter is therefore to challenge and undermine what are regarded as important lessons about knowledge and knowledge creation. In another sense, I wanted to show an other method, a method of approaching others, to cultivate a healthy sense of disrespect for what certain central views we as teachers, thinkers, and writers of methods hold.

Among these varieties of ways, or methods, tools, and techniques of data gathering and analysis, there is one purpose though: to get to know the chosen object. In the human sciences, this object is a human being. Given the nature of our historical and social reality, scientists are, to a large extent, of one race, class, and sex, and those they study are more often than not of another race and class. In considering our methods and our tools, this must be borne in mind. But this identification affects the entire research logic, from the statement of the problem through research design to conclusions drawn.

There is another less obvious similarity between divergent ways of getting to knowledge. There is to be found in both quantitative and qualitative research a certain mode of knowing and of dissemination that is an element of or concomitant to structures, institutions, and relations of inequality. This is a form of knowing and knowledge that refuses others their ordinariness. That is to say, it is an approach to and reading of others which, at its core, can never allow them an own consciousness, but insists on modes of knowledge and analyses that turn others into ghosts, refusing them that strange ordinariness which the self takes for granted.

So what do postcolonial methodologies do differently? They try to show that such traditionalist approaches to, and analysing of, lives of 'others' and their relations are an antecedent of, and at the same time perpetuate, the colonial and apartheid relations of domination and subjection, this time played out between investigator and investigated. Postcolonial-minded researchers understand that there is contained in such colonially-minded approaches to knowledge, though they may look dissimilar (for example, qualitative versus quantitative) a far more important commonality: an assumption about the place of the researcher in relation to what she or he is studying, in other words, an assumption about power. At the most basic, but not unimportant, level the assumption is in how the researcher looks at the object of study, and how he is never looked at. When he remembers to look at himself, it is called **reflexivity**. Even here though, it is the researcher who is looking at himself, it is not those he is studying looking at him.

Ultimately then, what postcolonial thinking brings to our methods with regard to 'others' concerns the issue of how to understand ghost knowledge. It is to think on the possibility and productivity of finding *different* techniques, languages, and frames, to understand 'an *other* life' as well as to develop research relations which might bring researchers to this other life in a less alienating manner.

Both quantitative and qualitative approaches assume modes of knowing that reproduce structures, institutions, and relations of inequality. This form of knowing and knowledge refuses others their ordinariness.

Postcolonial methodologies show how traditionalist analyses of lives of 'others' may perpetuate colonial and apartheid relations of domination and subjection, now played out between investigator and investigated.

Conclusion about 'an other life'

The methodological work and analytics that have been argued for here are those that make it difficult to evade the fact that, even while one observes others, one cannot escape the fact that these others are observing one right back. Social scientists are very unsteady and all too often belligerent when this is brought to their attention. Not many orthodox researchers are comfortable when shown the routes, meanings, and effects of their power as social scientists on the lives of those they study. Let me make this point once again as a way of ending.

Research in the human sciences ought to focus on what, for a lack of the words, I have elsewhere called, in the words of the French philosopher and novelist and only writer to reject the Nobel Prize, Jean-Paul Sartre, 'an other life'. More radically, researchers have to move to showing how others' lives are no more 'other' than the life of the self, no more strange than the life taken as 'normal'. 'An other life' is in fact what research in the human sciences is always concerned with. It is just that researchers do not wish to face up to the hard question of admitting what they do, and how they have to justify their conclusions. The trouble is, objects of the research of psychologists and anthropologists and sociologists are people. This is a simple but crucial point to take in. People have lives – maybe I need to say that. Much of people's lives they will not bring to the research encounter. People will look at us as we look at them. By other life, I thus wish to indicate the surplus meanings and secreted experiences of the subjects of the studies we undertake in the human sciences. There are immense and unused possibilities of good, socially worthy, and applicable work if this is admitted. We have to aim at clearing the overgrown paths and figuring the possible hidden existences of the subjects of studies we undertake, and particularly of these lives' relations to the cultural and racial economies of the past and to freedom. In this way, we are enabled to face up to the violence that is contained in studies that social scientists have conducted on African subjects for a long time.

In this chapter, 'an other life' refers to the surplus meanings and secreted experiences of subjects in the studies we undertake in the human sciences.

In addition to the aim of pointing out the evasions and wilful neglect in social and psychological research, a second purpose here has been to indicate a way to finding and understanding other lives underneath the public ones when studying African subjects. Both these aims, I have said, are based on the understanding that fudging and carelessness are not outliers in the enterprise of the social sciences. Evasions and neglect to take adequate care for those seen as not of one's group (whether the group the researcher identifies with at the moment of formulating his problem, selecting his sample, administering his instruments, analysing his data, and writing his study is that of scientists, researchers, white persons, or males) are not chance occurrences. They are in fact an integral part of systematic disrespect if not systematic abuse. The idea of abuse is derived from the conception of violence offered by, among others, the Martinican postcolonial psychiatrist Frantz Fanon and the Somali-born psychologist Hussein Bulhan. Abuse does not refer only to the presence of physical violence, but to any condition or act that supports the inhibition of optimal relations or communication between a person and others. This inhibition leads to psychological and social underdevelopment.

Abuse refers to any condition or act that supports the inhibition of optimal relations or communication between a person and others. This inhibition leads to psychological and social underdevelopment.

If social researchers disrespect, fudge, or neglect to take care in their interpretations, problem formulation, participant selection, procedures, and administration of method, and continue with their research business as usual, there will continue to be a violation against others under the pretext of social science. If there is a moment when objectivity in human sciences is not characterised by a lack of respect for the object of study, it takes a great deal of training, for a defining element in objectification is de-identification, and the latter usually is characterised by antipathy. Hence, researchers have to learn disrespect.

Exercises

1. Certain social science disciplines or subdisciplines continue to privilege a hypothetico-deductive model (as opposed to inductive models), quantifiable measures (rather than textual), and statistics (over discursive analysis) in their research practices. It is possible to make a case (and base it on a body of supportive literature) that these disciplines or subdisciplines will gain from using the tools of ethnography.

    (a) If you agree that there is such a case to be made for the social science discipline or subdiscipline in which you work, what would the gains be? What are the limitations of the hypothetico-deductive model, quantification, and statistics, and how can these limitations be addressed by adopting ethnography?

    (b) If you think that there is not much to be gained from adopting an ethnographic approach in the social science discipline or subdiscipline in which you work, offer supporting reasons for the continued privileging of the hypothetico-deductive model, quantification, and statistics in your disciplines.

    [To execute this task, you may want to consult the chapters in this book as well as published studies on ethnography.]

2. Some research studies demand a nonanthropological researcher to live among his or her subjects for extended periods, learn their language, and adapt to their ways of life. Using HIV/Aids as an example, formulate a study that would demand the researcher to live among HIV-positive 'others' for extended periods, stating a physical place in South Africa where such a study might be necessary, the rationale of the investigation, a research question, and the aim of such a study. Consult at least three kinds of material: studies on HIV/Aids prevalence and incidence rates using representative sample, Census data, and a map of South Africa.

3. Much of postcolonial critique is concerned with the politics of representation – how 'others' are represented (in research, literature, art, popular culture) or how, through the circulation of ideas and images, some people are made into 'others', usually meaning that they are distorted, marginalised, rendered into 'ghosts'. Break up into small groups and discuss the following: In what ways have you been subjected to such 'othering' processes, or, in what ways has such a process determined your perception of other South Africans or Africans? In which institutions or social

contexts did you feel 'othered'? How was or is this 'othering' supported by ideas and images circulated in the media, in literature, or in the social science research? How can such ideas and images be disrupted?

4. Discuss the following question in small groups: Is it possible for a white researcher to study black people, and for a male researcher to study women? Why do you think some people answer 'no' to the above? If you believe the answer should be 'yes', how would you motivate it?

Key readings

Fanon, F. (1967). *Black Skin, White Masks*. New York: Grove.

Fanon, F. (1965). *The Wretched of the Earth*. New York: Grove.
Together with Albert Memmi, Frantz Fanon was one of the earliest and most prominent contributors to postcolonial studies. In these two classic texts, he offers an uncompromising analysis of race and subjectivity in colonial and postcolonial contexts.

Glossary

Ability assessment The assessment of intellectual, physical, or artistic abilities.

Accountability The responsibility between parties, e.g., of those receiving resources to account for the uses to which these have been put.

Action research Research involving intervention in the functioning of the real world, and close examination of the effects of this action.

Anonymity Research which is anonymous does not record the identifying details of the participant on any research records. The participant is thus not identifiable or traceable after the research.

Applied research Research to solve a particular problem. A distinction is sometimes made between basic and applied research, although this is now increasingly viewed as arbitrary. See *Basic research*.

Audit trail Notes and other mechanisms for indicating critical decisions made while collecting and analysing research material; this enables later researchers to retrace the research path followed.

Authorship agreement A contract outlining the authorship sequence, reflecting the particular involvement of all contributors to a study.

Autonomy A philosophical ethical principle that embodies respect for persons and emphasises the right of individuals to make their own independent decisions without undue influence or coercion.

Basic research Research aimed at accumulating knowledge or developing theory, rather than solving particular real-life problems. The distinction between basic and applied research is however fairly arbitrary. See *Applied research*.

Beneficence A philosophical ethical principle that underlines the ethical obligation to do good or generate benefits for the participants in research.

Bibliographic access The identification of relevant literature or sources of relevant information.

Bourgeoisie A Marxist term for the middle-class stratum of society.

Central limit theorem A statistical principle that defines the mean, standard deviation, and shape of the sampling distribution of the mean.

Chi square statistic An estimate of the degree to which the observed frequencies in all the cells of a bivariate frequency table differ from the expected frequencies if the two variables were in fact independent.

Clinical research Any research applied in a context associated with health, health care, or medicine.

Closed questions Questions that do not allow the respondent to provide answers in his or her own words, but force the respondent to select one or more choices from a fixed list of answers provided.

Clusters Groups of elements into which very large populations are subdivided in order to facilitate random sampling.

Conceptualisation The process whereby a researcher develops a clear and explicit theoretical image or idea of the construct that matches the attribute that is to be measured or understood.

Concurrent validity A form of validity where scores on a new measurement and a criterion measure are collected at the same time.

Confidence interval A range of values within which a population mean is expected to fall with a known probability.

Confidentiality An undertaking by the researcher to protect the anonymity of research participants.

Confounding variable An uncontrolled 'extraneous variable' that co-varies with the experimental manipulation, thus undermining the internal validity of the experiment.

Coherence/Design coherence A criterion of a good research design which is attained by ensuring that the research purposes and techniques are arranged logically so as to 'fit' within the research framework provided by a particular paradigm.

Consent Permission given by individuals agreeing to participate in research. See *Informed consent*.

Control The isolation and regulation of elements of the research environment, in order to ensure the singularity of the relationships under study; in other words, to eliminate the possible influence of extraneous and confusing variables.

Constructionism A research paradigm premised on the idea that social and psychological phenomena do not have a pre-given reality but are socially constructed and can be understood through 'deconstructing' the elements that go into making them appear meaningful. See also *Positivism*.

Constructs Phenomena that researchers wish to turn into observable variables. Constructs are conceptual understandings of these variables that have been defined in language and theoretically elaborated in terms of how they are related in various ways to other constructs.

Convenience samples Using any participants who are available to participate in a study.

Correlation The degree of association, or the strength of the relationship between two variables. Correlations are usually represented by a correlation coefficient (r) which is a number that can range from -1 to 1. When r = 0 there is no relationship between variables. As r approaches 1 the strength of the positive relationship increases, and as r approaches -1 the strength of the negative relationship increases.

Co-variation The extent to which scores on measures relate to each other. For example, height and weight co-vary because taller people tend also to weigh more than shorter people.

Criterion measure A form of validity established by comparing different measures of the same construct.

Cronbach's Alpha A coefficient ranging from 0 to 1, indicating the internal consistency of a scale.

Cultural politics A form of politics emerging from multicultural contexts, often involving struggles about the role and meaning of tradition, lifestyle, and identity.

Data Plural for datum. A collection of information, often in the form of numerical measures of a group of people. Also sometimes used to refer to other kinds of raw material used in research, such as a collection of texts or images.

Defamiliarisation The act of making apparently everyday and unremarkable objects or events seem unusual.

Dependent variable The variable that registers the effect of variation or manipulation in a research study.

Descriptive data analysis Analysis that aims to describe data by investigating the distribution of scores on each variable, and by determining whether the scores on different variables are related to each other.

Descriptive studies Studies that aim to describe phenomena without providing causal explanations of the phenomena.

Derived etics Understanding that pulls together both Emic and Etic perspectives.

Design validity A criterion of a good research design, which is attained by identifying and eliminating plausible rival hypotheses.

Dialectics A Marxist term referring to points of tension in social relations and formations as well as to the interrelationship between various aspects of capitalist systems.

Dichotomous item An item that can have only one of two possible answers (e.g., Yes or No).

Discourse analysis A form of textual analysis that shows how language is deployed to achieve particular effects in specific contexts.

Dismantling The research technique used in intervention or psychotherapy research to evaluate the relative importance of different subcomponents of a therapeutic intervention. This involves the careful operationalisation of a therapeutic procedure, and the gradual removal of certain components in order to determine which components are necessary and sufficient for therapeutic change.

Distanciation A term used by Ricoeur to indicate understanding a context from outside the context; i.e., understanding the subjective limits of the context. See also *Verstehen*.

Document delivery Physically accessing and having in hand the relevant literature or information traced in an information search.

Double blind study An experimental technique used in clinical trials, where neither the researchers nor the subjects know whether the subject is in the experimental or control group.

Ecological fallacy A logical error in reasoning that occurs when the units of analysis do not correspond to the objects about which conclusions are being drawn.

Economies of knowledge The idea that, in a globalising world, trade is dominated by products with high technological content; i.e., knowledge-intensive products.

Effectiveness The positive effects or success of an intervention as measured in real-world, and therefore less rigorously controlled, contexts. See also *Efficacy*.

Efficacy The positive effects or success of an intervention as measured in highly controlled, or laboratory, situations. See also *Effectiveness*.

Emic perspective Understanding phenomena on their own terms; a commitment to everyday forms of understanding. See also *Etic perspective*.

Empathic Experiencing, analysing, or describing a phenomenon in a way that shows empathy.

Empathy 'Feeling with' a person or situation. Placing oneself 'in their shoes'.

Empowerment Raised awareness in people of their own abilities to mobilise for social action.

Enumerator areas Geographic areas or pockets of land used for sampling in a census.

Epistemology Theory of the grounds of knowledge, i.e. how things can be known. The rules or premises by which it is accepted that knowledge is generated.

Ethical review A formal process in which a legally constituted and accredited research ethics committee reviews research proposals and examines the ethical and scientific aspects of the proposal to ensure that the welfare of research participants is not compromised.

Ethnography The study of cultures and sub-cultures, usually by immersing oneself in the culture studied over a period of time.

Etic perspective The use of theory to understand phenomena. See also *Emic perspective* and *Derived etics*.

Euclidean distance Euclidean distance expresses the distance between two points in n-dimensional space. Thus, it will tell us the distance between the tuples (1, 4, 8) and (3, 2, 9) in three-dimensional space.

Expectancy effects In an experimental design, the bias introduced by the researcher's expectations about the effect of an experimental treatment.

Experiments Studies that seek to identify cause-effect relationships by manipulating the hypothesised causal variable (independent variable) in a controlled environment, and observing the effect of this manipulation on an outcome variable (dependent variable).

Explanatory studies Studies that aim to provide causal explanations of phenomena.

Exploratory studies Studies that make preliminary investigations into relatively unknown areas of research.

External validity The degree to which research findings can legitimately be generalised to other similar contexts. This is determined by the representativeness of the research participants and the measures used in the research.

Field research Immersing oneself in the actual set of events in order to gain first-hand knowledge of the situation.

Focus group A discussion conducted by a researcher with a group of research participants, and usually focused on a particular issue or set of issues.

Force-field analysis A technique for diagrammatically plotting the forces that support or oppose a particular issue or policy in order to assess the risks of implementing that policy.

Formative evaluation The process of undertaking evaluation research aimed at ongoing programme improvement. See also *Summative evaluation*.

Frequency distribution A graphical representation of the number (frequency) of subjects who obtained a particular score on a variable.

Gatekeeper A person who is in a position to give or deny permission for a researcher to gain entry to a group or setting.

Grounded knowledge The idea that research should be directed toward the development or discovery of knowledge that is not derived from previous assumptions or theoretical speculations.

Grounded theory A qualitative method which has as a goal the development of theoretical accounts on the basis of a close, inductive engagement with the context of study.

Hawthorne effect An effect produced in research participants by the mere presence of an interventional research programme, regardless of whether the intervention has any real effect.

Hegelian Tradition of philosophy inspired by the nineteenth-century German philosopher G.W.F. Hegel. In social and critical theory, the term is often used to refer to dialectical reason or when theorising dialectical oppositions, e.g. male–female, self–other.

Hegemonic A neo-Marxist or Marxist term referring to the ascendance or domination of a particular structure or idea which serves to invalidate other forms.

Hermeneutic Concerned with interpretation.

Hermeneutics The science or study of interpretation. The study of meaning.

Hermeneutical circle A process of interpretation conceived of as a circular movement between the parts and the whole.

Histogram A graphical frequency distribution, in which bars are used to represent the frequency of cases in each category.

Human Sciences Research Council (HSRC) A large, partially government-funded organisation doing research in the social sciences and humanities.

Hypothesis A formal statement postulating a relationship between variables.

Hypothesis testing The use of statistics to determine the probability that a hypothesis is true.

Idealism The tendency of constructionist work to reduce everything to language, and therefore to the world of ideas.

Ideologies Beliefs that explain the world, bind together their adherents, and suggest desirable activities and outcomes. When used in a Marxist or neo-Marxist sense 'ideology' refers to 'false beliefs' or socially sanctioned ideas, which operate to support dominant relations of power and prevent more critical awareness of inequities.

In-betweenity Term from postcolonial theory that describes the way colonised people find themselves suspended between different (dominant and dominated) cultural traditions, and subsequently internalise negative and distorted cultural self-descriptions.

Incommensurable Used to describe ideas or practices that cannot be evaluated with reference to the same set of standards.

Independent variable The variable that produces an effect in a causal explanation.

Inferential data analysis Statistical analyses that allow the researcher to draw conclusions about populations from sample data

Information search The development of a search strategy, use of specific criteria and skills to identify various sources of information, and accessing and selecting relevant literature and information.

Informed consent The process of seeking the explicit and uncoerced agreement from subjects to participate in a research project, based on their full understanding of the procedures involved and their likely effects.

Interaction effect The effect in a factorial ANOVA, where the pattern of mean differences for one level of a factor (across a second independent variable) are not the same as the pattern of mean differences for another level of the factor.

Internal validity The coherence of a research design; the evidentiary adequacy of a piece of research, assessed in terms of its premises, observations, and conclusions.

Internal consistency In relation to narrative, the extent to which one part of the narrative does not contradict another. In relation to quantitative measures, the degree to which each item in a scale correlates with each other item. See also *Reliability*.

Interpretive meaning The interpretation of intended meaning, for example, by a researcher. See also *Intended meaning*.

Inter-rater reliability The degree to which the evaluations made by two or more individuals (e.g., the marks given by two lecturers to students' essays) correlate. See also *Correlation* and *Reliability*.

Intersubjective Refers to that which is shared between subjects; especially group understanding.

Item A question or statement in a test or questionnaire to which a testee is expected to give a response.

Item analysis A procedure for deciding which items to discard from a test or questionnaire, usually because the item is unrelated to other items, too easy, too difficult, or biased against certain groups.

Justice in research This is a complex philosophical principle which when applied to research requires researchers to exercise fairness in all aspects of the research so that participants are not exploited and receive a fair return for their efforts and risks.

Key informant A person who provides a researcher with important orienting information about a group or setting being studied.

Knowledge workers People who use their research skills as capital in various domains of the knowledge economy, often not confined to the discipline they come from.

Kuder-Richardson coefficient See *Cronbach's Alpha*. Usually used with scales containing dichotomous items.

Langue A term introduced by Saussure to describe language as a 'system of differences without any positive terms'. See also *Parole*.

Library catalogue A listing of books, journals and other materials that a library has in its collection, indicating the location of these materials within the library.

Literature review The identification and analysis or review of the literature and information related to what is intended to be, or has been, studied.

Literature search See *Information search*.

Logocentrism The idea that actual, physical presence in the moment (as opposed to being distanced from it in time and space) allows for more valid observation of what is really happening.

Longitudinal study Any research study which follows up a particular individual or group (cohort) over time, observing or measuring changes in the phenomenon of interest with time.

Matrix A matrix is a collection of data points, ordered in dimensions. The dimensions typically reflect the number of variables (k) in a data set, and the number of observations per variable (N). An Nxl matrix is a collection of data points from just one variable, whereas a 10x30 matrix is a collection of data points from 10 variables, and 30 subjects.

Mean The arithmetic average of a set of scores.

Measurement Assigning numbers to objects in a rule-like manner to represent quantities of attributes that the objects possess.

Measurement validity The degree to which a measure does what it is intended to. This includes both the fact that the measure should provide a good degree of fit between the conceptual and operational definitions of the construct, and that the instrument should be usable for the particular purposes for which it was designed.

Median The middlemost score in a set of scores.

Meta-analysis A method for summarising and comparing statistical effects across a number of different studies.

Metanarratives Used by postmodern theorists to refer to the grand narratives of modernity, e.g., that society will continue to progress through a combination of science, technology, and humanism.

Methodology The study of procedures (methods) used in research to create new knowledge.

Mode The most frequently occurring value in a set of scores.

Modernity See *Postmodernity*.

Multiple regression A multivariate statistical procedure used to model complex phenomena and relationships.

Multivariate Multivariate = multi(ple) variate(s). Multivariate methods study several variables simultaneously; i.e., they consider joint functions of variables (distributions, statistics, and other properties).

Narrative analysis A qualitative research method based on the notion of life as narrative, which seeks to reveal the way in which people construct life narratives around particular experiences, like disease.

Needs assessment The process of identifying whether there is a need for a particular type of social intervention.

NGO Non-governmental organisation. It has been estimated that there are around 54 000 NGOs operating in South Africa, and many of these do social research work.

Nonmaleficence The ethical obligation not to do harm (in research).

Nonparametric statistics Inferential statistical analyses that require few assumptions about the population.

Nonprobability sampling Any kind of sampling where the selection of elements is not determined by the statistical principle of randomness. See *Probability sampling*.

Normal distribution A model population frequency distribution with characteristic bell curve shape.

Ontology Theory of the essence of things, their true nature. The philosophical understanding of what aspects of human existence are available to study.

Open-ended questions Questions that do not provide respondents with a predetermined set of responses, but allow respondents to formulate responses using their own ideas and words. See *Closed questions*.

Operationalisation/Operational definition The process whereby the researcher translates a conceptual (linguistic, theoretical) under-standing of a construct into observable indicators.

Panel A sample of people whose opinions on particular issues are repeatedly canvassed. Panel studies are used to gather data on a continuous basis about public opinion.

Paradigm An all-encompassing system of practice and thinking, which defines for researchers the nature of their enquiry; i.e., those things that can be taken for granted about the social world they are studying and the correct ways of going about studying it.

Parameter A value (e.g., for the mean) that is a property of a population. For example, the value of the population mean.

Parametric statistics Statistical analyses in which sample statistics can be used as estimates of population parameters.

Parole A term introduced by Saussure to describe the act of using language. See also *Langue*.

Participant observation A form of observation where researchers become fully involved in the setting being studied. See *Ethnography*.

Participatory action research Research that aims to produce knowledge in an active partnership with those affected by that knowledge, and for the express purpose of improving their social, educational and material conditions.

Participatory research Research which involves the 'subjects' of a research study in the planning and implementation of the study.

Pastiche The act of creating a collage, that is, creating a picture or other work by pasting together apparently unconnected bits and pieces – newspaper cuttings, pieces of cloth, leaves, tea bags. Used to describe any postmodern text put together from disparate elements, often with scant regard for the original contexts from which the elements were drawn.

Patriarchy Strictly speaking refers to 'the rule of the father', but used more broadly to refer to societies which are structured to ensure men's domination of women.

Peer review A widely accepted practice in science and knowledge creation whereby a panel of experts reviews research proposals or research results to determine and comment on their scientific merit and feasibility. Journal editors implement peer review to assist them in deciding whether a paper warrants publication on scientific or technical grounds.

Percentiles The percentage of individuals in a group who received the same or lower score as each possible raw score.

Personality assessment The assessment of what people are like, by providing general descriptions of people along one or several dimensions.

Phenomenology An approach to research which aims to understand human experience in context. A number of quite specific phenomenological research techniques have been developed, but the term phenomenology is also used more broadly to signal a commitment to understanding human phenomena in context, as they are lived, using context-derived terms and categories. Phenomenology typically involves suspension of one's own prior theoretical commitments.

Phonocentrism The belief that speech, because it supposedly happens spontaneously, is more authentic and true than writing.

Placebo A treatment given to a group of research participants that is known to be ineffective (e.g., an injection of distilled water). Participants do not know that the treatment is ineffective. The purpose of administering a placebo is typically to control for reactivity effects – in particular, to determine whether any intervention at all on the part of the researcher will produce an effect, regardless of whether it has effective properties or not.

Placebo effect The phenomenon by which a subject may bias the findings of an experimental study (often a clinical trial) by expecting the intervention being studied to be effective, with the expectancy itself producing some of the actual effects.

Plagiarism The unacknowledged and fraudulent copying of another author's work or ideas.

Plausible rival hypotheses Alternative interpretations of research findings. These are factors that the researcher has not identified and eliminated, but which can explain the findings of an investigation.

Policy A set of principles or course of action adopted by, for example, a government department.

Policy research Any research intended to influence or facilitate policy development.

Poll A survey that seeks to elicit information about individual opinions and intentions.

Population The larger pool of cases from which a sample is drawn.

Positivism A research paradigm concerned with gathering information about social facts in an objective and detached manner, often making use of quantitative indices.

Postcolonial Literally the era after colonialism, but also a critical theoretical concept referring to the study of continued cultural and political domination after colonialism.

Post-hoc test Statistical procedures, similar to t-tests, which detect a pattern of differences in a set of means.

Postmodernity Both a critique of modernity and a global cultural phenomenon which is said to have (partially) replaced modernity. Where modernity believes in the possibility of a unifying synthesis or whole, postmodernity playfully exposes as sham the apparent coherence in scientific or political programmes, works of art, and texts of all sorts. Among the 'grand narratives' of modernity which are starting to unravel in postmodernity is the idea that each individual has a clear-cut identity and that society progresses through the rational application of scientific principles.

Predicitive validity A form of validity established by correlating a measure with some future event.

Principipilism The term used to describe approaches to bioethics which are based on the following four principles: Autonomy and respect for persons, Beneficence, Nonmaleficence, and Justice.

Probability There are several definitions of this important statistical concept. The *relative frequency* definition is the ratio of the frequency of occurrence of an event to the total possible number of events (in that class). For example, the probability that a fair die will show a 5 when cast is 1/6 (there is only one '5' out of six possible outcomes). An everyday understanding of the concept is as likelihood (of an event occurring).

Probability sampling A procedure for ensuring that every element in a target population has a known chance of being selected into a sample.

Probability theory A branch of mathematics that is used to determine to what extent a sample represents the parameters of a population.

Purposive sampling Sampling based on careful selection of cases that are typical of the population being studied. Often used to create small, relevant samples in qualitative research or case studies.

Qualitative research In contrast to quantitative research, qualitative research seeks to preserve the integrity of narrative data and attempts to use the data to exemplify unusual or core themes embedded in contexts.

Quantitative research Research in which data are collected or coded into numerical forms, and to which statistical analyses may be applied to determine the significance of the findings.

Quasi-experimental methods Experimental-type research designs involving limited control of the independent variable; where random assignment of persons is not possible, or a control or comparison group cannot be included in the design.

Random error Random disturbances in performance on a measure; i.e., an individual could score higher than his or her true score on one occasion and lower on another.

Randomisation/Random assignment Assignment of participants (or other entities) to conditions such that participants have an equal (or an other determinate) and independent chance of ending up in any particular condition.

Random selection A random procedure of selecting a sample.

Range A measure of dispersion in a set of scores, which is calculated by determining the difference between the largest and smallest score.

Reflexivity The explicit recognition and examination of the researcher's role in the research process, including the assumptions with which they operate, their identifications and disidentifications, and their possible influence on the research process.

Regression line A straight line that is drawn through the middle of the distribution of dots on a scatterplot, and thus summarises the distribution of cases along the two variables.

Relativism The idea that there are many truths, and that there is no objective way to privilege one account of reality over another.

Reliability The dependability of a measurement instrument, that is, the extent to which the instrument yields the same results on repeated trials. See also *Internal consistency* and *Inter-rater reliability*.

Representativeness The extent to which a sample resembles the population from which it is drawn on dimensions that are relevant to the study (e.g., sex, age, home language).

Research design A strategic framework or plan that guides research activity to ensure that sound conclusions are reached.

Research ethics A field of applied ethics that seeks to ensure that the welfare of research participants is protected.

Research ethics committee (REC) A committee that is formally established and accredited as competent to examine the ethical aspects of research proposals to ensure that the welfare of research participants is not compromised.

Research ethics guidelines Documents which contain ethical guidance for researchers and RECs. There are several local, national, and international guidelines for various types of research. Some institutions also develop their own research ethics guidelines. Ideally, all guidelines should harmonise with each other, but many conflicting guidelines do exist.

Response format The type of answer that it is possible to give to an item.

Sampling Sampling involves selection of the specific research participants from the entire population, and is conducted in different ways according to the type of study.

Sampling distribution of means A frequency distribution showing all possible sample means that occur when samples of a particular size are drawn from the raw score population described by the null hypothesis.

Sampling error The (calculable) extent to which a sample diverges from the parameters of a population.

Sampling frame A 'list' of all the members in the population who are eligible for inclusion into a sample.

Sampling interval The fixed distance, calculated by dividing the sampling frame size by the size of the sample, between elements to be selected according to the process of systematic sampling. See *Systematic sampling.*

Sampling to redundancy Instead of a predetermined sample size, this approach to sampling entails the continued selection of cases for inclusion into a study until further selection no longer yields significant new information. It is often used in qualitative research.

Saturation The point in an interpretive study where the researcher has explored the data to satisfaction and has a clear sense of what conclusions can be drawn from the data analysis.

Scales Psychological tools developed to measure, *inter alia*, knowledge, attitudes, and beliefs. Examples are attitude questionnaires and intelligence tests.

Scatterplot A graphical representation of the correlation between two variables.

Search strategy The identification of key concepts that describe and set parameters on the topic about which literature or information is sought, and the identification of relevant sources of information from this literature.

Significance level A conventionally agreed level of improbability, denoted by the symbol α, and typically having the values 0.05, 0.01 or 0.001.

Simple random sampling A procedure of selecting a probability sample where each element of the sampling frame has a known, equal probability of selection.

Single case experimental design A form of case study of individuals, families, organisations or communities in which independent and dependent variables are carefully defined, and in which the effect of the independent variable on the dependent variable is carefully monitored over time.

Snowball sampling Sampling by means of a gradual accumulation of relevant cases through contacts and references.

Standard deviation A measure of dispersion or variation in a set of scores, which is calculated by determining the square root of the variance.

Standard normal distribution See *Normal distribution.*

Statistical analysis The summarisation and analysis of numerical data.

Statistical inference The use of statistical theory and methods to draw (probabilistic) conclusions from data.

Statistical power The ability (likelihood) that a study is sensitive enough to detect an hypothesised effect that does actually exist.

Stratified sampling A procedure of selecting a probability sample where a heterogeneous population is first divided into subgroups (known as strata) on the sampling frame, and simple random samples are drawn from each of the strata.

Structured transformation In participatory action research, the goal of the collaborative researchers and participants. See *Empowerment.*

Subaltern Literally refers to an inferior military commissioned officer's rank, or, in logic, to a particular rather than a universal proposition. Used in postmodernist and especially postcolonial discourse to refer to a class of people or an individual regarded as inferior to another, combined with the more positive sense of their particular identity.

Summative evaluation The process of undertaking evaluation research aimed at establishing programme impact, outcomes, value, and cost/benefit. See also *Formative evaluation*.

Survey research The application of questionnaires or interviews to relatively large groups of people.

Systematic observation Observation that is planned, and seeks to answer a specific research question through a valid and coherent research design.

Systematic error Nonrandom bias that impacts on the reliability of a measure.

Systematic sampling A procedure of selecting a probability sample where every n-th element of a randomly ordered list is included in the sample.

Temporal That which relates to or exists in time.

Therapy manuals Standardised therapeutic procedures.

Ubuntu A Zulu word which has come to signify a commitment to values of communality, sharing, and unconditional positive regard for others of humankind. Associated with respect for and tolerance of others, generosity of spirit, and working towards common goals.

Units of analysis The object of investigation which is determined by who or what the researcher wishes to draw conclusions about.

Univariate Univariate = uni(tary) variate. Univariate methods study one variable at a time; i.e., they consider variables (their distributions, statistics, and other properties) independently of other variables.

Validity See *Measurement validity*.

Values An explicit preference for courses of action and outcomes.

Variable A concept or empirical measure that can assume two or more values, e.g., age, sex or weight.

Variance A measure of dispersion or variation in a set of scores, that is calculated by determining the average squared deviation of each score from the mean.

Verstehen A term introduced by Dilthey to indicate empathic, contextual understanding of phenomena. Often equated with empathy.

Vicious circularity of understanding An inevitable tendency in research to project ideas onto the world and then to rediscover them as findings.

Victim-blaming The assumption that people cause their own misfortune. For example, implying that poor people are lazy (i.e., failing to take unequal social opportunities into consideration).

References

Abelson, R.P. (1995). *Statistics as principled argument*. Hillsdale, New Jersey: Erlbaum.

Abercrombie, N., Hill, S., & Turner, B. (1980). *The dominant ideology thesis*. London: George Allen and Unwin.

Abrahams, F., & Mauer, K.F. (1999a). The comparability of the constructs of the 16PF in the South African context. *Journal of Industrial Psychology, 25*(1), 53–59.

Abrahams, F., & Mauer, K.F. (1999b). Qualitative and statistical impacts of home language on responses to the items of the Sixteen Personality Factor Questionnaire (16PF) in South Africa. *South African Journal of Psychology, 29*, 76–86.

Adler, P.A., & Adler, P. (1994). Observational techniques. In N.K. Denzin & Y.S. Lincoln (Eds), *Handbook of qualitative research*. London: Sage.

Adorno, T.W., Frenkel-Brunswik, E., Levinson, D.J., & Sanford, N. (1950). *The authoritarian personality*. New York: Harper.

Agresti, A. (1990). *Categorical data analysis*. New York: John Wiley.

Alinsky, S. (1971). *Rules for radicals: A practical primer for realistic radicals*. New York: Vintage.

Altheide, D.L., & Johnson, J.M. (1994). In N.K. Denzin & Y.S. Lincoln (Eds), *Handbook of qualitative research*. London: Sage.

Althusser, L. (1971). *Lenin and philosophy and other essays*. London: NLB.

Amdur, R. (2003). *Institutional review board member handbook*. Sudbury, Massachusetts: Jones & Bartlett.

American Academy of Pediatrics (2004). Policy statement: Ethical considerations in research with socially identifiable populations. *Pediatrics, 113*, 148–151.

American Psychological Association (APA) (1994). *Publication manual of the American Psychological Association*. Washington, DC: APA.

Anastasi, A. (1997). *Psychological testing*. (7th edn). Upper Saddle River, New Jersey: Prentice Hall.

Appel, S.W. (1989). Outstanding individuals do not arise from ancestrally poor stock: Racial science and the education of black South Africans. *Journal of Negro Education, 58*, 554–557.

Appiah, K.A. (1996). African identities. In L. Nicholson & S. Seidman (Eds), *Social post-modernism: Beyond identity politics*. London: Cambridge University Press.

Argyris, C, & Schon, D. (1996). Action research in professional psychology. *American Behavioral Scientist, 32*, 612–623.

Ashcroft, B., Griffiths, G., & Tiffin, H. (1995). (Eds). *The postcolonial reader*. London/New York: Routledge.

Ashcroft, R., & Parker, M. (2003). The ethical review of student research in the context of the governance arrangements for research ethics committees. In S. Eckstein (Ed.), *Manual for research ethics committees* (pp. 53–56). Cambridge: Cambridge University Press.

Ashley, M., Padayachee, M., & Holderness, W.L. (1996). *The implementation of the Thousand Schools Project during 1995: An evaluation*. Cape Town: Independent Development Trust.

Atkin, J.M. (1979). Educational accountability in the United States. *Educational Analysis, 1*(1), 5–21.

Austin, J.L. (1975). *How to do things with words*. Cambridge, Massachusetts: Harvard University Press.

Azar, B. (1997). APA task force urges a harder look at data. *APA Monitor*, March. Available online at www.apa.org/monitor/rnar97/stats.html

Babbie, E.R. (1989). *The practice of social research*. Belmont, California: Wadsworth.

Babbie, E., & Mouton, J. (2001). *The practice of social research*. (South African edn). Cape Town: Oxford University Press.

Bakhtin, M.M. (1981). *The dialogical imagination*. Minneapolis: University of Minnesota Press.

Bakhtin, M.M. (1986). *Speech genres and other late essays*. Austin: University of Texas Press.

Ball, M.S., & Smith, G.W.H. (1992). *Analyzing visual data*. London: Sage.

Ballen, L., Koloane, D., Potter, C.S., Ramogase, A., & Siwani, J. (1991). *An evaluation of the Khula Udweba Project: 1989–1990*. Centre for Continuing Education, Report and Reprint Series No. 104. Johannesburg: University of the Witwatersrand.

Banister, P., Burman, E., Parker, I, Taylor, M., & Tindall, C. (1994). *Qualitative methods in psychology: A research guide*. Buckingham: Open University Press.

Barsdorf, N., & Wassenaar, D. (2005). Racial differences in public perceptions of voluntariness of medical research participants in South Africa. *Social Science & Medicine, 60,* 1087–1098.

Basson, R.B. (1992). Integrated studies: An idiographic perspective. Unpublished PhD thesis. University of Oregon, Eugene.

Baudrillard, J. (1983). *Simulations.* New York: Semiotext(e).

Beauchamp, T., & Childress, J. (2001). *Principles of biomedical ethics.* (5th edn). New York: Oxford University Press.

Becher, R.A. (1974). *Styles of curriculum development and curriculum evaluation.* Edinburgh: Scottish Council for Research in Education.

Becker, H.S. (1986). *Writing for social scientists: How to start and finish your thesis, book or article.* Chicago: University of Chicago Press.

Bedell, B., & Phayane, O. (1998). *Employment opportunities for post-graduates in research psychology.* Reports from the Psychology Department, No 33. Pretoria: University of South Africa.

Bedell, B., Van Eeden, R., & Van Staden, F. (1999). Culture as moderator variable in psychological test performance: Issues and trends in South Africa. *Journal of Industrial Psychology, 25*(3), 1–7.

Behrens, S.J. (1994). *Bibliographic control and information sources.* Pretoria: University of South Africa.

Belar, C.D. (1998). Graduate education in clinical psychology. *American Psychologist, 53,* 456–464.

Beloff, H. (1997). Making and un-making identities: A psychologist looks at artwork. In N. Hayes (Ed.), *Doing qualitative analysis in psychology.* Hove, Sussex: Psychology Press.

Belsky, L., & Richardson, H. (2004). Medical researchers' ancillary clinical care responsibilities. *British Medical Journal, 328,* 1494–1496.

Berger, J. (1978). *Ways of seeing.* Harmondsworth: Penguin.

Berger, J., & Luckman, T. (1976). *The social construction of reality: A treatise in the sociology of knowledge.* New York: Anchor Books.

Berger, S. (1990). An 'inside story': The illness experiences of women with breast cancer. Unpublished master's dissertation. University of Cape Town.

Bergstralh, E.J., Kosanke, J.L., & Jacobsen, S.L. (1996). Software for optimal matching in observational studies. *Epidemiology, 7,* 331–332.

Bhaskar, R. (1979). *The possibility of naturalism.* Brighton: The Harvester Press.

Bickman, L., & Rog. D. J. (Eds). (1998). *Handbook of applied social research methods.* Thousand Oaks, California: Sage.

Bickman, L., Rog, D.J., & Hendrick, T.E. (1998). Applied research design: A practical approach. In L. Bickman & D. J. Rog (Eds), *Handbook of applied social research methods.* Thousand Oaks, California: Sage.

Biko, S.B. (1978). *I write what I like.* Harmondsworth: Penguin.

Blass, T. (Ed.). (1999). *Obedience to authority: Current perceptions on the Milgram paradigm.* Hillsdale, New Jersey: Erlbaum.

Bleicher, J. (1980). *Contemporary hermeneutics: Hermeneutics as method, philosophy and critique.* London: Routledge.

Bless, C., & Higson-Smith, C. (1995). *Fundamentals of social research methods: An African perspective.* Cape Town: Juta.

Boal, A. (1992). *Games for actors and non-actors.* London: Routledge.

Bogdan, R., & Taylor, S.J. (1975). *Introduction to research methods: A phenomenological approach to the social sciences.* New York: Wiley.

Bottomore, T. (Ed.). (1983). *A dictionary of Marxist thought.* Oxford: Blackwell.

Bowie, M. (1991). *Lacan.* London: Fontana.

Brandt, A.M. (1978). Racism and research: The case of the Tuskegee syphilis study. *Hastings Center Report, 8*(6), 21–29.

Braver, M.C.W., & Braver, S.L. (1988). Statistical treatment of the Solomon four-group design: A meta-analytic approach. *Psychological Bulletin, 104,* 150–154.

British Psychological Society (2003). *Guidelines for minimum standards of ethical approval in psychological research.* Leicester: Author.

Broadfoot, P. (1996). *Education, assessment and society.* Buckingham: Open University Press.

Brown, D.L. (1993). Social change through collective reflection with Asian non-governmental development organizations. *Human Relations, 46,* 249–272.

Brown, D.L., & Tandon, R. (1983). Ideology and political economy in inquiry: Action research and participatory research. *Journal of Applied Behavioral Science, 19,* 277–294.

Brown, L. (1997). A discursive analysis of the role of tertiary educational institutions in reproducing racism. Unpublished Master's Dissertation. University of Natal, Pietermaritzburg.

Brown, L.M., Tappan, M.B., Gilligan, C, Miller B.A., & Argyris, D.E. (1989). Reading for self and moral voice: A method for interpreting narratives of real-life moral conflict and choice. In M.J. Packer & R.B. Addison (Eds), *Entering the circle: Hermeneutic investigations in psychology*. Albany: State University of New York Press.

Budlender, D. (Ed.). (1996). *The women's budget*. Cape Town: Idasa.

Budlender, D. (Ed.). (1997). *The second women's budget*. Cape Town: Idasa.

Budlender, D. (Ed.). (1998). *The third women's budget*. Cape Town: Idasa.

Bulhan, H. (1977). Reactive identification and the formation of an African intelligensia. *International Social Science Journal, 39,* 149–164.

Bulhan, H.A. (1980). Dynamics of cultural in-betweenity: An empirical study. *International Journal of Psychology, 15,* 105–121.

Bulhan, H.A. (1993). Imperialism in studies of the psyche: A critique of African psychological research. In L.J. Nicholas (Ed.), *Psychology and oppression: Critiques and proposals*. Johannesburg: Skotaville.

Burman, E. (Ed.). (1998). *Deconstructing feminist psychology*. London: Sage.

Buros, O.K. (1988). *The mental measurements yearbook*. Highland Park: Buros Institute of Mental Measurement.

Butchart, A. (1998). *The anatomy of power: European constructions of the African body*. London: Zed Books.

Butchart, A., Lerer, L.B., & Terre Blanche, M.J. (1994). Imaginary constructions and forensic reconstructions of fatal violence against women: Implications for community violence prevention. *Forensic Science International, 64,* 21–34.

Callahan, J. (Ed.). (1988). *Ethical issues in professional life*. New York: Oxford.

Campbell, D.T. (1969). Social reforms as experiments. *American Psychologist, 24,* 409–429.

Campbell, D.T. (1988). *Methodology and epistemology for social science*. Chicago: University of Chicago Press.

Campbell, D.T., & Fiske, D.W. (1959). Convergent and discriminant validation by the multitrait-multimethod matrix. In D.T. Campbell, *Methodology and epistemology for social science*. Chicago: University of Chicago Press.

Campbell, D.T., & Stanley, J.C. (1966). *Experimental and quasi-experimental designs for research*. Chicago: Rand-McNally.

Campbell, D.T., Webb, E.T., Schwartz, R.D., Sechrest, L., & Belew Grove, J. (1981). Approximations to knowledge. In D.T. Campbell, *Methodology and epistemology for social science*. Chicago: University of Chicago Press.

Carmines, E.G., & Zeller, R.A. (1979). *Reliability and validity assessment*. Beverly Hills, California: Sage.

Carr, W., & Kemmis, S. (1982). *Becoming critical: Knowing through action research*. London: The Falmer Press.

Centre for the Study of Violence and Reconciliation (1996). *Truth and reconciliation*. Johannesburg: The Storyteller Group.

Chelimsky, E. (1997). The coming transformation in evaluation. In E. Chalinsky & W. Shadish (Eds), *Evaluation for the 21st century*. Thousand Oaks, California: Sage.

Choudhary, A., & Tandon, R. (1988). *Participatory evaluation*. New Delhi: Society for Participatory Research in Asia.

Claassen, N.C.W., & Hugo, H.L.E. (1993). *The relevance of the general Scholastic Aptitude Test (GSAT) for pupils who do not have English as their mother tongue* (Report ED-21). Pretoria: Human Sciences Research Council (HSRC)

Claassen, N.C.W., Krynauw, A.H., Holtzhausen, H., & wa ga Mathe, M. (2001). *A standardisation of the WAIS-III for English-speaking South Africans*. Pretoria: HSRC.

Claassen, N.C.W., & Schepers, J.M. (1990). Groepverskille in akademiese intelligensie verklaar op grond van verskille in sosio-ekonomiese status (Group differences in academic intelligence that can be explained by differences in socio-economic status). *South African Journal of Psychology, 20,* 294–302.

Clandinin, D., & Connelly, F. (1994). Personal experience methods. In N. Denzin & Y. Lincoln (Eds), *Handbook of qualitative research*. Thousand Oaks, California: Sage.

Clark, K.B., & Clark, M. P. (1947). Racial identification and preference in Negro children. In T.M. Newcomb & E.L. Hartley (Eds), *Readings in social psychology*. New York: Holt.

Cleaver, G. (1988). A phenomenological analysis of victimization. The experience of having one's house attacked and damaged. *South African Journal of Psychology, 18,* 76–83.

Cleaver, G., & Pallourios, H. (1994). Diabetes mellitus: Experiencing a chronic illness. *South African Journal of Psychology, 24,*175–183.

Clifford, J., & Marcus, C. (1986). *Writing culture.* London: Sage.

Cloete, N., & Muller, J. (1991). Human Sciences Research Council Incorporated (Pty) Ltd: Social science research, markets and accountability in South Africa. In J. Jansen (Ed.), *Knowledge and power in South Africa: Critical perspectives across disciplines.* Johannesburg: Skotaville.

Cloete, N., Muller, J., & Orkin, M. (1986). How we learned to stop worrying and love the HSRC. *Psychology In Society, 6,* 29–46.

Coetzee, J.K., & Wood, G.T. (1995). Local odyssey in search of a new space for freedom: Biographical accounts of the political struggle in the Eastern Cape (South Africa) in the 1980s. *South African Journal of Sociology, 26,* 1–8.

Cohen, J. (1988). *Statistical power analysis for the Behavioral Sciences.* Hillsdale, New Jersey: Erlbaum.

Cohen, J. (1990). Things I have learned (so far). *American Psychologist, 45,* 1304–1312.

Cohen, J., Cohen, P., West, S.G., & Aiken, L.S. (2003). *Applied multiple regression/correlation analysis for the behavioral sciences.* (3rd edn). Hillsdale, New Jersey: Erlbaum.

Cole, M.B. (1987). User-focused evaluation of training programme effectiveness in a South African industrial company. Unpublished M.Ed thesis. University of the Witwatersrand, Johannesburg.

Cole, E., & Coultrap-McQuin, S. (Eds). (1992). *Explorations in feminist ethics: Theory and practice.* Bloomington: Indiana University Press.

Collins, A. (1997). Review of social psychology: A critical agenda. *South African Journal of Psychology, 27,* 123–124.

Comer, J.P. (1988). Educating poor minority children. *Scientific American, 259,* 42–48.

Comstock, D.E. (1994). A method for critical research. In M. Martin & C. McIntyre (Eds), *Readings in the philosophy of social science.* Cambridge, Massachusetts: MIT Press.

Concise Oxford Dictionary, 9th edition. (1993). Oxford: Oxford University Press.

Cook, T.D. (1985). Postpositivist critical multiplism. In L. Shotland & M.M. Mark (Eds), *Social science and social policy.* Beverly Hills, California: Sage.

Cook, T.D., & Campbell, D.T. (1979). *Quasi-experimentation.* Chicago: Rand McNally.

Cribb, A. (2003). Approaching qualitative research. In S. Eckstein (Ed.), *Manual for research ethics committees.* (pp. 40–48). Cambridge: Cambridge University Press.

Cribb, R. (2004). Ethical regulation and humanities research in Australia: Problems and consequences. *Monash Bioethics Review, 23*(3), 39–57.

Crocker, L., & Algina, J. (1986). *Introduction to classical and modern test theory.* Orlando, Florida: Holt, Rinehart & Winston.

Cronbach, LJ. (1963). Course improvement through evaluation. *Teachers College Record, 64,* 672–683.

Cronbach, LJ. (1982). *Designing evaluations of educational and social programs.* San Francisco: Jossey-Bass.

Cronbach, L.J., Ambron, S.R., Dornbusch, S.M., Hess, R.D., Philips, D.C., Walker, D.F., & Weiner, S.S. (1980). *Toward reform of program evaluation.* San Francisco: Jossey-Bass.

Danziger, K. (1963). The psychological future of an oppressed group. *Social Forces, 42,* 31–40.

Danziger, K. (1986). The methodological imperative in psychology. *Philosophy of the Social Sciences, 16,* 1–13.

Danziger,K. (1990). *Constructing the subject.* Cambridge: Cambridge University Press.

Davidoff, S., & Van den Berg, O. (1990). *Changing your teaching: The challenge of the classroom.* Pietermaritzburg: Centaur.

Davies, S., & Terre Blanche, M. (1997). Training to care: An evaluation of a bereavement counselling course. *Journal of Educational Evaluation, 5,* 49–55.

Dawson, J., & Scott, J. (1996). Elevator etiquette. Paper presented at the 2nd Annual South African Qualitative Methods Conference, 3–4 September, Johannesburg.

De Beer, A.S. (1998). *Mass media – towards the millennium: The South African handbook of mass communication.* Pretoria: Van Schaik.

De Koning, K., & Martin, M. (Eds). (1996). *Participatory research in health: Issues and experiences.* Johannesburg: NPPHCN.

De la Rey, C, & Eagle, G. (1997). Gender and mental health policy development. In D. Foster, M. Freeman, & Y. Pillay (Eds), *Mental health policy issues for South Africa.* Pinelands: MASA Press.

De Beer, M. (1998). Learning potential assessment: Comparison of dynamic and standard cognitive psychometric test results. Paper presented at the annual Industrial Psychology Conference (Incorporating the Psychometrics Conference), Pretoria.

Delius, P. (1996). *A lion amongst the cattle: Reconstruction and resistance in the Northern Transvaal*. Johannesburg: Ravan.

Denzin, N.K. (1970). *The research act: A theoretical introduction to sociological methods*. Chicago: Aldine.

Denzin, N.K. (1989). *The research act*. Englewood Cliffs, New Jersey: Prentice Hall.

Denzin, N.K., & Lincoln, Y.S. (Eds). (2005). *Handbook of qualitative research*. (3rd edn). Thousand Oaks, California: Sage.

Dey, I. (1993). *Qualitative data analysis: A user friendly guide for social scientists*. London: Routledge and Kegan Paul.

DfID. (2003). Output to purpose review (OPR) for DfID support to Open Learning Systems Education Trust (OLSET), 24–28 November 2003. Johannesburg: Open Learning Systems Education Trust.

DfID. (2004). DfID project progress report: July 2004. Johannesburg: Open Learning Systems Education Trust.

Diallo, D., Doumbo, O., Plowe, C., Wellems, T. Emanuel, E., & Hurst, S. (2005). Community permission for medical research in developing countries. *HIV/AIDS, 41*, 255–259.

Dickert, N., & Grady, C. (1999). What's the price for a research subject? Approaches to payment for research participation. *New England Journal of Medicine, 341*, 198–203.

Dixon, J.A., Foster, D.H., Durrheim, K., & Wilbraham, L. (1994). Discourse and the politics of space in South Africa: The 'squatter crisis'. *Discourse & Society, 5*, 277–296.

Dixon, J., Tredoux, C.G., Durrheim, K., & Foster, D. (1994). Attributions of guilt as a function of speech accommodation and crime type. *Journal of Social Psychology, 134*, 465–475.

Duckitt, J. (1991). The development and validation of the subtle racism scale in South Africa. *South African Journal of Psychology, 21*, 233–239.

Duncan, N. (1996). Discourses on public violence and the reproduction of racism. *South African Journal of Psychology, 26*,172–182.

Duncan, N., Seedat, M., Van Niekerk, A., De la Rey, C, Gobodo-Madikizela, P., Simbayi, L.C.,

& Bhana, A. (1997). Black scholarship: Doing something active and positive about academic racism. *South African Journal of Psychology, 27*, 201–205.

Durrheim, K. (1997a). Social constructionism, discourse and psychology. *South African Journal of Psychology, 27*,175–182.

Durrheim, K. (1997b). Cognition and ideology: A rhetorical approach to critical theory. *Theory & Psychology, 7*, 749–770.

Durrheim, K., & Dixon, J. (2001). Geographies of racial exclusion: Beaches as family spaces. *Ethnic and racial studies, 24*, 333–350.

Durrheim, K., & Foster, D. (1995). The structure of sociopolitical attitudes in South Africa. *Journal of Social Psychology, 135*, 387–402.

Durrheim, K., & Mokeki, S. (1997). Race and relevance: A content analysis of the South African Journal of Psychology. *South African Journal of Psychology, 27*, 206–213.

Eagle, G.T., & Pillay, Y. (1988). Meeting the challenge: The St Wendolin's project. In G. Eagle, G. Hayes, & A. Bhana (Eds), *Mental health: Struggle and transformation*. OASSSA 3rd national conference proceedings. Durban: OASSSA.

Easter, M., Davis, A., & Henderson, G. (2004). Confidentiality: More than a linkage file and a locked drawer. *Ethics and Human Research, 26*(2), 13–17.

Eckstein, S. (2003). Research involving vulnerable participants: Some ethical issues. In S. Eckstein (Ed.), *Manual for research ethics committees* (pp. 105–112). Cambridge: Cambridge University Press.

Edwards, D., & Potter, J. (1992). *Discursive psychology*. London: Sage.

Eisner, E.W. (1975). *The perceptive eye: Toward the reformation of education evaluation*. Stanford, California: Stanford Evaluation Consortium.

Eisner, E.W. (1977). On the uses of educational connoisseurship and educational criticism for evaluating classroom life. *Teachers College Record, 78*, 345–358.

Elster, J. (1986). *Sour Grapes: Studies in the subversion of rationality*. Cambridge: Cambridge University Press.

Emanual, E., Crouch, R., Arras, J., Moreno, J., & Grady, C. (Eds). (2003). *Ethical and regulatory aspects of clinical research: Readings and commentary*. Baltimore, Ohio: Johns Hopkins University Press.

Emanual, E., Wendler, D., Killen, J., & Grady, C. (2004). What makes clinical research in developing countries ethical? The benchmarks of ethical research. *Journal of Infectious Diseases, 189*, 930–937.

Emanual, E., Wood, A., Fleischman, A., Bowen, A., Getz, K., Grady, K., Levine, C., Hammerschmidt, D, Faden, R., Eckenwiler, L., Tucker Muse, C., & Sugarman, J. (2004). Oversight of human participants research: Identifying problems to evaluate reform proposals. *Annals of Internal Medicine, 141*, 282–291.

Euvrard, G.E. (1996). An exploration of the factors which mediate the experience of parenting in an open adoptive parenting system. Unpublished honours research project. Rhodes University, Grahamstown.

Evans, S. (1998). Contextual interpretations of sexual fantasy. Unpublished master's dissertation. University of the Witwatersrand, Johannesburg.

Eysenck, H.J. (1952). The effects of psychotherapy: An evaluation. *Journal of Consulting Psychology, 16*, 319–324.

Fairclough, N., & Wodak, R. (1997). Critical discourse analysis. In T.A. van Dijk (Ed.), *Discourse as social interaction*. London: Sage.

Fals-Borda, O., & Rhaman, M.A. (Eds). (1991). *Action and knowledge: Breaking the monopoly with participatory action-research*. New York: The Apex Press.

Fanon, F. (1963). *The wretched of the earth*. New York: Grove.

Fanon, F. (1967). *Black Skin, White Masks*. New York: Grove.

Fanon, F. (1968). *Toward the African revolution*. New York: Grove.

Fanon, F. (1970). *A dying colonialism*. New York: Grove.

Fay, B. (1987). *Critical social science: Liberation and its limits*. Ithaca, New York: Cornell University Press.

Ferreira, M. (1988). A sociological analysis of medical encounters of aged persons at an outpatient centre: A qualitative approach. In M. Ferreira, J. Mouton, G. Puth, E. Schurink & W. Schurink (Eds), *Introduction to qualitative research*. Pretoria: HSRC.

Fetterman, D.M. (1989). *Ethnography: Step by step*. Beverly Hills, California: Sage.

Fetterman, D.M. (Ed.). (1993). *Speaking the language of power: Communication, collaboration and advocacy (translating ethnography into action)*. London: Falmer Press.

Fetterman, D.M. (1994). Empowerment evaluation. *Evaluation Practice, 15*,1.

Fetterman, D.M. (2001). *Foundations of empowerment evaluation*. Thousand Oaks, California: Sage.

Fetterman, D.M., Kaftarian, S.J., & Wandersman, A. (Eds). (1996). *Employment evaluation: Knowledge and tools for self-assessment and accountability*. Thousand Oaks, California: Sage.

Fetterman, D.M., & Wandersman, A. (Eds). (2005). *Empowerment evaluation principles in practice*. New York: Guilford.

Feuerstein, M. (1986). *Partners in evaluation: Evaluating development and community programmes with participants*. London: Macmillan.

Feyerabend, P.K. (1988). *Against method*. (Revised edn). London. Verso.

Finch, J. (1984). 'It's great to have someone to talk to': The ethics and politics of interviewing women. In C. Bell & H. Roberts. (Eds), *Social researching: Politics, problems and practices*. London: Routledge.

Finn, G.P.T. (1997). Qualitative analysis of murals in Northern Ireland: Paramilitary justifications for political violence. In N. Hayes (Ed.), *Doing qualitative analysis in psychology*. Hove, Sussex: Psychology Press.

Fisher, M., Friedman, S., & Strauss, B. (1994). The effects of blinding on acceptance of research papers by peer review. *Journal of the American Medical Association, 272*,143–146.

Fletcher, R. (1990). *Science, ideology, and the media: The Cyril Burt scandal*. New Brunswick: Transaction.

Flury, B., & Riedwyl, H. (1988). *Multivariate statistics: A practical approach*. London: Chapman & Hall.

Foster, D. (1991). 'Race' and racism in South African psychology. *South African Journal of Psychology, 21*, 203–209.

Foster, D., Davis, D., & Sandier, D. (1987). *Detention and torture in South Africa: Psychological, legal and historical studies*. Cape Town: David Philip.

Foster, D., Freeman, M., & Pillay, Y. (Eds). (1997), *Mental health policy issues for South Africa*. Pinelands: MASA Press.

Foster, D., & Nel, E. (1991). Attitudes and related concepts. In D. Foster & J. Louw-Potgieter (Eds), *Social psychology in South Africa*. Johannesburg: Lexicon.

Foucault, M. (1970). *The order of things*. London: Tavistock.

Foucault, M. (1972). *The archaeology of knowledge*. New York: Pantheon.

Foucault, M. (1977). Preface. In G. Deleuze & F. Guattari, *Anti Oedipus: Capitalism and schizophrenia*. London: The Athlone Press.

Foucault, M. (1977). *Discipline and punish: The birth of the prison*. Harmondsworth: Penguin.

Foucault, M. (1980). *Power/Knowledge: Selected interviews and other writing 1972–1977*. Worcester: The Harvester Press.

Foxcroft, C.D. (1997). Psychological testing in South Africa: Perspectives regarding ethical and fair practices. *European Journal of Psychological Assessment, 13*, 229–235.

Foxcroft, C., & Roodt, G. (Eds). (2006). *Introduction to psychological assessment in a South African context*. (2nd edn). Cape Town: Oxford University Press.

Franklin, R.S. (1991). *Shadows of race and class*. Minneapolis: University of Minnesota Press.

Freeman, M. (1989). *Paving the road towards a primary mental health care approach in South Africa*. Paper No. 18, Centre for the Study of Health Policy. Johannesburg: University of the Witwatersrand.

Freire, P. (1970). *Pedagogy of the oppressed*. Harmondsworth: Penguin.

Freire, P. (1973). *Education for critical consciousness*. New York: Seabury Press.

Freud, S. (1923). Remarks on the theory and practice of dream interpretation. *Standard Edition*. (Vol. 12). London: The Hogarth Press.

Freud, S. (2001/1901). *The interpretation of dreams*. London: Vintage/The Hogarth Press.

Fulford, K., Dickenson, D., & Murray, T. (Eds). (2002). *Healthcare ethics and human values*. Oxford: Blackwell.

Gadamer, H. (1975). *Truth and method*. London: Sheed & Ward.

Gale, G.W. (1938). *A suggested approach to the health needs of the native rural areas of South Africa*. Benoni: Record Printing Company.

Game, A., & West, M.A. (2002). Principles of publishing. *The Psychologist, 15*(2), 126–129.

Garbers, J. (1996). Group or team research. In J. Garbers (Ed.), *Effective research in the human sciences: Research management for researchers, supervisors and master's and doctoral candidates*. Pretoria: Van Schaik.

Gasa, N. (1998). Cultural notions of research and informed consent. Paper presented at the 4th annual conference of the Psychological Association of South Africa. University of Cape Town.

Geertz, C. (1973). *The interpretation of cultures*. New York: Basic Books.

Geertz, C. (1979). From the native's point of view: On the nature of anthropological understanding. In P. Rabinow & W.M. Sullivan (Eds), *Interpretive social science: A reader*. Berkeley: University of California Press.

Geertz, C. (1988). *Works and lives: The anthropologist as author*. Stanford, California: Stanford University Press.

Geldenhuys, P. (1989). *National service and you*. Pretoria: SADF.

Geras, N. (1989). Fetishism in Marx's Capital. *New Left Review, 65*, 79.

Gergen, K.J. (1985). The social constructionist movement in modern psychology. *American Psychologist, 40*, 266–275.

Germond, S., Schomer, H., Meyers, O., & Weight, L. (1993). Pain management in rheumatoid arthritis. *South African Journal of Psychology, 23*, 1–9.

Gibbs, W. (1995). Lost science in the third world. *Scientific American*, August, 76–83.

Gilligan, C. (1982). *In a different voice: Psychological theory and women's development*. Cambridge, Massachusetts: Harvard University Press.

Gilovitch, T. (1991). *How we know what isn't so: The fallibility of human reason in everyday life*. New York: The Free Press.

Giorgi, A. (1985). Sketch of a psychological phenomenological method. In A. Giorgi (Ed.), *Phenomenology and psychological research*. Pittsburgh: Duquesne University Press.

Goffman, E. (1979). *Gender advertisements*. Basingstoke: Macmillan.

Graham, P.M., & Zungu, V.E. (1987). *Edendale Lay Ecumenical Centre evaluation report*. Pietermaritzburg: University of Natal Centre for Adult Education.

Grundy, S. (1987). *Curriculum: Product or praxis*. London: The Falmer Press.

Grundy, S., & Kemmis, S. (1982). Educational action research in Australia: The state of the art. In S. Kemmis (Ed.), *The action research reader*. Waurn Ponds, Australia: Deakin University Press.

Guba, E.G., & Lincoln, Y.S. (1981). *Effective evaluation: Improving the usefulness of evaluation results through responsive and naturalistic approaches*. San Francisco: Jossey-Bass.

Guba, E.G., & Lincoln, Y.S. (1983). Epistemological and methodological bases of naturalistic inquiry. In G.F. Madaus, M. Scriven, & D.L. Stufflebeam (Eds), *Evaluation models: Viewpoints on educational evaluation*. Boston, Massachusetts: Kluwer-Nijhoff.

Guba, E.G., & Lincoln, Y.S. (1989). *Fourth generation evaluation*. Newbury Park, California: Sage.

Gulle, G., Tredoux, C.G., & Foster, D.H. (1998). Inherent and organizational stress in the SAPS: An empirical survey in the Western Cape. *South African Journal of Psychology, 28,*129–134.

Haag, D.E. (1996). *Guidelines for writing a dissertation or thesis*. Van der Bijl Park: Vaal Triangle Technikon.

Haag, D., & Van Vuuren, A. (1991). *Where to find research funding*. Pretoria: Foundation for Research Development/Centre for Science Development.

Haas, L.J., Malouf, J.L., & Mayerson, N.H. (1986). Ethical dilemmas in psychological practice: Results of a national survey. *Professional Psychology, 17,* 317–321.

Habermas, J. (1971). *Knowledge and human interests*. Boston, Massachusetts: Beacon.

Habermas, J. (1980). The hermeneutic claim to universality. In J. Bleicher (Ed.), *Contemporary hermeneutics: Hermeneutics as method, philosophy and critique*. London: Routledge & Kegan Paul.

Habermas, J. (1984). *Theory of communicative action*. (Vol. 2). Boston, Massachusetts: Beacon.

Habermas, J. (1991). *On the logic of the social sciences*. Cambridge, Massachusetts: MIT Press.

Haeck, W., & Yeld, N. (1993). Academic potential: Can tests deliver? Challenges in identifying students from poor educational backgrounds for admission to university study. Unpublished report, Alternative Admissions Research Project, University of Cape Town.

Haffajee, F. (1988). Are you a member of The Network? *Mail & Guardian, 24*(30), 8.

Hall, B.L. (1976). Participatory research: An approach for change. *Convergence, 8,* 2, 24–32.

Hall, B.L. (1978). Breaking the monopoly of knowledge: Research methods, participation and development. In B.L. Hall, & J. Roby Kidd (Eds), *Adult learning: A design for action*. Oxford: Pergamon.

Hall, B.L. (1981). Participatory research, popular knowledge, and power: A personal reflection. *Convergence, 14,* 6–17.

Handy, C. (1994). *The empty raincoat: Making sense of the future*. London: Arrow.

Haraway, D. (1990). A manifesto for cyborgs. In L. Nicholson (Ed.), *Feminism/Postmodernism*. London: Routledge.

Harland, R. (1987). *Superstructuralism*. London: Routledge.

Hay, W. (1998). Discourse as power relations: Concepts of self within situations of abuse of women in the traditional Roman Catholic marriage. Unpublished master's dissertation. University of the Witwatersrand, Johannesburg.

Hayes, G. (1996). The psychology of everyday life: Some Marxist reflections. In I. Parker & R. Spears (Eds), *Psychology and society: Radical theory and practice*. London: Pluto Press.

Hays, W. (1994). *Statistics*. (5th edn). New York: Harcourt Brace.

Heiman, G.A. (1995). *Research methods in psychology*. Boston, Massachusetts: Houghton Mifflin.

Henwood, K., & Pidgeon, N. (1995). Remaking the link: Qualitative research and feminist standpoint theory. *Feminism and Psychology, 5,* 7–30.

Herrera, C.D. (2000). Integrating research ethics and undercover hospital fieldwork. *IRB: A Review of Human Subjects research, 22*(1), 1–4.

Herrera, C.D. (2003). A clash of methodology and ethics in 'undercover' social science. *Philosophy of the Social Sciences, 33*(3), 351–362.

Herson, M., & Barlow, D.H. (1984). *Single-case experimental designs: Strategies for studying behavior change*. New York: Pergamon.

Heuchert, J.W.P., Parker, W.D., Stumpf, H., & Myburgh, C.P.H. (2000). The five-factor model of personality in South African college students. *American Behavioral Scientist, 44*(1), 112–125.

Hoeyer, K., Dahlager, L., & Lynöe, N. (2005). Conflicting notions of research ethics: The mutually challenging traditions of social scientists and medical researchers. *Social Science & Medicine, 61,* 1741–1749.

Holderness, W.L., & Altman, M.E. (1992). The PEUP: Factors contributing to sustainable innovation. *Journal of Educational Evaluation, 2*(1), 41–50.

Hollway, W. (1989). *Subjectivity and method in psychology: Gender, meaning and science*. London: Sage.

Hollway, W. (1995). A second bite at the heterosexual cherry. *Feminism and Psychology, 5,*126–130.

Hook, D. (2004). (Ed.) *Critical psychology*. Cape Town: UCT Press.

Hopa, M., Simbayi, L.C., & Du Toit, CD. (1998). Perceptions on integration of traditional and Western healing in the new South Africa. *South African Journal of Psychology, 28,* 8–14.

Hope, A., & Timmel, S. (1984). *Community workers' handbook*. (Vol. 1, 2, 3). Zimbabwe: Mambo Press.

Hoshmand, L.T., & O'Byrne, K. (1996). Reconsidering action research as a guiding metaphor for professional psychology. *Journal of Community Psychology, 24,*185–200.

House, E.R. (1983.) Assumptions underlying evaluation models. In G.F. Madaus, M. Scriven, & D.L. Stufflebeam (Eds), *Evaluation models: Viewpoints on educational and human sciences evaluation.* Boston, Massachusetts: Kluwer-Nijhoff.

Howell, D.C. (1988). *Fundamental statistics for the behavioral sciences*. (4th edn). Belmont, California: Duxbury.

Howell, D.C. (1997). *Statistical methods for psychology*. (4th edn). Belmont, California: Duxbury.

Howlett, M., & Lindegger, G. (1996). Attributional style and illness behaviour in chronic fatigue syndrome. *South African Journal of Psychology, 26,* 39–46.

Hugo, P. (Ed.). (1990). *Truth be in the field: Social science research in Southern Africa*. Pretoria: University of South Africa (UNISA) Press.

Hurt, K., & Budlender, D. (Eds). (1998). *Money matters: Women and the government budget.* Cape Town: Idasa.

Huysamen, G.K. (1996). Some methodological issues in health psychology research. *South African Journal of Psychology, 26,* 10–15.

International Health Policy Program (1996). Untitled newsletter.

Israel, M. (2004). *Ethics and the governance of criminological research in Australia*. Sydney: New South Wales Bureau of Crime Statistics and Research.

Israel, M., & Hay, I. (2006, in preparation). *Research ethics for social scientists*. London: Sage.

Ivey, G., & Simpson, P. (1998). The psychological life of paedophiles: A phenomenological study. *South African Journal of Psychology, 28*(1), 15–20.

Jacobson, P. (2001). Evaluation of a radio programme teaching English as a second language to South African primary school learners. Unpublished master's thesis. University of the Witwatersrand, Johannesburg.

Jameson, F. (1991). *Postmodernism, or, the cultural logic of late capitalism*. London: Verso.

Janesick, V.J. (1994). The dance of qualitative research design: Metaphor, methodolatory, and meaning. In N.K. Denzin & Y.S. Lincoln (Eds), *Handbook of qualitative research*. London: Sage.

Jansen, J. (Ed.) (1991). *Knowledge and power in South Africa: Critical perspectives across disciplines*. Johannesburg: Skotaville.

Jay, R. (1995). *How to write proposals and reports that get results*. New York: Prentice Hall.

Jelsma, J., & Singh, S. (2005). Research protocols: Lessons from ethical review. *South African Medical Journal, 95*(2), 107–108.

Jennings, R., Mulaudzi, J., Everatt, D., & Orkin, M. (1995). Human sciences research performed by NGOs. In *Directory of Human Science Research Organizations and Professional Associations in South Africa*. Pretoria: HSRC.

Jesani, A., & Beraji, T. (Eds). (2000). Ethical guidelines for social science research in health. Available online at www.hsph.harvard.edu/bioethics/guidelines/ethical.html (Accessed on 5 September 2005).

Joint Committee on Standards for Educational Evaluation (1981). *Principles and bylaws*. Michigan: Western Michigan University Evaluation Center.

Kalat, J.W. (1996). *Introduction to psychology*. (4th edn). Pacific Grove, California: Brooks/Cole.

Kaminer, D., & Dixon, J. (1995). The reproduction of masculinity: A discourse analysis of men's drinking talk. *South African Journal of Psychology, 25,* 168–174.

Kanjee, A., & Van Eeden, R. (1998). Item response theory and measurement equivalence in personality assessment: A South African example. Paper presented at the XIV congress of the International Association of Cross Cultural Psychology, Bellingham, USA.

Kantor, L., Schomer, H., & Louw, J. (1997). Lifestyle changes following a stress management programme: An evaluation. *South African Journal of Psychology, 27,* 16–21.

Kark, S.L. (1944). A health unit as family doctor and health advisor. *South African Medical Journal, 18,* 39–46.

Kark, S.L., & Steuart, G.W. (1957). Health education and neighbourhood family practice. *Health Education Journal, 15,* 1–10.

Kark, S.L., & Steuart, G.W. (Eds). (1962). *A practice in social medicine*. London: E. & S. Livingstone.

Katzenellenbogen, J.M., Joubert, G., & Abdool Karim, S.S. (1997). *Epidemiology: A manual for South Africa*. Cape Town: Oxford University Press.

Kazdin, A. (1998). *Methodological issues and strategies in clinical research*. (2nd edn). Washington: APA.

Kelly, K.J. (1996). Method evaluation: Dramaide, Eastern Cape Pilot Project. Report submitted to Dramaide, Durban.

Kelly, K. (1998). *Training evaluation report, national training project: Theatre for development, theatre of the oppressed*. Grahamstown: Social Research Africa.

Kennedy, G., Moen, D.R., & Ranly, D. (1993). *Beyond the inverted pyramid: Effective writing for newspapers, magazines and specialized publications*. New York: St Martin's Press.

Kerlinger, E.N. (1973). *Foundations of behavioral research*. (2nd edn). New York: Holt, Rinehart & Winston.

Kieffer, C. (1984). Citizen empowerment: A developmental perspective. In J. Rappaport, C. Swift & R. Hess (Eds), *Studies in empowerment*. New York: Haiworth Press.

Kim, M. (1992). A comparison of 3 measures of journal status: Influence Weight, Importance Index, and Measure of Standing. *Library and Information Science Research, 14*, 75–96.

Kinsey, A. (1953). *Sexual behavior in the human female*. Philadelphia: Saunders.

Kinsey, A.C., Nortin, C.E., & Pomeroy, W.B. (1948). *Sexual behavior in the human male*. Philadelphia: Saunders.

Kohlberg, L. (1966). A cognitive-developmental analysis of children's sex-role concepts and attitudes. In E. Maccoby (Ed.), *The development of sex differences*. Stanford, California: Stanford University Press.

Korber, I. (1990). Indigenous healers in a future mental health system: A case for cooperation. *Psychology in Society, 14*, 47–62.

Kosslyn, S.M., & Rosenberg, R.S. (2005). *Fundamentals of psychology: The brain, the person, the world*. Boston/Cape Town: Pearson.

Krog, A. (1996). Overwhelming trauma of the truth. *Weekly Mail & Guardian*, December 20.

Krog, A. (1998). *Country of my skull*. Johannesburg: Random House.

Kruger, D. (1979). *An introduction to phenomenological psychology*. Cape Town: Juta.

Kruger, D. (1990). The question of knowing and truth in psychology and psychotherapy. In J. Mouton & D. Joubert (Eds), *Knowledge and method in the human sciences*. Pretoria: HSRC.

Kuhn, T.S. (1962). *The structure of scientific revolutions*. Chicago: The University of Chicago Press.

Kuper, H. (1947). The concept of social medicine applied to some Bantu-speaking tribes. *The Leech, 25*(1), 55–58.

Kvale, S. (1996). *Interviews: An introduction to qualitative research interviewing*. London: Sage.

Lachenicht, L. G. (1997). Resourcing and costing applied research projects. Paper presented at the 3rd Annual Conference of the Psychological Society of South Africa, 10–12 September, Durban.

Last, J. (1988). *A dictionary of epidemiology*. (2nd edn). New York: Oxford University Press.

Lather, P. (1986). Issues of validity in openly ideological research: Between a rock and a soft place. *Interchange, 17*, 63–84.

Lather, P. (1995). Adventures with angels. *Qualitative Inquiry, 1*, 13–24.

Latour, B. (1987). *Science in action*. Cambridge, Massachusetts: Harvard University Press.

Lea, S., & Foster, D. (Eds). (1990). *Perspectives on mental handicap in South Africa*. Durban: Butterworths.

Lee, P. (1998). South African scientists try to marry western and traditional medicines. *Independent Online*, 18 May. Available online at www.inc.co.za/online/hero/1997/may18/featpetal60597.html

Leikin, S. (1993). Minors' assent, consent, or dissent to medical research. *IRB: A Review of Human Subjects Research, 15*(2), 1–7.

Levett, A. (1988). Psychological trauma: Discourses of childhood sexual abuse. Unpublished doctoral thesis. University of Cape Town, Cape Town.

Levett, A., Kottler, A., Burman, E., & Parker, I. (1997). *Culture, power and difference: Discourse analysis in South Africa*. London: Zed Books.

Li, X., & Crane, N.B. (1993). *Electronic style: A guide to citing electronic information*. New York: Meckler.

Library of Congress. (2003). *Library of Congress subject headings*. (4 vols.) (26th edn). Washington, DC: Cataloguing Distribution Services.

Lidz, C.S. (Ed.). (1987). *Dynamic assessment: An interactional approach to evaluating learning potential*. New York: Guilford Press.

Lightfoot, N. (1997). This is not a pipe. *South African Journal of Psychology, 34*, 4–9.

Lincoln, Y.S., & Denzin, N.K. (1994). The fifth moment. In N.K. Denzin, & Y.S. Lincoln (Eds), *Handbook of qualitative research*. London: Sage.

Lincoln, Y.S., & Guba, E.G. (1985). *Naturalistic inquiry*. Beverly Hills, California: Sage.

Lincoln, Y. (1995). Emerging criteria for quality in qualitative research. *Qualitative Inquiry, 1*, 275–289.

Lipnack, J., & Stamps, J. (1993). Networking the world: People, corporations, communities and nations. *Futurist, 27*, 9–12.

Lipsey, M.W., Crosse, S., Dunkle, J., Pollard, J., & Stobart, G. (1985). Evaluation: The state of the art and the sorry state of the science. In D.S. Cordray (Ed.), *Utilizing prior research in evaluation planning: New directions for program evaluation*. San Francisco: Jossey-Bass.

Lipsey, M.W. (1998). Design sensitivity: Statistical power for applied experimental research. In L. Bickman & D.J. Rog (Eds), *Handbook of applied social research methods*. Thousand Oaks, California: Sage.

Llosa, M.V. (1987). *The storyteller*. London: Faber and Faber.

Louw-Potgieter, J., & Giles, H. (1987). Afrikaner identity: Diversity among the right. *Journal of Multilingual and Multicultural Development, 8*, 283–292.

Lyotard, J-F. (1984). *The postmodern condition: A report on knowledge*. Manchester: Manchester University Press.

MacDonald, A. (1993). *Commitments and constraints: Evaluating the Science Education Project in South Africa*. Cape Town: Oxford University Press.

Macklin, R. (2002). Unresolved issues in social science research. In F. Lolas & L. Agar (Eds), *Interfaces between bioethics and the empirical social sciences*. Buenos Aires: World Health Organisation and PAHO.

Malaka, M.L. (1995). Assessment skills of teachers: A study of black South African teachers. Unpublished doctoral dissertation. University of Massachusetts, Amherst.

Manganyi, N.C. (1973). *Being-black-in-the-world*. Johannesburg: Ravan.

Marais, H. (1996). Human sciences technology. In J. Garbers (Ed.), *Effective research in the human sciences: Research management for researchers, supervisors and master's and doctoral candidates*. Pretoria: Van Schaik.

Maree, D.J.F. (2002). *Properties of and South African norms for the 16PF Fifth Edition (Technical Report)*. Johannesburg: Jopie van Rooyen and Partners.

Marks, D.F., Murray, M., Evens, B., & Willig, C. (2000). *Health psychology: Theory, research and practice*. London: Sage.

Martins, J., Loubser, M., & Van Wyk, H. de J. (1996). *Marketing research: A South African Approach*. Pretoria: University of South Africa Press.

Marx, K. (1975). Concerning Feuerbach. In *Karl Marx: Early Writings*. Harmondsworth: Pelican.

Marx, K. (1978). *Capital*. (Vol. 2). (Reprint) Harmondsworth: Penguin.

Marx, K. (1979). *Capital*. (Vol. 1). (Reprint) Harmondsworth: Penguin.

Marx, K. (1981). *Capital*. (Vol. 3). (Reprint) Harmondsworth: Penguin.

Masuku, S. (2000). Evaluation of the Radio Learning Project – self-efficacy, locus of control and teacher involvement: An exploratory study. Unpublished master's thesis. University of the Witwatersrand, Johannesburg.

Mathonsi, E.N. (1988). *Black matriculation results: A mechanism of social control*. Johannesburg: Skotaville.

Mauch, J., & Birch, J. (1993). *Guide to the successful thesis and dissertation: A handbook for students and faculty*. New York: Marcel Dekker.

Mauer, K. (1996). The art of scientific writing. In J. Garbers (Ed.), *Effective research in the human sciences: Research management for researchers, supervisors and master's and doctoral candidates*. Pretoria: Van Schaik.

Maxwell, J.A. (1998). Designing a qualitative study. In L. Bickman & D.J. Rog (Eds), *Handbook of applied social research methods*. Thousand Oaks, California: Sage.

Mayekiso, T.V., & Bhana, K. (1997). Sexual harassment: Perceptions and experiences of students at the University of Transkei. *South African Journal of Psychology, 24*, 230–243.

Mazibuko, K. (1990). *Final evaluation report on the Youth Leader Development Programme*. Centre for Continuing Education, Report and Reprint Series No 97. Johannesburg: University of the Witwatersrand.

McCormick, R. & James, M. (1983). *Curriculum evaluation in schools*. London: Routledge.

McCourt, F. (1996). *Angela's ashes*. London: Harper Collins.

McCoy, D. (1996). *Free health care for pregnant women and children under six in South Africa: An impact assessment.* Durban: Health Systems Trust.

McDonald, D., Gay, J., Lovemore, Z., Mattes, R., & de Fletter, F. (1998). *Challenging xenophobia: Myths and realities about cross-border migration in Southern Africa.* Migration Policy Series, No.7. Cape Town: Idasa.

McNaught, C, & Raubenheimer, D. (Eds). (1991). *Critical reflections on teachers in action: An evaluation report of the Natal Primary Science project.* Durban: The Urban Foundation.

Mead, M. (1943). *Coming of age in Samoa: A study of adolescence and sex in primitive societies.* Harmondsworth: Penguin.

Medical Research Council (2001). *Guidelines on ethics for medical research: General principles.* Cape Town: MRC. Available online at www.sahealthinfo.org/ethics/ethicsqualitative.htm (Accessed on 5 September 2005).

Meer, F. (Ed.). (1984). *Factory and family: The divided lives of South Africa's women workers.* Durban: Institute for Black Research.

Meiring, D., Van de Vijver, F., & Rothmann, I. (2003). Personality tests are no longer controversial in South Africa: 'Weeding out bias'. Paper presented at the 6th Annual Industrial Psychology Conference, Johannesburg.

Memering, D. (1983). *The Prentice Hall guide to research writing.* Englewood Cliffs, New Jersey: Penguin.

Memmi, A. (1965). *The colonizer and the colonized.* Boston, Massachusetts: Beacon Press.

Meyer, S., & Hofmeyr, J. (1994). Educational reconstruction in South Africa: Evaluation needs. *Journal of Educational Evaluation,* Special Conference Edition, 19–28.

Meyer, M.I., & Pinto, D. (1982). *Perspectives on an intervention programme for pre-university commerce students.* Centre for Continuing Education, Report and Reprint Series No. 2. Johannesburg: University of the Witwatersrand.

Miles, M.B., & Huberman, A.M. (1984). *Qualitative data analysis: A sourcebook of new methods.* London: Sage.

Miles, M.B., & Huberman, A.M. (1994). *Qualitative data analysis: An expanded sourcebook of new methods.* Thousand Oaks, California: Sage.

Miller, W.L., & Crabtree, B.F. (1992). Primary care research: A multimethod typology and qualitative roadmap. In B.F. Crabtree & W.L. Miller (Eds), *Doing qualitative research.* Newbury Park, California: Sage.

Miller, A. (1989). *Thou shalt not be aware: Society's betrayal of the child.* London: Pluto.

Mina, L. (1986). The ideology of rape in Newlands East: A feminist perspective. Unpublished master's dissertation. University of Natal, Durban.

Minnaar, A., & Wentzel, M. (1997). Witch-purging in the Northern Province. *In Focus Forum, 4,* 25–29.

Mishler, E.G. (1986). *Research interviewing: Context and narrative.* Cambridge, Massachusetts: Harvard University Press.

Mkhize, N.J. (2004). *Psychology: An African perspective.* In D. Hook (Ed.), *Critical psychology* (pp. 24–52). Cape Town: UCT Press.

Moeketsi, A. (1998). Psycho-cultural factors mediating the acquisition and use of condoms amongst Black male university students. Unpublished honours project. Rhodes University, Grahamstown.

Molyneaux, C., Wassenaar, D.R., Peshu, N., & Marsh, K. (2005). '...even if they ask you to stand under a tree all day you will do it!' (laughter). Community voices on the notion and practice of informed consent for biomedical research. *Social Science & Medicine, 61,* 443–454.

Moodley, P. (1998). An exploration of the psychological significance of soap opera viewing. Unpublished master's dissertation. Rhodes University, Grahamstown.

Morar, N.S., & Abdool-Karim, S.S. (1998). Vaginal insertion and douching practices among sex workers at truck stops in Kwazulu Natal. *Women's Health News and Views: Newsletter of the Women's Health Project, 25,* 26.

Morphet, A.R., Schaffer, A.J., & Millar, C.J. (1986). *Innovative policy study in education: An evaluation of the Science Education Project in South Africa.* Cape Town: University of Cape Town, Department of Adult Education and Extra-Mural Studies.

Morris, D. (1985). *Bodywatching: A field guide to the human species.* London: Jonathan Cape.

Morris, D. (1992). *Manwatching: A field guide to human behaviour.* London: Triad Granada.

Morrow, R.A. (1994). *Critical theory and methodology.* Thousand Oaks, California: Sage.

Motsei, M. (1993). Women battering. *Agenda, 16,* 99–101.

Mouton, J. (1995). Second language teaching for primary school students: An evaluation of a new teaching method. *Evaluation and program planning, 18*(4), 391–408.

Mouton, J. (2001). *How to succeed in your master's and doctoral studies*. Pretoria: Van Schaick.

Mouton, J., & Marais, H.C. (1990). *Basic concepts in the methodology of the social sciences*. Pretoria: HSRC.

Mulenga, D. (1997). *Knowledge, empowerment and social transformation: Participatory research in Africa*. Atlantic Hills, California: Zed Books.

Murphy, K.R., & Davidshofer, C.O. (1998). *Psychological testing: Principles and applications*. (4th edn). Englewood Cliffs, New Jersey: Prentice Hall.

Namuddu, K. (1997). Capacity building in research. *Bulletin: News for the Human Sciences, 4*, 10–14.

National Research Council. (2003). Protecting participants and facilitating social and behavioral sciences research. Panel on institutional review boards, surveys, and social science research. In C.F. Citro, D.R. Ilgen, & C.B. Marrett (Eds), *Committee on National Statistics and Board on Behavioral, Cognitive, and Sensory Sciences*. Washington, DC: The National Academies Press.

Ndebele, N. (1996). *Death of a son*. Johannesburg: Viva.

Nel, P. (1996). The globalisation of science, technology and research. In J. Garbers (Ed.), *Effective research in the human sciences: Research management for researchers, supervisors and masters and doctoral candidates*. Pretoria: Van Schaik.

Nel, C.M. (1987). Creative conflict handling in marriage. *South African Journal of Sociology, 18*, 39–42.

Nell, V. (1997). Science and politics meet at last: The insurance industry and neuropsychological norms. *South African Journal of Psychology, 27*(1), 43–49.

Nembahe, M. (1998). An investigation of mourning amongst urban Zulus in relation to Worden's model of mourning. Unpublished master's dissertation. University of the Witwatersrand, Johannesburg.

Neuman, W.L. (1997). *Social science methods: Qualitative and quantitative approaches*. Boston, Massachusetts: Allyn & Bacon.

Neuman, W.L. (2005). *Social research methods: Qualitative and quantitative approaches*. (6th edn). Boston, Massachusetts: Allyn & Bacon.

Nicholas, L.J., & Cooper, S. (Eds) (1990). *Psychology and apartheid*. Johannesburg: Vision/Madiba.

Ntshoe, I. (1999). Implementation and institutionalisation of innovation and change in science education: The case of SEP. Unpublished doctoral dissertation. University of the Witwatersrand, Johannesburg.

Nunnaly, J. (1978). *Psychometric theory*. (2nd edn). New York: McGraw-Hill.

Nzimande, B. (1995). To test or not to test. Paper presented at the annual Industrial Psychology Conference (Incorporating the Psychometrics Conference), Pretoria.

Oakley, A. (1981). Interviewing women: A contradiction in terms. In H. Roberts (Ed.), *Doing feminist research*. London: Routledge.

Ollman, B. (1993). *Dialectical investigations*. New York: Routledge.

Orne, M.T. (1962). On the social psychology of the psychological experiment: With particular reference to demand characteristics and their implications. *American Psychologist, 17*, 776–783.

Orpen, C. (1975). Authoritarianism revisited: A critical examination of 'expressive' theories of prejudice. In S. Morse & C. Orpen (Eds), *Contemporary South Africa: Social psychological perspectives*. Johannesburg: Juta.

Owen, K. (1996). Test bias and test fairness. In K. Owen & J.J. Taljaard (Eds), *Handbook for the use of psychological and scholastic tests of the HSRC* (pp. 77–96). (Revised edn). Pretoria: HSRC.

Packer, M.J., & Addison, R.B. (1989). Introduction. In M.J. Packer & R.B. Addison (Eds), *Entering the circle: Hermeneutic investigations in psychology*. Albany, New York: State University of New York Press.

Palmary, I., & Barnes, B. (1998). Bad boys and cool dudes: A study of school bullying. Paper presented at the 4th Annual Qualitative Methods Conference, 3–4 September. University of the Witwatersrand, Johannesburg.

Parker, I. (1989). *The crisis in modern social psychology – and how to end it*. London: Routledge.

Parker, I. (1992). *Discourse dynamics: Critical analysis for social and individual psychology*. London: Routledge.

Parker, I. (Ed.) (1998). *Social constructionism, discourse and realism*. London: Sage.

Parker, I. (2005). *Qualitative psychology: Introducing radical research*. Maidenhead, Sussex: Open University Press.

Parker, I., & Burman, E. (1993). Against discursive imperialism, empiricism and constructionism: Thirty-two problems with discourse analysis. In E. Burman & I. Parker (Eds), *Discourse analytic research: Repertoires and readings of texts in action*. London: Routledge.

Parry, C. (1997). Alcohol, drug abuse and public health. In D. Foster, M. Freeman, & Y. Pillay (Eds), *Mental health policy issues for South Africa*. Pinelands: MASA Press.

Parry, C.D.H., Bhana, A., & Bayley, J. (1998). South African Community Epidemiology Network on Drug Use (SACENDU). Monitoring alcohol and drug abuse trends in South Africa (July 1996–December 1997). *Research Brief, 1*, 1–16.

Patterson, O. (1979). On slavery and slave formation. *New Left Review, 117*, 32–33.

Patton, M.Q. (1980). *Qualitative evaluation methods*. Beverly Hills, California: Sage.

Patton, M.Q. (1987). *Analysing qualitative data*. Beverly Hills, California: Sage.

Patton, M.Q. (1990). *Qualitative evaluation and research methods*. Newbury Park, California: Sage.

Pauw, I. (1995). Sex workers' perceptions of AIDS and safe sex. Unpublished master's dissertation. University of the Western Cape, Cape Town.

Pauw, J. (1997). *Into the heart of darkness*. Cape Town: Jonathan Ball.

Pawson, R. (1989). *A measure for measures: A manifesto for empirical sociology*. London: Routledge.

Payze, C. (1997). An overview of computer-aided qualitative data analysis techniques. In M.J. Terre Blanche (Ed.), *The body politic*. Conference proceedings of the 2nd Annual South African Qualitative Methods Conference. Johannesburg: UNISA.

Pidgeon, N., & Henwood, K. (1997). Using grounded theory in psychological research. In N. Hayes (Ed.), *Doing qualitative analysis in psychology*. Hove, Sussex: Psychology Press.

Pike, K.L. (1967). *Language in relation to a unified theory of the structure of human behaviour*. The Hague: Mouton.

Pillay, Y. (1995). The politics of separation: Health policy in South Africa, 1910–1990. Unpublished doctoral thesis. Johns Hopkins University, Baltimore, Ohio.

Pillay, Y., Freeman, M., & Foster, D. (1997). Postscriptum update. In D. Foster, M. Freeman, & Y. Pillay (Eds), *Mental health policy issues for South Africa*. Pinelands: MASA Press.

Pityana, N.B., & Ramphele, M. (1991). *The bounds of possibility: The legacy of Steve Biko and black consciousness*. Cape Town: David Philip.

Polanyi, M. (1962). The republic of science. *Minerva, 1*, 54–73.

Pollock, K. (1988). On the nature of social stress: Production of a modern mythology. *Social Science and Medicine, 26*, 381–392.

Porter, R.W. (1995). Knowledge utilisation and the process of policy formulation: Towards a framework for Africa. Unpublished manuscript.

Posavac, E.J., & Carey, R.G. (2003). *Program evaluation: Methods and case studies*. (6th edn). Englewood Cliffs, New Jersey: Prentice-Hall.

Potter, C.S. (1991a). An analytical case study of a pre-university project. Unpublished doctoral thesis. University of the Witwatersrand, Johannesburg.

Potter, C.S. (1991b). Charting progress in large-scale innovation: Two case studies. Part one: A longitudinal evaluation of curriculum development in a pre-university project. *Journal of Educational Evaluation, 1*, 30–59.

Potter, C.S. (1996). Four white men and a dog: The implications of the ANC's draft policy framework for education and training for the training of evaluators in South Africa. *Journal of Educational Evaluation, 4*, 23–38.

Potter, C.S. (1998). Evaluation, knowledge and human interests. *Journal of Educational Evaluation, 7*, 1–15.

Potter, C.S. (2003). Nine years on: Ethnographic multimethod evaluation of a radio learning project. In C.S. Potter, G. Naidoo & A.S.F. Silva (Eds), *The long haul: OLSET's 'English in Action' 1995–2002*. Johannesburg: Open Learning Systems Education Trust.

Potter, C.S. (Ed.). (2005). *Case studies of interactive radio learning in South African primary schools*. Washington: Learn Tech, and Johannesburg: Open Learning Systems Education Trust.

Potter, C.S. (in press). Psychology and the art of programme evaluation. *South African Journal of Psychology*.

Potter, C.S., & Kruger, J. (2001). Social programme evaluation. In M. Seedat, N. Duncan, & S. Lazarus (Eds), *Community psychology in South*

Africa. (pp. 189–211). Cape Town: Oxford University Press.

Potter, C.S., & Leigh, S. (Eds). (1995). *English in Action in South Africa 1992–1994: A formative evaluation.* Washington: LearnTech.

Potter, C.S., & Moodie, P. (Eds). (1991). *The urban foundation primary science programme: A formative evaluation.* Johannesburg: University of the Witwatersrand, Centre for Continuing Education.

Potter, C.S., & Moodie, P. (1992). Charting progress in large scale innovation: Two case studies – Part two: A formative evaluation of curriculum development in a Primary Science Project. *Journal of Educational Evaluation, 1,* 50–70.

Potter, C.S., & Naidoo, G. (2005). *OLSET's 'English in Action': Using interactive radio to enhance classroom learning.* Johannesburg: Open Learning Systems Education Trust.

Potter, C.S., & Naidoo, G. (in press). Using interactive radio to enhance classroom learning: Reaching schools, classrooms, teachers and learners. *Distance education.*

Potter, C.S., & Silva, A.S.F. (Eds). (2002). *Teachers in action: Case studies of radio learning in South African primary schools.* Johannesburg: Open Learning Systems Education Trust.

Potter, C.S., & Van der Merwe, E. (2003). Perception, imagery, visualisation and engineering graphics. *European Journal of Engineering Education, 28*(1), 117–133.

Potter, C.S., Van der Merwe, E., Kaufman, W., & Delacour, J. (in press). A longitudinal study of student difficulties with engineering graphics. *European Journal of Engineering Education.*

Potter, J., & Wetherell, M. (1987). *Discourse and social psychology: Beyond attitudes and behaviour.* London: Sage.

Pretorius, T.B. (1994). Using the Maslach Burnout Inventory to assess educator burnout at a university in South Africa. *Psychological Reports, 75,* 771–777.

Pretorius, T.B. (1997). Salutogenic resistance resources: The role of dispositional and environmental factors in stress-resistance. Unpublished doctoral dissertation. University of the Orange Free State, Bloemfontein.

Prinsloo, C. (1995). The availability of human resources: professional researchers in the human sciences. In *Directory of Human Science Research Organizations and Professional Associations in South Africa.* Pretoria: HSRC.

Prinsloo, C.H. (1998). *The factor structure and readability of the South African English version of the fifth edition of the American 16PF.* (Internal Report). Pretoria: HSRC.

Prinsloo, C.H., & Ebersohn, I. (2002). Fair usage of the 16PF in personality assessment in South Africa: A response to Abrahams and Mauer with special reference to issues of research methodology. *South African Journal of Psychology, 32,* 48–57.

Prinsloo, R., Marais, H., & Maree-Snijders, A. (1996). The free market in research and the funding of projects. In J. Garbers (Ed.), *Effective research in the human sciences: Research management for researchers, supervisors and masters and doctoral candidates.* Pretoria: Van Schaik.

Pritchard, I. (2001). Searching for 'Research involving human subjects': What is examined? What is exempt? What is exasperating? *IRB: Ethics and Human Research, 23*(3), 5–13.

Putt, A.D. (1989). *Policy research: Concepts, methods, and applications.* Englewood Cliffs, New Jersey: Prentice Hall.

Rabinow, P., & Sullivan, W.M. (1979). The interpretive turn: Emergence of an approach. In P. Rabinow & W.M. Sullivan (Eds), *Interpretive social science: A reader.* Berkeley: University of California Press.

Rahman, M.A. (1991). Glimpses of the 'Other Africa'. In O. Fals-Borda & M.A. Rahman (Eds), *Action and knowledge. Breaking the monopoly with participatory action research.* New York: The Apex Press.

Ramcharan, P., & Cutcliffe, J.R. (2001). Judging the ethics of qualitative research: Considering the 'ethics as process' model. *Health and Social Care in the Community, 9*(6), 358–366.

Rapaport, R. (1970). Three dilemmas in action research. *Human Relations, 23,* 499– 513.

Raskoai, M.A. (1993). Effects of culture, age and gender on pictorial depth perception using the Hudson test. Unpublished master's dissertation. University of the Witwatersrand, Johannesburg.

Ratele, K. (2001). Between 'ouens': Everyday makings of black masculinity. In R. Morrell (Ed.), *Changing men in Southern Africa.* Pietermaritzburg: University of Natal Press and London: Zed Books.

Ratele, K. (2005). Proper sex, bodies, culture and objectification. *Agenda,* 63.

Ray, J.J. (1976). Do authoritarians hold authoritarian attitudes? *Human Relations, 29*, 307–325.

Reekie, J. (1997). An evaluation of the effectiveness of an AIDS prevention play for high school students. Unpublished master's dissertation. University of the Witwatersrand, Johannesburg.

Rennie, D., Yank, V. & Emanual, L.L. (1997). When authorship fails: A proposal. *Journal of the American Medical Association, 278*, 579–585.

Renzetti, C.M., & Lee, R.M. (1993). *Researching sensitive topics*. London: Sage.

Republic of South Africa. (2004a). National Health Act, Act 61 of 2004. *Government Gazette, 469*, 1–48.

Republic of South Africa. (2004b). *Ethics in health research: Principles, structures and processes*. Pretoria: Department of Health. Available online at www.doh.gov.za/docs/facts-f.html (Accessed on 21 September 2005).

Richter, L., Griesel, R., Durrheim, K., Wilson, M., Surendorff, N., & Asafo-Agyei, L. (1998). Employment opportunities for psychology graduates in South Africa: A contemporary analysis. *South African Journal of Psychology, 28*, 1–7.

Ricoeur, P. (1976). *Interpretation theory: Discourse and the surplus of meaning*. Fort Worth: Texas Christian University Press.

Ricoeur, P. (1979). The model of the text: Meaningful action considered as a text. In P. Rabinow & W.M. Sullivan (Eds), *Interpretive social science: A reader*. Berkeley: University of California Press.

Ricoeur, P. (1981a). Appropriation. In J.B. Thompson (Ed.), *Hermeneutics and the human sciences*. Cambridge: Cambridge University Press.

Ricoeur, P. (1981b). Phenomenology and hermeneutics. In J.B. Thompson (Ed.), *Hermeneutics and the human sciences*. Cambridge: Cambridge University Press.

Ries, J.B., & Leukefeld, C.G. (1998). *The research funding guidebook: Getting it, managing it and renewing it*. Thousand Oaks, California: Sage.

Robertson, B., Zwi, R., Ensick, K., Malcolm, C, Milligan, P., Moutinho, D., Uys, L., Vitas, L., Watson, R., & Wilson D. (1997). Psychiatric service provision. In D. Foster, M. Freeman & Y. Pillay (Eds), *Mental health policy issues for South Africa*. Pinelands: MASA Press.

Robinson, J.P., Shaver, P.R., Wrightman, L.S., &

Andrews, F.M. (1991). *Measures of personality and social psychological attitudes*. San Diego: Academic Press.

Roediger, H. (1997). Teaching, research and more: Psychologists in an academic career. In R. Sternberg (Ed.), *Career paths in psychology: Where your degree can take you*. Washington: American Psychological Association.

Rose, N. (1990). *Governing the soul: The shaping of the private self*. London: Routledge.

Rosenthal, R. (1966). *Experimenter effects in behavioral research*. New York: Appleton-Century-Crofts.

Rosenthal, R., & Rosnow, R.L. (1991). *Essentials of behavioral research*. (2nd edn). New York: McGraw-Hill.

Rosnow, R., & Rosenthal, R. (1989). Statistical procedures and the justification of knowledge in social science. *American Psychologist, 44*, 1276–1284.

Rossi, P.H., Freeman, H.E. & Lipsey, M.W. (1999). *Evaluation: A systematic approach*. (6th edn). Thousand Oaks, California: Sage.

Royce, D., Thyer, B.A., Padgett, D.K., & Logan, T.K. (2006). *Program evaluation: An introduction*. (4th edn). Belmont, California: Thomson Brooks/Cole.

Rudenberg, S.L., Jansen, P., & Fridjohn, P. (1998). The effect of exposure during an ongoing climate of violence on children's self-perceptions, as reflected in drawings. *South African Journal of Psychology, 28*, 107–115.

Ryan, W. (1976). *Blaming the victim*. New York: Vintage Books.

Sabate, M. (1997). A report on the feasibility study for the adaptation and standardisation of the junior South African individual scale for African language speaking pupils. Unpublished report. Pretoria: HSRC.

Schenk, K., & Williamson, J. (2005). *Ethical approaches to gathering information from children and adolescents in international settings: Guidelines and resources*. Washington, DC: Population Council.

Schiano, D.J. (1997). Convergent methodologies in cyber-psychology: A case study. *Behavior Research Methods, Instruments and Computers, 29*, 270–273.

Schrijvers, J. (1991). Dialectics of a dialogical ideal: Studying down, studying sideways and studying up. In L. Nencel & P. Pels (Eds), *Constructing knowledge: Authority and critique in social science*. London: Sage.

Schurink, W., & Schurink, E.M. (1988). Illustration: Participant observation at a gay club. In M. Ferreira, J. Mouton, G. Puth, E. Schurink & W. Schurink (Eds), *Introduction to qualitative research*. Pretoria: Human Sciences Research Council.

Schutz, A. (1967). *The phenomenology of the social world*. Evanston: Northwestern University Press.

Schwandt, T.A. (1994). Constructivist, interpretivist approaches to human inquiry. In N.K. Denzin & Y.S. Lincoln (Eds), *Handbook of qualitative research*. London: Sage.

Scriven, M. (1973). Goal-free evaluation. In E.R. House (Ed.), *School evaluation: The politics and process*. Berkeley, California: McCutchan.

Seedat, M. (1997). The quest for liberatory psychology. *South African Journal of Psychology, 27,* 261–270.

Seedat, M., Terre Blanche, M.J., Butchart, A., & Nell, V. (1992). Violence prevention through community development: The Centre for Peace Action Model. *Critical Health, 41,* 59–64.

Sehlapelo, M., & Terre Blanche, M. (1996). Psychometric testing in South Africa: Views from above and below. *Psychology in Society, 21,* 49–59.

Seidman, I.E. (1991). *Interviewing as qualitative research: A guideline for researchers in education and the social sciences*. New York: Teachers' College Press.

Seligman, M.E. (1995). The effectiveness of psychotherapy: The consumer reports study. *American Psychologist, 50,* 965–974.

Sellitz, C, Jahoda, M., Deutsch, M., & Cook, S.W. (1965). *Research methods in social relations*. New York: Holt, Rinehart & Winston.

Shadish, W.R. (1990). What can we learn about problems in community research by comparing it with program evaluation? In P. Tolan, C. Keys, F. Chertok, & L. Jason (Eds), *Researching community psychology* (pp. 201–223). Washington, DC: American Psychological Association (APA).

Shotter, J., & Gergen, K. (Eds). (1989). *Texts of identity*. London: Sage.

Siegel, S., & Castellan, N.J. (1988). *Nonparametric statistics for the behavioral sciences*. (2nd edn). New York: McGraw-Hill.

Silva, A.S.F. (2003). The OLSET teachers speak: Questionnaire analysis spanning 2001 to 2003. In C.S. Potter, G. Naidoo, & A.S.F. Silva (Eds), *The long haul: OLSET's 'English in Action' 1995–*

2002. Johannesburg: Open Learning Systems Education Trust.

Silva, A.S.F. (forthcoming). Organisational theory and community development: The case of the Open learning Systems Education Trust (OLSET). Unpublished doctoral dissertation. University of the Witwatersrand, Johannesburg.

Simon, M.A. (1982). *Understanding human action*. Albany, New York: SUNY press.

Simons, H. (Ed.). (1980). *Towards a science of the singular*. Norwich: University of East Anglia Centre for Applied Research in Education.

Simons, H. (1987). *Getting to know schools in a democracy: The politics and process of evaluation*. London: Falmer Press.

Siwani, J. (1986a). *An evaluation of a pilot course for training art teachers run under the auspices of the African Institute of Art*. Centre for Continuing Education, Report and Reprint Series No 35. Johannesburg: University of the Witwatersrand.

Siwani, J. (1986b). *An evaluation of a pilot programme for training community leaders*. Centre for Continuing Education, Report and Reprint Series No 36. Johannesburg: University of the Witwatersrand.

Siwani, J., Dzebu, M., & Gentin, J.C. (1990). *A review of the Youth Leadership Development programme*. Centre for Continuing Education, Report and Reprint Series No 101. Johannesburg: University of the Witwatersrand.

Skinner, B.F. (1988). Methods and theories in the experimental analysis of behaviour. In A.C. Catania & S. Harnad (Eds), *The selection of behaviour: The operant behaviourism of B.F. Skinner*. Cambridge: Cambridge University Press.

Slone, M., Kaminer, D., & Durrheim, K. (2000). The contribution of political life events to psychological distress among South African adolescents. *Political Psychology, 21,* 465–487.

Smaling, A. (1992). Varieties of methodological intersubjectivity: The relations with qualitative and quantitative research, and with objectivity. *Quality and Quantity, 26,* 169–180.

Small, S.A. (1996). Collaborative, community-based research on adolescents: Using research for community change. *Journal of Research on Adolescence, 6,* 9–22.

Smith, C.P. (1992). *Motivation and personality: Handbook of thematic content analysis*. Cambridge: Cambridge University Press.

Smith, J.A., Flowers, P., & Osborn, M. (1997). Interpretive phenomenological analysis and the psychology of health and illness. In L. Yardley (Ed.), *Material discourses of health and illness*. London: Routledge.

Smith, M.A., & Brant, L. (1997). Virtual subjects: Using the internet as an alternative source of subjects and research environment. *Behavior Research Methods, Instruments and Computers, 29*, 496–505.

Smith, M.L. (1986). The whole is greater: Combining qualitative and quantitative approaches in evaluation studies. In D.D. Williams (Ed.), *Naturalistic evaluation: New directions for program evaluation*. San Francisco: Jossey-Bass.

Snow, C.P. (1965). *The two cultures: A second look: An expanded version of the two cultures and the scientific revolution*. Cambridge: Cambridge University Press.

Sodi, T. (1996). Phenomenology as a viable methodological approach to the study of indigenous healing. Paper presented at the 2nd Annual South African Qualitative Methods Conference, 3–4 September, Johannesburg.

Soley, L. (1995). *Leasing the ivory tower*. Boston, Massachusetts: South End Press.

Solomon, R.L. (1949). An extension of control group design. *Psychological Bulletin, 46*, 137–150.

Spence, D. (1983). Narrative persuasion. *Psychoanalysis and Contemporary Thought, 6*, 457–468.

Spinewine, A., Swine, C., Dhillon, S., Franklin, B.D., Tulkens, P.M., Wilmotte, L., & Lorant, V. (2005). Appropriateness of use of medicines in elderly inpatients: Qualitative study. *British Medical Journal*. Published 10 August 2005 (E-publication ahead of print). Available online at www.bmj.bmjjournals.com/cgi/content/abstract/bmj.38551.410012.06v1 (Accessed on 6 October 2005).

Spradley, J. (1980). *Participant observation*. New York: Holt, Rinehart and Winston.

Squire, C. (1989). *Significant differences: Feminism in psychology*. London: Routledge.

Stake, R.E. (1974). *Responsive evaluation: New trends in evaluation*. Goteborg: University of Goteborg.

Stake, R.E. (1983). Program evaluation, particularly responsive evaluation. In G.F. Madaus, M. Scriven, & D.L. Stufflebeam (Eds), *Evaluation models: Viewpoints on educational and human services evaluation*. Boston, Massachusetts: Kluwer-Nijhoff.

StatSoft, Inc. (1995). *STATISTICA for Windows*. Tulsa, Oklahoma: Statsoft.

Stead, G.B., & Watson, M.B. (1998). The appropriateness of Super's career theory among black South Africans. *South African Journal of Psychology, 28*, 40–43.

Stenhouse, L. (1975). *An introduction to curriculum research and development*. London: Heinemann.

Stenhouse, L. (1981). What counts as research? *British Journal of Educational Studies, 29*(2).

Stenhouse, L. (1983). The curriculum as hypothetical. In J. Rudduck & D. Hopkins (Eds), *Research as a basis for teaching: Readings from the work of Lawrence Stenhouse*. London: Heinemann.

Sternberg, R. (1993). *The psychologist's companion: A guide to scientific writing for students and researchers*. (3rd edn). Cambridge: Cambridge University Press.

Steuart, G.W. (1962). Community health education. In S.L. Kark & G.W. Steuart (Eds), *A practice in social medicine*. London: Livingstone.

Stevens, C.T. (2000). *Bioethics in America: Origins and cultural politics*. Baltimore, Ohio: Johns Hopkins University Press.

Stevens, G., & Lockhat, R. (1997). 'Coca-Cola kids': Reflections on black adolescent identity development in post-apartheid South Africa. *South African Journal of Psychology, 27*, 250–254.

Stevens, M. (1998). Factors impacting on the development of the Pregnancy Termination Bill. Research report submitted to the Faculty of Management, University of the Witwatersrand.

Stevens, R.E., & Tighe Doerr, B. (1997). Trauma of discovery: Women's narratives of being informed that they are HIV-infected. *AIDS Care, 9*, 523–538.

Stevens, S.S. (1946). On the theory of scales of measurement. *Science, 103*, 667–680.

Stewart, D.W., & Shamdasani, P.N. (1990). *Focus groups: Theory and practice*. London: Sage.

Storr, A. (1989). *Freud*. Oxford: Oxford University Press.

Strauss, A.L., & Corbin, J. (1990). *Basics of qualitative research: Grounded theory, procedures, and techniques*. Newbury Park, California: Sage.

Stufflebeam, D.L. (2001). Evaluation models. *New Directions in Program Evaluation, no. 89*. San Francisco: Jossey-Bass.

Stufflebeam, D.L., Foley, W.J., Gerhart, W.J., Guba, E.G., Hammond, R.L., Merriman, H.O., &

Provus, M. (Eds). (1971). *Educational evaluation and decision-making*. Itasca, Illinois: Peacock.

Suffla, S. (1997). Experiences of induced abortion among a group of South African women. *South African Journal of Psychology, 27*, 214–222.

Swanevelder, C. (2003). The construct equivalence of the OPQ32n for Black and White subgroups in South Africa. Paper presented at the 6th Annual Industrial Psychology Conference, Johannesburg.

Swartz, L. (1989). Aspects of culture in South African psychiatry. Unpublished Ph.D dissertation. University of Cape Town, Cape Town.

Swartz, S. (1995). Changing diagnoses in Valkenberg Asylum, 1891–1920. *History of Psychiatry, 6*, 431–451.

Swartz, S. (1996). Shrinking: A postmodern perspective on psychiatric case histories. *South African Journal of Psychology, 26*,150–161.

Tabachnick, B.G., & Fidell, L.S. (2001). *Using multivariate statistics*. (4th edn). Needham Heights, Massachusetts: Allyn and Bacon.

Tallis, R. (1989). A cure for theorrhea. *Critical Review, 3*, 7–39.

Tandon, R. (1996). The historical roots and contemporary tendencies in participatory research: Implications for health care. In K. de Koning & M. Martin (Eds), *Participatory research in health: Issues and experiences*. Johannesburg: NPPHCN.

Taylor, I. (2000). The construct comparability of the NEO PI-R Questionnaire for Black and White employees. Unpublished doctoral thesis. University of the Free State, Bloemfontein.

Taylor, T.R. (1994). A review of three approaches to cognitive assessment, and a proposed integrated approach based on a unifying theoretical framework. *South African Journal of Psychology, 24*, 184–191.

Teffo, L.J. (1996). The other in African experience. *South African Journal of Philosophy, 15*, 101–104.

Terre Blanche, M.J. (1997). 'The knowledge that one seeks to disinter': Psychiatry and the discourse of discourse analysis. In A. Levett, A. Kottler, E. Burman, & I. Parker (Eds), *Culture, power and difference: Discourse analysis in South Africa*. London: Zed Books.

Terre Blanche, M.J., & Seedat, M. (2001). Martian landscapes: The social construction of race and gender at the National Institute for Personnel Research, 1946–1984. In N. Duncan, A. van Niekerk, C. de la Rey, & M. Seedat (Eds), *Race,* *Racism, knowledge production and psychology in South Africa*. (pp. 61–82). New York: Nova Science.

Thatcher, A., & Feldman, A. (1998). Cybersex: No mess, no fuss? The search for the virtual orgasm. In M.J. Terre Blanche (Ed.), *Touch me I'm sick. Proceedings of the 3rd Annual South African Qualitative Methods Conference*. Pretoria: UNISA.

Thornton, R. (1988). Culture: A contemporary definition. In E. Boonzaier & J. Sharp (Eds), *South African keywords*. Cape Town: David Philip.

Thornton, R.J., & Ramphele, M.R. (1988). The quest for community. In E. Boonzaaier & J. Sharp (Eds), *South African keywords: The uses and abuses of political concepts*. Cape Town: David Philip.

Tolan, P., Keys, C. Chertok, R., & Jason, L. (1990). *Researching community psychology: Issues of theory and methods*. Washington: APA.

Tredoux, C., & Durrheim, K. (Eds). (2002). *Numbers, hypotheses and conclusions*. Cape Town: UCT Press.

Trocco, F. (1998). How to study weird things. *Skeptical Inquirer*, September 1998. Available online at www.csicop.org/si/9809/weird.html

Tse-tung, M. (1943). Some questions concerning methods of leadership. In *Selected readings from the works of Mao Tse-tung*. Peking (Beijing): Foreign Language Press.

Tshwete, L.M. (1998). Group differences in performance in an admission test: What do they tell us? Implications for equity and access to higher education for students from unequal educational backgrounds. Paper presented at the annual conference of the International Association for Educational Assessment. Bridgetown, Barbados.

UNESCO. (1993). *World science report*. Paris: UNESCO.

University of Chicago Press. (1993). *The Chicago manual of style*. Chicago: University of Chicago Press.

Unrau, Y.A., Gabor, P.A., & Grinnell, R.M. (2001). *Evaluation in the human sciences*. Belmont, California: Thomson Brooks/Cole.

Van der Berg, H., Maree-Snijders, A., & Prinsloo, R. (Eds). (1996). *South African human sciences research networking directory*. Pretoria: HSRC.

Van der Merwe, H. (1996). The research process: Problem statement and research design. In J.G. Garbers (Ed.), *Effective research in the human sciences*. Pretoria: Van Schaik.

Van Dijk, T.A. (1987). *Communicating racism: Ethnic prejudice in thought and talk*. Newbury Park, California: Sage.

Van Eeden, R., & Visser, D. (1992). The validity of the Senior South African Individual Scale – Revised (SSAIS-R) for different population groups. *South African Journal of Psychology, 22*, 163–171.

Van Eeden, R., & Van Tonder, M. (1995). *The validity of the Senior South African Individual Scale – Revised (SSAIS-R) for children whose mother tongue is an African language: Model C schools*. Pretoria: HSRC.

Van Eeden, R. (1996). *Manual for the senior South African individual scale – revised (SSAIS-R): Part I*. Pretoria: HSRC.

Van Eeden, R., Taylor, T.R., & Du Toit, R. (1996). *Adaptation and standardization of the Sixteen Personality Factor Questionnaire Fifth Edition (16PF5) in South Africa: A feasibility study*. (Client Report). Pretoria: HSRC.

Van Eeden, R., & Prinsloo, C.H. (1997). Using the South African version of the 16PF in a multicultural context. *South African Journal of Psychology, 27*, 151–159.

Van Vlaenderen, H., & Gilbert, A. (1993). Participatory research for human capacity building in rural development. In P. Styger & M. Cameron (Eds), *Development in the transition*. Pretoria: Development Bank of South Africa.

Van Vuuren, C.P., Maree, A., & De Beer, A.S. (1998). Mass media research: The quest for certain knowledge. In A.S. De Beer (Ed.), *Mass media: Towards the millennium*. Pretoria: Van Schaik.

Velleman, R.E, & Wilkinson, L. (1993). Nominal, ordinal, interval and ratio typologies are misleading. *The American Statistician, 47*, 65–72.

Vogelman, L., Lewis, S., & Segal, L. (1994). Life after death row: Post traumatic stress and the story of Philip Takedi. *South African Journal of Psychology, 24*, 91–99.

Vogt, W.P. (1993). *Dictionary of statistics and methodology*. Newbury Park: Sage.

Wainer, H. (1990). *Computerised adaptive testing: A primer*. Hillsdale, New Jersey: Erlbaum.

Walby, S. (1990). *Theorizing patriarchy*. Oxford: Blackwell.

Walker, M. (1990). Action research in South African schools: Gilding gutter education or transforming schooling. *Perspectives in Education, 11*, 57–64.

Walker, M. (1991). Action research and transformation of teaching for people's education. Unpublished doctoral dissertation. University of Cape Town.

Walker, M. (1994). Research-based staff development. *South African Journal of Higher Education, 8*, 49–53.

Walker, A. (Ed.) (1997). *Thesaurus of psychological index terms*. (8th edn). Washington: APA.

Walt, G.W. (1994). *Health policy: An introduction to process and power*. Johannesburg: Witwatersrand University Press.

Walters, S., & Manicom, L. (Eds) (1996). *Gender and popular education: Methods for empowerment*. London: Zed Books.

Wa' Thiongo, N. (1986). *Decolonising the mind: The politics of language in African literature*. Harare: Zimbabwe Publishing House.

Weijer, C., Shapiro, S., Fuks, A., Glass, K., & Skrutkowska, M. (1995). Monitoring clinical research: An obligation unfulfilled. *Canadian Medical Association Journal, 152*, 1973–1979.

Weinstein, R.S., Soule, C.R., Collins, E., Cone, J., Mehlhorn, M., & Simontacchi, K. (1991). Expectations and high school change: Teacher–researcher collaboration to prevent school failure. *American Journal of Community Psychology, 19*, 333–364.

Weiss, C.H. (1983a). Toward the future of stakeholder approaches in evaluation. *New Directions for Program Evaluation, 17*, 83–96.

Weiss, C.H. (1983b). The stakeholder approach to evaluation: Origins and promise. *New Directions for Program Evaluation, 17*, 3–14.

Weiss, C.H. (1998). *Evaluation: Methods for studying programs and policies*. (2nd edn). Upper Saddle River, New Jersey: Prentice Hall.

Weitzman, E.A., & Miles, M.B. (1995). *Computer programs for qualitative data analysis*. Thousand Oaks, California: Sage.

Westen, D., Novotny, C., & Thompson-Brenner, H. (2004). The empirical status of empirically supported psychotherapies: Assumptions, findings and reporting in controlled clinical trials. *Psychological Bulletin, 130*, 631–663.

Wetherell, M., & Potter, J. (1992). *Mapping the language of racism: Discourse and the legitimation of exploitation*. London: Harvester Wheatsheaf.

White, H. (1980). The value of narrativity in the representation of reality. *Critical Inquiry, 7*, 5–28.

Whiteley, S. (Ed.) (1994). *The American Library Association guide to information access: A complete research handbook and directory.* New York: Random House.

Whyte, W.F., Greenwood, D.J., & Lazes, P. (1989). Participatory action research. *American Behavioral Scientist, 32,* 513–551.

Wilbraham, L. (1996). 'Few of us are potential Miss South Africas, but...': Psychological discourses about women's bodies in advice columns. *South African Journal of Psychology, 26,* 162–171.

Wilkins, N. (1988). *Poverty and inequality in South Africa.* Summary report prepared for the Office of the Executive Deputy President and the Inter-Ministerial Committee for Poverty and Inequality. Available online at www.sacs.org.za/pubserv/1998/pirsum.htm

Williams, B., & Campbell, C. (1996). Mines, migrancy and HIV in South Africa: Managing the epidemic. *South African Medical Journal, 86,* 1249–1251.

Williamson (1978). *Decoding advertisements.* London: Marion Boyars.

Wolf, R.L. (1974). Evidence and evaluation: The metaphors of law. Paper presented at the Annual Meeting of the American Educational Research Association. Chicago: AERA.

Wolf, R.L. (1983). The use of judicial evaluation methods in the formulation of educational policy. In G.R. Madaus, M. Scriven, & D. Stufflebeam (Eds), *Evaluation models: Viewpoints on educational and human services evaluation.* Boston, Massachusetts: Kluwer-Nijhoff.

Woolfolk, R.L., & Messer, S.B. (1988). Psychoanalytic interpretation and the question of validity: Commentary on Richard J. Bernstein. In S.B. Messer, L.A. Sass, & R.L. Woolfolk (Eds), *Hermeneutics and psychological theory: Interpretive perspectives on personality, psychotherapy, and psychopathology.* New Brunswick: Rutgers University Press.

World Health Organisation. (1993). *The health of young people.* Geneva: WHO.

Worthen, B.R., Sanders, J.R., & Fitzpatrick, J.L. (1997). *Program evaluation: Alternative approaches and practical guidelines.* (2nd edn). New York: Addison Wesley Longman.

Wright, M.L. (1997). An investigation into the impact of warnings on cigarette packets on the smoking behaviour of a student population. Unpublished master's dissertation. University of the Western Cape, Cape Town.

Wright, E.O. (1979). *Class, crisis and the state.* London: Verso.

Yardley, L., & Beech, S. (1998). 'I'm not a doctor': Deconstructing accounts of coping, causes and control of dizziness. *Journal of Health Psychology, 3,* 313–328.

Young, A. (1980). The discourse of stress and the reproduction of conventional knowledge. *Social Science and Medicine, 14,* 133–146.

Zerzan, J. (1995). The catastrophe of postmodernism. *Kaspharaster, 14,* 1–25.

Index

Please note: Page numbers in *italics* refer to figures and tables.

A

ability assessment 481–482
abstract of journal article 123
academic publication 119–120
action/intervention research 469
action-oriented research 382
action research (AR) 431
action(s) 43
  research in 10–12
African humanity vs objectification 511–512
African social science 539
aims of research in proposal 84
alienation vs relevance and familiarity 513
Alpha Problem 236–237
analysis 52
  units of 41–42
Analysis of Variance (ANOVA) 227, *230*
analytic errors 338
ANOVA, *see* Analysis of Variance
applied research 45–46
assessment 477
  computerised applications 495–496
  instruments 480–483
  research applications 479–484
  research practice 483–484
  in South Africa 478–479
associating 356, 358–359
association
  direction of *204*
  strength of *205*
attachments to journal article 126
attitudes 482
attributes of objects 140, 141
attributional style 457
audience watching 308–309
audit, conducting an 376–378
autonomy of persons 67

B

basic research 45–46
beneficence 67
bias in clinical assessment 484
bibliographic access 22
bibliographic database 29–31
bibliographic sources 26
bibliography 29–31
binary oppositions 337
bivariate cross-tabulation *232*
bivariate relationships 200–212
bivariate tables 206–208
Black/African scholarship 507
  history and foundations 508–509
  methods and practice 511–514
  principles of 509–510
blog (weblog) 114
body mass index (BMI) 146
Boolean searches 25
brain capacity index 146
browsing 24

C

calculator statistics functions 200
Campbell's schema 174–175
capitalism 533
cartography 11–12
cases 290
  confirming and disconfirming 290
  tracing 290–292
case study research 460–461
CAT testing, stages in *495*
causal attributions 39
causal direction 171
causal explanation 171
causality 56
causal modelling 259–263
causal/'path' diagram *260*
causation 168–169

centrality of research question 359
Central Limit Theorem 219, 221
  graphical depiction *221*
central tendency 196–197
chaos physics 526
checking 326
checklists 487–488
Chi-square
  analysis of data *233*
  test 232–234
class 518–519
clinically applied research 456–461
clinical research 469
  regulation of 474
clinical trials 458–460
closed questions 301, 487
cluster 137–138
  analysis 244, 245, 246–248
  sampling 138–139
coding 324–326
coherence 383
  of design 38–39, 89
  principle of 40
collaborative partnership 69
communality 514
communicative validity 381
community
  entry for research 470–471
  feedback meetings 118
  research 403–404
community-based clinical research 471–474
Comparative Fit Index (CFI) 263
comparative research 167, 172–174
complexity 255
  level of 324
  simplifying of 242–245
computerised catalogues 24–25
computers 324

positivist research 278
postcoloniality 551
postcolonial theory 530, 539
post-hoc tests 229
postmodernism 524–525, 530–532, 534–535
post-test measures 43
pragmatic proof 381–382
predictive validity 148
predictors 256–257
principilism 67
private sector 401
probability 216–217
   sampling 134, 135, 168
probing questions 301
problem(s)
   anticipated in proposal 86
   research 19–20
procedure of proposal 85
process research 467
programme
   evaluation 412
   planning 411–412
project title in proposal 84
proposal, research 81
   assessment form 82–83
   examples of 95–109
   rhetoric of 88–89
   science of 89
psychological intervention, evidence-based 468
psychologising 339
psychotherapy
   effectiveness vs efficacy 466
   outcome research 465–468
publication
   alternate forms of 118–119
   forms of 113–117
public health research 472–474
publishing tips 120
purpose of research 40
   in proposal 84
purposive sample 139

Q

qualitative inquiry, themes of 48
qualitative practice 379–380
qualitative research 47–48, 76–77
   common-sense perspective

272–273
data collection 286
ethics 76
ethics committees 64
methods 462–463
social constructionist paradigm 277–278
validity 90
quantitative research 47–48
   ethics committees 64
   strengths 132
   validity 90
quantitative variables 141
quantity of material 288–290
quasi-experimental designs 182
quasi-experimental research 172-173
quasi-experiments 172, 182
questioning errors 301
questionnaire
   assembling of 489–490
   development 484–495
   evaluating measures 490–493
   example *190–191*
questions, research 540–541
   banished 545
   context of answering 545–546
   good 541–545
   importance 541–545
   measurability 541
quotations 365

R

race 511, 514
random assignment 175
random error 152
randomised controlled experimental studies 458–460
random selection 134
range 198
rationale of research in proposal 84
ratio scales 156
reactive effects 176
reality effects 332
Reconstruction and

Development Programme (RDP) 444
recording
   focus groups 307
   interviews 298–299
   observations 311
record keeping 315–316
recurrent terms 334
references in journal article 125
referencing styles 125
reflexivity 506, 553
refusal
   manifold 551
   methodological and analytical 552
regression
   line *206, 256*
   to the mean 177
relational research 167, 169–172
relativism 283
reliability 89, 152–154, 493
reliability/dependability 92–94
repeated measures design 465
replication 237
representation
   of population 133
   visual 360
representativeness
   of sampling 49, 132
   validity 166
repression, notion of 548
research
   national and international 395–396
   practicality of 514–515
   question 359–362, 540–549
   reports 117, 453
   trail 376–378
researcher, becoming a 404–405
research ethics committee (REC) 61
respect for participants 69, 73
respondent characteristics 293
response format, choosing a 486–490
results in journal article 124
reversal designs 181–182